Therapist's Guide to Clinical Intervention

Therapist's Guide to Clinical Intervention

The 1-2-3's of Treatment Planning

Third Edition

SHARON L. JOHNSON

ELSEVIER

ACADEMIC PRESS
An imprint of Elsevier

Academic Press is an imprint of Elsevier
125 London Wall, London EC2Y 5AS, United Kingdom
525 B Street, Suite 1800, San Diego, CA 92101-4495, United States
50 Hampshire Street, 5th Floor, Cambridge, MA 02139, United States
The Boulevard, Langford Lane, Kidlington, Oxford OX5 1GB, United Kingdom

Notices
Knowledge and best practice in this field are constantly changing. As new research and experience broaden our understanding, changes in research methods, professional practices, or medical treatment may become necessary.

Practitioners and researchers must always rely on their own experience and knowledge in evaluating and using any information, methods, compounds, or experiments described herein. In using such information or methods they should be mindful of their own safety and the safety of others, including parties for whom they have a professional responsibility.

To the fullest extent of the law, neither the Publisher nor the authors, contributors, or editors, assume any liability for any injury and/or damage to persons or property as a matter of products liability, negligence or otherwise, or from any use or operation of any methods, products, instructions, or ideas contained in the material herein.

Library of Congress Cataloging-in-Publication Data
A catalog record for this book is available from the Library of Congress

British Library Cataloguing-in-Publication Data
A catalogue record for this book is available from the British Library

ISBN: 978-0-12-811176-5

For information on all Academic Press publications visit our website at
https://www.elsevier.com/books-and-journals

Working together
to grow libraries in
developing countries

www.elsevier.com • www.bookaid.org

Publisher: Nikki Levy
Developmental Editor: Nate McFadden
Editorial Project Manager: Barbara Makinster
Production Project Manager: Lisa M. Jones
Designer: Greg Harris

Typeset by TNQ Books and Journals

CONTENTS

Chapter 1
TREATMENT PLANNING: GOALS, OBJECTIVES, AND INTERVENTIONS

Chapter 2
ASSESSING SPECIAL CIRCUMSTANCES

Chapter 3
SKILL BUILDING RESOURCES FOR INCREASING SOCIAL COMPETENCY

Chapter 4
PROFESSIONAL PRACTICE FORMS CLINICAL FORMS BUSINESS FORMS

INTRODUCTION

THIS third edition, like the first and second, is intended to serve as a comprehensive resource tool. Behavioral health industry changes continue to evolve with the development of evidence-based treatment, DSM 5, electronic health care records, telepsychology, and the documentation transition for clinicians to the diagnostic coding of the ICD-10 system of the World Health Organization. Regardless of the continuing evolution, the clinician providing behavioral health services operates within a formal ethical framework. It is likely that no other health treatment is so stringently founded on privacy and confidentiality than psychotherapy. Providing behavioral health interventions is a complex process that takes into consideration evidence-based practices, multifaceted individualized aspects of the individual, and institutional demands of the insurance industry.

Clinicians are sensitive to the needs of the individual, and the *Therapist's Guide to Clinical Intervention* provides best practice interventions in an easy-to-use manner that provides the clinician the evidence-based treatment necessary to meet the patient where they are while respectfully incorporating personal need/desire, time, and resources. Case management demands continue to increase with documentation being more important than ever resulting in potentially more indirect service required by the clinician. Additionally, the consumer has become more sophisticated—often inquiring about the type(s) of interventions a clinician uses, thus making commensurate educated decisions regarding the type of therapy they are seeking for a specific problem. Therefore, in many cases, both the consumer of services and the contractor of services expect the therapist to provide refined diagnostic skills, brief evidence-based treatment planning with defined goals and objectives, crisis intervention, case management with collateral contacts, contracting with the client for various reasons, and discharge planning that is well documented and research supported. The *Therapist's Guide to Clinical Intervention* facilitates the ease of accomplishing these expectations by combining the aforementioned significant aspects of practice. All of this is provided in a single resource, versus a considerable number of review texts necessary to encompass a commensurate amount of information.

The third edition of the *Therapist's Guide to Clinical Intervention* has retained the original format while updating organization to improve utility and evidence-based treatment supported by a thorough literature review. Changes in the DSM 5 played a role in both the organization associated with diagnostic categorization as well as diagnostic criteria. However, from a common sense perspective, specifically with regards to pediatrics, there was a break from DSM 5. The divergence in no way interferes with treatment planning, but it did increase ease of developmental clinical treatment planning and intervention with maximum ease of utilization. Additionally, the third edition will be structured into four sections consistent with prior editions.

The first chapter of the book is an outline of evidence-based cognitive behavioral treatment planning. This organization of goals and objectives associated with specific, identified problems supports thoroughness in developing an effective intervention formulation that is individualized to each client. The treatment planning section was designed to be user-friendly and to save time. There is a list of central goals derived from identified diagnostic symptoms and the associated treatment objectives for reaching those goals from a cognitive behavioral perspective. It goes without saying that not all individuals or diagnoses are amenable to brief therapy interventions. However, cognitive behavioral interventions can still be very useful in the limited time frame for developing appropriate structure and facilitating stabilization. Often the brief intervention will be used as a time for initiating necessary longer-term treatment or making a referral to an appropriate therapeutic group or psychoeducational group.

The second chapter of the book offers a framework for assessing special circumstances, such as those involving a danger to self, danger to others, danger to the gravely disabled, spousal abuse/domestic violence, and so forth. Additionally, this section offers numerous report outlines for various assessments with a brief explanation of their intended use. The assessment outlines provide a thorough, well-organized approach resulting in the clinical clarity necessary for immediate intervention, appropriate referrals, and treatment planning. The goal is to save the general clinical practitioner time needed for direct services by providing adaptable assessment formats to fulfill the demand of a variety of clinical demands.

The third chapter of the book offers skill-building resources for increasing client competency. The information in this section is to be used as an educational resource and as homework related to various issues and needs presented by clients. This information is designed to support cognitive behavioral therapeutic interventions, to facilitate the client's increased understanding of problematic issues and to serve as a conduit for clients to acknowledge and accept their responsibility for further personal growth and self-management. Skill-building resources, whether offered verbally or given in written form, promote the use of client motivation between sessions, enhancing goal-directed thoughts and behaviors.

The fourth chapter of the book offers a continuum of clinical/business forms. The time-consuming endeavor of creating forms is eliminated by the presentation of basic forms necessary for a clinical practice. Some of the forms have only minor variations due to their specificity, and in some cases they simply offer the therapist the option of choosing a format that better suits his or her professional needs. Many of the forms can be utilized as is, directly from the text. However, if there is a need for modification to suit specific or special needs associated with one's practice beyond what is presented, having the basic framework of such forms continues to offer a substantial time-saving advantage. This text is a compilation of the most frequently needed and useful information for the time-conscious therapist in a general clinical practice.

To obtain thorough utilization of the resources provided in this text, familiarize yourself with all of its contents. This will expedite the use of the most practical aspects of this resource to suit your general needs and apprise you of the remaining contents, which may be helpful to you under other, more specific circumstances.

While the breadth of the information contained in this book is substantial, each user of this text must consider his or her own expertise in providing any services. Professional and ethical guidelines require that any therapist providing clinical services be competent and have appropriate education, training, supervision, and experience. This would include a professional ability to determine which individuals and conditions are amenable to brief therapy and under what circumstances. There also needs to be knowledge of current scientific and professional standards of practice and familiarity with associated legal standards and procedures. Additionally, it is the responsibility of the provider of psychological services to have a thorough appreciation and understanding of the influence of ethnic and cultural differences in one's case conceptualization and treatment and to see that such sensitivity is always utilized.

Level of Patient Care and Practice Considerations

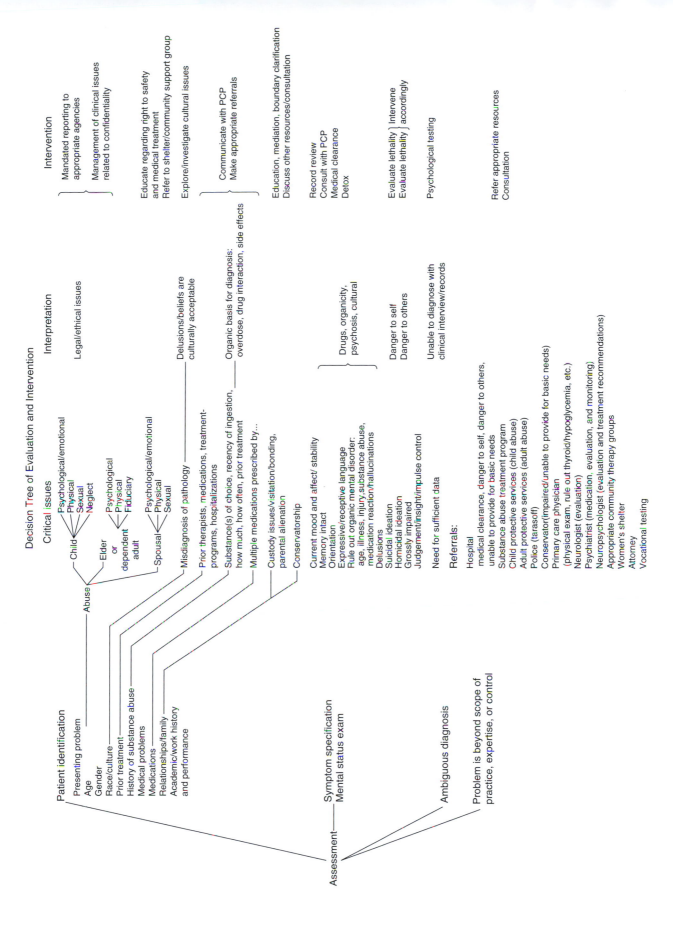

Decision Tree of Evaluation and Intervention

Levels of Functioning and Associated Treatment Considerations

Level of Functioning	Treatment Goals[a]	Focus of Treatment	Possible Treatment Modalities
1. Patient demonstrates adaptive functioning with minimal-to-no symptomology	Increase Knowledge Understanding Problem solving Choices/alternatives	Self-efficacy Education Prevention	Didactic/educational groups Community/church-based support groups Therapeutic classes/groups focused on developmental issues Recommended reading
2. Patient demonstrates mild-to-moderate symptomology that interferes with adaptive functioning	Cognitive restructuring Behavior Modification	Decrease symptomology Self-care Improve coping Improve problem solving and management of life stressors	Individual therapy Conjoint therapy Family therapy Group therapy dealing with specific issues and/or long-term support
3. Patient demonstrates moderate symptomology warranting higher level of care	Improve daily functioning and self-management	Stabilization Daily activity schedule Productive/pleasurable activities Symptom management Development and utilization of social supports	Urgent care Intensive outpatient (OP) Reinitiate OP treatment with possible increased frequency Medication evaluation/monitoring Therapeutic/educational groups Case management
4. Patient demonstrates severe symptomology: danger to self; danger to others; grave disability	Monitor and provide safe environment	Stabilization All aspects of patient's life and environment (family, social, medical, occupational, recreational) Decrease symptomology Psychopharmacology Monitoring Improve judgment, insight, impulse control	Increased OP therapy contact Urgent care Intensive OP Partial hospitalization 23-h unit Inpatient treatment Safely maintained in structural/monitored setting with adequate social support Home health intervention Reinitiate individual treatment when adequately stabilized
5. Patient demonstrating acute symptomology	Provide safe environment and rapid stabilization	Stabilization Decreased symptomology Psychopharmacology Monitoring	Increased OP therapy contact Urgent care Intensive OP 23-h unit Partial hospitalization Support group Medication monitoring Case management
6. Patient demonstrating acute symptomology with difficulty stabilizing	Provide safe environment Protection of patient Protection of others	Psychopharmacology Monitoring	Inpatient treatment 23-h unit Urgent care Partial hospitalization Intensive OP Individual therapy Support group Medication monitoring Case management

[a]Treatment goals are cumulative, i.e., a patient at a functioning level of 6 with acute symptomology may include treatment goals of previous, less acute levels, as symptomology decreases and level of functioning increases.

HIGH-RISK SITUATIONS IN PRACTICE

You can substantially reduce or eliminate risk in the following situations by giving heed to the track record of liability insurance companies. To gain perspective in these issues, plan to take a Risk Management Continuing Education course when available in your area.

1. Child Custody Cases
2. Interest Charges
3. Service Charges
4. Patients Who Restrict Your Style of Practice (e.g., Do Not Want You to Take Notes)
5. Release of Information without a Signed Form—To Anyone
6. Collection Agencies
7. Answering Service
8. Interns or Psychological Assistants to Supervise
9. Patient Abandonment
10. Dual Roles
11. High-Risk Patients, Such As Borderline Patients, Narcissistic Patients, or Multiple Personality Patients
12. Repressed Memory Patients or Analysis
13. High Debt for Delayed Payment
14. Appearance of a Group Practice without Group Insurance
15. Sexual Impropriety
16. Evaluations with Significant Consequence
17. Over or Under Diagnoses for Secondary Purposes
18. Failure to Keep Session Notes

Printed by permission from Allan Hedberg, PhD

The Treatment Plan formulation serves as the guide for developing goals and for monitoring progress. It is developed specifically to meet the assessed needs of an individual. The Treatment Plan is composed of goals and objectives, which are the focus of treatment. The following is an example of how to use the treatment planning information to quickly devise a clear Treatment Plan. Listed in the example are five identified treatment goals and the corresponding objectives.

A 12-year-old boy is referred for treatment because of behavioral problems. He is diagnosed as having an Oppositional Defiant Disorder.

Goals and Objectives

TREATMENT PLAN

Goal 1
Parent Education

Objectives

A. Explore how family is affected, how they respond, and contributing factors such as developmental influences, prognosis, and community resource information.

B. Parent Effectiveness Training Limit setting, natural consequences, positive reinforcement, etc.

Goal 2
Develop Appropriate Social Skills

Objectives

A. Role-model appropriate behaviors/responses for various situations.

B. Identify manipulative and exploitive interaction along with underlying intention. Reinforce how to get needs met appropriately.

C. Identify behaviors which allow one person to feel close and comfortable to another person.

Goal 3
Improved Communication Skills

Objectives

A. Teach assertive communication.

B. Encourage appropriate expression of thoughts and feelings.

C. Role-model and practice verbal/nonverbal communication responses for various situations.

Goal 4
Improved Self-Respect and Responsibility

Objectives

A. Have person define the terms of self-respect and responsibility, and compare these definitions to their behavior.

B. Have person identify how they are affected by the behavior of others and how others are affected negatively by their behavior.

C. Work with parents to clarify rules, expectations, choices, and consequences.

Goal 5
Improved Insight

Objectives

A. Increase understanding of relationship between behaviors and consequences.

B. Increase understanding of the thoughts/feelings underlying choices they make.

C. Facilitate problem solving appropriate alternative responses to substitute for negative choice.

SOLUTION-FOCUSED APPROACH TO TREATMENT

1. Meet people where they are psychologically and emotionally
   A. Listen
   B. Validate
   C. Reflect
2. Reframe
   A. When necessary/helpful
   B. To facilitate the ability to see alternatives/new possibilities
   C. "Planting seeds"
3. Clarify
   A. Clear descriptions of feelings
   B. Clear descriptions of situations and associated responses
   C. Patterns (relationship between thoughts, feelings, and behaviors)
   D. What are they motivated to work on or change?
4. Develop realistic expectations and limitations
   A. Establish appropriate/obtainable goals
   B. Identify markers of progress
5. Evaluate the response and outcome of prior crises
   A. What/who was helpful?
   B. What does the person think was a turning point?
   C. What did the person learn?
6. Facilitate development of problem solving and decision making
   A. Teach basic skills (Johnson, 1997)
7. Develop a plan of action
   A. Requires specifics that can be broken down
   B. Mutually agreed on plans/goals
   C. Integrate empirically supported treatments
   D. Self-monitoring
8. Homework
   A. Designed to continue treatment progress
   B. Facilitate personal growth and recovery
9. Follow up
   A. Follow up on homework assignment to clarify
      1. What did or did not work
      2. Motivation
      3. Associated increased awareness and associated choices
10. Reinforce efforts and encourage continued growth
    A. Reinforce efforts throughout the course of treatment

Case Conceptualization
(Given nothing; hypothesize everything)

Part 1: Foundations of
professional practice

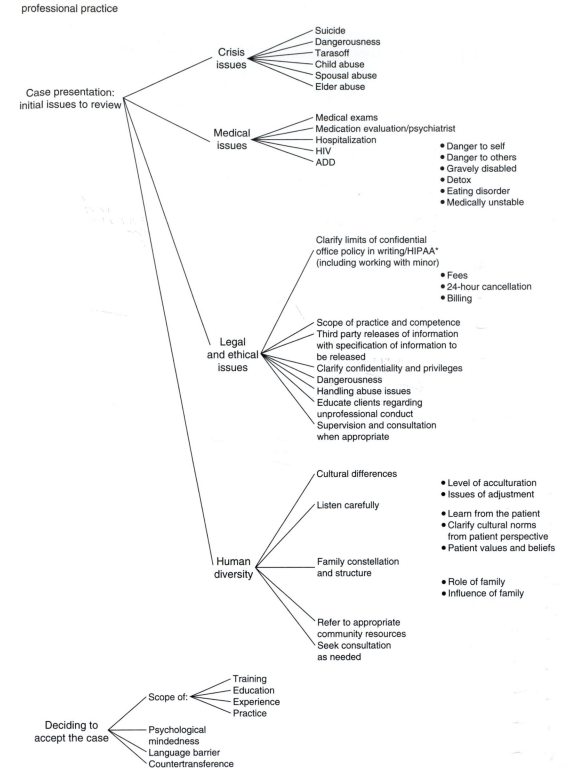

Case presentation:
initial issues to review

Crisis issues
- Suicide
- Dangerousness
- Tarasoff
- Child abuse
- Spousal abuse
- Elder abuse

Medical issues
- Medical exams
- Medication evaluation/psychiatrist
- Hospitalization
- HIV
- ADD

  • Danger to self
  • Danger to others
  • Gravely disabled
  • Detox
  • Eating disorder
  • Medically unstable

Legal and ethical issues
- Clarify limits of confidential office policy in writing/HIPAA* (including working with minor)
  • Fees
  • 24-hour cancellation
  • Billing
- Scope of practice and competence
- Third party releases of information with specification of information to be released
- Clarify confidentiality and privileges
- Dangerousness
- Handling abuse issues
- Educate clients regarding unprofessional conduct
- Supervision and consultation when appropriate

Human diversity
- Cultural differences
  • Level of acculturation
  • Issues of adjustment
- Listen carefully
  • Learn from the patient
  • Clarify cultural norms from patient perspective
  • Patient values and beliefs
- Family constellation and structure
  • Role of family
  • Influence of family
- Refer to appropriate community resources
- Seek consultation as needed

Deciding to accept the case
- Scope of:
  - Training
  - Education
  - Experience
  - Practice
- Psychological mindedness
- Language barrier
- Countertransference

*HIPAA: Health Insurance Portability and Accountability Act. Protecting the privacy of patient's health information.

Part 2:
Treatment planning

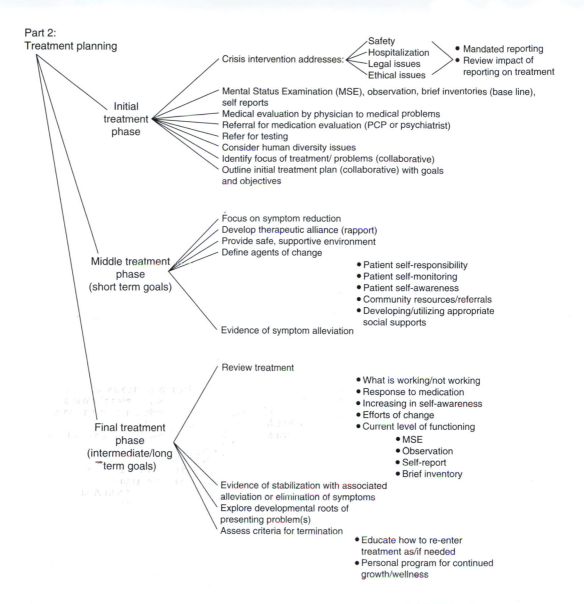

Initial treatment phase
- Crisis intervention addresses:
  - Safety
  - Hospitalization
  - Legal issues
  - Ethical issues
    - Mandated reporting
    - Review impact of reporting on treatment
- Mental Status Examination (MSE), observation, brief inventories (base line), self reports
- Medical evaluation by physician to medical problems
- Referral for medication evaluation (PCP or psychiatrist)
- Refer for testing
- Consider human diversity issues
- Identify focus of treatment/ problems (collaborative)
- Outline initial treatment plan (collaborative) with goals and objectives

Middle treatment phase (short term goals)
- Focus on symptom reduction
- Develop therapeutic alliance (rapport)
- Provide safe, supportive environment
- Define agents of change
  - Patient self-responsibility
  - Patient self-monitoring
  - Patient self-awareness
  - Community resources/referrals
  - Developing/utilizing appropriate social supports
- Evidence of symptom alleviation

Final treatment phase (intermediate/long term goals)
- Review treatment
  - What is working/not working
  - Response to medication
  - Increasing in self-awareness
  - Efforts of change
  - Current level of functioning
    - MSE
    - Observation
    - Self-report
    - Brief inventory
- Evidence of stabilization with associated alleviation or elimination of symptoms
- Explore developmental roots of presenting problem(s)
- Assess criteria for termination
  - Educate how to re-enter treatment as/if needed
  - Personal program for continued growth/wellness

COMMON DIAGNOSES AND ASSOCIATED CODES

For a behavioral health provider the DSM 5 remains the primary diagnostic resource. ICD-10 provides increased diagnostic specificity. ICD-10 does not contain information that can be used to guide diagnosis—that is derived from the DSM. To learn more about the transition to DSM 5 and ICD-10, see www.psychiatry.org/ICD10transition.

According to NIMH the five most common diagnoses are as follows:

1. **Anxiety issues.** This is the most common behavioral health condition presented in the United States. Approximately 18% of the American adult population (40 million) experience anxiety per year. Social phobia is the most common anxiety disorder experienced.

2. **Mood issues.** Approximately 9% of the American adult population (21 million) experience a mood disorder per year. Of these the most common mood disorder is depression.

3. **Attention deficit.** Approximately 11% of children and 4% of adults are diagnosed with ADD or ADHD.

4. **Personality issues.** There are numerous personality diagnoses in the DSM. Approximately 9% of the American adult population experience personality issues. The most common personality disorder is avoidant personality disorder (5% of adults diagnosed with personality dysfunction determinants).

5. **Substance use disorders.** Approximately 23 million Americans experience a substance use disorder in any given year. As challenging as this is, with extensive social cost, only about 10% of those with an addiction receive appropriate treatment interventions.

Source: http://www.nimh.nih.gov/health/publications/the-numbers-count-mental-disorders-in-america/index.shtml.

Behavioral Health Code Crosswalk From DSM to ICD-10

309.9 Unspecified adjustment reaction	**F43.20** Adjustment disorder, unspecified
	There are more specific code choice selections available in ICD-10-CM. These include:
	F43.21 Adjustment disorder with depressed mood **F43.22** Adjustment disorder with anxiety **F43.23** Adjustment disorder with mixed anxiety and depressed mood **F43.24** Adjustment disorder with disturbance of conduct **F43.25** Adjustment disorder with mixed disturbance of emotions and conduct **F43.29** Adjustment disorder with other symptoms
300.4 Dysthymic disorder	**F34.1** Dysthymic disorder
311 Depressive disorder not elsewhere classified	**F32.9** Major depressive disorder, single episode, unspecified
	There are more specific code choice selections available in ICD-10-CM. These include:
	F32.0 Major depressive disorder, single episode, mild **F32.1** Major depressive disorder, single episode, moderate **F32.2** Major depressive disorder, single episode, severe without psychotic features **F32.3** Major depressive disorder, single episode, severe with psychotic features **F32.4** Major depressive disorder, single episode, in partial remission **F32.5** Major depressive disorder, single episode, in full remission **F32.8** Other depressive episodes

296.31 Major depressive affective disorder recurrent episode mild degree	**F33.0** Major depressive disorder, recurrent, mild
296.32 Major depressive affective disorder recurrent episode moderate degree	**F33.1** Major depressive disorder, recurrent, moderate
296.36 Major depressive affective disorder recurrent episode in full remission	**F33.42** Major depressive disorder, recurrent, in full remission
296.80 Bipolar disorder, unspecified	**F31.9** Bipolar disorder, unspecified

There are more specific code choice selections available in ICD-10-CM. These include:

F31.0 Bipolar disorder, current episode hypomanic
F31.10 Bipolar disorder, current episode manic without psychotic features, unspecified
F31.11 Bipolar disorder, current episode manic without psychotic features, mild
F31.12 Bipolar disorder, current episode manic without psychotic features, moderate
F31.13 Bipolar disorder, current episode manic without psychotic features, severe
F31.30 Bipolar disorder, current episode depressed, mild or moderate severity, unspecified
F31.31 Bipolar disorder, current episode depressed, mild
F31.32 Bipolar disorder, current episode depressed, moderate
F31.4 Bipolar disorder, current episode depressed, severe, without psychotic features
F31.5 Bipolar disorder, current episode depressed, severe, with psychotic features
F31.60 Bipolar disorder, current episode mixed, unspecified
F31.61 Bipolar disorder, current episode mixed, mild
F31.62 Bipolar disorder, current episode mixed, moderate
F31.63 Bipolar disorder, current episode mixed, severe, without psychotic features
F31.64 Bipolar disorder, current episode mixed, severe, with psychotic features
F31.70 Bipolar disorder, currently in remission most recent episode unspecified
F31.71 Bipolar disorder, currently in partial remission, most recent episode hypomanic
F31.72 Bipolar disorder, currently in full remission, most recent episode hypomanic
F31.73 Bipolar disorder, currently in partial remission, most recent episode manic
F31.74 Bipolar disorder, currently in full remission, most recent episode manic
F31.75 Bipolar disorder, currently in partial remission, most recent episode depressed
F31.76 Bipolar disorder, currently in full remission, most recent episode depressed
F31.77 Bipolar disorder, currently in partial remission, most recent episode mixed
F31.78 Bipolar disorder, currently in full remission, most recent episode mixed

296.90 Unspecified episodic mood disorder	**F39** Unspecified mood [affective] disorder
300.00 Anxiety state unspecified	**F41.9** Anxiety disorder, unspecified

There are more specific code choice selections available in ICD-10-CM. These include:

F41.1 Generalized anxiety disorder
F41.8 Other specified anxiety disorders

300.3 Obsessive compulsive disorders	**F42** Obsessive-compulsive disorder
314.9 Unspecified hyperkinetic syndrome of childhood	**F90.0** Attention-deficit hyperactivity disorder, predominantly inattentive type
	F90.1 Attention-deficit hyperactivity disorder, predominantly hyperactive type
	F90.2 Attention-deficit hyperactivity disorder, combined type
	F90.8 Attention-deficit hyperactivity disorder, other type
	F90.9 Attention-deficit hyperactivity disorder, unspecified type

Common DSM "V" Codes

V Code	Diagnoses
V15.81	Noncompliance with Treatment
V61.1	Partner Relational Problem Physical/Sexual Abuse of a Adult
V61.20	Parent-Child Relational Problem
V61.21	Child Neglect Physical/Sexual Abuse of a Child
V61.8	Sibling Relational Problem
V61.9	Relational Problem Related to Mental Disorders or General Medical Condition
V62.2	Occupational Problem
V62.3	Academic Problem
V62.4	Acculturation Problem
V62.81	Relational Problems
V62.82	Bereavement
V62.89	Borderline Intellectual Functioning Phase of Life Problem Religious or Spiritual Problem
V65.2	Malingering
V71.01	Adult Antisocial Behavior
V71.02	Child or Adolescent Antisocial Behavior
V71.09	No Diagnosis or Condition on Axis I

Chapter 1

Treatment Planning: Goals, Objectives, and Interventions

A diagnosis holds value in conceptual communication, multidisciplinary collaboration, and the development of an individualized treatment plan that improves the quality of life for a person. Commensurate with that defining foundation is evidence-based practice (EBP), which is weighted in the cognitive-behavioral therapy (CBT) realm. As with many diagnoses today, CBT is specialized to specific diagnostic challenges. For example, CBT for anxiety and depression, dialectical behavioral therapy for personality disorders, and for schizophrenia, CBT for psychosis is referred to as "CBT-P." CBT has been shown to be as useful as antidepressant medications for some individuals with depression and may be superior in preventing relapse of symptoms. For decades it has been accepted that those in therapy who receive CBT in addition to treatment with medication have better outcomes than those who do not receive CBT as an additional treatment.

The literature review foundation for the treatment section was based upon: The Center for Implementation-Dissemination of Evidence-Based Practices Among States (IDEAS) (2015), SAMHSA Behavioral Health–Evidence-Based Treatment and Recovery Practices (2012), SAMHSA Evidence-Based WEB GUIDE (2014) were used as a review sources in identifying EBP treatment goals and objectives. The last resource was a comprehensive collection of EBP collaborations [Campbell Collaboration, Child Trends, Cochrane Collaboration, Effective Child Therapy EB MH Treatment for Children and adolescents, National Guidelines Clearinghouse (AHRQ)] and many others.

There are three essential principles to CBT:

1. Set specific goals
2. Provide rewards and consequences (life is about choices)
3. Consistency of rewards and consequences is a key

Therapist's Guide to Clinical Intervention. http://dx.doi.org/10.1016/B978-0-12-811176-5.00001-2

INTELLECTUAL DISABILITY

Intellectual disabilities are described by learning, cognitive, and social characteristics. An intellectual developmental disorder is characterized by deficits in intellectual functioning (IQ of 70 ± 5 or below) with concurrent deficits in adaptive functioning, which includes social skills, communication, daily living skills, age-appropriate independent behavior, and social responsibility "without ongoing support." However, in contrast with most other disability categories, children with mild intellectual disabilities are inclined to have more general, delayed development in academic, social, and adaptive skills. This delayed development is reflected in low achievement across content and skill areas as well as significantly lower scores on measures of intelligence and adaptive behavior when compared to their peers who do not demonstrate intellectual disabilities.

Cognitive performance influences acquisition of language and academic skills, specifically associated to attention, memory, and generalization. Attentional difficulties such as orienting to task, selective attention, and sustaining attention to a task present the need for creative interventions to increase effectiveness (Beirne-Smith, Patton, & Kim, 2006). Short-term memory deficit is benefitted from rehearsal strategies (Kirk, Gallagher, Anastasiow, & Coleman, 2006) and focusing on meaningful content during instruction to facilitate remembering information [i.e., rehearsal, clustering information, and mnemonic devices (Smith, Polloway, Patton, & Dowdy, 2012)]. Generalization difficulties interfere with generalized material learned in one setting and transferred to another (i.e., school to home and community) (Smith et al., 2012). These challenges benefit from:

1. Present initial stimuli that vary in only a few dimensions
2. Direct attention to these critical dimensions
3. Initially remove unnecessary/inessential stimuli that may result/increase distractibility
4. Increase difficulty of task over time
5. Teach decision-making rules for discriminating relevant from irrelevant stimuli/factors

There are four degrees of severity in impairment: mild, moderate, severe, and profound.

Differential diagnoses include learning disorders, medical cause, and autism spectrum disorder (ASD). Other diagnoses identified as developmental include:

1. Global developmental delay
2. Unspecified intellectual disability
3. Communication disorder
4. Language disorder
5. Speech sound disorder
6. Childhood onset fluency disorder
7. Social (pragmatic) communication disorder (new disorder)
8. Autism spectrum disorder

A medical exam, neurological exam, or evaluation by a neuropsychologist is important to rule out organicity, vision/hearing deficits and to determine the origin of the presenting problems. Another valued evaluation from which to gather important functional information is an occupational therapist to determine regulatory disorders that play a significant role in coping. With the information yielded from such exams, a thorough individualized program can be developed and implemented. An individualized treatment and educational plan addresses the individual needs along with the identification of intelligence level and strengths for the facilitated development of the highest level of functioning for that individual (Bhaumak, Gangadharan, Hiremath, & Russell, 2011; Schalock et al., 2010; Stein, Blum, & Barbaresi, 2011).

As per Grey and Hastings (2005), applied behavior analysis (ABA), psychopharmacology, and service evaluation are the traditional sources of practice guidelines. ABA continues to be the research focal point with positive outcome as a service model for associated behavior disorders. However, questions persist when it comes to behavior disorders that reaffirm respectful individualized treatment planning. Intervention and support include the resources and clinical strategies to encourage and reinforce the development, education, interests, and well-being of an individual identified for treatment. Behavior problems, especially underlying mental illness with those diagnosed with intellectual disability, are generally multifactorial in origin. A therapist specializing in the treatment of those with intellectual disability identifies them as functioning as part of a treatment team that seeks to provide services matching skill level. Therefore, their input may be valuable in areas such as case management, vocational programs, day programs, residential options, early intervention, special education, and transitional services—in addition to individualized clinical intervention. Parents should be an integral part of the planning and treating/teaching team. APA (retrieved from the web, September 2015) asserts, evidence-based assessments from multidisciplinary perspectives (e.g., developmental pediatricians, psychologists, speech-language pathologists, occupational and physical therapists) are recommended to guide intervention efforts. Additionally, early intervention is more effective waiting for demonstrations of critical levels of need when it comes to mitigating the effects of disabilities. Finally, Wehmeyer and Obremski (2010) assert the assumption, "the positive outcomes of people who received personalized supports over a sustained period of time, emphasizes both the significant impact such personalized supports can have on the functioning of people with intellectual disability, but also on the fact that people with intellectual disability can, with adequate supports, live lives of quality and contribute to society by their presence and productivity…"

Additionally, appropriate educational services that begin as early as possible and continue throughout the developmental stages will facilitate a child/individual's fullest potential. To offer an individualized treatment plan the clinician must be prepared to modify instruction to meet individual needs as an integral process to successful learning and cognitive-behavioral change (Johnson, 2004, 2013).

INTELLECTUAL DISABILITY

Goals

1. Establish developmentally appropriate daily living skills
2. Develop basic problem-solving skills
3. Decrease social isolation and increase personal competence
4. Develop social skills
5. Support and educate parents on management issues

Treatment Focus and Objectives

1. Daily Living Skills (Waking by Alarm, Dressing, Hygiene/Personal Care, Finances, Taking the Bus, Etc.)
   A. Realistic expectations and limitations
   B. Repetition of behaviors
   C. Modeling of desired behaviors
   D. Breaking down behaviors into stepwise sequence (shaping)
   E. Positive feedback and reinforcement
2. Improve Problem Solving
   A. Role-play solutions to various situations
   B. Develop a hierarchy of responses for potential problem/crisis (enlist help of caretaker, parents, neighbor, or 911)
   C. Practice desired responses by role-playing pertinent scenarios
   D. Focus on efforts and accomplishments
   E. Positive feedback and reinforcement
3. Social Isolation
   A. Appropriate educational setting
      1. Most communities have a vocational rehabilitation program and volunteer bureau to offer jobs in the community related to their level of functioning. Every routine of social participation serves as a positive reinforcer of skill development and provides structure to counter social isolation.
   B. Special Olympics or community sporting activities
   C. Programmed social activities
   D. Camps for the intellectually challenged
   E. Contact local association for intellectually challenged persons for identified community resources
   F. If older, evaluate for vocational training, living arrangement away from family, which includes social agenda (independent living or group home), if low functioning, a day treatment program may be helpful

4. Impaired Social Skills
   A. Realistic expectations and limitations identified through assessment and caretaker observation.
   B. Teach appropriate social skills (developmental, age appropriate). Primarily utilizing opportunities to practice in vivo and role-playing to practice when opportunities are not available via real-time experiences. Repetition is imperative for adequate skill development and refinement.
      1. Collaboration
      2. Cooperation
      3. Follow rules
      4. Etiquette/manners
      5. Appropriate expression of emotions
   C. Games that practice social skills. Creativity and repetition are important.
   D. Programmed experiences (play date, community activity, etc.).
   E. Practice/repetition.
   F. Focus on efforts and accomplishments.
   G. Positive feedback and reinforcement.
5. Family Intervention/Education
   A. Educate regarding realistic expectations and limitations
   B. Review options and alternatives to various difficulties
   C. Identify and work through feelings of loss, guilt, shame, and anger; it is not uncommon for parents/families of severely, handicapped children to feel resentment toward the child, who may be disruptive to the family
   D. Facilitate other children in the family to deal with their feelings or concerns
   E. Encourage acceptance of reality that everyone is different along with appreciation for differences
   F. Encourage identification and utilization of community support organizations and other associated resources
   G. Teach parents behavior-modification techniques

Additional Considerations

During Assessment
1. If there are adequate verbal skills, utilize open-ended questions
2. Clarify with concrete, simple, tightly structured interview questions
3. Be careful to accurately assess for a rich fantasy life versus a diagnosis of psychosis/perceptual distortions
4. Be sensitive to depression and low self-esteem as clinical issues

Levels of intellectual disability by intelligence test range

Mild	50–70
Moderate	35–49
Severe	20–34
Profound	Below 20

Behavior competency expectations associated with degree of intellectual challenge (Gluck, 2014)

Mild

Preschool (0–5 years)	Able to develop social and communication skills. The minimal sensory–motor disability may not be evident until later.
School age (6–18 years)	Academic proficiency up to 6th grade level. Able to take the lead to social conformity.

Moderate

Preschool	Able to talk/learn to communicate. Poor social awareness. Adequate motor skills. Benefits from self-help skill training with supervision.
School age	Able to benefit from social and occupational skill training. Not likely to advance beyond 2nd grade level. Some independence in familiar setting.

Severe	
Preschool	Poor language development. Minimal language skill/little communication. Unlikely to benefit from self-help training.
School age	Able to learn to talk/communicate. Training beneficial for basic self-help skills. Benefits from systematic habit training (applied behavior analysis/CBT).
Profound	
Preschool	Minimal capacity in sensory–motor functioning. Requires intense care.
School age	Some evidence of motor development. May respond to very limited range of training in self-skill development.

Any condition that impairs the development of the brain prior to birth, during birth, or in the childhood years can result in a child becoming intellectually challenged. NIH (2013) asserts that intellectual disability is diagnosed before the age of 18 years, includes below-average intellectual function and a deficit in ability to effectively execute daily living skills.

Intellectual disability affects about 1%–3% of the population. The causes of intellectual disability are numerous, but in only about 25% of the cases are a specific reason identified. Risk factors are related to the causes. Causes of intellectual disability can include (NIH, 2013):

1. Infections (present at birth or occurring after birth)
2. Chromosomal abnormalities (such as Down syndrome, fragile X)
3. Environmental
4. Metabolic (such as hyperbilirubinemia, i.e., very high bilirubin levels in infants)
5. Nutritional (such as malnutrition/malabsorption)
6. Toxic (fetal alcohol exposure, cocaine, amphetamines, and other drugs)
7. Trauma (before and after birth)
8. Unexplained (the greatest number is for unexplained occurrences of intellectual disability)

Associated Deficits

Experiencing a mild intellectual challenge is generally an isolated condition. However, when severe it is often accompanied by associated deficits such as:

1. Cerebral palsy
2. Visual deficits
3. Seizures
4. Communication deficits
5. Feeding problems
6. Attention-deficit hyperactivity disorder (ADHD)

Dual Diagnosis (Developmentally Disabled With Psychiatric Disorder)

Dual diagnosis (developmentally disabled with psychiatric disorder) expounds on the challenges faced in caring for and treating those with cognitive/intellectual disabilities and co-occurring mental illness. The complexities of dual diagnosis with this population are better understood integrating the following clinical contributions (Tang et al., 2008):

1. **Psychosocial masking:** Due to the reality that people with developmental disabilities have limited social experiences, their psychiatric symptoms may be very different than those of the "normal" population.
2. **Intellectual distortion:** Since there are deficits in abstract thinking, receptive and expressive language skills, emotional symptoms may be difficult to elicit. In fact, emotional symptoms may manifest behaviorally.
3. **Cognitive disintegration:** Those with developmental disabilities have decreased ability to tolerate stress resulting in anxiety-induced behavior, which may be misinterpreted as psychosis.

4. **Baseline exaggeration:** Onset of psychiatric illness may increase the severity or frequency of chronic maladaptive behavior. This factor can influence the diagnosis of mental illness if the biopsychosocial model has not been employed to understand the context of behavior.

Therefore, when working with people who have developmental disabilities it is essential to always consider the possibility that they have a mental health disorder. As a result, clinicians of all disciplines serving as a part of a treatment team encounter the task of confronting the need for accurate diagnosing and providing effective interventions and resources.

Jacobson (1982a, 1982b) surveyed intellectually challenged children from infancy to adolescence and found that 9.8% had significant psychiatric impairment, which was categorized into four areas based on features and severity:

1. Cognitive
   A. Major thought disorder
   B. Hallucinations
   C. Delusions
2. Affective
   A. Significant depression
   B. Dysphoric affect
3. Minor behavioral problems (on a continuum to major problems)
   A. Hyperactivity
   B. Tantrums
   C. Stereotypies
   D. Verbal abusiveness
   E. Substance abuse
4. Major behavioral problems
   A. Physical aggression/assault
   B. Property destruction
   C. Coercive sexual behavior
   D. Self-injurious behavior

Parents and siblings must be evaluated in association with their own risk for significant difficulties (any identified difficulties may or may not be related to the intellectually disabled child in the family system). Additionally, the family system may lack cohesiveness and harmony.

Parents	Increased risk for depression
	Decreased satisfaction in parenting
	Potential for negative attitude toward retarded child
	Marital stress
	Increased social isolation
Siblings	Behavioral problems
	Feelings of guilt/anger
	Psuedoadult responsibilities (loss of their childhood associated with assuming adult-type responsibilities in the family system)

AUTISM SPECTRUM DISORDER

The concept of ASD results from the overlap among the different forms of autism. ASD affects 1 in 68 American children (WebMD, 2015). APA (2013) identifies ASD, "tend to have communication deficits, such as responding inappropriately in conversations, misleading nonverbal interactions, or having difficulty building friendships appropriate to their age." In addition, individuals with ASD may be overly dependent on routines, highly sensitive to change in their environment, or intensely focused on inappropriate items. Again, the symptoms of those with ASD will fall on a continuum, with some individuals showing mild symptoms and others having much more severe symptoms. This spectrum will allow clinicians to account for the variations in symptoms and behaviors in an individualized manner.

1. Reciprocal social interaction: not aware of others' feelings, doesn't imitate, doesn't seek comfort at times of distress, and impairment in ability to make peer relationships.
2. Impaired communication: abnormal speech productivity, abnormal form or content of speech, and impaired initiating or sustaining conversation despite adequate speech.
3. Restricted repertoire of activities and interests: stereotyped body movements, marked distress over trivial changes, and restricted range of interests.

As per DSM 5, severity needs to be identified and documented:

1. "requiring very substantial support for deficits in social communication and requiring substantial support for restricted, repetitive behaviors"
2. "with accompanying intellectual impairment" or "without accompanying intellectual impairment"
3. "with accompanying language impairment-no intelligible speech" or "with accompanying language impairment-phrase speech"

A medical exam to rule out physical problems such as hearing and vision impairments should be performed prior to the assignment of this diagnosis. ASD shows severe qualitative abnormalities that aren't normal for any age in comparison to intellectual disability, which demonstrates general delays and behaviors indicative of an earlier stage of normal development. However, intellectual disability may coexist with ASD.

NIH (2013; NIMH, 2011) assert that those with ASD have increased potential of using all of their abilities and skills if they receive appropriate therapies and interventions that are individualized to the person's needs, and early intervention is imperative. It is further stated that as a result of the symptom overlap between ASD and other diagnoses (such as ADHD) that treatment should focus on the specific needs of the person rather than the diagnostic label.

Treatment Goals

1. Child will not harm self
2. Child will demonstrate trust in his/her caretaker
3. Shaping child's behavior toward improved social interaction
4. Child will demonstrate increased self-awareness
5. Child will develop appropriate means of verbal and nonverbal communication for expressing his/her needs
6. Identifying and facilitating self-regulation and sensory processing and reactivity
7. Support and educate parents regarding behavioral management

Treatment Focus and Objectives

Applied behavioral analysis has become an identified treatment framework that has been adopted to encourage positive behaviors and discourage negative behaviors in an effort to develop, improve and reinforce desired skills (CDC, 2015). The Treatment and Education of Autistic and Related Communication model used visual cues, such as picture cards, to teach basic skills such as getting dressed by breaking the task down into small manageable steps (CDC, 2015). Additionally, Greenspan (2001) and Johnson (2013) provide the "Greenspan Floortime Approach," also referred to as DIR (developmental individual differences), a Relationship-Based Approach which focuses on emotional and relational development (feelings, relationships with caregivers) and how the child deals with sights, sounds, and smells.

D = Functional developmental stages
I = Individual differences in the areas of auditory processing, motor planning, and sensory modulation
R = Relationship dynamics, evolving/ever-changing learning interactions and family patterns

1. Risk of Self-harm
   A. Intervene when child demonstrates self-injurious behaviors
   B. Determine precipitators of self-injurious behaviors (such as increased tension in environment or increased anxiety)
   C. Make efforts to assure, comfort, or give appropriate structure to child during distressful incidents to foster feelings of security and trust
   D. Offer one-to-one interaction to facilitate focus and foster trust
   E. Use safety helmet and mitts if necessary
   F. Modify environment to assure safety

2. Lack of Trust
   A. Consistency in environment and interactional objects (e.g., toys, etc.) fosters security and familiarity.
   B. Consistency in caretaker to develop familiarity and trust.
   C. Consistency in caretaker responses to behavior to facilitate development of boundaries and expectations; behavioral reinforcement.
   D. Caretaker must be realistic about limitations and expectations. Prepare caretaker to proceed at a slow pace and to not impose his/her own wants and desires of progress on the child who will have to move at his/her own slow pace.
   E. Proceed in treatment plan with the lowest level of desired interaction to initiate positive behavioral change. Low-level behaviors could include eye contact, facial expression, or other nonverbal behaviors. Development of these types of behaviors requires one-to-one interaction.
   F. Keep environmental stimuli at a minimum to reduce feelings of threat or being overwhelmed.

3. Dysfunctional Social Interaction
   A. Requires objectives 1 and 2 to be in practice.
   B. Support and reinforce child's attempts to interact. Provide consistent guidance toward goal behaviors.
   C. Consistently restate communication attempts to clarify and encourage appropriate and meaningful communication that is understandable (be careful to not alter the intended communication, just clarify it).
   D. Friendship training is the basic social skill needed to interact with peers.
      1. Conversation
      2. Handling teasing
      3. Being a good sport
      4. Showing good host behavior during play dates

4. Identity Disturbance
   A. Utilize activities that facilitate recognition of individuality, such as difference in appearance and choices. Begin with basic daily activities of dressing and mealtime.
   B. Increase self-awareness and self-knowledge. This can be initially facilitated by having the child learn and say the name of the caretaker, his/her own name and learning the names of his/her own body parts. These types of activities can be done through media such as drawing, pictures, or music. Providing necessary repetition and making it fun.
   C. Reinforce boundaries and individuality.

5. Impaired Communication
   A. Consistently make efforts to clarify intent/need associated with communication.
   B. Caretaker consistency will facilitate increased understanding of child's communication patterns.
   C. When clarifying communication, be eye to eye with child to focus on the communication in connection with the issue of need being presented by the child.

6. Self-regulation, Sensory Processing, and Reactivity
   A. Parent report measures are selected by the treatment team (e.g., The Infant-Toddler Symptom Checklist in addition to clinical observation instruments)
   B. Relationships

1. Clarifying the concept of family
   a. Make a poster of the family tree
   b. Use social gatherings/holidays and phone calls as opportunities to clarify the meaning of family
   c. Make a collage—let the child cut out and glue family pictures on a poster board and label them
2. Understanding the perspective of others
   a. Facilitate understanding that relationships are bidirectional (the golden rule, thinking about you–thinking about me)
   b. Facilitate the child to list why listening is important
3. Identifying friends
   a. Make a list about friends and add what they like about friends

C. Learning to listen
   1. Using eye contact "I look at the person I am listening to with my eyes"
   2. Don't interrupt
      a. "Don't interrupt." When the child is talking, interrupt them. Ask them what it was like to be interrupted (ignored, frustrated, angry).
      b. Practice being a statue (statues don't move, they make eye contact, and listen).
      c. Practice appropriate responding; take turns talking.

D. Personal space
   1. Identify personal space. Have a child take a hula hoop and stand in the middle of it to help them identify the physical feeling of the parameter of personal space.

E. Waiting: sometimes a child experiences difficulty waiting
   1. Identify when to wait. Make a list together. Practice.
   2. What is hard to wait for? Make a list of situations where they have a hard time waiting (e.g., taking turns in class, waiting their turn to play, etc.).
      a. Role-play the identified circumstances for practice

F. Dealing with anger
   1. The anger thermometer. Draw a thermometer and indicate the intensity of emotion by graded levels. For example, the lower level is frustration and the top is furious.
   2. Management tools.
      a. Take a deep breath.
      b. Count to 10.
      c. Walk away/go to a safe place.
      d. Make a list of trigger that result in an angry outburst and brainstorm options.
      e. Make a list of replacement behaviors to substitute for the behaviors they engage in when they lose their temper.
      f. Practice, practice, practice. "Let's pretend you are angry…" Then working together to problem-solve a positive solution. Making this practice fun may also benefit by a change in emotional perspective that motivates change
      g. Catch them being good and demonstrating management of frustration/anger.
      h. Teach the turtle technique; recognize feelings of anger, think "stop," go inside "shell" and take three breaths. Think calm, think solution, do it!

G. Using your voice: learning to speak more quietly and with appropriate emotion
   1. Using musical instruments (like a drum) to demonstrate loud versus quiet
   2. Practice volume being low, medium, high
   3. Sound examples, i.e., tones associated with different emotions (angry, sad, happy, etc.)

H. Cooperation
   1. Make an activity chart demonstrating the tasks that require cooperation (going to bed, sitting at the table, brushing teeth).
   2. When to be a helper (it feels good to be a helper and appreciated). Identify how we help each other.

3. Taking turns. Explain how taking turns provides the opportunity for everyone to do something they want to do.

4. Explain the reason for limits and requests. Point out how rules help everyone.

5. Take the time to problem-solve. Identify the problem, brainstorm solutions, make a choice and redirect. Sometimes they need help in finding ways to channel their desires or goals.

6. Assign chores at an early age to learn the benefits of cooperation. "Together we can set the table, then we will have time later to read a book together."

7. Offer suggestions or choices—not commands while maintaining the rules.

I. Behavior management

1. Help the child identify triggers for the problem behaviors (could happen in a single significant situation or in multiple situations).

2. Determine if the triggers can be eliminated by environmental modifications.

3. Replacement behaviors. Make a list of things the child could do as "choices" instead of the problem behaviors.

4. Practice the replacement behaviors, using role-playing or simulations.

5. Connect the use of the replacement behaviors with a reward/reinforcement. Self-regulation works toward internalizing the problem-solving process of a child asking themselves, "What is my problem?" "What is my plan?" "Am I following my plan?" "How did I do?"

J. Impulse control

1. Identify situations where impulsive behaviors occur (such as making the transition from one activity to another).

2. Agree on a rule for the situations. The rule should focus on what the child can do to control impulses (i.e., use their quiet voice, wait their turn, keep their hands to themselves).

3. Use a story board to tell the story of the steps for how the child is "going to do it differently." For example, if they think they are going to lose control in a situation what are the agreed-upon strategies for backing away.

4. Practice using the choices to see what works best in what situations. It will help the child understand themself better and improve their self-confidence.

K. Flexibility: helping a child to accept changes without distress

1. Using well-rehearsed routines to decrease anxiety/distress. Predictable is comforting.

2. Informing a child ahead of time when changes are being made and prepare them for making the adjustment.

3. Use time ranges when possible to increase flexibility.

4. Use a schedule board showing the child activities for the day or week. It can be done using pictures.

5. Review the schedule at the beginning of the day with the child.

7. Parental Intervention/Education

As per Johnson (2013), treatment strives to create a useful dynamic picture of the family system by identifying:

- Safety and protection issues
- Strengths
- Areas of relative weakness/limitations/needs to be problem-solved and/or strengthened if possible
- Reframing when possible to highlight the value of learning and benefitting from "challenging" situations and when things do not turn out "right"
- Resources within the nuclear family, extended family, community resources (formal and informal resources)
- Coping skills and capabilities
- Fit between parent(s) and child—a reality issue not a guilt or shame provocation

NIMH offers a Parent's Guide to ASD: www.nimh.nih.gov/health/publications/a-parents-guide-to-autism-spectrum-disorder/index.shtml.

A. Educate regarding realistic understanding of expectations and limitations. The CDC provides a developmental factsheet that offer a brief summary of age-related milestones and accompanying parenting skills. The parenting information is a progression that highlights the type of parent activities that promotes child development caregiver skill building (Johnson, 2013).

B. Identify and work through feelings of loss, guilt, shame, and anger.

C. Facilitate other children in the family to deal with their feelings and concerns.

D. Encourage acceptance of reality.

E. Encourage identification and utilization of community support organizations and other associated resources.

F. Identify additional support and respite care.

G. Teach parents specific behavioral management techniques to fit their needs, such as how to solve practical problems (within family, between child/school, family/school, and with other services), how to celebrate progress, and how to establish reinforcers.

H. Recognize that parents may be at increased risk for depression or stress-related illnesses.

Some conditions produce ASD symptoms, therefore, if a formal diagnosis has not previously been assigned, the following information should be given to the parents and appropriate referral considerations be communicated to the primary care physician.

Medical Assessment

1. History
2. Examination
3. Rule out associated medical conditions (pica and associated lead intoxication)
4. Visual/audiology exams
5. Neurological assessment important to evaluate for seizures
6. Genetic screening
7. Language/communication assessment, such as articulation/oral motor skills and receptive/expressive skills

Developmental Stage

1. Preschool
   A. Early intervention
   B. Parental education and training
   C. Some eligibility of services
2. School age
   A. Increased eligibility for services (public, social, educational)
   B. Continued education and support of parents, including a focus on problem-solving skills and behavior management
3. Adolescence
   A. Expanding eligibility for services by focusing on adaptive skills development, prevocational skills, and vocational programming/education
   B. Clinical clarification of strengths/weaknesses as related to vocational training
   C. When possible include adolescent in treatment planning
   D. Monitor for development of comorbid diagnoses such as depression or seizures
4. Adult
   A. Identification of community resources
   B. Support in planning long-term care, including employment, residential care, social support/activities, and family support

DISRUPTIVE BEHAVIOR DISORDERS

Though ADHD is a part of the neurodevelopmental disorders section it has been annexed into the disruptive behavior disorders section because it is characterized by the feature of impulsivity. Therefore, from a treatment perspective, treatment planning focuses on behavioral self-control as does oppositional defiant disorder (ODD) and impulse control disorders.

ATTENTION-DEFICIT HYPERACTIVITY DISORDER AND OPPOSITIONAL DEFIANT DISORDER

There is somewhat of a continuum and overlap between manifestations of ADHD and ODD. ADHD may be an underlying issue in ODD. A careful assessment taking this into consideration will allow the therapist to rule out the ADHD diagnosis in these instances. Because of the commonality in behavioral symptomology, the treatment focus and objectives will be offered as a single section to draw from based on the needs of the case. Both of these diagnoses include emotional and behavioral symptoms that can vary in severity. Risk factors, for different reasons, include child temperament, parenting issues (child experience of abuse, neglect, harsh or inconsistent discipline, or lack of adequate parental supervision) and other family issues (parental/family discord, mental health problems, or substance use disorders, SUDs) (Mayo Clinic February 6, 2014). The clinical challenge is separating the active and deliberate argumentativeness and defiance versus impulsivity.

Medscape (2015) sets forth that in circumstances where a child with a difficult temperament or ADHD grows up in an environment with harsh, punitive, or inconsistent parenting, there is an escalated risk of the child developing ODD. Additionally, Zwi, Jones, Thorgaard, York, and Dennis (2011) highlight the importance of educating parents for a positive effect on child behavior.

ADHD children are at risk for delinquent behaviors because they do not consistently demonstrate behaviors that will naturally elicit positive reinforcement. Instead they tend to receive negative feedback from their peers and adults. In an effort to fit in with a peer group, they may find acceptance with children/adolescents who have obvious behavioral problems. Generally, there is behavioral evidence of difficulties associated with ADHD in all settings (home, work, school, social), and symptoms are usually worse in situations requiring sustained attention. Although the excessive motor activity characterizing ADHD often subsides prior to adolescence, the attention deficit frequently persists. For more information on ADHD visit the following websites:

1. National Resource Center on ADHD (www.help4adhd.org)
2. Children and adults with attention-deficit/hyperactivity disorder (CHADD) (www.chadd.org)

In cases where ADHD is suspected, first refer to a physician for a medical exam to rule out endocrine problems or allergies and to address the issue of medication. Rule out mood disorders and abuse. In cases where ODD is a potential diagnosis, rule out family systems/high contact relationships/caretaker issues such as substance abuse, sexual abuse, physical/emotional abuse, and ADHD.

Disorders of behavior are treated with a focus on behavioral interventions. Therefore, therapy encompasses these basic features:

1. Highly structured
2. Moderate in supportiveness (some attention to past patterns/difficulties)
3. May include modalities of individual, family, and self-help groups
4. Physical examination with minimal use of medication (not a substitute for modifying inappropriate behavior)
5. Brief duration of treatment

Treatment Goals

1. Assess for referral for medication evaluation
2. Enhance parent education regarding familial and clinical aspects of the disorder and behavioral management

3. Collateral cooperation in behavioral management with teaching staff
4. Develop responsible behavior and self-respect
5. Develop appropriate social skills
6. Improve communication
7. Decrease defensiveness
8. Improve self-esteem
9. Improve coping
10. Improve problem solving
11. Improve insight
12. Improve impulse control
13. Anger management
14. Eliminate potential for violence

Treatment Focus and Objectives

1. Assess and Refer for Medication Evaluation
   A. If parents have a negative or resistant response to medication, direct them to some appropriate reading material and suggest that they meet with a physician specializing in this disorder before they make a decision.
2. Parent Education
   A. Overview giving the defining criteria of the specific disorder, explore how the family is affected and how they respond, etiology, developmental influences, prognosis, a selection of reading materials, and information on a community support group, if available.
   B. Parent effectiveness training. Training to include parenting skills in behavioral modification, contingency planning, positive reinforcement, appropriate limit setting and consequences, encouraging self-esteem, disciplining in a manner that fosters the development of responsibility and respect for others. Consistency is imperative to successful behavioral change and management. In addition to this parenting skill set the repertoire for boundaries with children should be addressed. Conceptually this reinforces self-responsibility with the associated recognition that every choice bears a consequence—some positive and some negative, but that the child plays the essential role in selecting the outcome from their environment. The lesson is a very positive one regarding personal power and choices.
   C. Dysfunctional family dynamics.
      1. Explore and identify family roles
      2. Identify modification and changes of person's role in family
      3. Identify the various roles played by family members and the identified patient, and modify or change as needed in accordance with appropriate family dynamics and behavior
      4. Facilitate improved communication
         a. Slow down and listen. Encourage a habit of slowing down by taking a few breaths before you talk.
         b. Observe others. Learn from others who have good skills such as being a good listener or making positive statement to others.
         c. Allow for equal time. The best conversations allow for equal exchanges. Have fun practicing to increase awareness for the pattern of each person in a conversation speaking for approximately equal lengths of time.
         d. Practice echoing/reflecting. Learn to listen by reflecting to others what they have said. This skill also allows for direct feedback and correcting errors of interpretation.
         e. Role-play. Rehearse communication techniques to instill new skills. Make it fun by integrating the practice into fun and interesting activities.
      5. Clarify differences between being a parent and a child in the family system, along with role expectation. "Boundaries with children" exemplifies role expectations and self-responsibility. Boundaries can be conceptualized as a line draw around one person which defines where they begin and end. Calm, thoughtful, constructive parenting takes place with clear boundaries. For example:
         a. Avoid doing for a child what they can do for themselves.
         b. Be interested in their thoughts and ideas, but avoid influencing them by intrusiveness or manipulation.

      c. Be consistent in maintaining boundaries as parents with a child.
        1. Parents need to be aligned as one. They are on the same page and consistently set limits.
        2. Avoid making a child the focus all the time.
      d. Don't share adult information with a child—allow a child to be a child and not worry about adult concerns or issues. Children are not a parent's friend or confidant.
      e. When a child is experiencing emotional distress and the parent(s) respond with similar distress, it makes the parent someone to take care of rather than to rely on.
      f. Every challenge is an opportunity. A child needs to be allowed to learn from its own experiences.
  6. Explore the necessity of out of home placement if parents are unable to effectively manage and support behavior change or are actual facilitators of antisocial behaviors. Depending on severity of behaviors, it may require placement for monitoring to prevent risk of harm to self or others.

3. Teachers and Parents
   A. Define classroom rules and expectations regularly.
     1. Make a list of expectations
     2. Educate and reinforce the principle of "respect"
     3. Identify and reinforce positive choices, and the consistency of being held accountable will increase understanding, empathy, and thinking first
   B. Break down goals into manageable steps and time frames depending on the task. Time frames could be 15 min, 30 min, 1 h, a day, or a month. Be encouraging by providing frequent feedback.
   C. Give choices whenever possible.
   D. Provide short exercise breaks between work periods.
   E. Use a time to encourage staying on task. If they finish a task before the allotted time, reinforce their behavior and direct into rewarding activities.
   F. Facilitate the development of social skills.
     1. Support friendships.
     2. Model respectful behavior.
     3. Facilitate development of relationship management skills. For example, taking time to cool down and learning to apologize.
     4. Role-model how to give compliments.
   G. Encourage specific behaviors associated with identified individualized needs.
   H. Develop contracts when appropriate. It will also help parents reinforce the teacher's program.
   I. Develop a secret signal that can be used as a reminder to stay on task, which will avoid embarrassment and low self-esteem.
   J. Facilitate the development of self-monitoring so that students can pace themselves and stay on task, as well as self-reinforce for progress.
   K. Structure the environment to reduce distracting stimuli.
   L. Separate these students from peers who may be encouraging inappropriate behavior.
   M. Highlight or underline important information.
   N. Use a variety of high-interest modes to communicate effectively (auditory, visual, hands-on, etc.).
   O. Position these students close to resources/sources of information.
   P. Consistency is imperative.
   Q. Work collaterally with all professionals to develop an individualized cognitive-behavioral program.
   R. "Green time" (Weider & Greenspan, 2001). Exercising is one of the easiest and most effective ways to reduce the symptoms of attention-deficit disorder (ADD)/ADHD. Physical activity immediately boosts the brain's dopamine, norepinephrine, and serotonin levels—all of which affect focus and attention. Activities that require close attention to body movements, such as dance, gymnastics, martial arts, and skateboarding, are particularly good for kids with ADD/ADHD. Team sports are also a good choice. The social element keeps them interesting.

4. Lack of Respect and Responsibility
   A. Have the child define these terms accurately (may need support or use of external resources) and compare the working definitions to his/her behavior as well as developing appropriate behavioral changes. This may be beneficial in facilitating thoughts associated with "how they want to be known."
   B. Facilitate the concept of choices related to consequences, and acceptance of consequences as taking responsibility for one's own actions.

C. Have the child identify how they are affected by the behavior of others and how others are affected negatively by their behaviors. Clarify that they only have control over their own behaviors.

D. Work with parents to clarify rules, expectations, choices, and consequences.

E. An aspect of self-respect and self-responsibility are good self-care behaviors/routines.

    1. Sleep (HelpGuide.Org—retrieved from the web, September 15, 2015)

    Regular good quality sleep can lead to significant improvement in the symptoms of ADD/ADHD. However, it is not uncommon that children with ADD/ADHD to have problems getting to sleep at night. Sleep difficulties may be due to stimulant medications. Regardless of the underlying reason the following may help:

      a. Set a regular bedtime (and make it consistent).

      b. If sleep is disturbed by background noise, try a sound machine or a fan for white noise.

      c. No electronics (TV, computer, video games, iPhone) at least an hour before bed.

      d. Limit physical activity in the evening to minimize overstimulating.

    2. Nutrition (HelpGuide.Org—retrieved from the web, September 15, 2015)

    Just as with sleep hygiene, consistency in mealtime can make a difference when it comes to managing ADD/ADHD.

      a. Schedule regular meals or snacks no more than 3 h apart. This will help maintain a child's blood sugar level, thus minimizing irritability and supporting concentration and focus.

      b. Including a little protein and complex carbohydrates at each meal or snack is beneficial. These foods will help a child feel more alert while decreasing hyperactivity.

      c. It may be beneficial to get a referral to a dietician from the primary care physician to identify healthy choices and assure a balanced diet, reinforcing is the important role of their physician.

5. Dysfunctional Social Interaction

    A. Model appropriate behaviors/responses for a variety of situations and circumstances. Provide situations or vignettes to learn from.

    B. Provide positive feedback and constructive education about their interaction.

    C. Identify manipulative or exploitive interaction. Explore intention behind interaction and give information and reinforcement on how to get needs met appropriately.

    D. Focus on the positive demonstrations of interaction over negative ones when reinforcing behavioral change.

    E. Identify reasons for inability to form close interpersonal relationships to increase awareness and to develop choices for change.

    F. Identify behaviors that allow one person to feel close or comfortable with another person versus distancing behaviors.

6. Impaired Communication Skills

    A. Teach assertive communication skills

    B. Encourage appropriate expression of thoughts and feelings

    C. Model and practice communication responses (verbal and nonverbal) for various situations and circumstances

    D. Positive feedback and reinforcement

7. Defensive Behaviors

    A. Increase awareness for defensive tendencies by defining with examples and encouraging the identification of similar behaviors of his/her own

    B. In a nonthreatening way, explore with these individuals any past feedback that they have been given from others about how others perceive them and what contributes to that perception

    C. Focus on positive attributions to encourage positive self-esteem

    D. Encourage acceptance of responsibility for one's own behavior

    E. Identify the relationship between feelings of inadequacy and defensiveness

    F. Improve management of disappointment

      1. Facilitate putting things in perspective

        a. Facilitate appropriate reactions versus overreactions

        b. Facilitate realistic expectations

        c. Model how and when to appropriately express strong emotion

2. Acknowledge feelings, but focus on the positive
   a. Encourage them to put their disappointment into words
   b. Acknowledge their point of view (sad, angry, etc.), but help them to use a difficult situation to learn from or create new opportunities
G. Positive feedback and reinforcement

8. Low Self-esteem (Worth and Capability)
   A. Through a positive therapeutic relationship, be accepting, respectful, and ask them often what their views are about issues, affirming the importance of what they have to offer and that they are valued.
   B. Support and encourage appropriate risk taking toward desired goals.
   C. Encourage their participation in problem solving.
      1. Identify what the problem is, choices for resolving, make a decision, take action
      2. Identify what they can and cannot control
      3. Recognize that mistakes are opportunities—learn something new (small success can bring feelings of competence)
   D. Reframe mistakes in an effort toward change as an opportunity to learn more and benefit from experiences. Encourage taking responsibility for one's own mistakes.
   E. Encourage self-care behaviors: grooming/hygiene, exercise, no use of substances, good nutrition, engaging in appropriate pleasurable activities.
   F. Identify self-improvement activities; behavioral change, education, growth experiences.
   G. Identify and develop healthy, appropriate values.
   H. Identify strengths and develop a form of daily affirmations for reinforcing positive self-image.
   I. Identify desired changes. Be sensitive, realistic, and supportive in development of shaping changes.
   J. Facilitate assertive communication and positive/appropriate body language.
   K. Educate about the destructiveness of negative self-talk.
      1. Identify negative self-statements and create beneficial substitute statements
   L. Create opportunities for child to show his/her abilities.
   M. Notice examples of ability and point them out. Build on strengths.
   N. Positively reinforce their efforts and accomplishments. Praise is essential to behavior shaping.
   O. Recognizing and modifying negative self-talk. Clarify associated realistic expectations and limitations.

9. Ineffective Coping
   A. Provide appropriate physical activity to decrease body tension and offer a positive choice with a sense of well-being
   B. Set limits on manipulative behavior and give appropriate consequences
   C. Facilitate change in coping by not participating in arguing, debating, excessive explaining, rationalizing, or bargaining with the person
   D. Develop realistic expectations and limitations
   E. Facilitate how to effectively deal with feeling to run away
   F. Encourage identification of improved coping strategies
      1. Identify the nature and extent of running away
      2. Clarify and interpret the dynamics of running away (why?)
      3. Work through the identified dynamics
      4. Facilitate the individual to identify the signs of impending runaway behavior
      5. Facilitate identification and implementation of alternative solutions to running away
   G. Lying
      Educate parents that an attitude "that they will grow out of it" is a dangerous attitude. Lying is an unacceptable behavior that warrants zero tolerance. To help a child connect choice-consequences associated with lying. Privileges should be removed and consistency is essential. Trust is an imperative factor in healthy relationships. As is the case in most discipline issues, it may be harder for the parent than the child, but the child is depending on the parent to reinforce their development as a respectful, responsible, and trustworthy family member and person.

1. Identify the nature and extent of lying.
2. Confront lying behavior. Assert the importance of behavior matching what is verbalized.
3. Clarify and interpret the dynamics of lying.
4. Work through the dynamics of lying.
5. Facilitate the development of a behavioral management program for lying. Monitor accurate reporting of information and encourage the person to make amends with those lied to whenever possible.

H. Focus on positive coping efforts
I. Encourage honest, appropriate, and direct expression of emotions
J. Facilitate the development of being able to delay gratification without resorting to manipulative or acting-out behaviors
K. Have child verbalize alternative, socially acceptable coping skills

10. Ineffective Problem Solving
A. Encourage the identification of causes of problems and influencing factors.
B. Encourage the identification of needs and goals. Facilitate, with the individual's input, the objectives, expected outcomes, and prioritization of issues.
C. Encourage the exploration of alternative solutions.
D. Provide opportunities for practicing problem-solving behavior.
E. Explore goals, and problem-solve how to reach goals.
F. Teach comprehensive thinking that encompasses creative and critical thinking. Learning new ways of thinking is best accomplished when it is associated with some cognitive exercise or behavioral activity to reinforce it being used in real time.
   1. Creative thinking—the ability to look at a situation in many different ways, thus becoming a flexible thinker with willingness to take appropriate risks, to experiment, and to even make mistakes.
      a. Brainstorm—this can be a fun activity. One way to proceed is to ask a question that has many solutions.
      b. Reflect—this concept requires flexible thinking, which can be encouraged by requesting comment on the possibilities or view of an object or situation in new ways.
   2. Critical thinking
      a. Challenge—encourage the practice critical and logical thinking. This can be done by asking open-ended questions, thus reinforcing approaching an answer with a variety of possibilities.
      b. Listen instead of responding and allow time for thinking. Asking questions that don't make sense encourages critical thinking and the expression of ideas.
   3. The role of a parent or teacher in fostering problem solving by having a responsive and accepting attitude
      a. Provide time everyday for making choices, choosing activities based on interests, etc.
      b. Observe their interactions and dilemmas to encourage problem-solving efforts and help them accomplish their goals
      c. Reinforce their solutions—as a validation that their ideas and efforts are valued
      d. Ask open-ended questions about activities as a way to extend the practice of creative problem solving
   4. Nurturing problem-solving skills
      a. As an observer step back and watch independent problem solving to reinforce confidence in their ability to problem-solve. Let the process unfold.
      b. Acknowledge their effort, demonstrating that what they are doing is important.
      c. Create a safe and encouraging environment to increase the freedom to express ideas without fear of being wrong or embarrassed.
      d. Provide opportunities for open-ended play activities to facilitate solving their own problems and plenty of time to test out the possibilities.
      e. Watch for when they are involved in problem solving and interject thought provoking questions to encourage new ways of thinking.
      f. Emphasize the vocabulary of problem solving such as problem, think, ideas, brainstorm, choices, goals, solve.
      g. As a role model be willing to make mistakes so that it can be seen that adults make mistakes, and ask them to help find a solution to the problem.

11. Poor Insight
   A. Increase understanding of relationship between behaviors and consequences
   B. Increase understanding of the thoughts/feelings underlying choices made
   C. Facilitate problem solving appropriate alternative responses to substitute for negative choices
   D. Encourage thinking before acting

12. Poor Impulse Control
   A. Increase awareness and give positive feedback when the person is able to demonstrate control.
   B. Explore alternative ways to express feelings. Developing an understanding of the difference between feelings and behaviors, i.e., it is okay to feel mad, but not okay to hit.
      1. Identify choices of dealing with feelings without reacting.
   C. Facilitate the identification of particular behaviors that are causing problems.
      1. Identify option for appropriate behaviors.
   D. Facilitate identification of methods to delay response and encourage thinking of various responses with associated consequences.
   E. Teach listening skills. Learning to listen to direction will decrease impulsivity. Have them repeat back what they heard before they take action.
   F. Teach problem solving—it will help them to think before they act. It will also support developing the skill to develop several solutions to a problem and analyze which solution is likely to have the best outcome.
   G. Teach anger management so that they can learn to calm themselves down when upset.
   H. Provide structure that is consistent and routine = less opportunity for chaos.
      1. Set clear limits and repeat the rules often.
   I. Practice delayed gratification. Tell them about something fun coming up to give a child the needed opportunity to practice waiting in patience.
   J. Encourage physical activity to improve their ability to manage impulses. Being a bundle of energy increases the likelihood of acting without thinking.
   K. Play impulse control games that provide a child a fun way to practice impulse control (Simon Says, Red Light Green Light, Follow the Leader, etc.).

13. Poor Anger Management
   Anger is a normal emotion. Uncontrolled anger can lead to aggression.
   A. Identify antecedents and consequences of angry outbursts.
   B. Facilitate understanding of anger within the normal range of emotions and appropriate responses to feelings of anger.
      1. Expressing anger and understanding emotion
      2. Encourage the appropriate use of words to express their emotions
      3. Create additional understanding about the difference of emotions by inquiring how they are feeling when they are calm and happy
   C. Suppressing anger and letting go. Identify issues of anger from the past and facilitate resolution or letting go or dealing with a real-time issue causing anger.
      1. Recognize anger and convert the anger into something positive and constructive
      2. Draw a picture of how the emotion feels
      3. Facilitate learning how to calm down—taking time out to let anger go while thinking about constructive choices
         a. Taking deep breaths
         b. Going for a walk or participating in other physical activity
         c. Spending time alone being quiet
         d. Doing yoga or martial arts
      4. Finding a solution to the anger. Do not reward temper tantrums which is reinforcing. If they break a toy it is not replaced. If they break something belonging to someone else they must pay/earn by chores to replace the object.
   D. Identify the difference between anger and rage.
   E. Identify affect of anger on close, intimate relationships.
      1. Talk about the importance of using words appropriate to express emotion
      2. Discuss the two outcomes of behavior—pushing people away or bringing them closer

    F. Identify role of anger as a coping mechanism or manipulation.

    G. Facilitate the taking of responsibility for feelings and expressions of anger.

    H. Problem-solve current issues of anger to resolve conflicts.

    I. Positive feedback and reinforcement for efforts and accomplishments.

14. Potential for Violence

    A. Assess for signs and symptoms of acting out

    B. Maintain a safe distance and talk in a calm voice

    C. Provide a safe, nonthreatening environment with a minimum of aversive stimulation

    D. Use verbal communication and alternative stress and anger releasers to prevent violent acting out

    E. Anger management

        1. Identify the nature, extent, and precipitants of the aggressive behavior (i.e., is the behavior defensive, etc.)

        2. Facilitate identification and increased awareness of the escalators of aggressive behavior

        3. Clarify and interpret the dynamics of aggressive impulses and behavior

        4. Work through the dynamics of aggression

    F. Reinforce the use of the skills that the person has developed

    G. Identify and discuss alternative ways of expressing their emotion appropriately to avoid negative consequences

    H. Encourage the individual to verbalize the wish or need to be aggressive rather than to act on the impulse

    I. If the child demonstrates the tolerance of intervention, provide a recreational outlet for aggressive impulses

    J. Facilitate the implementation of alternative actions to aggressive behavior

    K. At a later time when the threat of acting out has passed, help the child to benefit from the experience by reviewing the circumstances, choices, and different points of possible intervention and what would have been helpful to reinforce problem-solving efforts

Additional Considerations

Regarding culturally diverse and inner-city dwellers, it is imperative to obtain information on the family and neighborhood:

1. Inquire about the possibility of lead intoxication and malnutrition
2. Ask about parental abuse of substances and antisocial behavior/personality disorder (including family members and peer reference group)
3. In the culturally diverse, assess the level of cultural tolerance for certain behaviors
4. Determine if their environment demands physical strength and aggression as survival factors
5. What is the impact of social/economic pressures on lying, truancy, stealing, early substance abuse, sexual behavior, inconsistent/absent parental figures (i.e., single parent who works and is not available), and their values/beliefs

    For the caveat of ODD the challenge for parents is to persevere, redirect, and conquer. Just as with ADHD it requires a commitment and consistent follow-though. Improving parent skills to more effectively manage ODD and necessary behavior-modification requirement

1. Give effective time outs and pursue time out in a nonemotional–nonreactive manner
2. Avoid power struggles
3. Remain calm and nonemotional when confronting opposition
4. Recognize and praise good behavior and positive attributes (catch a child being good)
5. Offer acceptable choices, providing the child with some control

*Most importantly is the lesson that comes with understanding that every choice bears a consequence—some positive and some negative. It is the value found that comes with the responsibility of having the freedom of making choices.

6. Limit consequences to ones that can be consistently reinforced and to last for a reasonable and limited amount of time
7. Recommend consideration of family therapy to support the family system structure, alignment of parents, and reinforcing boundaries
8. Encourage the development of cooperative family activities both work (chores) and play that are a consistent part of family routines

Many children diagnosed with ADD, ADHD, or other behavioral disorders may actually be manic depressive. Bipolar disorder in children (Medscape, 2015):

1. May strike as early as age 7
2. May be prone to rapid cycling
3. May go untreated for years

Similarities between hyperactivity and mania in children are that the children are

1. Excessively active
2. Irritability
3. Easily distracted

However, children with bipolar disorder may also exhibit

1. Elated mood
2. Inappropriate giggles
3. Grandiosity
4. Flights of ideas
5. Racing thoughts
6. Decreased need for sleep

*Children are not prone to suicide. Caution parents that if they suspect suicidal ideation or self-destructive behaviors that it is essential to seek professional help as quickly as possible.

IMPULSE CONTROL DISORDERS

The essential feature of impulse control disorders is the failure to resist an impulse, drive, or temptation that is harmful to the person or to others. DSM 5 (APA, 2013) defines these disorders as demonstrating problems in the self-control of emotions and behaviors. Unique to impulse control disorders is a manifestation of behaviors that violate the rights of others that places them in conflict with societal norms and authority figures. Even though there is an increasing sense of tension prior to the act, the act may or may not be premeditated. Additionally, there may or may not be an awareness for resistance to the impulse.

IMPULSE CONTROL DISORDERS

Goals

1. Eliminate danger to others
2. Eliminate danger to self
3. Improve coping skills
4. Improved stress-management skills
5. Improve self-esteem
6. Relapse prevention

Treatment Focus and Objectives

1. **Risk for Violence Toward Others**
   A. Reduce environmental stimuli
   B. Clarify positive regard and support, but stress that aggressive behaviors are unacceptable
   C. Remove all potentially dangerous objects
   D. Facilitate identification of the underlying source(s) of anger
   E. Remain calm when there is inappropriate behavior to support and role-model containing impulses
   F. Encourage use of physical exercise to relieve physical tension
   G. Facilitate recognition of warning signs of increasing tension
   I. Facilitate identification of choices
   J. Clarify the connection between behavior and consequences
   K. Positive feedback and reinforcement

2. **Risk for Self-destructive Behavior**
   A. Assess
      1. Mental status
      2. History of self-destructive behaviors
      3. Recent crisis, loss
      4. Substance abuse
      5. Plan
      6. Means
      7. Quality of support system
   B. Provide safe environment and intervene to stop self-destruction
   C. Provide behaviors (remove dangerous objects, monitor, etc.; the person may require hospitalization)
   D. Facilitate identification of environmental or emotional triggers associated with self-destructive impulse
   E. Facilitate person to identify areas of desired change
   F. Develop a plan for behavior modifications to reach goals of desired behavior change
   G. Encourage appropriate venting of thoughts and feelings
   H. Avoid focus and reinforcement of negative behaviors
   I. Focus on efforts and accomplishments
   J. Positive feedback and reinforcement

3. **Ineffective Coping**
   A. Increase awareness and insight of their behaviors
   B. Facilitate clarification of rules, values—right and wrong
   C. Encourage the person to take responsibility
   D. Confront denial related to behaviors/choices
   E. Facilitate development of understanding the relationship of behaviors to consequences
   F. Explore and clarify the person's desire and motivation to become a productive member of society
   G. Clarify for person socially acceptable behaviors versus nonsocially acceptable behaviors

H. Facilitate increased sensitivity to others

I. Facilitate increased awareness for how others experience the person and how they interpret the person's behaviors

J. Clarify that it is the person but rather the person's behavior that is unacceptable

K. Facilitate increasing ability to delay gratification

L. Model and practice acceptable behaviors over a range of situations

M. Positive feedback and reinforcement for efforts and accomplishments

4. Ineffective Stress Management

A. Teach relaxation techniques
   1. Progressive muscle relaxation
   2. Visual imagery/meditation

B. Self-care (exercise, nutrition, utilization of resources)

5. Low Self-esteem

A. Focus on strengths and accomplishments

B. Avoid focus on past failures (unless utilized in a positive manner to facilitate hopefulness and the learning of new behaviors)

C. Identify areas of desired change and objectives to meet those goals

D. Encourage independent effort and accepting responsibility

E. Teach assertive communication and appropriate setting of limits and boundaries

F. Positive feedback and reinforcement for efforts and accomplishments

6. Relapse Prevention

A. Self-monitoring

B. Reframe regression issues as an opportunity for taking responsibility and effectively problem solving necessary for behavioral change

C. Journal writing to monitor progress and any other changes in behavior

D. Participation in community groups or utilization of other supportive resources

It is necessary to delineate separate characteristics and clarify commonality among the disorders of impulse control to determine the course of treatment. Additionally, impulse control disorder(s) and obsessive–compulsive disorder (OCD) have traditionally been viewed as two very different disorders, the former one is generally driven by the desire to avoid harm whereas the later one driven "by reward seeking behavior," and they are driven by different processes. Impulse control disorder and SUDs are driven by the compulsive process whereas OCD is a progressive dysfunction of the ventral striatal circuit (AHRQ, 2008, 2011).

These individuals do not often present for treatment of their own volition. As per the DSM 5 (APA, 2013), five behavioral stages characterize impulsivity: an impulse, growing tension, pleasure on acting, relief from the urge, and finally guilt. The signs and symptoms of impulse control disorders will vary based on the age of the children or adolescents suffering from them, the actual type of impulse control that they are struggling with, the environment in which they are living, and whether they are male or female. The psychosocial treatment approach is CBT.

Behaviors characterized by impulsivity and impulse control include the following:

1. Pathological Gambling.

A. Systematic desensitization

B. Aversive therapy

C. Cover sensitization

D. Imaginal desensitization

E. Stimulus control

F. Psychoeducation
   1. Cognitive restructuring
   2. Relapse prevention

G. Refer for medication evaluation

2. Kleptomania is characterized by an impulsive urge to steel for the sake of gratification. Kleptomania is thought to be the underlying cause of a small percentage of acts of shoplifting.
   A. Pattern of being unable to resist the impulse to steal, even with items of no immediate use or monetary value
   B. Increasing sense of tension before acting
   C. No planning or assistance from others

3. Pyromania is characterized by impulsive and repetitive urges to deliberately set fires. Under 5% of children and adolescents suffer from pyromania and more prominently in juvenile and adolescent males than females.
   A. Pattern of behavior to resist impulse to set fires
   B. Increasing sense of tension before acting
   C. An experience of intense pleasure/release at time of committing the act
   D. No motivation such as political action/monetary gain involved
   E. CBT treatment of children may be effective

4. Intermittent explosive disorder is the experience of recurrent aggressive episodes that are out of proportion to the identified stressor associated with the episode.
   A. Several discrete episodes of extremely aggressive acts or destruction of property
   B. Act is grossly out of proportion to precipitating social or psychological stressors
   C. No impulsivity or aggressiveness between episodes
   D. No specific organic disorder associated (such as a brain tumor)
   E. Psychosocial treatment
      1. Facilitate understanding and control of thoughts and behaviors
      2. Focus on conscious thought patterns and overt behaviors
         a. Recognize onset of urge or impulse to explode
            1. May uncover underlying feelings and reasons behind anger and rage
         b. Identify the triggers or circumstances associated with onset
         c. Develop ways to prevent explosive behavior from occurring
      3. Family or marriage counseling
      4. Attending 12-step meeting such as Alcoholics Anonymous (AA) if alcohol is involved or other pertinent support groups
      5. Refer for medication evaluation

5. Sexual compulsion is associated with an increased urge in sexual thoughts and behaviors. Partner selection may be risky with an increased possibility of contracting a sexually transmitted disease (STD) and becoming depressed. More males than females engage in sexual compulsion. This compulsion may be integrated with various media including the Internet.
   A. Identify triggers to sexual behaviors
   B. Reshaping cognitive distortions
   C. Explore core conflicts; themes of shame avoidance, anger, and impaired self-esteem
   D. Focus on controlling compulsive sexual behaviors
   E. Relapse prevention
   F. Family or conjoint therapy to restore trust, minimize shame/guilt, and establish a healthy sexual relationship between partners
   G. Refer for medication evaluation

6. Internet addiction is the most recently acknowledged impulse control disorder seen as excessive and damaging use of the Internet and increased amount of time involved in social media at a pathological degree and involving chatting, web-surfing, gambling, shopping, or exploring pornographic websites. Though more evident in males, females are increasingly engaging in this impulse control disorder as well. The cognitive-behavioral approach to treatment would include the following:
   A. Practice opposite time of Internet use to disrupt schedule and patterns
   B. Use external stoppers, i.e., real events or activities that disrupt patterns of use
   C. Set goals with regard to amount of time of Internet use

D. Abstain from specific applications/sites

E. Use reminder cards to serve as a cur to remind the person of the cost of the behavior and the benefit of changing it

F. Develop personal inventory listing all activities used to engage as a deflection from compulsive behavior

G. Family or marriage therapy for accountability and regaining trust

H. Support group

7. Compulsive shopping demonstrated by a frequent irresistible urge to shop even if the purchases are not needed or cannot be afforded. Vastly, more females than males engage in this impulse control disorder.

A. Exposure and response prevention

B. Cognitive-restructuring

C. Covert sensitization

D. Stimulus control

E. Relapse prevention

SEPARATION ANXIETY

The most prominent feature of this disorder is excessive anxiety concerning separation from those to whom the child is attached. Additional symptoms of separation anxiety include irrational fears, nightmares, emotional conflicts, and refusal to attend school. Explore the presence of domestic issues that are related to or are exacerbating the child's emotional and behavioral problems. Separation anxiety is manifested in a range between children from becoming hysterical for a brief period of time once they lose sight of a parent to a more chronic anxiety state.

Separation anxiety is normal in very young children (those between 8 and 14 months old). They often go through a phase when they are "clingy" and afraid of unfamiliar people and places. When this fear occurs in a child aged over 6 years, is excessive, and lasts longer than 4 weeks, the child may have separation anxiety disorder. In other words, separation anxiety is viewed as being normal up through the toddler stage of development. However, it is inappropriate for older children and may suggest the diagnosis of separation anxiety disorder. Some children also develop physical symptoms, such as headaches or stomachaches, at the thought of being separated. Functionally, the fear of separation causes great distress to the child and may interfere with the child's normal activities, such as going to school or playing with other children (ADAA, 2015; APA, 2015; WebMD, 2015).

SEPARATION ANXIETY

Goals

1. Support and educate parents regarding age-appropriate separation issues
2. Identify and resolve the events precipitating the anxiety
3. Decreased worrying
4. Improved coping
5. Consistent school attendance
6. Resolution of emotional conflict
7. Foster cooperative efforts with school personnel to effectively manage behavior
8. Parent education

Treatment Focus and Objectives

1. Educating parents regarding age-appropriate emotional separation. General parental patterns are helpful:
   A. Timely "good-bye" rituals. Provide the special aspects of good-bye.

*If parents linger in their good-bye, they are increasing the transition time and that equals increased anxiety. Children whose parents are overprotective may be more prone to separation anxiety.

    B. Be consistent. Avoid unexpected factors in the daily transition ritual. It needs to be the same "predictable" everyday. Predictability brings comfort. A routine builds trust. The consistency comforts because it is predictable which decreases fear—hence anxiety.

    C. Attention. During the process of separation provide full attention to the child. Be caring, loving, and affectionate. Then be timely—quick with the goodbye. Do not reinforce crying or tantrums. Leave as if that were not taking place and maintain the ritual.

    D. Keep your promise. To build trust and facilitate independence require that a child develop feelings of confidence in their ability to be without their parent. Do not "visit" to make sure everything is okay following a difficult transition. That will reinitiate the process and is very unfair to a child who has finally been calmed.

    E. Be specific using child terminology. For example, telling a child you will be returning at 12:30 would not carry the same meaning as "I will be here after lunch." That is time that a child can understand. If a parent is going to be gone for several days the terminology would be, for example if a parent was going to be gone 3 days it would be more meaningful for a child to say "I will be back in three sleeps" (or three nights sleep).

    F. Practice being apart. Make regular arrangements/playdates for a child to stay with a grandparent, family, family friends, or other trusted adults on a regular basis. This will prepare a child for developmental transitions such as daycare, preschool, or school.

*Reinforcing a child's independence and self-esteem through support and approval may help prevent future episodes of anxiety.

2. Exploring precipitating events such as recent losses, stressors, and changes
    A. Explore the issues of substance abuse in the home or other contributors of instability
    B. Explore parental conflict and spousal abuse issues
    C. Explore possible nightmares or fears associated with separation
    D. Explore the fear of being alone
3. Excessive worrying
    A. Explore fears related to concerns—rational and irrational
    B. Deal with issues related to rational fears and problem-solve more adaptive coping responses
    C. Confront irrational fears and beliefs
4. Ineffective coping
    A. Challenge irrational self-talk ("This is difficult but I can do it")
    B. Help the child identify what they can do (brainstorm possibilities with the child)
    C. Coping card (small index card) with short sentences of coping skills
        1. Reminder that physical symptoms are just anxiety
        2. Name the anxiety (pest, Mr. Worry, etc.)
        3. Anxiety won't hurt you and it doesn't last forever
        4. Positive coaching statements ("I can get through this")
        5. Reminder to use coping skills ("I can do my breathing," "I can decide the best way to do it")
    D. Distraction
        1. Cognitive distractions
            a. Humming
            b. Reading aloud
        2. Behavioral distraction
            a. Conscious effort to interact with others
            b. Redirect attention
        3. Physiological distraction
            a. Relaxation strategies

b. Exercise

c. Listening to music with headphones/ear buds.

5. Refusal to attend school

    A. Child needs to attend school

        1. Contact school to prepare the staff for the situation

        2. Parents and teachers to be consistent with a mutual understanding of the plan to manage the child

6. Difficulty dealing with emotional conflict

    A. Play therapy to identify and work through issues

    B. Relaxation training (with reaffirming messages such as "mommy is at work, but will be home at…, Everything is the way it is supposed to be…")

    C. Keeping a journal for venting feelings and for problem solving

    D. Encourage appropriate behavior; do not focus on negative behavior

    E. Explore presence of physical symptoms associated with anticipation of separation. Facilitate development of management skills to decrease symptoms

    F. Positive feedback and reinforcement

7. Teacher

    A. Inform teacher of difficulties that child is experiencing

    B. Coordinate consistency between efforts of school personnel and parents in being supportive to the child

8. Parent

    A. Acknowledge a child's fears and anxieties, but try to focus on any positive steps they may be taking

        1. Encourage them to take small steps toward facing fears

        2. Reinforce efforts and accomplishments

    B. Avoid labeling the child as shy or anxious

    C. Do not punish a child when they fail at their attempts

    D. Talk to the child about times they have been anxious

For separation anxiety this can be quite distressing for parents when they are leaving as they need to (i.e., work) and they hear the painful crying of their child and they feel they are abandoning their child. Most of the time the child adjust pretty quickly to their leaving, however, there are things to help both the parent and the child make this transition smoother. Offer parents the following recommendations:

1. Tell their child they are leaving and when they will be back.

2. Despite the temptation to sneak out, this is not recommended as it can add to fear and they will be more clingy next time and less prepared to let them out of their sight.

3. Make the goodbye quick and don't drag it out with long explanations they have no way of grasping nor are capable of rationalizing.

4. If the child is going to someone else's home or a play date at a park, etc., allow them to take something from home such as a teddy or blanket. These items (transitional objects that are comforting) will gradually phase out as the child becomes more comfortable with the setting.

5. Also spend a little time with them at the initial visit so that they have memories of it being safe and fun place to be left.

6. Remind parents that some anxiety is a normal part of child development.

While separation anxiety is seen as a normal response in young children, when it interferes with age-appropriate tasks (school attendance, peer interaction, daily activities, etc.), it needs to be dealt with.

Additional Considerations

For children residing in inner-city settings there may be legitimate issues of safety associated with high crime rates. Parents may be reluctant to let their children go outside and play without adult supervision, feeling anxious, and unsafe themselves. Therefore, the parents' level of anxiety and coping must be carefully evaluated. If there is an instance of actual harm or abrupt separation from a caretaking figure, a child's anxiety may increase.

Note that a diagnosis of anxiety disorder is only appropriate when a child's fear, anxiety, worries are persistent and unrealistic.

PEDIATRIC GENERALIZED ANXIETY DISORDER

To build upon the separation anxiety disorder, it may be beneficial to the clinician to highlight some additional treatment objectives for their work with children dealing with anxiety disorders. Therefore, this section will be a modified presentation of treatment goals and objectives from which the clinician can draw from and integrate into their treatment-planning framework. Education regarding the nature of anxiety will prepare parents to support their child's management of symptoms. For example, to identify and challenge irrational thinking, relaxation training, challenging fear and avoidance. It is also important to role-model for parents to implement and practice the management skills with their children.

Medscape (2015) defines pediatric generalized anxiety disorder as persistent, excessive, and unrealistic worry that is not focused on a particular object or situation. This disorder is characterized by irrational anxiety where there is no identifiable situation linked to the fear. Symptoms include worry about the future, low self-esteem (self-confidence), inability to effectively cope, need for reassurance, and somatic complaints.

PEDIATRIC GENERALIZED ANXIETY DISORDER

Goals

1. Correct irrational thinking
2. Improve coping
3. Decrease anxiety
4. Improve self-esteem
5. Improve self-management through identifying personal goals
6. Decrease avoidance
7. Improve peer relationships
8. Family education and intervention
9. Collateral contact with school personnel

Treatment Focus and Objectives

1. Irrational Beliefs
   A. Rule out trauma/abuse
   B. Explore parental experience of the world (e.g., mother may be over anxious, therefore the world is a dangerous place)
   C. Challenge irrational thoughts with reality
      • understand fear
      • normalize fear
      • manage fear
      1. Substitute irrational thoughts with rational thoughts
      2. Encourage appropriate risk taking (plugging in some guaranteed successes)
   D. Encourage appropriate risk taking
      1. Playtime plays a key role in the development of future life choices and satisfaction
      2. Encourage an increasing repertoire of physical, emotional, and social skills to increase confidence in problem solving that is challenging or risky
      3. What is a good risk? It is action, activity, or behavior that involves a "leap" toward the edge of safety and danger that maximizes learning, improves skill, self-esteem, and self-confidence
         a. Identify the risk, physical, social, emotional, intellectual
         b. Stay aware of potential dangers, and benefits, of moving forward or staying still and not finding out more

        c. Think through options

        d. Evaluate one's actions afterward. It is so important that children learn to take smart/calculated risks and to minimize taking poor risks

    E. Educate about anxiety symptoms

        1. Anxiety and worry are associated with restlessness or feeling keyed up or on edge, being easily fatigued, difficulty concentrating, irritability, muscle tension, and sleep disturbance

        2. Use positive self-talk to challenge and modify incorrect assumptions

        3. Educate parents

            a. Their coping styles will be modeled (social learning) so that they can assess and correct their styles of coping if it is negatively impacting their child

            b. Importance of practicing skills with their children

            c. Reinforcing efforts and accomplishments

2. Ineffective Coping

    A. Facilitate identification of feelings

        1. Give words to feelings to make them understandable and manageable

    B. Encourage appropriate venting of feelings

        1. Learning how to effectively use words

        2. Taking a time out to calm down to help thinking before acting

        3. Identifying what the goal is/outcome ("To talk about doing something different or taking turns?", "To let them know you did not like that behavior?)

            a. Facilitating conflict resolution and a constructive outcome, constructive outcome helps develop increased skills

    C. Identify effective solutions to anxiety-provoking situations

        1. Identify triggers

            a. If possible give a warning so that they can prepare and increase predictability

        2. What are the choices and what are the likely outcomes for each choice

        3. Take a quiet time to calm

            a. Talk through and process the strong emotion experienced

            b. Have they experienced a similar situation? If so, what did they learn? What will they do differently?

        4. Brainstorm strategies to deal with different anxiety-provoking situations

    D. Practice positive thinking and effective behaviors in a variety of situations

        1. Focus on the child and what they are going through. Be present and understanding.

        2. Model active listening. When they are done speaking, restate what they have said back to them—which will increase feelings of validation/understanding.

        3. Ask related questions to facilitate processing, identifying choices, and making a decision about how they want to respond to stressful/anxiety-provoking situations.

    E. Focus on efforts and accomplishments

    F. Positive feedback and reinforcement

3. Elevated Anxiety

    A. Teach relaxation techniques

        1. Progressive muscle relaxation

        2. Deep breathing

        3. Visualization that creates a feeling of calm, reassurance, and safety

        4. Imagining/in vivo exposure

        5. Model the successful management of anxiety (use of role-modeling)

    B. Challenge irrational beliefs and behavior

        1. Reframing and finding new interpretations

        2. Distinguishing facts from assumptions

        3. Teaching objective thinking which increases the ability to tolerate frustration and anxiety

        4. Determine if parents are "anxious worriers" and assess their ability to carry out interventions

        5. Predict resistance. What do the parents believe the child or others will do to sabotage efforts of change

    C. Facilitate development of appropriate substitute self-statements and behaviors for irrational ones

D. Create mastery experiences; they may need to be broken down into successive approximations

E. Educate/teach how to recognize early somatic and cognitive signs/manifestations of anxiety

F. Exercise encouraged to promote a sense of well-being

G. Limit caffeine intake

4. Low Self-esteem

A. Support and encourage appropriate risk-taking behavior

1. Let a child make their own age-appropriate choices to help them begin to connect their choices to consequences and feel more powerful

2. Encourage them to take the time to think of various choices and associated consequences to increase their decision-making skills

3. Allow a child to struggle with failure and disappointment

B. Encourage participation in problem solving

C. Reframe mistakes in an effort toward change and an opportunity to learn more

1. Allow a child to struggle with failure and disappointment

2. Offer appropriate support, encouragement, and praise their efforts

3. Encourage them to talk through what they learn

D. Identify desired areas of change

E. Identify strengths and develop daily affirmations for reinforcing positive self-image

F. Improve confidence and optimism

1. Don't rescue the child—kids need to know that it is okay to fail, as well as it being normal to feel sad, anxious, or angry

a. Children learn to succeed by overcoming obstacles, not by having them removed

b. Encourage the opportunity to play and take risks without feeling their parents will criticize or correct them for doing something wrong

c. Parents can make their own little mistakes (purposefully for learning) so that it can be witnessed by a child and normalized

2. Allow them to make decisions to gain confidence in their own judgment

a. Children can be overwhelmed by having too much control; therefore, decision-making options should be age appropriate.

1. Provide three options for them to choose from

b. Exercise boundaries with children. There are some decisions they don't get to make.

3. Focus on the glass half full principle

a. When disappointed help them look on the bright side

b. Encourage thinking about specific ways to improve a situation and bring them closer to their goals

c. Explain that everyone learns at their own pace and offer to spend extra time with them as needed

d. If they are disappointed acknowledge and validate their feelings, "I can see how you are disappointed, let's come up with a plan to improve or increase your chances for what is important to you"

4. Nurture special interests

a. It is important that a child be exposed to numerous activities

b. When they find something they love (have a passion for) feel proud of their expertise—it will benefit their success in other areas of their life

c. Quirky hobbies may be particularly helpful for a child who has a hard time fitting in

5. Promote problem solving

a. A child is confident when they are able to negotiate getting what they want

b. If a child asks for a solution ask them what they think would be a good way to deal with it

c. Create opportunities for problem solving

d. Reinforce efforts

6. Encourage helping others

a. Helping others and making a difference results in feelings of confidence

b. Assign household responsibilities

c. Request a child to assist in a project ("I could really use your help")

7. Find opportunities for a child to spend more time with adults

a. Spending time with older people expands a child's world

b. Encourage conversation with other adults, besides parents to offer a different way of thinking

c. Having a close relationship with a special grown-up (teacher, aunt/uncle, friend's parent, etc.) makes a child more resilient

8. Fantasize about the future

a. A child envisioning themselves doing something important or fulfilling when they grow up increases confidence.

b. It is mind enriching to talk to parents and other adults about how they chose their career.

c. Let a child dream about the possibilities—don't try to lower their expectations. Time and experience will help them develop more realistic goals over time.

G. Facilitate development of assertive communication

1. Support healthy risks. Cheer them on and avoid rescuing. Teach them to speak appropriately out loud about their thoughts and feelings.

2. Role-play scripts—making eye contact, speaking in a confident voice, and expressing their needs effectively.

a. Asking the teacher for help

b. Saying "no" to a peer regarding something they do not want to do

c. Appropriately saying what they want. Coach a child on how to speak up for themselves

H. Create opportunities for children to demonstrate strengths/desired changes

I. Feedback and positive reinforcement for efforts and changes

5. Overwhelmed and Lack of Focus

A. Identify strengths and interests

B. Identify goals

C. Break down objectives to goal into manageable steps

D. Focus on efforts and accomplishments

E. Positive feedback and reinforce

6. Avoidance

A. Teach assertive communication

B. Teach appropriate social skills

C. Role-play responses to variety of social situations

D. Systematic desensitization

1. Develop hierarchy of increasing anxiety-provoking situations to facilitate feelings of being in control

2. In vivo desensitization may work faster for some individuals than imaginal desensitization

E. Positive feedback and reinforcement for efforts and accomplishments

7. Difficult Peer Relationships

A. Encourage participation in activity where additional benefit is time shared with peers who have the same interest

B. Encourage participation in engaging situations or activities that offer distraction, thereby increasing mastery over anxiety while in the company of peers

C. Parents may have to be more accommodating and lack demonstrations of distress associated with accommodating

8. Family Intervention/Education

The importance of parent/family participation in treatment should not be minimized for its significant benefit for challenging irrational beliefs, skill development, symptom management, encouragement, and reinforcing efforts/progress/change.

A. Refer to primary care physician for a physical examination if somatic complaints are present to rule out any organic basis for complaints

B. Explore what they may be doing to reinforce the beliefs and behaviors

C. Explore possibility of parental overconcern on child as a deflective response to avoid their own relationship issues, or is this the only method they have for joining?

D. Strengthen the relationship with siblings, if present

E. Facilitate appropriate parental focus on the child's behaviors

F. Educate parents regarding needs for emotional availability, limits/boundaries, encouragement, and positive reinforcement

9. Collateral Contact With Teacher (WebMD, August 2015)
   A. Monitor withdrawal from age appropriate activities and collaborate with parents to problem-solve
   B. Work with school toward mastery behavior versus concern for anxious behavior
   C. Reinforce for efforts and accomplishments

According to Keeton, Kolos, and Walkup (2009)

1. Fears and anxieties of family members constitute a factor in whether or not to treat the fears and anxieties of a child (could be sabotaging/unconsciously undermining)
2. In the vast majority of cases of child anxiety, there is a positive correlation between parental anxiety and child anxiety
3. This correlation between parental and child anxiety demonstrates stronger lies for younger children than older children

Additional Considerations

1. Assess parental response to new people and situations
   A. Modeling responses to children is significant in teaching children how to cope
   B. Level of anxiety of parents and their response
2. Assess
   A. Parental encouragement/reassurance of appropriate risk-taking behavior
   B. Resolution to distressing situations—learning/increased awareness versus appropriate distrust
3. Work with parents to help them understand their child's behavioral and emotional reactions and the role they can play in modification of dysfunctional behavior and ineffective coping

FEEDING AND EATING DISORDERS

Eating disorders are complex illnesses, and concurrent diagnoses are very common. As a result, eating disorders often require more than one type of treatment. All eating disorders feature serious disturbances in eating behaviors and weight regulation. Additionally, they are associated with a vast range of adverse psychological, physical, and social consequences. The psychological effects of an EDO on mood and feelings are often seen in depression, panic, obsessions, and compulsions. The most effective and long-lasting treatment for an eating disorder is some form of psychotherapy or counseling, coupled with careful attention to medical and nutritional needs. Some medications have been shown to be helpful. Ideally, whatever treatment is offered should be tailored to the individual; this will vary according to both the severity of the disorder and the patient's individual problems, needs, and strengths. Treatment must address the eating disorder symptoms and medical consequences, as well as psychological, biological, interpersonal, and cultural forces that contribute to or maintain the eating disorder. NIMH (2014) cites that eating disorders affect both genders, although rates among women and girls are 2½ times greater than among men and boys. Eating disorders frequently appear during the teen years or young adulthood but also may develop during childhood or later in life. Family-based treatment is a well-established method for families with minors. Recovery from eating disorders involves learning to:

1. Listen to one's body
2. Listen to one's feelings
3. Self-trust
4. Self-acceptance
5. Self-love
6. Enjoying life and living in the moment

DSM 5 sets forth changes in clinical descriptions of EDOs (NIH, 2014).

1. **Binge-eating disorder (BED)**: BED is defined as "recurring episodes of eating significantly more food in a short period of time than most people would eat under similar circumstances, with episodes accompanied by feelings of lack of control." Someone with BED may eat quickly and uncontrollably, despite hunger signals or feelings of fullness. The person may have feelings of guilt, shame, or disgust and may binge eat alone (sometimes at night) to hide the behavior. To be diagnosed with BED, the behavior will have typically taken place at least once a week over a period of 3 months.
   A. Treating BED
      1. Similar to the treatment for bulimia nervosa
2. **Anorexia nervosa**: Characterized by emaciation, a relentless pursuit of thinness and unwillingness to maintain a normal or healthy weight, a distortion of body image and intense fear of gaining weight.
   A. Treating anorexia nervosa involves three components (CBT):
      1. Restoring the person to a healthy weight
      2. Treating the psychological issues related to the eating disorder
      3. Reducing or eliminating behaviors or thoughts that lead to insufficient eating and preventing relapse
3. **Bulimia nervosa**: Characterized by recurrent and frequent episodes of eating unusually large amounts of food (e.g., binge eating), and feeling a lack of control over the eating. This binge eating is followed by a type of behavior that compensates for the binge, such as purging (e.g., vomiting, excessive use of laxatives, or diuretics), fasting and/or excessive exercise. The frequency of binge-eating and compensatory behaviors that people with bulimia nervosa must exhibit once a week.
   A. Treating bulimia nervosa (CBT)
      1. Changing binge-eating and purging behaviors and eating attitude
      2. Facing current problems and learning to effectively cope with them
      3. Identify distorted or unhelpful thinking patterns
      4. Relate to others in more positive ways

Due to the overlap in symptoms and the blending of features from more than one diagnosis of eating disorder, the goals and objectives will be presented as one section instead of separated according to the specific diagnosis.

As a result of the relationship of EDO behaviors to physical etiology and consequences, it is important to refer the person to a physician initially (and monitoring if necessary) to rule out the presence of organic problems such as those associated to the endocrine system, gastrointestinal complications, cancer, hypothalamus brain tumor, electrolyte imbalance, assessing the need for hospitalization, etc. A treatment team for a person with an eating disorder would comprise, in addition to a therapist skilled in treating eating disorders:

1. A registered dietitian to provide nutritional counseling.
2. A psychiatrist for medication prescription and management, when medications are necessary. Some psychiatrists also provide psychological counseling.
3. Medical and dental specialists to treat health or dental problems that result from an eating disorder.
4. Partner, parents, or other family members. For young people still living at home, parents should be actively involved in treatment and may supervise meals.
5. There are times when hospitalization may be needed to effectively intervene to treat problems resulting from malnutrition or to ensure they get adequate nutrition if they are clinically underweight.

When working with individuals diagnosed with an EDO, be aware of the possibility of a general problem with impulse control. Compulsive behaviors can be oriented around stealing, sex, self-destructive behaviors, and substance abuse. It is not uncommon for individuals diagnosed with an EDO to trade compulsions (even the EDO behaviors) when they are in treatment and are making efforts to alter their behaviors. Additionally, assess the comorbidity of a mood disorder and personality disorder with these individuals, with the associated complications to the clinical picture and effective treatment planning goals and objectives.

FEEDING AND EATING DISORDERS

Goals

1. Medical stability
2. Assess for referral for medication evaluation
3. Improve coping
4. Facilitate appropriate autonomy
5. Improve body image
6. Improve rational thinking
7. Improve interpersonal relating
8. Improve communication
9. Improve self-esteem
10. Identify feeling states
11. Differentiate between internal sensations and emotional states
12. Family intervention
13. Self-monitoring
14. Assess psychiatric status and safety

Treatment Focus and Objectives

1. Inadequate Nutrition
   A. Evaluation by physician/dietitian to determine adequate fluid intake and number of calories required for adequate nutrition and realistic weight. These professionals will have to monitor the medical side of the disorder. For the therapist to become involved, serious complications must arise in the therapeutic relationship.

      As adequate nutrition and normal eating patterns are established, begin to explore with the person the emotions associated with his/her behavior.

      In instances in which intervention has taken place early and the weight loss is not extreme, it may be adequate to do dietary education: the nutritional needs of the body, the effects of starvation, what purpose(s) the illness serves, and contracting for stabilization of weight and normalizing eating patterns. If these limits are transgressed, refer for medical intervention.

      If 15% of body weight is lost, refer to physician for monitoring. According to the World Health Organization, normal weight is considered to be a BMI of 18.5–24.99. A BMI of 17–18.49 is considered to be mild thinness, 16–16.99 is considered to be moderate thinness, and less than 16 is considered to be severe thinness. Because anorexia is defined as having a below normal body weight for height, a BMI below 18.5 would meet the criteria for anorexia. This condition puts the body at risk for additional medical complications and severely compromises quality of life. In considering the issues of hospitalization: Hospitalization is identified as a treatment choice when determined to be medically necessary by a physician. However, anytime a person is experiencing medical complications from their eating disorder or they are unable to make progress on an outpatient basis, inpatient hospitalization may be considered appropriate. Other factors that may deem hospitalization appropriate is when someone is suicidal, they live far away from treatment providers or they have other complicating factors.
   B. Rapid weight fluctuation. This is rarely a problem so extreme to be life threatening. With severe engagement of the bulimic binge–purge cycle, there can be electrolyte imbalance and dehydration. Additional physical complications are hair loss, pimples, esophageal tears, gastric ruptures, and cardiac arrhythmias.

      Ask directly about behaviors of restriction, bingeing, purging, and laxative/diuretic use.

2. Assess for Referral for Medication Evaluation
   A. Presence of mood disturbance (depression/anxiety)
   B. Potential benefit of psychotropic medication for EDO symptoms
3. Ineffective Coping
   A. Identify person's anger or other feelings associated with loss of control of his/her eating pattern.
   B. Explore family dynamics. Facilitate the recognition that maladaptive behaviors are related to emotional problems due to family functioning/structure.
   C. Explore fears that interfere with effective coping.
   D. Explore history of sexual abuse, physical abuse, emotional abuse, neglect.
   E. Identify problem situations and develop alternative responses.
   F. Identify manipulative responses.
   G. Encourage honest, appropriate expression of emotions.
   H. Identify eating rituals and the role they play.
   I. Identify the fears associated with stopping the purging behavior.
   J. Identify the reasons to choose not to binge and purge.
   K. Identify what the bulimics behaviors protect the individual from.
   L. Assertive communication.
   M. Relaxation training.
      1. Progressive muscle relaxation
      2. Visualization
      3. Meditation
      4. Breathing techniques
      5. Yoga
   N. Grounding to separate from emotional distress, and to regain balance (Najavits, 2015).
      1. Mental grounding (examples)
         a. Using all senses—describe the environment in detain (colors, shapes, contents, temperature, textures)
         b. Describe a daily activity in detail (First I...)
         c. Repeat a favorite and comforting saying over and over again (i.e., Serenity Prayer)
         d. Say a safety statement out loud. "My name is…, I am safe right now. I am in the present, not in the past. I am located in…the date is…"
      2. Physical grounding (examples)
         a. Focus on your breathing. Note each inhale and exhale. Repeat a favorite or soothing word on each inhale (i.e., calm, safe).
         b. Run cool or warm water over the hands.
         c. Walk slowly, focusing on each step and saying out loud left foot, right foot…
         d. Stretch; extend fingers, arms, legs, as far as possible; roll the head around paying attention to all the physical sensations.
      3. Soothing grounding
         a. Rehearse the imagery of a safe and soothing place (beach, mountains, special room). Focus on every detail using all of the senses.
         b. Identify a statement that affirms the ability to cope, "I can handle this," "This will pass."
         c. Practice grounding for a long time period (20–30 min). Repeat, repeat, repeat. Practice, practice, practice.
4. Difficulty With Autonomy
   A. Teach response options to increase choice and feelings of responsibility.
   B. Encourage increased confidence and self-esteem.
   C. Encourage self-care and being good to oneself.
   D. Explore ways to identify and work through underlying fears.
   E. Encourage appropriate risk taking.
   F. Reframe mistakes as opportunities for learning and encourage related problem solving.
   G. Encourage appropriate separation from family.

H. Resolve developmental fears.
I. Encourage the person's collaboration and input in treatment.
J. Identify confusion.
   1. Separate self-acceptance from performance and the evaluation of others
   2. Encourage the validation of the person's own thoughts and feelings
   3. Explore the meaning of weight
   4. Facilitate accurate perception of self
   5. Through positive feedback, help these individuals to accept themselves as they are
   6. EDO's insidious nature wreaks havoc with a person's negative self-perception. Recovery essentially involves learning to the following:
      a. Listening to one's body
      b. Listening to one's feelings
      c. Trusting oneself
      d. Self-acceptance
      e. Self-love
      f. Enjoying life
K. Respecting autonomy. A part of healing is "restoring autonomy." At times EDO treatment can be intrusive and seizing the person's control to prevent self-harm. These experiences are challenging to self-esteem and self-determination. Therefore, once an episode of risk of harm has been negotiated, it is imperative to refocus the emphasis of treatment of giving the person their respected position as part of the treatment team. This ensures that choices, wishes, and goals are understood and taken into consideration in treatment decisions.

5. Distorted Body Image
A. Develop realistic expectations
B. Explore relationships and the belief of needing to be a certain way to maintain the relationship
C. Encourage appropriate grieving for loss of central focus of preoccupation with body and food
D. Increase awareness and expression through guided imagery and art
E. Utilize experiential therapy to examine the role EDO plays in their life
   1. To challenge their physical and emotional body image distortions
   2. To develop trust, self-esteem, and confidence
F. Utilize creative expression, guided imagery, relaxation, and grounding techniques to develop skills to effectively manage anxiety and triggers associated imbalanced physical fitness
G. Dance and movement therapy can be beneficial in developing greater trust and appreciation of one's body
H. Reconnecting the mind and body to develop personal boundaries and a sense of self
   1. Write a letter from one's mind to their body and from their body to their mind
I. Positive affirmations and mirror work
   1. Take photos of one's body (themselves) and label the photos with positive body affirmations (to associate their own image with positive characteristics)
J. Collage of images, words, advertisements that contribute to negative rituals, self-harm/eating disorder behavior
   1. Burn the image as a symbol of release of external control and emotional pain
   2. Reframe the symbolism as a means of using positive affirmations or learning to identify and challenge negative thought patterns

6. Irrational Thinking (EDO Thinking)

*EDO's are not about willpower but irrational thinking. An anonymous quote, "the best way to keep yourself from relapsing into old habits is to remove yourself from the mindset that causing your anxiety in the first place."

A. Negative self-talk, all or nothing thinking, overgeneralizations, and perfectionistic: should statement need to be explored and replaced with honest, useful, and rational substitute statements.
B. Confronting fear of weight, fear of growing up, and autonomy.

C. Replacing negative thoughts with realistic and constructive thoughts. Educating regarding the impact of the compulsive insidious nature of an EDO on self-perception.

D. Recognizing and correcting irrational thinking is to be reinforced for the empowerment, gains/progress in self-care, and improved emotional balance.

E. Relax before challenging irrational thinking.

    1. Breath (there are numerous techniques to choose from).

    2. Create time to relax (drink a cup tea slowly, take a long hot bubble bath, do arts/crafts, listen to favorite music, meditate, take a walk, organize, etc.).

    3. Practice intentional thought.

        a. Allow choosing to think about irrational thought

        b. Ask self, "What is the truth?" "Why am I thinking this?" etc.

    4. Identify encouraging and trusting support and practice using it. It is vital to not rely on one person. A network is the best support.

    5. Recognize when it is important to seek help—instead of waiting past the time and creating an unnecessary crisis.

7. Impaired Interpersonal Relations

    A. Identify trust and honesty issues in relationships

    B. Identify fear of "being found out" and of being rejected

    C. Encourage appropriate risk-taking behavior in developing relationships

    D. Assertive communication

    E. Boundaries; appropriate boundaries are a part of healthy and mutually respectful relationships

8. Dysfunctional Communication

    A. Teach assertive communication.

    B. Encourage appropriate ventilation of thoughts and feelings.

    C. Model and role-play appropriate responses to various situations.

    D. Practice listening and reflecting. Validating that someone has been heard does not mean that there is an agreement or submission to the view of another.

9. Low Self-esteem

    A. Explore ways to change faulty self-perceptions

    B. Encourage the persons to develop trust in themselves and their abilities

    C. Encourage their participation in problem solving

    D. Encourage self-care behaviors and positive self-talk

    E. Create opportunities for success

    F. Identify strengths and develop daily affirmations for reinforcing a positive self-image

    G. Identify personal growth activities

    H. Promote feelings of control within the environment through participation and independent decision making

    I. Positively reinforce their efforts and successes

10. Identify Feeling States (Feelings Are Often Complex and It Is Hard to Identify Them)

    A. Explore ways for these individuals to separate and maintain their own emotions from the emotions of others.

    B. Facilitate accurate identification and acknowledgment of feelings.

    C. Expression of feelings.

        1. Talk it out: It is very therapeutic to share feelings with a trustworthy person (therapist, safe friend/family member, or a support person). They should be a person who are willing to listen to their feelings without evaluating them and who will encourage them to express feelings. An outlet for feelings might result in feeling relieved and lighter.

        2. Write it out: Sometimes it is helpful to make a feeling journal to vent feelings in a written manner. It is good to periodically review this journal and see if there is a pattern emerging. This is a healthy and positive outlet for feelings. Other examples of healthy outlets are creative artwork, writing poems, and songs.

        3. Discharging sadness: Withholding sadness can cause a heavy load on the body and mind. It is important to instruct asking questions such as: Do I ever cry? Under what circumstances do I

cry? Do I cry because someone hurt me, I am lonely or afraid, or no apparent reason? Do I cry alone or do I allow others to see me crying? Also explore the potential issue of feeling sad but having trouble expressing tears. In this situation it is advisable to listen to some evocative music, watch an emotional movie, or read literature to provoke the sad feelings and be able to shed tears. Encourage the ventilation of sadness because holding it in can result in more sadness and anger toward those they identify as hurting them.

4. Discharging anger: Anger is the most pervasive emotion that leads to anxiety. Anger ranges from mild irritation to extreme rage. Withheld anger can cause the development of a vulnerability to being anxiety prone and also cause symptoms of OCD. When a person is frustrated and angry, they can become more preoccupied with their obsessions and phobias but often they are unaware of these angry feelings. Those who are prone to anxiety have a strong need to control so when they feel threatened by a sense of loss of control, they give in to their anger and it frightens them.

D. Assist person in dealing effectively with feelings.

E. Facilitate understanding of feelings such as despair and guilt.

F. Identify people pleasing patterns—fearing their honesty will result in hurting someone's feelings. Those who are, by nature, people pleaser, are prone to having anxiety disorders. They always want to present themselves as pleasant and nice. They are also dependent on relationships with significant others. Outward expression of feelings can risk the relationship of phobic people so they tend to suppress their anger.

G. Tune in to the somatic experience. Understanding how feelings are. Instruct the person in the following manner.

1. Physically relax your body for 5–10 min doing progressive muscle relaxation or meditation, to slow down your mind. Practicing mindfulness is great skill development.

2. Encourage asking the question, "What am I feeling right now?"

3. Identify where your body experiences that feeling. Tune in to that place in your body where you feel emotional sensations such as anger, fear, or sadness. This is your inner place of feelings.

4. Listen to their body. Take time and listen to whatever they can sense in their place of feelings. Do not analyze or judge… just observe. If you begin to evaluate then they may not be able to get a sense of their real feeling.

5. Once they have obtained a general sense of what they are feeling, and then ask the following questions: "Where is this feeling in my body? What is the shape of this feeling? If I have to give a color to this feeling, what would it be?"

H. Encourage daily journal entry related to feelings identification.

*The complexity of emotions warrants education. Before a person can learn to accurately and effectively identify their feelings is important to understand.

- Feeling states are a part of an overall body reaction (mind–body).
- Feelings are influenced by a person's thoughts and perceptions.
- There is a tendency to suppress feelings. When suppression of feelings becomes a habit, the result is a person being out of touch with their feelings. When feelings are withheld or ignored they can be overpowering and depressing.
- Feelings can be simple and complex. Simple feelings do not require a lot of explanation, they are anger, fear, grief, sadness, joy, excitement, love. Complex feelings are seen as a combination of basic feelings influenced by thoughts and images. From a mental health perspective, fear and panic can be seen as basic or simple emotions while free floating anxiety exemplifies a more complex feeling.
- Feelings are energizing. Honest expression of feelings by a person who is in touch with how they feel may feel more energetic whereas suppressed/unaware feelings can lead a person to feel numb, fatigued, or even depressed.
- It is possible to experience more than one feeling at the same time. For example, if feeling threatened there could be feelings of fear and anger.
- Feelings are contagious. We can be influenced by the feelings of others. You can be encouraged and enthusiastic by positive people and feel sad and even cry when spending time with a depressed person. Hence, it is important being in touch with one's own feelings.
- Feelings simply exist, they are not right or wrong (though the perception or judgment of them can be right or wrong). When it is learned to appropriately express feelings, it tends to feel better—a relief.

11. Differentiation Between Internal Sensations and Emotional States

Feelings involve a body reaction. For example, during moments of emotional distress, body reactions such as increased heart rate, respiration, perspiration, trembling, and even shaking may take place.

A. Explore eating patterns in relationship to denial of feelings, sexuality, fears, concerns, self-comforting, approval, and so on

B. Facilitate development of acknowledging hunger and eating in response to internal hunger cues

C. Identify ritualistic behaviors and substitute appropriate eating patterns (learn and practice healthy eating)

12. Family Therapy

A. Approach family in a nonblaming manner

B. Assume that families have done their best (rule/out)

C. Assume that families want to help (rule/out)

D. Recognize that families are tired and stressed

E. Facilitate age-appropriate separation

F. Identify person's role in the family

G. Identify how family maintains the dysfunctional behavioral/emotional patterns

H. Identify the role of the family in recovery

I. Identify community resources

1. Referral to group therapy and/or self-help groups

Physical signs of poor nutrition and inadequate self-care

Body areas	Nutrient deficiency or other cause of problem	Signs associated with poor nutrition or other cause
Hair	Protein	Lack of natural shine: hair dull and dry; thin and sparse; hair fine; color changes; easily plucked
Face	Protein, calories, niacin, zinc, riboflavin, vitamin B6, essential fats (A, D, E, and K)	Skin color loss; skin dark over cheeks and under eyes; lumpiness or flakiness of skin on nose and mouth; scaling of skin around nostrils
Eyes	Vitamin A	Dryness of eye membranes; night blindness
Lips	Riboflavin, vitamin B, folate	Redness and swelling of mouth or lips, especially at corners of mouth
Tongue	Riboflavin, niacin	Swelling; scarlet and raw tongue; magenta color; swollen sores
Teeth	Fluoride, sugar	Missing or erupting abnormally; gray or black spots; cavities
Gums	Vitamin C	"Spongy" and bleed easily; recession of gums
Glands	Iodine, protein	Thyroid enlargement; parotid (cheeks) enlargement
Skin	Protein, niacin, zinc, vitamin B6, C, and K, essential fats (A, D, E, and K)	Dryness; sandpaper feel of skin; red swollen pigmentation of exposed areas; excessive lightness or darkness; black and blue marks due to skin bleeding; lack of fat under the skin
Muscles	Protein, calories, thiamin	Lack of muscles in temporal area, hand between thumb and index finger and calf muscles; pain in calves; weak thighs

13. Self-monitoring/Relapse Prevention

A. Identify "red flag" patterns of behavior

B. Identify resources and support system

C. Encourage regular review of their program for recovery

D. Journal writing (thinking, feeling, behaving)

1. Expressing thoughts and feelings honestly; venting, clarification, and use for problem solving

2. Record keeping of food consumption, vomiting, purging, and laxative use

3. Encourage identification of behavioral patterns and related emotional states
4. Facilitate identification of the kinds of thinking that leads to trouble
5. To provide a more objective record of changes those do or do not occur
   E. Maintain increased awareness for the role of negative emotional states in relapse
   F. Planning for follow-up with various professionals
14. Assess Psychiatric Status and Safety
   A. Suicidality
   B. Mood/anxiety disorders
   C. Substance use/dependence
   D. OCD/symptoms
   E. Personality disorders
   F. Posttraumatic stress disorder (PTSD)

Additional Considerations

If an eating disorder is suspected for an individual from a culturally diverse group, it is important to determine the eating behavior and dietary habits that are culturally acceptable, the acculturation issues negatively impacting the individual, and the person's internal struggle with adjustment. The individual's efforts of personal growth and success in a new culture may create significant cognitive dissonance as well as family pressure, disappointment, or alienation.

Possible signs and symptoms of anorexia nervosa, bulimia nervosa, and compulsive overeating (age 13 to adult)

	Physical symptoms	Psychological symptoms
Anorexia nervosa	Skin rashes Blueness in extremities Poor circulation Fainting spells Anemia Chronic low body weight Irregular thyroid Postpubertal absence of menses Decreased gastric emptying Water retention	Perfectionist expectations Avoidance of relationships Preoccupation with weight History of sexual abuse/assault Euphoria Sense of omnipotence Views self as "fat" Overly compliant Highly motivated Ritualized behaviors
Bulimia nervosa	Swollen glands Susceptibility to infections Irregular heart rate Persistent acne Menstrual irregularity Frequent diarrhea or constipation Water retention Dental erosion Ipecac poisoning Aspiration pneumonia	Impulsive behaviors Intense attachments Preoccupation with weight Alcoholic parent(s) Depression Suicidal thoughts Poor self-esteem Extreme sense of guilt Mood swings History of excessive exercise
Compulsive overeating	Shortness of breath Frequent constipation Irritable bowel syndrome Elevated blood sugar Water retention Nausea Sleep disturbance Weight fluctuation Joint inflammation	Compulsive behavior Dependent attachments Preoccupation with weight Alcoholic parent(s) Depression Suicidal thoughts Distorted perception of body Sense of inadequacy History of frequent dieting

   In addition to forwarding a letter that outlines recommendations for treatment, include this laboratory assessment chart for patients with eating disorders when a consultation note is sent to primary care physicians. It will offer them information on assessment in a manner in which they are familiar.

A dental examination should also be performed. In younger patients it is generally useful to assess growth, sexual development, and general physical development. A standard pediatric growth chart is useful for identifying patients who have failed to gain adequate and expected weight or who have experienced a disturbance in normal growth trajectory.

The American Psychiatric Association recommends the following laboratory assessments for patients with eating disorders:

1. Consider the following recommended assessments for all patients with eating disorders;
   A. Basic analyses
      1. Blood chemistry studies
         a. Serum electrolyte levels
         b. Blood urea nitrogen levels
         c. Creatinine level
         d. Thyroid function
      2. Complete blood count (CBC)
      3. Urinalysis
2. Consider for malnourished and severely symptomatic patients
   A. Additional analyses
      1. Blood chemistry studies
         a. Calcium level
         b. Magnesium level
         c. Phosphorus level
         d. Liver function
      2. Electrocardiogram
3. Consider the following medical intervention recommendations for those individuals who have been underweight for more than 6 months
   A. Osteopenia and osteoporosis assessments
      1. Dual-energy X-ray absorptiometry
      2. Estradiol level
      3. Testosterone level (male)
4. The following are nonroutine assessment procedures
   A. Consider only for specific unusual indications
   B. Possible indicator of persistent or recurrent vomiting
      1. Serum amylase level
   C. For persistent amenorrhea at normal weight
      1. Luteinizing hormone (LH) and follicle-stimulating hormone levels
   D. For ventricular enlargement correlated with degree of malnutrition
      1. Brain magnetic resonance imaging
      2. Computerized tomography (CT)
   E. For blood
      1. Stool sample analysis

PREVENTING WEIGHT AND BODY IMAGE PROBLEMS IN CHILDREN

Increased stress, ever-present media involvement, convenience food and soda, and decreased physical activity have led to an epidemic of obesity in children. Children are becoming more concerned about their weight and body image at an earlier age. Whatever their size or weight, children can develop either a positive or negative view of their bodies. And, body image disturbances can begin as early as preschool, so parents and other adult role models need to play a pivotal role in promoting a positive body image for children. Children with a positive body image feel more comfortable and confident in their ability to succeed. Contrary, children with a negative body image feel more self-conscious, anxious, and isolated. These children are at greater risk for excessive weight gain/obesity and for developing eating disorders (Academy of Nutrition and Dietetics, 2015).

Obesity among children has now become a health concern that can make some medical issues worse and lead to others (such as diabetes, joint problems, hypertension, premature onset on periods, and irregular periods, etc.). Both genetic and environmental factors affect a child's potential for obesity. Therefore, it may be important to change some habits of your child and yourself. Consult with your family physician or nutritional specialist, attend nutrition classes, and educate yourself by reading about how to eat healthfully. Continuously bringing up exercise and dieting to children and adolescents can create conflicts, resistance, and negative self-esteem. Therefore, problem-solve what changes you will make that sets the tone for nutrition and exercise. Your children will learn from you. Be a more active family. Make activity fun and an important part of your lifestyle.

Obsession With Weight

While being obsessed is not necessarily related directly to lower self-esteem, there is still warranted concern.

1. Peer cruelty
2. Parental focus on weight
    A. Feelings of inadequacy
    B. Potential precursor to eating disorders
3. Media continuously portraying cultural perception of thin as attractive

Obesity and Self-esteem

1. Obesity is not always related to the lowering of self-esteem
2. Self-esteem is more likely to be associated with the following:
    A. How family members respond to weight issues
    B. Social experiences
    C. Development of effective coping skills

What Parents Can Do

1. Set a healthy example
    A. Physical activity
    B. Nutrition
2. Make sure that children know and feel they are loved regardless of their weight
    A. Do not focus on their weight or counting calories
    B. Focus on spending time with them, engaged in fun, educational, and physical activity
    C. Focus on teaching them effective life-management skills

RECOMMENDATIONS FOR FAMILY MEMBERS OF ANOREXIC INDIVIDUALS

1. With child/adolescent anorexics, demand less decision making from the anorexic. Offer fewer choices, less responsibility. For example, they should not decide what the family eats for dinner or where to go for vacation.
2. With child/adolescent anorexics, in conflicts about decisions, parents should not withdraw out of fear that their child/adolescent will become increasingly ill.
3. Seek to maintain a supportive, confident posture that is calming yet assertive. Maintain awareness to avoid being controlling, or the perception of being controlling.
4. Express honest affection, both verbally and physically.
5. Develop communication/discussion on personal issues rather than on food and weight.
6. Do not demand weight gain or make negative comments to the individual for having anorexia.
7. Do not blame. Avoid statements such as "Your illness is ruining the family." The person is not responsible for family functioning.

8. Do not emotionally abandon or avoid the anorexic family member. Remain emotionally available and supportive. Utilize clear boundaries.

9. Once the individual is involved in treatment, do not become directly involved with the weight issues. If there is any observed change in the individual's appearance, the clinician would have previously prepared, with necessary discussions about appropriate sharing of information and releases to allow for contact with the therapist or other pertinent professional such as the person's physician and dietitian.

10. Do not demand that they eat with you, and do not allow their eating problem to dominate the family's eating schedule or use of the kitchen. Be consistent.

11. For child/adolescent anorexics, do not allow them to shop or to cook for the family. This puts them in a nurturing role and allows them to deny their own needs for food by feeding others.

12. Increase giving and receiving of both caring and support within the family. Develop clear boundaries, and allow each person to be responsible for themselves and setting their own goals.

NEUROCOGNITIVE DISORDERS

Major neurocognitive disorders (NCDs) correspond to the condition referred to in *DSM-IV* as dementia. The most substantial changes in this category of disorders is the addition of "mild NCD" and the elimination "cognitive disorder not otherwise specified" category. Those disorders that do not cause sufficient impairment to qualify for a diagnosis of dementia are now defined as NCDs and placed on a spectrum with the more severe conditions. The concept of social cognition is also introduced as one of the core functional domains that can be affected by an NCD. Conceptually this may be particularly significant in the evaluation of patients with non-Alzheimer dementias (such as frontotemporal dementia). With an aging population and the increasing recognition of the possibility of long-lasting cognitive deficits after traumatic brain injury, the need for forensic assessments of cognitive disorders is likely to increase (Regier, Kuhl, & Kupfer, 2013).

Because of the term "dementia" having a long medical history and its familiarity among clinicians and patients, DSM 5 (APA, 2013) recognizes the term "dementia" as an acceptable alternative for the newly preferred and more scientifically accurate term "NCD" that is subtyped into *major or mild* degrees of impairment. This range of decline is important and consistent with research indicative that treatments for declining cognition may be phase-specific, with certain medications and approaches possibly only working early in the disease course. It may seem challenging to the clinician to distinguish mild from major impairment, but the DSM 5 does attempt an objective distinction. Diagnostic clarification will ultimately be determined by a neuro specialist substantiated by validating assessments.

Unlike the old term (dementia), NCDs include dementia and amnestic disorder diagnoses as well as recognizing specific etiologic subtypes of neurocognitive dysfunction, such as Alzheimer disease, Parkinson disease, HIV infection, Lewy body disease, and vascular disease. Each subgroup can be further divided into *major or mild* degrees of cognitive impairment on the basis of cognitive decline, specifically the inability to perform daily living functions independently. In addition, a subspecifier "with" or "without behavioral disturbances" is offered. The clinical implications for the distinction of major versus mild impairment are set forth with the reasoning that the new classification will increase research in the areas of prevention and early intervention.

Cognitive decline meets the "major" criteria when "significant" impairment is evident or reported and when it does interfere with a patient's independence to the point that assistance is required. Cognitive decline meets the "major" criteria when substantial impairment is evident/reported and when it does interfere with a patient's independence to the point that assistance is required. Whereas, mild NCD requires "modest" cognitive decline that does not interfere with capacity for independence in everyday activities (e.g., paying bills, taking medications correctly, able to provide for their own basic needs). In other words, the diagnostic distinction relies heavily on observable behaviors. Furthermore, DSM 5 recognizes specific etiologic subtypes of neurocognitive dysfunction, such as Alzheimer disease. The new manual defines six key domains of cognitive function:

1. Complex attention
2. Executive function
3. Learning and memory
4. Language

5. Perceptual-motor function
6. Social cognition

Psychosocial intervention for treatment of Alzheimer disease is one approach that is best accomplished in a collaborative care network. Psychosocial interventions include cognitive and social stimulation, behavioral-oriented therapies, and caregiver support. Other approaches include validation therapy, reminiscence therapy, and reality orientation. Studies have demonstrated improved self-care, emotional well-being and cognitive function as well as a reduction in risk for, or delay in, nursing home placement. It is also universally recommended as initial approach for behavioral symptoms of NCDs (Johnson, 2004; Regier, Narrow, et al., 2013).

The various NCDs are manifested in disturbances of cognitive, behavioral, and personality changes. The presented symptoms, history, and observations obtained during assessment are crucial in determining the origin of symptom presentation. Just with the symptoms of hallucinations and delusions, the clinician must take into consideration organicity, psychosis, depression with psychotic features, and substance abuse or drug reaction (which can happen easily with the elderly). Substance abuse or drug reaction will be the easiest way to clarify because of lab results and history and change in symptom presentation as the person detoxes. Therefore, for the initial refinement in diagnosis the following general comparisons are helpful:

Organicity	Depression	Psychosis
History of failing memory	Difficulty concentrating	History of personality disturbance
Disorientation for time	More precise onset	Auditory hallucination/delusions
Perseverations	Low motivation	Disoriented to people and place
Visual/olfactory hallucinations	Self-critical	Perseveration of bizarre thoughts
Neurological signs	Mood congruent hallucinations	Mood inappropriate
Worse at night	Vegetative symptoms (sleep/appetite)	

Depression can lead to symptoms that may appear to be NCD/dementia. However, depression can also be the response to early signs of NCD/dementia. Because of the potentially confusing presentation, clinical suspicion is imperative. To clarify whether you are dealing with NCD/dementia or depression/pseudodementia, the following guidelines may be helpful (Clinical Concerns, 2012; Johnson, 2004):

Indicator	NCD/dementia	Depression/pseudodementia
Age onset	Age is nonspecific Onset is vague (over months or years)	Elderly ≥60 More precise onset (days or weeks)
Course	Slow course, worse at night	Rapid, uneven course (not worse at night)
Presentation	Dysphasia, agnosia, apraxia	Sadness, somatic symptoms of depression
Impairment	Increased cognitive impairment —Memory —Disoriented to time/date	Increased impairment in personality features in —Confidence —Interests —Drive
Mental status	Keeps making same mistakes	Same mistakes
Mood	Usually normal but can become transiently unhappy in relation to events	Develop a persistently sad mood over a period of weeks
Behavior and affect	Congruent with degree of impaired thought processes and affect	Incongruent mood/affect Self-deprecating
Sense of guilt/worthlessness	Rare	Common
Suicidal ideation	Rare	Common
Anxiety/agitation	Seen as dementia progresses. Often worse later in day (sundowning) and in unfamiliar surroundings	Can develop over weeks. Often worse in the morning
Cognition	Progressive, gradual decline in memory and other domains. Concentration normal early on	Problems with concentration and focus that develops over weeks. Indecisiveness and anxiety about making mistakes.
Concerns about cognitive deficits	Show little concern minimizes and often denies	Seem to exaggerate severity. Preoccupied with deficits
Physical symptoms	Gradual weight loss over years. Gradual disruption of normal sleep/wake cycle often less active but rare to see psychomotor retardation until dementia is advanced	Changes in appetite over weeks sleep disruption over weeks more/less than usual frequent complaints of fatigue and, if depression is severe, can psychomotor retardation evident
Cooperativity	Cooperative but frustrated	Cooperative effects poor
Responses to questions	Confabulated	Response to questions a pathetic, "I don't know"
Emotional response	Response to funny/sad situations is situation's normal/exaggerated	Little or no response to sad or funny
Med assessments	Neuroevaluations abnormal (CT, EEG)	Neuroevaluations normal (CT, EEG)

While the diagnostic generalities fit the elderly population, there are differences that warrant clarification because of the impact on treatment plan formulation and care. Those presenting with NCD exhibit a broad range of cognitive impairments, behavioral symptoms, and mood changes; thus, necessitating an individualized, multimodel treatment plan, and multidisciplinary treatment team. Since NCD is often progressive, and in conjunction with its evolution is the emergence of new issues to address, the clinician must closely monitor for changes, and whenever possible predict impending change for the individual and/or their family. The following mnemonic provides a useful overview for diagnostic consideration.

DEMENTIA

D drug interaction
E emotional disturbances/current crises or losses
M metabolic/endocrine problems such as diabetes or thyroid dysfunction
E eyes and ears
N nutritional deficiencies
T tumor or trauma
I infection/brain abscess
A arteriosclerosis or other arteriosclerotic problems

This mnemonic (Perry, Frances, & Clarkin, 1985) can be utilized while doing a mental status exam and making a thorough diagnostic assessment to rule out reversible dementia such as depression, anemia, hypothyroidism, alcoholic dementia, and so on. Refer for a complete physical that includes a recommendation for a neurological exam, drug screen, endocrine panel, a neuropsychological testing if appropriate.

A family session can be used to educate family members and encourage their consulting with the physician on the case. This will be helpful for increasing their understanding of the medical situation, prognosis, indications, and contraindications of treatment. They need to be educated on how to manage perceptual disturbances and disruptive behaviors, and the importance of medication compliance and signs of toxicity.

NCDs may have various origins. However, the symptomatology does not vary other than for nuances of case individuality and the progression of deterioration. NCDs demonstrate evident symptoms through cognitive, behavioral, and personality changes. There may also be evidence of depression, delirium, or delusions. A person with NCDs may feel anxious, agitated, restless associated with their experience of profound loss of ability to negotiate new information and stimulus. Fear and fatigue are a natural result of trying to make sense out of an increasingly confusing world.

The dysfunction of NCDs tends to be chronic in that the related physical disorders attributed to these changes are progressive, except in some cases of psychoactive substance–induced NCDs. In other words, in some cases, there is no cure for an NCD. However, there are various forms of neurological damage from injury, illness, substance abuse, stroke, anoxic brain injury, and cardiac events that can benefit from behavioral treatment.

Because of the unique qualities of each person, and the variations in family circumstances, there is not a one size fits all treatment approach. Therapy for NCD can help train those with enduring problems in cognitive ability to compensate for many kinds of damage. By working to strengthen and enhance memory creation and retrieval, promote problem solving, and build responsible and reliable habits for dealing with the world around them, clinicians can help ensure that those experiencing NCDs lead the fullest lives possible. Cognitive retraining seeks to restore thinking, communication, and memory skills affected by brain injury. Cognitive rehab teaches strategies to compensate for memory problems and improve safety.

The level of functioning must be thoroughly assessed for treatment planning, which includes placement if necessary.

NEUROCOGNITIVE DISORDERS

Goals

1. Refer for medical evaluation
2. Stabilization and thought processes are intact
3. Deal with sensory perceptual

4. Improve self-care
5. Decrease social isolation
6. Improve self-esteem
7. Improving mood states
8. Cognitive rehabilitation
9. Person will not experience physical injury
10. Managing behavioral symptoms
11. Person will not harm self or others
12. Reduce stress of caregiver

Treatment Focus and Objectives

1. Refer for immediate medical examination to rule out drug interactions, metabolic or endocrine problems, problems with hearing or vision, presence of tumor, infections, and so on, which could be contributing to the symptom presentation. Additionally medical treatments are available for cognitive symptoms, which offer modest benefit.
   A. Medications to boost neurotransmitter levels
   B. Referral to occupational therapy that focuses on teaching strategize to minimize the effect that cognitive impairment has on day-to-day living
   C. Steps to develop successful nonmedication treatments
      1. Recognizing that the person is not just acting ornery or agitated, but also experiencing further symptoms of the disease
      2. Identifying the cause and how the symptom may relate to the experience of the person with the NCD
      3. Changing the environment to resolve challenges and obstacles to comfort, security, and ease of mind
2. Altered Thought Processes
   A. Assist in reality testing. Encourage person to interrupt thoughts which are not reality based.
   B. Instruct caretaker on facilitating person's orientation to time, place, person, and situation.
   C. Discourage pattern stabilization of false ideas.
   D. Offer simple explanations when necessary, and talk slowly and face to face to increase effective communication.
   E. Reinforce accurate reality testing with positive feedback, while maintaining realistic expectations.
3. Sensory-Perceptual Changes
   A. Decrease environmental stimuli
   B. Assist in reality testing
   C. Discourage pattern stabilization of false ideas by talking to the person about real people and situations
   D. Provide reassurance for increased feelings of security
   E. Instruct caretaker on facilitating reality testing when person demonstrates inaccurate sensory perception
4. Inadequate Self-care
   A. Encourage daily independent living skills
      1. Bathing
      2. Cleaning hair, cutting when necessary, and styled appropriately
      3. Brushing teeth
      4. Dressing adequately and appropriately
      5. Cleaning self adequately after using bathroom and washing hands
   B. Occupational therapy that focuses on strategies that minimize the effects of cognitive impairment on day-to-day living and helps to create a schedule of activities of daily living (ADLs) and how best to accomplish them
5. Social Isolation
   A. Supportive psychotherapy in early stages of dementia to address issues of loss
   B. Reminiscence therapy
   C. Stimulation oriented treatment

1. Recreational activity
2. Art therapy
3. Pet therapy
6. Low Self-esteem
   A. Encourage honest expression of feelings loss related to deterioration in functioning
   B. Encourage all levels of communication and self-care
   C. Problem-solve ways of dealing with cognitive deficits (making labels large and easy to read, signs identifying rooms, etc.)
   D. Focus on abilities and accomplishments
   E. Reinforce accurate reality testing with positive feedback
   F. Identify, challenge, and create useful substitutes for destructive thought patterns
   G. Identify and correct distorted thinking
   H. Reinforce accurate reality testing with positive feedback
7. Difficult Mood States
   A. Depression

*The most common treatment for depression associated dementia involves a combination of medication, counseling, and a gradual reconnection with activities and people, that feel safe and lift their mood.

1. Support groups, especially an early stage when they are aware of their diagnosis and prefer an active role in seeking help or helping others
2. Schedule a predictable daily routine, taking advantage of their best time of day to undertake challenging or difficult tasks
3. Make a list of activities, people, or places that the person enjoys, and schedule these more frequently
4. Facilitate regular exercise as part of their schedule, particularly in the morning
5. Acknowledge and validate their frustration or sadness, while continuing to express hope that they will feel better/less depressed soon
6. Celebrate small successes and occasions
7. Problem-solve with family how the person can contribute to family life and be sure to recognize their contributions
8. Provide reassurance that the person is important to their family and loved, respected, and appreciated as part of the family, and not just for what they can do now but for the family member they have been
9. Reassure them that they will not be abandoned
   B. Anxiety and Agitation
   1. Determine possible causes
   2. To prevent or decrease anxiety and agitation
      a. Create a calm environment. Environmental approaches, such as reducing clutter and noise around the person to make it easier to focus on tasks and reduce confusion and frustration
         1. Remove stressors
         2. Create a quiet and safe environment
         3. Offer a security object, rest, or privacy
         4. Offer soothing rituals and limiting caffeine use
      b. Avoid environmental triggers
         1. Noise, background distraction (TV/radio), glare of sunlight
      c. Monitor personal comfort
         1. Check for basics—pain, hunger, thirst, full bladder, constipation, infection, skin irritation
         2. Make sure the room is at a comfortable temperature
         3. Be sensitive to fears, misperceived threats, and frustration with expressing what is wanted
      d. Simplify tasks and routine
         1. Predictable is comforting and reassuring
      e. Provide an opportunity for exercise
         1. Go for a walk, put on quiet music and dance, community gardening

8. Cognitive Rehabilitation (CR) (Bird, 2000; Clare, 2008; Mateer, 2005)

CR is a process of relearning cognitive skills that have been lost or altered as a consequence of damage to brain cells/chemistry. If skills cannot be relearned, then new ones must take their place. Learning new skills enable a person to compensate for lost cognitive functions. CT is a systematic, functionally oriented therapeutic intervention of cognitive activities based on a person's brain–behavior deficits. Be thoughtful and creative in developing an individualized program focused on a person's thinking, attention, perception, memory, problem-solving skills, and decision-making skills. With hard and dedicated work from the patient, significant improvement in cognitive functioning can be achieved that can lead to significant improvement in daily functioning and meaningful participation in activities of daily living.

The process of identifying and addressing goals is defined by stages. The approach needs to be flexible and the goals measurable:

- Work with the person to determine whether the person is able to identify something that she/he would like to be different.
- Identify the area(s) to focus on—for example, memory difficulties, participation in activities, or family relationships.
- Identify the specific issue to focus on—for example, remembering the names of people met when participating in an activity, when to take medication, going out on errands.
- Establish the baseline level of performance.
- Identify the goal expressed in clear behavioral terms.
- Identify what level of performance will indicate that the goal is.
- Completely or partially achieved.
- Plan the intervention to address the goal, using appropriate methods and techniques. Be patient and flexible
- Implement the intervention, with appropriate attention to emotional responses and contextual issues.
- Monitor progress and adjust the intervention if necessary.
- Evaluate the outcome of the intervention(s) and decide on any further steps to be taken.

A. Education
   1. Developing awareness for the problem(s)
      a. attention skills
      b. executive skills
      c. memory skills
      d. visual spatial skills
      e. problem-solving skills
      f. communication
   2. Cognitive strengths and weaknesses
B. Process training
   1. Identify the problem(s) to be resolved
   2. Development of skills through direct retraining (compensatory) or practicing the underlying cognitive skills
   3. Improve functional competence in daily life situations by direct retraining, compensatory strategies, or cognitive tools
   4. Involve the person in experiences that require individuals to interact, analyze, question, reflect, and connect with what they have learned in new situations in their daily life experiences
   5. Reinforcing, strengthening, or reestablishing previously learned patterns of thinking and behaving or compensatory mechanisms to replace them
C. Strategy training
   1. Focus on compensating rather than resolving the problems
   2. Utilize environmental, internal, and external strategies
D. Functional activities training
   1. Improving real-life experiences
   2. Combines education, process training, and strategy training
E. Memory enhancement strategies
   1. Accept their explanation—believe what they tell you
      a. validate that it can be painful to acknowledge that lack of recollection for personal and family history

2. Use a log and/or an appointment book
   a. A log is a simple and effective device to recap where they went, who they talked to and current event topics
   b. At the end of the day writing the plan down for the next day
   c. Encourage the expression of personal thoughts and feelings associated with their daily experiences
3. Tell stories and share their history
   a. Telling stories can be an encourager of memories and over time it may help in remembering the details
4. Use all of the senses to make memories
   a. Look through photos. Don't overwhelm to too many.
   b. Watch home videos.
   c. When in a favorite place utilize all of the senses. Describe smells, tastes, and sounds in simple terms.
5. Develop a booklet or use note cards of written instructions utilizing a few steps
6. Use external memory devices to enhance independence (in addition to log book and instructions)
   a. An alarm system as a reminder for taking medication of other routine and scheduled activities (could be a watch with an alarm)
   b. Using a calendar to be prepared for a scheduled activity and to "check off" what was accomplished at the end of the day
   c. Each day write out the schedule on an index card and carry it in a pocket or purse (whatever routine is created)
7. Construct a life history "autobiography"
   a. Choose specific events from childhood—interview family and friends for their memories of the event
   b. May be useful to utilize early life photos (again not too many to prevent overload)
8. Build on memory strengths (for procedural memory and working memory)
   a. An example would be a good retained memory for sport activities. Use this memory and skill by joining in a sports club. It is a positive way to build self-esteem associated with "ability"
9. Rehearsal; rehearse important events
   a. Prior to new or anxiety-provoking events, talk about the event, what will happen, and discuss how they can feel in control
   F. Environmental modifications
9. Risk for injury
   A. Assess
      1. Psychosis
      2. Disorientation
      3. Wanders off
      4. Agitation unmanageable
      5. Excessive hyperactivity
      6. Muscular weakness
      7. Falling
      8. Seizures

*Agitation and psychosis are a common presentation in individuals with NCDs. If these symptoms are present, a thorough evaluation to determine what may underlie the disturbance is recommended.

   B. Precautions
      1. Caretaker to remain in close proximity for monitoring, check frequently
      2. Objects/furniture in room should be placed with function and safety in mind
      3. Remove potentially harmful objects
      4. Padding of certain objects may be necessary
      5. Educate caregiver on safety and management issues

10. Manage behavioral symptoms (Alzheimer's and Dementia Care Center, 2015)
   A. Anxiety and agitation can be related to numerous medical conditions, medication interactions, or by any circumstance that negatively impacts a person's ability to think. Ultimately, the person experiencing an NCD is biologically experiencing a profound and intense loss of their ability to process and deal with new information and stimuli as a consequence of their disease. To help manage anxiety and agitation.
      1. Create a calm environment. Eliminate or decrease stressors
         a. Move to a quieter, less stimulating environment
         b. Provide a security object
         c. Provide privacy and rest
         d. Try calming/soothing rituals (and limiting or eliminating caffeine)
      2. Avoid environmental triggers
         a. Noise, glare, background distractions (TV, etc.)
      3. Monitor personal comfort
         a. Check for pain, hunger, thirst, full bladder/constipation, fatigue, infections, skin irritation
         b. Make sure environment is at a comfortable temperature
         c. Be sensitive to fears, misperceived threats, and possible frustration with expressing what a person want
      4. Simplify tasks and routines
      5. Structure opportunity for exercise in the daily schedule
   B. Recommended manner in which to respond to identified anxiety/agitation
      1. Listen in an interested and caring manner to frustration
         a. Determine, if possible the underlying cause/try to understand
      2. Offer reassurance
         a. Use calming words and phrases, assuring that you are there to help them
            1. "You are safe here," "I am sorry you are upset," "I will stay with you until you feel better"
      3. Create opportunities to involve them in activities
         a. Utilize art, music, or other activities to help engage the person and divert their attention away from their distress
      4. Modify the environment
         a. Eliminate or decrease noise and distractions, or relocate
      5. Identify outlets for the person's energy
         a. The person may feel bored and looking for something to do. Take them for a walk or go for a car ride
      6. Self-monitor (by caregiver)
         a. Maintain self-awareness to avoid raising their voice, overreact/show alarm, corner, crowd, restrain, criticize, ignore, or argue with the person. Be thoughtful to not make sudden movements in the periphery/out of their view to avoid startle
      7. Medical consult
         a. Visit the primary care provider to rule out any physical/medical causes or medication related side effects
   C. Common sleep changes. Many people with dementia experience changes in their sleep patterns that include
         a. Difficulty sleeping. Many people with Alzheimer wake up more often and stay awake longer during the night. Brain wave studies show decreases in both dreaming and nondreaming sleep stages. Those who cannot sleep may wander, be unable to lie still, or yell or call out, disrupting the sleep of their caregivers.
         b. Daytime napping and other shifts in sleep–wake cycle. Individuals may feel very drowsy during the day and then be unable to sleep at night. They may become restless or agitated in the late afternoon or early evening, an experience often called "sundowning." In extreme cases, people may have a complete reversal of the usual daytime wakefulness–nighttime sleep pattern.

c. Contributing medical factors. A person experiencing sleep disturbances should have a thorough medical exam to identify if any treatable illnesses that may be contributing to the problem.
   1. Depression
   2. Restless leg syndrome
   3. Sleep apnea
11. Risk of violence
   A. Assess level of agitation, thought processes, and behaviors indicative of possible episode of violent acting outing potentially directed toward self or others
   B. Keep environmental stimuli to a minimum and remove all dangerous objects
   C. Encourage caregiver to maintain a calm manner
   D. Gently correct distortions of reality
   E. Evaluate need for higher level of care
12. Caregiver stress

   Being a caregiver can be very stressful. Caregiving a person who has memory impairment can be challenging. It is a role that requires a lot of patience.
   A. Encourage appropriate expression of feelings such as anger and depression
   B. Coping tips—identify ways to effectively deal with emotions
      1. Monitor personal comfort. Check for pain, hunger, thirst, constipation, full bladder, fatigue, infections, and skin irritation. Maintain a comfortable room temperature.
      2. Avoid being confrontational or arguing about facts. For example, if a person expresses a wish to go visit a parent who died years ago, don't point out that the parent is dead. Instead, say, "Your mother is a wonderful person. I would like to see her too."
      3. Redirect the person's attention. Try to remain flexible, patient, and supportive by responding to the emotion, not the behavior.
      4. Create a calm environment. Avoid noise, glare, insecure space and too much background distraction, including television.
      5. Allow adequate rest between stimulating events.
      6. Provide a security object.
      7. Acknowledge requests.
      8. Look for reasons behind each behavior.
      9. Explore various solutions
      10. Don't take the behavior personally, and share your experiences with others.
   C. Identify feelings of stress and loss in relationship to the person they are taking care of
   D. Identify family conflict related to issues of care
   E. Identify how their own lives have been interrupted/interfered with by caregiver role
   F. Develop rotations of time off to take care of own needs and have time to themselves
   G. Refer to community support group focusing on caregiver situation

SUBSTANCE-RELATED AND ADDICTIVE DISORDERS

This diagnostic section is identified by personality, mood, and behavioral changes associated with the use of substances. These changes are manifested by impairments in the following areas of functioning: social, emotional, psychological, occupational, and physical. Instead of using the terms tolerance and withdrawal to describe substance dependence it may be more helpful to conceptualize "addiction" by the following criteria:

1. Obsessive–compulsive behavior with the substance
2. Loss of control, manifested by the person being unable to reliably predict starting and stopping his/her use of the substance
3. Continued use despite the negative consequences associated with substance use

The following are the four pathways of use:

1. Oral—absorption in the bloodstream
2. Injection—IV use
3. Snorting—absorbed through the nasal membrane
4. Inhaling—absorbing through the lung

Brown's (1985) developmental model for the stages of alcohol recovery offers a conceptual framework for identifying where an individual is in his/her recovery so that the developmentally appropriate interventions can be made. The stages are as follows:

1. Substance abuse. The internal and external conflicts of addiction lead the individual to a point of loathing, fear, self-hatred, losses, and other consequences. The individual hits bottom.
2. Transition. The individual makes a shift from using to not using. If the individual does not fully accept and believe that he/she is addicted, the person may slip back and forth between stages 1 and 2. At this stage, work with the resistance as much as possible. Without a constant focus on the substance, the individual is enticed back into the belief that he/she can control use and may initiate the cycle of use once more.
3. Early recovery. The individual begins social integration by interacting with others without the use of a substance. With continued abstinence the person begins to recover some of his/her losses with a return to work, family relationships, and other adjustments. This is a period of new experiences for the individual, which requires the support of others. The individual benefits from participation in a 12-step group.
4. Late recovery or ongoing recovery. This is the developmental stage of recovery where the more typical psychotherapeutic issues are evident. During this period, there is a move from the self-centered view of the world to a view in which the individual exists in relation to others.

SUDs are evident when a person needs a substance (alcohol or other substance) to function normally. The clinical intervention begins with determining if there is concern of an SUD. All patients should be screened for substance (alcohol and other substances) misuse. There are numerous evidence-based screening tools for specific identified populations. If a positive screen is given, provide a brief intervention that includes an assessment and follow-up care, including a referral to specialty services and systematic monitoring as needed. Utilize motivational interviewing techniques to result in a collaborative effort as treatment decisions, and treatment, progress via psychosocial interventions.

To optimize the SUD treatment outcome a comprehensive understanding of a person's life experience and repair of the damage or losses need to be assessed and addressed for developing effective interpersonal, vocational, educational, coping skills, and family system issues. Of particular importance is the comprehensive treatment of co-occurring psychiatric or medical conditions that may negatively impact the risk of relapse such as chronic pain, mood disturbances, anxiety disorders, impaired thought processes, and impulse control disorders.

A SUD is a serious condition and difficult to treat (NIMH, 2014). For outpatient treatment SAMHSA (2015; NQF, 2005) recommends an IOP program, medication if indicated, additional recovery support services, 12-step fellowship and peer support (Smart Recovery is an alternative). While some programs are developed for specific populations, common therapy interventions include the following;

1. Motivational interviewing utilizes techniques that promote a patient to move closer to a stage of readiness to change substance use behaviors.
2. Motivational enhancement therapy is an empathic approach of motivating a patient regarding the pros/cons of abstinence and recovery and their ambivalence about reaching the recovery identified goals. It is imperative to understand the person's stage of readiness to change (precontemplation, contemplation, preparation, action, or maintenance stage) for effectively

determining what motivational strategies to utilize at a specific time of intervention. A primary goal of motivational enhancement is to reinforce the person's reasons for change and provide the necessary treatment assistance.

3. CBT teaches individuals in treatment to recognize and stop negative patterns of thinking and behavior. For instance, CBT might help a person be aware of the stressors, situations, and feelings that lead to substance use so that the person can avoid them or act differently when they occur.

4. Structured family and couples therapy goal is to enlist concerned significant others to foster treatment seeking and retention in family members who are unmotivated to change substance abuse behaviors, and increase their likelihood of following through and demonstrating better treatment results.

5. Contingency management is designed to provide incentives to reinforce positive behaviors, such as remaining abstinent from substance use.

6. Community reinforcement therapy aims to provide individuals with SUDs with natural alternative reinforcers by rewarding their involvement in the family and social community.

7. 12-Step facilitation therapy seeks to guide and support engagement in 12-step programs such as AA or Narcotics Anonymous.

*To increase compliance requires a signed/initiated/dated meeting/appointment attendance list.

Kleber et al. (2010) assert that psychosocial treatments are the foundation for a spectrum of intervention methods for the process of recovery:

1. Sustained motivation
   A. avoid the rewards of substance use
   B. tolerate the discomforts of withdrawal symptoms
   C. maintain the drive to avoid relapse despite episodic craving
2. Coping skills
   A. manage and avoid situations that place the individual at high risk for relapse
3. Alternative sources of reward or symptom relief must be sought and used to fill the place previously filled by substance use
4. Dysphoric affect (anger, sadness, anxiety) needs to be managed in a manner that does not involve continued substance use

Recovery is not a linear process. It is the up, down, and sideways flow of interaction between all of the experiences. This includes new ideas, new behaviors, new belief system, and the shaping of a new identity integrating the culmination of where the individual has been and where he/she is. This foundation of integrating experience 1 day at a time is what will take the individual to tomorrow.

SUBSTANCE-RELATED AND ADDICTIVE DISORDERS

Goals

1. Complete assessment with appropriate referrals
2. Encourage abstinence
3. Break through denial
4. Support cognitive restructuring
5. Improve behavioral self-control
6. Develop refusal skills

7. Improve social skills
8. Improve communication skills
9. Improve coping skills
10. Improve problem-solving skills
11. Improve self-esteem
12. Relapse prevention
13. Support and educate family

Treatment Focus and Objectives

1. Thorough Assessment for Referral and Treatment
   A. Evaluate substance use (how much, how often, substances of choice, family history, patterns of use, prior treatment, level of impairment in major life areas, inability to control use, etc.) (NICE, 2011).
   B. Refer for general physical examination and consultation with primary care physician. Refer for specific assessment of physiological impairment if warranted by history.
   C. Referrals (assuming detox is not an issue or is completed).
      1. If unable to remain in recovery, refer to residential program
      2. Outpatient chemical dependency program
      3. 12-Step meetings or other supportive groups and programs

*Provide motivational intervention as part of the assessment process. Key factors in motivational interviewing include (NICE, 2011):

   - facilitating recognition of problems/potential problems related to substance use
   - facilitating the resolve of ambivalence and encourage positive change and belief in one's ability to change
   - utilize support, persuasiveness, and encouragement while avoiding confrontation/argumentativeness

   D. Evaluate cognitive deficit
      1. Establish baseline assess of fund of knowledge, take into consideration level of education and level of development
      2. Identify strengths and weaknesses
   E. Inadequate nutrition
      1. Facilitate identification of prior eating patterns
      2. Develop and establish eating three balanced meals a day
   F. Recovery support services
      1. Transportation to recovery activities
      2. Employment/educational support
      3. Peer to peer affiliation, accountability coach, mentor, sponsor
      4. Faith-based support
      5. Self-help support group (AA, NA, Smart Recovery, Secular Recovery, etc.)
      6. Education about strategies that promote wellness and recovery
2. Abstinence
   During this phase, it can be helpful to encourage new experiences and roles consistent with a substance free lifestyle and to discourage major life changes and disruption to early stabilization.
   A. Individual has made a commitment to abstain from substance use
   B. Individual is participating in an outpatient program
   C. Individual has worked with therapist to develop own program for abstinence recovery

D. Active engagement in 12-step program with sponsor, weekly meetings/affiliation and step work (or other similarly structured program)
1. Discussing ambivalence and emotional distress associated with "giving up" substance use
2. Identifying emotional and environmental triggers of craving and substance use, i.e., social influences (friends), economic influences (unemployment), medical influences (chronic pain, fatigue), and psychological influences (hopelessness, despair, mood disorders, anxiety, etc.)
3. Developing and reviewing specific coping strategies to deal with internal and external stressors
4. Exploring the decision chain leading to reinitiation of substance use
5. Learning from brief episodes of relapse (slips) about triggers leading to relapse such as relapse risk situations, thoughts, or emotions they must learn to recognize triggers for relapse and learn to manage unavoidable triggers
6. Developing effective techniques for early intervention (preventing a slip/lapse/relapse)

3. Denial
A. Convey an attitude that is not rejecting or judgmental, that is focused on their goals. Motivational enhancement is characterized by an empathic therapeutic approach in which the therapist helps to motivate the patient by asking about the pros and cons of specific behaviors, exploring their goals and associated ambivalence about reaching those goals, and practicing reflective listening to the patient's responses. This technique may be particularly useful for those who are not highly motivated to change.
B. Confront denial with reality of use and education to correct misconceptions
C. Identify the relationship between substance use and personal problems
D. Do not accept or ignore the use of other defense mechanisms to avoid reality, redirect using information they have shared regarding change
E. Encourage person to take responsibility for choices and associated consequences
F. Provide positive feedback and reinforcement for insight and taking responsibility, encourage and reinforce growth

4. Negative/Irrational Thinking
Cognitive strategies are essential for fostering the determination to abstain by exploring positive/negative consequences of continued substance use.
A. Educate regarding positive self-talk to challenge negative self-statements and negative self-fulfilling prophecy
B. Identify differences in statements prefaced as "can," "can't," "will," and "wont't"
C. Seek clarification "Does my style of thinking help or hinder me?"
D. Challenge beliefs with factual information
E. Accurately reflect reality to individual

5. Lack of Self-control
Self-control is integral to relapse prevention. Teaching individuals to anticipate and avoid substance-related cues, training them to monitor their affective/cognitive states associated with increased craving and substance use. Also there is significant value to educating and training cue extinction, relaxation techniques and developing coping skills, and lifestyle changes that support abstinence and recovery.
A. Facilitate individual's analysis of substance use patterns and monitoring.
1. Identify situations, people, emotions, and beliefs associated with substance use
2. Monitor currently or through recollection of past behaviors
3. Facilitate preparation for anticipated difficult situations and planning strategies either to avoid or cope with these situations (strategies should be both cognitive and behavioral)/preparing for emergency or crisis situations
4. Encourage active participation in group affiliation and other self-care behaviors
5. Build in "reminder" statements or affirmations about the individual's commitment to abstinence
6. Coping with cravings
B. Facilitate development of assertive communication.

C. Offer relaxation training with positive self-statements attached.

D. Increase repertoire of coping skills through modeling, rehearsal, and homework assignments. This can also be a positive use of planned distraction.

E. Challenge processes that underlie substance use.

  1. Identifying and modifying dysfunctional thinking patterns

  2. Develop coping strategies that serve as an effective alternative to substance use

    a. Exploring positive and negative consequences of continued use

    b. Recognizing decisions that could result in high-risk situations

    c. Identifying and confronting thoughts about substance use

    d. Developing strategies for coping with cravings, preparing for emergencies, and coping with a slip, lapse or relapse

6. Lack of Refusal Skills

  A. Goal is to develop the skills needed to refuse substances, refuse invitations to participate in activities or be in the company of others associated with substance abuse

  B. Specific tasks to develop to strengthen refusal skills

    1. Rehearsal—asking for help

    2. Honestly expressing thoughts and feelings

    3. Confronting and dealing with fear(s)

    4. Standing up for their rights

    5. How to deal with being left out

    6. How to deal with group pressure and persuasion

7. Ineffective Social Skills

  A. Teach social skills through role-modeling, rehearsal, and role-playing

  B. Teach effective communication

    1. Nonverbal communication such as positioning, eye contact, and personal space

    2. Verbal communication

      a. Initiating conversation

      b. Listening and reflecting

      c. Giving and accepting compliments

      d. Using "I" statements

      e. Dealing with criticism or teasing

      f. Assertive communication

  C. Develop and utilize social supports

    1. Recovery supportive social relationships

    2. Recovery supportive activities

    3. Recovery supportive community structure

  D. Developing close and intimate relationships

    1. Steps of getting to know someone

    2. Disclosure (how much/what/how soon)

    3. Setting limits and boundaries

    4. How to be close to someone and not lose focus on your goals

    5. Being able to imagine someone else's feelings and thoughts

    6. Being able to monitor and modify one's own nonverbal communication

    7. Being able to adapt to circumstances to maintain relationships

    8. Establish trusting relationship reciprocating respect by keeping appointments, being honest, etc.

      a. Facilitate person to clarify the impact that substance abuse/dependence has had on their significant relationships, financial implications, work, physical health, and social supports/ interaction, or peer reference group

      b. Once these issues are identified, facilitate insight, understanding, and the development of choices in dealing with these various situations

8. Ineffective Communication
   A. Assertive communication. Educate using comparisons of assertive communication to aggressive-passive/aggressive-passive. Use vignettes and role-play.
   B. Facilitate awareness for inappropriate behaviors and verbal expressions as ineffective attempts to communicate.
   C. Identify feelings behind inappropriate behavioral and emotional expressions and facilitate problem solving.
   D. Use "I" statement to avoid blaming and manipulation.
   E. Use vignettes, role-modeling, rehearsal, and role-play for developing communication skills.

9. Ineffective Coping
   A. Facilitate identification of feelings.
   B. Encourage appropriate ventilation of feelings.
   C. Set limits on manipulative behavior (be consistent).
   D. Facilitate development of appropriate and acceptable social behaviors.
   E. Educate person regarding the effects of substance use on social, psychological, and physiological functioning.
   F. Explore alternatives for dealing with stressful situations. Problem-solve appropriate responses to replace substance use behaviors.
   G. Facilitate the development of a self-care plan that outlines resources, skills to use in various situations, daily structure, red flags to regression, and so on.
   H. Encourage person to take responsibility for choices and associated consequences.
   I. Positive feedback for independent and effective problem solving.

10. Ineffective Problem Solving
    A. Teach problem-solving skills
    B. Develop some sample problems and give homework to practice new skills
    C. Identify secondary gains which inhibits progress toward change

11. Low Self-esteem
    A. Be accepting and respectful of person
    B. Identify strengths and accomplishments
    C. Encourage a focus on strengths and accomplishments
    D. Facilitate identification of past failures and reframe with a perspective of how the person can benefit and learn from previous experiences
    E. Identify desired areas of change and facilitate problem solving the necessary objectives to meet the defined goals
    F. Facilitate self-monitoring of efforts toward desired goals
    G. Encourage and positively reinforce appropriate independent functioning
    H. Facilitate development of assertive communication
    I. Facilitate clarification of boundaries and appropriate limit setting in relationships

12. Relapse Prevention (refer to the section "List of Symptoms Leading to Relapse")

*Prevention means watching for warning signs. Therefore, the best way to prevent relapse is to understand warning signs and factors that commonly lead to relapse.

   A. An important factor in planning relapse prevention is to understand that not everything can be controlled
   B. Create a relapse prevention plan
      1. Create an index card to be carried in a wallet, purse, or pocket
         a. On one side of the card write names and phone numbers for safe and supportive people who can be called if craving or emotional distress is experienced
         b. Include sponsor(s), accountability partners, and hotlines
         c. Include contact information for supportive family members and friends

      d. On the other side of the index card write down "five" things that can be done if cravings are experienced (such as attending a meeting, engaging in recovery supportive activity, call their sponsor/recovery partner, etc.)

    C. Avoidance as an effective tool

*Avoiding a situation where temptation may arise, recommend the consideration of using the buddy system by asking a close friend, family member, or sponsor to attend the event with them.

      1. Locations where the substance was easy to access (bars/clubs, certain people, events)
      2. Spending time with anyone who actively in their disease or not supportive of recovery
    D. Identify high-risk situations that increase likelihood of relapse

*Generally these situations involve negative emotional states.

    E. Identify interpersonal conflicts such as marriage, friendship, family members, or employer–employee relations, and how they can deal with each category versus using it as an excuse to relapse
    F. Identify social pressure
      1. Direct sources such as interpersonal contact with verbal persuasion
      2. Indirect sources such as being in the presence of others who are engaging in the same target behavior, even though no direct pressure is involved
    G. Understanding that symptoms of relapse can be experienced even long after expected withdrawal
      1. Postacute withdrawal "PAW"—a protracted withdrawal that might lead to relapse
      2. Inability to cope with high-risk situations
        a. Never acquired the coping skills necessary for these situations
        b. Appropriate responses are inhibited by fear or anxiety that they will relapse
    H. Abstinence violation effect which is defined by the following cognitive–affective elements
      1. Cognitive dissonance (conflict and guilt)
      2. Personal attribution–blaming self as the cause of the relapse
      3. Perceived positive effects of the alcohol/substance
    I. Cognitive distortions
      1. Denial and rationalization make it much easier to set up a relapse episode
    J. Addictive preoccupation consisting of obsessive thought patterns, compulsive behaviors, and physical cravings
    K. Lack of lifestyle balance between perceived external demands (should) and activities perceived as pleasurable and self-fulfilling
13. Dysfunctional Family Interaction
    A. Evaluate how family has been affected by behavior of this person (fear, isolation, shame, economic consequences, guilt, feeling responsible for the behavior of others)
    B. Explore how family may help sustain or reinforce this dysfunctional behavior
    C. Teach communication skills
    D. Refer family members to appropriate 12-step groups, other community resources, or therapy. Decrease isolation.

CATEGORIES OF PHARMACOLOGICAL INTERVENTION

1. Medications to treat intoxication and withdrawal states
2. Medications to decrease the reinforcing effects of abused substances
3. Medications that discourage substance abuse by
    A. Inducing unpleasant consequences through drug–drug interaction
    B. Coupling substance use with an unpleasant drug–induced condition

4. Agonist substitution therapy
5. Medications to treat comorbid psychiatric conditions

TREATMENT SETTINGS

As in all cases, individuals should be treated in the least restrictive setting that provides safety and effectiveness. General treatment settings include the following:

1. Hospitalization
   A. Danger to self, others, gravely disabled
   B. There has been an overdose
   C. There is risk of severe/medically complicated withdrawal
   D. Comorbid medical condition(s) prohibits a safe outpatient detox
   E. Psychiatric comorbidity impairs ability to comply and benefit from a lower level of care
2. Residential treatment facility—sober living facility
   A. Does not meet criteria for hospitalization
   B. Lacks adequate social and vocational skills to maintain abstinence
   C. Lacks of social support
3. Partial hospitalization
   A. Requires intensive care but is able to abstain.
   B. Requires a transitional level of care following discharge from inpatient care when risk of relapse remains relatively high.
   C. Lacks sufficient motivation to continue in treatment.
   D. Requires a high level of support (for those returning to high-risk environments). There has not been a positive response to intensive outpatient.
4. Outpatient Programs
   A. Clinical conditions/environmental circumstances do not require intensive care

*Duration of treatment is individualized to the specific needs of the person in treatment and may last from several months to several years.

HOW TO PREVENT AN OPIOID OVERDOSE AND OPIOID-RELATED OVERDOSE (NIAAA, 2015; SAMHSA, 2013)

1. Identify opioids: Illegal drugs such as heroin, as well as prescription medications such as morphine, codeine, methadone, oxycodone (Oxycontin, Percodan, Percocet), hydrocodone (Vicodin, Lortab, Norco), fentanyl (Duragesic, Fentora), hydromorphone (Dilaudid, Exalgo), and buprenorphine (Subutex, Suboxone).
2. Educate those at risk: An overdose can occur when a patient purposefully misuses a prescription opioid or an illegal drug such as heroin. Overdose can also happen when a patient takes the drug as directed, but the prescribing physician miscalculated the dose or an error is made by the pharmacy. An additional overdose caveat is when a person takes prescribed opioid medication belonging to someone else, or the combining of opioids with alcohol, or other central nervous system depressants (prescribed or over the counter).

HOW TO PREVENT AN ALCOHOL DETOX DEATH

1. Alcohol detox is the most dangerous. When a person stops drinking abruptly, the consequences can be deadly. Sudden alcohol cessation can result in hallucinations, convulsions, and even heart seizures that may result in death.

2. Initial alcohol detox symptoms may include anxiety, convulsions, delirium tremens, hallucinations, heart failure, insomnia, nausea, seizures, and shakiness. Professional alcohol detox generally includes prescribed medication(s) that increases the comfort and safety of detox. Medications require medical monitoring.

LIST OF SYMPTOMS LEADING TO RELAPSE

1. *Exhaustion*: Becoming over tired. Not following through on self-care behaviors of adequate rest, good nutrition, and regular exercise. Good physical health is a component of emotional health. How one feels will be reflected in their thinking and judgment.

2. *Dishonesty*: It begins with a pattern of small, unnecessary lies with those a person interacts with in family, in society, and at work. Dishonesty with others is followed by lying to themselves or rationalizing and making excuses for avoiding working their program.

3. *Impatience*: Things are not happening fast enough for them. Or others are not doing what they want them to do or what they think they should do.

4. *Argumentative*: Arguing small insignificant points that indicate a need to always be right. This is sometimes seen as developing an excuse to drink.

5. *Depression*: Overwhelming and unaccountable despair may occur in cycle. If it does, talk about it and deal with it. They must acknowledge and accept that they are responsible for taking care of themselves.

6. *Frustration*: With people and because things may not be going their way. Remind themselves intermittently that things are not always going to be the way that they want them.

7. *Self-pity*: Feeling like a victim, refusing to acknowledge that they have choices and are responsible for their own life and the quality of it.

8. *Cockiness*: "Got it made" compulsive behavior is no longer a problem. Start putting self in situations where there are temptations to prove to others that they don't have a problem.

9. *Complacency*: Not working their program with the commitment that they started with. Having a little fear is a good thing. More relapses occur when things are going well than when not.

10. *Expecting too much from others*: "I've changed, why hasn't everyone else changed too?" A person can only control themselves. It would be great if other people changed their self-destructive behaviors, but that is their problem. They have their own problems to monitor and deal with. They cannot expect others to change their lifestyle just because you have.

11. *Letting up on discipline*: Daily inventory, positive affirmations, 12-step meetings, meditation, prayer, and therapy. This can come from complacency and boredom. Because they cannot afford to be bored with your program, take responsibility—talk about it and problem-solve it. The cost of relapse is too great. Sometimes they must accept that they have to do some things that are the routine for a clean and sober life.

12. *The use of mood-altering chemicals*: They may feel the need or desire to get away from things by drinking, popping a few pills, and so on, and their physician may participate thinking that you will be responsible and not abuse the medication. This is the most subtle way to enter relapse. They must take responsibility for their life and the choices that they make.

Common drugs of abuse

Type of drug	Pharmaceutical or street name	Psychological dependence	Physical dependence	Tolerance	Methods of use	Symptoms of use	Withdrawal syndrome
Stimulant/uppers							
Amphetamines	Benzedrine				Swallowed pill/capsule or injected into veins, snorted, injected, smoked	Increased activity and alertness, euphoria, dilated pupils, disorientation, increased heart rate and BP, insomnia, loss of appetite	Apathy, long periods of sleep, irritability, depression
Amphetamines	Dexadrine						
Dextroamphetamine	Pep-pills, toot						
Methamphetamine	X-tops, Meth Crystal, Ice Bennies, Dexie Uppers, Speed						
Cocaine		High	Moderate to high	Yes			
Nicotine					Smoke Snuff Chew	Paranoia, hallucinations, anxiety, convulsions	
Caffeine					Swallowed pill/capsule or beverages		
Depressants/downers							
Barbiturates	Phenobarbital Seconal, Tuinal, Quaalude, Soper	High	High		Swallowed in pill or capsule form or injected into veins	Slurred speech, disorientation, drunken behavior, drowsiness, impaired judgment	Anxiety, insomnia tremors, delirium, convulsions, possible death
Sedative	Barbs, Yellow Jackets, Red Devils, Blue Devils	High	High	Yes			
Hypnotics							
Tranquilizers	Librium, Valium Equanil, Miltown						
Alcohol	Beer, Wine, Spirits	Moderate	Moderate		Swallowed in pill or liquid form, injected into veins, or smoked	Euphoria, drowsy, respiratory depression, constricted pupils, nausea chills, sweating cramps, nausea	Watery eyes, runny nose, yawning, loss of appetite, irritability tremors, panic
Opium	Paregoric (O)	High	High				
Morphine	(M) Hard Stuff	High	High				
Codeine	School Boy	Moderate	Moderate				
Heroin	H, Horse, Smack	High	High	Yes			
Hallucinogens							
Marijuana (Hashish)	Pot, Grass, Joint Reefer	Possible	Possible		Smoked, inhaled, or eaten	Illusions, hallucinations, poor perception of time and distance slurred vision confusion, dilated pupils, mood swing	
LSD	Acid, Lucy in the Sky with Diamonds	Possible	No	Yes	Injected or swallowed in tablets, sugar cubes		
PCP	Peace Pill, Angel Dust	Possible	No				
Psilocybin	Magic Mushrooms	Possible	No				
Inhalants/solvents							
Gasoline	Trash Drugs				Inhaled or sniffed often with use of paper or plastic bag or rag	Disorientation, slurred speech, dizziness, nausea, poor motor control	Restlessness, anxiety irritability
Taluene	Inhalants						
Acetone		Moderate	No	Yes			
Cleaning fluids							
Airplane cements							
Nitrous oxide	Laughing Gas	Moderate	No	Yes	Inhaled or sniffed	Light-headed	
Nitrites							
Amyl	Poppers, Locker Room	Moderate	No	Yes	Inhaled or sniffed from gauze/ampules	Slowed thought, headache	
Butyl	Rush, Snappers						

BP, blood pressure; *LSD*, lysergic acid diethylamide; *PCP*, phencyclidine.

SCHIZOPHRENIA SPECTRUM AND OTHER PSYCHOTIC DISORDERS

To increase the reliability of a schizophrenia diagnosis, a person is required to have at least one of three "positive" symptoms of schizophrenia.

1. Hallucinations
2. Delusions
3. Disorganized speech

Schizophrenia, if left untreated, can result in severe emotional, behavioral, and health problems, as well as legal and financial problems that affect every area of life. Complications that schizophrenia may cause or be associated with include:

1. Anxiety and phobias
2. Any type of self-injury
3. Depression
4. Abuse of alcohol, drugs, or prescription medications
5. Noncompliance with prescribed medications
6. Poverty
7. Homelessness
8. Family conflicts
9. Inability to work or attend school
10. Social isolation
11. Health problems, including those associated with antipsychotic medications, smoking, and poor lifestyle choices
12. Being a victim of aggressive behavior
13. Aggressive behavior, although it's uncommon and typically related to lack of treatment, substance misuse, or a history of violence
14. Suicide

Clinical case management defines an overview of intervention for this chronic complex diagnosis. Similar to other challenging diagnoses, treatment success requires integration of services from all involved disciplines. The clinician plays a vital role because it is likely there will be more contact with the clinician than anyone else on the treatment team, thus providing more opportunity to listen, observe, and utilize the information with the treatment team on behalf of assuring the most effective treatment for the person. The basics of counseling/clinical case management are the following:

1. Cognitive-behavioral strategies to enhance coping skills
2. Supportive counseling to foster linkage with community services
3. Assertive case management to ensure coordination of all medically and socially necessary services
4. Concurrent treatment of substance abuse, when present
5. Coordination of care between prescribing and nonprescribing behavioral health-care practitioners, as well as with the primary care physician

The goal of treatment is usually not to cure the individual but to improve the quality of life. Once psychosis recedes, psychological and social (psychosocial) interventions are important—in addition to consistent compliance with medication. These may include the following:

1. *Individual therapy.* Learning to cope with stress and identify early warning signs of relapse can help people with schizophrenia manage their illness.
2. *Social skills training.* This focuses on improving communication and social interactions.
3. *Family therapy.* This provides support and education to families dealing with schizophrenia.

*It is amazing how "infrequently" family is not included as part of the treatment team. This requires that the patient provides an appropriate HIPAA compliant release of information and honesty about how this resource is to be used for the benefit of the patient.

4. *Vocational rehabilitation and supported employment.* This focuses on helping people with schizophrenia prepare for, find, and keep jobs.

Most individuals with schizophrenia require some form of daily living support. Some communities have programs to help people with schizophrenia with jobs, housing, self-help groups, and crisis situations. A case manager (or someone on the treatment team) or conservator can help find resources. With appropriate treatment, support, and positive daily structure, most people with schizophrenia can manage their condition. As with many diagnoses today, CBT is specialized to specific diagnostic challenges. In this case, CBT for psychosis is referred to as "CBT-P."

As previously stated, treatment of schizophrenia requires integration of medical, psychological, and psychosocial factors. The majority of care occurs in an outpatient setting and probably is best carried out by a multidisciplinary team. It is important to keep the primary care physician apprised of mental status and to help maintain the medical care of the person with a schizophrenia spectrum disorder. Obesity, diabetes, cardiovascular disease, and lung diseases are prevalent in schizophrenia, and the person with schizophrenia often does not receive adequate medical care for such conditions (National Guidelines Clearinghouse, 2013).

SCHIZOPHRENIA SPECTRUM AND OTHER PSYCHOTIC DISORDERS

Goals

1. Ensure that person will not harm self or others
2. Provide safe environment
3. Refer for medication evaluation
4. Encourage stabilization with decreased/elimination of perceptual disturbances
5. Improve coping skills
6. Improve self-management skills (grooming/hygiene, sleep cycle, etc.)
7. Improve sleep pattern
8. Improve self-esteem
9. Decrease social isolation
10. Improve communication skills
11. Family intervention
12. Medication compliance
13. Educate person and significant others on side effects of medication
14. Vocational rehabilitation

Treatment Focus and Objectives

1. Evaluate for risk to self or others (psychotic thinking, rage reactions, pacing, overt aggressive acts, hostile and threatening verbalizations, irritability, agitation, perceives environment as threatening, self-destructive, or suicidal acts, etc.)

*Comorbidity and dual diagnosis are diagnostic considerations that serve as an important component of assessment—especially depression and substance abuse that would significantly impact the effectiveness and compliance of medication as well as therapeutic participation.

    A. Keep environmental stimuli low
    B. Monitor closely
    C. Remove dangerous objects from environment
    D. Redirect physical acting out through physical exercise to decrease tension
    E. Medication as directed/prescribed
    F. Call for crisis team or police of necessary to transport to psychiatric facility if a behavioral escalation occurs

2. Evaluate Environmental Safety
    A. Determine if person demonstrates adequate level of cooperativity
    B. Evaluate adequacy of social support
    C. Adjust level of care if necessary
        1. Day treatment program/partial hospitalization
        2. Inpatient setting→open unit
        3. Inpatient setting→closed unit

3. Refer for Medication Evaluation
    A. If this is an initial evaluation and symptoms of perceptual disturbances are identified, refer for a medication evaluation. If this is the first experience of being diagnosed with perceptual disturbances and referral for pharmacological treatment, there is an expectation of aloneness, fear, and other negative emotional states. Validate their experience and prepare them with the supportive understanding that they will not be making this journey alone and that therapy combined with medication is going to help them live the most fulfilling life possible.
        1. Psychoeducation
            a. General information on the nature of schizophrenia/psychotic disorder and its treatment
            b. Emphasizing medication compliance, avoidance of stress, identification of prodromal signs, increasing coping skills, increasing independent living skills
            c. Defining the disorder as a "no-fault" brain disease
    B. If this has been an ongoing case and the person is experiencing an exacerbation of symptoms, their functioning has deteriorated, or there are any other signs of decompensation, refer them to their prescribing physician. Additionally, consult directly with the physician to ensure optimal case management.
    C. To improve patient medication compliance, discuss their concerns, have more frequent visits, provide verbal and written education for the patient and their family.

4. Sensory-Perceptual Disturbance
    A. Identify the nature and etiology of delusions
        1. Encourage identity of their own delusions or paranoid beliefs
        2. Explore how these beliefs negatively impact their life
        3. Help them to engage in experiments to test these beliefs
        4. Treatment focus on thought patterns that cause distress and on developing more realistic interpretation of events
            a. For example, developing an understanding of the evidence base a person uses to support their delusional belief and encouraging them to recognize evidence that may have been overlooked—and does not support the belief (i.e., no hidden camera in the waiting room, alien controlled television remote, etc.)

B. Rule out the presence of concomitant medical conditions as etiology of delusions

C. Look for signs of person withdrawing into self

D. Keep stress and anxiety at a minimum and educate regarding the relationship between stress and anxiety to perceptual disturbance

E. Increase awareness for patterns of talking or laughing to self

F. Monitor for disorientation and disordered thought sequencing

G. Confront distortions and misinterpretations with reality testing and encourage person to define and test reality

H. Intervene early to correct reality if person is experiencing perceptual or sensory distortions

I. Distract the person away from the perceptual disturbance by engaging him/her in another direction of thinking or activity

J. Skill development for stress and anxiety management

1. Using progressive muscle relaxation

2. Listening to soft music

3. Walking or other appropriate activity

4. Utilizing support from others

5. Ineffective Coping

Coping with schizophrenia is challenging for the person with the condition and their family.

A. Learn about schizophrenia. Education about the condition can help motivate the person with the disease to stick to the treatment plan. Education can help friends and family understand the condition and be more compassionate with the person who has it.

B. Facilitate identification of stressors contributing to increased anxiety and agitation, which result in disorientation of person.

C. Be honest and open about what is or will be taking place so as to decrease suspiciousness and to increase trust.

D. Confront distorted thinking, facilitate reality testing.

E. Encourage consistency in environment.

F. Encourage verbalization of feelings.

G. Facilitate appropriate problem solving.

H. Encourage medication compliance.

I. Educate family to be supportive of appropriate responses, consistency in environment, medication compliance, emotional management, minimal stimuli, necessity for honesty and following through on promises, and so on.

J. Facilitate person's ability to adequately and effective appraise situations and to respond appropriately.

K. Encourage and facilitate appropriate interaction and cooperation.

L. Social skills training.

1. Engaging in conversation

2. Listening

3. Increased awareness for nonverbal communication

M. Encourage and facilitate remaining focused on goals. Managing thought disorder is an ongoing process. Keeping treatment goals in mind can help the person with thought disorder to say motivated.

N. Cognitive remediation (CR) (Frankenburg et al., 2015). CR is based on neuropsychological rehabilitation and is based on the premise of neuroplasticity and that "brain exercises" encourage neuronal growth and can develop the neurocircuitry underlying many mental activities. Different models of CR are available and work best when a patient is stable.

1. Drill-based practicing of isolated cognitive skills with the aid of a computer

2. Use of strategies developed to overcome areas of weakness

3. Cognitive enhancement or metacognitive therapy

6. Grooming and Hygiene

A. Encourage daily independent living skills

1. Bathing

2. Cleaning hair, cutting when necessary, and styling appropriately

3. Brushing teeth

4. Dressing adequately and appropriately
5. Cleaning self adequately after using the bathroom and washing hands
   B. Encourage appropriate independent efforts
   C. Role-model and encourage the practice of appropriate behavior
   D. Offer positive reinforcement for efforts and accomplishments of independent living s

7. Sleep Disturbance
   A. Log sleeping pattern to develop treatment plan
   B. Use sedative antipsychotic medications at night (if prescribed)
   C. Clarify if fear or anxiety plays a role in difficulty falling to sleep
   D. Develop a pattern for winding down and offer methods to promote sleep
      1. Warm soothing bath or shower
      2. Light snack
      3. Warm milk or herbal tea
   E. Discourage daytime sleeping
   F. Encourage exercise during the day
   G. Use relaxation techniques such as meditation, yoga, tai chi
   H. Use soft music or nature sounds
   I. Limit caffeine intake

8. Low Self-esteem
   A. Reinforce accurate reality testing with positive feedback
   B. Social skills training
      1. Engaging in conversation
      2. Listening
      3. Increased awareness for nonverbal communication
   C. Encourage assertive communication
   D. Problem-solve through modeling and role-play ways to deal with typical problems encountered by the person in their environment, when interacting in society, and in peer situations
   E. Encourage and positively reinforce self-care behaviors

9. Social Isolation
   A. Educate, role-model, and practice appropriate social skills.
   B. Brief, frequent social contacts to facilitate familiarity.
   C. Accepting attitude to facilitate trust and feelings of self-worth.
   D. Offer patience and support to increase feelings of security.
   E. Encourage respect of personal space.
   F. Initiate the development and understanding of social cues.
   G. Identify feelings or circumstances that contribute to desire or need to withdraw and isolate.
   H. Refer person to appropriate social gatherings/groups to practice appropriate social behaviors. Support groups for people with schizophrenia can help them reach out to others facing similar challenges. Support groups may also help family and friends cope.

10. Ineffective Communication
   A. Encourage person to stay on task with one topic
   B. Encourage appropriate, intermittent eye contact
   C. Clarify communication (I don't understand…, Do you mean…?, etc.)
   D. Help person understand how his/her behavior and verbal expression are interpreted and act to distance or alienate the person from others
   E. Encourage efforts and accomplishments with positive reinforcement
   F. Facilitate person's ability to recognize disorganized thinking
   G. Facilitate person's ability to recognize impaired communication
   H. Practice social skills training reinforcement
      1. Engaging in conversation
      2. Listening
      3. Increased awareness for nonverbal communication

11. Relapse Prevention
    A. Combine educational, behavioral, and cognitive strategies
        1. Multidisciplinary compliance therapy with reinforcement
        2. Psychosocial support
        3. Family support and schedule of activities to improve quality of life experience and decrease social isolation
        4. Identify and counter social withdrawal
        5. Monitor depression and worthlessness—feeling despair/suicidal and counter with support and structure that is valued by the person
        6. Maintain a positive sleep regimen
        7. Monitor for anxious/nervous feeling as this often is seen prior to relapse episodes
        8. Problem-solve alleviating distress, i.e., arguments, criticism, sudden increased responsibility
        9. Make a list of treatment providers and safe social supports to contact if early signs of relapse are experienced (psychiatrist, therapist, family, friends)

12. Dysfunctional Family Interaction
    A. Identify how family is affected by person's behavior
    B. Identify behaviors of family members that prevent appropriate progress or behavioral management
    C. Educate family
        1. Regarding appropriate management of behaviors, the impact of conflict, impact from level of environmental stimuli, importance of medication compliance, reality testing, and how to respond to self-injurious or aggressive behavior.
        2. The importance of a release of information (HIPAA compliance) with each provider of the identified patient to improve their ability to participate in effective support and management.
        3. Recommend family to speak with physician and pharmacist regarding the side effects of the medications, the issue of monitoring side effects, and how to respond to the various side effects.
        4. Recommend self-education about the diagnosis and participate in NAMI for their own additional support and education regarding resources.

13. Support Medication Compliance
    A. Educate person regarding role of medication in functioning
    B. Support and reinforce medication compliance as a self-care behavior
    C. There are new long acting injectables that can be beneficial for medication compliance
    D. Reinforce medication compliance by discussing the patient's concern, more frequent visits, verbal and written education for the patient and their family
    E. Refer patient to med-monitoring group if available

14. General Side Effects of Medication

    This is not just a significantly challenging disorder, but the medications have numerous side effects as well. Therefore, the therapist should take the time to familiarize with the side effects profile of the specific medications their patient is taking to increase the benefit of their observations as a treatment team member and supportive as well as validating the patient's experience. Review the following to become acquainted with the side effect experience.
    A. Antipsychotic medication—be familiar with side effect profiles to better understand the experience of the person and increase useful observations for consultation
        1. Nausea
        2. Sedation
        3. Skin rash
        4. Orthostatic hypotension
        5. Photosensitivity
        6. Anticholinergic effects
            a. Dry mouth
            b. Constipation
            c. Blurred vision
            d. Urinary retention

7. Extrapyramidal symptoms
    a. Pseudo-parkinsonism (shuffling gait, tremor, drooling)
    b. Akinesia (muscle weakness)
    c. Dystonia (involuntary muscular movements of face neck and extremities)
    d. Akathisia (continuous restlessness)
8. Hormonal effects
    a. Weight gain
    b. Amenorrhea
    c. Decreased libido
    d. Retrograde ejaculation
    e. Gynecomastia (excessive development of the breasts in males)
9. Reduced seizure threshold
10. Agranulocytosis (monitor CBC and symptoms of fever, sore throat, malaise)
11. Tardive dyskinesia (bizarre tongue and facial movements)
12. Neuroleptic malignant syndrome (monitor fever, severe parkinsonian rigidity, tachycardia, blood pressure fluctuation, and fast deterioration of mental status to stupor and coma)

B. Antiparkinsonian medication side effects
1. Nausea
2. Sedation
3. Intensifies psychosis
4. Orthostatic hypotension
5. Anticholinergic symptoms
    a. Dry mouth
    b. Constipation
    c. Urinary retention
    d. Paralytic ileus (monitor absent bowel sounds, abdominal distention, vomiting, nausea, epigastric pain)
    e. Blurred vision

If the person reports having any side effects from the medication, initiate an immediate consult with the prescribing physician and encourage the person to do so as well. The participation of the patient in contacting the physician is necessary practice in reaching out for needed intervention and support.

15. Vocational rehabilitation (Frankenburg et al., 2015)
    A. Most people with schizophrenia would like to work but can't get or maintain a job because of their lack of stability or "odd behavior." However, helping them to gain employment can have numerous positive consequences. Employment can improve income, self-esteem, and social status. There are supportive employment programs and those thought to be most effective are those that offer individualized, supported, and rapid job assignments and that are integrated with other services. Such programs are associated with higher rates of employment, but they are not to be found in every community.
    B. Facilitate/arrange for a transitional or supported employment program specialized for patients with severe mental illness, when clinically indicated and resources permit.

SUMMARY OF TREATMENT RECOMMENDATIONS FOR PATIENTS WITH PERCEPTUAL DISTURBANCES

For disorders involving loss of contact with reality, the following summary creates a useful overview of areas to consider. Prior to proceeding, be sure to review the specific disorder's diagnostic criteria because of the broad variations in this section.

1. Treatment objectives
    A. Alleviate/eliminate symptoms
    B. Restore contact with reality

    C. Maximize emotional/behavioral adjustment disorders

    D. Improve coping

    E. Prevent relapse

    F. Educate family

    G. Support family

      1. Appropriate referral

        a. Emotional support

        b. Problem solving

        c. Community programs

2. Assessment

    A. Medical: to clarify diagnostic picture, substance use

    B. Neurological: intellectual level, level of functioning

    C. Psychological/emotional

3. Treatment team

    A. Medical (PCP, psychiatrist, neurologist)

    B. Psychological (family therapy, individual therapy, group therapy)

    C. Rehabilitation

      1. Cognitive rehabilitation

      2. Vocational rehabilitation

4. Treatment setting

    A. Inpatient

    B. Residential

    C. Outpatient

5. Interventions

    A. Medication; monitor closely to limit side effects

    B. Level of care required

      1. Inpatient

      2. Residential

      3. Outpatient

    C. Therapy modality

      1. Behavior therapy

        a. Improve coping

        b. Manage stress

        c. Improve socialization/utilization of resources

      2. Family therapy

        a. Education

        b. Support

        c. Adjustment

      3. Group therapy

        a. Rehabilitation counseling

        b. Vocational therapy

        c. Socialization

        d. Respite care (structured time and activities for several hours to half day)

6. Prognosis

    A. Varies based on disorder and level of functioning

    B. While therapy typically plays a secondary role in the treatment of most organic disorders, it can be an important adjunct to medical treatment. This is particularly true in the early/mind stages of primary degenerative dementia, multiinfarct dementia, and so on. It can serve to do the following:

      1. Encourage active/independent living as long as possible.

      2. Focus on behavioral-cognitive adjustments.

      3. Facilitate compensation for changes in capacity by building on coping mechanisms.

4. Assist in the management of negative affective states and destructive impulses adapted from L. Seligman (1990) and Kashdan et al. (2005). Resilience, positive assessment, flexibility, and hopefulness play an important role in self-esteem and affective instability.
    a. Increase awareness of self-evaluations/self-worth impact feelings of vulnerability and/or increased impulsivity with later regret
    b. Subjective well-being (satisfaction with life and overall quality of emotional experiences)
    c. Acknowledgment of genuine gratitude involving mindful awareness of circumstances of one's life and not taking positives for granted.

MOOD DISORDERS

The mood disorders section is divided into depressive disorders including persistent depressive disorder that includes both chronic major depressive disorder and what was previously dysthymic disorder and bipolar disorder. Additionally, a new specifier was added to indicate the presence of mixed symptoms across both the depressive and bipolar disorders allowing for the possibility of manic features in individuals with a diagnosis of unipolar depression. Another specifier of both diagnostic and treatment significance acknowledges the importance of anxiety as relevant to prognosis and treatment decision making. This specifier "with anxious distress" provides the clinician with an opportunity to rate the severity of anxious distress in those experiencing these diagnoses (APA, 2013). A mood disorder affects a person's everyday emotional state. Treatments include medication, psychotherapy, or a combination of both (NIH, 2015).

According to the APA (2015), bipolar disorder is the medical/brain disorder that results in alterations of mood, energy, and ability to function. This diagnostic category includes bipolar I, bipolar II, and cyclothymic disorder. This section will deal more simply with the objects and goals related to depressive symptoms and the objectives and goals related to manic symptoms.

Regier, Kuhl, et al. (2013) asserts that the new specifier "with anxious distress," applied to depressive disorders and bipolar and related disorders, incorporates symptoms that are not a part of the criteria for most mood disorders (e.g., difficulty in concentrating because of worry), however, describe a specific variant of mood disorder that causes impairment and/or distress and warrants intervention. It provides additional clinically useful information for both treatment planning and tracking outcomes. Additionally, the DSM 5's introduction of severity specifiers contributes important details about the presentation and may provide valuable information for promoting more appropriate treatment, as treatment for certain mild disorders should differ from treatment regimens for moderate-to-severe disorders.

The objectives of treatment result in measurable goals.

1. Reduce symptoms and remove signs of depression
2. Restore occupational and psychosocial functioning to premorbid levels
3. Reduce the likelihood of relapse and recurrence

Intervention and practices considered (APA, 2010) are initially conceptualized during the course of a clinical evaluation considering the following:

1. Establishing and maintaining a therapeutic alliance
2. Psychiatric assessment
    A. Mental status examination
    B. Demographics
    C. Previous episodes of depression and/or mania
    D. Response to previous treatment
    E. Substance use/abuse
    F. History of suicidal ideation/attempts, homicidal ideation/actions
    G. Family history of mental illness
    H. Precipitating factors

3. Safety evaluation including evaluation of suicide risk, level of self-care and dependent care, and risk or harm to self and others
4. Establishing appropriate treatment setting including hospitalization if appropriate
5. Evaluation of functional impairment and quality of life
6. Coordinating care with other clinicians, monitoring status, and tailoring treatment to specific patient needs
7. Assessment and acknowledgment of potential barriers to treatment
8. Patient and family education

DEPRESSION

Goals

1. Assess danger to self and others
2. Provide safe environment
3. Assess need for medication evaluation referral
4. Improve problem-solving skills
5. Improve coping skills
6. Develop and encourage utilization of support system
7. Resolve issues of loss
8. Improve self-esteem
9. Cognitive restructuring
10. Improve eating patterns
11. Improve sleep patterns
12. Develop depression management program
13. Educate regarding medication compliance

Treatment Focus and Objectives

1. Suicide Risk Assessment
   A. Thoughts of killing self or persistent death wish
   B. Plan
   C. Means to carry out the plan
   D. Feelings of hopelessness
   E. Past history of suicide attempts/rehearsals, or someone close to them who has attempted or committed suicide
   F. Recent losses
   G. Substance abuse
   H. Comorbid diagnosis (for example, SUD, borderline personality disorder (BPD), perceptual disturbance/chronic mentally ill, intolerable/chronic pain, progressive/incurable disease)
   I. Poor impulse control
   J. Poor judgment

During the interview it may be possible to decrease the level of emotional distress by validating the difficulty that the person is experiencing and encouraging him/her to vent feelings and intentions of suicide. Talking about these issues, which have resulted in such despair and hopelessness, may not only decrease the level of distress, but may create some opportunity for intervention. As the person talks about his/her thoughts of suicide, he/she can be facilitated to begin to understand what a significant impact his/her suicide would have on family, friends, and others. Offering clients validation and reassurance may increase their ambivalence. Further, this process of engaging the person in problem solving can increase their ambivalence associated with suicide. Identify "safe" people who offer support without judgment, components of positive daily structure, identify all levels of social support, and triggers associated with negative/self-destructive/suicidal thinking.

This is the foundation of engaging the person in developing improved coping and a safety plan to interrupt the progression leading to suicidal ideation and potentially a fatal gesture.

If the person has resources and does not intend to commit suicide, but is vulnerable, consider increasing the frequency or duration of outpatient contacts for a brief period of time. If there are resources but they are not able to provide the necessary supportive contact consider an intensive outpatient program, or partial hospitalization. If the person is not currently being prescribed antidepressant medication, he/she should be referred for a medication evaluation.

If the person is not able to make any assurances that he/she does not intend to commit suicide, then hospitalization is necessary. Initially, approach the person about voluntary admission to a psychiatric facility. If the person is unwilling to voluntarily admit himself/herself, then an involuntary admission process will ensue. Providing a safe environment with monitoring and support is imperative.

While danger to self is often the critical clinical dilemma requiring immediate attention and intervention, it is also important to assess and rule out any homicidal thoughts and intentions that place others in a position of potential harm. If an assessment reveals the intention to harm another person, the appropriate clinical interventions and legal issue of the duty to warn must be dealt with immediately. A summary of assessing suicide includes the following:

- Ask and observe: identify factors associated with suicide risk
- Identify resilience—areas of relative strengths
- Clarify suicidality versus overwhelmed or death wish
- Define level of risk
- Define interventions
- Thoroughly document each of the steps above

*If it isn't documented it didn't happen.

2. Provide Safe Environment
   A. Evaluate whether person is demonstrating adequate cooperation (removal of firearms, medications, etc., that person may have considered for self-harm/suicide)
   B. Evaluate adequacy of social support
   C. Adjust level of care if necessary
      1. Urgent care; flexible time for meeting, along with extended meeting time to allow the person to ventilate their emotions and initiate problem-solving without additional pressure
      2. Partial hospitalization
      3. Inpatient-open unit
      4. Inpatient-closed unit
3. Referral Assessment for Medication Evaluation
   A. If this is an initial assessment and a history of depression is given that has clearly affected quality of life and functioning, refer for a medication evaluation.
   B. If this has been an ongoing case and acute depressive symptoms are present that are interfering with level of functioning, refer for medication evaluation.
   C. Assess for mood congruent psychotic features. They can be present and not identified. If positive, convey information to prescribing physician.
4. Ineffective Problem Solving
   A. Define the problem(s)
   B. Brainstorm all plausible solutions
   C. Identify the outcomes in relation to the various solutions
   D. Make a decision that appears to best fit the demands of the problem situation

E. Identify what has worked in the past

F. Prepare the person for the possibility that the solution may not work out as planned; therefore, have a contingency plan

5. Dysfunctional Coping

A. Help person recognize that he/she can only do one thing at a time

B. Teach person relaxation skills to use if feeling overwhelmed

C. Facilitate prioritizing issues that person must deal with

D. Facilitate clarification of boundaries, especially related to issues of pleasing others versus self-care

E. Rule out secondary gains

F. Helplessness

1. Encourage taking responsibility and making decisions

2. Include the person when setting goals

3. Provide positive feedback for decision making

4. Facilitate development of realistic goals, limitations, and expectations

5. Identify areas of life and self-care in which the person has control, as well as those areas where the person lacks control

6. Encourage expression of feelings related to areas of life outside person's control and explore how to let it go

6. Ineffective Development or Utilization of Resources and Social Supports

A. Resist desire to withdraw and isolate

B. Identify positive social/emotional supports that the person has have been avoiding

C. Make commitment to utilize resources and supports in some way every day

D. Educate regarding role of isolation in maintaining depression

E. Evaluate impaired social interaction

1. Convey acceptance and positive regard in creating a safe, nonjudgmental environment

2. Identify people in the person's life and activities that were previously found pleasurable

3. Encourage utilization of support system

4. Encourage appropriate risk taking

5. Teach assertive communication

6. Give direct, nonjudgmental feedback regarding interaction with others

7. Offer alternative responses for dealing effectively with stress-provoking situations

8. Social skills training in how to approach others and participate in conversation

9. Role-play and practice social skills for reinforcement and to increase insight for how the person is perceived by others

10. Daily structure to include social interaction

7. Dysfunctional Grieving

A. Evaluate stage of grief that person is experiencing

B. Demonstrate care and empathy

C. Determine if the person has numerous unresolved losses

D. Encourage expression of feelings

E. Use the empty chair technique or have the person write a letter to someone he/she has lost, which may provoke the resolution process

F. Educate person on stages of grief and normalize appropriate feelings such as anger and guilt

G. Support person in letting go of his/her idealized perception so that the person can accept the positive and negative aspects of his/her object of loss

H. Positively reinforce adaptive coping with experiences of loss (taking into consideration ethnic and social differences)

I. Refer to a grief group

J. Explore the issue of spirituality and spiritual support

8. Low Self-esteem
    A. Focus on strengths and accomplishments
    B. Avoid focus on past failures
    C. Reframe failures or negative experiences as normal part of learning process
    D. Identify areas of desired change and objectives to meet those goals
    E. Encourage independent effort and accepting responsibility
    F. Teach assertive communication and appropriate setting of limits and boundaries
    H. Teach effective communication techniques by using "I" statements, not making assumptions, asking for clarification, and so on
    I. Offer positive reinforcement for tasks performed independently
9. Distorted Thinking
    A. Identify the influence of negativism on depression and educate regarding positive self-talk
    B. Seek clarification when the information communicated appears distorted
    C. Reinforce reality-based thinking
    D. Facilitate development of intervention techniques such as increased awareness with conscious choice of what to focus on (positive thoughts), thought stopping, and compartmentalizing
    E. Facilitate person's clarification of rational versus irrational thinking
10. Eating Disturbance
    A. Evaluate eating pattern and fluid intake
    B. Educate regarding importance of good nutrition for energy and clear thinking
11. Sleep Disturbance
    A. Evaluate sleep pattern and overall amount of sleep
    B. Encourage appropriate and adequate sleep cycle
    C. Discourage daytime napping
    D. Avoid caffeine and other stimulants
    E. Perform relaxation exercises, meditation, or listen to relaxing music before sleep
    F. Daily aerobic exercising such as walking
    G. Administer sedative medications in the evening instead of other times during the day
    H. Suggest activities such as warm bath, massage, herbal tea, light snack, and so on, which promote sleep
12. Difficulty Consistently Managing Depression: This requires a thorough review of lifestyle. Managing depression requires a commitment by the person to take responsibility for improving his/her quality of life. Depression management is a significant deterrent to relapse.
    A. The components of a self-care plan to manage depression include the following:
        1. Structured daily activities
        2. Development and utilization of social supports
        3. Positive attitude and identification of the positive things in one's life
        4. Awareness
        5. Regular aerobic exercise
        6. Eating nutritionally
        7. Living in accordance with one's own value system
13. Educate Person (and Family if Appropriate) on Medication Issues
    A. Emphasize the importance of compliance. Encourage patient to clarify potential side effects including those that require immediate attention.
    B. Recommend that patients familiarize themselves with any restrictions related to medication use.
    C. Refer person to clarify medication issues with his/her physician and pharmacist.
    D. Educate regarding chemical imbalance related to depression.
    E. Educate regarding role of decompensation related to lack of medication compliance.
    F. Possible side effects of antidepressant medication.
        1. Consult with prescribing physician immediately and encourage the person to do the same

G. Since a therapist is likely to have significantly more contact with an individual in treatment who is being prescribed psychotropic medication than the prescribing physician, it is imperative to monitor the patient response to medication and communicate salient information to the prescribing physician.
   1. At least moderate improvement should be achieved in 6–8 weeks
   2. Monitor for presence of side effects (especially those that require immediate attention)
H. Risk factors for recurrence of major depressive episode.
   1. History of multiple episodes of major depression
   2. Evidence of dysthymic symptoms following recovery from an episode of major depression
   3. Comorbid nonaffective psychiatric diagnosis
   4. Presence of chronic medical disorder
I. Clinical features that influence the treatment plan.
   1. Crisis issues
   2. Psychotic features
   3. Substance abuse
   4. Comorbid axis I or axis II disorders
   5. Major depression related to cognitive dysfunction (pseudodementia)
   6. Dysthymia
   7. Severe/complicated grief reaction
   8. Seasonal major depressive disorder
J. Atypical major depressive disorder features (defined by reversal of vegetative symptoms).
   1. Increased sleep versus decreased sleep
   2. Increased appetite versus decreased appetite
   3. Weight gain versus weight loss
   4. Marked mood reactivity
   5. Sensitivity to emotional rejection
   6. Phobic symptoms
   7. Extreme fatigue with heaviness of extremities
K. If there is little to no symptomatic response by 4–6 weeks.
   1. Assess compliance
   2. Reassess diagnosis
   3. Reassess adequacy of treatment

14. Relapse Prevention (Tartakovsky, 2013)
   A. Treatment compliance
   B. Educated regarding commitment and management (identify reasons to actively following treatment recommendations)
   C. Actively pursue interests, passions, desires, talent
   D. Identify the ways in which they can take special care of their mind and body (sleep, nutrition, exercise)
   E. Educate the role of rumination in relapse
      1. Teach the importance of recognizing the who, what, whys, and whens of emotional and physical life.
      2. Identify difficult anniversaries so that they can be anticipated and planned for.
      3. Monitor physical status. If there is excessive fatigue, irritability or difficulty eating or sleeping they could be in the middle of a triggering event.
   F. Mindfulness to mitigate cognitive symptoms
   G. Navigating a relapse
      1. Tracking mood states to identify early signs
      2. Journaling for mindful reflection, use of apps on the computer
      3. Contacting physician and therapist at earliest sign of relapse

DEPRESSION CO-OCCURRING WITH OTHER ILLNESS

The co-occurrence of depression with other medical, psychiatric, and substance abuse disorders should always be considered. Awareness and treatment can improve overall health and decrease suffering. A thorough assessment and accurate diagnosis are imperative.

According to the National Institute of Mental Health, failure to recognize and treat co-occurring depression may result in increased impairment and decreased improvement in the medical disorder.

Co-occurrence With Psychiatric Disorders (NIH, 2015)

1. There is a 13% co-occurrence with panic disorder; in approximately 25% of these patients the panic disorder preceded the depressive disorder
2. 50%–75% of those with eating disorders have a lifetime history of major depression

*Detection of depression can result in clarifying the primary diagnosis and lead to more effective treatment and improved outcome.

Co-occurrence With Substance Abuse Disorders

1. Substance abuse disorders frequently coexist with depression
2. Over 30% of individuals with depression experience a substance abuse disorder
3. Over 25% of those with major depression experience substance abuse disorder
4. Over 50% of those with bipolar disorder experience a substance abuse disorder

*Substance abuse must be discontinued so that a clear diagnosis can be made and the appropriate treatment given. Treatment for depression may be necessary if it continues when the substance abuse problem ends.

BIPOLAR DISORDER

Bipolar disorder (NIH, 2015) often reveals itself in a person's late teen or early adult years. However, children and adults can also have bipolar disorder. The illness usually lasts a lifetime, and if not treated, can result in damaged relationships, poor job/academic performance, and even suicide. To help the clinician clarify a diagnosis of bipolar consider the following factors (Helpguide Treatment of Bipolar, updated August 2015):

1. The experience of repeated episodes of major depression
2. The first episode of major depression was experienced prior to age 25
3. There is a first degree relative with bipolar
4. When not depressed, their mood and energy levels are higher than most people's
5. When depressed there is a tendency to overeat and oversleep
6. Episodes of major depression are short (less than 3 months)
7. They have experienced a loss of reality while depressed
8. They experienced postpartum depression previously
9. They developed mania or hypomania while taking an antidepressant

10. Their antidepressant stopped working after several months
11. They have tried three or more antidepressants without success

MANIA

Goals

1. Provide safe environment
2. Eliminate danger to self or others
3. Stabilization and medication compliance
4. Thought processes intact
5. Eliminate perceptual disturbances
6. Improve social interaction/decrease isolation
7. Improve self-esteem
8. Improve self-management
9. Improve sleep pattern
10. Educate regarding medication issues and general side effects

Treatment Focus and Objectives

1. Risk for Injury
   A. Assess
      1. Destructive acting-out behavior
      2. Extreme hyperactivity
      3. Extreme agitation
      4. Self-injurious behavior
      5. Loud and escalating aggressiveness
      6. Threatening behavior
   B. If person lacks control and is a danger to himself/herself or others, hospitalization is necessary. Hospitalization provides a safe environment, monitoring, and an opportunity to stabilize medication. Depending on the level of mania, the person's admission to a psychiatric facility will be voluntary or involuntary (5150)
   C. Keep environmental stimuli at a minimum
   D. Remove hazardous objects
   E. Physical activity such as walking to discharge energy
   F. Medication compliance as prescribed
2. Risk for Violence (Directed Toward Self or Others)
   A. Assess
      1. Extreme hyperactivity
      2. Suspiciousness or paranoid ideation
      3. Hostility, threatening harm to self or others
      4. Rageful anger
      5. Aggressive body language or aggressive acts of behavior
      6. Provoking behavior (challenging, trying to start fights)
      7. Hallucinations or delusions
      8. Possesses the means to harm (gun, knife, etc.)
      9. Bragging about prior incidence or history of abuse to self or others
   B. Keep environmental stimuli at a minimum
   C. Monitor closely
   D. Remove all potentially dangerous objects
   E. Physical exercise to decrease tension

F. Maintain calm attitude with person and do not challenge

G. Medication compliance as prescribed

As with risk for injury or danger to self or others, hospitalization may be necessary during a manic phase if symptoms are escalating and unmanageable. If this is a first episode, the person should also be referred for evaluation of medical conditions and medications that can mimic the symptoms of bipolar disorder (NIH, 2015).

3. Medication Noncompliance

A. As a person's functioning improves, educate regarding importance of medication compliance and relationship between decompensation and lack of medication compliance. Medication is clearly the primary mode of treatment for mania/bipolar disorder. Medication compliance is imperative to symptom management. "If a risk factor for poor outcome is a common choice of patients (history of nonadherence), it is vital that clinicians are encouraged to ask proactively about problems with adherence and create an atmosphere where such issues can be discussed openly" (Pope, 2002). Research by Rasgon, Bauer, Glenn, and Whybrow, (2002) suggests that women with bipolar disorder may be more depressed and experience more frequent mood changes than men.

4. Altered Thought Processes

A. Do not argue with person or challenge him/her

B. Communicate acceptance of the person's need for the false belief, but let him/her know that you do not share the delusion

C. Use clarification techniques of communication (Would you please explain…? Do you mean…? I don't understand…)

D. Offer positive reinforcement for accurate reality testing

E. Reinforce and focus on reality by talking about real events

1. Reorient to person, place, and time as needed.

2. Address person by name.

3. Consistency of environment is important. In residing environment and office, maintain familiar objects, clock, etc., within view.

4. Maintain a fairly structured and consistent routine. Write out (or use a white-board) the schedule of activities, appointments to be used for reference.

5. Repeat instructions as necessary being clear and concise/brief.

6. Encourage the person to maintain lists of planned activities.

7. Assist as needed in problem-solve.

8. Maintain realistic expectations and limitations of current ability.

F. Facilitate development of intervention techniques such as thought stopping, slowing things down, and requesting the support of others in reality testing

5. Sensory-Perceptual Disturbance (Sensory Overload)

Auditory and visual processing dysfunctions are likely the most common and occupy the interface between sensory/perceptual and cognitive processing (Javitt, 2009)

A. Evaluate for hallucination or delusional thinking.

B. Let the person know that you do not share the perception. Point out that although what he/she hears or sees seems real to the individual, you do not hear or see what the person does.

1. Provide a low stimulation environment

2. Use a calm, unhurried approach when interacting

3. Speak in a slow, distinct manner with appropriate volume

4. Recommend to person and support system the need to have adequate rest, sleep, and daytime naps

C. Facilitate understanding between increased anxiety and reality distortions

D. Distract the person with involvement in an interpersonal activity and do reality testing

1. Use here and now activities (ADLs) that focus on something outside of the self that is concrete and reality oriented

E. Intervene when early signs of perceptual disturbances are evident

F. Help person recognize perceptual disturbances with repeated patterns and how to intervene

G. Offer positive reinforcement for efforts and maintenance of accurate reality testing

6. Impaired Social Interaction
   A. Increased awareness for how other people interpret varying forms of behavior and communication
   B. Role-model and practice appropriate responding to social situations
      1. Work with support system to also provide role-model and practice of practical social exchanges
   C. Encourage acceptance of responsibility for own behavior versus projecting responsibility onto others
   D. Encourage recognition of manipulative behaviors
   E. Set limits and boundaries; be consistent; do not argue, bargain, or try to reason; just restate the limit
   F. Positive reinforcement for recognition and accepting responsibility for own behavior
   G. Positive reinforcement for appropriate behaviors
   H. Facilitate appropriate ways to deal with feelings
   I. Facilitate understanding of consequences for inappropriate behaviors
   J. Identify and focus on positive aspects of the person
   K. Refer to a support group for bipolar disorder
7. Low Self-esteem (Johnson, 2004; NIH, 2015)
   A. Validate person's experience. Identify negative impact that disorder has had on the person's life.
      1. Explore what issues he/she controls versus issues involving lack of control.
      2. Identify difficulty that person has in accepting the reality of the disorder and as a result not accepting himself/herself.
      3. Help them separate the difference between their identified symptoms and true self. Encourage them to be open about behaviors they want to change and how to break those goals down to manageable objectives.
      4. Work with the person to identify healthy lifestyle choices.
      5. Encourage them to actively participate as a treatment team member by keeping a journal, maintaining awareness in symptomatic stability, and reporting changes early.
   B. Facilitate identification of strengths.
   C. Identify areas of realistic desirable change and break it down into manageable steps.
   D. Encourage assertive communication.
   E. Offer person simple methods of achievement.
      1. Carefully select tasks that are within realistic expectations
      2. Encourage the person to problem-solve some activities to accomplish
         a. Going to the library or other structured environment that is common and predictable
   F. Positive feedback and reinforcement for efforts and achievements.
8. Improved Self-management
   A. Increase awareness of mood changes and how to more effectively manage
   B. Increase understanding of developmental deviations and delays caused by chronic mental illness
   C. Confront and deal with the stigmatization associated with mental illness
   D. Challenge fear of recurrent episodes and associated inhibition of normal psychosocial functioning
   E. Problem-solve interpersonal difficulties
   F. Confront and develop appropriate resources to effectively deal with marriage, family, child-bearing, and parenting issues
   G. Improved understanding and development of effective interventions to deal with emotional, social, and legal problems
9. Sleep Disturbance (Johnson, 2004; Mago, 2009)
   The goal of sleep hygiene is to train the brain to feel sleepy and to feel awake at a regular and customary time to maximize quality of sleep–rest cycle in a normalized manner.
   A. Monitor sleep patterns
   B. Reduce stimulation, provide a quiet environment
      1. Use the bedroom for sleep and sex, not TV.
      2. Go to bed when sleepy.
      3. Restrict time in bed to actual sleeping time. Don't lay awake in bed. Gradually increase the time spent in bed as sleep time increases which should result in progressively longer periods.

C. Provide structured schedule of activities, which includes quiet time or time for naps

D. Monitor activity level. Avoid being overstimulated at bedtime
   1. Stop doing mental activity at least 1 h before sleep.
   2. Try to get some exercise in everyday.
   3. Create soothing bedtime rituals that are a progression to sleep time. Wind down, warm bath/shower, light reading, soothing music, etc.
   4. Practice meditation/mindfulness or consider learning some other relaxation techniques.

E. Increase identification and awareness for fatigue

F. Avoid caffeine or other stimulants (after about 3 p.m.) and/or alcohol as a calming technique to promote sleep

G. Administer sedative medications, as prescribed, at bedtime

H. Provide cues and methods to promote sleep such as relaxation, soft music, warm bath, and so on

10. Education Regarding Medication Issues

A. Person and his/her family should be educated about the disorder and management of the features of the disorder, and they possess a thorough understanding of medication issues.

B. Refer the person and family to the prescribing physician and pharmacist for clarification of medication issues.

C. Educate regarding the chemical imbalance relationship of mania. It is a medical disorder, and "no-fault," i.e., there is nothing they have done to themselves to develop bipolar.

D. Educate regarding the issue of decompensation and the lack of medication compliance.

E. General side effects of medication.
   1. It is important that the clinician familiarize themselves with the general side effect profile of the medication(s) the person is taking. The therapeutic relationship requires honesty and collaboration.
   2. Encourage the person to create a history of medications, dosages, and side effects. This is particularly beneficial upon changing prescribing physicians and when there is a need to change or add medications.
   3. Encourage the development of a spreadsheet format of current medications including name of medication, date prescribed, dosage, and time of day taken.

If the person reports having any side effects from the medication, consult the prescribing physician immediately. The consultation is important for integration of patient's care. Additionally, it is good practice for the person to get their needs met in a collaborative relationship with the prescribing physician.

Individual therapy is an extremely beneficial adjunctive treatment to medication for individuals diagnosed with mania/bipolar disorder. It is used to help individuals recover from the symptoms of their disorder, restore normal mood, repair relationship damage, repair career damage, and establish self-monitoring. Therapy is, of course, not attempted during a manic phase, which requires medical/medication stabilization. Family therapy and education are also important to help/support family members in their understanding of the nature of the illness and treatment.

CHILDREN

Bipolar disorder that starts during childhood or early teens is referred to as "early-onset" bipolar disorder. Bipolar disorder appears to be more severe in children. Geller et al. (2002) reported that bipolar disorder in young children is synonymous with the most severe experiences of bipolar disorder in adults. In adults, the typical bipolar experience involves episodes of either mania or depression that lasts a few months with relatively normal episodes of functioning. However, mania in children has been found to be a more severe, chronic course of illness. The report states that many children experience both depression and mania at the same time and may remain ill for years, enduring multiple daily highs and lows without intervening periods of relative normalcy. To treat children and adolescents with bipolar disorder, there is a significant reliance on information from the significant adults in their life (parents, close relatives, teacher, etc.).

WebMD (2014) asserts that while mood changes and other symptoms are extremely challenging to the children and their family, mood changes and other symptoms, they can be managed effectively. The following information is offered to be shared with parents in counseling for their child and associated family system issues; how to help your child prevent manic episodes:

1. Exercise, eat a balanced diet, establish a regular sleep schedule, and keep a consistent routine. This can help reduce minor mood swings that often lead to more severe episodes of mania.
2. Take medicines according to the doctor's instructions to help reduce the number of manic episodes.
3. Avoid triggers such as caffeine, alcohol and drug use, and stress to help prevent manic episodes.
4. Learn the warning signs and seek early treatment to avoid more severe, prolonged manic episodes.
5. Have a plan of action in place and a support system to help follow the plan when symptoms of a manic episode start.
6. Have certain people at school or at home who know how to help during a manic episode.
7. Maintain consistency and realistic expectations.
8. Set limits using self-responsibility and boundaries as the frame.
9. Stability requires consistency, compliance, and vigilance.

Though symptoms are more likely to appear during adolescence children as young as 7 or 8 years may develop bipolar symptoms. However, until recently children and adolescents were seldom diagnosed with this disorder. Additionally, as many as one-third of the 3.4 million children and adolescents with depression in the United States may actually be experiencing the early onset of bipolar disorder, according to the American Academy of Child and Adolescent Psychiatry (WebMD, 2014).

Psychosocial variables include the following:

A. Cross-cultural issues
   1. Culture may influence experience and communication of symptoms (as with all mental health issues)
   2. Culture may influence under diagnosis/misdiagnosis/delayed diagnosis
   3. There may be a differential response to antidepressant medications among ethnic groups
B. Environment
   1. During manic phase, a calm environment routine is helpful
   2. Manic individuals may need room to pace and exercise
   3. The individual may benefit from the support of someone in his/her environment who has been educated about realistic expectations and safety associated with mania
C. Stressors
   1. Psychosocial stressors may be associated with the precipitation of mania
   2. Many episodes of mania have no identifiable psychosocial stressor and as the illness progresses, episodes appear to occur spontaneously
   3. May be helpful for individuals with bipolar and their families to work with their therapist to develop an understanding of unique associations to stressful events and the onset of symptoms

BIPOLAR DISORDER HYPERSEXUALITY

For individuals with bipolar disorder, the extreme behaviors associated with mania can be devastating. While there is a listing of potential extreme behaviors in the DSM indicative of manic episodes, the review of one of those behaviors serves to highlight the damaging results. Hypersexuality is defined as an increased need or compulsion for sexual gratification. A person may be reluctant to expose his/her experience of hypersexuality in treatment because of the associated immense feelings of shame. With the decreased inhibition associated with hypersexuality, individuals find themselves engaging in sexual behaviors that they may consider "deviant or forbidden" and that results in feelings of shame. For some, the frequency of their compulsion is at an addictive level. In addition to feelings of shame, hypersexuality can destroy a marriage or a committed relationship and increase the risk of STDs.

Regarding the issue of the broad patterns of sexual addiction behavior, the Mayo Clinic defines sexual addiction as a loss of control with the focus on compulsion: "compulsive sexual behavior refers to spending inordinate amounts of time in sexual related activity, to the point that one neglects important social, occupational, or recreational activities in favor of sexual behavior." According to the National Council on Sexual Addiction and Compulsivity, sexual addiction is characterized as "loss of the ability to choose freely whether to stop or to continue…continuation of the behavior despite adverse consequences, such as loss of health, job, marriage, or freedom…obsession with the activity." The use of computers with this compulsion can be highly compromising and damaging.

Examples of the specific behaviors that are common to those who struggle with hypersexuality's compulsive and reckless behaviors include the following:

1. Fantasy sex
2. Fetishes
3. Inappropriate sexual touching
4. Sexual abuse and sexual assault
5. Compulsive masturbation
6. Compulsive sex with prostitutes
7. Masochism
8. Patronizing sex-oriented establishments
9. Voyeurism
10. Exhibitionism

The range of consequences associated with hypersexuality include the following:

1. Shame
2. Low self-esteem
3. Fear
4. Financial distress/ruin (cost of prostitutes/phone sex and items or activities in sex-oriented establishments)
5. Loss of job
6. Destruction of relationships
7. Health risk, loss of job (pornography on the computer, inappropriate behavior, etc.)

While evaluating and treating someone with bipolar disorder, the aforementioned information should clarify the importance of fully understanding the manic experience of the individual because of the potential deep-seated emotional damage resulting from extreme personally unacceptable behavior. Providing a safe environment (without judgment), education, and validation are important interventions.

ANTIDEPRESSANT MEDICATION AND OTHER TREATMENT FOR MAJOR DEPRESSION

Everyone views the treatment choices for depression in his or her own individual manner. Some individuals prefer an initial treatment modality for mild major depression to be antidepressant medication, while others will prioritize therapy as the initial treatment. There will be some who obtain the desired response in accordance with their treatment choice. Often an individual may be treated most effectively by combining these modalities, especially when there is a history of depression. A referral for an evaluation for antidepressant medication should be provided for those with moderate to severe major depression. If an individual presents with a major depression with psychotic features he/she is likely to be treated with an antidepressant and antipsychotic medication. If the depressive symptoms are difficult to treat and the person cannot stabilize or experience relief and improve quality of life, electroconvulsive therapy, repetitive transcranial magnetic stimulation, neurofeedback, a stimulant, or thyroid supplement may be considered for effectiveness in a given case.

According to the American Psychiatric Association Practice Guidelines (APA, October 2010), when determining the frequency of individual therapy contacts, multiple factors need to be considered:

1. Symptom severity (including suicidal ideation)
2. Co-occurring disorders
3. Cooperation and compliance with treatment
4. Availability of social supports
5. Goals of treatment

ADDITIONAL TREATMENT CONSIDERATIONS

1. *Treatment of Depression in the Elderly.* This complex and challenging clinical dilemma is related to the high degree of comorbidity with medical disorders. Some of the complications that confound treatment of depressive disorders in the elderly are as follows:
   A. Nonpsychotropic medications may cause depression, alter blood levels of antidepressant medications, and increase the side effects of antidepressant medication.
   B. Concurrent psychiatric conditions may result in depression, require the use of different medications, and reduce the response to antidepressant medication.
   C. Concurrent medical illnesses may cause biological depression, reduce the effectiveness of antidepressant medication, and change the metabolic rate of antidepressant medications.
   D. Complications related to stage-of-life issues include metabolic slowing, which requires lower dosing levels, fixed income with limited resources available to them, issues of loss, dependency and role reversal with children, social isolation, and illness.
2. *Treatment of Depression in Children.* Children and adolescents may not demonstrate the manifestations of depressions as the symptoms readily recognized in adults. Depression in this population is often masked by acting-out or behavioral problems. A careful and thorough diagnostic assessment is extremely important because of the high risk of suicide in troubled adolescents. If depression is diagnosed and psychotropic medication is prescribed it is crucial to monitor medication compliance.
3. *Coexisting Disorders and Conditions.* Diagnostic clarification. Unless the person has a long-standing history of depression (dysthymia), it is the general standard of practice to treat the coexisting disorders and conditions first. If the depression remains, then the depressive disorder is clearly diagnosed and treated. Possible associated disorders and conditions include substance abuse, side effects of other medications, the result of medical conditions, other psychiatric conditions, such as anxiety disorders, and medical conditions such as menopause.
4. *Coexistence of Depression and Anxiety.* A person may experience a depressive disorder that is accompanied by symptoms of anxiety. However, the symptoms of anxiety may not fully meet the criteria necessary for a diagnosis of an anxiety disorder. The reverse may also be true. A person may have an anxiety disorder accompanied by symptoms of depression. In this situation it is possible that the depressive symptoms are not sufficient to meet the criteria for the diagnosis of a depressive disorder.

ANXIETY DISORDERS

The DSM 5 (APA, 2013) presented a number changes to this diagnostic category. The category of anxiety disorders includes diagnoses of generalized anxiety, panic disorder, agoraphobia, specific phobias, social anxiety disorder, phobias, and separation anxiety (presented in neurodevelopmental disorders). OCD and PTSD have been defined as separate diagnoses.

The central features of these disorders include anxiety, fear, emotional distress, self-defeating cognitive and behavioral rituals, distressing physical symptoms evoked by intense distress and body tension, an inability to be still and calm, sleep and appetite disturbance, feeling out of control, and experiencing difficulty effectively coping. AHRQ EBPs (2008, 2011; Australian Psychological Association, 2015) recommends cognitive-behavioral therapy to teach psychosocial skills and management techniques as the behavioral treatment of anxiety disorders.

ANXIETY DISORDERS

Goals

1. Assess for need for medication evaluation referral
2. Identify source of anxiety and fears
3. Improve coping skills
4. Improve problem-solving skills
5. Improve self-care skills
6. Improve feelings of control
7. Improve communication skills
8. Cognitive restructuring
9. Improve self-esteem
10. Improve stress-management skills
11. Family education
12. Educate regarding side effects of medication

Treatment Focus and Objectives

1. Assess for Referral for Medication Evaluation
   Patients with heightened anxiety, withdrawal, lack of sleep, obsessive thoughts, and compulsive behaviors may benefit from the use of psychotropic medications. If there is comorbidity of depression, convey this information to the referred physician.
2. Feelings of Anxiety and Fear
   A. Validate person's emotional experience
   B. Identify factors contributing to anxiety
   C. Problem-solve factors contributing to anxiety
      1. What is the problem?
      2. Brainstorm various choices for dealing with the problem if it is within the person's control.
      3. Make a decision and follow through. Have a contingency plan.
      4. If it is out of the person's control, encourage the person to let go of it.
   D. Explore methods of managing anxiety
      1. Relaxation techniques, including deep breathing
      2. Distracting, pleasurable activities
      3. Exercise
      4. Meditation

5. Positive self-talk
6. Grounding

E. Assess medication for effectiveness and for adverse side effects

F. Educate regarding signs of escalating anxiety and various techniques for interrupting the progression of these symptoms (refer to section on Managing Anxiety). Also explore possible physical etiology of exacerbation of anxiety.

G. Fear

1. Explore the source of the fear.
2. Clarify the reality of the fear base. Encourage venting of feelings of fear. If the fear is irrational, the person must accept the reality of the situation before any changes can occur.
3. Develop alternative coping strategies with the active participation of the person.
4. Encourage the person to make his/her own choices and to be prepared with a contingency plan.
5. Use systematic desensitization to eliminate fear with gradual exposure to the feared object or situation (exposure can be real or through visual imagery).
   a. Graded exposure for increased control over feared object and personal comfort level
   b. Construct an exposure hierarchy in which feared stimuli are ranked according to their anticipated fear reaction

*Imaginal exposures can also be useful for confronting fears of worst-case scenarios (e.g., patients with OCD who imagine that they might contract a deadly illness, patients with social phobia who imagine that they are being ridiculed) to reduce the aversiveness of the thought.

6. Use implosion therapy where exposure to the feared object or situation is not graded but rather direct exposure.
7. Educate person regarding role of internal, self-talk to feelings of fear, and develop appropriate counterstatements.
8. Utilize grounding to decrease distress and anchor in the moment.

H. Manage obsessive thoughts and compulsive behaviors

1. Patients with obsessive thoughts should be encouraged to engage in reality testing and to redirect themselves into productive and distracting activity
2. Patients with compulsive behavior should develop a stepwise reduction in the repetition of ritual behaviors (medication can be very helpful for managing OCD)

I. Positive feedback and reinforcement for efforts and accomplishments

3. Ineffective Coping

A. Identify factors that escalate anxiety and contribute to difficulty coping

B. Identify ritualistic patterns of behaviors

C. Educate regarding the relationship between emotions and dysfunctional/compulsive behavior

D. Develop daily structure of activities

E. Gradually decrease time allotted for compulsive ritualistic behaviors, utilizing daily structure of activities that acts to substitute more adaptive behaviors

F. Positive feedback and reinforcement for effort and change to shape behavior

G. Teach techniques that interrupt dysfunctional thoughts and behaviors, such as relaxation techniques, meditation, thought stopping, exercise, positive self-talk, visual imagery, and so on

1. Distraction as a coping mechanism can come in different forms
   a. Cognitive distractions
      1. Reading aloud
      2. Listening to nature sounds
      3. Singing along with songs
   b. Behavioral distractions
      1. Spend time with people who are fun and interesting
      2. Work on a project with someone
      3. Volunteer or help someone less fortunate

    c. Physiological distractions
      1. Exercise
      2. Relaxation techniques
      3. Working on tasks
  H. Facilitate shaping of social interaction to decrease avoidant behavior

4. Ineffective Problem Solving
  A. Teach problem-solving skills
  B. Develop realistic sample problems and give homework to practice new skills
  C. Identify secondary gains that inhibit progress toward change

5. Self-care Deficiency
  A. Support person to independently fulfill daily grooming and hygiene tasks
  B. Adequate nutrition
  C. Regular exercise
  D. Engaging in activities and being with people, all of which contribute to feelings of well-being
  E. Use of positive self-talk and affirmations
  F. Positive feedback and reinforce efforts and accomplishments
  G. Time management
  H. Prioritize demands/tasks
  I. Develop and utilize support system

6. Feels Lack of Control Over Life
  A. Break down simple behaviors and necessary tasks into manageable steps
  B. Provide choices that are in their control
  C. Cognitive restructuring to identify and challenge irrational, unrealistic, or maladaptive beliefs
    a. Overestimation—or overprediction of unlikely outcomes
    b. Catastrophizing—the magnification of the consequences of aversive outcomes
  D. Support development of realistic goals and objectives
  E. Encourage participation in activities in which the person will experience success and achievement
  F. Facilitate development of problem-solving skills (four steps)
    a. Defining the problem
    b. Generating alternatives
    c. Evaluating and selecting alternatives
    d. Implementing solutions
  G. Facilitate shaping of social interaction to decrease avoidant behavior

7. Ineffective Communication
  A. Assertive communication
    1. Assess personal style (opinionated vs. silent/judgmental—or blaming/are they avoided or feared)
    2. Use "I" statements
    3. Practice saying "no"
    4. Rehearse what is desired to say
    5. Use body language effectively
    6. Keep emotions in check
    7. Start small with manageable practice opportunities
  B. Anger management
    1. Provide bibliotherapy to increase knowledge of anger and that anger is often masking other emotions
    2. Identify the warning signs and triggers associated with anger
    3. Identify negative thought patterns
    4. Avoid people, places, and situations that bring out the worst
    5. Learn ways to cool down
    6. Find healthier, appropriate, and more effective ways to express anger
  C. Role-play, rehearse, and problem-solve appropriate response choices in various situations
  D. Avoid manipulation, set limits and boundaries
  E. Positive feedback and reinforcement

8. Irrational Thinking/Beliefs
    A. Identify negative statements the person makes to themselves
        1. Some thought increase symptoms of anxiety
        2. Use the concept of the word thermometer to clarify the connection between thoughts and mood
        3. Keep a record of thoughts (tally positive vs. negative)
    B. Identify the connection between anxiety and self-talk
    C. Develop appropriate, reality-based counterstatements and substitute them for the negative ones
    D. Keep a daily record of dysfunctional thoughts to increase awareness of frequency and impact on emotional state
    E. Disrupt dysfunctional thoughts by increasing awareness for internal self-talk, distracting oneself through relaxation, exercise, or other positive activity, and using thought stopping
    F. Irrational Beliefs
        1. Identify false beliefs (brought from childhood, integrated parental statements)
        2. Challenge mistaken beliefs with rational counterstatements
        3. Identify effect that irrational beliefs have on emotions, relationship with self and others, and choices the person makes
        4. Increase awareness for the negative impact of anticipatory anxiety and its role in the cycle of anxiety
    G. Self-defeating Beliefs/Behaviors That Perpetuate Anxiety
        1. Identify needs or tendencies that predispose the person to anxiety
            a. Need to control
            b. Perfectionistic
            c. People pleaser with strong need for approval
            d. Ignoring signs of stress
            e. Self-critical
            f. Perpetual victim role
            g. Pessimistic, catastrophize
            h. Chronic worrier
            i. Anticipatory anxiety

9. Low Self-esteem
    A. Self-care
        1. Identifying needs
        2. Setting appropriate limits and boundaries
        3. Seeking a safe, stable environment
    B. Identify realistic goals, expectations, and limitations
    C. Identify external factors that negatively affect self-esteem
    D. Overcome negative attitudes toward self
    E. Address issues of physical well-being (exercise and nutrition) and positive body image
    F. Assertive communication
    G. Identify feelings that have been ignored or denied
    H. Positive self-talk, affirmations
    I. Focus on efforts and accomplishments
    J. Positive feedback and reinforcement

10. Ineffective Stress Management
    A. Facilitate development of stress management techniques
        1. Deep breathing
        2. Progressive muscle relaxation
        3. Visual imagery/meditation
        4. Time management
        5. Self-care

*Pleasant activities and exercise improve mood.

11. Educate Person/Family
   A. Facilitate increased understanding of etiology, course of treatment, and the family role in treatment. Taking medical exam to rule out any physical etiology.
   B. Encourage person's participation in treatment planning.
   C. Educate regarding the nervous system and explain that it is impossible to feel relaxed and anxious at the same time. Therefore, mastery of stress management techniques such as progressive muscle relaxation works to slowly intervene and diminish the symptoms of anxiety.
   D. Educate regarding the use of medication, how it works, the side effects, and the need to make the prescribing physician aware of the person's reaction/responses to the medication for monitoring (the anxious person may need the reassurance from the physician about the medication and how to use it on more than one occasion). Some antianxiety medications exacerbate depressed mood.

12. General Side Effects of Medication
   A. Clinician to be familiar with antianxiety medication side effects/risks
   B. Share monitoring responsibility with person to share with prescribing physician

*If the person reports having any side effects to the medication, consult the prescribing physician immediately and encourage the person to do the same. For individuals who suffer from an anxiety disorder, internal dialogue, interpretation of their experience, and feeling/belief that something negative is about to happen or will happen significantly affect their ability to effectively cope. Their cognitive distortions act, in part, as a setup for a self-fulfilling prophecy. That is what makes them difficult to treat. They believe that their fears have been validated by their experiences. However, it is actually their negative thinking and distorted beliefs that are keeping them stuck. If they can be supported to adhere to a program of cognitive-behavioral interventions, they are likely to experience a dramatic change in their level of distress. This requires a trusting therapeutic relationship so that the person feels confident of support and knowledge.

One thing all anxiety disorders share is the behavioral and emotional manifestations of avoidance. These individuals experience thoughts, beliefs, and internal dialogue (self-talk), which perpetuate a cycle of emotional distress. The person wants to participate but experiences fears, cognitive distortions, and emotional distress, which escalates and eventually leads to avoidance to escape the distress. In other words, their functional performance is compromised by their interpretation, distorted thoughts, and negative self-talk as it pertains to relational and environmental interaction.

CYCLE OF ANXIETY-PROVOKED EMOTIONAL DISTRESS

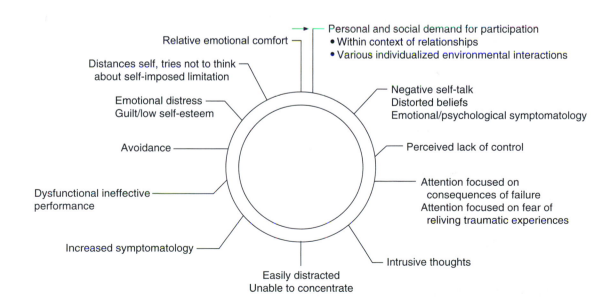

It is evident that unless cognitive-behavioral changes are made, the cycle of anxiety if self-perpetuating.

1. Functional impairment
   A. Sometimes a person is more focused on the panic attacks themselves than on such issues as avoidance, which significantly impacts his/her daily life (these issues become of secondary importance)
   B. It is important to determine how the individual defines a desired/satisfactory outcome, which influences motivation/compliance
   C. If the defined quality of life is not at an adequate functioning level, the individual should be encouraged to be more realistic
2. Monitoring progress
   A. While there is often an initial positive response in the control of panic attacks, subthreshold panic attacks may continue necessitating further treatment
   B. The fear that attacks may occur in the future often continue when panic attacks cease
   C. It is not uncommon to experience a panic attack after a period of no panic attacks
      1. Predict this possibility for patients
      2. Use as a monitoring tool to rule out the resumption of a poor self-care routine (i.e., increased stress/expanded demands, no exercise, lack of sleep, lack of progressive muscle relaxation)
   D. Be aware of comorbid issues of depression and substance abuse
   E. Be alert to emergent depression
3. Improving treatment compliance
   A. The anxiety associated/produced by treatment may result in noncompliance
      1. Fear side effects of medication (therefore, fear of taking medication)
      2. Sensitive to somatic sensations
   B. Treatment must be sensitive, supportive, honest, reassuring, and, whenever possible, predictive of what to expect (to reinforce choice/control and to validate)

*Anxiety disorders demonstrate a higher than average rate of suicide attempts (Anxiety and Depression Association of America, 2015).

TRAUMA RESPONSE

Everyone's reaction to trauma is unique. Potentially traumatic events are powerful and upsetting experiences that intrude upon daily life. Some will experience a minimal impact while others will experience PTSD. However, there are some generalities that may offer some benefit of understanding the significant impact trauma can have upon an individual. The sequential responses to trauma include the following stages: stressful event, outcry, denial, intrusion, working through, and resolution. Sometimes an individual will bypass the outcry stage and proceed from the traumatic event to denial. Corresponding to the stages of sequential responding are normal reactions or intensification/pathological reactions. Intensifications result when the normal reaction is unusually intense or prolonged.

1. Traumatic/Stressful Event
   A. Normal emotional response: anxiety, fear, sadness, distress

*If normal response is unusually intense or prolonged, the result is a pathological response.

   B. Pathological response: overwhelmed, confused, dazed
2. Outcry
   A. Normal emotional response: anxiety, guilt, anger, rage, shame, protest

*If normal response is unusually intense or prolonged, the result is a pathological response.

    B. Pathological response: panic, exhaustion, dissociative symptoms, psychotic symptoms

3. Denial
    A. Normal emotional response: minimizing, hypersomnia, anhedonia, depression, suppression, repression, obsession, fatigue/lethargy, denial

*If normal response is unusually intense or prolonged, the result is a pathological response.

    B. Pathological response: maladaptive avoidance, withdrawal, substance abuse, suicidality, fugue state, amnesia, rigid thinking, psychic numbing, sleep dysfunction, massive denial of initial trauma or current problems, somatization (headaches, fatigue, bowel problems/cramps, exacerbation of asthma, etc.)

4. Intrusion
    A. Normal emotional response: anxiety, somatization, decreased concentration and attention, insomnia, dysphoria
    B. Pathological response: flooded states, hypervigilance, exaggerated startle response, pseudohallucination, illusions, obsession, impaired concentration and attention, sleep/dream disturbance, emotional lability, preoccupation with the event, confusion, fight or flight activation (diarrhea, nausea, sweating, tremors, feelings of being on edge), compulsive reenactments of trauma, impaired functioning

5. Working Through
    A. Normal emotional response: find meaning in experience, grieve, personal growth

*If working through is blocked, the result is a pathological response.

    B. Pathological response: frozen states or psychosomatic reaction, anxiety/depression syndromes

6. Resolution
    A. Normal response: return to preevent level of functioning, psychological/personal growth/integration

*If not achieved the result is a pathological response.

    B. Pathological response: inability to work/act/feel, personality change, generalized anxiety, dysthymia

(Adapted from J.S. Maxmen and N.G. Ward, 1995—modified from M.J. Horowitz, 1986; Australian Psychological Society, 2015.)

SOMATIC SYMPTOMS AND RELATED DISORDERS

Somatoform DSM 5 (APA, 2013) redefines the criteria for somatoform disorders. By eliminating the concept of medically unexplained symptoms, the DSM 5 criteria prevent the easy assumption of a psychiatric diagnosis in patients who present with medical symptoms of unclear etiology. In the past, this disorder was believed to be related to emotional stress. The main symptom of somatoform disorder is chronic pain that limits a person's work, relationships, and other activities. The pain symptoms was often said to be "all in their head." However, those with somatoform pain disorder seem to experience painful sensations in a way that increases their pain level. Additionally, pain and worry create a cycle that is hard to break. There may be areas of relative weakness that predispose a person to a somatoform disorder, such as those who have a history of physical or sexual abuse. Unfortunately, historically, there have been many diagnosed with this disorder based on false assumptions. Now, the concept of the medically unexplained symptoms has been eliminated and the focus is on the degree to which patients' thoughts, feelings, and behaviors about their somatic symptoms are disproportionate or excessive. However, in cases where somatic symptoms are medically explained, DSM 5 requires that all other criteria for the disorder be met. The DSM 5 promotes a holistic perspective based on a comprehensive assessment with the acknowledgment that emotional well-being affects the way in which pain symptoms is perceived. The diagnosis is made when these diagnostic efforts do not reveal a clear source of the pain they experience (Medline Plus, 2015).

SOMATIC SYMPTOMS AND RELATED DISORDERS

Goals

1. Refer for medical review and rule out cognitive deficits
2. Increase awareness for relationship between emotional functioning and physical symptoms
3. Improve coping skills
4. Improve body image
5. Improve self-care
6. Decrease or eliminate perceptual disturbances
7. Improved self-esteem
8. Stress management

Treatment Focus and Objectives

1. Medical Referral, Consultation, and Initiating Treatment
    A. Consult with physician regarding a thorough medical evaluation, including lab work and radiology scans to determine the source of the pain, lab test, and so on to rule out possibility of organic etiology
        1. Antidepressant medications are often beneficial with both pain and worry surrounding pain
        2. Possible complications
            a. Addiction to prescription pain medication
            b. Complications from surgical procedures/anesthesia
            c. Depression, anxiety, history of abuse/trauma
    B. Acknowledge and validate that the pain/other physical symptoms experienced by the person as real
    C. Identify the factors that precipitate the pain/other physical symptoms
    D. Encourage the involvement in activities that help distract the person from symptoms
    E. Identify unresolved emotional and psychological issues
    F. Facilitate increased awareness and identification for relationship between anxiety and symptoms
    G. Identify alternative means of dealing with stress
    H. Identify ways of intervening to prevent escalation/management of symptoms in an effort to decrease physical distress, such as the following:
        1. Relaxation
        2. Guided imagery
        3. Breathing exercises
        4. Massage (consult PCP)
        5. Yoga (consult PCP)
        6. Physical exercise (consult PCP)
    I. Positive feedback and reinforcement for demonstrating effective, adaptive efforts and coping
2. Lack of Awareness and Knowledge or Cognitive Deficits
    A. Evaluate person's awareness and knowledge of relationship between psychological functioning and physical functioning.
    B. Encourage the person to keep a journal that focuses on psychological functioning (anxiety/stress/fears) to facilitate increased awareness and understanding of mind–body relationship.
        1. Recognize what seems to make the pain worse
        2. What helps alleviate/minimize discomfort

3. Develop ways of coping with painful body sensations
4. Identify ways to keep self more active, even if there is pain

C. Assess level of anxiety (which negatively affects learning) and motivation to learn.
D. Consult with physician regarding the results of treatment and tests. Explain to person the reason or purpose of all procedures and the results.
E. Encourage venting of fears and anxiety.
F. Facilitate identification of primary and secondary gains so that person can understand dysfunctional attempts to get needs met and manipulative behaviors.
G. Identify methods in which the person can get needs met appropriately, such as assertive communication.

3. Ineffective Coping

A. Confront irrational beliefs. Consult with physician regarding treatment, lab test, and so on to rule out the possibility of an organic etiology so that accurate medical information has be utilized in treatment.
B. Identify the extent of somatization.
1. Identify primary gains
2. Rule out secondary gain
3. Review degree of negative impact to all major areas of life
C. Identify other impairments that may be manifesting as somatizations.
D. Recognize and validate that the symptoms are experienced as real by the person, but confront the associated cognitive distortion that may precipitate, exacerbate, or maintain the symptoms.
E. In the beginning, while developing the therapeutic relationship, gratify the person's dependency needs to develop trust and decrease possibility of symptom escalation.
F. Identify primary and secondary gains of symptomatology experienced by the person.
G. Utilize identified primary and secondary gains to facilitate appropriate problem solving with person.
H. Gradually decrease focus and time spent on physical symptoms to discourage pattern of dysfunctional behaviors. Set limits in a stepwise progression if necessary to decrease focus on symptomatology and be consistent in not discussing physical symptoms.
I. Encourage venting of anxieties and fears.
J. Facilitate increased awareness and identification for the relationship between stress and symptom development or symptom exacerbation.
K. Inform patient that development of any new symptoms should be relayed to physician to rule out organic etiology.
L. Identify ways to intervene in dysfunctional pattern of symptomatology to avoid resorting to physical symptoms as a coping mechanism.
1. Appropriate and necessary confrontations
2. Overcoming avoidant patterns
3. Assertive communication, including saying "no"
M. Facilitate identification of how interpersonal relationships are affected by person's behavior.
N. Teach relaxation techniques.
1. Progressive muscle relaxation
2. Visualization
3. Meditation
O. Positive feedback and reinforcement for demonstrating effective, adaptive coping.

4. Body Image Disturbance

A. Identify misconceptions and distortions in body image
B. Decrease focus on distorted perception, as focus is increased on adaptive coping and positive self-care
C. Facilitate grieving for feelings of loss if person has experienced bodily changes
D. Facilitate self-care behaviors
E. Encourage person to strengthen self-esteem by engaging in productive, worthwhile contribution of effort
F. Positive feedback and reinforcement

5. Ineffective Self-care

A. Consult with physician regarding disabilities and impairment, and collaborate in developing adequate and effective self-care behaviors
B. Encourage independent fulfillment of daily activities related to hygiene, grooming, and other self-care behaviors (have patient write out a chart of daily behaviors)

C. Be accepting of person—the symptoms that they experience are real to them. Assure them with information from the physician regarding their *abilities* and what activities they can safely participate in

D. Positive feedback and reinforcement

6. Sensory-Perceptual Disturbance

    A. Consult with physician regarding treatment, lab tests, and so on to rule out possibility of organic etiology; perform regular mental status exam for ongoing assessment

    B. Identify primary and secondary gains that symptoms provide for the person

    C. Facilitate the person following through on independent daily activities for self-care

    D. Decrease focus on disturbances, as support and focus is increased on effective, adaptive behaviors

    E. Set limits and be consistent regarding manipulation with disabilities

    F. Reinforce with reality testing

    G. Encourage venting of fears and anxiety

    H. Teach assertive communication to increase appropriate means of getting needs met

    I. Facilitate identification of effective coping tools for dealing with stressful situations

    J. Facilitate the use of helpful supportive measures (PCP consult)

        1. Distraction techniques

        2. Hot and cold packs

        3. Hypnosis

        4. Eye movement desensitization and reprocessing (EMDR)

        5. Neuroreprocessing

        6. Massage

        7. Physical therapy

        8. Stress reduction exercises

        9. Support group focused on pain management

    K. Facilitate development and utilization of support system

    L. Positive feedback and reinforcement for efforts and accomplishments

7. Low Self-esteem

    A. Facilitate identification of strengths

    B. Focus on efforts and accomplishments

    C. Teach and encourage assertive communication

    D. Replace negative thinking with positive self-talk

    E. Encourage taking responsibility for one's own choices and behaviors

    F. Positive feedback and reinforcement for efforts and accomplishments

8. Ineffective Stress Management

    A. Relaxation techniques

    B. Time management

    C. Self-care behaviors

    D. Rational self-talk

*Part of this diagnostic category includes Psychological Factors Affecting Other Medical Conditions. Because of the added element of increased risk, it is important for the clinician to familiarize themselves with this caveat. When initially assessing an individual, particularly if medical issues are present, note if there appears to be a significant relationship between the individual's coping mechanisms and choices potentially (or are) negatively impacting the medical issue.

For instance, specific psychological factors interfere with treatment, affect the course of the medical issue, increase risk, or exacerbate symptoms of the medical condition. Therefore, the fundamental feature of this disorder, "is the presence of one or more clinically significant psychological or behavioral factors that adversely affect a medical condition by increasing the risk for suffering, death, or disability" (see DSM 5, p. 310). Guidi, Rafanelli, Roncuzzi, Sirri, and Fava (2013) set forth the results of a study demonstrating the association with dimensional measures of psychological distress and functioning in a population of medical patients; (1) 61.5% of the patients were diagnosed with Psychological Factors Affecting Medical conditions, (2) 41.4% most frequently were identified with the specifiers of illness denial, demoralization, and irritable mood, and (3) a greater number of significant associations with measures of psychological distress, global functioning, and stress.

DISSOCIATIVE DISORDERS

DSM 5 (APA, 2013) has provided a number of changes to dissociative disorders, including dissociative identity disorder. However, the update does not change the general treatment plan considerations for developing an individualized treatment plan. The central feature of dissociative disorders is a disturbance in the integration of identity, memory, or consciousness. Dissociation is a common response to exposure to a traumatic event—it is a way of organizing information that is referred to as compartmentalization of experience. Selected mental contents are removed or dissociated from conscious experiences; however, they continue to produce motor or sensory effects. The disturbance may have a sudden or gradual onset and may be temporary or chronic in its course. However, symptoms usually develop as a reaction to trauma. Additionally, episodes of stress can temporarily worsen symptoms. Depending on the mode of disturbance (identity, memory, or consciousness), the individual's life experience is affected in different ways. Conceptually, the course of treatment is to establish safety, stabilize, improve coping, maintain reality, and establish normal integrative functions. Suicidal and self-injurious/destructive behaviors are common with individuals with this diagnosis. Research (Foote, Smolin, Neft, & Lipschitz, 2008; Ross & Norton 1989) states that 67% of dissociative disorders, patients report a history of repeated suicide attempts and 42% report a history of self-destructive behavior. Additionally, BPD is diagnosed in approximately 30%–70% of those diagnosed with dissociative disorder (Korzewa, Del, Links, Thabane, & Fougere, 2009; Sar et al., 2003). However, Brand, Armstrong, Loewenstein, and McNary, 2009 and Lowenstein, 2007 assert that once the severe dysregulation associated with dissociative symptoms has been stabilized that the diagnosis of BPD is significantly decreased.

The basis of treatment is that an individual's own thoughts determine their behavior rather than the cause originating from external people or situations (International Society for the Study of Trauma and Dissociation, 2015). Successful treatment often takes significant time and persistence to effective treat underlying trauma and issues associated with dissociative disorders. Peterson (2010) highlights a phase or stage oriented approach to treatment.

1. Safety, stabilization, and symptoms reduction
   A. Safety from self-injury, substances, promiscuity, destructive relationships
   B. Stabilization of mood, affect tolerance, switching among alters, functioning in daily life, relationships
   C. Symptom reduction, learning to self-sooth, containment of reexperienced traumas
2. Processing traumatic experiences
   A. Reexperiencing, abreacting, desensitizing, and detoxifying traumatic events
   B. Reframing context of the abuse
   C. Tolerating feeling helplessness, confusion, grief, shame, horror, terror, anger, and rage
   D. Sharing traumatic memories among alters
3. Fusion and postfusion treatment
   A. Coming to terms with grief, loss, mourning
   B. Coming to terms with loneliness
   C. Practice new skills
   D. Tolerate not relying on dissociation
   E. Deal effectively with everyday problems

Throughout the stage-related treatment, there is a need and benefit to use behavior therapy that incorporates being in the moment (mindfulness), grounding, and self-soothing techniques. The outcome-oriented focus of treatment is to develop safety, stability, and increased adaptation to daily life demands.

DISSOCIATIVE DISORDERS

Goals

1. Establish safety and stabilize
2. Thought processes intact
3. Maintain a sense of reality
4. Improve coping skills
5. Stress management
6. Personality integration
7. Family education and support

Treatment Focus and Objectives

1. Address Safety Concerns and Initiate Stabilization. Skills development plays a significant role in safety and stabilization to address factors that undermine safety and stand in the way of stabilization.
   A. Identify and problem-solve safety issues
      1. Education regarding the necessity for safety
      2. Assess the history and function of unsafe/risky behaviors and impulses
      3. Identify and develop a repertoire of constructive/beneficial behaviors that sustain and reinforce safety
         a. Increase emotional awareness
         b. Improve emotional regulation
         c. Identify and utilize the predictability of safety and stability related issues
      4. Address safety issues associated with alter identities to help maintain safety
         a. A positive therapeutic alliance is essential, and when there is a history of therapist abuse, validate the negative impact and that they are in the position of making the decision of whom they are comfortable to work with (i.e., choosing their therapist, expressing boundaries, making choices)
   B. Address symptoms management
      1. Structure sessions to include education about the nature of dissociation and trauma treatment
         a. Predict and problem-solve that intense discomfort can be engendered during treatment
         b. Assure that the person will be helped when in therapy to pace the work to minimize becoming overwhelmed, i.e., the learning of skills for mastering symptoms and crises, separating the past from the present, and challenging/changing distortions
      2. Discuss the identified symptoms that establish the foundation of the treatment plan and the responsibility of each treatment team member—including the person being treated
      3. Self-monitoring and using resources to support emotional regulation
         a. Identify safe people (write them down on an index card for easy access in times of increased stress)
         b. Identify management choices to use when aware of escalating distress and write them on an index card (make duplicates and place them so that they are always available, because when distress increases, it is difficult to think clearly and remember such information)
         c. Facilitate development of basic and adequate coping strategies such as relaxation training, stress reduction exercises, and cognitive modulation of affect through self-talk
2. Altered Thought Processes
   A. In addition to assessing the person directly, gather information from family and significant others, which acts to broadly define the person (life, experiences, pleasurable activities, likes/dislikes, favorite music, places the person find relaxing, etc.)
   B. Expose person to positive past experiences and pleasurable activities
   C. Slowly elicit personal information from the person to prevent flooding, which could cause regression
      1. Asking for specific step by step details of trauma (visual, kinesthetic, auditory, etc.) memories of the event, what happened to them/their body

2. Clinicians can decrease intensity by asking content questions (How old are you?), using a calm/hypnotic tone of voice, ask them to stop talking about the trauma and anchoring them to the present and using relaxation techniques

D. As person allows memories to surface monitor closely for potential overstimulation, reinforcing trust in the clinician

E. Encourage the person to talk about situations that have posed significant stress

    1. Separate past from present

    2. Reinforce managing crisis when emotional distress is escalating but effectively intervened

    3. Challenging and changing distortions

F. Facilitate the person to verbalize stressful situations and to explore the feelings associated with those situations, reassuring them that they are in control of the processing time frame—taking it as slowly as they need and desire

*This careful awareness and slow titrating process, with repeated iterations, allows memories to be transformed from traumatic memories into narrative memories.

    1. Skills to help manage difficult memories and emotions

*Using a process similar to systematic desensitization the clinician is responsible for managing the level of emotional stimulation in sessions. Therefore, they teach basic skills for avoiding hyperarousal and feeling in control.

        a. Grounding

        b. Separating past from present

        c. Effectively utilizing distraction to prevent overstimulation and becoming overwhelmed

    2. Reinforce efforts

G. Facilitate increased awareness and understanding of all the factors that have contributed to the dissociative process

    1. Emotional distress, fear, loss

        a. Controlled and paced therapeutic process

        b. Understanding conditioned fear, anger, and shame in response to external and internal cues that foster dissociation

    2. Cognitive reframing of traumatic experiences

    3. Countering irrational guilt and shame through recognizing the adaptive responses present during trauma

    4. Bring together memories, sequence of events, the associated affects, and the physiological and somatic representations of the experience

        a. Intensive memory work should not be allowed to dominate session after session. Take time to avoid retraumatization and or destabilization.

    5. Develop a more complete and coherent history and sense of self

    6. Maintain awareness for trauma-based cognitive distortions and/or transference reactivity that may interfere

    7. Hypnosis may be a beneficial adjunct treatment for calming, soothing, containment, and ego strengthening

    8. Consider other specialized interventions that may be beneficial, i.e., family therapy, expressive therapy, DBT, EMDR, sensorimotor psychotherapy, substance abuse treatment, and/or eating disorder treatment

H. Facilitate identification of specific conflicts that are unresolved

    1. Allow the realization that past experiences belong to the past allowing the processing of memories to feel safe and manageable.

        a. Hypnosis or EMDR can be used for calming, managing stressful experiences, or impulsive behaviors

2. Acknowledging and understanding the impact of experiences on their life.
3. Identify the loss, grief, and mourning the trauma causes.
4. Develop interventions with the person for the purpose of becoming grounded in the present and ending the session. This can be done by cuing the person at an agreed amount of time before the end of the session to initiate the process of reorientation and self-calming.

I. Develop possible solution to the unresolved conflicts and bringing those skills into the here and now
   1. Being present and focused in the here and now
   2. Develop the ability to be not focused on the hurts of the past or possible negative outcomes of the future
   3. Able to attend to verbal and nonverbal communications of the other person
   4. Develop the ability to deal with conflicts as they occur, and do not avoid conflicts
   5. Becoming self-nurturing
      a. Develop ability to accurately reflect on their own inner experience and that of the other person
      b. Develop the ability to pay equal attention to the needs and wants of themselves and those of others
      c. Develop ability to regulate thoughts, feelings, and expectations

J. Identify time gaps/loss of time associated with recall for everyday events, not just traumatic experiences
   1. Clarify time sequence of experiences

K. Be supportive and offer positive feedback and reinforcement for the courage to work through these issues

3. Sensory/Perceptual Distortion
   A. Identify the nature, extent, and possible precipitants of the dissociative states
      1. Decrease or eliminate sensory/perceptual distortions
   B. Obtain a collaborative history of the nature and extent of the dissociative states from family/friends
   C. Educate the person regarding depersonalization experience, behaviors, and the purpose they generally serve for the person (or did serve originally)
   D. Be supportive and encouraging when the person is experiencing depersonalization
   E. Validate feelings of fear and anxiety related to depersonalization experience
   F. Educate the person regarding the relationship between severe anxiety and stress to the depersonalization experience
   G. Explore past experiences such as trauma and abuse
   H. Encourage the identification and working through of feelings associated with these situations
   I. Identify effective and adaptive responses to severe anxiety and stress
   J. Encourage practice of these new adaptive behaviors, this may be initiated through modeling and role-play
   K. Facilitate the person's ability to separate past from present to more effectively cope with the traumatic memories and feelings

4. Ineffective Coping
   A. Be supportive and reassuring
   B. Identify situations that precipitate severe anxiety
   C. Facilitate appropriate problem solving to intervene and prevent escalation of anxiety and to develop more adaptive coping in response to anxiety
   D. Explore feelings that the person experiences in response to stressful situations
   E. Consider using environmental manipulation to improve coping
   F. Whenever possible, encourage maintenance of employment as long as possible
   G. Facilitate understanding that the emotion experienced is acceptable and often predictable in times of stress
   H. Facilitate the development of improved coping abilities and encourage the identification of the underlying source(s) of chronic anxiety

I. Encourage identification of past coping strategies and determine if the response was adaptive or maladaptive

J. Develop a plan of action for effective, adaptive coping to predictable future stressors

K. Explore with the person the benefits and consequences of alternative adaptive coping strategies

L. Use of grounding

M. Identify community resources that can be utilized to increase the person's support system as he/she makes efforts to effectively manage

N. Facilitate identification of how the person's life has been affected by the trauma

O. Identify and reinforce the self-confidence that comes with increased self-understanding and effective use of coping strategies

P. Offer positive feedback and reinforcement for efforts and accomplishments

5. Ineffective Stress Management

   A. Relaxation techniques.

   B. Use grounding.

   C. Time management.

   D. Self-care (exercise, nutrition, utilization of resources, etc.).

   E. Expressive therapy may be useful in allowing the person to express the feelings without the cognitive self-judgment that may accompany "talk therapy."

   F. EMDR may offer accelerated information processing using alternating focus across the midline. Resource installation is used to bolster the patient's internal resources such as self-confidence.

   G. Educate regarding role of negative self-talk.

   H. Identify positive daily structure for predictability, practice of skill development, and enhancing self-confidence.

6. Identity Disturbance

   A. Develop a trusting therapeutic relationship. With a multiple personality, this means a trusting and honest relationship with consistency and boundaries. Educate person about multiple personality disorder to increase his/her understanding of subpersonalities.

   B. Facilitate identification of the need of each subpersonality, the role they have played in psychic survival.

   C. Facilitate identification of the need that each subpersonality serves in the personal identity of the person.

   D. Facilitate identification of the relationship between stress and personality change.

   E. Facilitate identification of the stressful situations that precipitate a transition from one personality to another.

   F. Decrease fear and defensiveness by facilitating subpersonalities to understand that integration will not lead to their destruction, but to a unified personality within the individual.

   G. Hypnotherapy.

   H. Facilitate understanding that therapy will be a long-term process, which is often arduous and difficult.

   I. Be supportive and reassuring.

7. Family Dysfunction and Negative Environment

   A. Family environment is essential to progress and success

      1. Decrease family chaos and violence

         a. Safety is essential. Be aware of impulsivity and dissociative processes in family members.

      2. Identify impulsivity and dissociative processes in family members

   B. Screen for dissociative symptoms in family members

   C. In unstable settings, focus on environment consistency and ego strengthening

      1. Problem-solve managing impact of unstable home environment

      2. Identify potential options for residential changes to safe environment

      3. Focus on areas of control

      4. Reinforce the use of stress-management skills

DSM 5 (APA, 2013) in changes this diagnostic category now requires more exact severity of the criteria to decrease the overdiagnosis of sexual dysfunctions. Subtypes for sexual dysfunctions in the DSM 5 include only "lifelong versus acquired" and "generalized versus situational." The DSM 5 deleted two subtypes: "sexual dysfunction due to a general medical condition" and "due to psychological versus combined factors." Additionally, there was some renaming of dysfunctions that were highly comorbid and difficult to differentiate.

The subtle but critical refinement that defines the line between an atypical sexual interest and disorder makes it possible for an individual to engage in consensual atypical sexual behavior without erroneously being labeled with a mental disorder (Regier et al., 2013). This DSM 5 revision makes a clear distinguished definition between atypical sexual interests and mental disorders involving these desires or behaviors.

DSM 5 (APA, 2013) diagnoses in this category require a person to feel extreme distress and interpersonal strain for a minimum of 6 months (excluding substance or medication-induced sexual dysfunction). The term sexual dysfunction may refer to physical sexual dysfunction as well as paraphilias (disorders of sexual preference). Therefore, a thorough sexual history and assessment of other health problems are very important for a comprehensive evaluation. This is in addition to a general health assessment. Sexual dysfunction is the difficulty experienced by an individual or a couple during any stage of a normal sexual activity, including physical pleasure, desire, preference, arousal, or orgasm. Many sexual dysfunctions are based on the human sexual response, but the emotional or psychological impact to sexual difficulties is very important and often associated to performance and feelings of anxiety, guilt, stress, and worry.

Once the diagnosis and underlying factors have been identified, if the issues require more than counseling, problem-solving life of relationship issues, or adjustment and resolution that do not alleviate the sexual dysfunction, it is then ethical and appropriate to refer to a certified sex therapist.

SEXUAL DYSFUNCTIONS

Goals

1. Clarify origin of disorder
2. Make appropriate referrals (physician, certified sex therapist, etc.)
3. Create a baseline for monitoring change
4. Promote education and treatment of emotional and psychological problems

Treatment Focus and Objectives

1. Assess for Predisposing Factors
    A. Review current medications that person is taking. Chronic alcohol and cocaine use have been associated with sexual disorders. Prescription medications that have been implicated include antidepressants, anxiolytics, antipsychotics, anticonvulsants, antihypertensives, cholinergic blockers, and antihistamines.
    B. Assess psychosocial factors. These factors are wide ranging and encompass age of experiences, developmental implications, belief systems, interpersonal issues, trauma or pain, and cultural conditioning. These factors may include shame, guilt, fear, anxiety, depression, disgust, resentment, anger toward partner, stress, fatigue, fear of pregnancy, ambivalence, fear of commitment, disease phobia, childhood sexual assault/abuse, moralistic upbringing with negative messages about sexual contact and sexual organs or rigid religiosity, moral prohibition, or inhibition.
    C. Consult with physician and refer for medical evaluation. Organic etiologies include the decreased estrogen levels associated with menopause, endometriosis, pelvic infections, tumors, cysts, penile infections, urinary tract infections, prostate problems, damage or irritation of the sexual organs, low levels of testosterone, diabetes, arteriosclerosis, temporal lobe epilepsy, multiple sclerosis (MS), blood pressure, medication reactions, substance abuse, and Parkinson disease. Pelvic surgery, genitourinary surgery, and spinal cord injuries may also be associated with sexual dysfunction.

2. Assess for Appropriate Referrals
    A. Refer to physician to rule out organic etiology
    B. Refer to other pertinent specialists such as a certified sex therapist if such expertise is needed
3. Establish Baseline Information of Sexual Dysfunction Experience
    A. Time frame associated with onset of dysfunction
    B. Persistent or recurrent (for diagnostic clarity assess whether life long, acquired, generalized, situational, with or without masturbations, with or without partner, due to psychological or combined factors)
        1. Frequency
        2. Setting
        3. Duration
        4. Level of subjective distress
            a. Insufficient lubrication
            b. Inadequate stimulation
        5. Effects in other areas of function
    C. Does not occur exclusively during the course of another disorder (major depression, acute anxiety, substance abuse, etc.)
    D. Life situation/stress level
    E. Causes marked stress or self-esteem/interpersonal difficulty
    F. Clarify and interpret the dynamics of sexual dysfunction
        1. Absence of orgasm
            a. Sexual inhibition
            b. Inexperience
            c. Lack of knowledge
            d. Psychological factors
                1. Guilt, anxiety, etc.
                2. History of sexual trauma or abuse
        2. Painful intercourse
            a. R/O by gynecological exam
                1. That is endometriosis, ovarian cyst, presence of scar tissue, STD, poor lubrication, etc.
    G. Work through the dynamics of sexual dysfunction
    H. Relationship issues
    I. Medical issues/medication
    J. Mood and emotion
    K. Misinformation or lack of knowledge
    L. Sexual history
    M. Belief system
4. Lack of Understanding Regarding Dysfunctional Sexual Issues
    A. Educate person regarding the potential for change in satisfaction through various interventions (medical, behavior, psychological)
        1. Educate regarding human anatomy, sexual function, and normal changes associated with aging
        2. Enhancing stimulation
            a. Erotic material (videos or books)
            b. Masturbation
            c. Changes in sexual routines
            d. Devices: A prescription device called the Eros can help with arousal by increasing blood flow to the genital area and enhancing sensation
        3. Providing distraction techniques
            a. Erotic or nonerotic fantasies
            b. Exercises with intercourse
            c. Music, videos, TV can be used to promote relaxation and eliminate anxiety

4. Encouraging noncoital behaviors
      a. Physically stimulating activity that does not include intercourse
         1. Sensate focus
      b. Sensual massage to promote comfort and increase partner communication
   5. Minimizing pain
B. Identify emotional responses to sex and intimacy
C. Explore how sensitive and caring the individual's partner is to the person's needs
D. Determine whether the individual has ever experienced sex as pleasurable or experienced orgasm
E. Identify the individual's goals, how to incorporate the partner in treatment, and invest the partner as a support and agent of change
   1. Boredom with regular sexual routines (lack of interest/enthusiasm)
   2. Lifestyle factors (career, care of children, care of ill parents, etc.)

Additional Considerations

1. Hormonal changes. For women the focus is often on estrogen. However, both females and males may experience sexual dysfunction associated with testosterone.
   A. Women. Testosterone, when used short-term (a year or two), may increase sex drive in some women. Testosterone products for women are approved in some countries but not in the United States. The long-term safety of testosterone for women has not been proven and is being studied.
   B. Men. Low blood testosterone levels may result diminished libido (sex drive), erectile dysfunction (impotence), decreased muscle mass, increased fat, and are at increased risk for thinning of the bones (osteoporosis). Treatment is designed to increase a man's testosterone level, libido, erectile function, and muscle mass; bone density usually improves as testosterone levels return to normal.

2. Menopause

   The loss of estrogen can result in numerous consideration associated with sexual function. Emotional changes that often accompany menopause can add to a woman's loss of interest in sex and/or ability to become aroused. Hormone replacement therapy or vaginal lubricants may improve some conditions (vaginal lubrication and genital sensation). Also, an oral medication taken once a day, ospemifene (Osphena), makes vaginal tissue thicker and less fragile thus improving comfort and likely associated desire. There are likely to be additional medications on the market in the future that improve sexual satisfaction.

   Interestingly, menopause does not always result in negative impact to sexual satisfaction. Some postmenopausal women report an increase in sexual satisfaction. This may be due to decreased anxiety over getting pregnant. Additionally, these women are likely to have fewer child-rearing responsibilities (and associated stage-of-life demands). Thus, allowing them to relax and enjoy intimacy with their partners.

3. Hysterectomy

   Many women experience changes in sexual function following a hysterectomy. These changes may include a loss of desire, and decreased vaginal lubrication and genital sensation. These problems may be associated with the hormonal changes that occur with the loss of the uterus. An additional concern is that nerves and blood vessels may be damaged during the course of surgery that is critical to sexual function.

GENDER DYSPHORIA

The development of the DSM 5 was sensitive to the stigma associated with choosing the right words whereby "dysphoria" replaced "disorder." Gender dysphoria refers to the distress that may accompany the incongruence between one's experienced or expressed gender and one's assigned gender. Additionally, gender dysphoria manifests itself differently in different age groups. Underlying these word choices, was the respect for those identified a more appropriate diagnostic name suited to the symptoms and behaviors experienced that did not result in decreasing their access to treatment options.

To varying degrees, adults with gender dysphoria may choose the behavior, clothing, and mannerisms of the experienced gender for emotional congruence. They are presented with basic associated issues for which to find a solution:

1. They feel uncomfortable being regarded by others, or functioning in society, as members of their assigned gender.
2. Some adults may have a strong desire to be of a different gender and treated as such, and they may have an inner certainty to feel and respond as the experienced gender without seeking medical treatment to alter body characteristics.
3. They may find other ways to resolve the incongruence between experienced/expressed and assigned gender by partially living in the desired role or by adopting a gender role neither conventionally male nor conventionally female.

Additionally, once the diagnosis and underlying factors have been identified, if the issues require more than counseling, problem-solving life of relationship issues, or adjustment and resolution that do not alleviate the sexual disorder, it is then ethical and appropriate to refer to a certified sex therapist or recognized specialist.

GENDER DYSPHORIA

Goals

1. Decreasing functional consequences
2. Make appropriate referrals (physician, certified sex therapist, etc.)
3. Create a baseline for monitoring change
4. Promote education and treatment of emotional and psychological problems/growth

Treatment and Focus Objectives

1. Identify and Validate Functional Consequences
   A. Preoccupation with cross-gender wishes
   B. Identify the impact upon peer relationship
   C. Identify the impact of interference with daily activities
   D. Identify negative social responses experienced
      1. Stigmatization, discrimination, and victimization resulting in negative self-concept
      2. Increase rates of comorbid mental disorders
      3. Economic marginalization (school drop-out, unemployment)
      4. Increased health risks
      5. Decreased social involvement
2. Assess for Appropriate Referrals (if person does not have resources identified)
   A. Refer to primary care physician for medication evaluation and sound referrals to other specialists to maintain safety and standards of care
   B. Refer to other pertinent specialists such as a certified sex therapist if such expertise is needed
3. Establish Baseline Information of Gender Dysphoria Experience
   A. Time frame associated with onset of gender dysphoria
   B. Differentiate simple nonconformity to stereotypical gender role behavior
      1. Rule out distress and impairment criteria specific
      2. Identify and treat comorbid anxiety and depression

3. Duration
4. Level of subjective distress
5. Effects in other areas of function
C. Assess for comorbidity
1. Depressive disorders
2. Anxiety disorders
3. SUDs
D. Life situation/stress level
E. Causes marked stress or self-esteem/interpersonal difficulty
F. Relationship issues
G. Psychosocial issues
1. Safety
2. Housing (i.e., living in a negative environment, positive independence, etc.)
3. Financial (lack of financial support, difficulty getting a job due to bias)
4. Access to health care
5. Positive social support
H. Medical issues/medication
I. Misinformation or lack of knowledge
J. Sexual experience history
K. Personal belief system
4. Lack of Education About Choices and Treatment
A. Educate person regarding the potential for change in satisfaction through various interventions (medical, behavior, psychological).
B. The current main psychiatric approaches to treatment for persons diagnosed with gender dysphoria are psychotherapy, supportive therapy, or to support the individual's preferred gender through hormone therapy, gender expression and role, or surgery.

*Keeping in mind that the diagnosis only applies to the discontent experienced by associated issues.

C. Identify and treat any adjustment or adaptation issues that may be related. If a person successfully completes gender reassignment surgery, it does not automatically mean any issue is resolved, and much psychotherapy may be needed after the procedure to improve outcome generally (Cohen-Kettenis & Pfäfflin, 2009; Royal College of Psychiatrists, 2013).
D. Reinforce the courage, self-honesty, assertiveness, and continued efforts to meet personal goals.

ADJUSTMENT DISORDERS

The hallmark of this DSM 5 disorder (APA, 2013) is a maladaptive reaction to an identifiable stressor(s). Adjustment disorder is a stress-related, short-term, nonpsychotic disturbance. The discomfort, distress, turmoil, and anguish to the patient are significant, and the consequences (i.e., suicidal potential) are extremely important.

The stressor may be single or multiple. The severity of the reaction cannot be extrapolated from the intensity of the stressor. Instead, the reaction is a function of the vulnerability and coping mechanisms of the individual. According to APA (2013; Medscape, 2015), therapy may substantially alleviate symptoms of adjustment disorder. The predominant mood accompanying adjustment disorder (e.g., depression or anxiety) is the central consideration for both pharmacologic and supportive behavioral interventions. Additionally, clinicians should consider both psychotherapy and pharmacotherapy for patients who have adjustment disorder with depressed anxious mood.

ADJUSTMENT DISORDERS

Goals

1. Analyze the stressors
2. Alleviate emotional, psychological, or behavioral distress
3. Improve coping skills
4. Improve problem-solving skills
5. Improve adjustment
6. Improve stress-management skills
7. Improve self-esteem
8. Improve social interaction
9. Develop social supports

Treatment Focus and Objectives

1. Assess the Origin Maladjustment
   A. Assess the stressors affecting the patient and determine whether they can be eliminated or minimized (problem solving)
   B. Clarify and interpret the meaning of the stressor for the person
   C. Reframe the meaning of the stressor
   D. Highlight, reflect, process the concerns and conflicts the patient experiences
   E. Identify means of reducing the stressor
   F. Maximize the person's coping skills (emotional self-regulation, avoidance of maladaptive coping, especially substance misuse)
   G. Facilitate the gaining of perspective on the stressor, establish relationships, mobilize support, and manage themselves and the stressor
2. Mood Disturbance
   A. Educate regarding relationship between mood and adjusting
   B. Identify predisposition/history of emotional response to stressors
   C. Review methods of coping in similar situations
   D. Reduce stimuli to decrease agitation/anxiety
   E. Develop appropriate daily structure
   F. Identify precipitating factors that exacerbate mood disturbance
   G. Educate regarding importance of good nutrition
   H. Regular physical exercise to release tension and decrease fatigue
   I. Journal writing to vent thoughts and feelings and to clarify and facilitate problem solving
3. Ineffective Coping
   A. Encourage appropriate venting of thoughts and feelings
   B. Identify physical activities that provide for a healthy outlet for negative feelings
   C. Encourage independent functioning
   D. Facilitate identification of factors that person has some control over and initiate problem solving, also identify factors that person has no control over and initiate letting go
   E. Increase awareness for person's response to feelings of powerlessness (victim role, manipulation of others, helplessness, etc.)
   F. Positive feedback and reinforcement toward improved coping
4. Impaired Problem Solving
   A. Facilitate identification of the issues
   B. Facilitate development of alternative ways to manage or resolve issues
   C. Facilitate individual to take action, being aware of the consequences and alternative choices should be necessary

5. Impaired Adjustment
   A. Have person describe his/her functioning prior to the change
   B. Have the person describe his/her "normal functioning"
   C. Encourage venting of thoughts and feelings associated with change or loss
   D. Encourage independent functioning
   E. Facilitate problem solving about how the person is going to incorporate the change or loss as a life experience
   F. Identify problems associated with the change or loss
   G. Utilize modeling and role-playing to prepare person to follow through on dealing with difficult areas
   H. Refer the person to appropriate community resources
6. Ineffective Stress Management
   A. Teach relaxation techniques
      1. Progressive muscle relaxation
      2. Visual imagery
      3. Mindfulness meditation
      4. Yoga
   B. Self-care (exercise, nutrition, utilization of resources)
   C. Educate regarding role of negative self-talk
   D. Stress inoculation (inoculate or prepare a person to become resistant to the effects of a particular stressor)
      1. Appraisal
         a. The clinician provides education about the general nature of the stress and that cognitive distortions play an essential role in shaping stress reactions
            1. Commonly and inadvertently, a stress is made worse through the unconscious use of ineffective coping behaviors
         b. Develop a clear understanding of the nature of the specific stressor that the person is facing
            1. Differentiate between aspects of their stressors and their stress-induced reactions that are changeable and aspects that cannot change, so that coping efforts can be adjusted accordingly
            2. Facilitate acceptance-based coping that are appropriate to situations that cannot be changed
            3. Facilitate more active interventions appropriate for changeable/modifiable stressors
      2. Skills acquisition and rehearsal
         a. Skills individually tailored to the specific needs of the person (strengths, vulnerabilities, etc.) for skills to be effective. For example,
            1. Emotion regulation
            2. Relaxation
            3. Cognitive appraisal
            4. Problem solving
            5. Communication
            6. Social skills
      3. Application and follow through
         a. Provide the person with opportunities to practice coping skills
         b. Encourage use of a variety of simulation methods to increase realism of coping practice
         c. Include visualization exercises, modeling and vicarious learning, role-playing of feared or stressful situations, simple repetitious practice of coping routines for desensitization and mastery
7. Low Self-esteem
   A. Be accepting and nonjudgmental toward person
   B. Facilitate identification of realistic expectations (goals) and limitations
   C. Facilitate identification of person's assets/strengths
   D. Facilitate identification of areas of desired change and develop a problem-solving framework that person can utilize in working toward those goals
   E. Encourage and support the person in confronting areas of difficulty
   F. Discourage repetition of negative thoughts

G. Encourage taking responsibility for choices and behaviors

H. Facilitate increased self-awareness
   1. Journal writing
   2. Exploration of thoughts and feelings

I. Facilitate self-acceptance
   1. Identify personal beliefs and value system.
   2. Encourage objectivity and positive regard to the self versus rejecting. Educate the person about the impact of negative self-talk on self-esteem.

J. Focus on the positive; reframe failures as opportunities to learn

K. Positive feedback and reinforcement

8. Impaired Social Interaction

A. Facilitate increased awareness of behavioral responses in relationship and how others experience and interpret the individual's behavior

B. Identify ineffective and inappropriate attempt to get needs met, such as manipulative, angry, or exploitative behavior

C. Identify appropriate verbal and behavioral responses

D. Role-model and practice appropriate verbal and behavioral responses for a variety of anticipated situations

E. Utilize resources

F. Positive feedback and reinforcement for efforts and accomplishments

9. Lacks Social Support

A. Educate and support regarding the development of an appropriate and adequate support system

*The primary goal of treatment is to facilitate the patient in returning to the precrisis level of functioning. The secondary goal is to capitalize on the emotional turmoil of the crisis to change preexisting maladaptive patterns into more useful and self-satisfying ways of responding to the environment. Overall, therapy is supportive in nature, focusing on an individual's strengths in an effort to help individuals adapt and cope effectively with stressors.

Medication might be utilized as a short-term intervention in adjustment reaction when there is a clear target symptom, such as depression, acute anxiety, or insomnia, which might impede recovery or impair functioning if not treated.

PERSONALITY DISORDERS

Personality disorder diagnoses were previously listed on a different axis than other disorders; however, they have now been added into a single axis with all other mental and medical diagnoses. According to the DSM 5 (APA, 2013), this was done to remove the insinuated distinction between conditions to benefit both clinical practice and research use. In other words, moving from a multiaxial to a monoaxial system eliminates the arbitrary delineation between personality disorders and other mental disorders. Stetka (2013) asserts, "the fact that borderline personality disorder had such good inter-rater reliability, whereas the other personality disorders did not, may support previously endorsed views that it could belong in the bipolar disorder spectrum rather than being classified as a personality disorder."

A person may meet the criteria for more than one personality disorder. Additionally, there is an overlap in the diagnostic criteria of various personality disorders. Because a person suffering a clinical crisis may demonstrate personality disorder features during the period of that crisis does not warrant the diagnosis of a personality disorder. A diagnosis of personality disorder is only given when enduring personality traits are inflexible and maladaptive and cause significant impairment in how the individual interacts with the environment.

Due to the nature of personality disorders (enduring and pervasive maladaptive behaviors), psychodynamic treatment, in conjunction with results-oriented brief therapy interventions and skills development (CBT), offers optimal results toward behavioral change (AHRQ, 2008; Brand et al., 2009; Mayo Clinic, 2014; NAMI, 2012; NHS.uk, 8/2014; NIH, 2015; NIM/NIH, 2015).

There are 10 types of personality disorders and the only one not included is antisocial personality disorder which is a psychiatric condition characterized by chronic behavior that manipulates, exploits, or violates the rights of others. Antisocial personality disorder is a condition in which people show a pervasive disregard for the law and the rights of others. The terms "sociopath" and "psychopath" are sometimes used to describe a person with antisocial personality disorder.

AVOIDANT PERSONALITY DISORDER

Individuals with avoidant personality disorder are particularly sensitive to scrutiny, even in a therapy situation. They may be reluctant to openly discuss their internal experience of thoughts and emotions for fear of criticism from the therapist and also for fear of embarrassment. The initial goal of therapy should be to establish the positive rapport necessary for these patients to be able to feel comfortable and begin to develop a therapeutic alliance that allows them to make a commitment to a course of treatment. If this is not accomplished, the patient is not likely to return for a second visit or terminate from treatment prematurely. Additionally, clinicians must carefully be thoughtful in determining the length of treatment necessary for the person to become fully functional. Given the challenges of this disorder, and the importance of developing a positive therapeutic alliance it may take at least a year before the avoidance is no longer significantly maladaptive, even though there may be noticeable improvement in functioning before that. Treatment gains may not appear immediately significant after a standard period of brief therapy. However, benefit will likely become evident after a longer course of exposure to avoidant situations. Predict for the person that it is not uncommon to have a relapse experience after termination from a course of treatment and that "maintenance" therapy of intermittent follow-up sessions will enhance the benefits of CBT.

The goal of cognitive therapy is to modify negative self-talk (self-critical thoughts and fear of the negative assessment of others), and to challenge the mistaken belief than any negative or unpleasant emotion or interaction is intolerable. Exposure practice experiences are important to challenge the tendency to negatively interpret social interactions and positively alter the person's general assessment of their social experiences.

This disorder shares numerous similarities with social phobia, as well as with agoraphobia. Avoidant personality disorder also shares characteristics with other personality disorders, particularly dependent personality disorder (DPD). An individualized treatment plan considers all of the factors that influence distressing symptoms and quality of life.

AVOIDANT PERSONALITY DISORDER

Goals

1. Decrease resistance to beneficial intervention/change
2. Develop goals
3. Improve social interaction
4. Decrease avoidant behavior
5. Resolve issues of loss
6. Improve coping skills
7. Cognitive restructuring
8. Decrease sensitivity
9. Improve self-esteem

Treatment Focus and Objectives

1. Therapeutic Resistance
   A. Establish a trusting therapeutic relationship
   B. Do not engage the person in clinical issues too quickly
   C. Do not pressure the person with expectations
   D. Encourage taking appropriate risk, such as entering therapy

1. Take the chance to develop new ways of thinking
2. Opportunity to practice new skills in a safe, judgment-free environment
3. Challenging irrational anxiety and self-consciousness in a social situation

2. Lack of Goals
   A. Develop appropriate goals for personal growth and behavioral change
      1. Explore what would the person "wish" they could do
         a. Identify limiting factors
         b. Problem-solve creating possibilities that are manageable and progressive
      2. Identify what has the person historically initiate but did not complete because of emotional distress, fear, or doing something wrong or being embarrassed

3. Impaired Social Interaction
   A. Facilitate identification of fears (rejection, etc.) and feeling that the environment is unsafe.
      1. Focus on overcoming fears
      2. Challenge their reluctance to become involved with activities and others for fear of rejection
      3. Challenge exaggeration of problems/limitations/fears
      4. Develop coping mechanisms associated with "choices" to decrease anxiety
      5. Systematic desensitization provides useful, progressive practice for overcoming fear
   B. Educate regarding effect of anxiety in avoidant behavior.
      1. Educate regarding "shyness"
         a. Exposure therapy to confront feared situations. Starting with the least feared/frightening situations, mastering them, moving on to more difficult situations, mastering them, and so on
         b. Social skills training
            1. New ways of thinking and behaving (using eye contact, asking appropriate questions)
            2. Use many different situations for practice and rehearsal
         c. Relaxation training. Learning to relax while in the situation they fear
            1. Meditation
            2. Breathing techniques
      2. Cognitive restructure/reframe fear of social settings and relationships
   C. Facilitate identification of realistic expectations regarding changes in avoidant behavior.
   D. Develop a slow-paced stepwise progression of social interaction.
      1. Identify desired social interactions
      2. Develop, with person, small steps to accomplish and reinforce progress
   E. Facilitate identification of fear of rejection and hypersensitivity. Increase awareness of alternative ways of viewing the responses of others versus personalizing.
      1. Practice exposure experiences are needed to desensitize reaction and reinforce the improved experience associated with appropriately modifying negative self-statements
      2. Reinforce efforts and accomplishment
      3. Use efforts and accomplishments as foundation for challenging negative self-concept and improving self-esteem
   F. Refer to group therapy and family therapy (if appropriate) to increase awareness for and practice dealing with hypersensitivity.
      1. Prepare the person in individual therapy to anticipate the positive and safe experiences of group therapy to facilitate and reinforce new attitudes/beliefs and skills
      2. Group therapy provides corrective emotional experiences that allow the person to pursue personal relationships outside of therapy where they will receive empathic support and appreciation of the courage to expose themselves to social situations they previously avoided due to fear and emotional distress
   G. Family therapy. This can be challenging because the avoidant personality disorder may be reinforced by the family or family context.
      1. Engage family members in the treatment process by educating them about the importance of behavior change for the identified patient.
         a. The family may be overprotective with the intent of being helpful but in fact may help to maintain the patient's unwillingness to take chances

2. Family members may become extremely helpful in encouraging the patient to engage in social situations and also may be able to give emotional support while prodding the patient to seek out new experiences.
    H. Facilitate small steps toward calculated risks for social/personal gratification.
    I. Positive feedback and reinforcement for efforts and accomplishments.
4. Avoidance of People and Situations
    A. Systematic desensitization/flooding
    B. Teach assertive communication
        1. Role-play and model effective, honest responses/behaviors
    C. Break down desired behavioral changes into manageable steps
    D. Be supportive, focusing on positives
    E. Positive feedback and reinforcement for efforts and accomplishments
5. Issues of Loss
    A. Facilitate identification of feelings of loneliness, being an outsider, and so forth
    B. Identify behaviors that contribute to isolation and aloneness
    C. Facilitate resolution of losses through venting of feelings, closure on issues where appropriate, problem-solving, and behavioral changes
6. Ineffective Coping
    A. Establish a trusting relationship, reciprocating respect by keeping appointments, being honest, genuine, and so on within the therapeutic frame
    B. Facilitate identification of feelings
    C. Encourage appropriate ventilation of feelings
    D. Explore alternatives for dealing with stressful situations instead of avoidance
        1. Refer to group and family therapy to practice new ways of thinking and behaving to develop improved coping and a willingness to take appropriate risks
    E. Identify goals for desired changes, and break down each goal into manageable steps for shaping new behaviors
    F. Educate regarding role of negative self-talk
    G. Teach relaxation techniques
        1. Progressive muscle relaxation
        2. Visual imagery/meditation
        3. Time management
    H. Positive feedback and reinforcement for efforts and accomplishments
7. Distorted Beliefs
    A. Challenge irrational thoughts, statements, and attributions
    B. Reframe beliefs and situations to provide rational, believable alternatives
    C. Refer to group and family therapy to challenge irrational and distorted beliefs
    D. Paradoxical interventions
        1. Prescribing avoidant behaviors. This intervention can sometimes be used to slow down avoidant responding by circumscribing and limiting avoidant patterns of behavior by assigning specific avoidant behaviors.
        2. Prescribing rejections. To fulfill this intervention, seek situations that are predictable and under control.
8. Overly Sensitive
    A. Facilitate increased awareness for acute sensitivity
        1. Difficult for the person to benefit from the feedback from others because it is viewed as criticism and disapproval
        2. Interferes with others feeling comfortable with being honest with the person, fears the person's negative response
    B. Role-play social situations to decrease fear/anxiety
    C. Initiate person to speak honestly about them

D. Explore issues of self-acceptance
E. Refer to group therapy to facilitate increased awareness for acute sensitivity and desensitization and family therapy to challenge reinforcing avoidant patterns

9. Low Self-esteem
    A. Be accepting and respectful to person
    B. Identify and focus on strengths and accomplishments
    C. Facilitate self-monitoring of efforts toward desired goals
    D. Facilitate development of assertive communication
    E. Refer to group and family therapy for the opportunity to challenge irrational beliefs and practice new ways of thinking and behaving
    F. Encourage and positively reinforce efforts and accomplishments

These individuals want affection, but not as much as they fear rejection. The slightest disapproval or critique is misconstrued as derogatory. They may ingratiate themselves to others in an effort to prevent rejection. A friendly, gentle, and reassuring approach is essential in developing a beneficial therapeutic relationship with someone who is hypersensitive to potential rejection and has low self-esteem. Depression and substance abuse should always be assessed with this diagnosis.

BORDERLINE PERSONALITY DISORDER

NAMI (2012) identifies BPD as a serious mental illness characterized by impulsivity and instability in mood, self-image, and personal relationships. NIH (2015) suggests that clinicians adapt psychotherapy to best meet the needs of the individual. And, indeed may switch from one type of therapy to another, mix various techniques, or use a combination of different therapy techniques. There is a high rate of self-injury without suicide intent, as well as a significant rate of suicide attempts and completed suicide in severe cases.

The person with BPD may experience intense bouts of anger, depression, and anxiety that may last only hours, or at most a day. These may be associated with episodes of impulsive aggression, self-injury, and drug or alcohol abuse. Distortions in cognition and sense of self can lead to frequent changes in long-term goals, career plans, jobs, friendships, gender identity, and values. They commonly feel unfairly misunderstood or mistreated by others, bored, empty, and have little idea who they are. Such symptoms are most acute when people with BPD feel isolated and lacking in social support and may result in frantic efforts to avoid being alone. Thus, the intense fear associated with abandonment.

BORDERLINE PERSONALITY DISORDER

Goals

1. Goal development
2. Appropriate expression of emotions
3. Increase awareness for intensity in relationships
4. Decrease self-destructive behaviors
5. Decrease manipulative behavior
6. Clarify boundaries
7. Improve communication
8. Improve self-esteem
9. Anger management

Treatment Focus and Objectives

1. Lack of Goals
    A. Facilitate development of appropriate goals for personal growth and behavioral change
        1. What have they previously tried and what has been beneficial to build upon
    B. Facilitate development of realistic expectations and limitations
        1. Develop a progressive breakdown of steps in meeting an identified goal
        2. Establish a framework of practice, mastering, and reinforcement for each step of progress toward a goal

2. Inappropriate Expression of Emotions
   A. Facilitate increased awareness for inappropriate, exaggerated expression of emotions (emotional instability)
   B. Facilitate increased awareness for how inappropriate emotional expression impacts relationships
   C. Facilitate increased awareness for how inappropriate emotional expression impacts person getting their needs met
   D. Facilitate increased awareness for how inappropriate emotional expression impacts self-esteem
   E. Positive feedback and reinforcement for efforts and accomplishments
3. Inappropriate Behavior and Lack of Awareness
   A. Facilitate increased awareness regarding appropriate behavior
      1. Identified desired behaviors, initially specified to specific situation, and then practice for generalization
   B. Facilitate increased awareness for how inappropriate behavior impacts relationships
      1. Use a journal to identify their responses and the consequent responses of others.
      2. How are the impacts to others contrary to what is desired.
      3. Give self-permission to take responsibility for their behavior as quickly as possible in the chain of behaviors. With practice it will support their behavior modification.
   C. Facilitate increased awareness for how inappropriate behavior interferes with getting needs met
      1. Reinforce efforts and accomplishments
      2. Frame efforts and accomplishments as self-reinforcing
   D. Facilitate increased awareness for how inappropriate behavior impacts self-esteem
   E. Role-play and model appropriate behavioral responses
   F. Positive feedback and reinforcement for efforts and accomplishments
4. Self-destructive Behavior
   A. Facilitate increased awareness for pattern of being easily overwhelmed by anger and frustration which often results in impulsive, manipulative, and/or self-destructive behavior
      1. Anger management
      2. Encourage appropriate expression of feelings and thoughts
         a. Identify choices of management to avoid escalation
   B. Self-mutilation
      1. Identify the nature and extent of self-mutilating behavior
      2. Assess the seriousness of the behavior(s) and provide a safe environment when necessary
      3. Clarify and interpret the dynamics of the behavior (gain attention, get close to others who try to soothe them vs a form of venting, control their emotions, etc.)
      4. Work through the dynamics of self-mutilation
      5. Encourage venting of thoughts and feelings associated with the behavior
      6. Facilitate development of appropriate alternatives for dealing with unpleasant affective states that precipitate self-mutilation behavior
         a. Identify choices to circumvent escalation
   C. Facilitate development of appropriate communication
   D. Facilitate clarification of wants and needs and how to appropriately get them met
   E. Clarify wants and needs to be met by the individual versus those to be met in a relationship
      1. Process and identify realistic wants/needs versus setup for failure
      2. Clarify limitations of others to know what the person wants and needs
         a. Responsibility to effectively communicate wants and needs
   F. Develop appropriate alternatives of behavioral responses
      1. Identify specific situations
         a. Generate appropriate choices to substitute ineffective behavioral responses
   G. Facilitate recognition of how self-defeating and self-destructive behaviors keep person from getting their needs met
   H. Facilitate increased awareness and understanding of the underlying meaning of self-destructive behaviors
      1. What do these behaviors mean to them, what do they want to do differently, and what are the goals of their behaviors?

    I. Positive feedback and reinforcement for efforts and accomplishments

    J. Identify use of substances to self-medicate, impulse control, and/or other underlying motivations that complicate and negative impact efforts and progress

5. Manipulative Behavior
    A. Increase awareness of use of manipulative behavior
        1. Use of manipulation as a means to avoid feelings of rejection and/or abandonment
        2. Even with family members, individuals with BPD are highly sensitive to rejection, reacting with anger and distress to such mild separations as a vacation, a business trip, or a sudden change in plans
        3. Fears of abandonment seem to be related to difficulties feeling emotionally connected to important persons when they are physically absent, leaving the individual with BPD feeling lost and perhaps worthless
        4. Suicide threats and attempts may occur along with anger at perceived abandonment and disappointments
    B. Increase awareness for goal behind manipulative behavior and the positives and negatives associated with it
    C. Facilitate awareness of benefits associated with eliminating manipulative behavior
    D. Role-play and model appropriate and inappropriate behaviors for clarification and to broaden repertoire of appropriate behaviors
    E. Educate regarding boundaries
    F. Positive feedback and reinforcement for efforts and accomplishments

6. Lack of Appropriate Boundaries
    A. Facilitate increased awareness for person's lack of boundaries
    B. Facilitate increased awareness of relationship difficulties associated with lack of boundaries
        1. Provide education on boundaries, reading materials, homework, and practice
    C. Facilitate increased awareness for fear of abandonment and role this plays in poor boundaries, as well as other inappropriate behaviors and inappropriate expression of emotion (all issues of appropriate boundaries in interpersonal interaction)
    D. Facilitate increased awareness for self-defeating relationship difficulties such as:
        1. Unstable and intense relating
        2. Idealization and devaluation
        3. Manipulation

7. Ineffective Communication
    A. Teach assertive communication
    B. Facilitate awareness for inappropriate behaviors and verbal expressions as ineffective attempts to communicate
    C. Identify feelings behind inappropriate behavioral and emotional expressions and facilitate problem solving with person for appropriate changes to accomplish their goal
    D. Role-play and model assertive communication
    E. Positive feedback and reinforcement for efforts and accomplishments

8. Low Self-esteem
    A. Identify and focus on strengths and accomplishments
        1. Identify emotions/behaviors that continue to negatively impact the development of self-esteem
            a. Negative emotions to replace with positive/honest effect substitutes
                1. Emotions spiral out of control, leading to extremes of anxiety, sadness, rage, etc.
                2. Extreme reactions to perceived slights or criticism (e.g., may react with rage, humiliation, etc.)
                3. Expresses emotion in exaggerated and theatrical ways
                4. Emotions change rapidly and unpredictably
                5. Feels unhappy, depressed, or despondent
            b. Antagonism
                1. Intense anger, out of proportion to the situation at hand (e.g., has rage episodes)

      2. Often angry or hostile
     c. Disinhibition
      1. Need for stimulation/proneness to boredom
      2. Impulsivity
      3. Promiscuous sexual behavior
      4. Irresponsibility
  B. Facilitate self-monitoring of efforts toward desired goals
  C. Facilitate development of appropriate behavior and verbal communication
  D. Positive feedback and reinforcement for efforts and accomplishments
9. Inappropriate and ineffective anger
  A. Increased awareness for the issues underlying the reactive anger
  B. Previously, suicide threats and attempts may have occurred along with anger at perceived abandonment and disappointments—to be substituted with honest and effective responses of anger, disappointment, fear
    1. Identify appropriate responses for managing anger
     a. Distraction.
     b. Take a break from the situation or person causing anger and regroup.
     c. Identify ways to be calm (soothing music, walking the dog, meditation, watching a favorite movie, yoga, etc.).
     d. Communicate feelings. People with BPD may have a difficult time communicating how they feel, causing anger to build up and turn into rage. Instead of letting your anger get to that point, find a way to communicate your emotions.
      1. Talking to a trusted friend
      2. Journaling
      3. Discussing the situation with the person who is the source of the anger
     e. Change environment
     f. Seek appropriate support
    2. Identify safe people, possibly an accountability partner for processing anger versus acting out

This disorder tends to run in families and has a high rate of association to mood disorders. A majority of borderlines have a history of physical, sexual, or emotional abuse by their caregivers who at times were also adequate in their care and were even nurturing. The result is loving and hating the caregiver in a vacillating manner (all good or all bad).

While splitting may be a normal and healthy defense in 18- to 36-month-old toddlers, when the mind is able to handle greater complexity, developmental adjustment facilitates the good/bad dichotomy diversity and is recognized and managed in the ambiguous shades of gray in which good and bad exist. Borderlines do not accomplish this developmental adjustment. It is imperative to assess those with BPD for depression, bipolar disorder, PTSD, feeding and eating disorders, neurocognitive deficits (i.e., ADHD, auditory processing difficulties, etc.) and SUDs.

DEPENDENT PERSONALITY DISORDER

Although DPD is common it often occurs with other personality disorders, especially borderline, histrionic, and avoidant personality disorders. According to DSM 5 (APA, 2013) cardinal symptoms include difficulty making decisions, need for others to make decisions for them, difficulty expressing disagreement with others, feel helpless when alone, go to excessive lengths to obtain support or nurturance from others, and preoccupied with fear of being left alone. Because dependency may be viewed as a sign of weakness and immaturity, many adults—especially men—are reluctant to acknowledge dependent thoughts and feelings. Interviewing knowledgeable informants can be enlightening. When this person enters treatment there may be repeated attempts to have the clinician take responsibility for their decisions and direct them in managing their life. CBT is useful for fostering the person's independent decision making. Separation issues may present a problem for the person anticipating termination, which involves mourning past losses or disappointments. Dependency's severity varies over time and across situations. Depressive episodes are associated with temporary increases in self-reported dependency and avoidance. Even modest mood changes can amplify dependency. Failure to confront the avoidance may result in a failure to make lasting, dynamic changes, leaving the patient at risk for a sense of betrayal after termination, followed by deterioration. The most effective interventions emphasize replacing unhealthy, maladaptive dependency with flexible, adaptive dependency.

DEPENDENT PERSONALITY DISORDER

Goals

1. Increase independent behavior
2. Develop goals
3. Improve decision-making skills
4. Improve communication skills
5. Improve stress-management skills
6. Promote cognitive restructuring
7. Decrease sensitivity
8. Improve self-esteem

Treatment Focus and Objectives

1. Dependent behavior
   A. Be careful not to push the person before the person is ready for change
   B. Identify fears associated with independent behaviors
      1. Distinguish healthy from unhealthy dependency
   C. Identify how dependent behaviors limit the person in getting needs met and/or participating in chosen interests
   D. Identify how dependent behaviors communicate a mixed or incorrect message to others
   E. Facilitate identification of own competence and self-worth
   F. Clarify that seeking autonomy will not be harmful to others
   G. Identify unsatisfying, punitive relationships and challenge self-defeating patterns
      1. Challenge the person to leave or assert themselves
      2. Prepare them for dealing with the predictable anxiety-provoking aspect of change
      3. Prepare for the realistic threat of a punitive response
      4. Refer to a support group for validation, reinforcement, and problem-solving punitive responses from a partner or others
   H. Education and homework for developing assertive communication
2. Lack of Goals
   A. Facilitate development of appropriate goals for personal growth and behavioral change
      1. Support and reinforce the engagement in developing goals
      2. Facilitate the development of a stepwise progression of tasks to complete identified goals
3. Difficulty Making Decisions
   A. Teach decision-making skills
   B. Teach problem-solving skills
   C. Facilitate decrease in self-critical behavior/internal dialogue (self-talk)
4. Ineffective Communication
   A. Teach assertive communication
      1. Predict and prepare person for feared responses
      2. Problem-solve choices in managing challenging situations
   B. Role-play and model assertive communication
      1. Identify feared situations
      2. Facilitate person to identify the anxiety-provoking responses they fear
      3. Model and role-play the identified scenarios
   C. Positive feedback and reinforcement for efforts and accomplishments

5. Ineffective Stress Management
   A. Expose the person to anxiety-provoking situations
   B. Develop situations that program person for success in accomplishing simple tasks that normally elicit stress/anxiety
   C. Educate regarding the influence on negative self-talk on stress
   D. Facilitate development of positive self-talk
   E. Educate the person regarding the stages of relations, which include loss and how to cope with it
   F. Facilitate identification of persons' fear of being alone
      1. Problem-solve constructive time along for brief periods
      2. Positive feedback and reinforcement for efforts and accomplishments
      3. Identify irrational thinking behind fear of being alone
   G. Teach relaxation techniques
      1. Progressive muscle relaxation
      2. Visual imagery/meditation
      3. Meditation/mindfulness
      4. Yoga
      5. Relaxing music or nature sounds
      6. Time management may be an important component for managing anxiety

6. Distorted Thinking
   A. Challenge irrational beliefs and offer plausible substitute statement
      1. Explore key relationships from the patient's past that reinforced dependent behavior; determine if similar patterns occur in present relationships
      2. Examine their "helpless self-concept" dependency's key cognitive component (asking the patient to write a self-description can be useful)
      3. Make explicit any self-denigrating statements that propagate the patient's feelings of helplessness and vulnerability; challenge these statements when appropriate
      4. Facilitate increased insight into the ways they express dependency needs in different situations (and more flexible, adaptive ways he or she could express these needs)
      5. Role-play in session and provide homework to help the patient build coping skills that will enable him or her to function more autonomously
   B. Facilitate clarification when the information communicated appears distorted
   C. Reframe situations previously viewed as negative as an opportunity for change and growth when appropriate
   D. Facilitate person's clarification of rational versus irrational thinking
   E. Reinforce reality-based thinking

7. Overly Sensitive
   A. Facilitate increased awareness for difficulty that the person has accepting feedback from others and in viewing it as critical or disapproving
   B. Increase understanding for the effect of being overly sensitive in the context of a relationship and how it limits honest communication
      1. Identify reasonable and rational responses to coping with losses
      2. Identify losses as reasonable and expected aspects of life
   C. Facilitate identification of fear of abandonment and how this fear affects person and how they relate to others
   D. Reframe fears and integrate effective coping
   E. Identify, model, and role-play coping skills needed for more effective control of dependency-related impulses

8. Low Self-esteem
   A. Identify and focus on positives and accomplishments
   B. Identify goals and break them down into manageable steps so that the person can see progress and feel positive about it (self-esteem is activity based)
      1. Provide practice that is self-reinforcing

    C. Facilitate development of assertive communication

    D. Positive feedback and reinforcement for efforts and accomplishments

    E. Facilitate identification of the person's own competence and self-worth

    F. Challenge self-defeating thought patterns

        1. Helplessness-inducing automatic thoughts (reflexive thoughts that reflect the person's lack of self-confidence)

        2. Negative self-statements (self-deprecating internal monologues in which dependent persons reaffirm their perceived lack of competence and skill)

        3. Ask them to write a self-description

It is not unusual for individuals with DPD to call their therapist constantly clarifying appointments and asking advice or seeking guidance. Clear limits established at the onset of treatment regarding the regularity of appointments and therapist availability is necessary. Assess persons with DPD for depression, history of trauma, and SUDs.

DSM (APA, 2013) identifies that people with histrionic personality disorder (HPD) often seek treatment when they have depression or anxiety from failed romantic relationships or other conflicts with people. HPD may affect a person's social or romantic relationships. The person may be unable to cope with losses or failures. The person may change jobs often because of boredom and not being able to deal with frustration. They may crave new things and excitement, which leads to risky situations. All of these factors may lead to a higher chance of depression. All of this being said, people with this disorder are usually able to function at a high level and can be successful socially and at work.

HISTRIONIC PERSONALITY DISORDER

Goals

1. Goal development
2. Appropriate affect and expression of emotion
3. Appropriate social behavior
4. Appropriate emphasis on appearance
5. Improve communication skills
6. Improve self-esteem

Treatment Focus and Objectives

1. Lack of Goals
    A. Facilitate development of appropriate goals
    B. Constantly seeking reassurance and approval interferes with own goals
    C. Refer to appropriate group to facilitate clarification of goals as well as efforts toward progress

2. Inappropriate Affect
    A. Facilitate increased awareness for exaggerated emotional display
    B. Facilitate increased awareness for seductive behavior
        1. Identify seductive behavior (acting or looking seductive)
        2. Being overly dramatic and emotional
        3. Need for being the center of attention
    C. Explore need for attention and excitement
    D. Facilitate increased awareness for how emotional overreaction affects his/her relationships
    E. Encourage anger management
        1. Develop tolerance for frustration
    F. Promote clarification of feelings and appropriate, congruent expression
    G. Encourage person to take responsibility for the consequences of his/her actions
    H. Positive feedback and reinforcement for efforts and accomplishments

3. Dramatized Social Interaction
   A. Facilitate increased awareness for inappropriate social responding and the effect that it has on others in the person's relationships
      1. Being easily influenced by others versus true to the self
      2. Being overly sensitive to criticism or disapproval
      3. Needing to be center of attention
      4. Quickly changing emotions
   B. Role-play appropriate responses to various social situations
   C. Facilitate identification of particular areas of difficulty the person experiences in expressing himself/herself (e.g., how does the person respond when he/she feels ignored)
   D. Increase awareness for manipulative behavior
   E. Be supportive and empathic toward person's emotional/social difficulties
   F. Positive feedback and reinforcement for efforts and accomplishments
   G. Increase awareness and improve accuracy in self-image (inflated/distorted)
   H. Address provocative attention-seeking behavior
4. Overemphasis on Appearance
   A. Facilitate identification of distorted beliefs and overinvestment in appearance
   B. Increased awareness and understanding of lack of congruence between looking good on the outside and internal emptiness/lack of fulfillment
   C. Facilitate identification of fears associated with aging, which will affect appearance
   D. Facilitate identification on lack of development of internal resources because the person's energy is consistently used to "look good," whether by physical appearance or by collecting things
   E. Facilitate increased awareness for self-centered actions to gain immediate satisfaction
   F. Positive feedback and reinforcement for efforts and accomplishments
5. Ineffective Communication
   A. Teach assertive communication
   B. Encourage the person to keep a journal to increase awareness for honesty, self-centeredness, and tendency toward shallowness
   C. Role-play and model appropriate, assertive communication
   D. Facilitate increased understanding for shifting emotions, inappropriate exaggerations, and the need to be the center of attention, which are communicated to others. Explore the impact that this has on the person getting needs met and having fulfilling relationships.
   E. Positive feedback and reinforcement for efforts and accomplishments
6. Low Self-esteem
   A. Identify and focus on strengths and accomplishments
   B. Facilitate the development of goals
   C. Facilitate self-monitoring of efforts toward desired goals
   D. Facilitate the development of assertive communication
   E. Positive feedback and reinforcement for efforts and accomplishments

Since those with HPD think in terms of impression not fact, trying to get detailed information during the interview process becomes an arduous task. However, presentation in combination with acting in an overly dramatic or emotional way (usually as a bid to draw attention) provides the clinical intuition for further assessment.

NARCISSISTIC PERSONALITY DISORDER

Named for the figure from Greek mythology, narcissistic personality disorder (NPD) causes patients to have an inflated view of self or their importance, often at the expense of others. CBT also has the potential to benefit those with NPD that centers on repairing narcissistic schemas and the defective moods and coping styles associated with them. This highly active and work-intensive form of treatment encourages patients to confront narcissistic cognitive distortions (e.g., black-and-white thinking and perfectionism) and has yielded some promising results in the treatment of NPD.

NARCISSISTIC PERSONALITY DISORDER

Goals

1. Develop goals
2. Increase sensitivity toward others
3. Improve problem-solving skills
4. Increase self-awareness
5. Improve self-esteem

Treatment Focus and Objectives

1. Lack of Goals for Personal Growth and Development
   A. Facilitate development of appropriate goals
   B. Break down goals into reasonable steps
   C. Identify and problem-solve factors that previously inhibited reaching goals
   D. Develop realistic expectations and limitations (these individuals often feel inadequate and helpless when they fail to meet unrealistic goals)
   E. Positive feedback and reinforcement for efforts and accomplishments
2. Lack of Sensitivity Toward Others
   A. Encourage the person to put himself/herself in the place of others to increase understanding
      1. Facilitate improved ability to relate so that relationships are more intimate, enjoyable, and rewarding
      2. Facilitate the person to accept and maintain real personal relationships and collaboration with coworkers
   B. Encourage the person to appropriately express how he/she feels when people are insensitive to the person's needs
   C. Positive feedback and reinforcement for efforts and accomplishments
3. Ineffective Problem Solving
   A. Teach problem-solving skills
   B. Develop sample problems to practice new skills on
   C. Facilitate increased awareness of how feelings of entitlement interfere with appropriate, effective problem solving
   D. Identify secondary gains that inhibit progress toward change
   E. Improve coping by increasing awareness for the power struggle between the person's intense need to be admired by an individual he/she views as important and, at the same time, feeling rage at being disappointed by that person
4. Lacks Self-awareness
   A. Encourage journal writing to identify thoughts, feelings, and behaviors
   B. Encourage honest self-evaluations
   C. Facilitate increased awareness for how these individuals' constant seeking of love, admiration, and attention from others impedes them taking responsibility for themselves and learning to fill their sense of emptiness on their own
   D. Facilitate insight into feelings of inadequacy and vulnerability
   E. Facilitate ability to recognize and accept actual competencies and potential in an effort to improve tolerance to criticism and failures
   F. Facilitate increased ability to understand and regulate their feelings
5. Low Self-esteem
   A. Identify and focus on strengths and accomplishments
   B. Facilitate self-monitoring of efforts toward desired goals
   C. Facilitate development of assertive communication

D. Facilitate development and support maintenance of realistic concept of the individual's own self-worth

    1. Understand and tolerate the impact of issues related to their self-esteem

E. Facilitate the release of desire for unattainable goals and ideal conditions and gain an acceptance of what's attainable and what they can accomplish

F. Positive feedback and reinforcement for efforts and accomplishments

If this individual presents for treatment, it is not likely associated with insight about the need for taking responsibility and making necessary changes. Instead, it is likely due to depression, pressure from a partner, adjustment/loss, or is associated with a medical condition. When a therapist exposes these individuals' issues of grandiosity/self-importance, it should be done in a gentle way with guidance into a proper perspective. Otherwise it will illicit strong resentment. Their self-centeredness is a shield of protection that when fractured exposes insecurity.

The suffering from other mental-health problems has been found to be associated with a lower likelihood of symptoms of NPD being alleviated with treatment. One of the major complications to treatment and therefore to a good prognosis for those with NPD is the perception by these individuals that their problems are caused by others rather than by their own self-centered tendencies.

OBSESSIVE–COMPULSIVE PERSONALITY DISORDER

Individuals with obsessive–compulsive personality disorder tend to be constricted in many aspects of their lives. Relationships may be uncomfortable, stiff, formal, and distant, and affects are shallow. Although often devoted to their work, these individuals have doubts about their performance and are perfectionist and indecisive, which limits the amount of satisfaction they may derive from their efforts. They experience significant anxiety when confronted with situations marked by uncertainty or unpredictability. These traits are often chronic and egosyntonic and only present for treatment when confronted with a disruptive crisis (APA, 2013).

Treatment focusing on validation of the patient's current feelings will help to relieve guilt, self-doubt, and fear and that growth and change are possible within the limits of short-term therapy. Brief CBT may result moderate changes in personality, a decrease in negative and ambivalent self-references, and an increase in positive self-references. Procrastination and narcissism may also be decreased with a course of treatment.

OBSESSIVE–COMPULSIVE PERSONALITY DISORDER

Goals (Issues Control Orderliness and Perfectionism)

1. Assess for referrals
2. Develop goals
3. Decrease perfectionism
4. Decrease ritual behaviors
5. Decrease obsessive, ruminative thoughts
6. Increase functional, constructive behavior
7. Improve communication skills
8. Improve self-esteem

Treatment Focus and Objectives

1. Assess Regarding Appropriate Referrals
   A. Refer for medication evaluation
   B. OCD group or other appropriate community resources (for developing increased awareness for maladaptive coping mechanisms and for reinforcing of positive efforts and change)

2. Lack of Goals
   A. Facilitate development of appropriate goals for personal growth and behavioral change.
   B. Facilitate understanding and acceptance that therapy can be a long, slow process when dealing with such issues. Avoid power struggles. These individuals can be highly resistant to change and have difficulty dealing with issues of power and authority.
3. Perfectionism
   A. Facilitate identification of feelings and tendency to minimize feelings
   B. Facilitate venting of feelings
   C. Explore issues of control and frustration associated with perfectionism
4. Compulsive Rituals
   A. Identify the nature and extent of compulsions
   B. Identify the internal and external triggers for compulsions
   C. Facilitate the individual in learning to interrupt the compulsions and to substitute with appropriate behavior
   D. Identify the dynamic of the compulsions
   E. Work through the dynamics of the compulsions
   F. Systematic desensitization of increase tolerance for associated anxiety
   G. Explore unacceptable thoughts and intense feelings that are not expressed
   H. Explore fear associated with expression of feelings and thoughts
   I. Facilitate use of behavioral journal
      1. To develop baseline
      2. To develop a reasonable program for decreasing the frequency of ritual behaviors
      3. Reinforce focus on positives and accomplishments
5. Obsessive Ruminations
   A. Identify the nature and extent of obsessions
   B. Identify the internal and external triggers for obsessions
   C. Facilitate the individual in learning to interrupt the obsessions and substitute with rational thinking
   D. Identify the dynamics of the obsessions
   E. Work through dynamics of the obsessions
   F. Encourage decision making
   G. Confront irrational thinking with reality
   H. Facilitate rational, positive self-talk
   I. Facilitate the use of thought stopping using distraction (redirecting focus)
   J. Encourage making of choice of distract self from ruminative thoughts by utilizing physical activity or other activities.
   K. Explore relationship of the obsessive thoughts and compulsive behaviors
   L. Maintain focus of treatment on the person's feelings (because these individuals tend to intellectually defend against threatening feelings)
6. Ineffective Coping
   A. Facilitate increased awareness for how obsessions and compulsions interfere in normal daily functioning
      1. Facilitate identification of losses, activities the person does not have time to participate in, or fears that prevent participation in otherwise desirable activities
      2. Develop daily structure of activities
      3. Person to make support system aware of his/her goals and how the support system can help in efforts toward change
      4. Capitalize on positive effect experienced when the person breaks the OCD and pattern such as improved self-esteem, enjoyment of life, and feelings of control over his/her life
   B. Validation of their feelings of guilt, self-doubt, and fear coupled with associated stepwise progression of change for challenging the presented problems
   C. Refer to group therapy where confrontation of defenses may be more effective (adjunctively and reinforcing of individual therapy goals)
      1. Modification of cognitive style
      2. Assist with decision making

3. Increase comfort with affective experience
4. Modification with harsh self-statements
5. Resolution of control issues
6. Modification of interpersonal style
7. Ineffective Communication
    A. Teach assertive communication
    B. Teach anger management
    C. Role-play and rehearse, problem-solving appropriate responses to a variety of situations
    D. Learn to say no, avoid manipulation, set limits and boundaries
    E. Positive feedback and reinforcement for efforts and accomplishments
8. Low Self-esteem
    A. Identify realistic goals, expectations, and limitations
    B. Identify factors that negatively affect self-esteem
    C. Overcome negative feelings toward the self
        1. Examine personal relationships
            a. Social relationships can also be examined, reinforcing strong, positive relationships while having the person reexamine negative or harmful relationships
        2. Properly identify feeling states than just intellectually or distancing from their emotions
            a. Writing feelings down in a journal
            b. Identify feelings
    D. Assertive communication
    E. Positive self-talk and affirmations
    F. Identify feelings that have been ignored or denied
    G. Focus on efforts and accomplishments
    H. Positive feedback and reinforcement for efforts and accomplishments

Compulsives are a difficult population to treat. Their obsessiveness can paralyze attempts of clinical progress. They often want complete explanations of what will happen during the evaluation and course of treatment. Additionally, they often lack insight to initiate change because their thinking is highly concrete. Progress is measured in terms of behavioral change.

COMPULSIVE PERSONALITY DISORDER

Goals

1. Assess for referrals
2. Develop goals
3. Decrease perfectionism
4. Decrease ritual behaviors
5. Decrease obsessive, ruminative thoughts
6. Increase functional, constructive behavior
7. Improve communication skills
8. Improve self-esteem

Treatment Focus and Objectives

1. Assess Regarding Appropriate Referrals
    A. For medication evaluation
    B. OCD group or other appropriate community resources (for developing increased awareness for maladaptive coping mechanisms and for reinforcing of positive efforts and change)

2. Lack of Goals
    A. Facilitate development of appropriate goals for personal growth and behavioral change.
    B. Facilitate understanding and acceptance that therapy can be a long, slow process when dealing with such issues. Avoid power struggles. These individuals can be highly resistant to change and have difficulty dealing with issues of power and authority.
3. Perfectionism
    A. Facilitate identification of feelings and tendency to minimize feelings
    B. Facilitate venting of feelings
    C. Explore issues of control and frustration associated with perfectionism
4. Compulsive Rituals
    A. Identify the nature and extent of compulsions
    B. Identify the internal and external triggers for compulsions
    C. Facilitate the individual in learning to interrupt the compulsions and to substitute with appropriate behavior
    D. Identify the dynamic of the compulsions
    E. Work through the dynamics of the compulsions
    F. Systematic desensitization of increase tolerance for associated anxiety
    G. Explore unacceptable thoughts and intense feelings that are not expressed
    H. Explore fear associated with expression of feelings and thoughts
    I. Facilitate use of behavioral journal
        1. To develop baseline
        2. To develop a reasonable program for decreasing the frequency of ritual behaviors
        3. Reinforce focus on positives and accomplishments
5. Obsessive Ruminations
    A. Identify the nature and extent of obsessions
    B. Identify the internal and external triggers for obsessions
    C. Facilitate the individual in learning to interrupt the obsessions and substitute with rational thinking
    D. Identify the dynamics of the obsessions
    E. Work through dynamics of the obsessions
    F. Encourage decision making
    G. Confront irrational thinking with reality
    H. Facilitate rational, positive self-talk
    I. Facilitate the use of thought stopping
    J. Encourage making of choice of distract self from ruminative thoughts by utilizing physical activity or other activities
    K. Explore relationship of the obsessive thoughts and compulsive behaviors
    L. Maintain focus of treatment on the person's feelings (because these individuals tend to intellectually defend against threatening feelings)
6. Ineffective Use of Time
    A. Facilitate increased awareness for how obsessions and compulsions interfere in normal daily functioning
        1. Facilitate identification of losses, activities the person does not have time to participate in, or fears that prevent participation in otherwise desirable activities
        2. Develop daily structure of activities
        3. Person to make support system aware of his/her goals and how the support system can help in efforts toward change
        4. Capitalize on positive affect experienced when the person breaks the OCD and pattern such as improved self-esteem, enjoyment of life, and feelings of control over his/her life
7. Ineffective Communication
    A. Teach assertive communication
    B. Teach anger management

    C. Role-play and rehearse, problem-solving appropriate responses to a variety of situations

    D. Learn to say no, avoid manipulation, set limits and boundaries

    E. Positive feedback and reinforcement for efforts and accomplishments

  8. Low Self-esteem

    A. Identify realistic goals, expectations, and limitations

    B. Identify factors that negatively affect self-esteem

    C. Overcome negative feelings toward the self

    D. Assertive communication

    E. Positive self-talk and affirmations

    F. Identify feelings that have been ignored or denied

    G. Focus on efforts and accomplishments

    H. Positive feedback and reinforcement for efforts and accomplishments

Compulsives are a difficult population to treat. Their obsessiveness can paralyze attempts of clinical progress. They often want complete explanations of what will happen during the evaluation and course of treatment. Additionally, they often lack insight to initiate change because their thinking is highly concrete. Progress is measured in terms of behavioral change.

PARANOID PERSONALITY DISORDER

Individuals with paranoid personality disorder (PPD), however, rarely present themselves for treatment. Early termination is quite common because of the difficulty associated with developing the rapport necessary for a positive therapeutic alliance. According to the DSM 5 (APA, 2013), those with PPD are always vigilant, believing that others are constantly trying to demean, harm, or threaten them. These generally unfounded beliefs, as well as their habits of blame and distrust, might interfere with their ability to form close relationships. It is important is be genuinely supportive, client-centered, and offering common sense problem solving. Social isolation along with problems at work or school is possible treatment complications.

PARANOID PERSONALITY DISORDER

Goals

1. Decrease treatment resistance
2. Develop goals
3. Decrease paranoid thinking
4. Improve social skills
5. Manage anger
6. Decrease fear with supportive therapeutic relationship
7. Improve self-esteem

Treatment Focus and Objectives

1. Treatment Resistance
    A. Develop a trusting therapeutic relationship
    B. Explain purpose for a cooperative effort
2. Lack of Goals
    A. Facilitate development of appropriate goals for personal growth and behavioral change
3. Distorted Paranoid Thinking
    A. Identify the nature and extent of paranoia
    B. Facilitate the individual's development of awareness for the presence of paranoia

C. Explore thoughts and feelings
   1. Identify that person expects to be used or exploited
   2. Identify personal impact/losses for being unable to trust
   3. Identify that the person is always looking for hidden meaning/conspiracy
D. Be careful to avoid any ambiguity in communication with this person
E. Medication compliance
   1. Suspiciousness. Encourage the person to ask questions and read literature on medication.
   2. Prepare the person for the various side effects that he/she may experience.
F. Facilitate increased awareness for inability to relax, and work with person to develop plausible alternatives for relaxing (and clarify benefit)

4. Ineffective Social Skills
   A. Determine range of paranoid thinking (i.e., within normal limits—paranoid)
   B. Educate and role-play regarding appropriate limits and boundaries within various relationships
   C. Educate regarding appropriate level of disclosure in various relationships
   D. Problem-solve with person about how to deal with paranoid thinking in a social context
   E. Facilitate increased awareness for restricted affect
   F. Positive feedback and reinforcement for efforts and accomplishments

5. Underlying Anger
   A. Encourage venting of underlying anger/jealousy
   B. Validate feelings of anger/jealousy
   C. Increase person's awareness for role he/she plays in situations and support his/her in taking responsibility for that behavior
   D. Facilitate person recognizing that withholding of anger is not in his/her best interest
      1. Teach anger management
      2. Role-play the appropriate expression of feelings
      3. Teach other constructive methods for dealing with anger and frustration (exercising, finding a trustworthy person to vent to, journal writing with a problem-solving component)
   E. Positive feedback and reinforcement for efforts and accomplishments

6. Fear and Lack of Support
   A. Supportive psychotherapy
   B. Be clear, respectful, honest, open
   C. Challenge denial and projection in a supportive manner
   D. Empathize (genuine and caring) with the person's difficult life experience, while encouraging him/her to take responsibility
   E. Facilitate increased awareness for relationship ambivalence
   F. Facilitate increased awareness for the projection of the person's own unacceptable thoughts
   G. Facilitate increased awareness of how the person's distorted perspective interferes in his/her life
   H. Facilitate increased awareness for over involvement in fantasy and private belief system
   I. Through problem solving with person, develop minimally threatening situations for practice and programmed success
   J. Positive feedback and reinforcement for efforts and accomplishments

7. Low Self-esteem
   A. Be accepting and respectful to the person
   B. Identify and focus on strengths and accomplishments
   C. Facilitate self-monitoring efforts toward desired goals
   D. Positive feedback and reinforcement for efforts and accomplishments

These individuals rarely present for treatment on their own simply because they do not perceive weakness or faults in themselves. They tend to be guarded in sharing personal information. The central goal of treatment is to minimize the distrust of the therapist and the therapy process. With regard to almost all issues, the paranoid expects the worst but feels assured in being given all the details beforehand. Therefore, it is imperative to give adequately detailed and accurate information.

SCHIZOTYPAL PERSONALITY DISORDER

Those diagnosed with schizotypal personality disorder work best alone, experience detachment (social withdrawal, intimacy avoidance, inability to feel pleasure, restricted emotional expression), suspiciousness, and tend to be irrational, eccentric, odd beliefs, and perceptual distortions (DSM 5). As can be determined by the core issues of this disorder, a central feature is the experience of discomfort with close relationships. They have little reaction to emotionally arousing situations and restricted emotional expression. Thus they may appear indifferent or cold. They may have social withdrawal with avoidance of social contacts and activity. Individuals with this disorder may have undue suspiciousness and feelings of persecution (Mayo Clinic, 2015). They may have excessive social anxiety with these paranoid fears. While they do not have psychotic symptoms such as delusions or hallucination, they do experience ideas of reference and odd beliefs that appear similar to delusions. Additionally, they may demonstrate unusual perceptual experiences, such as bodily illusions, that are almost hallucinations. They may demonstrate odd speech (i.e., vague, circumstantial, overelaborate, or stereotyped) that is almost grossly disorganized. These are pervasive and enduring patterns manifesting in a broad range of personal and social situations. These individuals rarely present for treatment.

*The ICD 10 does not classify schizotypal personality disorder as a personality disorder, but does identify it as the developmental trajectory of schizophrenia (because it generally converts to schizophrenia), and as such, treats it as a mind, arrested or premorbid form of schizophrenia. The best therapy for this diagnosis is antipsychotic medication and the development of a trusting relationship with the prescribing physician and a skilled therapist.

Fundamental reasons that this diagnosis benefits little from psychotherapy:

1. In schizophrenia and related disorders, there is malfunctioning of the brain's "detachment" function. This causes social withdrawal, intimacy avoidance, inability to feel pleasure, and restricted emotional expression.
2. Guilt is an inherent emotion. Individuals who lack guilt and show a callous disregard for the feelings and rights of others demonstrate malfunctioning of this anger–guilt function. Other diagnoses who lack guilt include ODD, conduct disorder, and antisocial personality disorder.
3. There is a dearth of wisdom, which is sign of inability to be adaptive. There are four adaptive factors that interfere with development of wisdom; irrationality, forgetfulness, distractibility, and apathy (lack of interest).
4. Malfunctioning of self-control which causes impulsivity (related to eating disorders and substance-related disorders).
5. Fear and courage are fundamental to survival instincts which are negatively impacted as evidenced by response patterns

SCHIZOTYPAL PERSONALITY DISORDER

Goals

1. Decrease treatment resistance
2. Develop goals
3. Improve social skills
4. Decrease isolation
5. Improve communication skills
6. Improve self-esteem

1. Treatment Resistance
   A. Explain purpose of therapy intervention
      1. Encourage them to identify what is distressing to them that they feel would be beneficial to work on
   B. Explain that the person is at risk for premature termination from therapy because of difficulty trusting the therapist and others, and encourage them to express their thought about therapeutic content
   C. Assess disordered thinking
2. Lack of Goals
   A. Identify what the person wants and needs
      1. Problem-solve appropriate ways to meet needs
   B. Develop and utilize resources that support efforts toward identified goals
   C. Positive feedback and reinforcement for efforts and accomplishments
3. Ineffective Social Skills
   A. Facilitate increased awareness for overinvolvement in fantasy and private belief system
   B. Increase awareness for odd and eccentric behavior
   C. Increase awareness for how others experience the person
   D. Role-play various social situations to demonstrate appropriate and effective responses
   E. Positive feedback and reinforcement for efforts and accomplishments
4. Social Isolation
   A. Problem-solve ways to decrease isolation with a minimal amount of distress
   B. Participation in regular activities to facilitate development of comfort level with familiarity
5. Ineffective Communication
   A. Teach assertive communication
   B. Role-play and model assertive communication
   C. Refer to appropriate group or other social interaction to provide opportunity for practice
   D. Positive feedback and reinforcement for efforts and accomplishments
6. Low Self-esteem
   A. Identify and focus on strengths and accomplishments
   B. Facilitate development of assertive communication
   C. Identify goals and break them down into manageable steps for programmed success
   D. Positive feedback and reinforcement for efforts and accomplishments. Schizophrenia should always be considered in those under the age of 35. If there is a clear diagnosis, continue to monitor for decompensation
      1. They may become transiently psychotic under stress
      2. The condition may evolve into schizophrenia
      3. They may develop fanatic beliefs

Medication (antipsychotics) may be beneficial in alleviating some of the intense anxiety and cognitive symptoms (such as odd speech and unusual perceptual experiences). Therefore, consider the referral for a medication evaluation:

SCHIZOID PERSONALITY DISORDER

While schizoid personality disorder is not nearly as incapacitating as schizophrenia it does share many of the same risk factors, but does not cause the same disconnection from reality (hallucinations or delusions). Schizoid personality disorder usually does not improve over time, identifying it as a long-term chronic illness. Additionally, social isolation generally prevents the person from seeking support or treatment (APA, 2013)

SCHIZOID PERSONALITY DISORDER

Goals

1. Decrease treatment resistance
2. Develop goals
3. Improve social interaction
4. Decrease social isolation
5. Improve communication skills
6. Improve self-esteem

Treatment Focus and Objectives

1. Treatment Resistance
   A. Explain purpose of therapy
   B. Encourage the person to discuss mixed feelings about participating in therapy
2. Lack of Goals
   A. Facilitate development of appropriate goals
   B. Assess disordered thinking
3. Ineffective Social Interaction
   A. Increase awareness for how others experience the person (cold, detached)
   B. Role-play appropriate and effective responses for various social situations
   C. Facilitate increased awareness for emotional experience in relating to others
   D. Facilitate identification for consequences of cold, aloof responding to others
   E. Positive feedback and reinforcement for efforts and accomplishments
4. Social Isolation
   A. Facilitate identification of the person's experience.
   B. Facilitate development of goals. They must be realistic and broken down into manageable steps.
   C. Communicate respect for the person's need for privacy.
5. Ineffective Communication
   A. Teach assertive communication
   B. Role-play and model assertive communication
   C. Positive feedback and reinforcement for efforts and accomplishments
6. Low Self-esteem
   A. Identify and focus on strengths and accomplishments
   B. Facilitate development of assertive communication
   C. Positive feedback and reinforcement for efforts and accomplishments

Because social isolation is such a prominent feature with this disorder, these individuals are not likely to seek treatment.

PHYSICAL FACTORS AFFECTING PSYCHOLOGICAL FUNCTIONING

The following is an example of how a person's emotional and psychological functioning is affected by a health issue. This section is meant to highlight for clinicians the importance considering the functioning of the entire person when engaging in the diagnostic process. As will be seen and understood, it is imperative to communicate with a person's primary care provider for integrated care and the most beneficial outcome for those in treatment.

1. Vignette

   An individual is referred for therapy by the person's primary care physician. While the person has been experiencing various symptoms for some time, the individual has recently been diagnosed with MS. For some, a diagnosis of MS being presented months or even years after the onset of symptoms is a relief from the standpoint that the person now knows what is wrong. For others, this diagnosis is a terrible shock.

2. Symptoms of MS possibly experienced prior to diagnosis
   A. Weakness
   B. Fatigue
   C. Low self-worth (associated with the decreased productivity from fatigue)
   D. Depression
   E. Impaired memory
   F. Difficulty concentrating

3. Common reactions to being given the diagnosis of a chronic illness
   A. Disbelief
   B. Fear
   C. Anger
   D. Depression
   E. Guilt
   F. Fear of losing control over one's life
   G. Grieving (grieving losses in functioning as part of adjustment)
   H. Denial

4. Central emotional crisis issues associated with a medical crisis
   A. Control
   B. Self-image
   C. Dependency
   D. Stigma
   E. Abandonment/rejection
   F. Anger
   G. Isolation/withdrawal
   H. Death

*Refer to information on crisis counseling.

Additionally, some fears associated with a long-term illness where there is decompensation over time include fear of pain, imposed changes in lifestyle, alteration of social patterns, and fear of the future. The impact of such a significant crisis is stressful to clarify, speak about, and, initially, to problem-solve how to deal with imposed changes in the level of physical and cognitive functioning as the illness progresses.

STAGES OF ADJUSTMENT

Adjusting to MS is an ongoing process that evolves over a period of time (which varies among individuals). Some people proceed through cycles of progression and remission, others decompensate with little remission, and yet others may remain in remitted states for a very long period of time. Initially, if there is little evidence of disability, the individual may not experience denial because he or she is not currently confronted with changes in functioning. Evidence of psychological stress and efforts to cope may be evidenced as follows:

1. Denial is a normal defense reaction in not wanting to accept and acknowledge such stressful information. Denial is easily validated with a remission of symptoms ("I don't really have MS").

2. Resistance to letting "this illness" control one's life is an action-based response against the illness. While this may be a positive demonstration of will, it may also be an unrealistic expectation of personal control, which could lead to significant depression if the individual is confronted with the reality that he/she cannot conquer the illness (i.e., symptom presentation and decompensation).

3. Affirmation is the acknowledgment that the diagnosis is real.
   This allows the individual to open up, process, and develop resources. It also facilitates a reevaluation of life priorities.

4. Acceptance is the realistic recognition of what the diagnosis means and coming to terms with it.

5. Personal growth is the silver lining in the cloud—responding to a difficult crisis with the attitude that with every experience in life there is the opportunity to grow and continue to evolve in new ways. There may be more appreciation for life in general and genuine gratitude for the things that are "right" in one's life.

There is an unfortunate history of nonintegrated treatment between practitioners of physical health and mental health. As a result, there is often negligence in acknowledging and educating patients regarding the emotional and psychological impact associated with various medical disorders and disease states. The following table presents a brief review used to highlight this significant relationship. Such information, when shared with a patient, acts to validate one's experience and leads to appropriate problem solving and interventions.

Medical causes of psychiatric illness

Medical problem	Depression mood disorders	Anxiety disorders	Personality change	Psychosis	Dementia
Adrenal insufficiency	✓	✓		✓	
AIDS	✓	✓		✓	✓
Altitude sickness		✓			✓
Amyotrophic lateral sclerosis	✓				✓ rare
Antidiuretic hormone inappropriate secretion					✓
Brain abscess		Range of cognitive symptoms			
Brain tumor	✓		✓		✓
Cancer	✓	✓			
Cardiac arrhythmias		✓			
Cerebrovascular accident	✓		✓	✓	
COPD (chronic obstructive pulmonary disease)	✓	✓			
Congestive heart failure	✓	✓			
Cryptococcosis				✓	✓
Cushing's syndrome	✓	✓		✓	
Deafness		Paranoid ideation			
Diabetes mellitus	✓	✓			

Medical causes of psychiatric illness (Continued)

Medical problem	Depression mood disorders	Anxiety disorders	Personality change	Psychosis	Dementia
Epilepsy	✓			✓	
Fibromyalgia	✓	✓			
Head trauma	Mood swings		✓	✓	✓
Herpes encephalitis		✓		✓	
Homocystinuria					✓
Huntington disease	✓		✓	✓	✓
Hyperparathyroidism	✓	✓	✓	✓	
Hypoparathyroidism	✓	✓	Paranoid ideation		✓
Hypothyroidism	✓	✓		✓	
Kidney failure	✓				
Klinefelter's syndrome	✓			✓	
Liver failure	✓				
Lyme disease	✓	✓		✓	
Meniere disease	✓	✓		✓	
Menopause	✓	✓			
Migraine	✓	✓			
Mitral valve prolapse		✓			
Multiple sclerosis	✓	Cognitive impairment			✓
Myasthenia gravis		✓			
Neurocutaneous disorders	✓	✓			✓
Parkinson disease	✓	✓			✓
Pheochromocytoma		✓			
Pneumonia		✓			
Pernicious anemia					
Porphyria	✓	✓		✓	
Postoperative states	✓	✓		✓	
Premenstrual syndrome	✓	✓			
Prion disease		✓			✓
Progressive supranuclear palsy	Labile mood				✓
Protein energy malnutrition		Cognitive change		✓ occasional	
Pulmonary thromboembolism		✓			
Rheumatoid arthritis	✓			✓ rate	
Sickle-cell disease	✓	Substance dependence			

Continued

Medical causes of psychiatric illness *(Continued)*

Medical problem	Depression mood disorders	Anxiety disorders	Personality change	Psychosis	Dementia
Sleep apnea	✓				
Syphilis	✓				
Systematic infection					
Wilson disease		Cognitive disorder			

Chapter 2

Assessing Special Circumstances

Some topics in this chapter provide an intervention/treatment addendum that either embellishes information offered in the treatment chapter or, because the assessment is not associated with a specific diagnostic category, reinforces varying aspects of relevance and importance to the assessment process. Additionally, the initial section of this chapter serves as a general foundation to the special assessment process. This is essential given the degree of influence an assessment may have upon choice(s), intervention(s), and disposition in the lives of others.

ASSESSING SPECIAL CIRCUMSTANCES

There are numerous screenings, assessments, and evaluations that clinicians can use for private practice and forensic settings. The following examples are provided as a sample of the more common clinical issues that a therapist may determine that an assessment will provide desired validation or clarity. Additionally, this section differentiates "crisis assessment" and "cognitive-behavioral therapy (CBT) assessment for mental illness." A crisis is a disruption in someone's normal functioning rendering their coping mechanisms ineffective versus mental illness, which presents multiple facets of chronic dysfunction. However, those who experience chronic mental illness (CMI) also experience crises or psychiatric emergencies. Because of the multifaceted complexity of mental illness, a conceptual foundation of what a mentally ill individual experiences must be considered to reinforce that basic intervention needs to be broad based clinically and inclusive of all resources. For both a crisis or mental illness assessment, integrated behavioral health is essential to recovery and relapse prevention.

Since the most consistent evidence-based practices are cognitive-behavioral interventions, a cognitive-behavioral assessment (CBA) structure is offered. The most common clinical presentations of distress are depression and anxiety; therefore these diagnostic categories were selected as the starting point for CBA although they do not represent "special circumstances." Tantamount to CBT is the avoidance of pathologizing diagnostic labels, instead focusing on the quality of thought, feelings, and behaviors that serve as the measure to problem-solve effective treatment planning.

The focus on thoughts, feelings, and behaviors requires careful assessment, treatment considerations regarding level of care and providing a safe environment, legal and ethical issues, and often a family system intervention. Furthermore, this section addresses other important clinical presentations in which the therapist may be engaged clinically to assess, provide evaluative reports, and/or to make appropriate interventions, referrals, and recommendations.

Guidelines for assessment/evaluation provide the framework from which the therapist can establish a valuable diagnostic foundation needed to proceed with standards of care and evidence-based interventions. For example, while there is no fail-safe method of establishing the issue of risk of violence, using standard assessment criteria in combination with clinical judgment and issues of immediate management offers numerous points of intervening, thereby decreasing risk while increasing safety. Having a crisis intervention protocol provides necessary risk management and facilitates treatment planning with associated effective evidence-based intervention. Roberts (2005) states that every year, millions of people are confronted with crisis-inducing events and experiences that they cannot resolve on their own. These individuals are dependent on the clinical expertise of those who assess and treat them—behavioral health professionals who possess a high level of clinical skill paired with an empathic understanding for those who experience mental illness and are in crisis.

When providing any of the aforementioned services, there are guidelines of education, training, supervision, and experience that are necessary.

UNDERSTANDING THE INDIVIDUAL IN CRISIS

Understanding crisis *requires* a biopsychosocial perspective. For example, consider the factor of lifespan developmental influence and the geriatric patient. Assessing cognitive deficits and problems with memory of a geriatric patient is complicated. It requires diagnostic sophistication to determine if the clinical presentation is due to emotional distress with associated acute psychosis and cognitive impairment or underlying medical issues (Borja, Borja, & Gade, 2007). Additionally, it is essential to consider medical conditions that mimic psychiatric illness. Overall, the primary challenge of a clinician is differentiating an emergent versus nonemergent psychiatric situation. Emergent situations are danger to self, danger to others, grave disability, and the need for medical clearance when necessary (for example, overdose of medication). Assessing the patient in an individualized and client-centered manner is necessary to assess symptoms, determine the level of dangerousness to self and others, and to provide the information needed to direct patient disposition.

The definition of crisis offered by Roberts (2005) establishes an understanding of the experience of someone presenting in crisis:

> *An acute disruption of psychological homeostasis in which one's usual coping mechanisms fail and there exists evidence of distress and functional impairment. The subjective reaction to a stressful life experience that compromises the individual's stability and ability to cope or function. The main cause of a crisis is an intensely stressful, traumatic, or hazardous event, but two other conditions are also necessary: (1) the individual's perception of the event as the cause of considerable upset and/or disruption; and (2) the individual's inability to resolve the disruption by previously used coping mechanisms. Crisis also refers to "an upset in the steady state." It often has five components: a hazardous or traumatic event, a vulnerable or unbalanced state, a precipitating factor, an active crisis state based on the person's perception, and the resolution of the crisis.* Roberts (2005, p. 778).

UNDERSTANDING THE INDIVIDUALIZED JOURNEY OF MENTAL ILLNESS

While evidence-based treatments have been identified, primarily CBT, it does not negate the value of psychodynamic understanding of the development of dysfunctional thinking and associated behavior. Psychodynamic case conceptualization provides an understanding of context, motivation, and ineffective coping that often has roots in early-life experiences making them "relative" to the individual and potentially serving as predisposing factors. The therapist as a client-centered instrument provides genuine interest and positive regard that creates a safe and trusted environment where effective patient–therapist collaboration can take place. The therapeutic frame offers one of the greatest gifts that one person can bestow upon another—to "listen."

THE INDIVIDUALIZED JOURNEY OF MENTAL ILLNESS

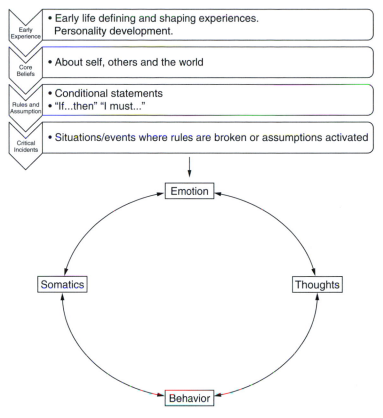

Early Experience	• Early life defining and shaping experiences. Personality development.
Core Beliefs	• About self, others and the world
Rules and Assumption	• Conditional statements • "If...then" "I must..."
Critical Incidents	• Situations/events where rules are broken or assumptions activated

*These elements interact in a vicious cycle and are highly reliant upon personality structure, coping mechanisms, internal resources and external resources.
Cognitive Formulation adapted from Beck (1976)

GENERAL CONCEPT OF INTERVENTION

Commensurate with the value of a thorough psychological assessment or evaluation for danger to self, others, and/or gravely disabled is the initial goal defined as the individualized treatment plan that provides the initial needs of safety and stabilization. The treatment team (clinician, psychiatrist, primary care physician, identified safe people, family/friend, clergy, and anyone else or any other socially supportive community resource) in association with a structured inpatient or outpatient program work together to provide supportive, respectful relationships and environments that encourage and reinforce positive behaviors that promote recovery, develop needed skills and resources, reinforce resilience, and prevent relapse. Successful outcome is accomplished by developing (and reinforcing) the following factors:

1. Goal setting
2. Relapse prevention
3. Trust
4. Accountability
5. Problem solving
6. Positive thinking
7. Positive peer relationships
8. Respect for authority
9. Expression of feelings

10. Impulse control and delayed gratification
11. Expression of feelings (regarding self and others)
12. Conflict resolution

The following are the variety of therapies that could be utilized to accomplish the treatment plan:

1. Process groups
2. Support and didactic groups
3. Individual and family meetings
4. Recreational therapy
5. Chemical dependency interventions (such as intensive outpatient, "IOP")
6. Anger and aggression management
7. Education and social skills
8. Medication management and education
9. Aftercare planning development

FAMILY AND COMMUNITY INVOLVEMENT

As previously mentioned, an essential factor of comprehensive treatment is the identification of external resources. During the challenging circumstances of a crisis, external resources and social supports offer additional information to help explore ways to prevent future crises while working with collateral supports. In the most difficult cases, teaching positive reinforcement methods/approach to closely aligned family and friends to benefit the needs and safety of the identified patient may be warranted.

CRISIS ASSESSMENT

Much like a CBA, the crisis assessment is a biopsychosocial assessment that considers internal and external supports, stressors, the need for medical treatment, the current use and influence of substances, and coping mechanisms. Prior to determining whether to proceed with a crisis intervention assessment versus a CBA associated with mental illness, the clinician must verify whether presenting for treatment is the result of a functional person in a crisis state as a consequence or an interpersonal conflict or a crisis-inducing event/ experience or originating from a preexisting mental illness issue.

CRISIS ASSESSMENT OUTLINE

Establishing a positive therapeutic relationship with the patient is an expected inherent quality of the crisis assessment and therapeutic process. Providing support, offering unconditional acceptance and reassurance in a nonjudgmental frame, identifies the clinician as the source of support that can be trusted for successfully problem solving and working through a crisis (Roberts, 2005; Wiger & Haroski, 2003).

1. Presenting problem(s) and precipitating crisis
   A. Assessing the situation
   B. Asking questions and determining what the individual needs to cope effectively with the crisis
   C. What were the overwhelming factors of the crisis event/experience
2. Assessing current imminent risk and potential risk for danger to self

(*Imminent risk/danger would assess domestic violence, sexual abuse/assault, stalker, violent stalker, etc.)

A. Clarifying suicidal thoughts and feelings
B. Clarifying determination of intent
C. Evaluating viability of plan and lethality
   1. Plan
   2. Feasibility of plan
   3. Plan lethality
   4. Access to means to carry out plan
D. History of suicidal thoughts and enactments
E. Identifying specific risk factors
   1. Depression/acute anxiety
   2. Social isolation
   3. Significant loss (e.g., close death, divorce, layoff from job, etc.)

3. Identify what precipitated the crisis
   A. Why seeking treatment now (the last straw phenomenon)
   B. Prioritizing identified clinical problems
   C. Review of coping ability "style" and associated modification(s) needed to resolve current crisis

4. Coping with emotions
   A. Challenge maladaptive beliefs by offering information for consideration, reframing, interpretation, playing the devil's advocate, utilizing paradoxical intervention
   B. Provide options, depending on the degree of dysfunction/risk associated with the crisis
      1. No-harm/suicide contract
      2. Increase frequency of brief clinical contacts
      3. Brief hospitalization
      4. Use of accountability partner and/or structured family–friend monitoring and support to ensure safety
      5. Generate and discuss alternative to satisfy current needs (medical treatment, housing, use of community supports, use of government entitlement support, etc.)
   C. Reinforce history of positive coping when previously confronted with a crisis
      1. Reinforce effective coping mechanisms, problem solving, and resilience
      2. Educate regarding steps they can take to minimize the damage or assault to the integrity of normal functional coping
      3. Reinforce that they will eventually return to normal function (homeostasis)

5. Substance use history including treatment and last use, history of blackouts, withdrawal syndromes, and the impact it has had upon their overall functioning—including legal problems

6. Current health status and health history (including last physical examination) over the counter medicines and supplements, medical problems, recent/past head trauma or accidents, and any known allergies

7. Family history for medical, psychiatric issues, and substance use problems

8. History of abuse or trauma—either as a victim or a perpetrator

9. Legal history, i.e., violence [including domestic violence (DV)] arrests, incarceration, probation, restraining order(s)

10. Quality of current support systems and availability
    A. Social history—present relationships
    B. Community supports and involvement
    C. Work history—current employment

11. Reestablishing emotional balance (dependent on achievements in prior stage of)
    A. Reflecting history of effective coping
    B. Reframe the crisis as an opportunity for increased self-awareness, added coping skills, reinforcing the successful negotiation through a crisis reinforcing resilience, and better understanding of how to approach the negative impact to personal coping should they experience a similar crisis

12. Development and implementation of agreed-on treatment plan
   A. Implementing strategies identified as safety issues (crisis intervention with high risk, suicidal youth, etc.)
   B. Identifying resources and safe/supportive people
   C. Decrease isolation and increase use of social supports
   D. Positive daily schedule
   E. Self-care
13. Relapse prevention
   A. Identify early warning signs of symptoms returning or escalating (for example)
      1. Poor sleep or not getting enough sleep
      2. Loss or grief
      3. Conflict in significant relationships
      4. Decreased tolerance and increased distractibility
      5. Negative experience such as perceived failure, disappointment, or criticism
      6. Other stressful events
      7. Alcohol and other drug use
      8. Anniversary of crisis event/experience
      9. Not following through on your treatment plan (such as not taking prescribed medications)
      10. Other health problems or concerns
   B. Consciously utilizing healthy coping mechanisms
   C. Utilizing social supports
   D. Self-monitoring
   E. Self-care routines such as regular exercise, laughter, engaging in regular and sufficient sleep regimen, relaxation (meditation/mindfulness, deep breathing exercises, progressive muscle relaxation, yoga, etc.)
   F. Engaging in recovery supportive activities
      1. Talking with a friend or loved one
      2. Talking with your health-care professional
      3. Attending a peer support group
      4. Spending time in nature, such as going to a park
      5. Writing in a journal
      6. Spending time on a hobby
      7. Volunteering for your favorite organization or helping someone else
      8. Watching a funny movie
      9. Cutting back on a few nonessential responsibilities
      10. Writing down a list of thoughts or behaviors that increase risk of relapse to be monitored and avoided
14. Termination and follow-up
   A. Preparing for termination requires the integration of new ways of thinking and behaving and consolidating the experience of the successful negotiation through a negatively impacting crisis
   B. Follow-up serves as an inoculation to support continuous solution–focused thoughts and behaviors

COGNITIVE-BEHAVIORAL ASSESSMENT

CBAs seek to understand what problems afflict a patient and what underlying thoughts or behaviors might be causing or worsening the problems. Therefore, the foundation of CBT is the belief that many psychological disorders are caused by unhealthy thoughts and behavior patterns.

CBA is a systematic and structured conceptual model whereby each component relates to one another and helps the therapist to visualize the implications for crisis intervention resulting in CBT goal-directed treatment that is supportive contextually and collaboratively engaged in between the clinician and patient. A positive therapeutic alliance (positive rapport, safe environment, instilling hope and trust) is expected to result in a clinical frame or perspective of being collaborative, safe, and trusting that facilitates problem solving, goal attainment, and crisis resolution.

A positive affiliation between the patient and the therapist has long been determined to be a positive contribution to the therapeutic process. This factor also leads to the decreased likelihood of resistance and an increased openness to exploration and change when a highly skilled therapist engages the patient motivationally. Additionally, it is expected that as treatment progresses, the therapeutic alliance will become stronger, allowing the therapist and patient to gradually move into more complex and meaningful therapeutic issues.

The patient is encouraged to keep a structured journal of their thoughts, feelings, and behaviors to increase awareness for the detailed patterns and associations. Even though behavioral health presses the clinician to apply brief standardized interventions—the one-size-fits-all clinical application cannot be an assumptive intervention. The clinician must conceptualize the patient characteristics that identify them as a candidate for brief therapy and develop an individualized treatment plan.

FACTORS TO CONSIDER IN EVALUATING PATIENTS FOR BRIEF COGNITIVE-BEHAVIORAL THERAPY

1. Demonstrated strong motivation to change
   A. Increased distress or a recent crisis is often associated with increased motivation to change.
   B. Positive treatment expectations (i.e., awareness/knowledge of CBT and having perceived benefits of treatment is associated with improved outcomes).
   C. Patients presenting for treatment with clear goals.
2. Time commitment
   A. Patient is willing to devote the time needed for weekly sessions.
   B. Patient is willing to devote energy to out-of-session homework assignments.
3. Life stressors/situation
   A. Identified and discrete problem focus. The presentation of too many problems/life stressors can result in unfocused work as well as chronically presenting in crisis versus solution-focused interventions culminating in resolution.
   B. Patients who present with strong support by family and friends are more likely to benefit from solution-focused CBT.
4. Cognitive functioning and educational level
   A. Requires a cognitive and educational level of functioning that allows for independent reading and follows through on homework assignments. Those lacking these characteristics may not do well or as well with CBT.
   B. There is an increased probability that patients possessing the ability to work independently are more likely to carry out between-session homework.
   C. Patients who are motivated and psychologically minded are more likely to benefit from short-term CBT.
5. Severity of psychopathology
   A. Patients presenting with comorbid psychopathology offer a more complicated clinical picture and may be more difficult to treat in short-term CBT. Additionally, diagnoses such as substance abuse or serious mental illness require focused and more intensive interventions specific to their diagnostic conditions. Programs with additional support mechanisms aid in preventing relapse.
   B. Patients with a character disorder diagnosis are also less likely to benefit from short-term CBT. Long-standing interpersonal issues often require longer treatment durations. This issue plays a role in the protracted period of time necessary for developing a positive therapeutic alliance.

Adapted from Bond and Dryden (2002), Beck (1995), and Rollnick, Mason, and Butler (1999).

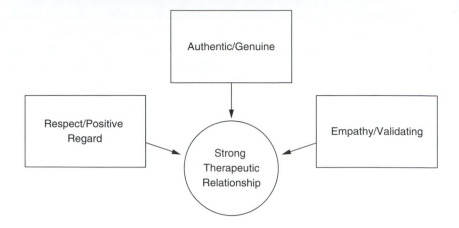

It may not be possible to assess all of the following points during the initial assessment. The assessment process continues throughout the course of treatment. The CBA has a general educational element that helps to focus the patient on internal and external variables that may not have appeared relevant to the problem.

CBT is generally offered as an integrated facet of a biopsychosocial assessment and case management approach especially for distorted thinking, altered behavior (withdrawal/altered levels of activity/avoidance), altered emotions (mood/feelings), life situations, relationships, and practical problems (Wright, Williams, & Garland, 2002). The underlying concept behind CBT is that thoughts and feelings play a fundamental role in behavior. The goal of CBT is to teach patients that while they cannot necessarily control what happens to them, they can take control of how they interpret and respond to what they experience. CBT is empirically supported and has been shown to effectively help patients overcome a wide variety of maladaptive behaviors (phobias, addiction, depression, anxiety) (Beck, 2011; Martin, 2013).

Cognitive-Behavioral Interview Outline

1. Succinct description of the presenting problem
2. Development of the problem

*Assessing risk is an initial task to ascertain current indications as well as potential risk.

    A. Behavior(s)
    B. Cognition(s)
    C. Affective response(s)
    D. Physiological reaction(s)
    E. To each of these, answer
        1. What
        2. When
        3. Where
        4. How often
        5. With whom
        6. Degree of distress
        7. Degree of disruption
3. Contextual variables or modulating variables
    A. Situation(s)
    B. Behavior(s)

C. Cognition(s)

D. Affective response(s)

E. Interpersonal response(s)

F. Physiological response(s)

4. Maintaining factors

A. Situation(s)

B. Behavior(s)

C. Cognition(s)

D. Affective response(s)

E. Interpersonal(s)

F. Physiological response(s)

5. Coping

A. History of responses to difficulty situations

B. Current resources

1. Intrapersonal

2. Interpersonal

3. Community

6. Psychiatric history

7. Medical history

8. Previous treatment

A. General course of treatment

B. How did they respond?

C. What was helpful?

9. Beliefs and interpretations associated with presenting issue

10. Mental status

11. Psychosocial factors

A. Family/social relationships

B. Psychosexual development

C. Occupation

D. Personal interests/leisure activities

E. Adjustment/accommodation

DEPRESSION AND ANXIETY SCREENING

While a complete clinical evaluation is necessary to establish a diagnosis of depression or anxiety, a simple screening instrument serves a useful purpose to do the following:

1. Clarify symptom presentation

2. Assess risk

3. Explore the history of symptoms

4. Explore treatment history

5. Explore history of effective coping in similar situations/levels of distress

6. Educate the patient regarding treatment choices

7. Initiate steps to provide safety and stabilization

8. Make appropriate referrals

DEPRESSION

Criteria for Major Depressive Episode

Five or more of the following symptoms have been present during the same 2-week period and represent a change from previous functioning. At least one of the symptoms is depressed mood or loss of interest/pleasure.

1. Fatigue or loss of energy
2. Feelings of worthlessness
3. Diminished interest/pleasure in all/almost all activities
4. Recurrent thoughts of death or suicide or suicide attempts
5. Significant weight loss or weight gain
6. Insomnia or increased need for sleep
7. Inability to concentrate
8. Depressed mood most of the day
9. Agitation or lethargy

The SAMHSA website offers recommendations for screening tools. For depression they suggested the Medicare Preventive Services "Screening for Depression" Booklet, the Patient Health Questionnaire (PHQ-9), and the MacArthur Foundation Depression Tool Kit (source: http://www.integration.samhsa.gov).

An additional consideration is the Beck Depression Inventory that is easy to administer and score.

ANXIETY

Many individuals with persistent anxiety present with somatic symptoms as well. For these individuals, consider a diagnosis of generalized anxiety disorder.

Generalized anxiety disorder is described as excessive anxiety and worry that occurs more days than not for a period of at least 6 months. The individual experiences difficulty controlling excessive worry. Anxiety and worry are associated with three or more of the following symptoms.

1. Feelings of restlessness/on-edge/keyed-up
2. Easily fatigued
3. Difficulty concentrating/maintaining attention
4. Irritability/low frustration tolerance
5. Muscle tension
6. Sleep disturbance

The SAMHSA website offers recommendations for screening tools. For anxiety they recommended the brief GAD-7 (Generalized Anxiety Disorder). The Beck Anxiety Inventory is another screening tool that many clinicians find easy to administer and score.

STRUCTURED INTERVIEW FOR DEPRESSION AND ANXIETY

When depression has been identified as the presenting or underlying issue, the next task is to clarify the nature of the depression and its severity so that appropriate treatment (including referrals for medication evaluation/hospitalization) can ensue.

1. Presenting problem and assessment of risk
   A. History of presenting problem/illness

    B. History of mental health issues

    C. History of substance use

2. Current level of functioning

    A. Symptoms

    B. Relationships

    C. Work/school

    D. Home

    E. Negative/self-defeating thoughts

    F. Onset of depression

    G. Development of depression

    H. Context of depression and/or anxiety

*Collaborate with the individual to develop a problem list from their perspective.

    I. Legal history

    J. Mental status

      1. Mood

      2. Affect

      3. Memory

      4. Processes

      5. Perceptual disturbances

      6. Judgment

      7. Insight

      8. Impulse control

        An example of examining mental status:

        a. What signs/symptoms of depression/anxiety are currently presented?

        b. Describe general appearance and behavior.

        c. Describe the characteristics of the patient's speech.

        d. Describe mood and affect, including the stability, range, congruence, and appropriateness of affect.

        e. Are thought processes coherent?

        f. Identify recurrent or persistent themes in the patient's thought processes.

        g. Describe any abnormalities of the patient's thought content (e.g., delusions, ideas of reference, overvalued ideas, ruminations, obsessions, compulsions, phobias).

        h. Identify thoughts, plans, or intentions of harming self or others.

        i. Identify evidence of experiencing perceptual disturbances (e.g., hallucinations, illusions, derealization, depersonalization).

3. Define treatment goals

    A. Collaborative

    B. Willingness to engage in process

4. Educate

    A. Regarding cycle of negative thinking and depression cycle

    B. Possibilities of change, offering hope

    C. Importance of self-care and self-responsibility

5. Homework/feedback

    A. Reinforce effort toward treatment goals and consistent management

    B. Awareness and interest

    C. Self-responsibility

    D. Preventative strategies developed/relapse prevention

6. Prepare for self-monitoring

    A. What to look for

    B. What process to use (journals, self-respect, survey, pre- and posttest instrument, etc.)

CYCLE OF DEPRESSION AND/OR ANXIETY: A COGNITIVE-BEHAVIORAL THERAPY ASSESSMENT

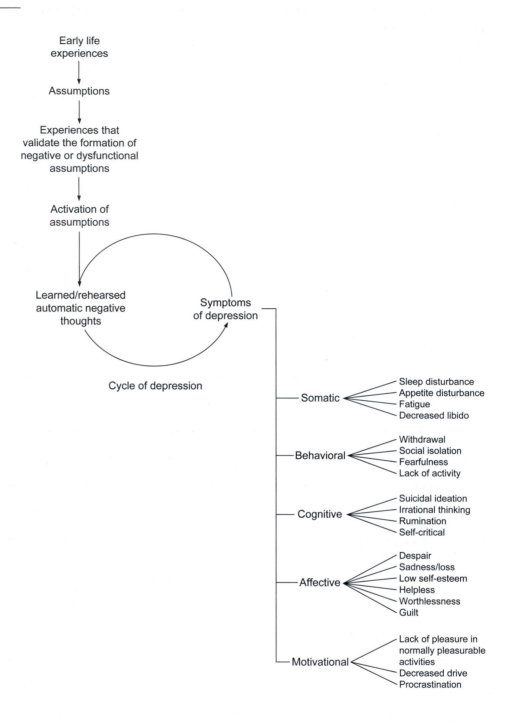

Please fill out the following by checking the correct space that applies

	None or a little of the time	Some of the time	A good part of the time	Most or all of the time
I feel downhearted and blue.				
I enjoy my time alone.				
I have crying spells or feel like having them.				
I have trouble sleeping at night.				
I eat as much as I used to.				
I enjoy sex.				
I notice that I am losing weight.				
I have trouble with constipation.				
My heart beats faster than usual.				
I get tired for no reason.				
My mind is as clear as it used to be.				
I find it easy to do the things I used to do.				
I am restless and cannot keep still.				
I feel hopeful about the future.				
I am more irritable than usual.				
I find it easy to make decisions.				
I feel that I am useful and needed.				
My life is pretty full.				
I feel that others would be better off if I were dead.				
I still enjoy the things I used to do.				
I spend time with friends.				
Describe your personality.				
What problem are you seeking help for?				

CYCLE OF DEPRESSION AND/OR ANXIETY: A COGNITIVE-BEHAVIORAL THERAPY ASSESSMENT

The patient takes the time to develop a narrative of their understanding of their life experience and the impact that it has had upon their emotional functioning. Included in this narrative is a description of their understanding of how their thinking and behavioral patterns have played a role in the cyclical experience of depression and/or anxiety. This practice is important as a demonstration of their self-awareness and motivation to change. It also provides the therapeutic process with rich information from which to develop an effective CBT treatment plan thoroughly collaborated in by the clinician and the patient.

A CBA may also be accomplished using a combination of standardized forms specifically developed by the clinician outlining the information in a manner they feel captures and reflects their strategic clinical process. When forms/worksheets are utilized, patients are requested to rate their thoughts, feelings, and behaviors as a foundation to gather more specific information. The purpose is to help them to gain a broader picture of their thoughts and behavioral patterns as well as to serve as the essential information from which a CBT treatment plan is developed.

COGNITIVE-BEHAVIORAL THERAPY INDIVIDUALIZED ASSESSMENT

The Depression Anxiety and Stress Scale, or DASS21, is a 21-question assessment that was developed to measure the degree of depression, anxiety, and stress in an individual. It includes seven questions for each, and the scores are calculated by adding up the scores for each item in the section. To adequately diagnose depressive disorders, anxiety and stress disorders that therapists take into account longer periods of time and many other factors such as family history, medications, drug and alcohol use, prior diagnosis, and many other factors. Therefore, the results of the scale can serve as a reference point indicating the importance of following through with a more thorough assessment to develop an effective treatment plan (http://depression-anxiety-stress-test.org is the official site).

COGNITIVE-BEHAVIORAL THERAPY ASSESSMENT

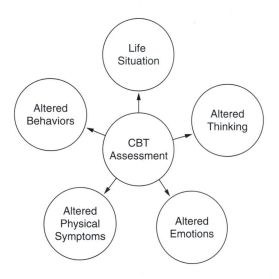

PSYCHIATRIC CRISIS EVALUATION

The presentation of a behavioral health crisis requires the clinician to avoid a narrow focus on the legal profile of danger to self or others. To accurately identify the foundation of a psychiatric crisis requires a clinical perspective of a whole person view. While the need of an emergency response is indicated, it is important to explore and clarify what may be underlying the crisis episode via a culmination or cascade of events resulting in a decompensation.

The crisis evaluation is utilized when urgent care is required as the consequence of the presentation of acute symptomology during the course of a behavioral health emergency assessment. The services and individualized needs of someone experiencing a psychiatric crisis require assessment and immediate intervention by behavioral health professionals/team of professionals specializing in the care of psychiatric emergencies and familiar with community resources. This information is necessary to effectively provide an in-depth psychiatric evaluation, crisis intervention, emergency behavioral stabilization, medication treatment, and brief observation. Treatment team members who are formally or informally affiliated offering urgent and emergency behavioral health services are highly trained in evaluating the safety risks to individuals in a crisis and providing referrals to the most appropriate and least intrusive level of care, including inpatient psychiatric or dual diagnosis units, partial hospitalization programs, substance use disorders (SUDs) rehabilitation, or outpatient therapy. A psychiatric evaluation determines whether hospitalization is needed or whether a less restrictive level of care may be more appropriate. The clinician must maintain awareness for behaviors that represent an imminent danger, thus indicating the need for some variation of an emergency response. Keeping in mind that only a fraction of presented psychiatric real-life crises may actually result in serious harm to self or others, an individualized response is activated when physical safety becomes an issue. Therefore, the psychiatric response must address the underlying crisis in a meaningful manner that facilitates recovery, resilience, relapse prevention as well as addressing legal and ethical concerns.

ESSENTIAL FACTORS TO CONSIDER

The foundation of responding to a mental health crisis includes the following 10 essential principles (Practice Guidelines, 2009):

1. *Avoid harm.* Timely access to support is essential to decreasing the intensity and duration of distress and is provided in the least restrictive manner utilizing routine networks and natural sources of support to provide necessary assistance during the course of crisis intervention and beyond. An appropriate and effective mental health crisis intervention considers risk, controlling danger sufficiently and addressing alternative crisis response in a manner commensurate with minimizing the negative impact of intervention. In other words, it is recognized that the application of some intervention measures results in a negative impact to be acknowledged and processed as part of recovery—thus the reason for applying the least restrictive intervention.

2. *Patient-centered intervention.* Patient-centered care provides a clinical frame that promotes the decision-making abilities and choices of treatment and recovery interventions. Patient-centered treatment strives for understanding of the whole life experience of the individual and that their goals and preferences be integrated as much as possible in the crisis response (IOM, 2006).

3. *Shared responsibility.* While a concentration on the precipitating/cascading crisis is necessary to address the urgent/emergent presentation, equal attention is given to the individuals' strengths and assets, which affirms their role as an active treatment team member. This is imperative to counter the discrete sense of helplessness associated with losing control over oneself and their life. The process of shared responsibility respects the patient's role in resolving the crisis and seeks to extrapolate and reinforce the long-term benefits.

4. *Identifying and addressing the crisis* (often a cascading event or buildup of unmanageable stressors with associated lack of control or inability to problem-solve/resolve). Experiencing a psychiatric crisis is a traumatizing event. An additional benefit of thoroughly identifying the crisis is its potential advantage for identifying the useful and healing elements of treatment and applying the information to mental health crisis planning (review the mental health crisis planning outline in Chapter 3).

5. *Establish and reinforce feelings of personal safety.* Feelings of fear and vulnerability, a common experience of a psychiatric crisis, are also challenged by interfacing with peers whenever possible. Peer support is beneficial because it offers the unique qualities of shared experiences that offer validation to the isolation and fear that accompany a behavioral health crisis. Validation is crucial to alleviating distress and creating a

foundation of relative response to the crisis that reinforces the essential role of the patient in maintaining the positive structure of internal and external resources that contribute to personal safety.

6. *Identify relative strengths and resources.* All interventions are strength based to further the treatment goals of building and reinforcing resilience. To accomplish this requires understanding precipitating factors and healing factors. Such understanding of their crisis and the beneficial interventions facilitate recovery from the current psychiatric crisis as well as serving as an inoculation to protect them from future decompensation.

7. *Use a whole person approach.* The label of "mental illness" can be a negative or even damaging influence to an individual's identity. Therefore, the whole person viewpoint rightfully (and beneficially) considers the multiple needs of the patient in psychiatric crisis and the interplay of other salient life factors. Many of these factors are common everyday factors associated with children, home, work, transportation, pets, etc.

8. *Respect the person as a credible source.* Once labeled as mentally ill, an individual may commonly experience a lack of faith in their abilities by others. A crucial issue is the *narrative* or life story that each person carries with them as their identity, experiences, and value as an individual. Therefore, the opportunity presented by a psychiatric crisis is to reframe their recovery as an opportunity for the meaningful life they desire and to work toward their full potential. DHHS (2004) asserts that the whole person response to crisis intervention highly values the patient as a credible source of factual and emotional information, thus highlighting personal strength and resourcefulness.

9. *Provide a clinical and social frame promoting recovery, resilience, and natural supports.* Effective crisis intervention places value on prior efforts by the individual and clinician/ treatment team. When a patient and their clinician/treatment team use prior and current management efforts to be prepared for emergencies, for instance, by having executed psychiatric advance directives or other crisis plans. Incorporating such measures in a crisis response requires that interveners be knowledgeable about these approaches, their immediate and longer-term value, and how to implement them.

10. *Relapse prevention.* Appropriate crisis interventions also include postevent reviews that may produce information that is helpful to the individual and his or her customary service providers in refining ongoing services and crisis plans that serve to decrease the potential, or duration and severity, of future psychiatric crisis events. This is best accomplished when psychiatric intervention identifies and addresses needed skill development, internal and external resources, and unmet needs.

*Thoroughly document assessment of risk and associated interventions, including mandated reporting events.

THE ASSESSMENT FRAME

The basic components of an initial psychiatric assessment are as follows:

1. Demographic information
2. Current and prior agency contacts (and associated releases for information)
3. Medical, psychiatric, and substance use history
4. Brief history of the patient and significant others
5. Summary of the patient's current situation
6. Presenting request for intervention (what is the patient seeking)
7. Presenting problem as identified by the patient

8. Treatment contract—agreement
   A. Basic treatment contract clarifying expectations and limitations of both the therapist and the patient.
   B. When a positive therapeutic relationship exists, there can be a benefit to developing a safety contract with a patient. The foundation of the contract is that the patient will contact the therapist for a clinical intervention should they begin to feel an escalation toward suicidality versus taking any negative actions. The essence of the contract is trust.
   C. Increased number of brief session appointments/increased contact.
   D. Medications appropriately secured and administered.
   E. A card for the wallet and refrigerator that lists all of the trusted clinical phone contact numbers and a list of "safe" people who have agreed to be part of the social support system or serve as accountability partners.
9. Agreed-on treatment plan
10. Agreed-on treatment goals

RISK MANAGEMENT

Risk management or the assessment of future behavior (specifically danger to self, other, or gravely disabled) requires a proactive openness to manage risk objectively and effectively. Risk assessment seeks to determine the potential threat that could be posed by an individual that must be managed to ameliorate (harm reduction) or eliminate harm. Melton, Petrila, Poythress, and Slobogin (2007) asserts that the role of clinicians in appraising risk requires the compilation of relevant clinical information and calculating the risk as components of clinical judgment. This assertion is supportive of the acknowledgment that risk management is not a dichotomous (all-or-nothing) issue. Instead risk exists on a continuum with a fluidity of vulnerability to dynamic interplay of both risk factors and protective factors.

Thorough documentation of risk management presentations and interventions is essential. *If it is not documented, it did not happen.* Risk assessment is applicable and essential not only to the endeavor to predict potential harm, but also in developing intervention strategies to help prevent future recidivism and potential dangerousness as well. Additionally, it is an opportunity to provide a positive insertion in the form of a constructive and encouraging reframe of preventive opportunity. The clinician identifying the issues of danger to self, others, or gravely disabled is cognizant of the imperative alliance of the treatment team in creating a matrix of support and mutual reinforcement of case management.

Primary care and psychiatry are highly valued treatment team members in these challenging cases. The common and practical interventions such as pharmacological and psychological treatments, along with educational and community awareness resourcefully, help promote prevention. Medications can help to relieve symptoms in psychiatric disorders and can provide a powerful early intervention serving to take the edge off of acute symptoms that interfere in effective daily functioning. They can relieve anxiety, depression, aggressive/violent behaviors, emotional and mood disorders, or suicidal and self-injurious behaviors. The therapist often plays a key role because of the increased contact with the patient in contrast to the other treatment team members thus being placed in the position of heightened responsibility to monitor and inform case dynamics to members of the treatment team and initiating treatment team problem solving.

Even though most therapists will not participate in the process of risk management beyond their outpatient practice, it is valuable clinically to review the legal process associated with the continuum of risk. The special assessment circumstances of risk of suicide (danger to self), dangerousness (danger to others), and gravely disabled constitute the most difficult and challenging situations with which the therapist will be presented. They require careful assessment, treatment considerations regarding level of care and providing a safe environment within prescribed legal mandates, as well as mandating reporting associated with safety to self or others.

DANGER TO SELF, OTHERS, OR GRAVELY DISABLED

The mental health process for a mentally ill person presenting with diagnostic indications requiring a psychiatric assessment regarding a danger to self, others, or gravely disabled is a complicated clinical picture associated with specific laws and evaluation process. Every clinician is responsible to be aware of the legal and ethical issues and respond accordingly. Aside from the legal issues a clinician must be apprised of, each county has designated personnel charged with the evaluation process of involuntary hospitalization. An overview of the process is provided in the diagram "Summary of Lanterman–Petris–Short Act (LPS)."

SUMMARY OF LANTERMAN–PETRIS–SHORT ACT

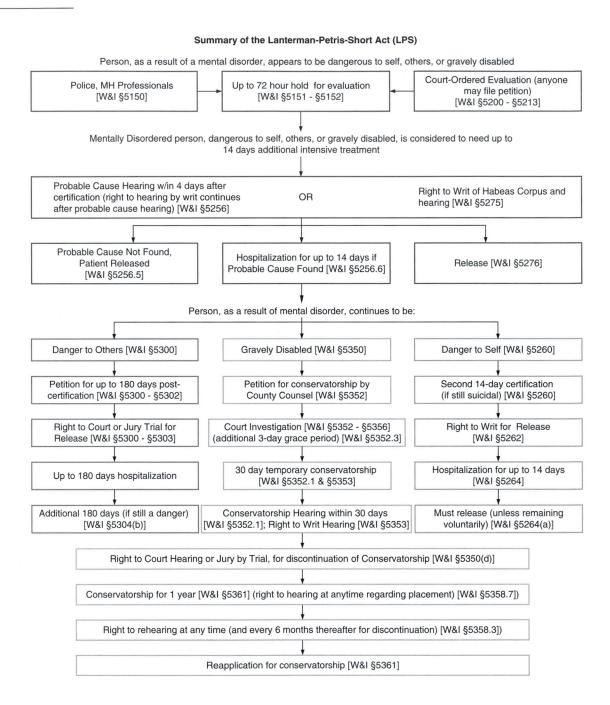

Summary of the Lanterman-Petris-Short Act (LPS)

Person, as a result of a mental disorder, appears to be dangerous to self, others, or gravely disabled

| Police, MH Professionals [W&I §5150] | Up to 72 hour hold for evaluation [W&I §5151 - §5152] | Court-Ordered Evaluation (anyone may file petition) [W&I §5200 - §5213] |

Mentally Disordered person, dangerous to self, others, or gravely disabled, is considered to need up to 14 days additional intensive treatment

| Probable Cause Hearing w/in 4 days after certification (right to hearing by writ continues after probable cause hearing) [W&I §5256] | OR | Right to Writ of Habeas Corpus and hearing [W&I §5275] |

| Probable Cause Not Found, Patient Released [W&I §5256.5] | Hospitalization for up to 14 days if Probable Cause Found [W&I §5256.6] | Release [W&I §5276] |

Person, as a result of mental disorder, continues to be:

| Danger to Others [W&I §5300] | Gravely Disabled [W&I §5350] | Danger to Self [W&I §5260] |

| Petition for up to 180 days post-certification [W&I §5300 - §5302] | Petition for conservatorship by County Counsel [W&I §5352] | Second 14-day certification (if still suicidal) [W&I §5260] |

| Right to Court or Jury Trial for Release [W&I §5300 - §5303] | Court Investigation [W&I §5352 - §5356] (additional 3-day grace period) [W&I §5352.3] | Right to Writ for Release [W&I §5262] |

| Up to 180 days hospitalization | 30 day temporary conservatorship [W&I §5352.1 & §5353] | Hospitalization for up to 14 days [W&I §5264] |

| Additional 180 days (if still a danger) [W&I §5304(b)] | Conservatorship Hearing within 30 days [W&I §5352.1]; Right to Writ Hearing [W&I §5353] | Must release (unless remaining voluntarily) [W&I §5264(a)] |

Right to Court Hearing or Jury by Trial, for discontinuation of Conservatorship [W&I §5350(d)]

Conservatorship for 1 year [W&I §5361] (right to hearing at anytime regarding placement) [W&I §5358.7])

Right to rehearing at any time (and every 6 months thereafter for discontinuation) [W&I §5358.3])

Reapplication for conservatorship [W&I §5361]

In general, once a referral/application is set forth, the Welfare & Institutions Code legally guides the process. Most clinicians do not play a role of these processes beyond the initial referral/application. However, it is important to be familiar with this journey of the mentally ill and the measures of legal safety provided. Whoever provides the application for emergency admission must state the specific nature of the danger and a summary of the observations upon which the statement of danger is based. Then the screening agency reviews the information presented on the application, gathers any other information they deem relevant, and conducts an interview with the individual to determine if there is reasonable cause to believe that the individual is, as a result of a mental disorder, a danger to self or to others, or is gravely disabled and if the person is unable or unwilling to receive an evaluation on a voluntary basis. At that juncture, if reasonable cause is determined, the screening agency examiner may submit a petition for a court-ordered mental health evaluation. If the individual is unwell or not able to undergo such an evaluation voluntarily, an order for involuntary hospitalization and evaluation results.

As can be easily understood, while the clinician as a mandated reporter must follow specific laws and guidelines, they are also responsible to thoroughly assess the patient so that no individual is subjected to this process unnecessarily. The intervention process demands being appropriately focused on specific information, being respectful and to use the least intrusive methods of intervention necessary.

CLARIFYING RISK OF HARM

Psychiatric disorders with high suicide risk factors (adults) include major depressive episode, bipolar disorder, anxiety disorders, schizophrenia, personality disorder, and SUDs. While the rate varies by age, ethnicity, and socioeconomic factors, it is a significant problem across all parameters. According to Nordentoft (2007), 90% of the people who kill themselves have a psychiatric diagnosis.

BASIC DOCUMENTATION

Current Risk Factors

Suicidality ____ None ____ Ideation ____ Plan ____ Intent w/o means ____ Intent w/means

Homicidality ____ None ____ Ideation ____ Plan ____ Intent w/o means ____ Intent w/means

If risk of suicide or homicide exists, patient is able to contract to not harm self or others and is willing to comply with recommendations: ____ Yes ____ No

Impulse control ____ Sufficient ____ Moderate ____ Minimal ____ Inconsistent ____ Explosive

Medical risks ____ None ____ Present If present, explain: _____

Substance use ____ None ____ Abuse ____ Dependence ____ Unstable remission ____ Stable remission

If substance abuse exists, specify substance, quantity, date of last use, ability to abstain, and prior CD treatment: _____

_____

Does significant substance abuse or dependence exist in client's living situation? ____ Yes ____ No

Current physical abuse, sexual abuse, and/or child/elder neglect? ____ Yes ____ No

If yes, client is: ____ Victim ____ Perpetrator ____ Both ____ Neither, but abuse exists in family

Does abuse involve a child and/or elder? ____ Yes ____ No

Legally reported? ____ Yes ____ No

Specifics _____

_____

History of Risk

Explain any significant history of suicidal and/or homicidal behavior, problems with impulse control, substance abuse, and/or medical risks that may affect client's current level of risk or may impair client's functioning.

_____

_____

Functional Impairments (*As applicable, explain how the symptoms affect daily functioning or place the client at risk.*)

Please rate severity of impairment. 1 = Mild   2 = Moderate   3 = Severe

Area	Severity	Description
Job/school	_____	_____
Relationships	_____	_____
Other	_____	_____

Disability? _____ None _____ Medical _____ Mental health

*Claiming workers' comp? _____ Yes _____ No

Current Medications _____ None _____ Psychiatric _____ Medical _____ No

Specify dosage, frequency, and compliance: _____

Prescribed by: _____ Psychiatrist _____Other physician

 This document (above) was provided as a potential format for case documentation and to engage the clinician to be thoughtful regarding the information to be sought and gleaned during the course of a clinical assessment associated with risk. The following information on suicide, dangerousness, and gravely disabled elucidates the complexity of risk management. In other words, a form may appear to be a series of check-offs and fill-ins, but that is far from the degree of integrated information, interpretation, and clinical decision making necessary for cases presenting risk.

SUICIDE

Assessing self-destructive threats, gestures, and suicide potential refers to the degree of probability that an individual may engage in harm or attempt to take their own life (complete suicide) in the immediate or near future. Suicidal thoughts and gestures are commonly identified in those identified with psychiatric disorders such as major depressive disorder, bipolar disorders, schizophrenia, posttraumatic stress disorder (PTSD), anxiety, SUDs, and personality disorders (e.g., antisocial and borderline). Not surprisingly, those presenting with psychiatric comorbidity are at increased risk for suicide. However, suicide risk is also seen in those with certain physical disorders that include (but are not limited to) HIV/AIDS, epilepsy, tumors, Huntington chorea, Alzheimer disease, multiple sclerosis, spinal cord injuries, traumatic brain injury, cancer, autoimmune diseases, and renal disease. Loss of ability, loss of hope, and overwhelming fear of being dependent on others can be a powerful foundation for considering suicide.

 Suicidal impulse and suicidal behaviors constitute a response by a person whose coping mechanisms have failed. They are often desperate and feel ashamed. If the person has attempted suicide, a medical evaluation and issues of medical stability supersede a clinical interview. Be calm and caring in your approach, establishing a setting conductive to eliciting the necessary information. Be reassuring in letting the person know how you plan to proceed regarding referral for medical evaluation if needed, and that you want to talk to them to understand what has been happening in their life which brought them to the point of suicidal intent and suicidal behavior.

SAMHSA SCREENING TOOLS FOR SUICIDE

SAMHSA provided consideration of the following screening tools associated with suicidality. The information by SAMHSA has been insignificantly modified/formatted to assure consistency with their publication:

1. The **Columbia-Suicide Severity Rating Scale (C-SSRS)** is a questionnaire used for suicide assessment. It is available in 114 country-specific languages. Mental health training is not required to administer the C-SSRS. Various professionals can administer this scale, including physicians, nurses, psychologists, social workers, peer counselors, coordinators, research assistants, high school students, teachers, and clergy.

    (Source: *http://www.integration.samhsa.gov/clinical-practice/Columbia_Suicide_Severity_Rating_Scale.pdf*)

2. **PHQ-9, SAFE-T,** and **SBQ-R** and other regular screenings in primary care and other health-care settings enable earlier identification of suicide risk and mental health disorders.

    (Source: *http://www.integration.samhsa.gov*)

3. QPR Institute's **risk audit** can help in your organization's current operational and training approach to suicidal patient safety.

    (Source: *http://www.qprinstitute.com/*)

4. **Stories Of Hope And Recovery** is a video guide for suicide attempt survivors and features inspiring stories from three people who survived an attempted suicide. Told through their voices and those of their families, the stories recount their journeys from the suicide attempt to a life of hope and recovery. Includes a video guide.

    (Source: *http://store.samhsa.gov/product/Stories-Of-Hope-And-Recovery-A-Video-Guide-for-Suicide- Attempt-Survivors/BackInStock/SMA12-4711DVD*)

5. The **MacArthur Depression Toolkit** is designed to be used by primary care clinicians with identifying and managing depression. This toolkit includes easy-to-use instruments to assist with identifying, diagnosing, treating, and monitoring depression.

    (Source: *http://www.integration.samhsa.gov/clinical-practice/macarthur_depression_toolkit.pdf*)

6. The **SAFE-T Card** guides mental health clinicians through five steps that address a patient's level of suicide risk and associated appropriate interventions. The goal is to provide an accessible and portable resource to the therapist whose clinical practice includes suicide assessment.

    (Source: *http://www.integration.samhsa.gov/clinical-practice/safe-t_card.pdf*)

7. **A Discussion Guide for Primary Health Care Providers.** This is an online guide designed for primary health-care providers with questions that fit easily into a discussion with a patient's primary care physician about alcohol, illicit drug, and mental health problems, as well as cooccurring disorders. While this is a brief guide, it also includes resources for patients who need an evaluation based on positive screening results (this was included as a potential benefit as a consultant to primary care physicians).

    (Source: *http://www.integration.samhsa.gov/A_Discussion_Guide_for_Primary_Health_Care_Providers.pdf*)

*In addition to the screening tools identified above, SAMHSA also offers recommendations for special populations that are readily accessible at their website.

DEPARTMENT OF HEALTH AND HUMAN SERVICES SUICIDE ASSESSMENT

This is available as "Suicide Safe mobile app" (www.samhsa.gov) on Google Play and the Apple App Store. Also available is the associated "Suicide Risk Assessment Guide." The assessment guide is printed below with minimal changes.

*National Suicide Prevention Lifeline 1-800-273-TALK (8255)

SAFE-T: SUICIDE ASSESSMENT FIVE-STEP EVALUATION AND TRIAGE

1. Identify risk factors
   A. Identify risk factors that can be modified to decrease risk
      1. *Suicidal behavior*: history of prior suicide attempts, aborted suicide attempts, or self-injurious behavior
      2. *Current/past psychiatric disorders*: especially mood disorders, psychotic disorders, alcohol/substance abuse, attention-deficit/hyperactivity disorder (ADHD), traumatic brain injury (TBI), PTSD, personality disorders, conduct disorders (antisocial behavior, aggression, impulsivity), comorbidity, and *recent onset of illness increase risk*
      3. *Key symptoms*: anhedonia, impulsivity, hopelessness, anxiety/panic, global insomnia, command hallucinations
      4. *Family history*: history of suicide attempts or psychiatric disorders with associated decompensation and/or requiring hospitalization
      5. *Precipitants/stressors/interpersonal*: triggering events leading to humiliation, shame, or despair (i.e., loss of relationship, financial, or health status—real or anticipated); ongoing medical illness (especially central nervous system disorders, pain); intoxication; family turmoil/chaos; history of physical or sexual abuse; social isolation
      6. *Change in treatment*: discharge from psychiatric hospital, provider, or treatment change
2. Identify protective factors (*Protective factors, even if present, may not counteract significant acute risk*)
   A. Identify protective factors that can be enhanced
      1. *Internal*: ability to cope with stress, religious/spiritual beliefs, frustration tolerance
      2. *External*: responsibility to children or beloved pets, positive therapeutic relationships, social supports
3. Conduct suicide inquiry
   A. Suicidal thoughts, plans, behavior, and intent
      1. *Ideation*: frequency, intensity, duration—in last 48 h, past month, and worst ever
      2. *Plan*: timing, location, lethality, availability, preparatory acts
      3. *Behaviors*: past attempts, aborted attempts, rehearsals (tying noose, loading gun) versus nonsuicidal self-injurious actions
      4. *Intent*: extent to which the patient (1) expects to carry out the plan and (2) believes the plan/act to be lethal versus self-injurious (3) access to firearms. Explore ambivalence: reasons to die versus reasons to live

*For youths: ask parent/guardian about evidence of suicidal thoughts, plans, or behaviors, and changes in mood, behaviors, or disposition.

*Homicide inquiry: when indicated, especially in character disordered or paranoid males dealing with loss or humiliation. Inquire in four areas listed above.

4. Determine risk level/intervention
   A. Determine risk. Choose appropriate intervention to address and decrease risk.
      1. *Assessment of risk* level is based on clinical judgment, after completing three steps above
      2. *Reassess* as patient or environmental circumstances change

Risk level	Risk/protective factor	Suicidality	Possible interventions
High	Psychiatric diagnoses with severe symptoms or acute precipitating event; protective factors not relevant	Potentially lethal suicide attempt or persistent ideation with strong intent or suicide rehearsal	Admission generally indicated unless a significant change reduces risk. Suicide precautions.
Moderate	Multiple risk factors, few protective factors	Suicidal ideation with plan, but no intent or behavior	Admission may be necessary depending on risk factors. Develop crisis plan. Give emergency/crisis numbers.
Low	Modifiable risk factors, strong protective factors	Thoughts of death, no plan, intent, or behavior	Outpatient referral, symptom reduction. Give emergency/crisis numbers.

(This chart is intended to represent a range of risk levels and interventions, not actual determinations.)

5. Document
   A. Assessment of risk, rationale, intervention, and follow-up
      1. Risk level and rationale; treatment plan to address/reduce current risk (e.g., medication, setting, psychotherapy, electroconvulsive therapy, contact with significant others, consultation); firearms instructions, if relevant (i.e., remove from access); follow-up plan. For youths, treatment plan should include roles for parent/guardian.

SUICIDE RISK ASSESSMENT POCKET CARD

The Suicide Risk Assessment Pocket Card was developed to assist clinicians in the assessment and care decisions regarding patients who present with suicidal ideation or provide reason to believe that there is cause for concern. This reference guide provides more specific information and the rationale for the sections on the pocket card. The sections of the guide correspond with the sections of the card. The reference guide may also be used as a teaching aid for new clinicians, residents, and students at all levels and disciplines as well as other caregivers. This introduction provides general information regarding the nature and prevalence of suicidal behaviors and factors associated with increased risk for suicide and suicide attempts.

Suicidal thoughts and behaviors (including suicide attempts and completed suicide) are commonly found at increased rates among individuals with psychiatric disorders, especially major depressive disorder, bipolar disorders, schizophrenia, PTSD, anxiety, chemical dependency, and personality disorders (e.g., antisocial and borderline). A history of a suicide attempt is the strongest predictor of future suicide attempts, as well as completed suicide/death by suicide. Intentional self-harm (i.e., intentional self-injury without the expressed intent to die) is also associated with long-term risk for repeated attempts as well as death by suicide.

Psychiatric comorbidity (greater than one psychiatric disorder present at the same time) increases risk for suicide, especially when substance abuse or depressive symptoms coexist with another psychiatric disorder or condition.

A number of psychosocial factors are also associated with risk for suicide and suicide attempts, including the following:

1. Recent stressful life events including losses (such as employment, careers, finances, housing, marital relationships, physical health, and a sense of a future).
2. Chronic or long-term problems (such as relationships problems, unemployment, and/or legal difficulties).
3. Psychological states of acute or extreme distress can be warning signs of vulnerability (such as humiliation, despair, guilt, and shame).
4. Certain physical disorders are associated with an increased risk for suicide including diseases of the central nervous system (such as epilepsy, tumors, Huntington chorea, Alzheimer disease, multiple sclerosis, spinal cord injuries, and traumatic brain injury), cancers (especially head and neck), autoimmune diseases, renal disease, and HIV/AIDS. Chronic pain syndromes can contribute substantially to increased suicide risk in affected individuals.

5. Patients with traumatic brain injuries may be at increased risk for suicide. In comparison to the general population, TBI survivors are at increased risk for suicide ideation (Simpson & Tate, 2002), suicide attempts (Silver, Kramer, Greenwald, & Weissman, 2001), and suicide completions (Teasdale & Engberg, 2001). TBI-related consequences can be enduring and may include motor disturbances, sensory deficits, and psychiatric symptoms (such as depression, anxiety, psychosis, and personality changes) as well as cognitive dysfunction. These cognitive impairments include impaired attention, concentration, processing speed, memory, language and communication, problem solving, concept formation, judgment, and initiation. Another important TBI consequence that contributes to suicidal risk is the frequent increase in impulsivity. These impairments may lead to a life-long increased suicide risk that requires constant attention.

Suicidal thoughts and behaviors are not uncommonly reported in the general population. A recent national survey (Kessler, Borges, & Walters, 1999) found that 13.5% of Americans report a history of suicide ideation at some point over the lifetime, 3.9% report having made a suicide plan, and 4.6% report having attempted suicide. Among attempters, about 50% report having made a "serious" suicide attempt. The percentages are higher for high school students asked about suicidal ideation and behavior over the preceding year: 16% report having seriously considered attempting suicide, 13% report having made a suicide plan, and 8.4% report having made an attempt during the prior 12 months (CDC, YRBS, 2005). These numbers are even higher when a psychiatric disorder is present.

Often there is a transition that takes place along the continuum from ideation to plan to attempts. 34% of individuals who think about suicide report transitioning from seriously thinking about suicide to making a plan, and 72% of planners move from a plan to an attempt. Among those who make attempts, 60% of planned attempts occur within the first year of ideation onset and 90% of unplanned attempts (which probably represent impulsive self-injurious behaviors) occur within this time period (Kessler et al., 1999). These findings illustrate the importance of eliciting and exploring suicidal ideation and give credence to its role in initiating and fueling the suicidal process.

LOOK FOR THE WARNING SIGNS

What are warning signs and why are they important?

There are a number of known suicide risk factors. Nevertheless, these risk factors are not necessarily closely related in time to the onset of suicidal behaviors—nor does any risk factor alone increase or decrease risk. Population-based research suggests that the risk for suicide increases with an increase in the number of risk factors present, such that when more risk factors are present at any one time, the more likely that they indicate an increased risk for suicidal behaviors at that time.

A recent review of the world's literature has identified a number of warning signs that empirically have been shown to be temporally related to the acute onset of suicidal behaviors (e.g., within hours to a few days). These signs should warn the clinician of *acute* risk for the expression of suicidal behaviors, especially in those individuals with other risk factors (Rudd et al., 2006). Three of these warning signs (bolded on the VA Suicide Risk Assessment Pocket Card) carry the highest likelihood of short-term onset of suicidal behaviors and require immediate attention, evaluation, referral, or consideration of hospitalization.

Common Warning Signs

The warning signs are as follows:

1. Threatening to hurt or kill self
2. Looking for ways to kill self; seeking access to pills, weapons, or other means
3. Talking or writing about death, dying or suicide

   The remaining list of warning signs should alert the clinician that a mental health evaluation needs to be conducted in the *very* near future and that precautions need to be put into place *immediately* to ensure the safety, stability, and security of the individual.

4. Hopelessness
5. Rage, anger, seeking revenge
6. Acting reckless or engaging in risky activities, seemingly without thinking

7. Feeling trapped—like there is no way out
8. Increasing alcohol or drug abuse
9. Withdrawing from friends, family, or society
10. Anxiety, agitation, unable to sleep, or sleeping all the time
11. Dramatic changes in mood
12. No reason for living, no sense of purpose in life

Other behaviors that may be associated with increased short-term risk for suicide are when the patient makes arrangements to divest responsibility for dependent others (children, pets, elders), or making other preparations such as updating wills, making financial arrangements for paying bills, saying goodbye to loved ones, etc.

SPECIFIC FACTORS THAT MAY INCREASE OR DECREASE RISK FOR SUICIDE

Risk and Protective Factors

Factors that may increase risk or factors that may decrease risk are those that have been found to be statistically related to the presence or absence of suicidal behaviors. They do not necessarily impart a causal relationship. Rather they serve as guidelines for the clinician to weigh the relative risk of an individual engaging in suicidal behaviors within the context of the current clinical presentation and psychosocial setting. Individuals differ in the degree to which risk and protective factors affect their propensity for engaging in suicidal behaviors. Within an individual, the contribution of each risk and protective factor to their suicidality will vary over the course of their lives.

No one risk factor, or set of risk factors, necessarily conveys increased suicidal risk. Nor does one protective factor, or set of protective factors, insure protection against engagement in suicidal behaviors. Furthermore, because of their different statistical correlations with suicidal behaviors, these factors are not equal and one cannot "balance" one set of factors against another to derive a sum total score of relative suicidal risk. Some risk factors are immutable (e.g., age, gender, race/ethnicity), while others are more situation specific (e.g., loss of housing, exacerbation of pain in a chronic condition, and onset or exacerbation of psychiatric symptoms).

Ideally, with the elucidation and knowledge of an individual's risk and protective factors as a foundation, the sensitive clinician will inquire about the individual's reasons for living and reasons for dying to better evaluate current risk for suicide.

The following are the factors that may increase a person's risk for suicide:

1. Current ideation, intent, plan, access to means
2. Previous suicide attempt or attempts
3. Alcohol/substance abuse
4. Current or previous history of psychiatric diagnosis
5. Impulsivity and poor self-control
6. Hopelessness—presence, duration, severity
7. Recent losses—physical, financial, personal
8. Recent discharge from an inpatient psychiatric unit
9. Family history of suicide
10. History of abuse (physical, sexual, or emotional)
11. Comorbid health problems, especially a newly diagnosed
12. Problem or worsening symptoms
13. Age, gender, race (elderly or young adult, unmarried, white, male, living alone)
14. Same-sex sexual orientation

The following are the protective factors that may decrease the risk for suicide:

1. Positive social support
2. Spirituality

3. Sense of responsibility to family
4. Children in the home, pregnancy
5. Life satisfaction
6. Reality testing ability
7. Positive coping skills
8. Positive problem-solving skills
9. Positive therapeutic relationship

ASK THE QUESTIONS

Some fear asking direct questions regarding suicide for fear of amplifying a problem. The opposite is true. It is an honest expression of concern and an initiation of the problem-solving process where risk of self-harm exists. Asking questions about suicidal ideation, intent, plan, and attempts is not easy. Sometimes the patient will be the one to provide the opening to ask about suicide, but usually the topic is not readily introduced as part of the presenting complaint while the clinician is gathering history related to the present illness. This can be particularly true in medical as opposed to behavioral health type settings. Nevertheless it is important to ask a screening set of questions whenever the clinical situation or presentation warrants it. Therefore, it is key to set the stage for the questions and to signal to the patient that they are naturally part of the overall assessment of the current problem. Successfully eliciting this information requires a clinician's familiarity with key screening questions and the ease and comfortableness he/she has with the topic and the asking of the questions. It is recommended that the clinical interaction introducing this discussion immediately follows the report and/or the elicitation of the patient (physical or psychic) and distress. Introductory statements that lead into the questions pave the way to ensuring an informative and smooth dialogue and reassure the patient that you are prepared for and interested in the answers.

For example: I appreciate how difficult this problem must be for you at this time. Some of my patients with similar problems/symptoms have told me that they have thought about ending their life. I wonder if you have had similar thoughts?

The questions on the pocket card are examples of the items that should be asked. They form a progressive questioning strategy where the answer would naturally lead to another question that will elicit additional important information.

1. Are you feeling hopeless about the present or future?
   If *yes* ask….
2. Have you had thoughts about taking your life?
   If *yes* ask….
3. When did you have these thoughts and do you have a plan to take your life?
4. Have you ever had a suicide attempt?

It is worth keeping in mind that suicidality can be understood as an attempt by the individual to solve a problem, one that they find overwhelming. It can be much easier for the provider to be nonjudgmental when he/she keeps this perspective in mind. The provider then works with the suicidal individual to develop alternative solutions to the problems leading to suicidal feelings, intent, and/or behaviors. The execution of this strategy can of course be more difficult than its conceptualization.

Why is it important to ask about a history of attempts? Most people who attempt suicide do not attempt again. However, about 16% repeat within one year and 21% repeat within 1–4 years (Beautrais, 2003; Owens, Horrocks, & House, 2002). The majority of repeat attempters will use more lethal means on subsequent attempts—increasing the likelihood of increased morbidity or mortality. Approximately 2% of attempters die by suicide within 1 year of their attempt. The history of a prior suicide attempt is the best known predictor for future suicidal behaviors, including death by suicide. Approximately 8–10% of attempters will eventually die by suicide.

Why is it important to ask about feeling hopeless? Hopelessness—about the present and the future—has been found to be a very strong predictor of suicidal ideation and self-destructive behaviors. Associated with hopelessness are feelings of helplessness, worthlessness, and despair. Although often found in depressed patients, these affective states can be present in many disorders—both psychiatric and physical. If present it is important to explore these feelings with the individual to better assess for the development or expression of suicidal behaviors.

Why is it important to ask about ideation? In most cases, suicidal ideation is believed to precede the onset of suicidal planning and action. Suicidal ideation can be associated with a desire or wish to die (intent) and a reason or rationale for wanting to die (motivation). Hence, it is essential to explore the presence or absence of ideation—currently, in the recent past, and concurrent with any change in physical health or other major psychosocial life stress.

Many individuals will initially deny the presence of suicidal ideation for a variety of reasons including the following:

1. The stigma that is associated with acknowledging symptoms of a mental disorder
2. Fear of being ridiculed, maligned, and/or judged negatively by the clinician
3. Loss of autonomy and control over the situation
4. Fear that the clinician might overreact and hospitalize the individual involuntarily

Even if denied, certain observable cues (affective and behavioral) should prompt the clinician to remain alert to the possible presence of suicidal ideation. Some signs and symptoms include the following:

1. Profound social withdrawal
2. Irrational thinking
3. Paranoia
4. Global insomnia
5. Depressed affect
6. Agitation
7. Anxiety
8. Irritability
9. Despair
10. Shame, humiliation, or disgrace
11. Anger and rage

The clinician may point out the apparent disparity between the current observable clinical condition (what is seen and felt in the examining room) and a denial of suicidal thinking on the part of the patient. Identifying and labeling the clinical concern may pave the way for an open and frank discussion of what the patient is thinking and feeling—and help shape a treatment response.

Asking about suicidal ideation and intent does not increase the likelihood of someone thinking about suicide for the first time or engaging in such behaviors. In fact, most patients report a sense of relief and support when a caring, concerned clinician nonjudgmentally expresses interest in exploring and understanding the patient's current psychological pain and distress that leads them to consider suicide or other self-injurious behaviors. All suicidal ideations and suicidal threats need to be taken seriously.

Why is it important to ask about timing of ideation and presence of a plan?

Although a minority of individuals are chronically suicidal, most people become suicidal in response to *negative life events* or psychosocial stressors that overwhelm their capacity to cope and maintain control, especially in the presence of a *psychiatric disorder*. Therefore, it is important to understand what elicits suicidal thoughts and the context of these thoughts. Knowing how much *time* has been spent thinking about suicide alerts the clinician to its role and influence in the daily life of the patient. Knowing what makes things better and what makes things worse regarding the *onset, intensity, duration*, and *frequency* of suicidal thoughts and feelings assists the clinician in developing a treatment plan. Also knowing what situations in the future might engender the return of suicidal thoughts helps the clinician and patient agree on a safety plan and techniques to avoid or manage such situations.

The presence of a suicide plan indicates that the individual has some intent to die and has begun preparing to die. It is important to know the possibilities and potential for implementation of the plan, the likelihood of being rescued if the plan is undertaken, and the relative lethality of the plan.

Although some research suggests a relationship between the degree of suicidal intent and the lethality of the means, the clinician should not dismiss the presence of suicidal planning even if the method chosen does not appear to be necessarily lethal (Brown, Henriques, Sosdjan, & Beck, 2004). It is also important to know whether the individual has begun to enact the plan, by engaging in such behaviors as rehearsals, hoarding of medications, gaining access to firearms or other lethal means, writing a suicide note, etc.

RESPONDING TO SUICIDE RISK

What is a crisis? A crisis is when the patient's usual and customary coping skills are no longer adequate to address a perceived stressful situation. Often such situations are novel and unexpected. A crisis occurs when unusual stress, brought on by unexpected and disruptive events, renders an individual physically and emotionally disabled—because their usual coping mechanisms and past behavioral repertoire prove ineffective. A crisis overrides an individual's normal psychological and biological coping mechanisms—moving the individual toward maladaptive behaviors. A crisis limits one's ability to utilize more cognitively sophisticated problem-solving skills and conflict resolution skills. Crises are, by definition, time limited. However, every crisis is a potentially high-risk situation.

Crisis intervention and management: The goals of crisis intervention are to lessen the intensity, duration, and presence of a crisis that is perceived as overwhelming and that can lead to self-injurious behaviors. This is accomplished by shifting the focus from an emergency that is life threatening to a plan of action that is understandable and perceived as doable. The goal is to protect the individual from self-harm. In the process, it is critical to identify and discuss the underlying disorder, dysfunction, and/or event that precipitated the crisis. Involving family, partners, friends, and social support networks is advisable.

The objectives are to assist the patient in regaining mastery, control, and predictability. This is accomplished by reinforcing healthy coping skills and substituting more effective skills and responses for less effective skills and dysfunctional responses. The goal of crisis management is to reestablish equilibrium and restore the individual to a state of feeling in control in a safe, secure, and stable environment. Under certain circumstances this might require hospitalization.

The techniques include removing or securing any lethal methods of self-harm, decreasing isolation, decreasing anxiety and agitation, and engaging the individual in a safety plan (crisis management or contingency planning). It also involves a simple set of reminders for the patient to utilize the crisis safety plan and skills agreed on by both the provider and the patient.

Referrals for mental health assessment and follow-up: Any reference to suicidal ideation, intent, or plans mandates a mental health assessment. If the patient is deemed not to be at immediate risk for engaging in self-destructive behaviors, then the clinician needs to collaboratively develop a follow-up and follow-through plan of action. This activity best involves the patient along with significant others such as family members, friends, spouse, partner, close friends, etc.

Here are some ways to be helpful to someone who is threatening suicide or engaging in suicidal behaviors:

1. Be aware—learn the risk factors and warning signs for suicide and where to get help.
2. Be direct—talk openly and matter-of-factly about suicide, what you have observed, and what your concerns are regarding his or her well-being.
3. Be willing to listen—allow expression of feelings, accept the feelings, and be patient.
4. Be nonjudgmental—don't debate whether suicide is right or wrong or whether the person's feelings are good or bad; don't give a lecture on the value of life.
5. Be available—show interest, understanding, and support.
6. Don't dare him or her to engage in suicidal behaviors.
7. Don't act shocked.
8. Don't ask "why."
9. Don't be sworn to secrecy.

10. Offer hope that alternatives are available—but don't offer reassurances that any one alternative will turn things around in the near future.
11. Take action—remove lethal means of self-harm such as pills, ropes, firearms, and alcohol or other drugs.
12. Get help from others with more experience and expertise.
13. Be actively involved in encouraging the person to see a mental health professional (MHP) as soon as possible and ensure that an appointment is made.

Individuals contemplating suicide often don't believe that they can be helped, so you may have to be active and persistent in helping them to get the help they need. And, after helping a friend, family member, or patient during a mental health crisis, be aware of how you may have been affected emotionally and seek the necessary support for yourself.

IMMEDIATE PSYCHOPHARMACOLOGICAL INTERVENTIONS

The most common psychiatric symptoms associated with acute risk for suicidal behaviors include agitation, anxiety, insomnia, acute substance abuse, affective dysregulation, profound depression, and psychosis. Thus, highlighting the importance of the multidisciplinary team approach as well as a referral for a psychiatric medication evaluation and obtaining a release of information to inform the primary care physician of the individual at risk of harm. Needless to say, the amount and type of medications to address such a clinical presentation needs to be carefully chosen and titrated when the individual is deemed to be under the influence of alcohol, illicit substances, or other medication in prescribed or overdose amounts. All of which highlights the importance of the multidisciplinary approach and thorough documentation of pertinent information and coinciding interventions.

Although depressive symptoms are often associated with risk for suicide, no antidepressant medication has yet to be shown to lower suicide risk in depressed patients. However, because of the relationship between low cerebrospinal fluid (CSF) serotonin levels and the emergence of aggression and impulsivity, the selective serotonin reuptake inhibitors (SSRIs) have been recommended for the treatment of depressive disorders when suicidal risk is present. However, treatment with SSRIs must be carefully monitored and managed during the initial treatment phase because of the potential for the possible emergence of suicidal ideation and behaviors during this time. The FDA has recently created a black box warning when prescribing SSRIs for persons under the age of 25.

MYTHS ABOUT SUICIDE

There are many myths about suicide and suicidal behavior that have been passed down through generations of health-care providers that some providers still believe today and may have actually been taught. Examples of these myths are as follows:

Myth: Asking about suicide would plant the idea in the patient's head.

Reality: Asking how your patient feels doesn't create suicidal thoughts any more than asking how your patient's chest feels would cause angina.

Myth: There are talkers and there are doers.

Reality: Most people who die by suicide have communicated some intent. Someone who talks about suicide gives the physician an opportunity to intervene before suicidal behaviors occur.

Myth: If somebody really wants to die by suicide, there is nothing you can do about it.

Reality: Most suicidal ideas are associated with the presence of underlying treatable disorders. Providing a safe environment for treatment of the underlying cause can save lives. The acute risk for suicide is often time limited. If you can help the person survive the immediate crisis and the strong intent to die by suicide, then you will have gone a long way toward promoting a positive outcome.

Myth: He/she really wouldn't kill themselves since _____.
  • he just made plans for a vacation
  • she has young children at home

- he signed a no-harm contract
- he knows how dearly his family loves him

Reality: The intent to die can override any rational thinking. In the presence of suicidal ideation or intent, the physician should not be dissuaded from thinking that the patient is capable of acting on these thoughts and feelings. No-harm or no-suicide contracts have been shown to be essentially worthless from a clinical and management perspective. The anecdotal reports of their usefulness can all be explained by the strength of the alliance with the care provider that results from such a collaborative exchange, not from the specifics of the contract itself.

Myth: Multiple and apparently manipulative self-injurious behaviors mean that the patient is just trying to get attention and are not really suicidal.

Reality: Suicide "gestures" require thoughtful assessment and treatment. Multiple prior suicide attempts increase the likelihood of eventually dying by suicide. The task is to empathically and nonjudgmentally engage the patient in understanding the behavior and finding safer and healthier ways of asking for help.

(American Psychiatric Association, 2004; Beautrais, 2003; Brown et al., 2004; CDC, 2005; Kessler et al., 1999; Owens et al., 2002; Russ et al., 2006; Silver, Kramer, Greenwald, & Weissman, 2001; Simpson & Tate, 2002; Teasdale & Engberg, 2001).

SUICIDE ASSESSMENT OUTLINE

1. Assessing suicidal ideation
   A. Ask directly if they have thoughts of suicide.
   B. Are the thoughts pervasive or intermittent with a definite relationship to given situation?
   C. Do they have a plan; if so, how extensive/detailed is their plan?
   D. Lethality of the means/method defined.
   E. Is there access to the identified means?
2. Individual risk factor review
   A. Demographics with highest risk:
      1. Age (teens, middle age, and elderly are at highest risk)
      2. Gender (males more often succeed at suicide attempts because of the lethality of means, but females make more attempts)
      3. Homosexuals (additional stressors/lack of social supports)
      4. Race (white)
      5. Bipolar disorder
      6. Marital status (separated, widowed, divorced)
      7. Social support (lack of support system, living alone)
      8. Employment status (unemployed, change in status, or performance)
   B. Family history: suicide, suicide behaviors, psychiatric disorder(s)
   C. Psychiatric history (past/present): mood, anxiety, psychotic, alcohol/drug, personality disorder
   D. Medical illness: chronic/acute, disabling, stigmatizing, dependency/self-care issues
   E. Poor social supports: isolated, living alone, poor social network, unhealthy relationships
   F. Domestic problems: exploitive/unhealthy relationships, abuse/violence, conflict, pressure, general dysfunction
   G. Poor stress tolerance: ineffective coping, poor self-management, ineffective problem solving, ineffective decision making
   H. History of suicidal behaviors: suicide attempts, planned but aborted attempts, self-harm/self-destructive behaviors
      1. Suicide attempts:
         a. Immediate referral for a medical evaluation for medical stability method of attempt warrants it
            1. Means, location, collaborator, rescuer, number of attempts
            2. Thoroughness of plan and its implementation
            3. Note signs of impairment and physical harm
            4. Level of treatment required (least restrictive for safety)

*Intention, plan, method, means, lethality, and prior attempts.

     I. History of abuse: recent or current abuse/violence, childhood abuse
     J. Exposure to suicide (direct/indirect): family, friends, community, culture, social media

3. Risk factors
    A. Intention and history
        1. Recent/prior attempts or gestures
        2. Direct or indirect communication of intent
        3. Extensiveness of plan
        4. Lethality of means
        5. Access to means
        6. Family history of suicidal behaviors
    B. Demographics with highest risk
        1. Age (teens, middle age, and elderly are at highest risk)
        2. Gender (males more often succeed at suicide attempts because of the lethality of means, but females make more attempts)
        3. Homosexuals (additional stressors/lack of social supports)
        4. Race (white)
        5. Bipolar disorder
        6. Marital status (separated, widowed, divorced)
        7. Social support (lack of support system, living alone)
        8. Employment status (unemployed, change in status, or performance)
    C. Emotional functioning
        1. Diagnosis (major depression/severe anhedonia, recovery from recent depression, schizophrenia, alcoholism, bipolar disorder, borderline personality disorder)
        2. Intense emotion (anxiety/panic, shame, humiliation, guilt, anger, isolation/loneliness)
        3. Shutdown (emotional withdrawal, disengaged, noncommunicative)
        4. Severe self-reproach/worthlessness
        5. Impaired reasoning (rigid thinking, poor judgment/problem solving/decision making) and ineffective coping ability
        6. Poor self-control (impulsivity, poor regulation of emotions/behaviors, violence/aggression)
        7. Psychosis (for example, auditory hallucination commanding death)
        8. SUD
        9. Recent loss or anniversary of a loss
        10. Fantasy to reunite with a dead loved one
        11. Stresses (chronic or associated with recent changes—severe legal/financial problems)
        12. Degree of hopelessness or despair
    D. Behavioral patterns
        1. Isolation
        2. Impulsivity
        3. Rigid
    E. Physical condition
        1. Chronic insomnia
        2. Chronic pain
        3. Progressive illness
        4. Recent childbirth
4. Cumulative interview risk overview
    A. *Suicidal ideation* (frequency, intensity, duration, persistence): One hypothesis is that many people who think about suicide are difficult to engage in treatment because they lack motivation to live and therefore lack interest in and energy for treatment
    B. *Suicide intent* (degree of ambivalence, commitment to die): Many individuals who think about suicide are ambivalent; they want to die, but they also want to live with less pain

C. *Suicide plan* (method, means, lethality, preparation)

D. *Concealed suicidality* (warning signs, verbal/nonverbal cues, collateral contact concerns/clinical intuition)

E. *Past suicide attempt* (number of attempts, trigger, context, method, lethality, consequences)

F. *Access to lethal means* (availability/access)

G. *Recent substance use/intoxication*

H. *Suicide trigger* (recent or unfolding crisis, anticipated crisis/conflict/loss, victimization, trauma)

I. *Unsolvable problem* (unable to see a solution, unable/unwilling to search for/identify solutions)

J. *Intolerable emotional state* (degree of emotional/psychological/physical distress is unbearable)

5. Resilience refers to the factors that safeguard or act as a shock absorber

A. Reasons for living

B. Internal strengths and resources

C. External resources

While many of these factors appear to be of a general nature, it is the clustering of these factors, which contribute to the person's mood, belief system, and coping ability that may lead to the risk of suicide.

MOTIVATIONAL INTERVIEWING

Motivational interviewing (MI) is essential to suicide prevention efforts. MI is a therapeutic approach that was developed to help individuals, presenting with substance use related with problems, find the motivation to change problematic behavior (Miller & Rollnick, 2002). MI is a client-centered method thoughtfully structured to engage the patient in the process of moving to a more functional clinical position of engaging in change. The principles of MI include (1) expressing empathy for clients' experiences, (2) rolling with resistance rather than confronting and escalating conflict, (3) developing discrepancy between actual and desired behavior, (4) and promoting self-efficacy that change is achievable. It is directive in that clinicians strategically guide their patients toward the desired outcome. Fundamental techniques of MI include (1) reflective listening to ensure that clients feel understood, (2) open-ended questions to encourage client elaboration, (3) affirmations to support clients' self-efficacy, (4) and summaries to help clients integrate and reinforce what was discussed. These techniques are strategically used to build the patent's motivation and commitment to change. Generally, clinicians avoid being directive during the interview process and course of treatment. However, in the case of MI the use of directive techniques, such as providing information and making recommendations, is viewed as appropriate and beneficial to eliminating or alleviating the risk of harm while increasing the buffers against harm (Hettema, Steele, & Miller, 2005).

Resolving ambivalence by increasing the motivation to live is critical to reducing engagement in life-threatening behavior and may also increase engagement in life-sustaining behavior such as treatment. The use of MI with suicidal clients is a logical precursor to CBT for suicide prevention. CBT for suicidal patients (Wenzel, Brown, & Beck, 2009) is an active, short-term intervention that is divided into three phases—an early phase that is focused on treatment engagement, an intermediate phase that is focused on the application of cognitive and behavioral strategies, and a later phase that is focused on relapse prevention.

ADOLESCENT SUICIDE

Suicide is the third leading cause of death for 15- to 24-year olds and the sixth leading cause of death for 5- to 14-year olds. Adolescents feel tremendous stress, pressure, confusion, fear, and self-doubt, perhaps more than at any other stage of life. For some teens, suicide may appear to be the only solution to their experience of emotional distress and other problems that result in feeling overwhelmed and hopeless. The prevalence of youth suicide attempts and completions is a clear indication of the importance of early identification and intervention to ameliorate risk. Of all of the risk factors for this population, depression presents the most significant biological and psychological risk.

Adolescents are endeavoring to navigate a confusing and challenging development stage of life that contributes to increased risk of becoming overwhelmed and an inability to effectively cope with the consequences of experimentation and questionable/poor choices that are specific to the angst of their stage of life. Since their presentation will be influenced by these developmental, social, and self-discovery issues, there are numerous relevant issues to be explored when a teenager has entered treatment.

Behavioral and Social Clues

1. Heavy drug use

2. Change in academic performance

3. Recent loss of a love object, or impending loss
4. Pregnancy
5. LGBT (additional stressors/lack of social support)
6. Running away
7. Prior suicide attempts or family history of suicide
8. Intense anger
9. Preoccupation with the violent death of another person
10. Impulsivity
11. Learning disability
12. Ineffective coping
13. Lack of resources and feelings of alienation
14. Hopelessness, depression
15. Risk-taking behaviors (playing in traffic, intentional reckless driving, etc.)
16. Loss of support system or being bullied (cyber bullying)
17. Recent move, change in school
18. Loss of family status (family member leaves or is removed from the home, change in economic level of family, abandonment by family due to completion of high school/turning 18 years of age)
19. Feeling anonymous and unimportant
20. Peer group activity associated with issue of death

Clinicians recognize the risk that can be associated with depression and that includes adolescent risk. In assessing adolescents, the symptoms of depression may not be indicated as directly as when assessing an adult. This is referred to as masked depression. Masked depression can be described in two ways:

1. *Classic*: Somatic complaints take the place of the general criteria of depression. There are chronic complaints of headaches, backaches, and stomachache.
2. *Behavioral*: Evidenced by acting out behaviors such as substance abuse, promiscuity, shoplifting. These are all representations of ways of converting affective state interpreted as boredom into something exciting. Young people are sometimes ineffective in expressing their depression. Therefore, they translate it into something else and project it outward, finding boredom in school, peers, and family. The use of substances may be an attempt to cope with emotional distress, lack of identity, or boredom. They may see the world as boring and unfulfilling. Males tend to act out more aggressively in their environments.

ADOLESCENT SUICIDE ASSESSMENT

Suicide assessments used for adult populations are inadequate seeking the individualized information needed to accurately understand an adolescent considering suicide (National Action Alliance for Suicide Prevention, 2013). When assessing adolescents who have been identified as being at imminent risk for suicide, there is no diagnostic tool validated at "predicting" the outcome of suicide. However, there are critical items, common risk factors, associated with suicidal ideation and adolescents. If the answer to any of the items below is yes, expand information, give time frames, identify symptoms, etc.

1. Family history of suicide ___yes ___no

   _____

   _____

   _____

2. Suicide of a friend ___yes ___no

_____

_____

_____

3. Depression ___yes ___no

_____

_____

_____

4. Overwhelmed by any problems that seem unresolvable ___yes ___no

_____

_____

_____

5. Lack of social support ___yes ___no

_____

_____

_____

6. Problematic family circumstances and/or social situations ___yes ___no

_____

_____

_____

7. Finding pleasure in normally pleasurable activities ___yes ___no

_____

_____

_____

8. Anger ___yes ___no

_____

_____

_____

9. Acts of impulsivity ___yes ___no

_____

_____

_____

10. History of psychiatric illness and treatment ___yes ___no

_____

_____

_____

11. Evidence of psychotic symptoms (ask directly about command hallucination for both suicidal and homicidal content)

_____

_____

_____

12. Suicidal ideation ___yes ___no

_____

_____

_____

13. Suicide plan, means, access to means ___yes ___no

_____

_____

_____

Plan: _____

Means: _____

Access to means: _____

14. Prior suicide attempts ___yes ___no

_____

_____

_____

15. Substance abuse ____yes ___no

_____

_____

_____

If yes—has most recent use/what substance(s) been within the last 24 h.

ASQ: SUICIDE-SCREENING QUESTIONNAIRE

Ask Suicide-Screening Questions (ASQ) is a screening instrument validated for pediatric as well as young adult populations. The screen consists of four questions and takes less than 2 min to administer (Horowitz et al., 2012).

Ask Suicide Screening Questions

1. In the past few weeks, have you wished you were dead?
   Yes ___ No ___ No response ___
2. In the past few weeks, have you felt that you or your family would be better off if you were dead?
   Yes ___ No ___ No response ___
3. In the past week, have you been having thoughts about killing yourself?
   Yes ___ No ___ No response ___

4. Have you ever tried to kill yourself?

    Yes ___ No ___ No response ___

    If yes, how? _____

    When? _____

TOOLS FOR SUICIDE ASSESSMENT AND SCREENING

*Tools for screening and assessing adolescent suicide risk (source: www.reconnectingyouth.com)

1. Identifying and assessing suicide risk level: National Action Alliance for Suicide Prevention (http://zerosuicide.actionallianceforsuicideprevention.org). This Web-based resource offers information on suicide screening in health-care and behavioral health settings as well as links to additional resources.
2. National Institutes of Health (www.nim.nih) offers the following information (retrieved from the web, July 17, 2016):
    A. Screening for Suicide Risk in Adolescents, Adults, and Older Adults in Primary Care (US Preventive Services Task Force)
    B. Suicide: What to Do When Someone Is Suicidal (Mayo Foundation for Medical Education and Research)

TREATMENT FOCUS AND OBJECTIVES

The goal of preventing suicide is initiated by the assessment of risk factors, covert messages, overt suicide clues, and a constructive intervention with the patient and their family (when appropriate). Suicide risk and despair/hopelessness decrease as the suicidal adolescent learns to identify and clarify problems, utilize social support, develop additional resources that address specific needs, and use safe coping/management strategies. Interventions include coping skill development, treatment for psychiatric disorders and SUDs, a no-suicide contract, family therapy and school suicide prevention programs (primary, secondary, and college age), and a comprehensive relapse prevention program.

The type of intervention is based on efforts to problem-solve and provide a safe environment for the suicidal person.

1. Outpatient therapy and management: Utilized when the risk of suicide is low, the precipitating crisis is no longer present, there is an adequate support system, and the person contracts that they will contact the therapist if they are unable to cope. Least restrictive and appropriate means of intervention are always utilized.
2. Hospitalization: Utilized if the person is at high risk for suicide, lacks adequate social supports, lacks adequate impulse control, is intoxicated, or is psychotic. For the benefit of the person, initially pursue the least restrictive course of a voluntary admission. If they are unwilling and the criteria are present, an involuntary admission is warranted, which will necessitate an evaluation by the appropriately designated persons/facility in your area.
3. Techniques (associated with least restrictive interventions and degree of risk).
    A. Alleviate the person's isolation by recommending that they stay with family or friends.
    B. Support the development and utilization of a support system, or the reestablishment of their support system.
    C. Facilitate the removal of weapons or other means of a suicide attempt from their environment. Deal with issues of substances (abuse) if necessary.
    D. Facilitate the appropriate expression of anger or other feelings that are contributing to self-destructive impulses.
    E. Validate the person's experience of the crisis, but also identify their ambivalence and the fact that suicide is a permanent solution to a temporary problem.

F. Refer for medication evaluation making sure that the physician is aware of the person's suicidal ideation/impulses.

G. Educate the person regarding the impact that a lack of sleep has on effectively coping, and reassure them that the depression can be managed or eliminated.

H. Identify irrational, negative beliefs. Help the person recognize that the associated negative self-talk contributes to keeping them in a state of hopelessness. Facilitate the identification of alternatives to the difficulties that they are currently experiencing.

I. Do not verbally or nonverbally express shock or horror.

J. Do not emphasize how much they have upset other people.

K. Do not offer psychological or moral edicts of suicide.

L. Explore with person what they hoped to accomplish by suicide.

M. Identify life issues that have contributed to person's emotional state.

N. Discuss the fact that suicide is a permanent solution.

O. Review resources and relationships (family, friends, family physician, clergy, employer, police, emergency response team, therapist, community support groups, 12-step groups, emergency room, psychiatric hospital).

P. Be reassuring and supportive.

Q. Facilitate improved problem solving and coping.

R. Facilitate development of a self-care program.
   1. Daily structure
   2. Inclusion of pleasurable activities
   3. Resources/support system (including therapy and medication compliance)
   4. Identify crisis/potential crisis situations and plausible choices for coping
   5. Identify warning signs (self-monitoring) that indicate that the person is not utilizing their self-care plan, medication difficulties, etc.
   6. Regular aerobic exercise and good nutrition

DEPRESSION RELAPSE AND SUICIDE RISK

People who are chronically depressed with an associated impact to quality of life or those who experience episodes of major depression, recurrent (ICD 10; F33) are at risk for suicide. Thoughts of suicide and at times intent is a key symptom of this impacting mental illness. Some studies show that the neurotransmitter serotonin plays a central role in the neurobiology of suicide. Researchers have found lower levels of serotonin in the brain stem and CSF of suicidal individuals suggesting it is associated with suicidality (WebMD, August 31, 2014).

Suicide does not begin with the self-destructive gesture. It begins with feelings of isolation, hopelessness, sleep disturbance, inability to cope, and other symptoms related to change, loss, or impulse control. Warning signs that serve as a potential red flag that there is an impending crisis include the following:

1. A general feeling that things are not going well "a pervasive negative outlook." They feel that life is not worth living, and they cannot manage day-to-day activities.

2. Denial. A belief by an individual that they lack control over their life, "there is no hope." Tendency to blame other people or situations for how they feel associated with an external locus of control. As a result of not dealing with what they are experiencing, there is a tendency toward decompensation.

3. Attempts to help others while disregarding the priority of self-care. They become involved in other people's issues and avoid dealing with their own resulting in a negative cumulative impact of overwhelming distress.

4. Defensiveness. Taking the position that they are doing fine and do not need the help of other people, resources, or medication.

5. Old behavior that the person has changed because of its negative role emotionally begins to surface as a result of personal neglect or a threshold of negative psychosocial stressors. This could be looking at pictures or listening to songs that make them sad, reading old love letters, etc.

6. Focus on negatives. The person focuses on a negative perspective rather than the positive view of things, which increases feelings of helplessness.

7. Impulsive behaviors. The person begins to make rash decisions and participates in risk-taking behavior. Decisions are often made under stress and without thinking through choices and consequences. Adds to the degree of distress experienced.

8. Isolation and withdrawal continue. The person makes up excuses and avoids socializing and utilizing much needed resources—even when a resource list has been developed.

9. Physical symptoms begin to appear such as appetite disturbance, sleep disturbance, fatigue, headaches, etc. Exacerbation of physical distress and somatization are not uncommon for those experiencing depression and anxiety that may be underlying suicidality.

10. The person does not maintain their daily schedule, finding it difficult to get everything done as they previously had been able to do, and this breakdown in effectiveness spreads to not being able to deal with daily life demands.

11. Hopelessness. The person feels that nothing will ever improve, that everything is a mess, and that life is not worth living. Hopelessness can escalate to despair.

12. The person is often confused and irritated. This low frustration tolerance affects all areas of life.

13. Breaking relations and associations. The person disengages from their support system. They may not feel the energy to participate or may believe that nothing and no one will make a difference in how they think and feel.

14. Energy level is diminished. The person does little or nothing, spends their time daydreaming/checked-out, and does not follow through on tasks.

15. Lack of sleep or poor sleep patterns begin to negatively impact their ability to effectively cope.

16. Depression becomes more severe in intensity and chronic. As a result, quality of life and relationships are significantly affected.

17. The person begins to miss therapy appointments. Self-care and treatment are a low priority.

18. The person expresses dissatisfaction with life, immersed in a negative perspective of everything going on around them. A negative self-fulfilling prophecy takes hold.

19. The person takes on the victim role that fosters helplessness and hopelessness.

20. Having thoughts of death or a "death wish." They do not want to kill themselves, but they want to escape their pain and see death as a state of not feeling the pain.

21. The person gets their life in order by making a will, giving things away, or saying goodbye as they emotionally detach.

22. The person appears to be doing much better following a depressive episode, which actually provides them with enough energy to attempt suicide.

23. Feeling overwhelmed and unable to cope. Not able to adequately problem-solve situations that normally would not present any difficulty.

24. Thoughts of suicide begin, and the person starts thinking about methods of suicide.

25. The person begins to demonstrate self-destructive patterns of behavior.

DANGEROUSNESS

Forensic psychiatrists and psychologists are increasing being requested to evaluate individuals demonstrating questionable/violent behavior to assess the risk of future danger. This forensic evaluation has become a proximate standard of the legal system, being essential to commitment hearings, capital sentencing proceedings, bail and parole determinations, assessing sexually violent predators, and sex offender registrants. The role of the MHP in assessing the potential for violence is to prevent injury and to provide the necessary care to people who are acting out violently or on the verge of losing control. The imminent concern of violent behavior is the potential harm of one person by another. Denial of an individual's civil liberties is a serious matter (Phillips, 2012).

Violence itself is not a diagnosable mental disorder or illness, but rather the symptom of an underlying disorder and problems with impulse control. It is important to not discount or disregard the signs of potential violence. Instead, it provides a crisis situation that requires effective control before further interventions can be made.

The central priority of dealing with the potentially violent person is to insure the safety of the person, other individuals within close proximity, and your own safety. If the person assumes an aggressive and hostile position, steps must immediately be taken to maintain a safe environment. Often these people are fearful of losing control over their violent impulses, and as a result, they are defending against feelings of helplessness or have learned intimidation serves as a method of perceived control when in emotional distress. The immediate goal in intervening is to help the person regain control over their aggressive impulses.

DANGEROUSNESS ASSESSMENT OUTLINE

Factors for Risk Assessments

Risk assessments must satisfy the following factors:

1. Prediction
   A. Probability of future acts of violence.
   B. Identification of risk factors associated with potential future acts of violence.
2. Management
   A. Problem-solve interventions to manage/decrease the probability of future violence.
   B. Identify and implement needed treatment interventions to decrease level of risk.
   C. Comprehensively review and predict scenarios of increased risk/recidivism.

Assessments associated with mandated reporting, thus the legal realm, include forensic psychiatric dangerousness and risk management.

1. Assess thoughts of violence
   A. Ask directly if they have thoughts of harming another person.
   B. Are the thoughts pervasive or transient (venting without intent) in relationship to a response to a given situation?
   C. Do they have a plan, if so, how extensive is their plan?
   D. What are the means to be used in harming someone?
   E. Do they have access to the planned means/method?
2. Do they have a history of violent behavior (have they ever seriously harmed another person)?
3. Does the person wish to be helped to manage aggressive impulses?
4. If you are in the process of interviewing someone with a history of violent behavior, be alert to signs of agitation and losing control:
   A. If it is determined that the person is at risk to harm another person, immediate steps need to be taken. If they demonstrate some semblance of being reasonable aside from their aggressive impulse toward another person, focus on their ambivalence and talk with them about voluntary admission to a hospital to gain control over the impulses and to learn appropriate means of dealing with their feelings. If there is concern that such a discussion would only escalate a person who is already demonstrating significant agitation, then contact the police for transport to a hospital.
   B. Remember: Having thoughts of wanting to harm someone and having the intention of acting on them are two different issues. If threats with intent to harm are present, there is a duty to contact the police and the intended victim so that precautions can be taken.
5. Risk factors—seeks to reveal insight into factors such as risk and *recidivism risk* for violence, DV, stalking, and sexual assaults/offenses. Absence of empathy for others.
   A. Intention and history
      1. Specific plan for injuring or killing someone
      2. Access or possession of the intended weapon of use
      3. History of previous acts of violence
      4. History of homicidal threats
      5. Recent incident of provocation
      6. Conduct disorder behavior in childhood/antisocial adult behavior
      7. Victim of child abuse

B. Demographics
   1. Gender (males are at higher risk to act out aggressive impulses)
   2. Low socioeconomic status (increased frustrations, general feelings of lack of control in life, aggressive environment, or survival issues)
   3. Social support (lack of support system)
   4. Overt stressors (marital conflict, unemployment)
C. Emotional functioning
   1. Diagnosis (depression with agitation, drug/alcohol intoxication or withdrawal, delirium, mania, paranoid or catatonic schizophrenia, temporal lobe epilepsy, antisocial personality disorder, paranoid personality disorder)
D. Behavioral patterns
   1. Poor impulse control
   2. Extreme lability of affect
   3. Excessive aggressiveness
   4. Easily agitated and signs of tension
   5. Loud or abusive speech
   6. Bizarre behavior or verbalization

FORENSIC PSYCHIATRIST DANGEROUSNESS AND RISK ASSESSMENT (THE FORENSIC PANEL)

As the subdiscipline of psychiatric risk assessment stands today, data on which judgments about dangerousness or recidivism are to be made should meet the following criteria:

1. "Dangerousness" or the potential for recidivism must be distinguished into clearly enumerating risk factors, nature of harm, and likelihood of occurrence. An array of psychiatric risk factors must be assessed from multiple domains in the offender's life, across the offenders' life span, including diagnostic considerations.
2. Risk assessment and recidivism prediction should incorporate what is known about the pertinent subpopulation, such as violent offenders, stalkers, or pedophiles.
3. More reliable predictions are available from actuarial research rather than mere clinical judgment alone.

*This final point is a testament to the importance than those who endeavor to provide forensic evaluations to be of the highest level of clinical psychology and psychiatry.

TREATMENT FOCUS AND OBJECTIVES

1. Outpatient setting
   A. Have a prior plan worked out with office staff for intervening with reinforcement of security guards or police if escalation is a concern.
   B. Establish a nonthreatening setting for the interview. Do not turn your back to the person, be aware of personal space, and position yourself close to the door in case an exit for safety is necessary.
   C. Provide supportive feedback, reflecting to them that you recognize that they are upset. Encourage them to talk about what is wrong.
   D. Set firm and consistent limits on violent behavior, and encourage the person to verbally express what they are feeling instead of acting on the aggressive impulses.
   E. Establish a collaborative environment, being respectful to the person.
   F. Be reassuring, calm, and if necessary assist in reality testing.
   G. Refer for medication evaluation.
   H. Identify personal and community resources.
   I. Encourage them to take responsibility and emphasize appropriate choices.

J. Clarify the connection between actions and consequences.

K. Initiate counseling on anger management or refer to a community group focusing on anger management.

L. Teach assertive communication.

M. Encourage appropriate physical exercise to discharge body tension.

N. Positive reinforcement for efforts and accomplishments.

O. Maintain keen awareness for your own reaction to the person.

P. End the interview if there are signs of increasing agitation. Inform the person that you sense the difficulty that they are experiencing in maintaining self-control.

2. Inpatient setting

If the person is hospitalized, the appropriate intervention selection will be based on the person's level of agitation and their ability to self-monitor and to respond appropriately. The basic goal is to provide a safe environment.

A. Give supportive feedback, and encourage appropriate ventilation and expression of feelings.

B. Maintain personal safety behaviors at all times (don't turn your back on the person, position yourself close to the door, leave the door open, maintain adequate distance).

C. Set clear and consistent limits. Educate the person about what is expected of them and how they will benefit by cooperation and collaboration.

D. Provide them with appropriate structure to discharge body tension.

E. Set physical limits on violent behaviors when verbal limits are not sufficient. Call for help immediately if there are signs of escalation with impending violent behavior. As attending you must assume a role of leadership to assure the staff and the person that you are prepared to take charge and direct the necessary step to insure safety of the person, unit peers, and staff. If possible, offer the person choices of self-restraint for regaining control. If they are not able to comply, seclude a patient demonstrating risk, and if warranted use restraints. At the very least the person should spend some time in the quiet room that is free of objects and easy to monitor, until they have time to regain composure and take responsibility for their behavior and be able to offer plausible alternatives for dealing with feelings of agitation or hostility. Consult with the treatment team psychiatrist regarding medication if person is unable to calm down and remains in an agitated state.

F. Provide education on assertive communication.

G. Provide education on anger management.

H. Provide education regarding the relationship between behavior and consequences.

I. Encourage the person to take responsibility for their behaviors.

J. Positive reinforcement for efforts and accomplishments.

GRAVELY DISABLED

Welfare and Institutions code section 5008(h)(1) (A) defines the term "gravely disabled" as a condition in which a person, *as a result of a mental disorder*, is unable to provide for his or her basic personal needs for food, clothing, or shelter. Note that, the existence of a mental disorder does not, in itself, justify a finding of grave disability (W&I Code 5008(3)).

In making a presentation to show grave disability, one should consider the following abilities of an individual:

1. Utilizing the means available to provide for his/her basic personal needs regarding food, clothing, or shelter

2. Voluntarily requesting and receiving assistance to meet his/her personal needs

3. Surviving safely, without involuntary detention, with the help of family members, friends, or others who are both willing and able to help provide for the person's basic needs regarding food, clothing, or shelter (W&I Code 5350(e))

An additional avenue of intervention could be a conservatorship. For this process to be initiated requires an evaluation by an authorized psychiatrist. A mental health (LPS) conservatorship makes one adult (called the conservator) responsible for a mentally ill adult (called the conservatee). These conservatorships are only for adults with mental illnesses listed in the Diagnostic and Statistical Manual of Mental Disorders (DSM).

The following are the most common illnesses that are serious, biological brain disorders:

1. Schizophrenia
2. Bipolar disorder (manic depression)
3. Schizoaffective disorder
4. Clinical depression
5. Obsessive compulsive disorder

*LPS conservatorships are not for people with organic brain disorders, brain trauma, retardation, alcohol or drug addiction, or dementia, unless they also have one of the serious brain disorders listed in the DSM.

"Gravely disabled minor" means a minor who, as a result of a mental disorder, is unable to use the elements of life, which are essential to health, safety, and development, including food, clothing, and shelter, even though provided to the minor by others. Intellectual disability, epilepsy, or other developmental disabilities, alcoholism, other drug abuse, or repeated antisocial behavior do not, by themselves, constitute a mental disorder (Section 5585.25 W&I Code).

FOUNDATION OF GRAVELY DISABLED

The gravely disabled individual is unable to provide for their basic necessities of food, clothing, and shelter. The gravely disabled state may be due to the following:

1. Confusion
2. Hallucinations
3. Delusional thinking
4. Impaired reality testing
5. Psychomotor agitation
6. Lack of motivation
7. Memory impairment
8. Impaired judgment
9. Undersocialization

Some behavioral indicators of being gravely disabled include the following:

1. Unable to dress self
2. Incontinent (without responsibly dealing with it)
3. Not eating/drinking
4. Deterioration of hygiene
5. Inability to maintain medical regime
6. Unable to provide residence for self

TREATMENT FOCUS AND OBJECTIVES

1. Inadequate hygiene [teach basic hygiene and activities of daily living (ADLs)]
   A. Person to seek assistance with bowel/bladder function

B. Person will bathe/shower on their own

C. Person will brush teeth, comb hair, shave, and dress appropriately daily

2. Uncooperative

   A. Person will be able to verbalize/demonstrate acceptance of daily assistance

   B. Person will comply with medication/medical regimen

   C. Person will accept assistance with living arrangement

   D. Person will accept long-term assistance

3. Inadequate nutrition/fluids

   A. Person will drink an adequate intake of fluids to maintain hydration

   B. Person will eat a balanced diet

4. Family nonsupportive or lacks understanding of needed intervention

   A. Family education regarding person's prognosis and necessary support/structure

   B. Community support group

5. Inadequate coping

   A. Consequences of noncompliance with medication

   B. Self-care management

   C. Facilitate problem solving and conflict resolution for practical situations that the person is likely to encounter

   D. Facilitate development of adequate social skills

      1. Provide opportunities for social interaction

      2. Model and role-play appropriate social behaviors

   E. Facilitate development of management of anger and frustration

   F. Teach relaxation training

   G. Identify leisure skills

6. Improved ability to manage and improve judgment

   A. Evaluate for conservatorship

7. Inadequate/inappropriate living arrangement

   A. Consider placement

      1. Board and care facility

      2. Planned senior citizen community with therapeutic and medical care

         a. Must ask permission of spouse for participation in appropriate adult activities

         b. Social isolation

         c. Reluctance of a spouse (offender) to allow spouse to be seen alone

         d. History of child abuse

         e. Behavior problems in children

ACTIVITIES OF DAILY LIVING

In evaluating competency as it pertains to self-care and self-sufficiency, there are standard behavioral issues to be assessed. This is a general review of ADLs, which need to be adapted to age-appropriate criteria when making an assessment. ADLs are the actions necessary for living independently, but not all are required activities on a daily basis.

Five Basic Categories of Activities of Daily Living

1. Personal hygiene—bathing, grooming, and oral care

2. Dressing—the ability to make appropriate clothing decisions and physically dress oneself

3. Eating—the ability to feed oneself though not necessarily to prepare food

4. Maintaining continence—both the mental and physical ability to use a restroom

5. Transferring—moving oneself from seated to standing and get in and out of bed

Whether or not an individual is capable of performing these activities on their own or if they rely on a family caregiver to perform the ADLs serves a comparative measure of their independence.

Other Activities of Daily Living

1. Basic communication skills—such as using a regular phone, mobile phone, email, or the Internet
2. Transportation—either by driving oneself, arranging rides, or the ability to use public transportation
3. Meal preparation—meal planning, preparation, storage, and the ability to safely use kitchen equipment
4. Shopping—the ability to make appropriate food and clothing purchase decisions
5. Housework—doing laundry, cleaning dishes, and maintaining a hygienic place of residence
6. Managing medications—taking accurate dosages at the appropriate times, managing refills, and avoiding conflicts
7. Managing personal finances—operating within a budget, writing checks, paying bills, and avoiding scams

LIVING SITUATION

Assessing the living situation encompasses the level of support needed in any given living situation/environment.

1. Does the individual live independently in their own home or apartment?
2. Do they reside with family members or other individuals, board and care facility, custodial care facility, residential drug treatment facility, nursing home, skilled care facility, etc.?
   A. Do they live there independently or require the care/support/monitoring of those with whom they reside?
3. Do they utilize community support services such as "meals on wheels," home health services, someone hired to care for them, etc.?
4. Do they attend school, sheltered workshop, day treatment, day activities center, social club, rehabilitation/training program?

SELF-CARE SKILLS

Assessing the level of knowledge of basic needs such as food, clothing, hygiene, grooming, compliance with treatment issues.

1. Feeds self appropriately, adequately
2. Bathes regularly, shaving if necessary, deodorant, hair cut/combed
3. Dresses self appropriately, buys clothes, does laundry
4. Medication and treatment compliance

LEVEL OF REQUIRED ASSISTANCE

Assessing the level of ability of assistance required.

1. Incapable or unable to provide sufficiently for some of own self-care needs
2. Limited by physical or mental condition
3. Can only carry out simple tasks
4. Can only carry out simple tasks under the supervision or direction of others
5. Can initiate and complete tasks without being reminded, assisted, or prompted by others

State/identify if ADLs are done by another individual for this person and to what degree assistance is required.

CARE OF ENVIRONMENT AND CHORE RESPONSIBILITIES

1. Individual takes care of all basic housecleaning tasks and yard tasks.
2. The qualities of care in these tasks are functional, neat, clean, (un)cluttered, (dis)organized, completion, done in an orderly manner.

Meals
Eats fast food, carryout, junk foods, snacks, prepared foods, sandwiches, simple cooking, boils/fries, full menu; is able to use all kitchen appliances; coordinates all aspects of a meal.

Childcare
Assesses for neglect, abuse, people living in the household and their contact with the child, issues related to entertainment. Additionally assesses for the positive, for example actively supervises child and does not leave them alone; teaches age-appropriate information/tasks; appropriately advocates for child.

Financial
Assesses ability to count, make change, recognition of coins and paper currency; is able to write checks, deposit checks/currency, do routine banking procedures; demonstrates ability to spend and save appropriately; effectively manages financial resources.

Shopping
Assesses ability to shop for personal toiletries, clothing, food, etc.

Transportation
Assesses ability to effectively available modes of transportation and to plan for necessary scheduling.

CRISIS ASSESSMENT

Numerous possibilities exist that could be placed under the conceptual umbrella of crisis assessment. However, the focus of the information in this section will be on the crisis of traumatic stress. The next two sections (Guidelines for Crisis Intervention and Crisis Assessment, Intervention, and Traumatic Exposure) are two different perspectives from which to approach assessment and intervention for a person exposed to a traumatic evident.

GUIDELINES FOR CRISIS INTERVENTION

Since the assessment of someone who has experienced traumatic exposure may also be their first behavioral health intervention, it is important for the therapist to think in terms of information that is important to both understanding and adjustment of the survivor. The following considerations are interventions that play a role in the crisis assessment and that are also going to be engaging the patient in thinking about what they have experienced and how they have been affected.

1. Explain the process, being sure that the patient understands that they are in control of the situation and if they need time to calm themselves, take a break or reschedule they can inform the therapist. If the patient is not able to complete the assessment and feels a need to leave, be sure they understand that problem solving associated with debriefing will take place before they leave the appointment location and reschedule for a later time.
2. Elicit the patient's description of what occurred. Encourage a thorough description of visual, auditory, and olfactory experience. Does the client play a role in what happened? If not, what do they know about it, and how did they learn about it.
3. Review their previous level of functioning, and rule out a cumulative effect from prior crisis experiences that have not been resolved.
4. What was the patient feeling and thinking before, during, or immediately after the event? What have been their feelings and thoughts about the situation since then?
5. Clarify the patient's reaction. Identify what had the most impact on them—the worst aspect of it for them—what part of the experience has made it the most difficult for them to deal with the situation.

6. What has been their emotional, mental, physical, and behavioral response to the crisis? Use the aforementioned symptoms to help them identify their response by breaking it down. Seeing that there are parts to what they are experiencing makes it more manageable and creates choices for them. They may feel more capable of dealing with one issue than another, and being in a position to make a choice gives a feeling of control that also contributes to progress toward working through and resolving the crisis.

7. Interventions
   A. Educate/validate the person regarding the range of experience accompanying a crisis.
   B. Identify strengths. Provide support for strengths and facilitate understanding how these can be utilized in the current situation.
   C. Identify vulnerabilities. Facilitate problem solving to avoid, strengthen, or reframe these issues.
   D. How have they coped with difficult situations and crises in the past?
   E. How do they view their own ability to cope, and why?
   F. Educate regarding how prior crisis experiences that are unresolved may act in concert with the current crisis to create a cumulative effect. In other words, not all of what they are currently experiencing may be due to the recent crisis.
   G. Educate regarding the working through stages for resolution of a crisis. Also, educate regarding the importance of developing a self-care program to improve coping while dealing with and resolving crisis issues.

8. Resolution
   As a client reaches the end stages of crisis resolution, summarize what they have experienced, what they have learned, and what they have resolved. Review their self-care plan, including resources and "red flags" that might be a signal to regression. Give feedback regarding their recovery within the context of a normal response and focus on the positives and internal resources as they prepare to bring this clinical contact is being brought to a close.

CRISIS ASSESSMENT OUTLINE

This is offered as a guide and not a rigid process that might circumvent any individualized situational factors/presentation from the patient. Meeting the patient "where they are" is a demonstration of astute clinical awareness and respect.

1. Crisis issues presenting risk
   A. Assess lethality regarding danger to self or others: Plan, intent, method, means
   B. Assess for gravely disabled
      1. Precautions to take (safety, legal, ethical)
      2. Level of care → least intrusive
         Current risk and safety concerns:

Current thoughts of self-harm/suicide	__yes __no
Past thoughts of self-harm/suicide	__yes __no
History prior suicide attempts	__yes __no
Current thoughts of harming another	__yes __no
Past thoughts of harming another	__yes __no
History of homicide/manslaughter	__yes __no
History of injuring another person	__yes __no
Current/history of harming animals	__yes __no
Recent/history of trauma exposure	__yes __no
Victim of violence/abuse	__yes __no
Perpetrator of violence/abuse	__yes __no

Current/past substance use disorder	__yes __no
Homeless	__yes __no
Other (specify)	__yes __no

2. Establish rapport

   Utilize attentive listening, paraphrasing, reframing, and the use of open-ended question to develop a positive clinical relationship.

3. Identify problems using a biopsychosocial framework to identify factors that play a role in the current and long-term symptom presentation. Encourage the patients to identify the problem(s) in their own words.
   A. Current health status
      1. Health issues, i.e., hypertension, diabetes, allergies, history of concussions/brain injury, medications, health and lifestyle behaviors (exercise, nutrition, sleep patterns, use of substances, etc.)
   B. Psychological status (mental status)
      1. Psychological issues, i.e., mental status, appearance and behavior, speech and language, mood and affect, cognitive functioning, concentration, memory insight, judgment, insight, general intelligence, perceptual disturbances, and the assessment of risk (suicidal ideation/homicidal ideation)
   C. Sociocultural experiences and cultural background
      1. Factors such as ethnicity, language, assimilation, acculturation, spiritual beliefs, environmental connections (community ties, neighborhood, economic conditions, availability of food and shelter), social networks, and relationships (family, friends, coworkers)
   D. Assess patient's participation in current and future treatment. Consider the following:
      1. Abilities/limitations (current/long-term)
      2. Willingness to participate in treatment
      3. Motivation
      4. Cooperativity

4. Identify prior effective interventions and practices/use of resources
   A. Encourage the patient to identify what interventions/personal efforts have been useful in the past when they have experienced similar difficulties

5. Identify and deal with feelings and issues of loss or lack of control
   A. Encourage the patient to tell their story to describe what has happened so that their emotions can be validated

6. Explore alternatives
   A. Encourage the patient to participate in a discussion about various options and interventions they believe would be useful and that they would be willing to engage in

7. Identify assets and reinforce resilience
   A. Internal resources
   B. External resources
   C. Identify and practice resilience factors

8. Develop a tentative diagnosis and associated treatment plan
   A. Multidimensional factors/influences underlying acute/symptomology
   B. What diagnostic issues are longer term to be confirmed/disconfirmed during the course of treatment

9. Identify goals

10. Follow-up
   A. Identify specific times to follow-up possibly by brief and specific phone check-in, tele-health, and/or in office sessions to reinforce stabilization and progress

CRISIS ASSESSMENT, INTERVENTION, AND TRAUMATIC EXPOSURE

When a person experiences an unexpected traumatic experience, an intervention is most beneficial when it follows the event as closely as possible. While the patient is being assessed, a discussion about what happened and the associated response facilitates working through and resolving the crisis experience by validating and normalizing their response and by reinforcing strengths/resilience/use of resources. Therefore, the following information is used to reframe and reinforce recovery, resilience, and consolidation of trauma exposure. The personal response to a traumatic crisis includes emotional, psychological, physical, and behavioral factors. The response pattern varies among individuals.

The individual response pattern is a function of the following:

1. Past experiences and how the person has coped
2. Access and utilization of a support system
3. Emotional health at the time of the crisis
4. Physical health at the time of the crisis
5. Beliefs
6. Attitudes
7. Values
8. How others/society respond to the individual and the event that the person experienced

Examples of common responses:

Emotional	Mental	Physical	Behavioral
Anxiety	Confusion	Fatigue	Angry outbursts
Fear	Forgetfulness	Exhaustion	Increased substance use
Agitation	Difficulty	Gastrointestinal	Isolation
Irritability	Concentrating	Problems	Withdrawal
Anger	Distractibility	Respiratory	Restless
Guilt	Intrusive thoughts	Problems	Interpersonal problems
Grief/loss	Flashbacks	Headaches	Appetite disturbance
Vulnerability	Nightmares	Twitching	Sleep disturbance
Fragility	Obsessing	Sweating	Change in libido
Disbelief	Hypervigilance	Dizziness	Easily agitated

In an effort to decrease the intensity of the emotional and psychological response, decrease physiological arousal, and facilitate resolution of the crisis with a return to previous level of functioning, discussion of the traumatic experience should be initiated as soon as possible following the crisis with a focus on safety, problem solving, self-care, positive daily schedule/routines, education of normal responses along with associated management skills, use of internal and external resources (highlighting and reinforcing strengths/resilience), and calming. Such early interventions will decrease the risk of developing PTSD for some individuals and decrease the length of time as well as intensity of symptom experience for others. Be careful to not overstimulate the individual and add to the experience of trauma-related distress.

1. Listen carefully and pay close attention to the responses of these individuals (detachment, agitation, emotional reactiveness, flashbacks, dissociation, etc.).
2. Decrease physiological arousal. For example, deep breathing is a natural relaxation response.
3. Facilitate appropriate support(s).
4. Normalize the response to the crisis. Their responses are relative to the individual, their life experiences, and their resources (internal and external).
5. Educate regarding the range of responses to the crisis, with care to avoid the following:
   A. Compounding social stigmatization of those with more symptoms
   B. Developing feelings of guilt for experiencing fewer symptoms than others, or feelings of shame for experiencing more symptoms than others
   C. Using confusing jargon/language not used by the general public
   D. Overpathologizing and focusing on disability
6. Assure that their response is temporary, while providing coping skills.
7. Let them know that there is not a specific time frame in which to recover from a crisis. However, if they engage in self-care behaviors and engage in positive self-talk, healing is likely to be expedited.
8. Foster resilience and recovery.
9. Assess for substance abuse and other behavioral health issues (comorbidity).
10. Follow up.

When providing psychological interventions to those recently traumatized and experiencing acute stress or individuals with PTSD validated treatment elements include direct therapeutic exposure and cognitive restructuring. Early cognitive-behavioral interventions include the following techniques:

1. Deep breathing
2. Progressive muscle relaxation
3. Imaginal and in vivo exposure therapy
4. Grounding techniques
5. Regular physical activity
6. Restorative sleep
7. Positive daily structure with natural and programmed reinforcers
8. Utilization of resources (internal and external)
9. Journaling
10. Self-monitoring

*Untreated and undertreated individuals with PTSD are especially susceptible to a deterioration of personal and work relationships, the development of substance abuse or dependence, and the development of depression.

TRAUMATIC STRESS AND PHYSICAL INJURY

This information applies to traumatic experiences of natural disasters, vehicular accidents, etc., where there has been harm to an individual's physical integrity or acute and intense fear of physical harm.

1. Physical review: What happened to the person physically?
   A. Physical trauma and near death/disfigurement
   B. Multiple injuries

C. Chronic/acute pain

D. Physical limitations

E. Continued medical treatment with associated physical recovery

1. Invasive procedure(s)

2. Experimental procedure(s)

3. Rehabilitation

F. Time that it takes to achieve stability where further procedures are not anticipated and the person is in a state of true adjustment in the recovery process

G. Time that it takes to heal (often someone who is released from medical treatment is in the initial stages of healing; healing can take a long time)

H. Effects/risks of medications

1. Dependence

2. Used as the only intervention for pain and acute anxiety management

2. Physical status affecting emotional and psychological functioning

A. Depression/anxiety/stress may be associated with the following:

1. Losses

2. Changes

3. Adjustment

4. Chronic pain

5. Continuing medical treatment

6. Medical instability

7. Rehabilitation challenges

8. Decompensation (feared or predicted/self-fulfilling prophecy)

B. The body may be depressed/fatigued struggling with healing and recovery—not solely psychological and emotional distress.

1. Fatigue

2. Low frustration tolerance

3. Stress/difficulty/pain associated with normal movement

4. Decreased stamina

C. Ongoing medical treatment may present the following issues:

1. How functional will the person be?

2. Will the physical integrity of the person's body be maintained?

3. Identity issues: "How have I been changed?"

a. Self-awareness

b. Others reflecting a change in personality/mood

3. Role of depression and PTSD

A. Depression

1. Decreased energy/fatigue

2. Sleep disturbance

3. Mood vulnerability

4. Increased potential for illness (people who are depressed are ill more often)

*Recovery is a lot of work. Depression slows the process, but it is also a normal part of adjustment.

4. PTSD (near death trauma/disfigurement with sustaining influence)

A. Ongoing medical treatment/continuing stress or trauma

B. Chronic pain

C. Physical limitations

D. Emotional vulnerability

E. Unpredictable good and bad days (may be emotion or pain related)

F. Additional health implications
  1. Musculoskeletal disorders
  2. Neurochemical changes resulting in an increased susceptibility to infection and immunological disorders (*addressed below under physiology of stress)
  3. Association of physical trauma and fibromyalgia
  4. Neurological impact of concussion and/or brain damage

5. Physiology of stress
  A. Stress negatively affects physiology
  B. Stress suppresses the immune system
    1. Stress impairs resistance to
      a. Infection
      b. Illness
  C. Stress accelerates metabolic activity
    1. Insomnia
    2. Nervousness (muscle tension)
    3. Fatigue/exhaustion

*Stress is four times as likely to precede infection, i.e., stress compromises the immune system enough for infection to take hold.

**An additional potential challenge to adjustment and recovery is when a person's face has been changed. For an individual to look in the mirror, even when completely physically recovered, and see even nuances of change in how they previously looked to themselves is a loss requiring adjustment. Be validating of their experience, these patients may have been told by their physician, family, and friends that their appearance is the same as before. Validate them by encouraging them to identify what has changed in their view and encourage them to process their experience and participate in identifying what will be helpful to their adjustment.

CRITICAL INCIDENT STRESS DEBRIEFING

Mitchell and Everly (2000) have suggested a seven-phase structured group discussion, which is provided within 10 days of a crisis (1–10 days). The purpose is to alleviate acute symptoms, assess for need of resources and follow-up, and provide a sense of closure to the crisis experience. However, critical incident stress debriefing (CISD) is not identified as an evidence-based treatment, and much controversy is associated with the efficacy of CISD. CISD does not prevent, treat, or cure PTSD. Therefore, clinicians are encouraged to educate themselves regarding the treatment guidelines and the case made for and against CISD and under what circumstances the consideration of its use would be made. The seven phases of CISD are as follows:

1. Introduction and guidelines for participation
2. Discussion of relevant facts
3. Discussion of thoughts
4. Discussion of reactions/emotions
5. Discussion of developing symptoms
6. Education about responses and coping strategies
7. Reentry
  A. Summarize
  B. Discuss additional available resources

SCREENING FOR SURVIVORS

The Institute of Medicine (IOM) offers screening program guidelines. The two websites below provide access such information:

http://books.nap.edu/books/0309068371/html/index.html
http://www.quic.gov/report/toc.htm

RECOVERING FROM TRAUMATIC STRESS

Traumatic stress results from a crisis that tends to be sudden and overwhelming, chronic, or cumulative. The psychological and emotional consequences range from a brief episode, which is acute but adequately coped with, to sustaining interference or a delayed response resulting in a compromised ability to adequately cope with normal daily stressors accompanied by significant intrusion of thought, emotional reactivity, avoidance, and physiological reactivity. Understanding the individualized experience of trauma is the first step to initiating recovery. It is crucial to reinforce the concept of healing and recovery. When trauma is associated with crisis assessment, it provides a potential opportunity to reinforce recovery and resilience. Working through the difficulties associated with adversity, as challenging as they can be, provide the double edge source of strengthening resilience.

OBSESSIONAL DISORDERS: AN OVERVIEW

Defined as unwanted and intrusive thoughts/images and impulses associated with attempts to neutralize the emotional discomfort

Triggering Stimuli
Provokes obsession
accompanied by

Feelings of discomfort,
Anxiety, Urge to neutralize ⟶ Often takes the form of
content compulsive behavior

Personally repugnant
topics such as
- Contamination
- Physical violence
- Death
- Accidental harm
- Sex
- Religion
- Orderliness

- Ascending to stereotyped pattern or idiosyncratic rules
- Associated with temporary anxiety relief *or* expectation that, had ritualizing not been carried out, anxiety would have increased
- Can include changes in mental activity such as:
  - Choosing to think differently in response to obsessional thoughts
  - Avoidance behavior (avoiding situations that could trigger obsessional thoughts)
- Sometimes accompanied by resistance to perform the compulsive behavior

Behavioral responses
- Urge to prevent
- Attempts to prevent

When calm, the individual usually can objectively regard his/her obsessional thought and compulsive behaviors as senseless or excessive (at least to some degree).

ASSESSMENT OF OBSESSIONAL DISORDERS

Obsessions are persistent thoughts, ideas, images, or impulses that are intrusive and cause marked anxiety or distress. The individual senses the obsessions are not normal, yet not within their control. Therefore, the obsessions and compulsions are "ego dystonic." However, in a smaller number of cases, the person is not aware that the obsessions and compulsions are excessive or unreasonable. In such cases the person could be misdiagnosed as psychotic when it is actually the result of poor insight. Many individuals afflicted by this disorder will not be forthcoming and disclose their symptoms unless they are specifically screened for this disorder. Additional diagnostic considerations include the distinction between impulse control disorders and obsessive-compulsive disorder (OCD) whereby there is never any gratification to the compulsions. There is a higher prevalence of cooccurring depressive and bipolar disorders in individuals with OCD than in the general population. Other anxiety and tic disorders are also commonly found in those with OCD. Cooccurring eating disorders as well may be more commonly seen in those with OCD.

An example of some general screening questions:

1. Do you ever have repeated unwanted or unpleasant thoughts that you are not able to control or unable to get rid of, such as:
   A. Fears of catching something?
   B. Fears of forgetting to do something like locking your door?
   C. Fear that something bad is going to happen?
   D. Fear that you might harm someone?
2. Do you ever feel the need to repeat things over and over again such as:
   A. Checking that you turned off the stove, lights, or locked the doors?
   B. Washing your hands repeatedly?

OBSESSIONAL DISORDERS ASSESSMENT OUTLINE

1. Presenting problem
   A. General description
      1. Recent and specific examples
      2. Description of situational trigger (nighttime, leaving the house, etc.)
2. Detailed cognitive, behavioral, physiological analysis
   A. Cognitive
      1. Form of obsession(s): thoughts/images/impulses
      2. Content of obsessions
      3. Cognitions that trigger obsessions
      4. Neutralizing
      5. Avoidance
      6. Perceived resistance to obsessions
      7. Senseless/excessive ruminations
   B. Emotional
      1. Mood changes associated with obsessions
         a. Anxiety
         b. Depression
         c. Other forms of distress_____
         d. Mood change before/after obsession
   C. Behavioral
      1. Triggers for obsessional thinking
      2. Avoidance
         a. Of situations in which obsessional thoughts might occur
         b. As an effort to control occurrence of obsessive thoughts
      3. Rituals
      4. Requesting reassurance
      5. Requesting others carry out tasks associated with their obsessions
   D. Physiological
      1. Triggers
      2. Changes associated with obsessions/compulsions

3. History of obsessional disorder
    A. Development of problem
        1. Obsessions
        2. Neutralizing
        3. Avoidance
    B. Negative impact on
        1. Intimacy/sex
        2. Personal growth and goals
        3. Work
        4. Social interactions/functioning
        5. Domestic role and functioning
        6. Significant relationships
            a. Patterns
            b. Dynamics
            c. Negative impact
        7. Benefits/costs associated with change

4. Monitoring
    A. For additional information
    B. For change
    C. Self-monitoring/reporting
    D. Questionnaire/survey/tests
        1. Maudsley Obsessive-Compulsive Inventory
        2. Compulsive Activity Checklist
        3. Beck Depression Inventory
        4. Beck Anxiety Inventory
        5. Yale-Brown screening and assessment tools are described in brief below as an example of instruments available for clinical consideration

5. Observation by others
    A. Significant other
    B. Relatives
    C. Friends
    D. In vivo home visits

OCD is both debilitating and difficult to treat. Therefore, consider the use of a screening tool and/or instrument to monitor symptom severity and changes in symptom severity over time. The following to be useful instruments to serve as treatment adjuncts:

1. Yale-Brown Obsessive-Compulsive Scale (Y-BOCS) is a universally used tool that consists of a 10-item severity rating scale with five dimensions of severity: time spent, interference, distress, resistance, and control with a maximum total score of 40 (the same five dimensions are used for obsessions and compulsions giving a total of a 10-item severity rating scale. For each of the 10-item severity scale, there is a rating from 0 to 4. A score of 16 and above is indicative of clinically significant OCD. Although it is not a diagnostic tool, it can be helpful as an additional screening tool. See the links below for obtaining the actual rating scale and the symptoms checklist. Y-BOCS Rating Scale and Checklist links:
    A. http://healthnet.umassmed.edu/mhealth/YBOCRatingScale.pdf
    B. http://healthnet.umassmed.edu/mhealth/YBOCSymptomChecklist.pdf

CYCLE OF PHOBIC ANXIETY

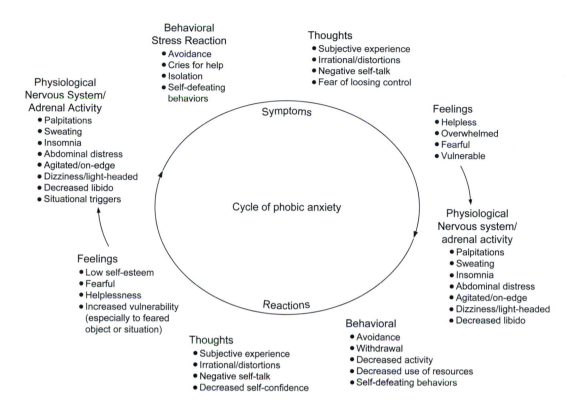

Behavioral Stress Reaction
- Avoidance
- Cries for help
- Isolation
- Self-defeating behaviors

Thoughts
- Subjective experience
- Irrational/distortions
- Negative self-talk
- Fear of loosing control

Physiological Nervous System/ Adrenal Activity
- Palpitations
- Sweating
- Insomnia
- Abdominal distress
- Agitated/on-edge
- Dizziness/light-headed
- Decreased libido
- Situational triggers

Feelings
- Helpless
- Overwhelmed
- Fearful
- Vulnerable

Symptoms

Cycle of phobic anxiety

Reactions

Physiological Nervous system/ adrenal activity
- Palpitations
- Sweating
- Insomnia
- Abdominal distress
- Agitated/on-edge
- Dizziness/light-headed
- Decreased libido

Feelings
- Low self-esteem
- Fearful
- Helplessness
- Increased vulnerability (especially to feared object or situation)

Thoughts
- Subjective experience
- Irrational/distortions
- Negative self-talk
- Decreased self-confidence

Behavioral
- Avoidance
- Withdrawal
- Decreased activity
- Decreased use of resources
- Self-defeating behaviors

This vicious cycle of symptoms and reactions mirror each other and validate or reinforce the self-fulfilling prophecy of expectations of the phobic individual. This cycle maintains and perpetuates fear-based symptoms and reactions (symptom-reaction list is not exhaustive—It is a sample list which can/should be individualized).

ASSESSMENT OF PHOBIC BEHAVIOR

The assessment of phobic behavior is associated with the fear(s) experienced by the individual and the identification of the practices, thoughts, or situations that reinforce and sustain phobic anxiety. Situational triggers alone influence physiology, thoughts, behavior, and feelings that perpetuate the cycle. When an individual is able to clarify the chain of experience, thought, physiology, behavior, and/or emotion that is specific to their phobic response, they will be able to problem-solve reaction management and behavior modification/change. Phobic disorders (social anxiety/phobias) are the most common forms of psychiatric illness, and severity can range from mild to severe regarding incapacitating one's ability to engage in daily functions and demands.

Signs and Symptoms
In obtaining a history from a patient with symptoms of a phobic disorder, the physician should inquire about the following:

1. History of symptoms and treatment
2. Other anxiety disorders (if present—history of symptoms and treatment)
3. Depression
4. Suicidal ideation
5. Substance-related disorders

6. Caffeine intake
7. Alcohol intake
8. Difficulties in social situations (in suspected social anxiety disorder)
9. Irrational and out-of-proportion fear or avoidance of particular objects or situations (in suspected specific phobia)
10. Intense anxiety reactions with exposure to specific situations (in suspected agoraphobia)

Anxiety is the most common feature in phobic disorders. Manifestations include the following:

1. Elevated heart rate
2. Elevated blood pressure
3. Tremor
4. Palpitations
5. Diarrhea
6. Sweating
7. Dyspnea
8. Paresthesias
9. Dizziness

*Because anxiety symptoms present with a number of physical manifestations, those presenting with physical symptoms suggestive of an anxiety disorder should be referred to their primary care physician to undergo a physical exam to rule out any physical conditions that could be the functional foundation of anxiety.

An assessment of phobia(s)/anxiety seeks to develop an accurate clinical picture and dynamic formulation from which an individualized treatment plan can be established.

PHOBIA ASSESSMENT OUTLINE

1. List of symptoms in the following areas:
   A. Physiology (nervous system/adrenal activity)
      1. Palpitations
      2. Sweating/chills
      3. Insomnia
      4. Abdominal distress
      5. Dizziness/light-headedness
      6. Decreased libido
      7. Others _____
   B. Behavior
      1. Stress reaction
         a. Avoidance (identify full range for developing hierarchy)
         b. Cries for help (decreased functionality)
         c. Isolation
         d. Self-defeating behaviors
   C. Thoughts
      1. Subjective experience
      2. Irrational thinking

3. Distortions of reality
4. Negative self-talk
5. Fear of losing control
   D. Feelings
      1. Helplessness
      2. Overwhelmed
      3. Fearfulness
      4. Vulnerability

2. Maintaining factors (interfere with progress)
   A. Avoidance
   B. Cognitive factors, thoughts of dangerousness of phobic stimulus
      1. Doubting the value of treatment
      2. Doubting one's ability to follow through on treatment decisions
   C. Presence of generalized (heightened) anxiety
      1. Associated depression (dysthymia)
   D. Possible underlying fear associated with overcoming the phobia
      1. Secondary gain
      2. Security associated with what is known eliminated, thereby increasing distress
      3. Would other problems develop?

3. Existing coping skills
   A. Methods of coping previously employed (may be helpful in treatment)
   B. Use of substances (alcohol/tranquilizers)
   C. What has been tried in an effort to overcome phobia?

4. Resources
   A. Hobbies
   B. Sources of pleasure
   C. Sources of success
   D. Helpful and caring family and friends
   E. Community resources
   F. Personal characteristics (persistent, sense of humor, intelligence, etc.)

5. Suitability for treatment
   A. Most cases improve with treatment
   B. Potential for noncompliant factors
      1. Severe depression
      2. Substance dependence requires prior treatment intervention
      3. Personality disturbance
      4. Other difficulties
         a. Fluctuating motivation
         b. Excessive emotional dependence
         c. Excessive hostility

6. Measures
   A. Baseline
   B. Information on progress
   C. Treatment plan and associated time frame
   D. Standardized rating scales
   E. Self-reports/self-monitoring

POSTPARTUM DEPRESSION, ANXIETY, AND PSYCHOSIS

Baby blues
Postpartum depression syndrome
Postpartum stress syndrome
Postpartum anxiety syndrome
    Postpartum panic disorder
    Postpartum obsessive-compulsive disorder

This syndrome refers to an illness that has a typical pattern of symptoms clustered together but does not have an identified specific single cause. Thus presenting the underlying reason why postpartum depression (PPD), postpartum stress, and postpartum anxiety syndromes often go undiagnosed and untreated. Screening and counseling for disorders such as PPD, anxiety, and OCD can prevent potentially serious consequences. Delay in receiving adequate treatment is associated with an increased duration (and perhaps severity) of PPD. Also, it is imperative that prior to treatment of postpartum emotional syndromes, there be a thorough medical examination to rule out other illnesses that may present similar symptoms but require very different treatment (such as thyroid dysfunction).

The Association of Reproductive Health Professionals (Updated July 2013 online) asserts the following information regarding postpartum counseling and emotional health:

Postpartum mood disorders are generally grouped accordingly:

1. *Baby blues*. Baby blues refers to commonly occurring mood swings or mild feelings of sadness after childbirth. Also called postpartum reactivity, these feelings usually peak approximately 3–5 days postpartum and disappear within a couple of weeks after the baby is born.

2. *Postpartum depression*. PPD, a far more serious disorder, usually develops within the first 3 months postpartum but may develop any time during the first year and includes symptoms such as low mood, sleep disturbance, and poor functioning. PPD affects up to 20% of postpartum women.

3. *Postpartum psychosis*. Potential for the development of postpartum psychosis (PPP) is highest within the first few weeks after childbirth. Onset is sudden and characterized by hallucinations, delusions, agitation, and other psychotic symptoms. Incidence is estimated at 1–3 per 1000 postpartum women.

4. *Postpartum anxiety (panic disorder, social phobia, generalized anxiety)*. Anxiety affects 5%–20% of new mothers; onset can be sudden or gradual. The patient may worry excessively or feel anxious, have a short temper, feel irritable and sad, or experience unusual symptoms of anxiety.

5. *Postpartum obsessive-compulsive disorder*. Approximately 3%–5% of postpartum women experience obsessive symptoms—intrusive, repetitive, and persistent thoughts or mental pictures (often about harming their baby), as well as behaviors targeted to reducing anxiety. Clinicians should maintain a heightened alertness for the range of possible symptoms that may indicate a mental health problem in a postpartum woman so that early treatment can be initiated.

*Postpartum anxiety and OCD are less well-recognized disorders and may occur on their own or in conjunction with depression.

Screening
Both provider-administered and patient self-report assessment tools have been recommended to identify women at risk for PPD. The Postpartum Depression Predictors Inventory (PDPI-Revised) provides a guide for interviewing a patient at any point between the preconception and postpartum periods. It includes questions

related to 13 predictors of PPD and assists the clinician in identifying issues for discussion and possible intervention.

Two well-tested, self-administered screening tools are available. The Edinburgh Postnatal Depression Scale (EPDS) assesses depressive mood in the past 7 days based on patient responses to 10 questions related to mood, anxiety, guilt, and suicidal ideation. The Postpartum Depression Screening Scale (PDSS) comprises 35 items that cover seven dimensions: sleeping/eating disturbances, anxiety/insecurity, emotional lability, mental confusion, loss of self, guilt/shame, and suicidal thoughts. Although the EPDS has fewer items than the PDSS, it can be completed by the patient within 5–10 min. The short-form Depression Anxiety Stress Scales (DASS-21) also can be used to diagnose depression or anxiety in postpartum women.

Postpartum Emotional Health Factors

The following are areas of life and socioemotional experience that have a significant impact on quality of life. All of these areas need to be explored with genuine care and interest.

1. Marital status
2. Self-esteem
3. Prenatal depression
4. Prenatal anxiety
5. Social support
6. Unwanted/unplanned pregnancy
7. Life stress
8. History of previous depression
9. Childcare stress
10. Marital/significant other—quality such as satisfaction, nurturance, support, etc.
11. Infant temperament
12. Maternity "blues"

One in four first-time mothers will experience PPD syndrome or postpartum stress syndrome. When postpartum anxiety syndromes are added, the number of women affected by postpartum emotional difficulties is one in three. Generally, there are no early warning signs or identified predispositions for postpartum disorders. Many women do not even present with a history of depression or anxiety. Also, postpartum syndromes can happen following any pregnancy (first, second, third, etc.). Therefore, it is not an exclusive experience for a first pregnancy; nor is there an assurance that a woman who experiences a postpartum disorder with one pregnancy will or will not experience this disorder following another pregnancy.

While postpartum syndromes are common, only a small number of women who experience some form of postpartum emotional distress will get help. Often postpartum difficulties are not identified by the woman or her physician. However, this has begun to change in recent years. Women have increased awareness and are seeking help.

Postpartum Depression Symptom Checklist

——— 1. I can't shake feeling depressed no matter what I do.
——— 2. I cry at least once a day.
——— 3. I feel sad most or all of the time.
——— 4. I can't concentrate.
——— 5. I don't enjoy the things that I used to enjoy.
——— 6. I have no interest in making love at all, even though my doctor says I'm now physically able to resume sexual relations.
——— 7. I can't sleep, even when my baby sleeps.
——— 8. I feel like a failure all of the time.
——— 9. I have no energy; I am tired all the time.
——— 10. I have no appetite and no enjoyment of food (or I am having sugar and carbohydrate cravings and compulsively eating all the time).

——— 11. I can't remember the last time I laughed.

——— 12. Every little thing gets on my nerves lately. Sometimes, I am even furious at my baby. Often, I am angry with my husband.

——— 13. I feel that the future is hopeless.

——— 14. It seems like I will feel this way forever.

——— 15. There are times when I feel that it would be better to be dead than to feel this way for one more minute.

Postpartum Stress Syndrome

This condition is also known as adjustment disorder. The level of emotional distress falls between minor baby blues and severe PPD. Approximately one in five women experience postpartum stress syndrome. Since symptoms are generally not as striking as PPD, no one may notice how awful the new mother feels.

Postpartum Anxiety/Panic Syndromes

Review the Postpartum Anxiety/Panic Disorder Symptom Checklist to see if you identify with the symptoms. Panic disorder symptoms occur without warning and generally last for about 10–30 min. Talk to your physician if you have these symptoms.

Postpartum Anxiety/Panic Disorder Symptom Checklist

——— 1. I can't catch my breath.

——— 2. My heart pounds, races, or skips a beat.

——— 3. My hands shake or tremble.

——— 4. I have stomach pains, nausea, or diarrhea.

——— 5. I get hot flashes or chills.

——— 6. I feel that something terrible is about to happen.

——— 7. I get dizzy or light-headed.

——— 8. Things appear "funny" or "unreal."

——— 9. I feel like I'm choking.

——— 10. I feel like I'm dying or about to have a heart attack.

——— 11. I am afraid to leave my house or be alone because I might have an anxiety attack and not be able to get help.

——— 12. I feel numb or tingly in my hands or around my mouth.

Postpartum Obsessive-Compulsive Disorder

While there may be many different symptoms, they all involve recurrent intrusive ideas or compulsive behaviors that cause significant distress or consume a great deal of time. There is the experience of certain repeated thoughts, urges, or images that are irrational and cannot be ignored, which result in discomfort and distress. Common examples include the following:

——— 1. Horrifying violent images (including thoughts of harming a child)

——— 2. Extreme doubts

——— 3. Severe fear of becoming contaminated by germs

——— 4. Compulsive housekeeping

——— 5. Checking and rechecking things

——— 6. Unnecessary repeated hand-washing, counting, or touching certain items

POSTPARTUM PSYCHOSIS

The rare and severe postpartum experience of PPP is when a woman experiences hallucinations or delusions with other symptoms. This is an overwhelming and terrifying experience. The outcome of a postpartum crisis is potentially tragic. If a patient is concerned that she may be experiencing the symptoms of PPP, she should contact her physician immediately so that she can receive appropriate treatment and support as quickly as possible.

Suicide is a potential consequence of PPP more often than harm to a child. There may not be adequate concern for a woman harming herself because the media have sensationalized the circumstances of a child(ren) being harmed by their mother (vs. the mother harming herself). As a result, equal weight may not be applied to potential risks of harm to a mother and child (children) associated with PPP. Below is a symptom checklist. If any of the symptoms are being experienced or the woman is concerned about her safety or the safety of the child, she should get medical and psychological intervention immediately.

Postpartum Crisis Symptom Checklist

———————— 1. I am afraid that I might harm myself to escape this pain.

———————— 2. I am afraid that I might actually do something to hurt my baby.

———————— 3. I hear sounds or voices when no one is around.

———————— 4. I do not feel that my thoughts are my own or that they are totally in my control.

———————— 5. I am hearing voices telling me to hurt my baby.

———————— 6. I have not slept at all in 48 h or more.

———————— 7. I do not feel loving toward my baby and can't even go through the motions of taking care of him or her.

———————— 8. I am rapidly losing weight without trying to.

———————— 9. I am being controlled by forces beyond myself.

———————— 10. I am thinking about hurting myself.

When a woman experiences difficulty coping effectively, hospitalization should be considered:

1. When medication requires very close monitoring
2. When necessary support of family and friends is not available
3. When outpatient treatment is not effective and a higher level of care is necessary
4. When symptoms are severe and unmanageable

Hospitalization is necessary when the individual is not able to adequately function and when there is a lack of support in the home environment to ensure appropriate care and supervision (not functioning adequately):

1. A woman is suicidal or experiencing perceptual disturbances
2. A child is at risk of harm
3. There are psychotic symptoms (heating voices, feeling paranoid, delusional beliefs)
4. A woman is not able to care for basic daily needs herself or her child
5. A woman cannot tolerate being left alone/or is not able to cope adequately with normal stressors

BREAKING THE POSTPARTUM SPIRAL

1. Seek professional help
   A. Physician for medication and appropriate referrals
   B. Group therapy
   C. Individual therapy
2. Seek support from caring family and friends
3. Accept that you are experiencing a postpartum syndrome so that you can deal with it
   A. "It is not my fault" (affirmation)
   B. "I will not always feel this way"
   C. "I will choose to participate in my treatment and help myself improve" (follow treatment recommendations)
4. Identify patterns of negative response; deal with "what is" not "what if"
5. Increase awareness for situations, mood changes, tasks, and so forth that trigger negative responses or escalate symptoms
6. Stop it with increased awareness of negative response patterns, problem-solve helpful and appropriate ways to respond
   A. Thought stopping
   B. Thought substitution
   C. Behavior change

7. Distract yourself
    A. Find something to replace negative response patterns such as going for a walk, calling a friend, meditating
8. Create options
    A. Give yourself permission to do what would be helpful and have a backup plan where a husband or someone else can take care of tasks while you
        1. Take a bath
        2. Exercise
        3. Engage in specific relaxation techniques
        4. Meditate
        5. Listen to music
        6. Pray
9. Be reasonable
    A. Remind yourself that it won't last forever
    B. Only do what needs to be done
    C. Get help
10. Set limits on telephone time
11. Limit visits from family and friends
12. Assert yourself to conserve energy, say no
13. Talk about your experience with someone you trust
14. Deal with difficult feelings
    A. Feelings of loss for the perfect pregnancy
    B. Feelings of loss for the perfect mother–baby experience
    C. Correct romanticizing childbirth and new motherhood
    D. Feelings of guilt
    E. Feelings of failure
    F. Low self-esteem
    G. Fear

Adapted from Kleiman and Raskin (1984). This Isn't What I Expected. Bantam Books.

CHRONIC MENTAL ILLNESS

This population can be described as individuals with disabling chronic conditions who are unable to sustain an adequate range of functional independent skills. Historically, most of the clinical focus has been on those diagnosed as schizophrenic. Hallucinations and delusions in these patients must be assessed (including the presence of command hallucinations) and treated. Additionally, there are a number of common medical conditions associated with secondary psychosis as well as medication side effects/interaction. Substance-induced psychosis (substance abuse consequence) must also be ruled out.

There is no question of the value of behavioral treatment in conjunction with the sensitive use of maintenance medication for many individuals. There is additional benefit to including the significant people in a patient's life for reinforcement of targeted behavior change, treatment compliance, and management. This population is observed as socially deteriorating, demonstrating poor hygiene and lack of self-care, slow speech and motor response, high rate of shouting or talking out loud (as they respond to internal dialogue, etc.), living in various residential settings (family home, board and care/institutional environments, etc.), and they are often homeless, delusional, and periodically violent in some cases. Many have an inability to participate in and maintain normal social interaction.

Clinically, their symptoms are classified as "positive" (for example, auditory hallucinations) or "negative" (for example, poverty of affect and apathetic). These behavioral deficits and excesses do not demonstrate correlation between individuals. Additional clinical descriptors associated with causation of symptomology include the following:

1. Premorbid deficits are the symptoms or difficulties experienced before the psychiatric illness existed, such as social stability and academic/vocational stability. The significant importance of this history is that it often has a predictive function in the final outcome or level of functioning of the individual with CMI.

2. Primary deficits are those that directly emerge as the fundamental nature of the disorder. It is these deficits that result in a diagnosis.

3. Secondary deficits are those experienced as a consequence of the illness or the adverse personal reactions that continue even when primary deficits are managed or eliminated—for example, property damage that results in lost opportunities for the individuals and possibly others as well (such as a wrecked car).

4. Institutional deficits are those that can be identified as the consequence of being institutionalized.

5. Iatrogenic deficits are the side effects of long-term medication use.

6. Pain deficit is experienced as an increased threshold for pain, or the individual may not present symptoms or illnesses to be treated medically, which is related to CMI individuals having a higher level of morbidity than the general population.

Therapists working with CMI patients recognize the importance of stimulation level in the individual's environment. Too much stimulation is agitating and can contribute to decompensation, while too little stimulation produces higher levels of social withdrawal and general apathy. When there is motivation and effort, appropriately include those with CMI in treatment planning outlining goals and objectives that relate to identified and perceived needs. Offer direct inquiry into personal desires of improvement, and offer to work with them to develop appropriate and helpful means of achievement. Encourage and facilitate as much social responsibility and opportunity as possible. As with all treatment, the lowest level of clinical intrusiveness should be applied along with adequate support. When the treatment plan has been established, there is the added clinical responsibility to educate and teach those involved in the direct care as to their role and necessary skill development for interaction with the identified patient.

Psychological treatments that have been demonstrated to be effective include cognitive-behavioral social skills training, pragmatic supportive therapy, personal therapy, the multimodal functional model, therapeutic contracting, case management, family therapy, and multiple family therapy. These innovative assessment and treatment techniques are described along with some experimental treatments for cognitive dysfunction (Beck, 2011; Bond & Dryden, 2002; NICE, 2016; Wright et al., 2002). As per NAMI (5/2016), interventions such as medication, psychotherapy, psychoeducation, psychosocial rehabilitation, assertive communication, self-help and support groups, vocational rehabilitation, and family support can result in the reduction of the symptoms of schizophrenia.

As with all assessments the goal is to guide treatment decisions to improve care and outcome; (1) identify areas of improvement/potential improvement, (2) develop improvement strategies, and (3) evaluate the nature and degree of improvements to monitor progress and to improve the quality of individualized interventions.

GENERAL GUIDELINES FOR ASSESSING THE CHRONIC MENTALLY ILL

1. General interview and demographic information
2. Current behavior
   A. Remaining skills/assets
   B. Deficits/losses
   C. Deviation/oddities/excesses
3. Past behavior
   A. Identified in prior treatment (hospital/outpatient)
   B. Self-reports
   C. Collateral reports
   D. Antecedents to episodes of decompensation (people, place, situation, timing)
   E. History of medication compliance
4. Potential target problems (those identified for treatment)
   A. Substance abuse
   B. Sexually exploited (poor judgment, etc.)

C. Medical treatment
5. The use of rating scales
   A. Standard measures (for general behavior/psychiatric rating)
6. Time sampling
   A. Observation at predetermined intervals
   B. Observation in specific environments/situations
7. Identifying community resources
   A. Applicable for unique needs of individuals
   B. Specific groups that encourage positive maintenance and desired changes
8. Changing sensitive treatment goals
   A. Checklist for specific steps of change
   B. Update goals as needed
9. Developing brief treatment planning
   A. When working with a motivated individual (avoid overwhelming them)
   B. When working with collateral contacts such as family members or other caregivers
10. Treatment team
    A. Consult as needed

In general, the results would be the development of the following:

1. A cognitive-behavioral program
2. Individualized treatment planning
3. Treatment in the context of larger groups that include
   A. Psychoeducation
   B. Skill development
   C. Social reinforcement and socialization opportunities
4. Treatment in the context of smaller groups (individuals with their families)

An example of an interview-based measure, the Positive and Negative Syndrome Scale (PANSS), is a measure of the severity of psychopathology in adults with psychotic disorders. The PANSS is a hand-scored instrument and is comprised of 30 items and 3 scales: the Positive scale contains seven questions to assess delusions, conceptual disorganization, hallucinations behavior, excitement, grandiosity, suspiciousness/persecution, and hostility; the Negative scale contains seven questions to assess blunted effect, emotional withdrawal, poor rapport, passive/apathetic social withdrawal, lack of motivation, and similar symptoms; and the General Psychopathology subscale addresses other symptoms such as anxiety, somatic concern, and disorientation.

MHS (2016) states that the PANSS provides a good diagnostic basis of schizophrenia comprising a minimum of two syndromes whereby the positive syndrome consists of productive symptoms while the negative syndrome is associated with deficits. This site offers basic information about the PANSS and how to use the assessment tool, Structured Clinical Interview for the PANSS (SCI-PANSS) and the Informant Questionnaire (IQ-PANSS).

SELF-CARE BEHAVIORS

Develop a personalized self-care plan for optimal results. This requires a commitment to health and consistent follow-through. It is recommended that there be a medical exam for medical clearance, as well as providing the opportunity for a medication evaluation that may be useful in dealing with unmanageable symptoms following a crisis.

1. Utilize relaxation techniques to decrease body tension and stress level.
2. Process the experience by the following:
   A. Utilize their support system. Talking about the experience and how they have been affected. Avoid isolation and withdrawal. Instead encourage spending time with people who offer a feeling of comfort and care.
   B. Initiate a journal. Instead of keeping thoughts and feelings inside where they build up, get them down on paper. Some individuals have difficulty expressing themselves to others or are afraid of being judged. To benefit a similar degree of relief as talking, journal writing can be useful.
   C. Enter therapy for a safe, nonjudgmental environment where they can speak freely about their thoughts and feelings without feeling how others will respond, or feeling the need to protect those close to them. Therapy can be extremely beneficial for resolving a crisis and receiving positive reinforcement.
3. Regular, moderate exercise. Aerobic exercise (such as walking) appears to be most helpful in alleviating and maintaining decreased body tension.
4. Approach each day with a purpose. Be productive by outlining daily structure that includes adequate sleep, good nutrition, exercise, relaxation, utilization of resources, and task accomplishment commensurate with level of functioning (no task is too small to feel good about).
5. Avoid anxiety-provoking talks or making significant life decisions during this time.
6. Relapse prevention is essential for the person with such vulnerability.
7. Encourage the avoidance of being self-critical. Being kind and understanding to oneself are important. Using positive self-talk is valuable for reassuring that the symptoms that are currently experienced will subside with time.

Ask: "What are some additional things that could add to a self-care plan to meet specific needs?"

MEDICAL CRISIS ASSESSMENT AND COUNSELING

Medical Crisis Assessment

All crisis presentations require a timely comprehensive assessment of the impact of the crisis upon coping and functioning, identifying relative strength and weakness, identifying internal and external resources. An additional clinical benefit is derived from a collaboration (patient–therapist) developing an associated treatment plan and goals (Roberts, 2000, 2002, 2005; Roberts & Otten, 2007).

Medical Crisis Counseling

Medical crisis counseling is a specialized approach to addressing the needs of individuals and families confronted by the difficulties of coping with losses or changes, as well as the challenge of living with long-term illness.

The goal for working with individuals presenting with a medical crisis is not to affect a cure, but to optimize quality of life by facilitating individuals and their families to cope with the emotional and psychological trauma that often accompany the medical crisis. As they learn to cope with the crisis and associated life changes, they will begin to integrate the illness as part of their life experience, to adjust to what has happened and/or will happen to them, and to live their life as fully as possible. For a therapist to intervene effectively requires that they be prepared to be:

1. Holistic in their approach of uniting mind and body
2. Aware and observant regarding the context of the family system and community in which the individual is a part of
3. Able to provide a perspective, which is able to assume that this is an individual with a healthy ego and defenses whose emotional equilibrium has been disrupted or affected by the intrusive force of a medical crisis versus an underlying psychopathology

Medical crises can be acute or chronic. In either case, appropriate interventions can help an individual avoid psychiatric complications and in some cases reduce the intensity or the onset of physical symptoms. While many of the issues being addressed would benefit an individual experiencing an acute medical crisis, the focus is on intervening with the individual experiencing a chronic medical crisis. The three heightened points of distress associated with a medical crisis where intervention is most effective are when a diagnosis has been made, an individual is released from the hospital, and/or there is an exacerbation in symptomatology. The initial focus of intervention is to reduce stress, address fears, and activate coping mechanisms.

Adaptive coping mechanisms are facilitated by the following factors:

1. Developing a clear picture of the situation. To process their medical condition, they must have accurate information about its progression and the prognosis. Other factors that need clarification include an understanding of financial issues, medical treatment and resources, and family resources.
2. Increasing emotional awareness. Asking questions of the self: How they feel and how they express their emotions?
3. Effectively managing emotions. Using clear communication to express themselves and to get their needs adequately and appropriately met. Making an effort to remain as flexible as possible regarding the possible changes of all conditions.
4. Ventilation of feelings and thoughts, verbally, with writing, drawing, or other expressive media.
5. Utilizing resources and support—both personal and professional. Creating a list of all personal and professional resources, their availability, specifically what context of resources or support is offered, and if possible put the list in order according to the associated difficulty for which the individual seeks an intervention. This will help alleviate frustration and other negative feelings unnecessarily initiated by dead ends and other limitations. It will also provide a beneficial resource to any enlisted helper.

The fears associated with long-term illness include fear of pain, body mutilation, imposed changes in lifestyle, alteration of social patterns, low self-esteem, fear of the future, and fear of death. The individual may experience many losses such as, loss of body parts, physical functioning, sexual functioning, job, home, relationships, self-image, feelings of control, and facing death itself. The fear of living with losses and limitations can be as overwhelming as the fear of death.

Intervening with an individual in a medical crisis requires that biopsychosocial issues be applied to the practical problems of daily living which confront an individual with a chronic illness such as medical management, treatment compliance, symptom control/management, dealing with social isolation and developing new resources and supports, adjusting to physical changes and loss of functioning, establishing some level of comfort in a new/changing lifestyle, dealing with financial consequences, and how those close to the individual respond. An entirely different issue not covered here, but of significant importance, are the needs and issues of family members, specifically those who may be the central caregivers. Similar to the individual they care for (emotionally and possibly figuratively), these people are also confronted with isolation, fear, uncertainty, and changes in their role.

TREATMENT FRAMEWORK AND CONCEPTUALIZATION

1. The focus of treatment is the medical crisis and condition (disease progression and prognosis).
2. Medical crises are often temporary, but if they appear to be of more a chronic nature (cycles of flare-ups or exacerbation), they still provide an opportunity for growth and learning.
3. The issues of adjustment facing people with chronic illness are often predictable (physical, emotional, financial, lifestyle, relationships, identity, etc.).
4. The focus is on an individual's capacity and ability to facilitate maximal coping.

The interventions for medical crisis are short term. However, there may be some individuals who will require more than one treatment of intervention due to underlying personality issues that interfere with their adjustment, the issue of secondary gains, or in response to a new crisis.

As previously stated, there are predictable issues that an individual experiencing a medical crisis associated with a chronic illness will experience. Support in confronting these issues will alleviate fear and make the issue less overwhelming. It is important to validate the reality basis for the identity of issues and the fear (or other emotions) associated with the medical crisis.

These issues are not experienced as a sequence of stages, but rather are assumed to be present all of the time. However, one issue may be dominant over another because of certain circumstances in a given time frame. Clinically, the therapist manages this by simply meeting the patient where they are emotionally at any given time. Take the cue from the individual as to what seems to be a prominent issue at the time, do as much resolution around the issue, and do not diffuse it by focusing on other issues at the same time. Distraction with focusing on other issues could be construed as an invalidation.

THE CENTRAL CRISIS ISSUES

1. Control
   A. How did they feel when a diagnosis was given? What did it mean to them? People do not know what the future will bring and often catastrophize, assuming/fearing the worst possible progression of the illness.
   B. Daily experiences of pain or other challenging symptoms.
   C. What is the expected course of treatment and treatment regimens?
   D. Facilitate venting of fears and uncertainty of outcome.
   E. Facilitate expressed feelings of loss.

2. Self-image
   A. Acknowledge the impact on an individual living in our society where there is a high social regard for good health and physical appearance.
   B. Validate feelings of loss and having to cope and adjust to the reality that they will never be the same again. "Who am I?"
   C. What are their personal strengths and resources that could help them cope?
   D. What was their life before the diagnosis? Medical treatments? Doing an inventory of what the individual perceives as valued qualities and abilities can facilitate the grieving process. This can in turn facilitate a modified version of the individual's original self-image so that other problem solving can transpire.
   E. Explore the individual's general feelings/belief system about impairments and disabilities prior to the illness. This clarification will help them correct how they assume the attitudes of others.

3. Dependency
   A. Threats to independence: emotional, physical, and financial security. This can contribute or lead to depression and suicidal ideation.
   B. Negative feelings associated with the need for support or additional resources in making the necessary adjustments and accommodations of change.
   C. Facilitate the cultivation of self-reliance within the limits of their capabilities. Validate their fear of loss of personal independence and to effectively deal with the fear of being a burden on their family. Encourage optimal independence.
   D. In evaluating issues related to fears of dependency, take into consideration the following factors: gender, age, psychosocial development, etc. Each factor presents constructs to explore.
   E. Spousal and/or family-related issues
      1. What was the type/degree of independence of each individual in the family system/couple prior to the illness?
      2. How troubling is the dependency to each (all) involved?
      3. How easy/difficult is it for the ill person to ask for help?
      4. How freely is support given by others?
      5. How difficult has it been to accept help/support from others?
      6. What are the practical demands of the situation (routines, needs, wants, financial stressors, time demands, time for self, etc.)?
      7. What are the helpful/useful community-based resources such as home health, church, specific support and education (for example, the MS Society), etc.?
      8. Role-play scenarios with individual and family members/partner.
      9. Facilitate reality checks for objective evaluations.
      10. Suggest talking to or meeting with the treating physician regarding limitations/prognosis.

4. Stigma
   A. Issues of self-acceptance.
   B. Facilitate development of social skills and belief system to deal with the attitudes of others.
   C. Be aware of the different social impact on the evaluation of men versus women. Males are more likely to be viewed as being more damaged and heroic, whereas there is a tendency to view females as weak, ineffective, and being self-absorbed or feeling sorry for themselves/trying to get sympathy.

5. Abandonment/rejection
   A. This issue may be more emotionally distressing than the fear associated with dying. There is a double bind for the individual. (1) There is a fear of abandonment, but they also feel bad about being a burden. (2) They want the care, but are aware of the difficulty that it poses on others. This is also a bind for caregivers who want to give the necessary care and offer comfort and feelings of security, but also wish that they did not have to deal with the problem.
   B. It is extremely important to facilitate clear communication and joint decision making as soon as possible.
   C. Awareness for the issue of caregiver burnout may prevent it from happening. With interventions such as acknowledging the caregiver's sacrifices and building in respite breaks into the regular routine, caregiver burnout can be circumvented. For this to be successful, the individual must be sensitized to the caregiver's need for time away/breaks and not personalize it in a negative manner.
   D. Reframe breaks as part of a functional pattern of long-term management to alleviate the interpretation of abandonment/rejection.
   E. Facilitate utmost self-reliance.

6. Anger
   A. Identify, validate, and constructively redirect the anger.
   B. Be aware of the possible lack of awareness or denial for feelings of anger.
   C. Reframe anger as a normal response to frustration when an individual is unable to control their life, the illness, and/or losses.
   D. Facilitate appropriate expression of anger. Possible modes of expressing anger include appropriate ventilation, humor, talking, activity, meditation, etc.
   E. Facilitate identification of the positive aspects of life: strengths, opportunities, and life pleasures.

7. Isolation/withdrawal
   A. Physically unable to continue in previous life activities such as work, social life, and other normal activities. Promote development of abilities.
   B. Be aware that the consequences of social, physical, and emotional isolation can include increased depression, hopelessness, and despair.
   C. Being cutoff from friends and family significantly increases the risk of sickness and death.
   D. Feelings of low self-esteem and unworthiness can lead to withdrawal and refusal of invitations to be with other people and being involved socially.
      This issue is just as important for the caregiver as the chronically ill individual. Their world has been radically decreased. Therefore, facilitate development and utilization of a support system. Also, facilitate identification of options and the setting of realistic goals. Lastly, recognize that isolation and withdrawal may be a consequence that of depression, fear, or rejection (real or perceived).

8. Death
   A. Facilitate acceptance.
   B. Recognize that the individual may vacillate between grief stages.
   C. Emphasize being in the here and now to maximize quality of life.
   D. Facilitate the individual to concentrate on living the life they have. Initiate conversations/discussions about life to promote living life to its fullest.
   E. Support the individual in accomplishing important and necessary tasks and to talk to family members/partner and other significant people in their life.
   F. Facilitate problem solving and resolution of practical issues that can contribute to their investment in living and decreasing a preoccupation with death.
   G. Facilitate clarification of priorities and values:
      1. Identifying the most meaningful aspects of life.
      2. If death is imminent, how does the individual want to be remembered?

3. What is important for them to take care of/get in order?
4. What are they able to let go of or resolve?
5. Facilitate exploration of beliefs about death and life.
6. Clarify philosophical and spiritual beliefs and resources.
7. Facilitate clarification of what gives them both strength and comfort.
8. Facilitate and support grieving.

This has been adapted and summarized from Pollin, I., & Kannan, S. B. (1995). *Medical crisis counseling*, New York: Norton.

DEALING WITH THE CHALLENGES OF LONG-TERM ILLNESS

(This could be printed and given to the person experiencing a long-term illness.)

1. Confronting your medical crisis: Recognize that you are not alone
    A. Learn skills to help you effectively cope. Instead of the goal to be cured, how do you learn to live with it and improve your quality of life.
    B. By confronting the illness and associated fears, you acknowledge what is happening and how it affects you. This is the path necessary for problem solving how you will live with the illness. Every experience you have becomes a part of you.
        1. Acknowledge it
        2. Accept it
        3. Learn how to cope with the illness and how it changes your life
        4. Learn to cope with how it has changed and is still changing you
    C. To accomplish this, review the eight central crisis issues associated with chronic illness with your therapist and consider the following general points for improved coping and management:
        1. Identify and accept adjustment as a normal part of life
        2. Identify the general style of coping with difficult circumstances
        3. Clarify
            a. Personal view of your illness
            b. The stress it creates
            c. Identify emotional reaction(s)
        4. Identify your strengths and weaknesses
        5. Maximize resources
            a. Personal (psychological and emotional endurance; physical strength)
            b. Social (support network such as family, friends, community participation, support groups, professional help)
        6. Decrease negative emotion, associated symptoms, and the impact to coping
            a. Stress
            b. Anxiety
            c. Depression
        7. Find ways to improve relaxation and being in the moment
            a. Prayer
            b. Visualization
            c. Meditation
            d. Stretching/yoga
            e. Formal relaxation techniques
            f. Deep breathing
        8. Improve positive daily structure and daily functioning

9. Be a positive and cooperative member of your treatment team
    a. Ask questions
    b. Make decisions
    c. Increase compliance with treatment by coidentifying the treatment plan and treatment goals
10. Decrease isolation/social withdrawal
11. Foster a sense of control (identifying ability and potential participation)
12. Continue to strive for quality of life and satisfaction in life

2. Impact of chronic illness on relationships

Once the diagnosis is made or onset of chronic illness is evident, relationships may change. Not only may it be a time of stress and adjustment, but it may also be a time when you require an increased level of attention and care from those closest to you. As a result, everyone experiences a greater degree of stress. This may be a time of extreme anxiety for you and your family. Because of the range of intense emotions for all involved, people sometimes try to avoid friction and pull away with "silencing" being a possible consequence.

A. Keep communication open.

B. It is normal to experience anxiety, depression, anger, fear, frustration, resentment, shame, guilt, and fatigue. Talking about it is the only way to find creative methods of dealing with such changes in yourself and significant relationships.

C. While you work at identifying how you are emotionally/psychologically responding, it is also important to understand how your loved ones feel. Don't wall yourself off. The consequences of the medical crisis you are experiencing, including loss and fear, are shared by all those close to you.

D. Take charge.
    1. Put problems in perspective
    2. Identify what is exacerbated or changed by the diagnosis/illness
    3. Avoid personalizing the illness

E. Facilitate a family discussion to address.
    1. Feelings
    2. Responses
    3. Fears
    4. Impact on the life of each person
    5. Problem solving for managing changes as a family
    6. Validating all feelings and thoughts
    7. Help others understand separating difficult behaviors associated with adjustment versus a personal problem of the person (you) experiencing the illness
    8. Expressing care and love

F. Develop realistic expectations and limitations for all family members (including yourself).

G. Clarify what you need from significant others.
    1. Tell them how you feel
    2. Tell them what you miss (and strive to deal with it too)
    3. Reassure their feelings about the medical crisis
    4. Give them guidance in how to help you
    5. Do not manipulate with your illness
    6. Share appreciation for help and support

H. Help significant others to do the following:
    1. Adjust to changes in responsibilities (some will feel others may feel displaced, so be aware and ready to talk about it and if possible, problem-solve it)
    2. Maintain as much responsibility and involvement in medical decisions as is possible
    3. Keep awareness for overprotectiveness from family

I. Don't use family guilt as an avenue to gain desired attention.

J. Make sure scheduling is structured so everyone gets respite care if necessary.

K. Develop an effective partnership with your physician(s) by getting as much information about your illness as possible. Create a personal list of questions for your physicians aimed at increasing knowledge and understanding:

1. Are you sure of the diagnosis? Did/do you feel you need for a second opinion?
2. How did I get the disease? What do you understand about the disease?
3. What factors make it worse or better?
4. How long must I stay in the hospital? How is hospitalization avoided?
5. What should I expect as far as disabilities?
6. Will the disease get worse?
7. Can the symptoms be controlled?
8. What treatments are available?
9. As the physician(s) if the treatment being recommended is the latest?
10. What is its success rate?
11. What are the risks of this treatment?
12. Do the benefits outweigh the risks?
13. Are there any experimental treatments I should know about?
14. If I take this medication for many years, what are the potential side effects?
15. If I have surgery, will it stop the disease or will the process continue?
16. What should I be doing to take care of myself?
17. What would make me feel better?
18. What would make me feel worse?

L. Clarify what you expect from your physician and what your physician expects from you.
M. Feel confident if you choose to do the following:
1. Seek a second opinion if you're dissatisfied with the specialist or feel uncertain about the diagnosis.
2. Get as much information about your disease as possible, but only as much as you are comfortable with. It should help with you being an informed member of the treatment team.
3. If you are anxious in your doctor's office, bring in prepared questions and take notes. Have someone accompany you.
4. Share your feelings and concerns with your doctor and his/her staff, especially if you feel you are being mistreated.
5. If you're going into surgery, put your surgeon's name on the release form. This will ensure that this particular surgeon will be performing the operation—not another member of the medical staff.
6. Get copies of your medical records if it helps you to keep track of your treatment.
7. Speak up clearly if you are dissatisfied with a nurse's treatment of you. Start by speaking with your nurse directly. If that doesn't work, speak to the head nurse and then with your doctor.

WORKING THROUGH THE CHALLENGES AND FEARS ASSOCIATED WITH LONG-TERM ILLNESS

1. Loss of control
    A. Acknowledge you may not be able to control what is medically happening to you, but that you have a choice in how you deal with it. Your emotional state can affect your physical state, and your physical state can affect your emotional and psychological functioning. So when you are confronted with some limitations and forced life changes, you still have power of choice over your psychological and emotional life. You may not have control over what happens to you, but you do have control over how you choose to interpret it and how you choose to deal with it.
    B. Find a way to come to terms with the loss of control and life changes.
    C. Evaluate what you do and do not have control over.
    D. Find ways to regain maximum control:
        1. Clarify and separate long-term from short-term issues
        2. Make your own decisions whenever possible
        3. Review your life before and after the diagnosis
            a. What was a priority?
            b. How have you changed?

       c. What part of your life remains intact?

       d. What changes do you need to make?

    4. Identify areas of stress

    5. Develop realistic expectations and limitations

    6. Continue using coping mechanisms that are or can be effective

    7. Explore new ways of decreasing stress

    8. Identify/develop your support system (determine who you can depend on and under what circumstances)

    9. Consider joining a support group that focuses on your specific health issue

   10. Be creative

   11. Be flexible

   12. Plan ahead to maximize choices and control in situations

   13. Never underestimate the power of how you think

   14. Live an attitude that strives for quality of life

2. Changes in self-image

   A. Identify what was familiar that is now changed or lost in appearance or in physical, emotional, or psychological functioning

   B. Determine if these changes are permanent, temporary, or progressive

   C. Grieve your losses, let go, and validate normal responses

   D. Identify what losses are ahead of you as a result of the illness

   E. Develop a self-image that currently fits your strengths

   F. Remind yourself that change is a normal part of life

   G. Encourage family and friends as partners in your efforts of change

   H. Do things that make you feel good about yourself

   I. Seek professional support

3. Dependency concerns

   A. Identify what you can do for yourself versus relying on others

    1. Emotionally

    2. Physically

    3. Financially

    4. Medically

    5. Daily life (shopping, house chores, childcare, etc.)

   B. Find a balance between autonomy, interdependence, and reliance on others

   C. Identify how the emotional impact associated by dependency issues associated with your illness

   D. Develop realistic expectations and limitations

   E. Develop new goals

   F. Give to others and participate in their lives

   G. Resolve financial issues or concerns as best possible

   H. Participate in your own medical decisions

   I. Maintain as much independence as possible

4. Stigma—real and perceived

   A. Have a realistic view of the world.

   B. Examine how you have dealt with the disabilities of others (insight into your own perceptions, which may result in your own distress with changes in you).

   C. Confront and resolve your own distortions of disabilities. It is extremely difficult to not allow emotion to play a role in interpretation. However, strive to be as objective as possible.

   D. Participate in a support group.

   E. Do not personalize the words or behaviors of others.

   F. Talk with your family and friends about your thoughts and feelings.

   G. Find ways to laugh at difficult situations and yourself. Laughter is the best medicine at times.

   H. Respond to others in an educative way—"I do things this way because…"

   I. Take control of how you present yourself. How do you want others to know who you are?

5. Abandonment
   A. Be aware of your sensitivity
   B. Avoid misinterpretations in family communication
   C. Confront your fear(s)
   D. Discuss your fears and concerns with family members and friends
   E. Identify negative thinking that is not reality based or shades of reality
   F. Be realistic and don't let your fear to control you
   G. Be sensitive to the needs of your family
      1. Be empathic
      2. Be appreciative
   H. Stay emotionally involved with those you care about
   I. Continue to participate as much as possible in the lives of family and friends (there are lots of ways to do the same thing or to be supportive)
   J. Do not withdraw and then distort it as a validation of abandonment by others

6. Anger
   A. Begin with self-evaluation
   B. Assess your feelings of anger and how you have learned to deal with anger throughout the course of your life
   C. Do not personalize normal responses of anger from those close to you
   D. Determine where feelings of rage are being focused
   E. Do not burden yourself with being "angry at you"
   F. Take responsibility for the future without blaming yourself for the past
   G. Talk rationally and appropriately about your anger
   H. Find appropriate and helpful ways to vent your anger
      1. Be creative
      2. Be forgiving
      3. Take action
      4. Find positive ways to use your energy
      5. Be helpful to others
   I. Acknowledge and accept reality

7. Isolation
   A. Identify the different forms of isolation
      1. Physical limitations (difficulty walking, wheelchair, bed-ridden, difficulty breathing, environmental sensitivities, etc.)
      2. Social isolation (fewer contacts)
      3. Emotional isolation
   B. Be empathic; family members may also experience isolation
   C. Prepare yourself to deal with issues of isolation (let people know you want to be included)
   D. Participate in a support group for encouragements validation, and problem solving
   E. Identify how much support you need and want
   F. Have realistic expectations about family and friends
   G. Problem-solve how to reintegrate yourself socially and develop new interests

8. Death
   A. Decrease your fear of death
      1. Talk about it with family and friends
      2. Be helpful to others to decrease self-focus
      3. Write about your thoughts and feelings
      4. Read
      5. Talk with clergy
      6. Plan for it—take control
   B. Ask the hard questions

C. Plan for the future

D. Face death as you have faced life

E. If death is imminent, confront your fear of death in your own way

F. Identify what is important to you and accomplish it on your own or with help

G. Continue to make your own decisions

H. Stay close to loved ones and invest yourself in important relationships

I. Remain hopeful and believe in miracles—they do happen

J. Live life to its fullest

K. Be in the moment and enjoy the moment

Adapted from Pollin, I., & Dutton, Donald, Susan, and Golant (1995). *"Taking charge": Overcoming the challenge of long term Illness*. New York: Times Books.

CHRONIC PAIN: ASSESSMENT AND INTERVENTION

Everyone suffers from acute pain when injured, but acute pain abates quickly. Pain is a feeling triggered by the nervous system. The experience of pain is subjective and very complex, involving a myriad of mechanisms. The quality of pain may be described in numerous ways such as sharp or dull, constant or intermittent. Pain is categorized as follows (www.StopPain.org 7/2/16):

1. *Nociceptive*: Two types of constant or enduring pain receptor activation:
   A. Somatic pain. The result of injury to the skin, bone, joint, connective tissue that often has associated inflammation. Descriptions of pain include dull, aching, sharp, burning, prickly.
   B. Visceral pain. The result of ongoing injury to internal organs or their supportive tissue. Descriptions are associated with the type of organ structure and may be cramping, deep pressure, stabbing.
2. *Neuropathic*: The result of changes in the nervous system that is initiated with an injury but continues after the injury has healed. Descriptions include burning or like electricity.
3. *Psychogenic*: Describes pain associated with psychological problems. There may not be an identifiable disease associated with the presentation of pain. Therefore, therapy is an integral component of treatment.

It is clear that there is a relationship between the experience of chronic pain and psychological factors. Therefore, it is recommended that all patients who present with chronic pain be psychologically assessed to determine if the underlying cause of pain is psychological.

Chronic pain is defined as pain that has not gone away or reoccurs often even after 6 months have passed. The management of chronic pain is so difficult because traditional methods of pain management frequently fail to bring relief. The most common types of chronic pain are back pain, headaches, and pain associated with arthritis. However, there are many other origins of chronic pain. Unfortunately, in many of these cases, the underlying cause of the pain is not identified.

The most common pain syndrome is myofascial pain, which refers to pain in the muscles or connective tissue. This pain tends to be diffuse and described as "achy" and is often associated with the muscles of the head, neck, shoulders, and lower back. The onset can be rapid or gradual and generally will diminish on its own. There can be a cycle with myofascial pain that (1) originates with muscle tension that produces pain; (2) focuses attention on the pain; (3) increased muscle tension; and (4) resulting in more pain. When an individual is not focusing on the pain, but instead doing other things and thinking about other things the distraction acts to minimize the experience and a normal alleviation or subsiding of the pain occurs.

Another pain syndrome, neuralgia, is similar to myofascial pain in that there appears to be a lack of tissue damage. The primary sign of neuralgia experienced by people is a severe sharp pain along a nerve pathway. This pain can occur suddenly with or without stimulation. It is transient and brief, but can reoccur and at times be intense enough to be incapacitating.

FACTORS AFFECTING THE EXPERIENCE OF PAIN

1. Cultural. Varying cultures offer different explanations of origin or meaning and expectation of pain. However, there are few differences in sensation thresholds cross culturally.
2. Cognitive response. The thoughts and beliefs that an individual has are one of the strongest influences on the perception of pain. Cognitive distortions such as excessive worrying, catastrophizing, negative self-fulfilling prophecy, overgeneralization, and personalization are common to individuals who suffer chronic pain. This type of thinking can play a role in the exacerbation of depression, requiring a thorough assessment of mood disturbance issues. The interpretation of pain will determine the overall experience of it, as well as feelings of control and self-efficacy in pain management.
3. Affect and stress. As stress increases, there is also an increase in the perception of pain. Psychogenic pain is chronic pain that lacks any physical etiology and is believed to be a response to psychological need or disturbance. Often, people with depression or other emotional distress will manifest their distress in pain.
4. Prior experiences of pain. Even though the reaction to pain is autonomic, earlier experiences influence pain perception. There is no cure or elimination for pain as an experience to injury; pain is a survival mechanism to prevent harm and death.

CLINICAL INTERVIEW

Individuals with pain often present with additional coping difficulties. Chronic pain is exhausting, physically limiting, and challenges an individual's identity and sense of control. Be sensitive to not minimize or invalidate their experience of pain.

1. Identifying information
2. Relationship history
3. Work/academic history
4. Relevant background information and developmental history
5. History of pain (intensity, frequency, quality)
6. Medical history (injuries, hospitalization/surgery, medication, etc.)
7. Psychiatric history (therapy, biofeedback, hospitalization, medication)
8. Mental status
9. Coping mechanisms and problem-solving ability
10. Strength and weakness
11. Diagnosis
12. Tentative treatment plan listing planned collateral contacts for further information and case management

Use of the MMPI 2. MMPI 2 scales can be very helpful when used as predictors of pain-coping strategies likely to be preferred by individuals with chronic pain.

ASSESSING AND MEASURING PAIN

1. Behavioral observation. Observed outward manifestations of pain may be offered by any significant person in the individual's life and by the therapist. These observations may include distorted posture, distorted ambulation, negative affect (irritable, fatigue, etc.), avoidance of activity, verbal complaints, and distressful facial expressions.

2. Subjective reports. The accuracy of subjective reports of pain is highly variable. It can be helpful to offer a conceptual range of pain from no experience of pain to pain that is intolerable (can't be any worse). This information can be clarified by using:

   A. A basic anatomical chart for identifying location/points of pain and type of pain.

   B. Facilitate the initiation of a journal for a brief period of time if clarification is necessary. **Concern is creating increased focus on the pain. However, information that can be gathered includes location, frequency, intensity, time of day which is worse, pain management techniques (what is helpful), etc.

   C. Create a pain diary to be used daily. The diary provides a record of the experience of pain and what was done to treat or manage the pain. This is valuable information for self-understanding and sharing recorded information with treating doctors during appointments for reviewing and problem-solving pain management/treatment.

THE PAIN SCALE

On a scale of-10 pain is identified as:

Pain at the worst it could be

Extreme Pain

Severe Pain

Moderate Pain

Mild Pain

No Pain

PAIN MANAGEMENT DIARY

PAIN MANAGEMENT DIARY

Please use this pain assessment scale to fill out your pain control log

```
0      1      2      3      4      5      6      7      8      9      10
No pain                                                        Worst pain you
                                                               can imagine
```

Date	Time	How severe is the pain? (use above scale)	Where is the pain?	Medicine or non-drug pain control method	How severe is the pain after 1 hour (use above scale)	Activity at time of pain

Adapted from: Clinical Guidelines Number 9. AHCPR Publication No. 94-0592: March 1994. Agency for Healthcare Research and Quality, Rockville, MD.

Using a pain diary worksheet shows the location where pain is experienced. Additionally, there are different symbols for making the location of pain on the diagram, which are descriptors of the type of pain that can be experienced. Every area that is marked as a location where pain is experienced should also be numbered between 0 and 10 to indicate the intensity of the pain experienced along with a corresponding symbol to identify the type of pain.

DAILY PAIN DIARY WORKSHEET

_____

Daily Pain Diary Worksheet		©Carrie Poole

Mark all places that hurt to day

Today's Date: _____ Time: _____

How do I feel right now? _____

S = Shooting pain
X = Stabbing pain
B = Burning pain
N = Numbness
A = Aching
P = Pins and Needles

Morning General Overall Pain Level	Afternoon General Overall Pain Level	Evening General Overall Pain Level
1 2 3 4 5 6 7 8 9 10 Low <------------> High	1 2 3 4 5 6 7 8 9 10 Low <------------> High	1 2 3 4 5 6 7 8 9 10 Low <------------------> High

Physical Symptoms

How well did I sleep?	What is my fatigue level?	How weak do I feel?
1 2 3 4 5 6 7 8 9 10 Rested <---------------> No Rest	1 2 3 4 5 6 7 8 9 10 Not tired <---------------> Exhausted	1 2 3 4 5 6 7 8 9 10 Not Weak <--------> Very Weak
How dizzy do I feel?	How is my eyesight?	How are my bowel movements?
1 2 3 4 5 6 7 8 9 10 Not dizzy <-----------> Very dizzy	1 2 3 4 5 6 7 8 9 10 Can read <------------> Can't focus	1 2 3 4 5 6 7 8 9 10 Constipated <-------------> Loose
How is my urination?	How is my hearing?	How is my walking?
1 2 3 4 5 6 7 8 9 10 Good <-------------------> Worst	1 2 3 4 5 6 7 8 9 10 Clear <------------------------> Worst	1 2 3 4 5 6 7 8 9 10 Good <---------------> Barely Walk

Mental/Cognitive/Emotional Symptoms

How is my thinking ability?	How anxious do I feel?	How depressed am I?
1 2 3 4 5 6 7 8 9 10 Clear <-----fuzzy-----> Who am I?	1 2 3 4 5 6 7 8 9 10 No fear <------shaky------> Extreme	1 2 3 4 5 6 7 8 9 10 None <---------------------> No hope
How angry do I feel?	How initable am I?	How happy am I?
1 2 3 4 5 6 7 8 9 10 Not angry <------------------> Livid	1 2 3 4 5 6 7 8 9 10 fine <-------------> leave me alone	1 2 3 4 5 6 7 8 9 10 Joyful <------------------> Unhappy

Possible Exacerbating Conditions

Current Temperatures	Current Pollen Count	Current Mold/Mildew Count
Indoor _____ Outdoor _____	1 2 3 4 5 6 7 8 9 10 Low <---------------------> High	1 2 3 4 5 6 7 8 9 10 Low <---------------------> High
Current Humidity	The Current Weather	Current Weather is Affecting Me
Indoor _____ Outdoor _____	Sunny Overcast Foggy Rainy Snowy	1 2 3 4 5 6 7 8 9 10 Not at all <------little------> Greatly

DAILY PAIN JOURNAL

Keeping a daily journal will help develop an understanding of the quality of the pain, the frequency, the association to activity, and what is most helpful in managing the pain. Therefore, use the information gathered by keeping a journal to identify the following and use it to improve communication with treating doctors as well as for improving self-care.

About how often do you get the pain?

__ more than once every day

__ once a day

__ at least once per week

__ at least once per month

__ less than once per month

__ only during specific activities (if yes, please explain)

_____

_____

_____

_____

_____

_____

How do other people try to help you when you have pain?_____

_____

_____

_____

How does the pain interfere in your life? What activities does it prevent you from doing?

_____

_____

_____

_____

_____

_____

If the individual is unable to use the 0 to 10 pain intensity scale, assess the following behavioral changes he/she experienced:

1. No behavioral/physiological changes indicating pain
2. Facial expressions (frowning, grimacing, fearful look)
3. Vocalizations (crying, moaning, grunting). Under what circumstances?
4. Sleep disturbance
5. Withdrawal or decreased social interaction
6. Guarding, rigidity, tension
7. Irritability, fidgeting
8. Physiological measures
   A. Increased heart rate/pulse
   B. Increased blood pressure

*The pain journal can be a comprehensive log that utilizes the resources of the pain scale, pain management diary, and pain chart.

INTERVENTIONS FOR CHRONIC PAIN

There are two perspective of intervention that must be addressed:

1. Understanding the physiological processes of the body
2. Taking into consideration the individuals' belief system, perspective, and response to pain
3. The importance of developing cognitive-behavioral management skills

*Case management requires a multidisciplinary, multimodal, and multilevel approach that offers individual flexibility and stepwise progression where possible (emotional and physical rehabilitation).

SIX STAGES OF TREATMENT

1. Assessment
2. Reconceptualization that offers an understanding of the multidimensional nature of the pain (psychological, emotional, cultural, social, and physical associations).
3. Skills development (cognitive and behavioral)
4. Rehearsal and application of skills developed
5. Generalization of new skills and effective management skills
6. Planned follow-up treatment sessions to maintain progress

INTERVENTIONS

1. Collateral contact(s) with treating physician(s) for clarification of etiology, lab results, and pharmacologic treatment.
   A. Assess patient's knowledge regarding their pain, its etiology, and its impact on their life and relationship. Let the patient verbalize in their own words their understanding of what is happening to them to cause the pain that they are experiencing and why it is happening. This practice of dialoging personal pain experience increases self-awareness.
2. During the initial phase of treatment, prepare an individual for their role in treatment planning and being the most significant person on the treatment team. Their compliance on recommendations and defined treatment interventions is imperative to the effective management of the case. Predict for them that, long term, there is a risk or tendency for regression due to the decrease in compliance and activity. Therefore, it is beneficial to schedule intermittent follow-up sessions for maintenance—and to serve as relapse prevention.
3. Refer for psychopharmacological evaluation if there is evidence of underlying emotional factors such as depression and anxiety.
4. Cognitive-behavioral interventions:
   A. Cognitive restructuring.
      1. Educate regarding the impact of negative thinking and negative self-talk. Develop calming self-talk and cognitive reappraisal.
      2. Facilitate development of compartmentalizing or being able to "put things away." In other words, not having to deal with something all of the time. It creates some experience of control.
      3. Facilitate a focus on "what is" versus "what if."
      4. Facilitate a focus on capabilities versus disabilities.
      5. Prayer helps some individuals alter their thinking patterns.
      6. Selective attention.
      7. Identify thoughts and feelings of helplessness, and in a supportive manner, confront with realistic information.

B. Relaxation training.
   1. Progressive muscle relaxation
   2. Visualization
   3. Hypnosis
   4. Meditation/mindfulness and breathing techniques (natural relaxation response)
   5. Systematic desensitization
C. Correcting maladaptive pain behavior patterns.
   1. Time contingent versus pain contingent programs (e.g., taking pain medication every 6 h as prescribed instead of "as needed").
   2. Functional rehabilitation through the use of physical therapy and occupational therapy to reclaim loss of functioning through a progressive hierarchy of task mastery.
   3. Decrease avoidant behavior and being self-absorbed/self-focused through increased interests and utilizing resources.
   4. Assess for abuse of pain management medication or other substances.
D. Biofeedback (review the literature for efficacy of treatment for specific etiology of pain). One example is use of the EMG.
E. Stress management.
   1. Relaxation training
   2. Stress inoculation training utilizing breathing techniques, imagery/visualization, progressive muscle relaxation, self-hypnosis or other focusing strategies, and cognitive restructuring
   3. Development and use of a self-care program
   4. Participation in pleasurable activities
   5. Regular, appropriate exercise
   6. Adequate nutrition
   7. Time management/prioritizing
F. Identify any precipitating stressors.
G. Encourage venting of feelings and explore the meaning that pain holds for the patient. This will help the patient connect symptoms of pain to emotional states.
H. To redirect the patient to other areas of their life, offer them reinforcing and engaging attention when they are not focusing on the pain. This serves as a reinforcer to encourage their adaptive behaviors. It may also act to facilitate as a transition to invest the patient in behaviors that distract them from the pain.
I. Explore with the patient various methods of intervention to utilize when symptoms intensify. Emphasize consistency in treatment compliance issues and the value of choosing constructive/supportive/interventions.
J. Facilitate effective coping.
   1. Validate patient's experience of pain. Acknowledgment and acceptance of their pain creates a foundation for improved coping.
   2. Identify any evident or presumed secondary gains related to pain experience such as attention, increased dependency, decreased responsibility, etc.
   3. Following initial fulfillment of dependency needs, begin to gradually withdraw attention from pain. Eventually any complaints of pain will be referred to the physician, therefore, reinforcing compartmentalization by the individual. Reframing it as part of their life experience—a life composed of many other factors.
   4. Encourage venting of anxiety and fears. Confront and problem-solve with reality-based information.
   5. Facilitate patient's insight into the relationship between psychosocial stressors and experience of pain.
   6. Explore and problem-solve the impact that chronic pain has had on relationships. Educate in a caring manner how the fears and frustration of others regarding their experience of pain create emotional distancing.
   7. Positive feedback and reinforcement for efforts and accomplishments.
   8. Encourage self-monitoring to develop self-reinforcement.
K. Issues of control.
   1. Facilitate identification of choices.
   2. Facilitate identification of how patient (can) manages issues which appear out of their control or are out of their control.
   3. Clarify what they "do" control over is how they choose to interpret their experience of pain and how they choose to manage it.

L. Body image issues.
  1. Encourage grieving for any issues of loss related to changes in functioning. This also affects personal identity and requires adjustment.
  2. Facilitate identification of distortion patient has regarding body image.
  3. Encourage self-acceptance.
  4. Encourage development and utilization of self-care program.
  5. Positive feedback and reinforcement for patient's acknowledgment of realistic body/physical perceptions.
  6. The development and utilization of a self-care program can serve to reorient the patient's perspective of the self and begin to heal damaged self-image.

SOMATIC PROBLEMS: A BRIEF REVIEW

The presentation of physical symptoms ranges from the consequences of acute or chronic stress on one end to somatoform disorders on the other. Somatic symptom disorders are a group of psychological disorders in which a patient experiences physical symptoms, which are inconsistent with or cannot be fully explained by any underlying general medical or neurologic condition. They can be represented by a wide spectrum of severity, ranging from mild self-limited symptoms, such as stomachache and headache, to chronic disabling symptoms, such as seizures and paralysis. These psychological disorders are often difficult to approach and complex to understand. It is important to note that these symptoms are not intentionally produced or under voluntary control. Medically unexplained physical symptoms account for as many as 50% of new medical outpatient visits. Physicians deal with the symptom presentation and engage in relative diagnostic procedures in an effort to clarify a diagnosis. When it becomes evident that there is not a functional, medical, or neurological basis for the symptoms, they often refer the patient to a therapist. *"The symptoms are not intentionally feigned or produced (as in Factitious Disorder or Malingering)" (psychcentral.com). Somatic presentation is characterized by the following:

1. Observable and identifiable disturbances of bodily functions
2. Disturbances of bodily functions, which are perceived rather than observed, or
3. Mixed (some combined presentation of items 1 and 2)

Somatic problems commonly seen in the mental health setting include these:

1. Headache
2. Insomnia
3. Abdominal distress
4. Irritable bowel syndrome
5. "Often ill" (as seen with some depressive individuals)
6. Illness anxiety disorder (along with somatic symptom disorder replaces hypochondriasis in DSM 5; Baller et al., 2016)

Both the causation and maintenance of somatic symptom conditions require exploration and treatment. Sometimes treatment is complicated by the presence of an actual physical condition. Such situations need a sophisticated direct psychological approach that does not focus on ruling out a physical condition, but instead frames in a positive psychological manner the problems experienced by the patient. A consultation with the treating physician is necessary to appropriately consider the following:

1. A realistic description of the patient's physical state
2. The course of the physical condition
3. Any physical limitations that affect psychological treatment

Patients presenting with somatic problems believe that their problems have a physical cause, which may be accurate or inaccurate. When this perception is distorted and exaggerated, it becomes a source of difficulty and anxiety. They look for evidence to support their perceptions and as a result misinterpret symptoms. Sometimes this may be an issue of miscommunication between the patient and a medical professional whereby the patient's physical functioning may vary from the norm but is considered as relative to the patient and not an impairment as the patient may believe. Regardless, when the therapist initially assesses the patient, they may likely to feel:

1. Fearful of the possibility of further decompensation
2. Fearful emotional distress of dependency
3. Dealing with issues of loss
4. Overwhelmed by the process of making associated adjustments
5. Angry
6. Depressed/anxious

Therefore, one's reaction to physical impairment, real or perceived, can be changes in thoughts, behavior, mood, and physiological functioning.

THE PATIENT WITH PSYCHOSOMATIC ILLNESS WHO HAS AN UNDERLYING PERSONALITY DISORDER

When a psychiatric problem, such as depression, anxiety, or another disturbance, manifests itself as seemingly unrelated physical symptoms, it is referred to a psychosomatic disorder. This diagnosis can only be given if there is no other medical explanation for the symptoms. Such a case will present numerous psychodynamic challenges and requires a sophisticated level of clinical expertise. Consider the following issues:

1. Psychosomatic symptoms associated with an underlying personality disorder present a significant challenge to the therapist. In this case, psychosomatic patients may demonstrate impulse-dominated modes of functioning utilizing the following defenses:
   A. Denial/splitting
   B. Magical thinking
   C. Feelings of omnipotence
   D. Demands of perfection versus worthlessness (extremes)
   E. Displacement/projection/projective identification
   F. Masochistic perfectionism
   G. Fantasized parental relationships (i.e., conflict-free mother–child relationship)
2. Psychosomatic *families* demonstrate a parental psychosocial profile that can be reviewed for problem solving diagnostically and in the treatment planning approach. The acronym for this system review is PRISES:
   Perfectionism—emphasis on:
   A. Good behavior
   B. Social conformity
   C. Exemplary childhood/adolescent developmental performance

*Results in indirect communication and separation attempts.

Repression of emotions caused by:

D. Parental hypermorality (evidenced by)
  1. Strict emotional control in front of children
  2. Aggressive behavior of children not allowed (in general aggression denied)
  3. Downplay/maximizing of successes
  4. Mother deferred to as moral authority

*The aforementioned serves as a demonstration of rigid internalization of good/bad (w/o rational review and growth in belief system).

Infantilizing decision-making control:

E. Everything has to be a noble purpose
  1. Major home activity is an intellectual discussion
  2. Scholarly reading
  3. Independent activity/assertiveness leads to consequences of humiliation

*Resulting in inability to make decisions with attempts to get others (therapist) to make decisions for them.

Organ-System choice:

F. Development of psychosomatic symptoms
  1. Ulcerative colitis
  2. Anorexia
  3. Asthma

Exhibitionism by parent(s):

G. Doors to bathrooms or bedroom left unlocked or open
  1. Facilitating child curiosity
  2. Overexposure paired with parental hypermorality
  3. Resulting inhibition in normal psychosexual development

Selection of one child (unconscious selection):

H. Treated differently than siblings
  1. Used as a confidant
  2. Infantialized (babied)
  3. Total devotion to selected child to exclusion of spouse/siblings

*Lack of individuality, poor boundaries, passive-aggressive.

Adapted from Wilson C.P., and Mintz, I.L. (1989). *Psychosomatic symptoms: Psychodynamic treatment of the underlying personality disorder.*

EATING DISORDER SCREENING AND ASSESSMENT

Eating disorders are a relatively common psychiatric disorder. Early detection and treatment improve the prognosis, but the presentation of eating disorders is often ambiguous. Eating disorders can be rooted historically in infant struggle with regulatory disorder associated with eating/food or developed in adolescence as dynamic of control.

EATING DISORDERS SCREENING QUESTIONNAIRE

1. Have you ever been diagnosed and treated for an eating disorder?

    _____ Yes _____ No

    If so, please explain _____

    _____

2. Height: _____

3. Weight: _____

4. Highest weight in the past 6 months: _____

5. Lowest weight at your current height: _____ How recently? _____

6. Have you missed two or more menstrual periods in the past 6 months?

    _____ Yes ___ No

For the following questions answer never (N), sometime (S), often (O), or always (A).

__Do you worry about gaining weight?

__Do you avoid certain foods because of calories, carbohydrate, sugar, or fat content?

__How often do you think about wanting to be thinner?

__Are you distressed about having fat on your body?

__Do you feel guilty after eating?

__Do you feel that food controls your life?

__During the past 6 months have you exercised to control your weight, even when you were not feeling well or against the recommendation of your physician?

__During the past 6 months, has exercising to control your weight interfered with other activities?

__Do your concerns or eating behaviors interfere with your relationships?

__Do your concerns or eating behaviors interfere with academic/work performance?

__Do your concerns, eating behaviors, or weight gain cause you a lot of distress?

During the past 6 months, have you had periods where you ate unusually large amounts of food within 2 h (bingeing), and have you felt unable to control how much you were eating at these times?   __Never

__Less than one time per month

__About one time per month

__About one time per week

__Two or more times per week

If you have experienced binge eating episodes (as described in the previous question), would you describe the experience as any of the following:

___ Yes ___No   Eating faster than usual?

___ Yes ___No   Eating until you felt uncomfortable?

___ Yes ___No   Eating a lot of food when you didn't feel hungry?

___ Yes ___No   Eating alone because you were embarrassed about the amount of food you were eating?

___ Yes ___No   Feeling depressed, guilty, or disgusted with yourself for overeating?

For the following statements, answer never (N), less than once a month (LM), about once a month (AM), about once a week (AW), or two or more times a week (MW).

__I have self-induced vomiting in an attempt to avoid gaining weight or to lose weight.

__I have taken laxatives in an attempt to avoid gaining weight or to lose weight.

____I have restricted my eating in an attempt to avoid gaining weight or to lose weight (eating less than 500 calories a day or skipping two or more meals a day).

____I have taken diuretics (water pills) in an attempt to avoid gaining weight or to lose weight.

____I have exercised in an attempt to avoid gaining weight or to lose weight.

How did these behaviors start? _____

_____

_____

_____

_____

_____

_____

_____

How do you feel when you engage in these behaviors? _____

_____

_____

_____

_____

_____

_____

_____

THE SCOFF QUESTIONNAIRE (MORGAN, REID, & LACEY, 2000)

THE SCOFF QUESTIONS*

1. Do you make yourself Sick because you feel uncomfortably full?
2. Do you worry that you have lost Control over how much you eat?
3. Have you recently lost more than One stone (14 lb) in a 3-month period?
4. Do you believe yourself to be Fat when others say you are too thin?
5. Would you say that Food dominates your life?

*The SCOFF questions may not provide a high level of sensitivity; however, it does provide clinical information warranting further exploration for the presence of an eating disorder.

THE MOOD EATING SCALE

If you agree with a statement, check it off.

___When I feel overwhelmed, eating can help me to feel relieved.

—Eating helps to calm me down when I feel nervous.

__If someone treats me badly, I find myself eating after it happens.

__If I am feeling frustrated, eating may not make me feel better.

__When I am feeling really happy, eating makes me feel even better.

__When I eat certain foods I feel guilty, but I find myself eating more of those foods than others (those foods are_____)

__When I am feeling stressed, I eat more food than usual (for example, when I have relationship problems, exams, or significant changes such as job, moving, school).

__If I had conflict with someone that I care about, eating would help to make me feel better.

__I generally do not eat when I am bored.

__If I feel inadequate, I find myself wanting to eat.

__If things feel out of control, I seem to eat more than usual.

__If I am angry with someone, eating doesn't make me feel better.

__If I am disgusted with myself, I feel like eating.

__I snack a lot while studying for tests.

__At times when everything seems to go wrong, I don't eat any more than usual.

__If someone makes fun of how I look, I find myself wanting to eat.

__When I feel like I am about to explode from stuffing my feelings, I feel better if I eat.

__If I fail at something I don't eat any more than usual.

__If someone has taken advantage of me, it will make me feel better if I eat.

__When I feel stressed and under pressure, I find myself eating more often.

__When I am lonely, I eat more.

Use this information for increasing your awareness for the connection between thoughts, feelings, and behaviors. Such information can be explored in journal writing and in therapy. Ask yourself the following questions about what you have learned regarding your eating patterns and how you use food to soothe your mood states:

1. **What insight did you gain from this exercise?**

   _____

   _____

2. **What are two things that you will do differently based on your experience with this exercise?**

   _____

   _____

(L. L. Jackson and R. C. Hawkins II, 1980; American Council on Exercise, 2014.)

EATING HISTORY

Please use the following form to record your eating history. Write about your loss of control associated with food use, rituals, and practices regarding the food you choose. When you have completed your eating history, share it with another person to break the cycle of secrecy and loneliness.

Consider the following:

1. Kinds, amounts, and frequency of food use

   Put this information in a timeline (at what age, what were/are the triggers)

2. Foggy memories or difficulty concentrating after eating too much

   Not able to think clearly

3. Feeling high after vomiting or starving
4. Feeling powerful and in control after vomiting or starving
5. Behavior changes
    A. Mood swings with eating/not eating
    B. Withdrawal from others to eat or starve
    C. Compulsive patterns, such as purchasing food to binge or changing to another compulsion when eating behavior becomes more healthy (trading compulsions)
6. Rituals surrounding food use
    A. Overeating or binge eating certain foods
    B. Frequent eating out
    C. Sneak eating
    D. Weighing self daily or more often
    E. Selecting specific foods and why
    F. Exercise
7. Preoccupation
    A. Thinking about eating/not eating
    B. Eating for relief from problems, boredom, frustration, etc. (using food as a coping mechanism)
    C. Protecting food supply; hiding food/hoarding
    D. Preoccupation with body size
    E. Carefully choosing clothes that mask starvation
    F. Preoccupation with secrecy and control
8. Beliefs
    A. What life changes are expected with weight loss/control of eating?
    B. How would the relationship with yourself change with weight loss/control of eating?
9. Attempts to control eating and/or weight
    A. Physician monitored diets
    B. Fad diets
    C. Diet pills and/or shots
    D. Starving, vomiting, laxative use, or manual extraction of stool
    E. Diet clubs or fat farms
    F. Hypnosis, acupuncture, stomach stapling, or gastric bypass surgery
    G. Spending money to control eating or weight
    H. Plastic surgery procedures

CHECKLIST OF OBSERVABLE EATING DISORDER BEHAVIORS

There are general observations made by a concerned friend or family member that can result in a referral to a physician or clinician specializing in the assessment and treatment of eating disorders. The following checklist offers a review of the types of observable behaviors that may be associated with an eating disorder:

1. Does anything to avoid hunger and avoid eating even when hungry
2. Is terrified about being overweight or gaining weight
3. Obsessive preoccupation with food
4. Eats large quantities of food secretly
5. Counts calories in all foods eaten
6. Disappears into the bathroom after eating
7. Vomits and either tries to hide it or is not concerned about it

8. Feels guilty after eating
9. Is preoccupied with a desire to lose weight
10. Must earn food through exercising
11. Uses exercise as punishment for overeating
12. Is preoccupied with fat in food and on the body
13. Increasingly avoids more and more food groups
14. Eats only nonfat or "diet" foods
15. Becomes a vegetarian (in some cases will not eat beans, cheese, nuts, and other vegetarian protein)
16. Displays rigid control around food: in the type, quantity, and timing of food eaten (food may be missing later)
17. Complains of being pressured by others to eat more or eat less
18. Weighs obsessively and panics without a scale available
19. Complains of being too fat even when normal weight or thin, and at times isolates socially because of this
20. Always eats when upset
21. Goes on and off diets (often gains more weight each time)
22. Forgoes nutritious food on a regular basis for sweets or alcohol
23. Complains about specific body parts and asks for constant reassurance regarding appearance
24. Constantly checks the fitting of belt, ring, and "thin" clothes to see if any fit too tightly

EATING DISORDER EVALUATION: ANOREXIA

1. Psychological evaluation
   A. Eating behaviors
   B. Weight
   C. Emotional symptoms
   D. Stressful life events
   E. Stressful life circumstances
   F. Parental verbal abuse
   G. History of mental/emotional illness
   H. Mental status
   I. Strengths/weaknesses
   J. Motivation for treatment
   K. Prior treatment experiences and outcome
   L. Collateral contact with family members/other treating professionals
2. Review diagnostic criteria
   A. Significant weight loss (less than 85% of ideal weight)
   B. Significant failure to gain weight normally
   C. Denial of the seriousness of weight loss or low body weight
   D. Excessive influence of body and weight on self-perception and self-evaluation
   E. Intense fear of gaining weight
   F. Loss of menstruation or delayed onset of menses
   G. Exploring other compulsive behaviors such as substance abuse
   H. Coexisting disorders (depression, anxiety disorders, PTSD, OCD, SUDs)
3. Physical symptoms and signs
   A. Dry skin

    B. Sallow skin/complexion

    C. Appearance/increase in fine hair on the body

4. Medical complications (physician review) (Note: This is not an exhaustive list.)

    A. Cardiac abnormalities (arrhythmia, slow heart rate)

    B. Low blood pressure

    C. Low body temperature

    D. Low white blood cell count

    E. Chronic constipation

    F. Osteoporosis

    G. Amenorrhea/infertility

    H. Hair loss

    I. Nail destruction

5. Referrals

    A. Physician's medical evaluation

    B. Registered dietician

    C. Family therapy

    D. Group therapy

    E. Specific eating disorder program

    F. Inpatient treatment

6. Treatment recommendations

    A. Psychotherapy (cognitive-behavioral, interpersonal, psychodynamic)

      1. Individual, family, conjoint, group

    B. Antidepressant medication

    C. Medical evaluation and possible monitoring

    D. Nutritional counseling

    E. Self-help groups

EATING DISORDER EVALUATION: BULIMIA

1. Psychological evaluation

    A. Eating behaviors

    B. Weight

    C. Emotional symptoms

    D. Stressful life events

    E. Stressful life circumstances

    F. Parental verbal abuse

    G. History of mental/emotional illness

    H. Mental status

    I. Strengths/weaknesses

    J. Motivation for treatment

    K. Prior treatment experiences and outcome

    L. Collateral contacts with family members/other treating professionals

2. Review diagnostic criteria

    A. Episodic binge eating (eating an extremely large amount of food within a specified period of time while feeling out of control)

    B. Episodic purging behavior, which includes vomiting, laxative use, diuretic use, enema use, fasting, or excessive exercise to prevent weight gain

C. Overconcern with body weight and shape

D. History of other compulsive behaviors such as shoplifting or substance abuse

E. Coexisting disorders (depression, anxiety disorders, PTSD, OCD, substance abuse)

*Binge eating disorder lacks purging behaviors

3. Physical symptoms and signs
    A. Dental enamel erosion and cavities
    B. Swelling of cheeks, hands, and feet
    C. Abdominal fullness, constipation, diarrhea
    D. Abrasions on knuckles
    E. Headaches
    F. Fatigue
    G. Hair loss

4. Medical complications (physician review) (Note: This is not an exhaustive list.)
    A. Electrolyte and fluid abnormalities (low serum potassium values)
    B. Dehydration
    C. Enlarged parotid glands (glands in the cheeks associated with salivation)
    D. Dental enamel erosion and cavities
    E. Bowel abnormalities

5. Referral
    A. Physician's medical evaluation
    B. Registered dietician
    C. Family therapy
    D. Group therapy
    E. Specific eating disorder program
    F. Dentist

6. Treatment recommendations
    A. Psychotherapy (cognitive-behavioral, interpersonal, psychodynamic)
    B. Individual, family, conjoint, group
    C. Antidepressant medication
    D. Medical evaluation and possibly monitoring
    E. Nutritional counseling
    F. Self-help groups

ATTENTION-DEFICIT DISORDER

Attention deficit may go unrecognized in childhood as a result of adequate compensation.

However, as stress and responsibilities increase, difficulty may become more evident. With education, support, and creative problem solving, symptoms can be managed. Undiagnosed adult attention-deficit disorder (ADD) can create problems in every major life area:

1. Physical and mental health issues
2. Work difficulties
3. Financial difficulties
4. Relationship problems

Some people are able to effectively manage the level of ADD symptoms they experience by challenging symptoms with structure, activities, and consistency:

1. Exercise and nutrition. Vigorous exercise can be a benefit to work off excess energy, and eating healthy foods (limiting sugar) can alleviate or eliminate mood swings. Structured activities, though struggling with distraction, can be beneficial.
2. Get adequate sleep. Without enough sleep, it is difficult to focus, manage stress, and remain on task with responsibilities. All of this negative impacts being effective and productive.
3. Keep a daily schedule of demands, and practice effective time management prioritizing time sensitive tasks.
4. Invest in relationships by scheduling activities with those that are important. Practice being "present" in conversations but avoid speaking too quickly. Relationships are cultivated by demonstrated interest and care.
5. Work smart by creating a supportive work environment using lists, reminders, color-coding, routines, and files. Pay attention to energy levels and workplace conditions to determine most effective times of the day and when energy is high, low, or flattens out. These factors are important to effectiveness and that means carefully scheduling what time of day to work on specific tasks with varying demands.

If symptoms are managed utilizing the factors previously identified, it is time to pursue intervention with an ADD specialist that can help:

1. Control impulsive behaviors
2. Manage your time and money
3. Get and stay organized
4. Boost productivity at home and work
5. Manage stress and anger
6. Communicate more clearly

ADULT ATTENTION-DEFICIT DISORDER SCREENING

A symptom checklist is a quick way to screen this specific diagnostic area and identify a constellation of symptoms that may warrant referral to an ADD specialist. The following areas of review will only take a few minutes. Check off areas identified as a problem and with each one checked "yes," explore the frequency of experience (never, rarely sometimes, almost always).

History

__Experienced ADD symptoms in childhood, such as difficulty maintaining attention, tendency to be easily distracted, impulsive, restless (it is a disorder that initiates in childhood not adulthood)

__Has not performed up to level of potential in school or work

__History of behavioral problems

__Experienced bed wetting beyond age 5

__Family history: ADD

                  Learning disabilities

                  Mood disorders

                  Substance abuse problems

                  Impulse control problems

Attention Span/Distractibility

__Short attention span, unless very interested and engaged

__Easily distracted

__Fails to pay adequate attention to detail

__Difficulty listening carefully to directions

__Often misplaces things

__Difficulty learning new games or tasks

__Easily distracted during intimacy

__Poor listening skills

__Tendency to space out

__Tendency to get bored

Problems Initiating and Following Through on Tasks

__General procrastination

__Does not complete tasks once started

__Motivated beginning, poor ending

__Tasks take longer due to inefficiency

__Inconsistent school/work performance

Poor Organizational Skills

__Poor organization and planning skills

__Difficulty maintaining organization in work/living
    environment

__Common to have piles of stuff

__Easily overwhelmed by daily tasks

__Poor financial management

__Able to be effective only with the organizational
    support of others

Restlessness

__Constant motion, fidgeting

__Needs to be moving to think about things

__Difficulty sitting still for too long (work, home, leisure)

__Feels anxious, nervous, on edge

Impulsivity

__Impulsive (spending, speaks before thinking)

__Difficulty following protocol/proper procedure

__Impatient

__Difficulty living beyond the moment

__Embarrasses others

__Lies or steals

__Frequent traffic violations

__Does not consider consequences associated with actions

__Tendency toward addictions (food, alcohol, substances, work)

Internal Feelings/Self-esteem

__Negative self-esteem

__Chronic bad feelings about self, which are associated with
    underachievement

__Unhappy with self for not having accomplished more at this stage of life

__Feelings that "the other shoe is about to drop"

__Negative thinking
__Mood swings
__Often feels demoralized
__Often feels that things will not work out well
__Tendency to worry needlessly and endlessly

Relationship Issues
__Difficulty maintaining relationships (friendships, significant relationships)
__Promiscuity
__Difficulty with intimacy
__Immature behavior
__Immature interests
__Difficulty empathizing with or understanding the needs of others
__Difficulty communicating within a relationship
__Self-focused
__Difficulty with authority
__Avoids group activities
__Verbally abusive

Anger Management
__Short fuse to real or imagined negative personal remarks
__Rageful outburst
__Damages property

Need for Stimulation
__May be argumentative
__May create conflicts
__Gravitates toward a high degree of stimulation (gambling, high-stress job)

Dyslexic Responses
__Switches numbers, letters, words
__Switches words in conversation

Coordination
__Poor writing skills (difficulty translating thoughts to written form)
__Often prints versus cursive handwriting
__General coordination difficulties

Pressure and Performance
__Performance deteriorates under pressure
__Tendency to go blank during tests (test anxiety)
__Tendency to shut down during social pressure/social situations
__Difficulty remaining focused during reading (may feel tired and fall asleep)
__No matter how hard one tries, it just gets worse
__Easily overwhelmed with pressure

Sensitivity
__Easily startled by unsuspecting noises
__Sensitive to noise
__Sensitive to touch
__Sensitive to the feeling of clothing
__Sensitive to light

Sleep/Wake Cycle
__Difficulty resting mind and falling asleep (continues to think about things)
__Does not awaken feeling alert
__Needs morning ritual of coffee or activity to get going

Energy Level
__Episodes of fatigue
__Energy low in morning and afternoon
__Often feels tired

A history of ADD symptoms in childhood, short attention span, and a high level of distractibility are necessary to consider a diagnosis of ADD.

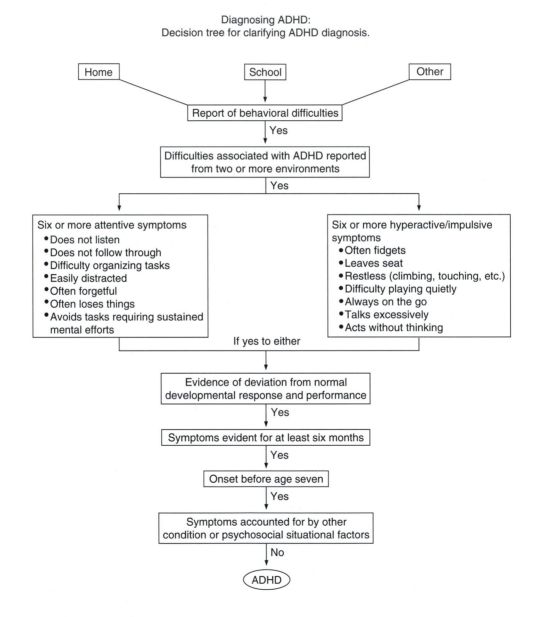

Diagnosing ADHD:
Decision tree for clarifying ADHD diagnosis.

ATTENTION-DEFICIT/HYPERACTIVITY DISORDER BEHAVIORAL REVIEW (CHILD)

Below find a list of behaviors one can review in establishing difficulties experienced by a child with a potential diagnosis of ADHD and referral for testing by a clinical specialist. When a therapist is consulting with teachers or parents, this information can be used to indicate the importance of an ADHD evaluation and referral for medical treatment. It is often valuable to assess parents for ADD when a child is being presented for a potential diagnosis of ASS/ADHD.

Child's name: _____

Gender: M F

Age: _____   Grade: _____

1. Does not give close attention to details.
2. Makes careless mistakes in schoolwork.
3. Squirms in seat and fidgets hands/feet.
4. Demonstrates difficulty maintaining attention on tasks/play activities.
5. Does not stay in seat or room as directed.
6. Does not appear to listen when being directly spoken to.
7. Exhibits behavior that is inappropriate to situations (climbing on things/getting into things when it is appropriate to be relatively quiet).
8. Does not follow instructions.
9. Fails to complete work.
10. Demonstrates difficulty playing quietly.
11. Demonstrates difficulty organizing tasks/activities.
12. Seems to be constantly on the go.
13. Avoids tasks that require consistent/sustained mental effort.
14. Talks constantly.
15. Constantly losing things that are needed for tasks/activities.
16. Is not able to wait his/her turn to talk or blurts out answers.
17. Is not able to wait for questions to be fully stated before answering.
18. Demonstrates difficulty waiting his/her turn.
19. Is easily distracted.
20. Demonstrates forgetfulness in daily tasks/activities.
21. Interrupts others.
22. Is intrusive in behavior/talking.

Adapted from Du Paul, G. J., et al. (1998). *ADHD Rating, Scale-IV*, School Version.

Adapted from Anastopolous, A. D., & Shelton, T. L. (2001). *Assessing Attention Deficit/Hyperactivity Disorder*. And DSM 5 (APA, 2013).

SUBSTANCE USE SCREENING AND ASSESSMENT

SUDs are common among those presenting in crisis. Substance use can exacerbate psychiatric symptoms and thus playing a role in crises developments. SUDs mimic numerous psychiatric and medical disorders. That and the prevalence of substance use underlie the reason that SUDs are to be assessed for with every clinical contact. Substance use has plagued society with tragic consequences to the lives of abusers, their family and friends, and society in general. Additional problems associated with substance use include risk of DV, sexual assault, and child sexual abuse (Bell, Harford, Fuchs, McCarroll, & Schwartz, 2006).

There are numerous evidence-based screening tools that can be accessed on government websites.

THE CAGE AND CAGE-AID QUESTIONNAIRE

1. Have you ever felt you ought to cut down on your drinking *or drug use*?
2. Have people annoyed you by criticizing your drinking *or drug use*?
3. Have you ever felt bad or guilty about your drinking *or drug use*?
4. Have you ever had a drink *or used drugs* first thing in the morning to steady your nerves or to get rid of a hangover?

Note. The plain text shows the CAGE questions. The italicized text was added to produce the CAGE-AID. For this study, the CAGE-AID was preceded by the following instruction: "When thinking about drug use, include illegal drug use and the use of prescription drugs other than as prescribed."

Adapted from "The prevalence and detection of substance use disorder among inpatients ages 18 to 49: An opportunity for prevention" by Brown RL, Leonard T, Saunders LA, Papasouliotis O. Preventive Medicine, Volume 27, pages 101–110, Copyright 1998, Elsevier Science (USA), reproduced with permission from the publisher.

THE CAGE AND CAGE-AID QUESTIONS

The original CAGE questions appear in plain type. The CAGE questions Adapted to Include Drugs (CAGE-AID) are the original CAGE questions modified by the *italicized text*.

The CAGE or CAGE-AID should be preceded by these two questions:

1. Do you drink alcohol?
2. Have you ever experimented with drugs?

If the patient has experimented with drugs, ask the CAGE-AID questions. If the patient only drinks alcohol, ask the CAGE questions.

1. In the last 3 months, have you felt you should cut down or stop drinking or *using drugs?*
   ____ Yes ____ No
2. In the last 3 months, has anyone annoyed you or gotten on your nerves by telling you to cut down or stop drinking or *using drugs?*
   ____ Yes ____ No
3. In the last 3 months, have you felt guilty or bad about how much you drink *or use drugs?*
   ____ Yes ____ No
4. In the last 3 months, have you been waking up wanting to have an alcoholic drink or *use drugs?*
   ____ Yes ____ No

Each affirmative response earns one point. One point indicates a possible problem. Two points indicate a probable problem.

Reference: The Society of Teachers of Family Medicine. Project SAEFP Workshop Materials, Screening and Assessment Module, page 18. Funded by the Division of Health Professionals, HRSA, DHHS, Contract No. 240-89-0038.

SUBSTANCE USE ASSESSMENT

_____

Date: _____

Name: _____

1. Description of Patient (identifying information):

   _____

   _____

   _____

   _____

2. Reason for Referral:

   _____

   _____

   _____

   _____

3. Patient's Perception of Substance Use:

   _____

   _____

   _____

   _____

4. Patient's Treatment Expectations and Goals:

   _____

   _____

   _____

   _____

5. Effects of Lifestyle/Symptomatology:
   A. Family (History of family problems in origin and/or present family including chemical dependency);

   _____

   _____

   B. Social (Description of peer association, isolation/hypersocialization):

   _____

   _____

   C. Occupational/Scholastic (Absenteeism because of chemical use, decreased performance, dismissal):

   _____

   _____

D. Physical (Emesis, blackouts/pass-outs, hallucinations, tremors, convulsions, serious injury/illness, surgery, handicaps):

_____

_____

E. Psychological/Emotional (Cognitive functioning, emotionality, paranoia, history of treatment, behavioral problems):

_____

_____

F. Spiritual (Change or conflict within belief system):

_____

_____

G. Financial:

_____

_____

H. Legal Implications (Underage consumption, driving while under the influence, dealing; include disposition if any):

_____

_____

6. Diagnostic Impression:

_____

_____

_____

7. Impressions and Recommendations:

Client's response to therapist: ☐ cooperative ☐ fearful ☐ suspicious ☐ hostile ☐ negative ☐ other _____

Mental status:

Mood	__normal __depressed __elevated __euphoric __angry __irritable __anxious
Affect	__normal __broad __restricted __blunted __flat __inappropriate __liable
Memory	__intact __short-term deficit __long-term deficit
Processes	__normal __blocking __loose associations __confabulations __flight of ideas __ideas of reference __grandiosity __paranoia __obsession __perseverations __depersonalization __suicidal ideation __homicidal ideation
Hallucinations	__none __auditory __visual __olfactory __gustatory __somatic __tactile
Judgment	__good __fair __poor
Insight	__good __fair __poor
Impulse Control	__good __fair __poor

Client's Attitude Toward Treatment: ☐ accepting ☐ neutral ☐ resistant

Communication: ☐ talkative ☐ satisfactory ☐ open ☐ guarded

☐ answers questions only ☐ other _____

Therapist _____   Date _____

SUBSTANCE USE PSYCHOLOGICAL ASSESSMENT

Date: _____   Age: _____

Name: _____

S.O. Name _____   Phone: _____

Religious/ethnic/cultural background: _____

_____

Marital Status: _____   Children: _____

Living with Whom: _____

Present Support System (family/friends): _____

Substance Use History:

Age	Last Dose	Length Chemical Use	Route	Age Started	Amt.	Freq.	Last Used	Length of Use

Description of Presenting Substance Use Problems (pt's view): _____

_____

Previous Counseling:

When	Where	Therapist/Title	Response To

Family/S.O. relationships/History of Substance Use: _____

_____

_____

_____

S.O. Relationships and History of Substance Use: _____

_____

_____

_____

Effects of substance use on Family/Support System: _____

_____

_____

_____

Daily Activities that: A. Support Abstinence: _____

                     B. Encourage Usage: _____

History of Sexual/Physical Abuse (victim/abuser): _____

_____

_____

Education: _____

Vocational History: _____

Leisure/Social Interests: _____

_____

Current Occupation: _____

Current Employer: _____

Impact of Substance Use on Job Performance: _____

_____

Socioeconomic/Financial Problems: _____

_____

_____

Legal: _____ DUI: Yes _____ No _____   Court Ordered: Yes _____ No _____

Patient's Perceptions of Strengths and Weaknesses: _____

_____

_____

Preliminary Treatment Plan: List presenting problems based on initial assessment of the client's physical, emotional, cognitive, and behavioral status

Detox: Yes _____ No _____ Explain: _____

Rehab: Yes _____ No _____ Explain: _____

Problem #1: _____

Problem #2: _____

Problem #3: _____

_____

Immediate treatment recommendations to address identifying problems:

_____

_____

_____

_____

Therapist _____   Date _____

SUBSTANCE USE HISTORY

Check if used	Chemical classification	Description of substance	Past history				Current use (last 6 months)			Comments (cost, chemical of choice)
			First use (onset)	Age of regular use	Frequency and amount	Range of frequency (include date of last use)	Range of amount	Route of administration		
	Alcohol									
	Amphetamines									
	Cannabis									
	Cocaine									
	Hallucinogens									
	Inhalants									
	Opiates									
	Phencyclidine (PCP)									
	Sedatives/Hypnotics/ Anxiolytics									

SUBSTANCE USE DISORDERS WITHDRAWAL

SUDs withdrawal is identified by two stages. The first stage is referred to as acute and generally does not last beyond a couple of weeks. Keeping in mind the *individualized* experience (the person and the substance) as everyone is different to some degree even though a broad view is commonly applied for the benefit of education in recovery group setting. The second stage is referred to as postacute withdrawal syndrome or PAWS. PAWS is experienced with fewer physical symptoms, but increased emotional and psychological withdrawal symptoms as a consequence brain chemistry incrementally returning to normal. The course of brain chemistry "recovery," i.e., approaching equilibrium, is not a linear progression but rather experienced by fluctuations that result in postacute withdrawal (PAW) symptoms. It is expected that each PAW episode will last for a couple of days and cannot be predicted by specific triggers. Commonly a person will wake up feeling under the weather and irritable, but just as it unexpectedly popped up it also comes to an end. As a patient processes these experiences in their recovery program, they develop confidence that the episode will last for a brief period and they can deal with it.

WITHDRAWAL SYMPTOMS CHECKLIST

Ratings: 0 = none   1 = mild   2 = moderate   3 = severe

PSYCHOLOGICAL

__ Drowsiness
__ Excitability (jumpiness, restlessness)
__ Unreality
__ Poor memory/concentration
__ Confusion
__ Perceptual distortion
__ Hallucinations
__ Obsessions
__ Agoraphobia/phobias
__ Panic attacks
__ Agitation
__ Emotionally overwhelmed
__ Depression
__ Fear
__ Paranoid thoughts
__ Rage/aggression/irritability
__ Craving

SOMATIC

__ Headache
__ Pain (limbs, back, neck)
__ Pain (teeth, jaw)
__ Tingling/numbness altered sensation (limbs, face, trunk)
__ Stiffness (limbs, back, jaw)
__ Weakness ("jelly legs")
__ Tremor
__ Muscle twitches
__ Ataxia (lack of muscle coordination)
__ Dizziness/light-headedness
__ Blurred/double vision
__ Ringing in the ears
__ Speech difficulty
__ Hypersensitivity (light, sound, taste, smell)
__ Insomnia/nightmares
__ Tantrums
__ Nausea/vomiting

__ Abdominal pain
__ Diarrhea/constipation
__ Appetite/weight change
__ Dry mouth
__ Metallic taste
__ Difficulty swallowing
__ Skin rash/itching
__ Stuffy nose/sinusitis
__ Influenza-like symptoms
__ Sore eyes
__ Flushing/sweating
__ Palpitations
__ Overbreathing
__ Thirst
__ Frequency/polyuria, pain on micturition
__ Incontinence
__ Abnormal heavy periods
__ Mammary pain/swelling
__ Other symptoms (specify)_____

COMMON POSTACUTE WITHDRAWAL SYNDROME SYMPTOMS

1. Mood swings
2. Anxiety
3. On-edge
4. Irritability
5. Tiredness or fatigue
6. Sleep disturbance
7. Variable energy
8. Apathy/decreased enthusiasm
9. Difficulty with concentration/increased distractibility

COPING WITH POSTACUTE WITHDRAWAL SYNDROME

As with all forms of emotional distress, being educated about what to expect along with being provided with management skills will improve coping ability, personal growth, and self-monitoring as well as providing a positive reinforcement to relapse prevention.

1. Develop a realistic expectation of symptoms and how long PAWS could continue to pop up.
2. Be patient. Recovery is a process lived 1 day at a time and while it is difficult it is survivable.
3. The more you resist the more it persists. This simply means go with the wave instead of being angry or resentful. Some days are rough and some days are good. Learn how to do the best you can to get through bad days.
4. Self-care behaviors are an essential factor in recovery and relapse prevention. It is a challenge to live the understanding that the recovery process is the opposite of addiction.
5. Relaxation and recreation. Because a feeling of fatigue and stress/tension is associated with PAWS, developing both relaxation and recreation choices is important. Making a choice of R & R is a positive way to avoid dwelling on the discomfort being experienced. *This too shall pass.*
   A. Relaxation could be listening to gentle music or nature sounds, practicing mindfulness, breathing techniques, etc.
   B. Recreation could take the form of getting out a coloring book, watching a humorous movie, etc.
6. Affiliation. Even though there may be the desire to withdraw socially and isolate, it is important to be around people who understand and talk about it. This will increase confidence and decrease the risk of relapse.
7. Expecting the unexpected. Weeks could pass without any PAWS, and then those uncomfortable symptoms can catch a person off guard. However, when a person knows this can happen, they can also plan how they will deal with it.

The National Institute on Drug Abuse (NIDA) website offers information from drugs of abuse, emerging trends of concern, and the latest science. NIDA provides a questionnaire "NIDA Quick Screen V1.O," which will take the clinician through a systematic interview assessment of substance use and can be found online at www.drugabuse.gov.

DOMESTIC VIOLENCE

The victim of DV is often reluctant to acknowledge and admit that abuse has occurred. They have been beaten down emotionally, suffer from low self-esteem, feelings of worthlessness or unworthiness, and convinced that they are incapable of managing their own lives. Therefore, the clinician needs to be astute in recognizing the signs of abuse and effectively intervening as a safe environment and therapeutic alliance are developed.

The cycle of abuse can be recognized by three loading factors. Stress and mounting tension are indicative of the first factor. There may be what is described as minor incidents (minimizing) of battering such as pushing. The individual facing abuse tries to cope by staying out of the way of the abuser and by making sure that they are not doing anything to upset the abuser. This stage can endure for a long time. The major coping mechanism for this stage is denial. The occurrence of an explosion is indicative of the second factor. There is a lack of control and predictability by the abuser. Acute battering occurs and can lead to the police being called or the abused individual seeking out a shelter/safe environment. Attempts to cope with these circumstances often include shock and denial. The third factor is referred to as the honeymoon. This is where the abuser is apologetic, loving, and promises to change. This leads to a denial of the violence, and the cycle repeats itself.

THE FAMILY SYSTEMS MODEL OF DOMESTIC VIOLENCE

The family systems model of DV, based largely on social learning theory, holds the offender accountable for the abuse instead of blaming the victim. DV, violence perpetrated within an intimate relationship, can be described as the coercive and violent patterns of behavior by one partner that are intentionally used to control or dominate the other partner by words, threats, activity, and tactics of power. While most DV is identified as being perpetrated by a male against a female, there are also female offenders and same sex offenders. DV is complicated by family system dynamics, social norms, substance abuse, and psychopathology. Because there is not a single underlying problem, there is not a single solution to the complex problem of DV. DV is not simply a male–female paradigm; it is much more complex socioculturally and must be challenged accordingly in an evidence-based manner.

The conceptual framework of systems theory is utilized to demonstrate the progression of the physically abusive relationship. Both the pattern of violence and the response to violence are learned early and can affect how a person deals with stress within a relationship. This is a process of adaptive change. The systems model of DV is understood by a system based on assessing family system dynamics and the associated social learning outcome:

1. The establishment of the family system
   A. How did earlier life history affect the new family system?
   B. How did family boundaries evolve?
   C. What are the rules of dominance and power?
   D. Did the abuse of substances play a role?
   E. Associated influence of mental illness (i.e., personality disorders, etc.)?
2. The first violent event
   A. How did the interaction between the couple during the first episode of violence affect the potential for future violence?
   B. How were boundaries shifted? How was the status quo changed?
3. Stabilization of violence
   A. What functions within the system allow violence to escalate?
   B. What role does internal goals between the couple play in the evolution of DV?
4. Pivotal crisis point
   A. At what point do patterns of violence become intolerable?
   B. What are the criteria for intolerance aside from the amount of violence?
5. Reorientation
   A. How do the boundaries that previously defined the system shift?
   B. How does leaving the system cause a shift in thinking and personal dynamics?
   C. How does the offender respond to the victim's attempts to change the boundaries of the system?

6. Reorientation and conversion or status quo
    A. Does the victim leave the relationship?
    B. Is the victim successful in developing new interactional patterns in a new system?
    C. If the victim remains in the relationship, will reorientation of system functioning and boundaries be successful, or will they remain the same?

Adapted from Giles-Sims, J. (1983). *Wife battering: A systems theory approach.*

THE CYCLE OF VIOLENCE

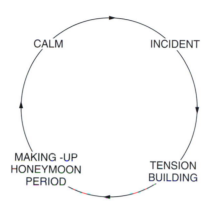

Adapted from Lenore Walker (1979).
Walker (1979) found that many violent relationships follow a common pattern or cycle. The entire cycle may happen in 1 day, or it may take weeks or months. It is different for every relationship and not all relationships follow the cycle—or little to know relief of abuse.

1. Incident
    A. Physical, psychological/emotional, sexual abuse
2. Tension building
    A. Anger begins to build in the abuser
    B. Communication begins to break down
    C. Victims feel the tension and try to keep the environment controlled and the abuser calm
    D. Tension continues to escalate and becomes too much
    E. Victim is walking on eggshells—and an explosion feels imminent
3. Honeymoon period (making-up)
    A. Abuser may apologize for the abuse (they may feel guilty)
    B. Abuser may promise the victim that it will never happen again, or
    C. The abuser may blame the victim for causing the abuse
    D. Abuser may deny the abuse (didn't happen) or minimize it (wasn't as bad as the victim claims)
4. Calm
    A. Abuser may give gifts to the victim
    B. Abuser acts as if the abuse never took place
    C. May not be any *physical* abuse taking place
    D. Promises made during the honeymoon period may or may not be fulfilled
    E. Victim may hope or fantasize that the abuse is over

THE DOMESTIC VIOLENCE ASSESSMENT PROCESS

According to the NASW (retrieved from the web, July 2, 2016), it is imperative that clinicians understand the dynamics of DV to effectively respond once a DV victim has presented for treatment. DV assessments, because of the risk factors require the clinician to gather adequate information, identify the presence of abuser and safety support factors, develop risk scenarios, work with the victim on their safety plan, and note priority actions.

INDICATORS OF DOMESTIC VIOLENCE

1. Obvious injuries at various stages of healing
2. Obvious erroneous explanation for their injuries
3. Repeated bruises and other injuries
4. Chronic depression, insomnia, nightmares, and anxiety
5. Fear and hypervigilance
6. Reluctance to offer more than general, superficial information
7. Vague somatic complaints
8. Overdependence on spouse
9. Complaints of marital problems
10. History of alcohol/substance abuse of the offender
11. Partner makes decisions of what they wear, who they see, and what they do

CORE FACTORS OF DOMESTIC VIOLENCE ASSESSMENT

Five core factors are associated with assessment of DV:

1. Patient's *immediate needs* of safety for the victim of DV presenting in a clinical environment
    A. *Safety*. Assess immediate danger/risk.
    B. Does their partner know where they are?
    C. What will happen when they are done with the appointment?
    D. Do they need police to be notified, or to take them home to retrieve some things?
2. The detailed pattern and history of DV
    A. When did DV begin?
    B. Have they been physically, psychologically, and/or sexually abused?
    C. What were the partner's tactics/behaviors for physical, psychological, and/or sexual abuse?
    D. Have they been controlled financially?
    E. Has the partner harmed or threatened to harm family, friends, or pets?
    F. Are the patient's activities controlled?
    G. If there are children, are they controlled?

*Using the calendar, do the best you can to identify the approximate dates during the past year when you were abused by your partner or ex-partner. Write on that date how bad the incident was.

1. Slapping, pushing; no injuries and/or lasting pain
2. Punching, kicking; bruises, cuts, and/or continuing pain
3. "Beating up"; severe contusions, burns, broken bones
4. Threat to use weapon; head injury, internal injury, permanent injury
5. Use of weapon; wounds from weapon

3. Determining if a potential connection exists between DV and health issues
   A. Do they believe that their health is being affected by the abuse? If so, how?
   B. Do they believe that the DV affecting their mental health? If so, how? (Stress, anxiety, depression, isolation, suicidal ideation, substance abuse, etc.)
4. Current access to advocacy and support resources
   A. What role if any, does culture play in the role of accessing social supports? If it does play a role strive to identify relevant social supports?
   B. What resources and social supports are available—including primary care physician, OBGyn?
   C. What resources; have they used in the past? Were they helpful or not? What resources are they willing to try?
5. Patient safety: Listen and respond to *general* safety issues
   A. Offer genuine concern for their safety and explore the partner's tactics, how often it happens, exactly what happens, has frequency increased, are there threats of suicide or homicide, use of substances, and have they required medical treatment or hospitalization as a consequence of DV in the past?
   B. Share with the patient safety planning. A brochure can be obtained from a local shelter or one you develop to give your patients. *Refer to Chapter 3.
   C. Review how to keep information private from the abuser.
   D. Offer a 24 h DV hotline number and the phone number to the local shelter.
   E. Offer to have them talk to an advocate now or at their next appointment.
   F. If the patient is in a high risk situation and planning to leave, reinforce that leaving without telling the partner is the safest way to proceed.
   G. Reinforce their strengths, resources, and resilience to making decisions regarding treatment.
   H. Ask direct and specific questions, such as:
      1. Is the abuse getting worse? How? Frequency?
      2. Have you been threated with a knife, gun, or other weapon?
      3. Has there been an attempt to choke or strangle you?
      4. Has your partner stalked you?
      5. Are you afraid for your life?
      6. Have you felt so much despair you thought about, planned, or tried to take your own life?
      7. Have your children been taken from you or held hostage as a means of your partner controlling you to get what they want?
      8. Has your partner threatened to hurt or hurt your children?

RISK-IDENTIFYING INSTRUMENTS

1. The **Lethality Screen** portion of the Domestic Violence Lethality Assessment Program (DVLAP), promoted by the Maryland Network against Domestic Violence, uses 11 of the 20 questions asked by the Danger Assessment. Law enforcement uses the Lethality Screen to identify high-risk victims and connect them with local advocates.
2. The **Duluth Police Pocket Card** has adapted several key questions from risk assessment instruments to guide responding officers in asking open-ended questions (instead of yes/no questions) of victims. The responses are included in the narrative of the police report and aren't intended to be viewed as a valid risk score, but rather to describe to the court possible danger to the victim.
3. The **Practitioner's Guide to Risk** contained within the Blueprint for Safety is based not only on risk and danger factors, but also on other research about violence against women.

Sources: Risk checklist/Psychological Violence Inventory (Sonkin, 2000); Spousal Assault Risk Assessment (SARA) (Kropp & Hart, 1997); Assessment for children: See Trauma Symptom Checklist for Children (TSCC) (Briere, 1996).

MEETING THE PATIENT WHERE THEY ARE

A clinician assessing DV must be highly skilled, genuinely empathic, and be knowledgeable about community resources. During the course of an assessment, there is also the opportunity to provide information and engage in some problem-solving interventions. To effectively respond to victims of DV:

1. Validate their experience
   A. "There are no excuses for domestic violence. You don't deserve this."
   B. "I am genuinely concerned about your safety and the safety of your children."
   C. "Domestic violence is complicated and requires problem solving."
2. Provide information and resources that increase safety and support for the victim and their children
3. Inform patients about the limits of confidentiality regarding mandated reporting requirements
4. The goal is to offer support, information, and resources—not to get them to leave their partner or for the therapist to save them and "fix" the problem

ASSESSMENT CHALLENGES

According to O'Leary, Vivian, and Malone (1992), less than 5% of couples seeking conjoint therapy report any incident of DV during intake. However, as many as 66% of those screened report some form of relationship violence experienced when given written self-report measures. Therefore, if specific questions are not asked during the interview, DV will not likely be identified and treated.

1. Reasons for not reporting DV
   A. Fear
   B. Shame
   C. Guilt/responsibility
   D. Belief that DV is not the problem
2. Complications of same-sex relationships
   A. Less likely to report DV than heterosexual couples
   B. May be more difficult to identify victim versus offender

*Advocates for Abused and Battered Lesbians have developed an assessment model to distinguish the victim from offender (Veinot, T.)

3. Complications for ethnic minority groups
   A. Language difficulties and associated limitations
   B. Isolated from their communities
   C. Obtaining services may result in increased community isolation
4. Children who are exposed to DV may present with the following concerns:
   A. Academic problems
   B. Social problems
   C. Low self-esteem
   D. Externalization demonstrated by behavioral problems
   E. Internalization of emotional effects
   F. Anger
   G. Aggressiveness
   H. Depression
   I. PTSD

5. Considerations to rule out in screening children (family history important):
   A. Other forms of trauma
   B. Depression
   C. ADD
   D. Conduct disorder
6. Victim symptom presentation

*When a patient presents with a consequence instead of a problem, the therapist is at an immediate disadvantage to correctly diagnose and develop an effective associated treatment plan. Therefore, it is expected that a physician may refer a patient, for their own treatment or the treatment of their child, for behavioral health issues or difficult symptoms while avoiding the reason serving as the foundation of the presentation.

   A. Depression
   B. Anxiety
   C. Sleep disorder
   D. Eating disorder
   E. SUD
   F. Somatization disorder
   G. Panic attacks
   H. Hypervigilance
   I. Intrusive thoughts
   J. Suicidality

Housekamp and Foy (1991) stated that most symptoms are PTSD related. As a result, one or more of the preceding symptoms/disorders would be a common presentation. Additionally, be aware of a misdiagnosis of borderline or histrionic personality disorder. According to Root (1992), the development of personality disorder symptoms is a normal reaction to abnormal situations, and the condition may have developed as a coping mechanism.

IMMEDIATE INTERVENTIONS

The primary goal is to protect the individual and their children.

1. Obtain medical treatment for the victim.
2. Provide the victim with the information for a shelter, and encourage them to call from your office.
3. Educate the victim regarding their right to safety and legal intervention.
   A. File a police report and press charges so that an intervention can be made with the abusive partner.
   B. Obtain a restraining order so that law enforcement can offer protection and enforce the law with the offender.
4. Offer support and understanding for what effects the experience has had on them and reinforce that they deserve better.
5. Educate the victim about the cycle of violence in their own life, and how continuing to live in that environment perpetuates the roles of victim and abuser for the children.
6. If the victim has a safe place to go to other than a shelter, strongly encourage them to participate in groups offered by the shelter for battered women.

7. Provide information about DV.
    A. DV is common and happens to all kinds of people
    B. Most violence continues and often becomes more frequent and severe
    C. Violence in the home can hurt children
    D. DV affects a person's health
    E. The perpetrator is responsible for ending DV not the victim
8. Positive reinforcement for efforts and accomplishments of self-care:
    A. Decrease feelings of responsibility for the abusive behavior
    B. Develop safety plans for the protection of self and children
    C. Develop and utilize support system
    D. Decrease isolation
    E. Decrease fear and feelings of helplessness
    F. Decrease dependency on relationship
    G. Increase constructive expression of anger and other feelings
9. Issues for the abused individual:
    A. Financial and emotional dependency
    B. Control of life is lacking
    C. Fear
    D. Isolation
    E. Distressing emotions, ambivalence
    F. Low self-esteem, shame, embarrassment
    G. Frustration
    H. Competency
    I. Minimizing
    J. Self-blame or low self-worth/value
    K. Harassment
    L. Learned acceptance, passivity, and submission

Because of the emotional distance, fear, and defenses of the abused individual, the therapist needs to be direct, honest, and genuinely caring. Use joining techniques and unconditional positive regard to reduce the resistance that will be innately present of this type of client.

Identify if the client has someone or something of value that he/she wants to protect (children, friends, job), and refer to this during treatment to empower the client. Clients may not feel motivated toward protecting themselves until sometime after this initial work is accomplished.

Identify faulty beliefs that keep patients in the victim role and instruct in cognitive reframing, thereby offering a healthy alternative to adopt and to utilize constructively as an agent of change.

Refer to other community resources that will assist patients in their independent functioning and separate from them the abusers, such as job training, childcare services, legal aid, AFDC [aid for dependent children (welfare)], self-help groups, and so on.

TWO COMPONENTS FOR ASSESSING THE PERPETRATOR OF DOMESTIC VIOLENCE

1. Assessing lethality
    A. Homicide risk (weapons, threats, degree of violence)
    B. Suicide risk (history and current status of risk factors)
    C. Frequency of violence (complete inventory of when violent behavior started, last episode of violence, typical degree of violence, most violent behavior, range of violent behavior, i.e., physical, sexual, property, emotional/psychological, cycle of violence, and current stage of violence)
    D. History of violence (own experiences of being abused, witnessing a parent being abused, violence in previous relationships)

    E. Substance use/abuse

    F. Mental health problems

    G. Assaults on other family members or other individuals

    H. Criminal history, criminal behaviors

    I. Isolation

    J. Proximity of abuser and victim

    K. Attitudes and beliefs related to violence; for example, negative attitudes about violence against women in relationships

    L. Ownership of partner, feelings of being entitled to partner's service, obedience, and loyalty

    M. Evaluation of life stressors; for example, employment or financial problems

    N. Psychiatric history and mental status

    O. Hostage taking

    P. Firearms available

2. Assessment of the offender's motivation for change

    A. Listen and carefully observe degree of interest in change.

    B. Is the motivation for change internally or externally driven?

    C. Does the person acknowledge having a problem with anger?

    D. Does the person acknowledge having a problem with violence?

    E. Is the person willing to discuss his/her violent behavior?

    F. Does the person minimize and deny violence?

    G. Are there any signs of remorse?

    H. Does the person feel his/her violent behavior is justified?

    I. Does the person acknowledge in any way a belief of being able to benefit from treatment, with any expression of wanting a violence-free relationship?

    J. Does the person have any insight into why he/she uses violence?

    K. Does the person see violence as a functional or integral part of the relationship?

    L. Is the person cooperative with treatment?

    M. What is the degree of externalization?

    N. Does the person keep appointments and arrive on time?

Issues related to motivation must be observed over time. The reasons for entering treatment are varied. Patients may not be presenting for treatment out of their own personal desire for change, but rather as a response to an external demand.

COUNSELING VICTIMS OF DOMESTIC VIOLENCE (LEE, 2007)

Sometimes clinicians struggle with what they perceive as weak and dependent behavior attributed to the victim of DV. Reasons a victim may remain connected to an abuser are numerous, with a few reasons being guilt, feeling responsible, helplessness/hopelessness, strong emotional and psychological forces, or situational realities such as financial limitations, lack of job skills, fear of losing custody of children, lack of alternative housing, cultural/religious restraints. Therefore, breaking free from abuse is not simply packing up and walking out the door. Leaving is a *process*.

Solution-focused interventions are imperative to DV counseling for stopping violence, establishing safety, empowering, reinforcing resilience, and healing. This approach encourages positive change in patients by focusing on solutions, strengths, and competencies instead of focusing on problems, deficits, and pathology. A stepwise progression can be seen in the value of assisting patients to think in terms of small, observable, and concrete behaviors so they can notice any small positive changes that make a difference in their situation.

Primary goal: To protect self and children.

OBJECTIVES

1. Enhance experience of self-empowerment
2. Decrease/eliminate responsibility for the behavior of others
3. Develop social support
4. Increase utilization of resources (medical, legal, welfare, social support)
5. Decrease isolation
6. Increase protection skills (for self and children)
7. Improve self-care skills
   A. Stress management
   B. Self-presentation
   C. Nutrition
   D. Self-affirmation
   E. Health care
8. Increase utilization of self-care skills
9. Decrease fear, immobilization, and helplessness
10. Decrease dependency on relationship with offender
11. Educate regarding family and social facilitators of DV
12. Improve assertive communication
13. Begin vocational training/education
14. Increase awareness of behavioral patterns and vulnerability

INTERVENTION FOR COUPLES OF DOMESTIC VIOLENCE

It is recommended that the individual participates in individual therapy, group therapy, and anger management class as modalities of intervention prior to the possibility of conjoint therapy, if that is an option. It is also important to assess for substance abuse. The modality or modalities used will be based on the needs of the client.

Requirements for conjoint therapy to proceed:

1. Maintenance of no violence
2. Successful completion of individual goals in prior treatment interventions
3. Both parties equally invested in safety for all parties involved as a priority over conjoint therapy and resolution of couple's issues

The literature is controversial regarding conjoint therapy. Some believe that conjoint therapy is prone to perpetuating further abuse; others believe that it is an essential intervention. Geffner and Mantooth (2000) have identified the following factors as being contraindicative for conjoint therapy:

1. Offender does not refrain from violence
2. Failure to accept responsibility for his/her actions
3. Failure to accept the discontinuance of abuse as the primary treatment objective
4. Inability to promote and preserve safety of all parties
5. High degree of fear and intimidation
6. Stalking or other obsessive behaviors
7. Use of alcohol or other substances
8. High degree of dangerousness and lethality
9. Disinterest or discomfort by either party to participate in conjoint therapy

COMPULSORY PSYCHOLOGICAL EVALUATION REFERRAL

A compulsory evaluation is used for a variety of circumstances. A common reason for referral is to establish the following:

1. Work-related problems
   A. Job performance
   B. Inappropriate behavior in the workplace
2. Determining remediation of difficulties and/or criteria for returning to work
3. A thorough assessment of psychiatric difficulties to clarify psychopathology and to offer treatment planning

A report template offers a general overview on what needs to be contained to produce report. However, the report that is based on individual needs and characteristics requires flexibility to tailoring the presentation. Sometimes sections can be simplified or omitted, and other times there is the need for further elaboration. Prior to initiation of the evaluation, informed consent must be obtained. Include a brief paragraph documenting the following sample process:

During the first meeting, the client is informed of the purpose of the assessment and the limits of confidentiality. The client is also informed that this psychological assessment report will include personal information, the examiner's clinical impressions, and treatment recommendations. The report will be sent to....... The patient is encouraged to ask questions regarding the evaluation and release of information process prior to signing any consent form(s).

COMPULSORY PSYCHOLOGICAL EVALUATION

Relevant Demographics and Sources of Data

1. Client Name.
2. Date of Birth.
3. Dates Tested.
4. Dates Interviewed.
5. Tests Administered: The utilization of integrated information from standardized tests offers a formal way to measure traits, feelings, beliefs, and abilities that can lead to people's problems. Some tests assess the presence of certain conditions, such as depression, anxiety, anger control, or susceptibility to stress. Other tests measure general well-being and provide an overall picture of a person's personality. A typical psychological assessment includes an interview with a mental health practitioner and one or more validated psychological test instruments.
6. Referral Source: Should include who will have access to the report and if the evaluator is to review the report with the patient once completed or is the patient directed to another clinical source for a review of the report upon completion.
7. Reason for Referral: To gain a deeper more complete understanding of a presenting problem(s). It may not be an overly complex clinical issue, just a desire for additional information to aid in refining the best fit of intervention for evidence-based practice.
8. Identifying Information: Age, marital status, children, occupation, etc.
9. Relevant Background Information (historical and of current problem):
   A. Psychological/psychiatric history (personal/family) medical history, i.e., significant illnesses, injuries, hospitalizations and dates (personal/family).
   B. Personal history: family history, brief description of childhood, adolescence, early adulthood.

C. Legal history: history of arrests and convictions, if any, including current status.

D. Military history: age at the onset of military career, dates, duration, and geographic locations of all deployments as well as occupation and rank during each circumstance of discharge and date.

E. Lifetime history of stressful events (if applicable). A brief documentation of stressful events reported by the patient. Indicate date, geographic location, the circumstances surrounding each, and the emotional response reported by the patient.

10. Behavioral Observations and Mental Status.

11. Assessment Validity: Provide a description of the validity of the assessment results (i.e., coherence, internal validity, symptom validity, symptom exaggeration/minimization, etc.).

12. Significant Test Results.

13. Summary.

14. Recommendations.

PSYCHIATRIC WORK-RELATED DISABILITY EVALUATION

This is a formal report format for the evaluation of an individual who is believed to be unable to work due to psychiatric disability. The essential elements of this assessment include a comprehensive clinical evaluation and appropriate standardized testing instruments to establish the diagnosis, clearly characterize the severity of impairment, and communicate the patient's abilities, restrictions, and need for accommodation (Soer, van der Schans, Groothoff, Geertzen, & Reneman, 2008; SSD retrieved from the web, June 18, 2016). According to Taiwo, Cantley, and Schroeder (2008), approximately 10.9 million people are not able to work and approximately 8.1 million people require some form of accommodation in the amount or type of work they can perform as a result of a chronic health condition.

Date of Report: _____

Name: _____

Date of Birth: _____

Date of Injury/DOI: _____

Case Number: _____

IDENTIFYING INFORMATION

A. Date, place, and duration of examination

B. Reason for referral and referral question(s)

C. Names of all individuals participating in the examination. Include the use of interpreter or any other party present and why they are present.

D. Sources of Information
1. Collateral contacts
2. Prior reports/progress notes/medical records
3. Clinical interview
4. Mental status exam
5. Psychological tests

DESCRIPTION OF CLIENT AT TIME OF INTERVIEW

A. Appearance (include any physical variance)

B. General behavior, demeanor, presentation

C. Cooperative with the process

DESCRIPTIONS OF CLIENT'S CURRENT COMPLAINTS

A. Subjective complaints, described in their own words
B. The client's view of the impairment created/resulting from the described complaint

HISTORY OF PRESENT ILLNESS

A. Client's description of work-related/industrial stressors, onset of the complaints, and the alleged injuries/illness associated with the onset
B. Psychological/emotional response to the alleged injury situation
C. History of mental health problems since the alleged injury
D. History of treatment since the alleged injury
E. Current treatment
   1. Medication (including medication taken on the day of the interview)
   2. Psychotherapy
   3. Group therapy
   4. Alternative approaches used for management of complaints

OCCUPATIONAL HISTORY

This section includes work events prior to injury, concurrent with injury, and after injury.

A. Educational level and profession, technical, and/or vocational training
B. Sequence of work experience/occupations pursued including military and internship trainings
   1. Training and skills required
   2. Management/supervisory responsibilities
   3. Career mobility (vertical or lateral moves)
C. Accomplishments and/or difficulties in each position and occupational setting
D. Previous occupational injuries, time lost, leaves of absence, and outcome to all situations addressed

PAST PSYCHIATRIC HISTORY AND RELEVANT MEDICAL HISTORY

A. Prior experiences in therapy
B. Hospitalizations
C. Psychotropic medication history/prescribed by whom
D. Medical history resulting from occupational setting or exacerbated by it

FAMILY HISTORY *AS IT APPLIES WITH PERTINENCE

A. Family of origin
   1. Parent's age, education, and occupational history
   2. Sibling's age, education, and occupational history
   3. Composition of family during client's childhood and adolescence
   4. Mental health history and relevant medical history of family members
   5. Family response to illness
   6. Relevant social history of family members
   7. Quality of family relations
B. Family of procreation
   1. Present marital status/history of previous marital relationships
   2. Spouse's age, education, occupational history
   3. Number of offspring (if offspring are of adult age, obtain same data as for spouse)

4. Mental health history and relevant medical history of family members
5. Relevant social history of family members
6. Quality of family relations

DEVELOPMENTAL HISTORY *AS IT APPLIES WITH PERTINENCE

A. Developmental milestones (met at appropriate ages/delays/difficulties)

SOCIAL HISTORY (DISTINGUISH PRIOR TO DISABILITY, DISABILITY CONCURRENT, AFTER INJURY)

A. Interpersonal relationships
B. Previous life changes/crises/losses and how responded to
C. Educational history
D. Relevant legal history (prior workers' compensation and personal injury claims with circumstances and outcome)
E. Relevant criminal history
F. Substance use and abuse
G. Client's description of a typical day

MENTAL STATUS EXAM

A. Hygiene, grooming, anything remarkable about appearance
B. Mood (normal, depressed, elevated, euphoric, angry, irritable, anxious)
C. Affect (normal, broad, restricted, blunted, flat, inappropriate, labile)
D. Memory (intact, short-term/remote memory)
E. Orientation (time, place, person, situation)
F. Speech (descriptors, expressive language, receptive language)
G. Processes (normal, blocking, loose associations, confabulations, flight of ideas, ideas of reference, grandiosity, paranoia, obsession, perseverations, depersonalization, suicidal ideation, homicidal ideation)
H. Hallucinations or delusions
I. Evidence of deficit (learning, problem solving, and judgment)
J. Impulse control
K. Behavioral observations/evidence of physiologic disturbance (somatoform or conversion symptoms, autonomic, skeletal muscle system)
L. Client's response to the examiner/appropriateness during course of interview

REVIEW OF MEDICAL RECORD

FINDINGS FROM PSYCHOLOGICAL ASSESSMENT

(Attach complete psychological report that has been completed as per workers' compensation guidelines.)

INTERVIEWS WITH COLLATERAL SOURCES AND REVIEW OF EMPLOYMENT OR PERSONNEL RECORDS (COMPARE DESCRIPTION OF INDUSTRIAL INJURY WITH CLIENTS DESCRIPTION)

ICD-10 DIAGNOSIS WITH APPROPRIATE MODIFIERS

SUMMARY AND CONCLUSIONS

A. Brief summary of relevant history and finding.
B. Present and justify an opinion concerning the current cause(s) of disability if present.
   1. The relationship of the work environment to the disability
   2. Nonindustrial causes of disability and preexisting causal factors
   3. Aggravating or accelerating factor (industrial and nonindustrial)
   4. Natural progression of preexisting disorder
   5. Active or passive contribution of the workplace to the disability
   6. Client's subjective reaction to stress at work
C. Indicate any diagnostic entities that were work disabling prior to the alleged industrial injury and provide evidence.
D. State whether the disability is temporary or has reached permanent stationary status and cite evidence. If the condition is permanent and stationary, state on what date it became so and cite evidence. Consider the history of the disorder and the response to treatment. If the condition is not yet considered to be permanent and stationary, state when you expect it will be so. If the opinion is that reasonable medical treatment will improve the condition, then describe the treatment and the expected benefits.
E. If the disability is permanent and stationary, offer an opinion regarding the nature and severity of the disability. Describe the disabling symptoms (subjective and objective), citing symptoms, mental status findings, psychological test data, and history to support opinion.
F. Make an advisory apportionment of disability. Do this by describing the disability that would exist at this time in the absence of the workplace injury. Cite the evidence on which the estimated preinjury level is based on.
G. Recommend treatment and/or rehabilitation if indicated and define using the following:
   1. The effects of the injury, combined or not with any previous injury
   2. Whether the individual is permanently precluded or likely to be precluded from engaging in their usual and customary occupation, or the occupation in which they were engaged in at the time of the injury (if different)
H. Assure that all referral questions have been addressed, and address any questions and/or issues raised in the referral reports.
   1. Indicate whether or not actual events of employment were responsible for a substantial degree of the total causation from all sources contributing to the psychiatric injury (clarify if the state that you practice in stipulates a percentage of total causation related to employment for valid work-related disability claim).
   2. Address if case has reached maximal medical benefit.

Making a statement that maximum benefit of treatment has been reached is a significant issue with numerous implications. It is defined as the point in which a condition is stabilized and further improvement is unlikely (Florette, 2013; Taiwo et al., 2008).

Improved Assessment of Mental Health Impairment

1. Detailed specific information on diagnosis, symptoms/signs, and degree of impairment of illness
2. Utilize multiple, objective, and verified sources of information substantiating the patients functional assessment
3. Carefully review for any inconsistencies observed by the clinician or reported by the patient in the presentation, diagnosis, treatment, and course of the patient's condition
4. Rule out secondary gain and malingering

FUNCTIONAL CAPACITY EVALUATION

A clinical assessment could be used to provide a prediction of function with associated work recommendations, but the specificity of the functional capacity evaluation (FCE) may be selected instead, thus allowing for a "job-specific" evaluation that can be instrumental in assessing the physical tasks related to the physical demands of work (possibly leading to vocational training) or if a patient is ready to be released without restriction to specific work demands. As per Taiwo et al. (2008), physical therapist and occupational therapist generally provide this type of evaluation but a behavioral health specialist may be requested to assess functional capacity. Therefore, an FCE referral is based on indication and contraindications and recommendations that provide needed information in determining if it is reasonable for a patient to return to their customary work without restrictions (full duty) or if accommodations are necessary (modified duty). It is recommended to consider screening for physical and psychosocial factors that may impact the performance of a successful return to work. Examples of instruments that could be beneficial might include the Pain Disability Index or a visual analogue scale. Factors of concern include but are limited to pain intensity, pain-related fear, self-perception of disability, illness behavior, self-efficacy, internal versus external locus of control and motivation (including job stress, secondary gain, malingering).

INDICATIONS

1. Maximal medical improvement achieved; however, question remains regarding return to work capacity (full duty or modified duty)
2. Quantify physical capabilities for disability determination
3. Quantify functional abilities preceding vocational planning or release to return to work
4. Quantify functional abilities to aid
   A. Vocational planning
   B. Medicolegal settlement

CONTRAINDICATIONS

1. Patient medically unstable
2. Medical problems currently experienced may be negatively impacted by the testing process (i.e., cardiopulmonary problems)
3. Impairment or inability to communicate with evaluator, therefore negatively impacts the understanding of directions associated with tests or vocal concerns

CONSULTIVE EXAMINATION

The Social Security Administration (SSA) (retrieved from the web, June 18, 2016; Office of Disability Employment Department, June 18, 2016; Gerg et al., 2012; Soer et al., 2008) states that when a patient's medical sources cannot adequately supply disability information that additional information can be sought via a consultative examination (CE) or a diagnostic study.

CONSULTATIVE EXAMINATION OUTLINE

A complete CE report will contain all of the standard evaluation components in the *applicable specialty* and include:

1. Chief complaint(s).
2. Detailed description of the history of the chief complaint(s).

3. Description, and disposition, of pertinent "positive" and "negative" detailed findings based on the history, examination, and laboratory tests related to the major complaint(s), and any other abnormalities (or lack thereof) reported or found during examination or laboratory testing.

4. Results of laboratory and other tests (for example, X-rays) performed according to the requirements stated in the Listing of Impairments. Reporting is inclusive of all date and comprehensive.

5. Diagnosis and prognosis for the patient's impairment(s).

6. Statement regarding what the patient is capable of doing despite impairment(s), unless the claim is based on statutory blindness.

7. If the patient is an adult age 18 or over, this evaluation statement should describe the opinion of the consultant about the patient's ability, despite his or her impairment(s), to do work-related activities, such as sitting, standing, walking, lifting, carrying, handling objects, hearing, speaking, and traveling (i.e., using the job description, do a compare and contrast of ability and restrictions).

8. Adult cases involving mental impairment(s) or mental functional limitations, this statement should also describe the opinion of the consultant about the patient's capacity to understand, to carry out and remember instructions, and to respond appropriately to supervision, coworkers, and work pressures in a work setting to aid in decision making regarding case disposition.

9. If the patient is a child under age 18, this statement should describe the opinion of the consultant about the minor patient's functional limitations compared to children of their age who do not have impairments in acquiring and using information, attending and completing tasks, interacting and relating with others, moving about and manipulating objects, caring for yourself, and heath and physical well-being.

10. Consultant's consideration, and some explanation or comment, on the patient's major complaint(s) and any other abnormalities found during the history and examination are reported from the laboratory tests. The history, examination, evaluation of laboratory test results, and the conclusions will represent the information provided by the consultant who signs the report.

EVIDENCE RELATING TO SYMPTOMS

In developing evidence of the effects of symptoms, such as pain, shortness of breath, or fatigue, on a claimant's ability to function, SSA investigates all avenues presented that relate to the complaints. These include information provided by treating professionals and other sources regarding:

1. The patient's daily activities/daily structure
2. Location, duration, frequency, and intensity of the pain or other symptom; a pain chart with a diagram and rating information on it would be useful
3. Identify precipitating and aggravating factors
4. Class and name, dosage, effectiveness, and side effects of any medication
5. Treatments, other than medications, for the relief of pain or other symptoms
6. Interventions the patient uses or has used to relieve pain or other symptoms
7. Other factors concerning the patient's functional limitations due to pain or other symptoms

In assessing the patient's pain or other identified symptoms, the above referenced information benefits those in the decision-making capacity. Therefore, it is important that evaluating sources address these factors in the reports they provide.

CHILD ABUSE AND NEGLECT

Child abuse encompasses physical abuse, emotional/psychological abuse, neglect, and sexual abuse. The report of suspected child abuse is a written narrative describing the suspected abuse, a summary of statements made by the victim or person(s) accompanying the child, and an explanation of known history of similar incident(s) for the minor victim on a form that can be obtained from Child Protective Services (CPS) or other agency whose jurisdiction oversees and investigates suspected child abuse. The foundation of the report is based on the verbalized statements of alleged abuse as well as the physical and emotional indicators of child abuse.

A therapist may participate at various levels of prevention, intervention, and treatment. As mandated reporters of child abuse, all therapists should be familiar with identifying families at risk for abuse as well as the interdisciplinary and community resources available to victims of child abuse and their families.

PREVENTION

Primary Prevention

Primary prevention is community education aimed at improving the general well-being of families and their children. The focus is to facilitate the development of skills that improve family functioning and to prevent or alleviate stress or problems that could lead to child abuse.

Secondary Prevention

Secondary prevention is the available or specifically designed services that identify high-risk families and help them prevent abuse.

Tertiary Prevention

Tertiary prevention is defined as the intervention or treatment services that assist a family in which child abuse or neglect has already occurred and acts to prevent further abuse or neglect.

INDICATORS OF ABUSE

Indicators of Physical Abuse

1. Bruises
2. Burns
3. Bite marks
4. Abrasions, lacerations
5. Head injuries
6. Whiplash (shaken baby syndrome)
7. Internal injuries
8. Fractures

Indicators of Emotional/Psychological Abuse

1. The child is depressed and apathetic
2. The child is withdrawn
3. The child is overly conforming to authority figures
4. Demonstrates behavioral problems or "acting out"
5. Demonstrates repetitive, rhythmic movements
6. Overly concerned with detail
7. Unreasonable demands or expectations are placed on the child
8. The child is triangulated into marital conflicts

9. The child is viewed as property of the parent (referred to as "it" instead of by name)
10. The child is used to gratify parental needs
11. The child demonstrates exaggerated fears or antisocial behaviors
12. The child is unable to perform normal, age-appropriate behaviors/skills
13. Constantly seeking the attention and affection of adults

Indicators of Child Neglect

1. Lack of adequate medical/dental care
2. The child demonstrates poor personal hygiene
3. The child is always dirty
4. The child is inadequately dressed
5. Poor supervision/left home alone
6. Unsanitary environmental conditions
7. Lack of heating and plumbing
8. Fire hazards and other unsafe home conditions
9. Inadequate sleeping arrangements (cold, dirty, etc.)
10. Inadequate nutrition/children fend for their own nutritional needs

These conditions existing as chronic and extreme constitute the definition of an unfit home and neglect.

General Symptoms of Possible Child Sexual Abuse

1. Enuresis or fecal soiling
2. Eating disturbances
3. Fears/phobias/compulsive behaviors
4. Age-inappropriate behaviors (pseudomaturity or regressive behaviors)
5. Problems with school performance and attitudes
6. Difficulty concentrating
7. Sleep disturbance
8. Depression, low self-worth, and withdrawal
9. Overly compliant
10. Poor social skills
11. Acting out/runaway/antisocial behaviors
12. Substance abuse
13. Age-inappropriate excessive self-consciousness of body
14. Sudden possession of money, new clothes, or other gifts
15. Self-destructive behavior, self-defeating behavior
16. Suicidal thoughts, plans, attempts
17. Crying without apparent reason
18. Fire setting
19. Sexually transmitted diseases, genital infection
20. Physical trauma or irritation to the anal or genital area
21. Difficulty walking or sitting due to genital/anal pain
22. Pain on voiding/elimination
23. Psychosomatic symptoms
24. Age-inappropriate knowledge of sexual behavior

25. Inappropriate sexual behavior with siblings, peers, or objects
26. Compulsive masturbation
27. Excessive curiosity about sexual issues and/or genitalia
28. Promiscuity or prostitution

CHILD CUSTODY EVALUATION

When mediation has not been successful, a qualified psychologist is often called on to conduct a child custody evaluation. Requirements of standard of care following ethical and professional guidelines act to protect and preserve the rights of all with the best interest of the children being the central focus of outcome.

Child custody evaluations are a legal process requiring an identified specialist. A list of recognized and accepted evaluators is generally provided by the court in any given jurisdiction. The legal intrusion of family court carries significant consequences that continue long after the case is closed. AAML (2011) states the following regarding child custody evaluation standards:

> The Standards are designed to apply only to processes that lead to an analysis of the relative strengths and deficiencies of the parties or that offer an analysis of different parenting plans under consideration by the custody evaluator" (AAML c. Applicability). This concept should be beneficial guidance for the clinical observer and consultant to the family court process in providing useful information toward reaching the goal. The goal is to determine what is in the best interest of the child. The APA (2010) asserts the rationale, "The evaluation focuses upon parenting attributes, the child's psychological needs, and the resulting fit." (pg 864). In other words, the evaluator is focused on the parenting capacity of the custodial disposition pertaining to the developmental and psychological needs of a child. APA (2010) provides what is broadly entailed, "This involves (a) an assessment of the adults' capacities for parenting, including whatever knowledge, attributes, skills, and abilities, or lack thereof, are present; (b) an assessment of the psychological functioning and developmental needs of each child and of the wishes of each child where appropriate; and (c) an assessment of the functional ability of each parent to meet these needs, including an evaluation of the interaction between each adult and child.

GUIDELINES FOR PSYCHOLOGICAL EVALUATION

A. Examination of child
  1. Mental status with behavioral observations noted.
  2. Developmental milestones.
  3. Coping methods, especially with regard to issues of change in lifestyle, family constellation in their daily environment, use of transitional objects in lieu of absence of a parent, and dealing with loss.
  4. Degree of attachment to parents.
  5. Stage of development and what type of parenting indicative of each parent.
  6. Presence of psychosocial impairment, severity, and interventions recommended.
  7. Use of psychological testing instruments as deemed necessary.

B. Individual examination of parents
  1. Mental status with behavioral observations noted.
  2. Personality functioning and parenting skills. Are there issues/concerns related to parental functioning that could compromise and/or damage the child's well-being?
     a. Psychopathological states that are indicative or have demonstrated the fostering of delinquent/antisocial behavior.
     b. Pathology that impairs the ability to parent consistently and safely such as psychosis, substance abuse issues, character disturbances. Specifics of associated relationship impairment or child safety issues are the focal point with these difficulties.
     c. An unhealthy focus or unconscious concerns related to dependency, power, sexuality, anger, and using the child(ren) to meet their own needs.

3. Personal history with reference to their own childhood experiences, i.e., how did their family deal with anger, discipline, emotional needs met, parental relationship, etc.
4. Demonstration of flexibility in accepting feedback related to their parenting responsibilities, skills, and recommendations for change.
5. Likely method of restoring the relationship of the missing partner—cooperative or noncooperative in reinforcing positive relationships and collaborative parenting.
6. Ability and willingness to form treatment alliance serving the best interest of their child(ren).
7. Use of psychological testing instruments as deemed necessary.

C. Conjoint examination of parents
1. How do they complement each other in appropriate parenting ability?
2. How do personality dynamics affect minimal cooperative efforts in managing the needs of child(ren)?
3. How will they likely respond to their ex-partner's choices such as remarriage?

The purpose of the Bonding Study is to develop an understanding of the degree to which the child demonstrates an attachment with their perspective family.

BONDING

Attachment or bonded relationships are essential in child development. When the continuity of care and risk of transition in a bonded relationship takes place, trauma can result. Therefore, an interruption in bonding can exact a significant cost on health and well-being. The younger the child and the deeper the bond, the more devastating and long lasting the impact can be. As a result, great care is to be taken when the sensitive lives of children are of concern in legal processes. Barone, Weitz, and Witt (2005; DHS, 2000) highlight psychological testing of parents, observation of the parent's interaction with the child, a thorough review of records as essential components of a bonding evaluation. The following records for review are cited:

1. Child protection services records
2. The child's school records
3. Previous mental health evaluations
4. Prior criminal records
5. Prior medical records
6. Substance abuse screening records

A bonding evaluation is a specialized type of assessment where the goal is to determine the nature and quality of the child's attachments to birth parents, foster parents, or other caregivers. A key feature of this evaluation is to identify if there is a parental figure who holds the relationship of greatest importance in a child's emotional life. Bonding evaluations can be conducted in the context of child welfare cases, divorce, and custody cases, particularly when there are questions about the bond and relationship between a young child and a parent. Important elements of bonding include attachment theory and a thorough review of history. For example, children who are securely attached to a parent/caregiver usually appear relaxed, happy, and enthusiastic while interacting with that person. Likewise, a caregiver's ability to recognize and respond to the nonverbal cues put forth by the child (eye contact, smiling, reaching, crawling toward, seeking nurturance/interaction, etc.) is a reflection of a sounded bonded relationship. There are different instruments that can be utilized for a systematic approach to gathering information such as the Attachment History Inventory.

While bonding assessments can be conducted in different ways, there are common themes to be observed and identified. The following are typical examples of characteristics between a parent and child that the evaluator will focus on (Barone et al., 2005):

1. Parent is able to meet physical needs of the child (developmental)
2. Parent initiates behaviors that foster attachment and bonding
3. Parent's affect matches message being given
4. Parent initiates activities and games that are shared and encourages talking

5. The frequency and nature of touching between parent and child as an index of comfort level

6. Parent responds positively toward child's cues

7. Parent responds immediately to child's emotional distress

8. Comfort-seeking and guidance-seeking behaviors by the child

9. Ability of the parent to soothe their child

10. Parent uses appropriate response(s) toward child's negative behaviors

11. Parent reflects pleasure toward child in gaze, voice, and smile

12. The capacity of the parent to engage the child effectively and to respond to the child's expressed needs in an appropriate manner

13. Parent positions child to engage in physical and verbal exchange

14. Demonstrations of how the parent prepares the child for change and is reinforcing of effort

15. Whether the parent and child make eye contact and smile at each other

16. Whether the child displays signs of upset if a separation occurs during the session

17. How the parent responds to the child's signals of hunger, thirst, want of comfort, or need to use the bathroom

18. Whether the child is willing to explore the environment while the parent is in the same room

19. Parent recognizes and understands the child's need for time and attention and responds positively

Another way to conceptualize bonding and attachment is to consider what would be seen (behaviorally and emotionally) when a child is experiencing attachment difficulties:

1. Persistent detachment
   A. Pulling or pushing away when touched
   B. Does not want to be held or touched

2. Distancing and isolation
   A. Lack of facial expression
   B. Lack of eye contact
   C. Inappropriate affect

3. Attention seeking
   A. Resistant—behavioral control problems
   B. Noncompliance
   C. Sneaky dishonest behavior

4. Tendency to form multiple shallow relationships or the inability to identify the difference between acquaintances and long-term caregiver
   A. Superficial
   B. Avoid discussion of feelings
   C. Clingy
   D. Poor ability to give/receive affection

5. Learning delays
   A. Difficulty with schoolwork

6. Aggressive behaviors
   A. Poor conscience
   B. Destructive to self or others
   C. Cruelty to animals
   D. Passive aggressive

7. Strange or perplexing behaviors
   A. Poor impulse control
   B. Chronic lying
   C. Poor judgment and doesn't learn from mistakes
   D. Abnormal eating patterns
   E. Bizarre, irritating, nonsense chatter

ABILITY OF THE CHILD TO BOND

In the context of a custody evaluation, it may be important to assess the quality, of the attachment that exists between a child and a parent.

1. Is the child bonded to the parent(s)?
2. What is the quality of attachment?
3. Does the child have the capacity to bond to anyone?
4. If the child were removed from this home, would it result in psychological damage?
5. Are the visitations between child and parent(s) meeting developmental/psychological needs of the child?
6. Compare/contrast the relationship of the child to both parents and both parents to the child.
7. Observe leave-taking behavior and affect.
8. Be aware of any impediments to child bonding such as child or parent deafness.

Some children identified as "at risk" and requiring special care may need specific parental qualities of nurturance and positive regard. The potential parents must be thoroughly evaluated for their ability and desire to care for a special-needs child. In observing the child and interactions with the potential parents, it is necessary to have a clear picture of the level of child development and maturity.

Additional issues include the following:

1. History and current status of the child's health
2. Any changes in the child's behavior observed by the custodial/foster parent on the way to a visit, on the way home from a visit, or for the rest of the day following the visit
3. Be prepared by being familiar with the history of the child and the relationship being observed

ABILITY OF THE PARENT TO BOND AND OTHER PERTINENT INFORMATION

1. Thorough review of background and court-related history
2. Observation of parent's mental status
3. Clinical interview
4. Psychological testing if necessary for clarification on issues of functioning
5. Observe nature of family relationships
6. Collateral contacts for information related to history of child (number of caretakers, quality of care, history of abuse, previous psychological treatment, etc.) history of perspective parent(s) (similar issues)
7. Stage of development versus behavioral manifestations in various settings
8. Additional considerations if present related to cultural or familial factors, substance abuse, support system, reunification, etc.

The unique information required in a bonding evaluation can be applied to the report outline of a child custody evaluation.

PARENTAL BEHAVIOR

1. Eye contact
2. Age-appropriate structure/limit setting/discipline
3. Type of objects brought by parents for the child(ren): food, toys, clothing, etc.
4. Amount and emotional quality of physical contact
5. Initiative toward interaction
6. Age-appropriate expectations
7. Appropriateness of verbal interaction, questions, etc.
8. Attitude and behavior, before, during, and after interview

INTERACTION BETWEEN PARENT–CHILD(REN)

1. Child(ren) behavior toward parent, and parent's response to it
2. Eye contact or avoidance on the behalf of parent or child(ren)
3. Affectionate, positive, nurturing body language
4. Quality and type of physical contact between parent and child(ren), i.e., sit together in chair, together on floor, playful, engaged in any way
5. Verbal exchanges
6. Parent limit setting/structure and child(ren) response

CHILD CUSTODY EVALUATION REPORT OUTLINE

A. Identification of case
   1. Parties and minor children
   2. Legal issues and standards
   3. Referral source(s)
   4. Referral question(s)
   5. List of collateral contacts and cite the form of contact such as phone, record review, etc.
B. Schedule of appointments
   1. Individual(s) seen
   2. Date(s) of service
   3. Amount of time devoted to evaluation of each individual and the methods of evaluation utilized
C. Assessment
   1. Document the stated objectives of each party related to custody and visitation.
   2. What does each party view as the primary issues such as conflicts, and allegations?
   3. Parent statements, from their perspective, of their own strengths, weaknesses, and limitations as a parent and their view of the child(ren) in terms of needs and impairments—and their view on the same issue as it pertains to the other parent.
   4. Information gathered from prior findings (records, summary analyses, etc.) that establish a foundation of relevant background and context for the current evaluation.
D. Results of evaluation
   1. Statement of evaluation findings that includes the following details:
      a. Mental status exam
      b. Interview information as it pertains to child custody

  c. Observations

  d. Relevant psychological testing information

E. Interpretation of findings

 1. Parental abilities, strengths/concerns/impairments that either enhance or detract from competent parenting.

 2. Mental health of child(ren) clarifying developmental needs, special considerations, vulnerabilities, etc.

 3. Quality of parent–child interaction, parent–parent interaction with issues of consistency and congruence.

 4. Issues of credibility related to these findings.

F. Discussion of findings

 This section utilizes specific references to detail each parent's competencies as it pertains to the best interest of the child(ren). Address issues of health, safety, and welfare of the child(ren). Include relevant issues such as child abuse, neglect, etc. Use this section to integrate all relevant findings presented in the evaluation.

G. Opinions

 If requested regarding specific referral questions and legal issues in reference to legal and physical custody, visitation, activities, contact with other significant people in the support system of the child(ren), etc.

H. Parent–child interaction

 1. How does the child(ren) spontaneously respond to the parent—valued, devalued, close, distant—and the reason behind it?

 2. Does the parent appropriately engage with the child(ren), listen and communicate with them, facilitate appropriate self-management by the child(ren), provide them choices, etc.?

 3. Is the parent nurturing and resourceful to the child(ren)?

ATTACHMENT STUDY VERSUS CUSTODY EVALUATION

When the reference of attachment is related to the issue of adoption, an attachment study takes place. Bonding by definition is a complex, one-way process that begins in the birth mother during pregnancy and continues. Bonding provides an instinctive parental protection for their child. Attachment, however, is a two-way reciprocal process between parents and their children. In any family, attachment must be achieved for the child to flourish, and that requires time and interaction (Feeney, Pasmore, & Peterson, 2007; Pace & Zavattini, 2011). There are practical suggestions for behaviors that can be made to increase attachment:

1. Feeding. Being responsive to the feeding signals in an infant, and dependable in family meal routines for children. Age appropriately encouraging their participation in family mealtime activities and in helping with food. As animals with one of two drive states associated to food, our relationship with food and feeding is multifaceted.

2. Eye contact. Making eye contact while holding and nurturing an infant and child leads to an exchange of smiles leading to feelings of comfort and closeness.

3. Holding and nurturing (touching, cuddling, stroking, hugging, kissing, etc.) are demonstrations of affection.

4. Sound. Reciting nursing rhymes or poetry, singing together, and reading together are sharing time for mutual responding and positive experiences.

5. Playing. Encourage and enjoy playing, allowing an infant or child to feel safe and react positively. Be creative in finding what a child prefers not only better fits a child but also increases feelings of competency as a parent.

6. Reflecting. Taking the time to drink in the beauty of a child simply softens and opens a heart. A child can feel that love, nurturance, and positive regard.

7. Timing. Take the time to understand the cycles of interaction and soothing that are paired in a way that results in a child feeling calm and relaxed. An example could be a play time followed by cuddling.
8. Hypersensitivity. Every child is unique in how they shift from different emotional states. For example, the adjustment may be slow after experiencing stress. Recommend being gently, decreasing the stimuli in the environment and creating calm for the child to draw from.

Some parents experience an immediate emotional connection and for other parents that degree of emotional connection never develops. While it is rare that a child is sent back to an agency or foster home, adoption disruption does take place. Actually, the risk of adoption disruption increases with age. An attachment study minimally requires the following:

1. An observation of the minor
2. Interviews with the bonding parent(s)
3. Observations in combinations of parent, parents–child, parent–child, whole family
4. Some of the observations are to be made in the home environment
5. Psychological testing will be utilized if the perspective parents have not been previously evaluated
6. Interviews with anyone significant to the child's life: prospective siblings, teachers, etc.
7. Thorough review of available documents
8. Recommendations

Specify treatment recommendations, individual (parent or child), conjoint remediation between parent or between parent–child(ren), need of special programs, etc. Be sure that all issues and questions raised by the court have been addressed.

PARENTAL ALIENATION SYNDROME

Parental alienation syndrome (PAS) occurs when parental influence or programming is combined with a child's own disparaging views of a parent (Gardner, 1999, 2001; Meyer, 2016). Parental alienation is the process, and result, of the psychological manipulation of a child to reject the other parent. Overall, there are four contributing factors to PAS.

PARENTAL PROGRAMMING

1. Most often overt and obvious
2. Often there is an infrequency of visits or lack of contact with the alienated parent (which decreases opportunity to correct the alienating parent's distortions. Without actual experience, the child may completely accept the alienating parents criticisms. However, contact does not guarantee a challenge to the progression of alienation.)
3. Common complaints of the preferred parent
   A. He/she has to pay for everything
   B. He/she cannot depend on the alienated parent
      He/she "abandoned us"
      He/she destroyed the family
      He/she is mean, abusive, or sick

C. The preferred parent exaggerates the psychological problems of the alienated parent
   1. Uses sarcasm to highlight how undesirable the alienated parent is
   2. Interferes with phone calls from alienated parent
   3. Mentors child in being deceitful to alienated parent, making the child an accomplice in warfare (Message is that alienated parent is not worthy of honesty and respect. There is also the dynamic of elevated power for the child in the alliance with the alienating parent over the alienated parent.)
   4. Labels attempts of hated parents to contact child or be involved in their lives as harassment

SUBTLE AND UNCONSCIOUS INFLUENCING

1. Preferred parent may state that he/she never criticizes the other parent to the child, however, says things like "I could tell you some things (about the other parent), but I'm not the kind of parent who speaks badly about the other parent"
2. Respects the child's wishes to spend time with the alienated parent, but the child generally knows that the preferred parent doesn't want him or her to or uses subtle sabotage: "If you don't visit, he/she will take us to court"
3. Provokes feelings of guilt for abandoning the preferred parent when the child spends time with the alienated parent
4. Finds neutral ways to convey the inadequacies of the alienated parent
5. Undoing (i.e., criticizes the other parent and then says, "I didn't mean it" or "I was just kidding")

CHILD'S OWN SCENARIOS

These are experiences or perceptions of the child, which play a role in the alienation process by feelings of validation, juvenile punishment of the alienated parent, power dynamic experienced by the child associated with the alliance of the alienating parent toward the alienated parent, protectiveness of the preferred parent, experience of viewing emotional/physical abuse perpetrated by alienated parent toward the preferred parent, and so forth.

1. Lack of nurturance from alienated parent
2. Lack of bonding
3. Anger or disappointments
4. Seeing preferred parent as a victim or fragile
5. Experiencing parent as nongratifying
6. Seeing alienated parent as mean and rigid (difficult to get the child's needs met)

*It is important to not lose sight of the child's contribution in parental alienation process, albeit initiated by manipulation and reinforced by the alienating parent.

FAMILY DYNAMICS AND ENVIRONMENT/SITUATIONAL ISSUES

1. System structure; parents create (nurturer, disciplinarian, understanding, rigid rules, encouragement, controlling, etc.)
2. Closed versus open family system
3. History of colluding behavior
4. Poor health in a parent
5. Prioritizing (work, couple's time, individual time, family time, etc.)
6. Values/morality

For the alienated parent, PAS only applies when this parent has not engaged in any degree of abusive behavior that would warrant such a response from the child. Generally, these parents have provided relatively normal nurturing to the child. Sometimes there is evidence of minor weakness/deficiencies, which are exaggerated and become the benchmark of focus in the development of PAS. Children are preoccupied in an unjust and exaggerated manner on these deficiencies in the parent.

As instruments of manipulation, these children are often rewarded with parental "friendship" and thus power that reinforces the benefit of the relationship with this parent. As a result, the child unwittingly becomes an ally with the *preferred* parent in an effort to preserve what they identify to be the most desirable living arrangement. This happens without awareness, and in some situations primary custody by the alienated parent might actually be in the child's best interest. Here the child becomes a weapon, thereby enabling the preferred/loved parent to gratify his/her hostility toward the alienated/hated parent through the child. The loved parent is also preoccupied with the hated parent's defects, thus creating and reinforcing a distorted image.

It is unfortunate that family court does not sternly support that children will not be used by either parent as a pseudopartner, confidant, be given overtly or covertly a negative perspective of the other parent, or as an object of any parental personal gratification. The evidence of this taking place would be children not being aware of the legal and financial issues between the parents, the conflicts between the parents, no difficulties in the scheduling and transfer between homes, and both parents demonstrating a responsible effort for the child's homework, projects, and schedule of activities. Children deserve to have both parents present for their events without fear or concern for how they will behave. The obvious exclusions to this is where abuse, neglect, or the presence of mental illness obfuscating a parent's ability to care for their child(ren).

SIX SIGNS OF PARENTAL ALIENATION SYNDROME

Meyer (updated, March 8, 2016) states that the motivation of parental alienation is one parent trying to destroy the bond a child has with the other parent.

1. Promoting anger toward the other parent. One parent criticizing and saying negative things about the other parent. Can be direct or indirect.
2. Overt attempts to promote anger. One parent criticizing or saying negative things about the other parent—not to the child but within hearing range.
3. Using the child as a confidant—sharing grown-up details with the child. Confiding in the child their distress being a victim of the other parent. Unnecessarily burdening the child with the purpose to cause anger and other negative feelings toward the other parent (divorce/legal, financial, etc.).
4. Covert attempts to cast negativity on the other parent. Using body language to convey negative messages about the other parent to the child. A word need never be spoken about the other parent being wrong or stupid, body language quietly says it all.
5. Refusal to coparent in a reasonable and adult manner maintaining the best interest of the child as the focus. One parent refuses to be in the same environment as the other parent and the child being told it is because one parent cannot be around the bad behavior of the other parent in an effort to promote negative feelings toward the maligned parent.
6. Making false accusations or reports about abuse against the other parent. This behavior can have dire and long-lasting results for the child and the falsely accused parent.

THREE CATEGORIES OF PARENTAL ALIENATION

1. **Mild** (as evidenced by)
   A. Subtle attempts to alienate a child against the other parent may take place
   B. The child is influenced to take on the preferred parent's point of view with unconscious or conscious efforts and a lack of insight of how it makes a child feel
   C. The alienating parent maintains the importance of a relationship with both parents

D. Generally, both parents recognize that alienation from either parent is not in the best interest of the child
E. Communication between parents exists and there is a more conciliatory approach to requests by the alienated parent to be involved in the child's life
F. Even though the preferred parent wants sole custody and believes that it would be best for the child, he/she recognizes that protracted legal proceedings may cause more suffering for the child
G. Children develop their own views, with slight prodding from the preferred parent
H. Children though ambivalent regarding visitation are free to express their feelings

*For most children the consequences are minimal and include minor loyalty conflicts and anxiety; there is no fundamental change in the child's own view of the alienated parent.

2. **Moderate** (as evidenced by)
    A. Preferred parent often feels hurt, angry, and vengeful
    B. Preferred parent expects the child to take sides and be loyal to him/her
    C. Preferred parent actively interferes with visitation arrangements and relationship with the alienated parent
    D. Preferred parent supports the notion of a relationship with the other parent, yet consciously/unconsciously perpetrates sabotage
    E. Preferred parent may ignore court orders (if he/she can get away with it)
    F. There is some ability to differentiate between allegations that are dishonest/outlandish versus genuine complaints
    G. Significant desire to withhold child from the alienated parent as vengeful maneuvering
    H. Though unreceptive, the preferred parent complies with court orders under pressure, threat of sanctions, transfer of custody, and so on
    I. Psychological bond may be healthy but is compromised by anger/rage
    J. The preferred parent likely demonstrated good parenting prior to divorce

*Common consequences for children

    1. Insecurity
    2. Distortions (viewing the alienating parent as the good parent and the alienated parent as the bad parent with some integration of positives about the alienated parent)
    3. Anxiety
    4. Splitting/manipulating
    5. Limited relationship with the alienated parent

3. **Severe** (as evidenced by)
    A. Preferred parent is angry, bitter, and possibly feels abandoned and betrayed by the alienated parent
    B. Conscious, consistence disparaging programming of the alienated parent by the preferred parent and the child (initiated by parent and adapted by child)
    C. In most cases, the child and alienated parent had a relatively positive and healthy relationship previously
    D. The preferred parent will utilize every mechanism and opportunity to prevent visitation
    E. These parents are not logical, reality based, or appeal to reason
    F. Paranoid projections
    G. Impaired child rearing capacity prior to separation/divorce
    H. The alienated parent is outraged by the influence and changes in the child and blames the other parent for these issues

CRITERIA FOR ESTABLISHING PRIMARY CUSTODY

The best case scenario for custody is two emotionally healthy parents working together to create a plan of shared custody that best fits the needs of their child. However, this is often not the case, such as when PAS is taking place, along with mounting acrimony, the disposition of custody will be determined by family court and whatever means the court finds necessary for satisfying the court's need for adequate information in rendering a court order for custody. A custody order is a written order signed by a judge. It defines the amount of time the parent or other caretaker will spend with the child (physical custody) and how major decisions are made about the child (legal custody). There are generally three types of parental physical custody of a child:

A. **Sole custody** means one parent is primarily responsible for the care of the child. The other parent may have visitation time with the child.
B. **Joint (or shared) custody** means that both parents will share physical custody of the child, although they do not necessarily need to have the child an equal amount of time.
C. **Split custody** means one parent will have custody of one child and the other parent will have custody of the other child. Courts typically prefer to keep siblings together, but there are circumstances where split custody makes sense.

The other component of child custody is legal custody. The parent who has physical custody makes the basic daily decisions in the child's environment. However, **legal custody** pertains to parental rights and responsibilities and the ability to make decisions regarding the child's health, education, religion, and other important matters.

There are two types of legal custody:

1. Sole legal custody means that only one parent will be able to make the long-term parenting decisions.
2. Joint legal custody means that both parents will make mutual decisions and share legal custody. This is the most common type of legal custody, and most parents will share legal custody of their child even if one parent has sole physical custody.

When parents share legal custody, they need to develop a process that they can use to help them reach a mutual agreement.

BASIS FOR FAMILY COURT CHILD CUSTODY RECOMMENDATIONS

When it comes to making decisions in the *best interest of the child*, the values of the parents relevant to parenting, ability to adequately and effectively meet a child's emotional needs, ability to plan for the child's future needs, capacity to provide a stable and loving home, and any potential for inappropriate behavior or misconduct that might negatively influence the child are considered. Psychopathology may be relevant to such an assessment, insofar as it has impact on the child or the ability to parent, but it is not the primary focus.

Regarding family court, the court's primary purpose in child custody cases is to foster frequent and continuous contact between the child and both parents—asserting the importance for the child to have a healthy relationship with both parents. Implicit in this perspective is each parent's willingness (and ability) to foster a close relationship between the child and the other parent. This means the court will base decisions on what is determined to be best for the child's health, safety, and physical and emotional well-being.

The following are some examples of the factors the court may consider:

1. The history of the care of the child and if primary custody has been being practiced. If so, why bring a custody issue to family court at this time.
2. The child's relationships with each parent and other important people in the child's life. Who are the identified resources who offer positive contributions to the child's life.

3. Each parent's willingness and ability to properly care for the child.
4. The needs of the child and how well each parent is able to meet those needs (including curricular and extracurricular activities).
5. The child's adjustment to his or her home, school, and community.
6. Any factors that may be harmful to the child, such as DV or substance abuse and/or other demonstrations of poor judgment or impulse control.
7. Any other factors the court finds to be relevant.

*Some states take the wishes of the child under consideration, but many times parents feel it is best to keep their child out of the middle of their divorce proceedings. Know the laws that pertain to child custody in the state in which you practice.

Treating therapists are often consulted regarding their observations and understanding of family relational dynamics. Therefore, it is crucial for the therapist to be aware of what is clinically relevant as an objective reporter and maintain a heightened awareness for the associated risk management issues. Additionally, the therapist is responsible for maintaining objectivity and to avoid in engaging in a parallel process in the clinical relationship.

Unfortunately, child custody cases are not brought to family court as a consequence of collaborative parenting. Judges in family court are presented with acrimony, irreconcilable differences, power struggles, at times complicating reporting issues (Sometimes true which place a child at risk, i.e., abuse, neglect, substance abuse, etc. Sometimes there are false allegations.). These are the cases where relational dynamic between the parents and between the child and each parent must be carefully determined.

1. Preference is given to the parent with the stronger and healthier psychological/emotional bond. An important factor in assessing this issue is the appreciation that a parent has of the role of the other parent in the raising the child. Parents who try to exclude and denigrate the other parent from the child's life reveal a parental impairment.
2. The primary caretaker during the early formative years of a child's life is likely to exhibit the stronger/healthier bond; however, this should not be taken for granted. Developmental changes and parental strengths are also considered in custody evaluations.
3. The more extensive time between these formative years and the time of the custody decision, the greater the likelihood that other factors may influence custody in either direction. Again, developmental changes may necessitate a review with regards to best serving the needs of the child.

BEHAVIORS OF THE PARENTS

Sometimes a custodial parent of a minor child incorrectly assumes that the status of custody will continue until the child is of age. This viewpoint, when held by a parent engaging in PAS, is likely to contribute to a pattern of behaviors that harm the child's relationship with the other parent or sabotaging the custody arrangement (shared time with the other parent).

1. The preferred parent resents behaviors of concern to be explored
   A. Denies positives in relationship between the child and the alienated parent
   B. Describes behaviors in absolutes of "always" or "never"
   C. Emotional boundary disintegration
      1. Merges his/her own feelings/views with the child ("We won't let them take us to court and hurt us anymore")
   D. Makes direct/indirect attempts to interfere with the relationship between the child and the alienated parent
   E. When the child is with the alienated parent, creates intrusive interference by numerous phone calls

F. Involves the child in spying and information gathering

G. Uses child as confidant, sharing adult issues about divorce, blaming, and so on

H. Uses child as a messenger between parents

I. Creates family splitting and feuding

*The evaluator will need to take into consideration if the behaviors of the preferred parent are associated with real or perceived deficiencies of the alienated parent. Reasons underlying the foundation for decisions need to be evidence based. Depending on what is found, there needs to be recommendations that address these issues. If the issues are addressed in the recommendations in the form of intervention, to whom they are directed depends on whether they are genuine or not (i.e., does the alienated parent need to modify or cease certain behaviors, or does the alienating parent need to alter perceptions and acknowledge the ways in which a child is negatively affected by the situation?). As a consequence of conflicts, changes in parent behavior and changes in the child custody orders may be continually modified as per the *best interests of the child*.

2. The alienated parent
    A. Healthy relationship with child prior to separation
        1. Being shut out of the child's life
        2. Insightful, willing to accept responsibility and examine a range of possibilities associated with a child's behavior
        3. History of actively participating in his/her child's life
        4. Nurturing qualities with possible tendency toward passivity
        5. May experience some difficulty dealing with overwhelming emotion

*These factors provide an environment for alienation to take hold. In such family systems, the preferred or alienating parent is typically emotionally overreactive and extreme, whereas the alienated parent is empathic, sensitive, nurturing, and passive or avoidant of conflict (peacemaker). Therefore, when the alienation is put in motion, the alienated parent may initially respond in a more passive manner, feel overwhelmed, and not know what to do. Unfortunately, there may be a tendency to detach to avoid conflicts, and this reinforces the behavior of the alienating parent. Additionally, if the court system reinforces or rewards the alienating parent's behavior, it creates a momentum to the alienation that seems impossible to stop. In this situation, when the alienated parent has finally had enough and responds with repeated efforts to participate more in the child's life, he/she is easily labeled with harassment, and when he/she sets firm limits with the alienating parent, he/she is labeled vengeful and often reprimanded and told he/she is fueling the situation.

    B. The parent claims alienation is the source of estrangement; however, he/she is defensive, avoidant, externalizes blame, and has difficulty with self-responsibility, which are really the original sources of estrangement
        1. Had little to do with the child prior to separation (workaholics/self-centered)
        2. Quickly involved in a new relationship with an insensitivity to child's feelings and issues of adjustment and relationship building
        3. Controlling, powerful, dominating (blame/externalizing is common)
        4. Expectation of child exceeds their investment in the relationship (demanding without nurturing, but expects the child to be a certain way following separation)
        5. Less child centered and less empathic
        6. Parent–child relationship has a superficial quality due to years of neglect
        7. Has a keen sense for showing up at the right moments for credit as being supportive—"Kodak moments"
        8. May report being active in the child's life via encouragement in activities or coaching sports, but the child actually feels pushed into these activities or sabotages participation in activities with excuses and blaming the other parent
        9. May allege alienation as a means to continue to control and blame

*Identification of these parental patterns is initially challenging, but clarity can be achieved by exploring the history of their investment in family and the parent–child relationship coupled with defensiveness, control, self-focus, blaming/externalization, and overall superficial quality to the parent–child relationship.

CHILDREN AND CUSTODY

The relationship between parents and children can be fragile and tenuous, even if it were a positive one prior to separation. Children don't have the ability, let alone the power, to maintain the necessary boundaries for normal and healthy relationships with their parents. They are dependent on parents setting and maintaining the guidelines for healthy relationships. As a result, when parents lack respect and responsibility in guiding their own behaviors and making decisions that are truly in the best interest of their children, the children are eclipsed and caught in the middle. It is these dynamics in which parental alienation is initiated and encouraged. The child becomes a pawn in vengeance and in meeting the needs of the parent. The needs of the child are secondary.

As the war ensues, causation and reason for the conflicts are often not clearly discernible. What is clear is that anyone or anything that is not supportive of the preferred parent's perception is viewed as negative and rejected. The child may already have his/her own slightly tainted image of the alienated parent, but this is accelerated under the influence of the preferred parent. If a child is somewhat passive, dependent, and feels a need to care/protect/nurture the alienating parent, he/she is even more susceptible to alienating programming. This fusion of feelings lacking boundaries enmeshes the child and the alienating parent. Some of the psychological/emotional problems that these children are at risk for developing include the following:

1. Depression
2. Dependency
3. Psychological vulnerability
4. Abandonment issues
5. Splitting
6. Inability to tolerate anger/hostility
7. Anger and rage
8. Difficulty developing intimate relationships
9. Conflicts with authority figures
10. Psychosomatic symptoms
11. Eating disorders
12. Entitlement

Often when these children are evaluated, there is little evidence of them being placed in the middle. Many have experienced one parent being controlling or dictatorial, severe hostility, and spousal abuse. There is a quality of sadness in them and either ambivalence associated with a desire for a healthy relationship with the alienated parent or just the lack of a relationship with this parent. This would indicate being aligned to the preferred parent, but not total alienation for the other parent.

As the clarity of system dynamics develops, several other issues may become apparent regarding the quality of the relationship the child shares with each parent. There may be an alignment with one parent, but it is not due to alienation. Time is spent with a specific parent because of shared interest (sports, arts/music, outdoors). The child also spends a modified amount of time with the other parent. Second, alignment with one parent may be an adaptive maneuver that removes the child from the middle as conflict escalates in an effort to decrease anxiety and vulnerability. In this case, the child is demonstrating a desire to not be a part of parental conflicts, not as an instrument in parental alienation, and it may not even matter which parent it is. Therefore, it is the conflict (anxiety and vulnerability) that drives the parental alignment and splitting. However, it is important to familiarize oneself with the role a child might play in PAS in the denigration of the other parent:

1. The child denigrates the alienated parent with foul language and severe oppositional behavior.
2. The child offers weak, absurd, or frivolous reasons for his or her anger.

3. The child is sure of himself or herself and doesn't demonstrate ambivalence, i.e., love and hate for the alienated parent, only hate.
4. The child exhorts that he or she alone came up with ideas of denigration. The "independent-thinker" phenomenon is where the child asserts that no one told him to do this.
5. The child supports and feels a need to protect the alienating parent.
6. The child does not demonstrate guilt over cruelty toward the alienated parent.
7. The child uses borrowed scenarios or vividly describes situations that he or she could not have experienced.

Animosity is spread to the friends and/or extended family of the alienated parent.

*When a parent is able to say that a child does not want to spend any time with the other parent, even though the court order says otherwise it is likely that the child has been completely brain-washed against the alienated parent. An important point is that in PAS there is not parental abuse and/or neglect on the part of the alienated parent. If this were the case, the child's alienation would be understandable and justified. Another distinction is that it is not PAS if the child has a positive relationship with the parent even though one parent is attempting to alienate the child and destroy the bond with the other parent.

PREPARING A PARENT FOR CHILD CUSTODY EVALUATION PROCESS

Parents generally express anxiety about the child custody process and request the therapist for information about what to expect. The Association of Family and Conciliation Courts (web, June 17, 2016) offers information on how to prepare parents for a custody evaluation when they are unable to resolve disputes about child custody. Consider addressing the following questions and concepts about the child custody evaluation process.

How Do I Prepare for the Evaluation Process?
1. Separate your marriage problems from your parenting concerns. You may still have a lot of hurt and angry feelings toward the other parent, but marital issues may not be relevant to child custody issues.
2. Do not look at the custody evaluation process as a win/lose situation. This is a good time to try to put the past behind you and focus on the future.
3. Plan to be open and honest with the evaluator.
4. The evaluator can be an information resource. Ask about reading material, parent education classes, counseling, and other help.
5. Consult with your attorney as needed throughout the evaluation process.
6. Keep your appointments.
7. Organize school and health records, and other information that the evaluator asks to review.

What Is the Purpose of the Evaluation?
1. An assessment of the needs of your children and each parent's ability to meet those needs.
2. Directed toward helping your family make a positive adjustment to divorce.
3. Attentive to past events, present resources, and future needs of the family.
4. Concerned with the strengths and weaknesses of both parents.
5. Focused on the "best interests" of children.

What Is Involved in a Custody Evaluation?

1. How do I prepare for the evaluation?
    A. Clarify in your own mind that you have two separate issues: marriage problems and parenting concerns. You may continue to have unresolved feelings of loss, hurt, and anger toward the other parent, but marital issues may not be relevant to child custody issues. This is about your child(ren) not about the problems you experienced in your marriage.
    B. The custody evaluation process is not a win or lose situation. It is actually an opportunity to put the past behind you and focus on the future instead of being focused on problems in a marriage that is over.
    C. Be open and honest with the evaluator.
    D. Look at the evaluator as an information resource. Ask about reading material, parent education classes, counseling, and other help that can benefit your growth, how to improve your relationship with the other parent, and if there are any recommendations of how you could help your child(ren).
    E. Consult with your attorney as needed throughout the evaluation process.
    F. Keep your appointments, be on time and prepared.
    G. Organize school and health records, and other information that the evaluator asks to review.
    H. Make notes of the questions you want to ask.

2. The evaluation will be comprised of a number of interviews.
    A. Meeting with the evaluator alone so that there is the opportunity to present issues and concerns about the other parent and the child(ren).
    B. Meeting with the evaluator with the other parent to determine the ability of the parents to work together in the best interest of their child(ren).
    C. Meeting with each parent and the child(ren) to observe family relationships and the qualities of interaction.
    D. If there are additional parental figures (step-parents or domestic partner), they could also be included in the evaluation process.

3. It is a process of gathering information.
    A. The evaluator may request written consent to obtain school and health records, social service and police information, and any other documents that contribute to a complete understanding of the family.
    B. The evaluator may want to talk with some of these people who have the written documentation to clarify any questions to understand how others see the issues.
    C. The evaluator may also ask both parents to complete a detailed questionnaire asking about the self (parent) and the relationship with your child(ren) and the other parent.

4. Will there be tests?
    A. Psychological testing may be required when information about each parent's emotional and mental status would be helpful to the judge.
    B. The evaluator will meet with each parent to talk and may administer several tests.
    C. It is okay to ask the evaluator to explain more about the kind of psychological evaluation that is being requested and why.

5. Will my child be involved in the evaluation process?
    A. Custody evaluators regularly interview and observe children and their interaction with each parent.
    B. Additionally, depending on the age of a child, the evaluator may have the child participate in structured play, draw pictures, or tell stories to express their feelings. The process the evaluator uses to engage and evaluate them will be determined by the child's age, i.e., be developmentally appropriate.

6. Will the evaluator ask my children where they want to live?
    A. Children's thoughts, feelings, and experiences are important to understanding the child, the child in each parent's environment, and how they cope with each situation.
    B. Generally, the evaluator will not ask children to choose between parents, which could increase numerous feelings of distress and place them in the middle of parental conflict.

PREPARING PARENTS FOR THE CHILD CUSTODY EVALUATION: A CHECKLIST OF DO'S AND DON'TS

Treating therapists are often asked by parents about the evaluation process and what they should expect. The following checklists offer beneficial guidance for the **"do's"** and **"don'ts"**:

1. **Do's**
   A. Arrive on time at your evaluation interview.
   B. Dress neatly and conservatively.
   C. Be cooperative.
   D. Be honest. The custody evaluator will be reviewing numerous sources of information as they review information from a parent.
   E. The custody evaluator may elect to use psychological testing. If they do, be cooperative and answer **honestly**. Educate the parent that these tests are designed to detect defensiveness, lies, and the effort to make oneself to present more positive than they are. Therefore, the best policy is honesty
   F. Be sincere and genuine. The custody evaluator is trained to observe and identify exaggeration and insincerity.
   G. It's normal to be nervous.
   H. It's all right to cry and/or show emotion—that is genuine and sincere.
   I. Answer questions directly and to the point. Demonstrate that you are listening and trying to be helpful to the process.
   J. Make sure you pay attention to what the evaluator is asking. You are there to be evaluated.
   K. Take your time when answering a question. If you are not sure that you understand what is being asked, ask the evaluator to explain what they mean.
   L. If the custody evaluator asks that you provide additional documentation, be cooperative and prompt in delivering them. If you are concerned about why certain documentation is being requested, it is okay to express your concern.
   M. If you provide the custody evaluator with names of people to contact (collaterals), it is a good idea to inform them that they may be contacted so that they can prepare to speak on your behalf and not be caught off guard.
   N. If the evaluator is observing you with your children, be attentive to their needs and focus on their interests—not yours. This is an opportunity for the evaluator to see the interaction between you and each child.
   O. Present yourself as being reasonable and placing the concerns and needs of your children as the priority.

2. **Don'ts**
   A. Speak badly of your spouse/partner. Simply answer the evaluator's questions. Your purpose of being there is to teach the evaluator about who you are and what is important to you.
   B. Make threatening comments about your spouse/partner (or anyone else) to the evaluator.
   C. Bother or harass the evaluator with phone calls or messages.
   D. Drop by the evaluator's office without an appointment. They will let you know when they want you to come to their office.
   E. Contact the evaluator to see if the report is completed. Your attorney will inform you when they receive the completed report.
   F. Prep your children to say negative things about their other parent. If a child asks questions about it, just tell them to tell the truth. The custody evaluator can see when a child has been prepped.

EVALUATION AND DISPOSITION CONSIDERATIONS FOR FAMILIES WHERE PARENTAL ALIENATION OCCURS

The degree of parental alienation syndrome may be viewed as reflective or directly related to the degree of motivation demonstrated by parents who present or are court-ordered for psychological evaluations and treatment from family court. As a result, these are inherently difficult cases, which pose an issue for risk management on behalf of the therapist involved in such a case. Document your case well. The following information presents the mother as the loved or preferred parent and the father as the hated or alienated parent. However, this scenario works in the reverse direction as well. Consider the following points and questions in your evaluation and recommendations.

1. Proper placement of the child is imperative. Without proper placement, treatment will be futile.
2. Although the parental alienation syndrome is actually a continuum with discrete markers defining the severity, it is necessary that the therapist evaluating a case specifically differentiates between moderate and severe cases because of the implication on placement.
3. A guardian ad litem for the children at the center of a custody litigation may be useful. However, if the guardian ad litem is not familiar with the dynamics of PAS, his/her involvement could prove to be a detriment to the outcome of the disposition in the case.
4. If the situation does not render reasonable certainty as to what would be the best decision, offer a "tentative" recommendation subject to review and reevaluation. However, when possible, every attempt to make a permanent recommendation is preferred.
5. Create a balance sheet overview of assets and liabilities, including stepparents if they are in the current clinical picture being evaluated.
6. The parent who is going to discourage the child from visitation is most likely to deprive the child from important information from the other parent. The healthier parent, even with his/her own personal issues associated with the divorce, recognizes the importance of continuing as positive a relationship as possible with both parents. This is a very important issue in determining primary custody. The decision of custody is extremely difficult, and there is no completely satisfactory solution to this issue.

QUESTIONS TO ASK CHILDREN

1. Ask the children to describe one parent and then the other. If PAS is present, the children will describe one parent with a number of criticisms and the other with a clear delineation of positive responses.
2. Ask the child to describe each parent's family. If PAS is present, the responses will reflect a distinct similarity to the answers in the prior question—thus, preferring the family of the preferred parent and alienation toward the family of the alienated parent.
3. If PAS has been established by the information gathered and, for example, the mother is the preferred parent and the father has been alienated, ask the child if his/her mother interferes with visitation of the father. It is very likely that the child will describe his/her mother as being neutral and not interfering, stating that the decision of visitation is entirely the child's own.
4. Again, assuming that the father is the hated/alienated parent, ask the child why he/she does not want to visit the father. The response initially may be vague. When pressed for specifics, horrible abuses may be conjured, which are exaggerations not warranting concern. Sometimes there will be a proclamation that the child's desire is to have absolutely no contact with the hated/alienated parent.

5. If the mother is the loved/preferred parent, ask the child if the mother harasses them. Normally, it would be expected that a child would offer several situations where he/she is not gratified. When PAS is present, the mother is likely to be described more in terms of being a perfect parent. The alienated parent's attempts to have contact and be involved with the child are what would be viewed as harassment.

6. Ask the child if the hated/alienated parent harasses him/her. The response would generally validate the harassment with any attempt (phone calls, letters, legal intervention, etc.) identified as harassment.

QUESTIONS TO ASK THE PARENTS

1. What is their opinion of parent–child relationships?
   A. What is the history of each relationship?
      1. What has changed?
      2. How has the child been affected?
   B. How does each parent demonstrate support of the child's relationship to the other parent?
   C. What do the parents think the child should know about what has happened in the marriage?
2. What are their ideas of how to improve the circumstances?
3. How do they believe that their behavior has affected their child?
4. What are they willing to do differently?
5. If they make the change recommended, what would be the evidence of that change in 3 months, 6 months, or 1 year?

PARENTAL ALIENATION SYNDROME INTERVENTION

With the focus on the emotional and psychological welfare of the child, the goal of intervention is to alleviate and/or eliminate the consequences of PAS. If the court or the collaboration of attorneys can ensue with the psychologist, it may be possible to develop a plan to restore healthy interactions and relationships to a dysfunctional family. While there is only a chance that this could be an effective outcome, it is a chance worth pursuing.

1. Mild PAS
   A. Most cases do not require intervention. Over time, parents' hurt and anger is diminished and they move forward in their own lives, thus creating the opportunity to collaborate positively on behalf of their child(ren).
   B. Generally, a final court order will confirm the custody arrangement, often with the preferred parent due to history of being the primary caretaker and demonstrating a stronger bond with the child.
2. Moderate PAS
   A. It is recommended that there be one therapist for the family system who is to report to the court regarding progress toward the goals. Further, it is understood by both parents, which without demonstrated family system progress there will be imposed sanctions. The goals are as follows:
      1. Reducing fractionation/braking components of communication
      2. Decreasing antagonistic subsystems
      3. Improving the bond and relationship with the alienated parent beneficial if therapist
   B. Some parents in this category may involve themselves meaningfully in the treatment process. They may even pursue individual therapy in an effort to take responsibility for and work through unresolved issues.
   C. Because they are good at child rearing, the child is often to remain in custody of the preferred parent.
   D. Combined effort of therapist and court realigns children to resume normal visitation.

3. Severe PAS
   A. One therapist for the family system who is to report to the court regarding progress toward the identified goals. Further, it is understood, by both parents, without demonstrated family system progress, there will be imposed sanctions.
   B. The alienating parent who is not receptive to therapy will impede progress—refusing to comply with therapy recommendations.
      1. Will consider a therapist who believes his/her position or is at least passively supportive by not implementing necessary change or confrontive of the PAS he/she is instigating.
   C. The literature's view of how to proceed on the disposition of custody varies.
      1. Gardner (1999) has stated that the child should be removed from the custody of the alienating parent with custody being transferred to the alienated parent. He has recommended a period of decompression/debriefing where there is no contact from the alienating parent to allow for the reestablishment of a relationship with the alienated parent. If there is visitation, it is minimal and in the presence of a designated third party contracted with the court to formally monitor the interaction. Once there has been stabilization with parent–child realignment, the contact with the alienating parent is proceeded with slowly to prevent a reoccurrence of the previous level of dysfunction. The belief is that if no intervention has been made, the risk of lifelong alienation between the child and the alienated parent will result.

      Both parents are to be educated about the PAS and what is expected of them regarding their interaction with the child and issues associated with the other parent. Addressing the importance of a strong bond with both parents:
      a. Child's exaggerated hatred is generally a façade (not allowed to be honest, fear of displeasing, protective, etc.)
      b. The need to develop a thick skin to deal with negative outbursts from the child
      c. The importance of neither parent withdrawing from participation in the child's life
      2. Stahl (1999) stated that any abrupt custody change may have significant negative consequences on the child. Therefore, any proposed changes should be thoroughly problem-solved so as to not cause more problems for the child. He has advocated a more balanced custody arrangement of equal time sharing in larger chunks (2 weeks or more at a time). The belief is that in some families there may never be a viable relationship between the child and the alienated parent, even with structural changes in custody, therapy, and monitoring. In such cases, with guidance from the therapist, there may be recommendation that the alienated parent temporarily withdraws from the child's life to prevent the child from experiencing any pain due to being in the middle. The decision to withdraw is only to help their child. It is also made clear that the parent loves the child, highly desires a relationship with the child, and will make contact every several months. The parent further states that the child will always know where the parent is and how to contact him/her.

      Research has not been conclusive or consistent on what the right intervention is in severe PAS cases. Instead, it appears that there should be a thorough review about how to proceed on a case-by-case basis. One intervention that may be helpful in every case for monitoring of change and information that the court could concretely reinforce for outcome-oriented specified results would be to explain to each parent the effects of PAS on the child:
      a. Have the information reiterated in written form.
      b. Have both parents sign a form acknowledging their understanding.
      c. Develop a written treatment plan that breaks down the expected changes and outlines the associated consequences; if there is not compliance, have parents sign the form.
      3. Referral for individual therapy for resolution of personal issues is made, and a consultation is made with the individual therapist so that he/she understands the situation and what is expected.
      4. Meet intermittently to review progress or lack of progress.

The information on PAS was adapted from R.A. Gardner (1999, 2001) and P. Stahl (1999).

VISITATION RIGHTS REPORT

When there has been a marital separation, divorce, or out-of-the-home placement, it is sometimes necessary to evaluate the parents and child for the purpose of visitation rights. This is necessary because there is likely discontent about the situation for at least one of the parents. Either their ex isn't complying with the schedule or there are possibly more serious issues associated with concerns for a child's safety. Regardless, the goal is to serve the *best interest of the child* by assuring adequate contact with each parent in a safe environment under which the visitation occurs. If there is concern related to safety or a history of difficulties associated with the contact of either parent with the child, then appropriate steps must be taken to provide for the safety of the child.

VISITATION RIGHTS REPORT OUTLINE

1. Dates of gathering information for the report
2. Names of father, mother, and child
3. Referral source
4. Identifying information for each party
5. Relevant background information
6. Site of visitation (and reason for that selected site)
7. History of visitation, and compliance with court recommendations/orders
8. Child's relationship with mother/evaluation of mother
9. Child's relationship with father/evaluation of father
10. Conclusions
    A. Temporary arrangement pending further information, supervision, completion of recommended classes (anger management/parenting/first aid/etc.), or other identified issues to be resolved
    B. Trial visitation arrangements
    C. Permanent arrangement
    D. Other parameters/considerations
11. Recommendations

DISPOSITIONAL REVIEW: FOSTER PLACEMENT; TEMPORARY PLACEMENT

A primary responsibility of MHPs working with mistreated children and their families is to remedy difficult situations and prevent placement if possible. Placement of a child outside of the family home is indicated only as the last option or when a child is in danger of harm. The task of the MHP may be as a consultant to a child protective service agency in directing the appropriate disposition of the child and family, what necessary placement would be appropriate, and the monitoring of all parties participating in a place (Dispositional Review).

When there is the possibility of remediating family system problems before it is referred to CPS, it may be beneficial to educate the parent(s) about the process that is common in most jurisdictions. This could serve as a motivation to work to improve their situation and comply with recommendation that have been made to improve their ability to effectively and safely parent.

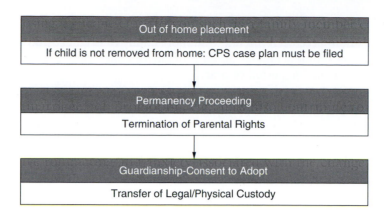

Out of home placement
If child is not removed from home: CPS case plan must be filed

Permanency Proceeding
Termination of Parental Rights

Guardianship-Consent to Adopt
Transfer of Legal/Physical Custody

This is a very basic initiation of change in custody disposition for placement. If the child is to remain at home, the judge generally imposes specific conditions on both the parents and the agency. In considering conditions to be imposed on the agency, the judge should determine what agency supervision will be needed for the child's protection and what services will be provided. There are several issues of parental responsibility when a child is allowed to remain at home. The court usually needs to impose specific behavioral directives upon the parents and to clarify their obligations to cooperate with the child welfare agency. In many cases, the judge must also establish or modify the child support obligations and visitation rights of the noncustodial parent. In some cases, the judge may need to issue a no-contact order for the child's protection. Whatever placement disposition is rendered, the foundation is found by the court to be suitable and in the best interests of the child. Once this step has been taken, the child cannot return home without a hearing in association with all outlined fact-finding presenting regarding factors related to proper care and supervision in a safe home.

*Know the laws and regulations governing this process in your jurisdiction.

In evoking the placement process, it is important to minimize traumatic disruption and replacement of caretakers as well as safe/familiar environments. Placements should be thoroughly screened to ensure that potential caretakers are prepared to cope effectively with the behaviors of troubled children. The last thing an abused or neglected child needs is the validation of rejection. Therefore, there should be continuity of care where the caretakers are consistent, dependable, and the basic needs of physical comfort, nurturance, affection, encouragement, gratification, intellectual development, and social development are offered and facilitated.

Because the court monitors such placements and because there can be planned or warranted charges in placement, there may be a request by the court for a Dispositional Review. The Dispositional Review is a thorough evaluation of all parties and the environment of the placement. Historically, it addresses the background leading to placement and the placement goals. The conclusion must address issues of adjustment, and status of goals and objectives. The last segment of the report is the area of recommendations. This report serves as a baseline for review and must lend itself to updated addendums to supply to the court with necessary information during the course of the placement (DHS, 2000; DHHS retrieved from the web, June 2016; Oregon Child Welfare Data Book, 2009). For questions or clarification on regional policy, contact your local county office.

DISPOSITIONAL REVIEW REPORT OUTLINE

1. Identifying information of minor/family court-appointed caretakers
2. Reason for referral
3. Relevant background information
4. Sources of data
5. Evaluation of
    A. Minor
    B. Mother
    C. Father
    D. Court-assigned caretakers
    E. Interaction/relationship functioning between minor and parents and minor and court-assigned caretakers
    F. Environment of placement

6. Criteria and written findings on review
    A. Services that have been offered to support family of origin custody, efforts to reunite if placed outside of the home—unless family cannot provide for child safety and need for a safe and permanent home within a reasonable period of time.
    B. When the child's return home is unlikely, the efforts that have been made to evaluate or plan for other methods of care.
    C. Goals for foster care placement and the appropriateness of the foster care plan.
    D. A new foster care plan, if continuation of care is sought, that addresses the role of current foster parent will play in the planning of the child.
    E. Reports on the placements the child has had and any associated services to the child and parent. For example:
        1. Where the child should be placed.
        2. What the child want to see happen in this case if they are old enough to participate as deemed by the court.
        3. The child's needs and what services should be offered to them.
        4. The parent's needs, what changes they must make, and the services that should be offered to them to support accomplishing the identified tasks. This will be stipulated in court orders, and by when these tasks/goals should be accomplished.
        5. Visitation between parent(s) and child, supervised or unsupervised.
        6. Visitation between siblings.
        7. Child support.
        8. If child is of school age, address whether placement would cause child to change schools and whether that is problematic. If so, offer a solution to avoid this additional distress and adjustment.
        9. If placement is with parents, stipulate limitations such as parents(s) having no contact with identified individuals suspected of harming the child or being an undesired influence, increase risk, etc.
        10. Whether CPS/DSS (Child Protective Services/ Department of Social Services) has made reasonable and extensive efforts to prevent or eliminate the need for placement outside of the home—and—what the response has been.
        11. Whether CPS/DSS has made a reasonable and extensive effort to identify family and/or friends as potential placement alternatives.
        12. Whether the case disposition should be moving toward reunification or termination—and—why.
        13. What is the position of CPS/DSS regarding disposition?
            a. Where are they requesting the child be placed?
            b. What arguments are made along with supporting evidence associated with the recommended placement?
            c. What are they stating must be changed, how the change will be achieved and when it is reasonable to expect the changes/improvement?
            d. What services have been offered to the child and the parents?
            e. What is the position regarding visitation and what evidence supports this position?
        14. Foster home placement is for the temporary care and nurturing of a child who has been placed outside their own home. During a time of disruption and change, foster parents are giving a child a safe home. The following are the roles of the foster parent(s)/home:
            a. Provide temporary care for children, giving them a safe, stable, nurturing environment.
            b. Cooperate with the caseworker and the child's parents in carrying out a permanency plan, including participating in that plan.
            c. Understand the need for, and goals of, family visits and help out with those visits.
            d. Help the child cope with the separation from his or her home.
            e. Provide guidance, discipline, a good example, and as many positive experiences as possible.
            f. Encourage and supervise school attendance, participate in teacher conferences, and keep the child's caseworker informed about any special educational needs.
            g. Work with the agency in arranging for the child's regular and/or special medical and dental care.

   h. If the child is of preschool or school age, it may be beneficial to work constructively with them through artwork/therapy to chronicle their life experience. For example, creating a "My Life Book"—a combination of a story, diary, and scrapbook (drawings and photos) that can help a child understand their past experiences so they can feel better about themselves and be better prepared for the future.

   i. Inform the caseworker promptly about any problems or concerns so that needs can be met through available services.

  15. When the case should be reviewed.

   a. An appropriate visitation plan.

   b. If the child is approaching major age (16 or 17 years of age), a report on an independent living assessment and, if appropriate, an independent living plan.

   c. When and if termination of parental rights should be considered.

   d. Any other criteria reports required by the court or that the court deems necessary.

7. Conclusions

8. Recommendations and follow-up review of plan

LEARNING DISABILITIES ASSESSMENT AND EVALUATION

Generally, only clinicians involved in the educational system are involved in the assessment and evaluation process of identifying disabilities. However, the following information is provided as an informational tool to familiarize a therapist with the process to reinforce the importance of why specialists are selected team members. Sometimes parents will go outside of the educational system to obtain testing believing that having an independent assessment and evaluation will be of greater benefit to their child. However, the participation of behavioral health clinicians outside of the educational system may complicate the process. Regardless, it is essential for clinicians to have at least a general perspective of what is entailed in identifying learning disabilities.

Diagnostic clarity in pediatric cases can be challenging due to the patient's ability (a child) to effectively express what they are experiencing. Additionally, clinicians strive to comprehensively incorporate developmental parameters to broaden their view of a child's ability to efficiently and successfully manage environment stimulation and emotional reactions. Therefore, a clinician's understanding of regulatory disorders, attachment, and communicative disorders (as per autistic spectrum disorders) is imperative to an accurate diagnosis and associated interventions. For a thorough review of these pediatric treatment topics (uncommon to behavioral health professional's education and training), along with further information on the legal and educational system aspects of education and pediatric disorders assessments and interventions, refer to *Therapist's Guide to Pediatric Affect and Behavior Regulation* (Sharon L. Johnson, 2013 Academic Press/Elsevier Science).

The National Joint Committee on Learning Disabilities (NJCLD, 2005/2016) strongly supports comprehensive assessment and evaluation of students with learning disabilities by a multidisciplinary team for the identification and diagnosis of students with learning disabilities. Comprehensive assessment of individual students requires the use of multiple data sources. These sources may include standardized tests, informal measures, observations, student self-reports, parent reports, and progress monitoring data from response-to-intervention approaches (NJCLD, 2005/2016). As with any assessment or evaluation, reliance on any single criterion or source of data for assessment or evaluation is viewed as not comprehensive.

As per NJCLD, the purpose of a comprehensive assessment and evaluation is to accurately identify a student's patterns of strengths and needs. The term assessment is used in many different contexts for a variety of purposes in educational settings including individual and group, standardized and informal, and formative and summative. Some professionals use assessment broadly to include both assessment and evaluation.

Assessment refers to the collection of data through the use of multiple measures, including standardized and informal instruments and procedures. These measures yield comprehensive quantitative and qualitative data about an individual student. The results of continuous progress monitoring also may be used as part of individual and classroom assessments. Information from many of these sources of assessment data can and should be used to help ensure that the comprehensive assessment and evaluation accurately reflects how an individual student is performing.

Evaluation follows assessment and integrates information comprehensively from all data sources. Evaluation refers to the process of integrating, interpreting, and summarizing the comprehensive assessment data, including indirect and preexisting sources. Whereas the central goal of assessment and evaluation is to provide sufficient information allowing team members to develop a profile of a student's strengths and weaknesses/needs. The student profile ultimately acts to inform decisions about identification, eligibility, services, and instruction. Comprehensive assessment and evaluation procedures are both essential for determining an accurate diagnosis of students with learning disabilities.

ROLE OF LEGISLATION

Legislation has played a significant role in determining process, intervention, outcome orientation, and disposition. There are two US federal education laws, the Elementary and Secondary Education Act (ESEA—referred to as the No Child Left Behind Act of 2001) and the Individuals with Disabilities Education Improvement Act of 2004 (IDEA, 2004). Both have had a major impact on instruction, as well as on the assessment, evaluation, identification, and eligibility of students suspected of having learning disabilities. A goal of IDEA 2004 was to position special education law more closely with ESEA, the general education law, so the two could work together. The 2004 reauthorization clarifies that a child may be determined to have a specific learning disability only when the child does not achieve adequately for the child's age or to meet State-approved grade-level standards in one or more of the following areas (when provided with learning experiences and instruction appropriate for the child's age or State-approved grade-level standards):

1. Oral expression
2. Listening comprehension
3. Written expression
4. Basic reading skill
5. Reading fluency skills
6. Reading comprehension
7. Mathematics calculation
8. Mathematics problem solving

DIFFERENTIAL DIAGNOSIS (LEARNING DISABILITIES VS. OTHER CONDITIONS)

Differential diagnosis is necessary to distinguish among disorders, syndromes, and factors that can interfere with academic performance. Teams including the child's parents need to determine the nature of the presenting problem and factors contributing to academic or behavioral difficulties. The following factors need to be considered to make an accurate differential diagnosis:

1. Definitions of learning disabilities always include acknowledgment of exclusionary factors, meaning that the students' learning needs are not due primarily to intellectual disabilities, sensory impairments, emotional/social difficulties, cultural and linguistic factors, or adverse environmental conditions.
2. Documentation of underachievement in one or more areas is a necessary, but not a sufficient, criterion for the diagnosis of learning disabilities.
3. Cultural and linguistic differences do not preclude the possibility that an individual also has learning disabilities.

4. Continued learning problems following high-quality, research-based instruction can be an indication of learning disabilities; however, inadequate instruction does not preclude the possibility that a student has learning disabilities.

5. Factors such as poor self-regulatory behaviors (e.g., inattention, lack of motivation, and impulsivity), poor social perception (e.g., inappropriate social judgment), and inappropriate social interaction (e.g., problems relating to peers) are not in themselves considered learning disabilities, but they may be concomitant with learning disabilities. A comprehensive assessment must address all areas of suspected disability, so if these conditions exist it is presumed that they would have been considered and addressed during the assessment. If this is the case, such information would be integrated into the comprehensive assessment report and may affect the program, curriculum, and/or instructional recommendations for the individual student.

6. Students with other conditions (e.g., autism, sensory impairment, emotional disturbance) also may be diagnosed as having concomitant learning disabilities.

7. Evidence of intraindividual differences in skills and performance can suggest learning disabilities.

8. Although a student with learning disabilities may show a severe discrepancy between ability and achievement, discrepancy formulas cannot be the sole basis for determining a learning disability under IDEA 2004.

9. Because scores on intelligence tests may not be an accurate reflection of intellectual ability, they may not be needed for a comprehensive assessment to determine the presence of a learning disability. Language impairment, for example, can reduce performance on intelligence tests and other achievement measures. Caution must be used in the selection of intelligence tests and interpretation of results for learning disability determination.

10. Sensitivity to validity and reliability issues must be considered when assessing students from culturally and linguistically diverse backgrounds, including ELLs (English Language Learners).

Chapter 3

Skill Building Resources for Increasing Social Competency

Cognitive-behavioral therapy (CBT) interventions have been identified as evidenced treatment that is beneficial for facilitating critical changes in cognition and behavior. In an effort to be efficient and effective, clinicians need to develop homework as skill building resources to support identified treatment plan–related changes. The following pages of information and homework on various clinical topics can be shared as they are presented or modified as necessary for individualized treatment needs. There is some overlap of information among documents with the purpose of providing similar information in a different way or with a different format. Additional goals of the following documents are that they serve as an introduction to various topics to encourage the initiation of important cognitive-behavioral change, a reinforcement of investment by the individual in treatment to participate as an active member of the treatment team (to investigate further on a given topic and learn more, take a class, etc.) and the encouragement and confidence that comes with symptoms alleviation and personal growth. Overall, identify cognitive-behavioral treatment as an empowering experience.

WHAT IS STRESS?

Stress is the body's physical, emotional, and psychological response to any demand. It is generally perceived mentally as pressure or urgency to respond, which is experienced as mental alertness. Stress is associated with the more primitive survival "fight" or "flight" response. When confronted with danger, the body responds physiologically with the release of adrenalin and hydrocortisone (cortisol). Short term, these chemicals shut down some biological mechanisms to conserve energy, which may be needed for fight or flight. After the challenge has been met and resolved, the body returns to normal. Normal body functioning is demonstrated by such measures as muscle relaxation, hands becoming dry, stomach/gastrointestinal relaxation, heart rate, and blood pressure returning to normal rates. Long-term exposure to adrenalin and cortisol can result in numerous negative influences physiologically, psychologically, and emotionally. One of these negative consequences is suppression of the immune system. Similarly, those who experience chronic stress or develop anxiety disorders are at risk for experiencing health problems. However, if managed effectively, stress is not necessarily bad for you. It can provide momentum to get things going and increase productivity. Review some differences between positive stress and negative stress. As you do so, be thoughtful about your own experiences and consequences.

1. Positive stress
   A. Short term
   B. Motivates
   C. May feel exciting
   D. Improves productivity
   E. Improves performance
   F. Is important to physical and mental fitness
   G. Focuses energy
   H. Sharpens the mind
2. Negative stress (referred to as distress)
   A. Can be harmful, especially if experienced for a long period of time
   B. Drains energy reserves
   C. Causes emotional depression or anxiety
   D. Suppresses immune system
   E. Builds over time instead of diminishing—impacting sleep and coping
   F. Can lead to mental and physical problems
   G. Can change the way a person thinks
   H. Can result in cumulative (buildup) negative impact [e.g., cumulative stress, posttraumatic stress disorder (PTSD), etc.]

Stress has no boundaries everyone experiences it. It is a part of daily life. Most individuals live a lifestyle and life circumstances at a moderate level of stress. This level is enough to keep one's attention sharp and motivation moderate to high. Being task oriented and productive generally manages stress and keeps it in check. It is when stress escalates beyond this moderate level that it can become harmful. Everyone is vulnerable to the negative effects of stress, and it may be cumulative if not effectively managed resulting in burnout and health issues.

Since everyone evaluates their experiences differently, no particular factors are identified as the causes of stress. Stress can come from pressures at home or work, from relationships from school, or as the result of other personal situations. Oftentimes, stress is associated with the "too much" phenomenon:

1. Too many changes
2. Too high of expectations
3. Too much responsibility
4. Too much information (overload)

The more stressors you have in a short period of time may have a buildup or "piling on" effect that makes it hard to manage. The result is referred to as a cumulative effect. In all likelihood, if one were able to experience these stressors over time allowing you to process and resolve each situation, then the stressors would be manageable. When there is not enough time between stressful events, however, the experience is overloading and debilitating.

There are generally two ways to define the source of stress: internal factors or external factors. Additionally, how each individual responds to stressful events can either increase or decrease the overall experience of stress. Failure to effectively cope with a stressful situation contributes to a feeling of things being more difficult, adding to the level of stress already felt from external sources. Skills such as self-care, use of resources, and self-talk form the foundation of effective stress management. The difference between being stressed and not being stressed is associated with the following three factors:

1. Individual perception of stress
   A. People often view the same situation very differently, depending on such factors as their life experiences, interpretations, self-concept, personality, and health. A visit to a personal physician for the same purpose may be stressful to one individual and not stressful to another.

*An individual's perception of stress will determine its effects on him/her.

2. Personal and family resources
   A. Time, skill (problem-solving ability), financial resources, family/friend resources all affect one's ability to handle stress. For example, money is double-edged: it can either be a stressor or a resource for resolving stress. Personal management style such as patience and perseverance also affects the way an individual or family system deals with stress.
3. Social support
   A. Your relationships with family, friends, and your community as well as access to professional resources can all offer opportunities for relieving stress. Aside from stress being derived from internal or external factors, there is another way to define the kinds of stress experienced.
      1. Ordinary daily life stressors
         a. Regular daily schedule (getting up, going to work/school, etc.). These stressors can be dealt with by setting priorities, following a schedule, having reasonable expectations, and delegating when possible.
      2. Developmental stresses
         a. Stage of life issues
         b. Learning new things/changing old habits
      3. Unexpected minicrises, i.e., car breakdown, unexpected health issue, etc.

Some experiences of stress can be effectively managed by identifying predictable developmental changes. When this is the case, look forward to the associated challenge, such as preparing for the empty nest or saving additional money for a rainy day. Being proactive in thinking through choices and how one wants to deal with things versus being forced to deal with the event when it happens can also minimize stress. One of the ways to accomplish this is making a *stress review*.

STRESS REVIEW

1. Keep a journal. Write what you think and feel to improve self-understanding
2. Identify the issues or situations that cause stress
3. Brainstorm a list of all possible ideas for dealing with these issues and situations
4. Clarify ideas
5. Evaluate all possible outcomes
6. Choose the best solution
7. Plan who does what (individual, family, outside resource); delegate, but be realistic
8. Create a trial period (day, week, month, etc.) for putting a plan into action
9. Evaluate the plan: What worked? What didn't work?
10. Integrate the new information you have to improve effectiveness of stress management

STRESS TOOLBOX

The foundation of stress management is the message offered by the serenity prayer. Regardless of whether or not you are a spiritual person the message offers the same benefit of evaluating what life brings you:

God grant me the serenity to accept the things I cannot change, courage to change the things I can, and the wisdom to know the difference. Reinhold Niebuhr

Make a list of the things you do or are learning to do to manage stress with the support of your therapist and other resources.

1. *Mental number line.* Visualize a thinking number line (3-2-1 –/+ 1-2-3). You must choose everyday "do you want to use your emotional energy thinking negatively (placing yourself on the negative side of the number line) or choosing to think realistically, rationally, and constructively on the positive side of the number line."

2. *Mental eraser.* Erase the old tapes of irrational and negative thoughts and substitute new positive ways of thinking

3. *Post-it notes.* Write affirmations and rational reminders that maintain constructive and positive energy

4. *Relaxation.* There are numerous relaxation techniques to reduce stress and anxiety that can be used as self-care maintenance and when distress begins to spiral out of control. The most benefit derived from using relaxation techniques is when they are used along with other coping methods, such as thinking positively, finding humor, problem solving, managing time, exercising, getting enough sleep, and reaching out to a positive support system. Several main types of relaxation techniques include the following:

   A. Deep breathing. When experiencing stress or anxiety it is beneficial to practice this 3 min/3x's a day. Inhalation and exhalation should be equal. One's ability to inhale deeply may depend on lack of exercise or disease (e.g., COPD). Inhale through the nose count of four, hold count of four, and exhale count of four. Inhale down into the diaphragm and if able exchange 7 s for 4 s.

   B. Autogenic relaxation. This relaxation technique uses both visual imagery and body awareness to reduce stress. You repeat words or suggestions in your mind to relax and reduce muscle tension. For example, you may imagine a peaceful setting and then focus on controlled, relaxing breathing, slowing your heart rate, or feeling different physical sensations, such as relaxing each arm or leg one by one.

   C. Progressive muscle relaxation. In this relaxation technique, you focus on slowly tensing and then relaxing each muscle group. This helps you focus on the difference between muscle tension and relaxation. You become more aware of physical sensations. One method of progressive muscle relaxation begins by tensing and relaxing the muscles in your toes and progressively working your way up to your neck and head. If you prefer, you can start at the head and work down to the toes. Tense your muscles for at least 5 s and then relax for 30 s, and repeat.

   D. Visualization. In this relaxation technique, you form mental images to take a visual journey to a peaceful, calming place, or situation. During visualization, try to use as many senses as you can (smell, sight, sound, and touch). For example, if you imagine relaxing at the ocean conjuring the smell of salt water, the sound of crashing waves, and the warmth of the sun on your body. You may want to close your eyes, sit in a quiet spot and loosen any tight clothing.

   E. Other relaxation techniques include the following:
      1. Deep breathing or slow controlled breathing
      2. Hypnosis
      3. Massage
      4. Meditation/mindfulness
      5. Tai Chi
      6. Yoga
      7. Biofeedback
      8. Music and art therapy

5. *Exercise.* Not only does it keep the heart healthy and get oxygen into the system, it also helps deplete stress hormones and releases mood-enhancing chemicals that help us cope with stress better.

6. *Positive social supports*. Benefit by offering a sense of belonging/decreased loneliness, increased sense of self-worth/positive reinforcement and feelings of security/comfort. Cultivate your developing social support system by staying in touch, not competing, being a good listener, and not overextending your social supports. They have to take care of themselves too.

7. *Develop goals*. Stress can actually be elevated by a lack of goals and direction. Break personal goal setting into four parts.
   A. Identifying and address problems (avoid unnecessary stress/let things go)
   B. Taking care of your body (the power of exercise, practice relaxation techniques, practice good nutrition, sleep well)
   C. Dealing with emotions (use visualizations to take "instant vacations," release emotional tension by dealing with one thing at a time by using creativity, talking to others, journaling, prayer, laughing, or crying)
   D. Contributing to making the world a better place—make a difference in other people's lives!

STRESS MANAGEMENT

Often, when a person enters therapy they are feeling overwhelmed by the stressors in their life. This crisis presents an opportunity for changes in thoughts and behaviors that are beneficial to the person's overall ability to cope effectively. During a period of crisis a person's normal defenses are down and emotional distress is high. The person feels an urgency to decrease the level of emotional distress. Because they are motivated toward alleviating emotional distress, they are open to new ways of thinking and behaving.

Some people have little awareness of the role that negative stress or too much stress plays in the complaints and physical ailments that they are reporting, which are reactions to the pressures and circumstances in their lives. The body generally offers several opportunities for the person to intervene via some method to decrease distress such as muscle tension telling the body the need for exercise and relaxation to decrease emotional and physical stress. Ignoring these signals often lead to emotional problems and physical ailments.

Change is stressful, even when it is beneficial. Change requires effort and conscious awareness. In preparing to engage someone in the process of change, it is important to understand how they normally interact with their environment. A life stress assessment includes a review of life events occurring in the last year, personality characteristics, and a review of significant historical life stressors, which have not been resolved and/or have contributed to how the person currently copes.

The responses to stress are numerous, and so are the approaches for dealing with it. What works for one person may not work for another. Therefore, it is necessary to be prepared with a number of strategies for handling stress.

The mind plays a powerful role in illness and in health. Because thoughts (cognitions or mental processes) have a strong influence, negative or positive, on the physical and emotional reactions to stress cognitive (thought) restructuring is an important intervention.

The five aspects of mental processing that play a significant role in stress include the following:

1. *Expectations/Self-fulfilling Prophecy*. What a person believes will happen or expects to happen sometimes influences their behavior in a way that makes that outcome more likely to happen. Negative expectations increase anxiety and stress. Identifying goals for change and facing such challenges with optimism and a positive attitude will facilitate optimal coping and management.

2. *Mental Imagery/Visual Imagery*. Along with expectations for a given situation a person will develop an accompanying mental picture and internal dialogue. This mental imagery can itself elicit emotional and physiologic responses. Negative mental imagery increases anxiety and stress reactions, whereas positive mental imagery minimizes the effects of life stressors and increases effective coping.

3. *Self-talk.* This is the internal dialogue that a person carries on with themselves all day and night (yes, even during sleep). Most people do not have a conscious awareness for self-talk or the influence it has on anxiety, stress, and self-esteem. Self-talk has a similar influence to that of mental imagery. Negative mental images and negative self-talk can result in anxiety and physical symptoms, whereas positive mental images and positive self-talk encourages self-confidence, effective coping, and a general feeling of well-being. Initially, an awareness for negative self-talk must be facilitated, followed by the development of rational substitute statements to replace the negative thoughts for cognitive restructuring.

4. *Controlling and Perfectionistic Behavior.* Perfectionism and unrealistic expectations often go together. Responses of controlling and perfectionistic behaviors are frequently an effort to avoid abuse, conflict, the unknown, or a feeling of uneasiness and inadequacy associated with perfectionism. Placing unrealistic expectations on others is a form of controlling behavior. It takes enough energy to manage yourself. Efforts to control the behavior of others lead to stress, anxiety, frustration, and anger. The goal is for the person to develop realistic expectations for themselves and accept that they have no control over the behavior of another.

5. *Anger.* Anger is a normal, healthy emotion when expressed appropriately. It can be damaging to the self and others when not expressed appropriately because of the internal stress and tension it causes as well as predisposing the person to "blow-ups" with others. This behavior results in low self-esteem and poor interpersonal relating. Chronic anger and hostility are related to the development or exacerbation of a number of physical symptoms, illnesses, and diseases. A person has a choice in how they evaluate a situation or what happens to them. Appropriate management of anger will decrease stress.

To effectively manage stress, persons must understand what they need and want emotionally, take responsibility for their own thoughts and behaviors, release themselves from the self-imposed responsibility of and efforts to control others, develop realistic expectations and limitations, have appropriate boundaries in relationships, express themselves honestly, and take care of themselves (by getting adequate sleep, eating nutritionally, exercising regularly, and utilizing relaxation techniques).

The central strategies for effective stress management focus on living healthy. This includes exercise, good nutrition, laughter and recreation, how stress is dealt with, relaxation skill development, helpful belief system, and positive attitude. Effective living requires goals, appropriate prioritization, and time management.

Given the pace of daily living and the demands placed on people it is not difficult to understand the level of stress experienced by the average person. Because it is physiologically impossible to be stressed and relaxed at the same time, developing techniques for alleviating distress (negative stress) is an important step in coping effectively with life stressors.

Excellent results have been found in the treatment of numerous physiological symptoms and emotional or psychological problems through the regular use of relaxation techniques. Regular use of relaxation techniques prevents the development of cumulative stress. Cumulative stress is generally associated with high levels of anxiety that have become unmanageable. The effective discharge of stress and tension associated with relaxation techniques creates the opportunity for the body to recover from the consequences of stress and places an individual in an optimal position for managing normal stressors, especially if they are engaging in regular exercise, getting adequate sleep, and eating nutritionally.

Difficulties leading to stress are often related to a person's style of managing or interacting with their environment. A lifestyle approach that results in unnecessary stress includes the following:

1. Attempting to do too much at one time.
2. Setting unrealistic time estimates, or poor time management.
3. Procrastinating on the unpleasant.
4. Disorganization.
5. Poor listening skills.
6. Doing it all yourself.
7. Unable to say "no."
8. Trouble letting other people do their job.

9. Impulsive, snap decisions.
10. Not taking responsibility for the quality of your own life. Blaming others.

EARLY WARNING SIGNS OF STRESS

Emotional Signs

1. Apathy, feelings of sadness, no longer find activities pleasurable
2. Anxiety, easily agitated, restless, sense of unworthiness
3. Irritability, low frustration tolerance, defensiveness, angry, argumentative
4. Mentally tired, preoccupied, lack of flexibility, difficulty concentrating
5. Overcompensating, avoiding dealing with problems, denial that you have problems

Behavioral Signs

1. Avoidance behavior, difficulty accepting/neglecting responsibility
2. Compulsive behaviors in areas such as spending, gambling, sex, substances
3. Poor self-care behavior (hygiene, appearance, etc.), late to work, poor follow-through on tasks
4. Legal problems, difficulty controlling aggressive impulses, indebtedness

Thought Changes

1. Experience of what feels like automatic thoughts
2. Negative influence on thinking
3. Thoughts about lack of control

A Life Events Survey can be administered to determine the specific stressors as well as a rough estimate of stress experienced by an individual. This can clarify acute crises and chronic problems that therapeutic interventions can seek to alleviate and resolve.

STRESS SIGNALS

The following messages from your body may indicate that you have a health problem or are on the road to developing a health problem. Also explore family history for any predisposition to a particular disease.

1. *Insomnia.* If you go to bed thinking about things or worrying, the physiological response is adrenaline, which is activating and interferes with getting to sleep or achieving restful sleep. Create a routine for winding down and putting your mind to rest. Before bed, swim, walk, meditate, drink warm milk or herbal tea (no caffeine), take a hot bath, or choose to think of peaceful, pleasant thoughts.

2. *Headaches and sore muscles.* When your body is in high gear, you are continuously on alert to respond and body tension accumulates. If tension is chronic, the result can be muscle soreness and rigidity. A tight neck, upper back, and shoulders can lead to a headache. Stretching and light exercise every couple of hours throughout the day may help to relieve these symptoms.

3. *Stomach problems.* When you are stressed, acid is secreted in the stomach, which can cause heartburn, stomach cramps, or other digestive problems. Over-the-counter antacids may alleviate the symptoms, but don't ignore the real culprits of irritation: stress, caffeine, smoking, alcohol, poor nutrition, inadequate sleep and relaxation, or spicy foods. Use physical activity, deep breathing, and self-soothing activities for calming your digestive track. Be sure to consult you physician. Don't ignore these symptoms.

4. *Addictive behavior.* Efforts to escape chronic stress by drinking too much, increased smoking, overeating, overspending, gambling, or other negative patterns lead to increased stress. Find helpful and healthful ways to deal with stress. Talk with your physician and seek professional help.

5. *Low sex drive.* While this can be a signal of stress and fatigue, a variety of other issues need to be explored with your physician:
   A. High blood pressure
   B. Sedentary lifestyle
   C. Hormonal imbalance
   D. Excessive salt consumption
   E. Excessive alcohol use
   F. Certain drugs/diseases that may cause high blood pressure

STRESS BUSTING—FIVE QUICK TIPS

1. Deal with stress when it strikes. Breathe slowly and deeply. Exercise to diminish adrenalin (stress chemicals).
2. Think positively. What causes stress is not the situation but how you think about it.
3. Practice improved management of stress by visualizing stressful situations and how you will manage them effectively. That way, when the stressful event occurs, it feels like you have already successfully dealt with it numerous times before.
4. Set limits. Create a "work" frame of time and when the time is up, shift gears and stop thinking about work. Consider how unfair it is to the people you care for if you are always thinking about work when you are with them, rather than being emotionally available and listening.
5. Be honest about what you have control over and what you don't control. If you have control, take action and plan for a resolution. If it belongs to someone else, let go of it.

EFFECTIVE MANAGEMENT OF STRESS

There are two approaches for coping with excessive stress:

1. Self-control, which requires taking responsibility for reactions to a situation.
2. Situation control, which includes problem solving, assertiveness, conflict resolution, and time management.

Factors that encompass managing stress effectively include the following:

CRITICAL PROBLEM SOLVING

1. Acknowledge and clarify the problem or issue.
2. Analyze the problem and identify the needs of those who will be affected.
3. Employ brainstorming to generate all possible solutions.
4. Evaluate each option, considering the needs of those affected.
5. Select the best option and implement the plan.
6. Evaluate the outcome or problem-solving efforts.

ASSERTIVENESS

To assert oneself positive includes the following:

1. Acting in your own best interest.
2. Standing up for yourself, expressing yourself honestly and appropriately.
3. Exercising your own rights without diminishing the rights of others.

CONFLICT RESOLUTION

Conflict resolution can be achieved cooperatively through a combination of problem-solving skills, assertiveness, good listening skills, and mutual respect until differing viewpoints are understood. This is followed by a course of action that satisfies the parties involved.

TIME MANAGEMENT

1. Clarify a plan of action, or tasks to be completed
2. Clarify priorities
3. Divide the plan of action into manageable goals and tasks
4. Allot a reasonable amount of time to complete all tasks

For optimal time management eliminate procrastination, combine tasks when possible, do things one time, and delegate when possible.

SELF-CARE

1. Adequate sleep and good nutrition
2. Good hygiene and grooming
3. Regular exercise
4. Relaxation techniques or other strategies for decreasing tension
5. Development and utilization of a support system
6. Use of community resources
7. Personal, spiritual, and professional growth
8. Self-monitoring for staying on task self-care behaviors to develop a routine

THE POSITIVE
STRESS CYCLE

STRESS

Positive
Behavioral
Response

Decreased
Stress
Symptoms

Improved
Mood

Beneficial
Thoughts

Relaxation
Self-talk

TIPS FOR STRESS MANAGEMENT

1. Learn to meditate and use other relaxation techniques (yoga, progressive muscle relaxation, visualization, etc.)
2. Practice good nutrition and physical activity
3. Review how you choose to think about things. How you think influences your stress level:
    A. Is your cup half empty or half full?
    B. Are you a chronic worrier?
    C. Do you catastrophize?
    D. Are you always thinking about "what if" instead of dealing with "what is?"
    E. Are you a perfectionist?
    F. Are you overly critical?
4. Take short breaks
    A. Reenergize with a short, refreshing time out
5. Manage your time
    A. Set priorities
    B. Be realistic about the amount of time it takes to do tasks
6. Talk about it
    A. Talk out your problems with a friend or family member to relieve stress and to put the problem in perspective
7. Live a balanced life
    A. Balance work with play
    B. Develop interests or hobbies
    C. Participate socially

*Make sure you have laughter in your life everyday.

8. Develop goals
    A. Set realistic goals
    B. Make sure you have what is required to successfully meet your goals

    C. When necessary, break tasks into small, manageable steps

    D. Reevaluate goals from time to time

9. Anticipate stress

    A. Use your awareness of situations coming up and plan ways to respond

    B. Review what you have control over and what you don't control

    C. Identify anything that can be done ahead of time to reduce the stress that will be a part of expectations associated with a given situation

10. Get help

    A. When you feel overwhelmed by stress, get professional help

    B. Identify supportive resources in the community

SIMPLIFYING LIFE AS A MEANS TO DECREASE STRESS

Are you exhausted? Do you feel overwhelmed and overworked? If you answered yes to these questions, take the time to step back, look at the choices you are making, and make simple changes. Small changes can often lead to an improved quality of life. Consider the following recommendations in reviewing life changes:

1. Reduce the "to do" list. Separate the following items:

    A. What needs to be done?

    B. What does not need to be done?

    C. What do you want to do?

    D. Clarify the difference between a want and a need

2. Stop procrastinating

    A. Be honest with yourself about what you are willing to do

    B. Acknowledge what needs to be done and just do it

    C. Accept that motivation is not something you "get" it is something you do

3. Take some time to yourself everyday

    A. Keep your lunchtime personal

    B. Do what you want to do during your brief "personal" time

    C. Try to increase personal time gradually

4. Set a stop time

    A. Set a time to stop working a task, and stick to it

    B. Move on to a restful enjoyable task to balance things

    C. Make others aware of your "stop time" so that it will be respected

5. Financial responsibility

    A. Consider how many hours you have to work to pay for a purchase and then ask yourself, "Is it worth it?"

    B. Disengage from "retail therapy" (buying to feel good for a while). Don't allow shopping to be a hobby—develop a real hobby.

    C. Get a handle on debt and create a special fund for desired purchases

6. Streamline

    A. Do not reinvent the wheel

    B. Do not do more than what is necessary to complete a task (get over perfectionism)

    C. Consider the purpose of a task and its importance

7. Organize

    A. Create manageable order to belongings

    B. Utilize time management

    C. Create a central information center for family demands

8. Identify quality-of-life issues
   A. Identify what matters most
   B. Enjoy the moment
   C. Spend time with people you enjoy or doing activities you enjoy
   D. Calm your soul—find peace

TEN RULES FOR EMOTIONAL HEALTH

1. Take care of yourself. Take time to relax, exercise, eat well, spend time with people you enjoy and activities that you find pleasurable. When you are the best, you can give your best to your relationships.
2. Choose to find the positives in life experiences instead of focusing on the negatives. Most clouds have a silver lining and offer opportunities for personal understanding and growth. When you accept that things are difficult and just do what you need to do then it doesn't seem so hard.
3. Let go of the past. If you can't change it and you have no control over it then let it go. Don't waste your energy on things that cannot benefit you. Forgive yourself and others.
4. Be respectful and responsible. Don't worry about other people; do what you know is right for you. When you take care of business you feel good. Don't get caught up in blaming others.
5. Acknowledge and take credit for your successes and accomplishments. Avoid false modesty.
6. Take the time to develop one or two close relationships in which you can be honest about your thoughts and feelings.
7. Talk positively to yourself. We talk to ourselves all day long. If your internal dialogue is negative and fearful, that is the way you will feel.
8. Remove yourself from hurtful or damaging situations. Temporarily walk away from a situation that is getting out of control. Give yourself some space and problem-solve a positive approach to dealing with it.
9. Accept that life is about choices and is always bringing change to you that requires adjustment.
10. Have a plan for the future. Develop long-range goals for yourself, but work on them 1 day at a time.

INDIVIDUALIZED TIME MANAGEMENT FOR DECREASING STRESS

Effective time management contributes to a balanced lifestyle. Review the following list and choose some time management tips that you can incorporate into your life to accomplish more and to feel less stress.

1. Be realistic with yourself regarding how much you can actually accomplish in a given span of time.
2. Say "no" to taking on additional responsibilities that infringe on personal/leisure or work time.
3. Prioritize your tasks because they are not equally important. Set priorities on a daily, weekly, and monthly basis for maximizing accomplishments.
4. Develop awareness for your peak energy periods and plan to do the activities with the highest energy demand at that time.
5. On a regular basis, review what the best use of your time is.

6. Striving for perfection is generally not necessary and can burn up time better spent in another way. Complete tasks well enough to get the results that you really need.

7. Delegate tasks and responsibilities to others whenever appropriate. Just be sure to communicate your expectations clearly.

8. Don't waste time thinking and rethinking the decisions for basic issues. Make those decisions quickly and move on.

9. If you have a difficult task to do that you are not looking forward to, do yourself a favor and approach it with a positive attitude. You will be surprised about how much stress that can relieve.

10. Break big overwhelming tasks into small manageable ones, that way it is easier to keep track of your progress and achievements.

11. Be prepared to make good use of "waiting" time by having small tasks or activities to do. Another way to deal with it is to always be prepared to take advantage of potential relaxation time when there are no demands on you.

12. When you need time to focus on your goals without interruption then request it. Take responsibility for creating a conductive work environment at home and at work.

13. Set goals and reward yourself when have accomplished them. If it is a big goal you may want to build in rewards at certain milestones of effort and accomplishment as a reinforcement of progress.

14. From time to time remind yourself how good it feels to accomplish tasks, what the benefits of accomplishment are, and the relief of having that weight off your shoulders.

15. Good use of time means more than completing "necessary" tasks. It means building in time for self-care such as leisure activities and exercise. You being the best that you can be is a priority.

SELF-CARE PLAN

For many a self-care plan will be the quintessential stress management program and a foundation block of self-responsibility. Develop a personalized self-care plan for optimal emotional health and a positive sense of well-being. This does require a commitment to health and follow through. It is recommended that there be a medical exam for clearance to participate in desired physical activity. Components of a self-care plan include the following:

1. Utilization of relaxation techniques to decrease body tension and to manage stress.
2. Review the social supports available to you. If necessary, work to develop an adequate and appropriate support system. Utilizing your social supports can offer relief, distraction, and pleasure. Make a list of your supports.
3. Initiate a journal. Instead of keeping thoughts and feelings inside, where they can build up and cause confusion and emotional/physical distress, get them down on paper. A journal is useful for venting thoughts and feelings, clarifying issues, and problem solving. It can also be helpful in determining patterns, relationships, health, and emotional functioning. Keeping a journal will help you monitor progress in life goals.
4. Get adequate sleep and rest.
5. Smile and have laughter in your life. Be spontaneous at times and playful.
6. Feed your body, mind, and spirit. Eat nutrition meals regularly. Practice good hygiene and grooming. Participate in life for personal, spiritual, and professional growth.

7. Approach each day with a purpose. Be productive by outlining daily structure. No task is too small to feel good about. Each step can be important to reach goals that you develop.

8. Avoid being self-critical. Be as kind and understanding of yourself as you would be to another person. Use positive self-talk to reassure yourself, to cope effectively, and to allow yourself to see that there are always choices.

9. Be sure to build in to your schedule time for relationships and pleasurable activities.

10. Take responsibility for your own life. Life is about choices. Understand yourself, your behaviors, your thoughts/beliefs, and your motivations.

HOW TO GET THE MOST OUT OF YOUR DAY

Whether you are simply considering a project or wanting to change something about your current lifestyle, the following tips will be useful.

1. Start your day right. Eat a light breakfast followed by some quiet time meditating or reading inspirational material.

2. Choose to greet the day with a positive attitude. You have the choice of setting the right tone for a positive outlook or a negative outlook everyday. You get back what you give out. What do you choose to create?

3. Organize your daily tasks on a list. You will feel great every time you put a line through an accomplished task. Be realistic about what is reasonable for you to accomplish and how much time a task requires to complete.

4. Inspire yourself by seeing yourself in a positive light. Overall, success is the adding up of all the little successes along the way. Each day, make a positive contribution.

5. Remind yourself of past successes. Tell yourself, "I am a capable person." Do not overwhelm yourself by thinking about all you had to do. Just do it. Life is genuinely difficult. However, it does not seem so bad when you just do what you need to do.

6. Work on your gratitude. Do you take the time to appreciate your blessings? Genuine gratitude offers a great attitude adjustment.

7. Be prepared. Break a task down into manageable steps if necessary and establish a routine for accomplishing it.

8. Practice self-improvement. From time to time, do a personal inventory. Work toward positive changes and personal growth while you actively make changes that you know will benefit you in all areas of your life.

9. Increase motivation. Enhance your actions by remembering this statement: "Motivation is not something you wait to get, motivation is something that you do."

10. Incorporate creativity into your life. Being creative leads to personal growth and is a great way to relax.

11. Bring out the child in you and play. Playing is a great way to rejuvenate and reenergize.

12. Be active. Use your body-walk or do some other activity. Walking is great for decreasing stress, increasing energy, improving sleep, and improving libido.

13. Have faith in yourself and your ability. The power of positive thinking works.

14. Practice self-discipline. Set goals. Decide what it is you need to do to accomplish the goals, and remind yourself on a daily basis of the importance of the goals that you set.

15. Convince yourself about the importance of your goals. Write a list about why it is important to you and why you believe you will accomplish it.

16. Make your vision a reality. Imagine yourself successful. Take that mental picture with you wherever you go.

17. Stay with it. Persevere. Never quit. Eventually you will accomplish what is important to you.

18. Be committed to being your best. If you stick with it, it will come true.

19. Reward yourself for your efforts. Sometimes the accomplishment is the reward itself. Creating a reward that is waiting for you at the finish line is a great motivator.

20. Always have things to look forward to. Anticipate things that are going to be.

Each day carries with it its own significance in our lives. It is not what happens to us that necessarily is the problem; it is the manner in which we interpret the event and choose to deal with it.

RELAXATION EXERCISES

DEEP BREATHING (5 MIN)

1. Select a comfortable sitting position.
2. Close your eyes and direct your attention to your own breathing process.
3. Think about nothing but your breathing, let it flow in and out of your body.
4. Say to yourself: "I am relaxing, breathing smoothly and rhythmically. Fresh oxygen is flowing in and out of my body. I feel calm, renewed, and refreshed."
5. Continue to focus on your breathing as it flows in and out, in and out, thinking about nothing but the smooth rhythmical process of your own breathing.
6. After 5 min, stand up, stretch, smile, and continue with your daily activities.

*3 min—3x's/day is a good practice for acute stress and anxiety management.

MENTAL RELAXATION (5–10 MIN)

1. Select a comfortable sitting or reclining position.
2. Close your eyes, and think about a place that you have been before that you found to be a perfect place for mental and physical relaxation. This should be a quiet environment, such as the ocean, the mountains, a forest, a panoramic view, etc. If you can't think of a real place, then create one.
3. Now imagine that you are actually in your ideal relaxation place. Imagine that you are seeing all of the colors, hearing all of the sounds, and smelling all of the different scents. Just lie back and enjoy your soothing, rejuvenating environment.
4. Feel the peacefulness, the calmness, and imagine your whole body and mind being renewed and refreshed.
5. After 5–10 min, slowly open your eyes and stretch. You have the realization that you may instantly return to your relaxation place whenever you desire, and experience a peacefulness and calmness in body and mind.

TENSING MUSCLES (5–10 MIN)

1. Select a comfortable sitting or reclining position.
2. Loosen any tight clothing.
3. Now tense your toes and feet. Hold the tension, study the tension, then relax.
4. Now tense your lower legs, knees, and thighs. Hold the tension. Study the tension, then relax.
5. Now tense your buttocks. Hold and study the tension. Relax.
6. Tense your fingers and hands. Hold and study the tension, then relax.
7. Tense your lower arms, elbows, and upper arms. Hold it, study it, relax.
8. Tense your stomach, hold the tension, feel the tension, and relax.
9. Now tense your chest. Hold and study the tension. Relax. Take a deep breath and exhale slowly.
10. Tense the lower back. Hold and study the tension and relax.
11. Tense the upper back. Hold the tension, feel the tension, then relax.
12. Now tense the neck, back, and front of your neck. Hold the tension, study the tension, then relax.
13. Now tense the shoulders. Hold and study the tension. Then relax.
14. Now tense your entire head. Make a grimace on your face so that you feel the tension in your facial muscles. Study the tension and then relax.
15. Now try to tense every muscle in your body. Hold it, study it, then relax.
16. Continue sitting or reclining for a few minutes, feeling the relaxation flowing through your body. Know the difference between muscles which are tensed and muscles which are relaxed.
17. Now stretch, feeling renewed and refreshed, and continue with your daily activities.

MENTAL IMAGERY (10–15 MIN)

Mental imagery can deepen relaxation when used with other techniques, or may be used by itself. The purpose is to calm your body, thoughts, and emotions. It gives you the opportunity to take a break from tension and stress. Mental imagery uses all of your senses to create and re-create a relaxing place, perhaps a meadow, a walk through the woods, along the beach, or perhaps a special place from your memory.

Prepare your environment so that you can complete this relaxation exercise without interruption. Spend sometime getting comfortable. Close your eyes, as you scan your body for any tension. If you find tension, release it. Let it go and relax.

Relax your head and your face.
Relax your shoulders.
Relax your arms and hands.
Relax your chest and lungs.
Relax your back.
Relax your stomach.
Relax your hips, legs, and feet.

Experience peaceful, pleasant, and comfortable feelings of being relaxed as you prepare to make an imaginary trip to a beautiful place.

Take a deep breath, and breathe out slowly and easily. Take a second deep breath, and slowly breathe out. Allow your breathing to become smooth and rhythmic.

Picture yourself on a mountaintop. It has just rained and a warm wind is carrying the clouds away. The sky is clear and blue, and the sun is shining down.

Below you are beautiful green trees. You enjoy the fragrance of the forest after the rain. In the distance you can see a beautiful white, sandy beach. Beyond that, as a far as you can see, it is crystal clear brilliant blue water. A fluffy cloud drifts in the gentle breeze until it is right over you. Slowly, this little cloud begins to sink down on you. You experience a very pleasant, delightful feeling. As the fluffy cloud moves down across your face, you feel the cool, moist touch of it on your face. As it moves down your body, all of the tension slips away, and you find yourself completely relaxed and happy.

As the soft cloud moves across your body, it gently brings a feeling of total comfort and peace. As it sinks down around you it brings a feeling of deep relaxation. The little cloud sinks underneath you, and you are now floating on it. The cloud holds you up perfectly and safely. You feel secure. The little cloud begins to move slowly downward and from your secure position on it, you can see the beautiful forest leading down to the beach. There is a gentle rocking motion as you drift along. You feel no cares or concerns in the world, but are focused completely on the relaxed feeling you experience. The cloud can take you any place you want to go, and you choose to go to the beach. As you move to the beach, the cloud gently comes to the ground and stops. You get off the soft cloud onto the beach, and you are at peace. You take some time to look around at the white sandy beach, and the beautiful blue water. You can hear sea gulls and the roar of the waves. As you feel the sun shining on you, you can smell the ocean air. It smells good. As you walk slowly on the beach, you enjoy the feeling of the warm clean sand on your feet. Just ahead on the beach is a soft blanket and pillow. You lie down and enjoy the feeling of the soft material on the back of your legs and arms. As you listen to the waves and the sea gulls and feel the warmth of the sun through the cool breeze, you realize that you are comfortable, relaxed, and at peace. You feel especially happy because you realize that you can return to this special and beautiful place anytime you want to. Feeling very relaxed, you choose to go back to the place where you started, knowing that you will take these peaceful and relaxed feelings with you. There is a stairway close by that leads you back to the room where you started. As you climb the five steps, you will become more aware of your surroundings, but you will feel relaxed and refreshed. You are at the bottom of the stairs now, and begin climbing.

Step 1 to Step 2: moving upward.
Step 2 to Step 3: feeling relaxed and more aware.
Step 3 to Step 4: you are aware of what is around you, and your body is relaxed.
Step 4 to Step 5: your mind is alert and refreshed, open your eyes and gently stretch.

BRIEF RELAXATION (5–10 MIN)

Get comfortable.
You are going to count backwards from 10 to 0.
Silently say each number as you exhale.
As you count, you will relax more deeply and go deeper and deeper into a state of relaxation. When you reach zero, you will be completely relaxed.

You feel more and more relaxed, and you can feel the tension leave your body.
You are becoming as limp as a rag doll, the tension is fading.
You are very relaxed.

Now drift deeper into relaxation with each breath, deeper and deeper.
Feel the deep relaxation all over and continue relaxing.
Now, relaxing deeper you should feel an emotional calm—letting go.
Feeling tranquil and serene, feeling of safety and security, and a calm peace.

Try to get a quiet inner confidence.
A good feeling about yourself and relaxation is coming over you.
Study once more the feelings that come with relaxation.
Let your muscles switch-off, feel good about everything and at peace.
Calm and serene surroundings make you feel more and more tranquil and peaceful.
You will continue to relax for several minutes.
When I tell you to start, count from one to three, silently say each number as you take a deep breath.
Open your eyes when you get to three. You will be relaxed and alert.
When you open your eyes you will find yourself back in the place where you started your relaxation.
The environment will seem slower and more calm.
You will be more relaxed and peaceful.
Now count from one to three.

BRIEF PROGRESSIVE MUSCLE RELAXATION

Clench both fists, feel the tension. Relax slowly…feel the tension leave. Feel the difference now that the muscles are relaxed.

Tighten the muscles in both arms. Contract the biceps…now relax the arms slowly.

Curl the toes downward until the muscles are tight up through the thigh…now slowly relax. Feel the tension ease.

Curl the toes upward until the muscles in the back of the legs are tight…now relax slowly. Feel the tension ease.

Curl the toes upward until the muscles in the back of the legs are tight…now relax slowly. Feel the tension ease.

Push the stomach muscles out and make it tight. Now slowly…relax. Your arms are relaxed, your legs are relaxed, and your even breathing gives you a feeling of calmness and releases stress.

Pull your stomach in up until your diaphragm feels the pressure. Now…slowly relax…slowly. Feel the tension ease.

Pull your shoulders up to your ears. Feel the tension in your back and chest. Now…slowly relax. Let your arms relax. You are feeling good. Your beating is easy and restful.

Tilt your head backward as far as you can. Stretch the muscles. Feel the tenseness. Now…slowly…relax. Feel the tension go.

Wrinkle your forehead. Hold it. Feel the tension. Now, relax. Feel the tension go.

Squint your eyes as tight as you can. Hold it. Now…relax.

Make a face using all of your face muscles. Hold it. Now relax…slowly…let it go. Your arms are relaxed… your breathing is easy and you feel good all over.

In a perfect state of relaxation you are unwilling to move a single muscle in your body. All you feel is peaceful, quiet, and relaxed. Continue to relax. When you want to get up count backward from four to one. You will feel relaxed and refreshed, wide awake and calm.

PROGRESSIVE MUSCLE RELAXATION (20–25 MIN)

Prepare your environment so that you can complete this relaxation exercise without interruption. Spend a little time getting as comfortable as you can. Prepare yourself for a pleasant and comfortable experience. Lie down or recline in a comfortable chair. Uncross your legs, loosen any tight clothing, and remove your shoes and glasses. Your arms should be placed comfortably at your sides. Slowly open your mouth and move your jaw gently from side to side. Now let your mouth close, keeping your teeth slightly apart. As you do this, take a breath, and slowly let the air slip out.

As you tighten one part of your body, try to leave every other part limp and relaxed. Keep the tensed part of your body tight for a few seconds and then let the tension go and relax. Then take a deep breath, hold it for a moment, and as you breathe out, think the words, "let go and relax." You don't have to tense a muscle so hard that you experience discomfort or cramping. The goal of this technique is to recognize the difference between tension and relaxation. It's time to begin progressive muscle relaxation.

First, tense all the muscles in your body. Tense your jaw, eyes, shoulders, arms, hands, chest, back, legs, stomach, hips, and feet. Feel the tension all over your body. Hold the tension briefly, and then think the words, "let go and relax." Let your whole body relax. Feel a wave of relief come over you as you stop tensing. Experience feelings of calm and peace.

Take another deep breath, and study the tension as you hold your breath. Slowly breathe out and think the words, "let go and relax." Feel the deepening relaxation. Allow yourself to drift more and more with this relaxation. We will continue with different parts of your body. Become aware of the differences between tension and relaxation in your body.

Keeping the rest of your body relaxed, wrinkle up your forehead. Feel the tension. Your forehead is very tight. Be aware of the tense feeling. Now let the tension go and relax. Feel the tension slipping away. Smooth out your forehead and take a deep breath. Hold it for a moment, and as you breathe out, think the words, "let go and relax."

Squint your eyes as if you are in bright sunlight. Keep the rest of your body relaxed. Feel the tension around your eyes. Now, let the tension go and relax. Take a deep breath and think the words, "let go and relax," as you breathe out.

Open your mouth as wide as you can. Feel the tension in your jaw and chin. Experience the tension. Now, let your mouth gently close. As you do, think the words, "Let go and relax." Take a deep breath, and as you breathe out, think the words, "let go and relax."

Close your mouth. Push your tongue against the roof of your mouth. Feel the tension in your mouth and chin. Hold the tension for a moment, then let it go and relax. Take a deep breath. Now think the words, "let go and relax" as you breathe out. When you breathe out, let your tongue rest comfortably in your mouth, and let your lips be slightly apart.

Keeping the rest of your body relaxed, clench your jaw. Feel the tension in your jaw muscles. Hold the tension for a moment. Now let it go and relax. Take a deep breath out, think the words, "let go and relax."

Focus now on your forehead, eyes, jaw, and cheeks. Are these muscles relaxed? Have you let go of all the tension? Continue to let the tension slip away and feel the relaxation replace the tension. Your face will feel very smooth and soft as all the tension slips away. Your eyes are relaxed. Your tongue is relaxed. Your jaw is loose and limp. All of your neck muscles are also very relaxed.

The muscles of your face and head are becoming more and more relaxed. Your head feels as though it could roll gently from side to side. Your face feels soft and smooth. Allow your face, head, and neck to continue becoming more and more relaxed as you now move to other areas of your body.

Become aware of your shoulders. Lift your shoulders up and try to touch your ears with each of your shoulders. Become aware of the tension in your shoulders and neck. Hold on to that tension, now let the tension go and relax. As you do, feel your shoulders joining the relaxed parts of your body. Take a deep breath. Hold it, and think the words, "let go and relax" as you slowly breathe out.

Notice the difference between tension and relaxation in your shoulders. Lift your right shoulder up and try to touch your right ear. Become aware of the tension in your right shoulder and along with the right side of your neck. Hold on to that tension, and now, let it go and relax. Take a deep breath and think the words, "let go and relax" as you slowly breathe out.

Now lift your left shoulder up and try to touch your left ear. Notice the tension in your left shoulder and along the left side of your neck. Hold on to that tension. Now, let the tension go and relax. Take a deep breath, and think the words, "let go and relax" as you slowly breathe out. Feel the relaxation spread throughout your shoulders. Feel yourself become loose, limp, and relaxed.

Stretch out your arms in front of you and make a fist with your hands. Feel the tension in your hands and forearms. Hold that tension. Now, let the tension go and relax. Take a deep breath and think the words, "let go and relax" as you slowly breathe out.

Press your right hand down into the surface it is resting on. Be aware of the tension in your arm and shoulder. Hold the tension. Now, let the tension go and relax. Take deep breath and as you slowly breathe out, think the words, "let go and relax."

Now push your left hand down into whatever it is resting on. Experience the tension in your arm and shoulder. Hold on to that tension. Now let go and relax. Take a deep breath and think to yourself, "let go and relax" as you slowly breathe out.

Bend your arms toward your shoulders and double them up as if you were showing off your muscles. Feel the tension and hold on to it. Now let it go. Take a deep breath and think the words, "let go and relax" as you slowly breathe out.

Move your attention to your chest. Take a deep breath that completely fills your lungs. Feel the tension around your ribs. Think the words, "let go and relax" as you slowly breathe out. Feel the relaxation deepen as you continue breathing easily, freely, gently.

Take another deep breath. Hold it and again experience the difference between relaxation and tension. As you do, tighten your chest muscles. Hold on to that tension and as you slowly breathe out, think the words, "let go and relax." Feel the relief as you breathe out and continue to breathe gently, naturally, and rhythmically. With each breath, you are becoming more and more relaxed.

Keeping your face, neck, arms, and chest relaxed, arch your backup (or forward if you are sitting). Feel the tension along both sides of your back. Hold that position for a moment. Now, let the tension go and relax. Take a deep breath and think the words, "let go and relax" as you breathe out. Feel the relaxation spreading up into your shoulders and down into your back muscles.

Feel the relaxation developing and spreading all over your body. Feel it going deeper and deeper. Allow your entire body to relax. Your face and head are relaxed. Your neck is relaxed. Your shoulders are relaxed. Your arms are relaxed. Your chest is relaxed. Your back is relaxed. All of these areas are continuing to relax more and more, as you are becoming more deeply relaxed and comfortable.

Move your attention to your stomach area. Tighten your stomach muscles, and briefly hold that tension. Let the tension go and relax. Feel the relaxation moving into your stomach area. All the tension is being replaced with relaxation, and you feel the general well-being and peacefulness that comes with relaxation. Take deep breath and think the words, "let go and relax" as you breathe out.

Now push your stomach out as far as you can. Briefly hold that tension. Now let it go and relax. Take deep breath. Hold it, and think the words, "let go and relax" as you breathe out.

Now pull your stomach in. Try to pull your stomach into your backbone. Hold it. Now, relax and let it go. Take a deep breath and think the words, "let go and relax" as you breathe out.

You are becoming more and more relaxed. Each time you breathe out, feel the gentle relaxation replace the tension in your body. As you continue to do these exercises, your body will relax more and more. Check the muscles of your face, neck, shoulders, arms, chest, and stomach. Make sure they are still relaxed. If they are not as relaxed as they can be, just tense and release them again. You are experiencing control over your body. Whatever part is still less than fully relaxed is starting to relax more and more. You are learning to recognize when you have tension in any part of your body. You are learning that you can become relaxed and let go of the tension you may find in any part of your body.

Now, focus your attention on your hips and legs. Tighten your hips and legs by pressing your heels down into the floor or couch. While you are tightening these muscles, keep the rest of your body as relaxed as you can. Hold on to the tension. Now, let the tension go and relax. Feel your legs float up. Take a deep breath and think the words, "let go and relax" while breathing out. Feel the relaxation pouring in. Be aware of the differences between the tension and relaxation. Let the relaxation become deeper and deeper. Enjoy the comfortable feeling.

Keeping your feet flexed toward your knees, tighten your lower leg muscles. Feel the tension, and hold on to that feeling. Now, let it go and relax. Take a deep breath and think the words, "let go and relax" as you breathe out.

Now, very gently, curl your toes downward toward the bottom of your feet. Be careful that you don't use so much tension that you experience cramping. Feel the tension. Now, let go of the tension. Feel the relaxation taking the place of the tension. Take a deep breath and think the words, "let go and relax" as you breathe out.

Keeping your lower legs relaxed. Bend your toes back the other way, toward your knees. Feel the tension. Hold on to the tension. Now let it go and relax. Feel the tension slip away. Take a deep breath, and think the words, "let go and relax" as you slowly breathe out. Feel the tension leaving your body and the relaxation coming in.

You have progressed through all of the major muscles in your body. Now, let them become more and more relaxed. Continue to feel yourself becoming more and more relaxed each time you breathe out. Each time you breathe out, think about a muscle and think the words, "let go and relax." Your hands are relaxed. Your chest is relaxed. Your back is relaxed. Your legs are relaxed. Your hips are relaxed. Your stomach is relaxed. Your whole body is becoming more and more relaxed with each breath.

Focus on the peaceful, comfortable, and pleasant experience you are having. Realize that this feeling becomes more readily available to you as you practice becoming aware of your body.

In a moment, I will start counting from five to one. At the count of three, I will ask you to open your eyes. On the count of two, just stretch your body as if you were going to yawn. And at the count of one, you have completed this relaxation exercise and can feel well rested and refreshed. 5…4…3…open your eyes…2… stretch your muscles gently…1…you have completed the progressive muscle relaxation exercise.

When a relaxation technique has been completed, visual imagery can be utilized while the person is still in the relaxed state. The visual imagery can range in emotional intensity from neutral to overwhelming anxiety. Its utility can be in the form of a hierarchy or in the repetition of a single troubling scene for the person that they are striving to master and resolve. In this form of imagined rehearsal, the person gains more practice in coping with anxiety-provoking situations. This acts to build behavioral repertoire and confidence.

The following example (from Navaco as cited in Meichenbaum and Turk, 1976, pp. 6–9) is a demonstration of the type of statements that can be used in conjunction with stress management and relaxation training to enhance or facilitate behavioral change. This particular example counters the negative self-statements indicative of an anger reaction. Because the individual is in a relaxed state with their defenses down they are psychologically less resistant to changing their schemata or plans. This is a beneficial way to increase coping in a variety of anxiety-provoking situations.

What can you tell yourself to control your feelings?

PREPARING FOR THE PROVOCATION

What is it that you have to do to?
You can work out a plan to handle it.
You can manage the situation.
You know how to regulate your anger.
There won't be any need for argument.

Take time for a few deep breaths of relaxation. You are feeling comfortable, relaxed, and at ease.

Confronting the Provocation

Stay calm. Just continue to relax.
As long as you keep cool, you're in control.
Don't take it personally.
Don't get all bent out of shape, just think of what to do here.
You don't need to prove yourself.
There is no point in yelling.
You're not going to let them get to you.
Don't assume the worst or jump to conclusions.
Look for the positives.
It's really a shame this person is acting the way they are.
For a person to be that irritable, they must be really unhappy.
There is no need to doubt yourself, what they say doesn't matter.

Your muscles are getting so tight, it's time to slow things down and relax.
Getting upset won't help.
It's just not worth getting so angry.
You'll let them make a fool of themselves.
It's reasonable to get annoyed, but let's keep a lid on it.
Time to take a deep breath.
Your anger is a signal of what you need to do.

IT'S TIME TO TALK TO YOURSELF*

You're not going to get pushed around, but you're not going to be aggressive and out of control either.
Try a cooperative approach, maybe you're both right.
They'd probably like you to get angry. Well, you're going to disappoint them.
You can't get people to act the way you want them to.

It worked!
That wasn't as hard as you thought it would be.
You could have gotten more upset than it was worth.
You're doing better at this all of the time.
You actually got through that without getting angry.
Guess you've been getting upset for too long when it wasn't even necessary.

The components of the last paragraph can progressively change in accordance with behavioral and cognitive modification and change.

A GUIDE TO MEDITATION (THE TIME FOR MEDITATION IS DECIDED BY THE INDIVIDUAL)

Meditation is a silent, internal process in which an individual attempts to focus their attention on only one thing at a time. It doesn't matter what the focus of attention is, only that all other stimuli are screened out. There are a variety of ways to practice meditation. Different meditation techniques are suited for specific purposes. Therefore, it is necessary to determine the needs or desired goal prior to determining the meditation technique to be utilized. The following meditation technique is general in nature and may be altered accordingly. Meditation does not eliminate the problems in a person's life. However, the resulting decrease in stress and tension would be an obvious contribution to an improved ability to cope.

Five steps of instruction on meditation will be presented. It is suggested that an individual experiment with the various techniques to determine which step they elicit the most comfort, ease, and benefit from. During periods of experimentation make an effort to increase the awareness for changes in both internal and external experiences.

Step 1: Preparation and Determining Your Posture.

Find a quiet place. Practice daily, at the same time each day, for at least 5 min. Choose a comfortable sitting position. Sit with your back straight and remain alert. Be sure that you are comfortable, your clothing fits loosely, and the environment lacks distractions.

Step 2: Breathing.

Close your eyes and focus on the sensations you are experiencing. With your eyes closed take several deep, cleansing breaths. Notice the quality of your breathing. Notice where your breath resides in your body, and how it feels. Try to move your breath from one area to another. Breathe deeply into the stomach (i.e., the lower area of the lung) and continue up until you reach the chest (i.e., the upper lung region). Likewise, when you exhale, start at the bottom, gently contracting the abdomen and pushing the air out of the lower lung. During this process be focusing on how you feel and how the breathing feels. This technique takes the shortest amount of time.

Step 3: Centering.

There are focal points, or centers in the body that enhance certain abilities when focused on. The middle of the chest is the heart center, the center of the forehead is the wisdom center, and the navel is the power center. There are other focal points, but these are most commonly used. Concentrating on the heart center increases and intensifies a person's compassion and offers the experience of being one with the universe. Focusing on the wisdom center expands wisdom and intuition. Focusing on the power center enhances the experience of personal power. The collective focus on all three centers represents compassion, wisdom, and power.

Step 4: Visualization and Imagery.

Visualization creates mental imagery impressions that can consciously train your body to relax and ignore stress. The use of visualization is wide ranging. It has been used to improve athletic performance and can be a powerful contributor toward the goals of self-development and self-exploration. To fully experience the varying sensations associated with different images meditate on the following topics, adding others to expand your experience if you choose:

1. A mountain lake
2. A forest
3. A happy time in your life or pleasing experience
4. Having as much money and success as you want
5. Radiating physical health
6. White light
7. Nirvana
8. A spiritual icon (Jesus, Buddha, Mohammed)

Choose a visualization that symbolizes what you want or are looking for in your life and mediate on that symbol daily.

Step 5: The Word.

Words are powerful, and focusing your meditation on certain words or phrases can be enlightening. The word or phrase is similar to what was described for visualization and imagery except, instead of a mental picture, the power of words are used instead. Most people are familiar with associating the power of words with positive affirmations.

Meditation words/phrases are generally utilized by repeating the word or phrase that have personal meaning and are affirming. Some examples are the following:

1. Love, God, peace, or creator
2. I am prosperous or my life is spiritually filled
3. Relax and feel the peacefulness

MANAGING DEPRESSION AND ANXIETY

Although no single cause of depression or anxiety has been identified, it appears that genetic, biological, environmental, and psychological factors may play a role.

These are both common conditions that many people will experience at some time during their life. With all the responsibilities in a busy life, managing depression and anxiety can be even more overwhelming.

Although anyone can develop depression or anxiety, the conditions seem to run in families. Whether or not they are genetic, the disorders are believed to be associated with changes to brain chemistry. Both of these disorders are treatable. Talk with your primary care physician, psychiatrist, or therapist regarding treatment. Medication may be discussed as part of a treatment plan to be considered along with numerous management skills that may include lifestyle changes.

You may be asked to identify the source(s) contributing to the disorder(s), the symptoms, triggers, or factors that intensify distress, internal resources, and external resources. Additional cognitive-behavioral management skills can be acquired through education and guidance by a therapist. Ultimately, you will be the most important factor in managing depression and/or anxiety because you will apply the effort and persistence to recover.

THE OVERLAP BETWEEN DEPRESSION AND ANXIETY

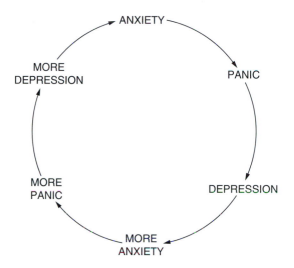

It is not uncommon for a person presenting with depression to also experience anxiety and vice versa. This overlap is called comorbidity. The National Comorbidity Survey states that the co-occurrence of anxiety disorders and depressive disorders was at least 58% (over half). Those with depression and anxiety generally have a sad mood, are nervous, are easily agitated, are tense, experience difficulties with sleep, and have a decreased ability to feel pleasure in normally pleasurable experiences and activities. A major science validation of the overlap between the symptoms of depression and anxiety is that a number of medications effectively treat them both. The basic management cognitive-behavioral tools, including challenging negative/irrational thinking (which includes identifying automatic negative thoughts or *ANTS*), self-care, positive daily structure, development and use of resources, etc. are utilized to support a person to learn to identify and change the problem thoughts and behavior patterns that perpetuate depression and anxiety. These techniques, which focus on behavior, have the potential to address underlying behavior and root causes of other, physical and mental health problems as well. Some of the most common comorbidities experienced in addition to depression and anxiety include bipolar disorder, panic disorder, avoidant personality disorder, and the use of alcohol and other drugs to relieve symptoms.

The causes of depression and anxiety include the following:

1. Environmental or situational factors. This depression is triggered by the stress of changes or losses such as losing a job, divorce, or death of a family member or friend.

2. How one chooses to interpret what happens to them, how they choose to deal with what they experience, what kind of self-talk they use (positive or negative), how resilient they are, etc.

3. Biological Factors. There are chemicals in the brain called neurotransmitters that communicate messages between the nerve cells of the brain. If there is an imbalance in these brain chemicals the result can be changes in thought, behavior, and emotion. Other biological relationships to depression and anxiety could be a thyroid dysfunction, medications, chronic pain or other medical illness, and the long-term experience of stress with a component of hopelessness, losses, or lack of choices.

4. Genetic Factors. There appears to be a relationship between family history of depression and/or anxiety. This suggests that if there are family members who have a history of depression or anxiety there may be a predisposition to having depression and/or anxiety. If you experience depression and/or anxiety there a number of interventions that you can use which can improve the quality of your life experience. Therapy is a key factor in understanding the source of your depression/anxiety and making the appropriate interventions. Also, discuss the possibility of medication management with your physician.

EIGHT STEPS OF TAKING RESPONSIBILITY

1. Make a commitment to change to improve the quality of your life.
2. Be aware of how the behavior of others affect you. Seek activities that are pleasurable and beneficial to you. People who feel good about their lives are less negative and angry. They are happy, practice positive/optimistic thinking, accept responsibility, avoid being judgmental of others, and take good care of themselves.
3. Self-care is the core of taking responsibility for yourself. Balance your life; nutrition, adequate rest, regular exercise, people and activities that you enjoy, personal growth, things to look forward to, etc.
4. Broadening your resources and support system is a lifelong endeavor. Don't limit yourself with minimal resources. Create as many choices for yourself as possible. Remember, change is always taking place, i.e., people move, availability of resources may be altered, etc. This makes it even more important to always be making the effort to develop new relationships and resources.
5. Clear boundaries and setting limits reinforces everyone being responsible for themselves. Don't do things just to please others. Give yourself permission to say "no." If you ignore this step you are likely to feel used, taken advantage of, and resentful.
6. Define your goals. Break each goal down into manageable steps. Regularly check on the progress you have made toward your goals. You create your own destiny.
7. Accept that if you are going to recover you will need to do things differently. It is acknowledged that you will not feel like exercising, not staying in bed, bathing, eating right, keeping your environment neat, sharing time with family and friends. No one can live a healthy and functional lifestyle for you.
8. Let go. If something is unresolved then take care of it and move on. If there is something that you don't have any control over then make peace with it, accept it, and let go. Letting go is also important if you choose to remain in situations or relationships that are frustrating to you. You only have control over yourself. You are responsible for your own health (emotional and physical) and happiness.

USING A MOOD AND THOUGHT CHART AS A MANAGEMENT TOOL

Improve control, increase awareness, decreased avoidance and distress by increasing your accountability by using a mood chart. This is a simplified method for the self-reporting of the relationship between moods—events–thoughts that are experienced to share with your treatment team (prescribing physician and therapist). This information will be useful to challenge irrational thinking that plays a significant role in maintaining negative mood states.

	Mood	Intensity (1-10)	Events	Thoughts
example	Depressed Happy Anxious	4 3 6	Criticized by friend Joe Went to see a movie at theatre Got bank statement	"I just can't do anything right recently." "Nice to get my mind off things." "If I can't get out of debt, I'll lose my family."
Mon				
Tue				
Wed				
Thu				
Fri				
Sat				
Sun				

DEPRESSION SYMPTOM CHECKLIST

The symptoms of depression vary widely from person to person. Which of the following feelings and symptoms do you experience?

__ feeling low	__ tense	__ fatigue
__ feeling sad	__ agitated	__ heaviness
__ difficulty with sleep	__ quiet	__ fear
__ compulsive eating	__ withdrawn	__ disorganized
__ no appetite	__ guilty	__ cries easily
__ low self-esteem	__ hateful	__ like a failure
__ obsessed with the past	__ hoping to die	__ unbearable
__ hating my life	__ plan to kill self	__ dead inside
__ helplessness	__ self-critical	__ body aches
__ anxious	__ no motivation	__ miserable
__ apathetic	__ worthless	__ alone
__ difficulty concentrating	__ excessive worrying	__ feelings of loss

If there are other symptoms that you experience please list them.

_____

_____

It is important to identify the symptoms that you are experiencing so that a course of intervention can be determined. Often, when someone is depressed they have numerous physical symptoms. These symptoms or sensations can be purely related to stress and depression or may have a physical basis. Therefore, if you have not been recently examined by your physician it is a good idea to make an appointment to rule out any physical complications that are contributing to your experience of depression.

Possible medical causes could be the following:

__ endocrine system problems (such as a malfunctioning thyroid)
__ medication interactions

__ acute or chronic stress reactions
__ allergies
__ premenstrual syndrome
__ chronic health problems
__ drug/alcohol abuse or dependence
__ recently stopped smoking
__ recent surgery
__ seasonal affective disorder (shorter days/less light)

MANAGING DEPRESSION

Managing depression requires that you gain some sense of control over depression. Because everyone's experience is unique to them it is necessary that you take the time to increase your awareness, take the risk of trying some interventions, and make the commitment to follow-through. Managing depression requires that you take responsibility for improving the quality of your life. If your depression has been chronic and/or severe, discuss antidepressant medication with your physician. There may be a biological or genetic factor influencing your mood that requires a medical intervention. Once this is determined then you must decide what you are going to do. This is accomplished by developing a self-care plan. The significant components of a self-care plan include the following:

1. *Daily Structure.* Structure your day to include the factors or interventions of taking care of yourself. This can be easily established by using a daily activity chart until you are able to consistently engage in self-care without constant reminders.

2. *Support.* Develop and utilize resources to eliminate social isolation and withdrawal. Having regular contact with family, friends, support group, etc. also brings new information to you, promotes problem solving, and reinforces self-responsibility.

3. *Positive Attitude.* Choosing positive thoughts instead of negative ones, reminding yourself that depression is a temporary emotional state, and focusing on taking 1 day at a time. Choosing to interpret events in a positive manner and taking action where possible has a significant impact on quality of life.

4. *Awareness.* To maintain and continue the progress that you make in managing your depression requires that there be an increased awareness for what works and is beneficial and what does not help you. Keeping a journal can be useful for self-monitoring. You will want to identify the "red flags" of potential regression and any patterns of behavior that affect you negatively.

5. *Exercise.* Before you initiate any exercise program check with your physician. Walking aerobically (quick paced 35–40 min) at least every other day is helpful in reducing body tension, improving sleep, creating a sense of well-being, increasing energy, and decreasing stress.

6. *Nutrition.* Eating well-balanced meals. If you are unsure of what it means to eat healthy, consult your physician, dietitian, or go to a bookstore where you will find many resources. People who are depressed often experience some disturbance in a normal healthy eating pattern, and as a result, there can be weight loss or weight gain.

7. *Value System.* Clarify what your values are and do an inventory. If you are not living in accordance with your value system this could be contributing to your experience of depression.

As you can see managing depression means total self-care. If you neglect to take care of yourself, once you begin to feel better, you will likely begin to reexperience some symptoms of depression. Emotional health, as well as physical health, is about lifestyle.

CHALLENGING DEPRESSION

Is it possible that your experience of depression is the result of not being true to yourself? If so, think about the following statement: If you are not true to yourself and are denying yourself, you lose yourself, and when you lose yourself you become depressed.

The following is a list of feelings that are associated with depression. Read through the list and identify your feelings. With this awareness you will then begin to monitor these feelings and take responsibility for the appropriate self-care practices to decrease or eliminate these feelings and therefore decrease or eliminate your experience of depression.

1. Withdrawn and lack of effort to engage with others
2. Fatigue and inactivity
3. Sad/melancholy
4. Difficulty with concentration and attention
5. Difficulty making decisions
6. Sleep disturbance
7. Decreased enthusiasm or pleasure in normally pleasurable activities
8. Social isolation/lonely
9. Irritability
10. Anxiety
11. Sense of helplessness and hopelessness
12. Feeling overwhelmed
13. Despair
14. Sexual dysfunction
15. Suicidal thought

*Self-medication with alcohol or other drugs.

DECREASING THE INTENSITY OF DEPRESSION

1. Clarify your needs, thoughts, and feelings.
   A. Express them and problem-solve necessary "what do you need to do to feel better?"
   B. If others are not supportive or caring, problem-solve appropriate ways to get your needs met and how to find the support you need
2. Be assertive; say "no" to certain activities and people.
3. Identify and change negative self-talk. It takes you down and keeps you there.
4. Get regular exercise; walk, it relieves stress, increases energy, and changes brain chemistry to decrease depression.
5. Prioritize tasks and do not overload yourself.
6. Engage in creative projects that are fun and distracting from other stressors.
7. Practice good nutrition.
8. Get adequate rest (not too much or too little).
9. Ask for help and delegate when possible.
10. Develop a supportive social network.
11. Develop goals and get focused.
12. Pamper yourself with a pedicure or manicure, get a massage, buy yourself a small gift, and so on.

BREAKING THE DEPRESSION CYCLE

The Depression Cycle

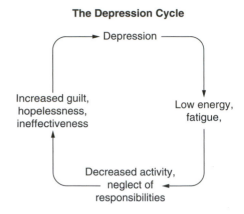

Some people have a good level of resilience, or the ability to deal with the good and bad that comes their way. It just seems to roll off them, but in truth they are dealing with stress and crisis in a healthy way. If you are a person who lacks resilience, you are more likely cast into a spiral when a stressful event occurs. The more you understand the causes underlying your depression the better able you will be to identify those triggers and problem-solve how to effectively cope with them.

1. Family history of depression (genetic vulnerability)
2. History of trauma
3. Lack of coping skills with specific situations
4. Lack of self-care and social connections
5. Lack of goal directedness, etc.

As you identify your triggers develop strategies for coping with them. For example, when something stressful or bad happens "don't shut down."

1. Get activated, reach out to resources, and start problem-solving immediately. Shutting down assures initiation of the depression cycle. When you know what doesn't work get busy finding something that does. To make sure that you are in the best shape possible to maximize a positive outcome, engage in good self-care behaviors, use your resources, get involved socially (social connectedness is imperative to good mental health), even volunteer. Volunteering is a good way to get out of self-focus, feel good about being helpful to others, and often a way to recognize the things you have in life to be grateful for.
2. Plan for the predictable. For example, changes that come with developmental stages of life—such as the kids leaving home, retirement, moving to a smaller home to accommodate changing income, etc.
3. Losses are hard and it is important to reach out. Grief can be a selfish experience leaving your feeling alone and those close to feeling discounted, not important and rejected. Medication may also be beneficial in getting through a rough time.
4. Marital problems/separation/divorce can be stressful, scary, and overwhelming even when you are exiting a toxic or abusive relationship. Starting over is hard. Get involved in social resources immediately, i.e., therapy, a divorce care class, or other support groups.
5. Boredom. This one is definitely a signal of isolation and not taking responsibility for developing skills or interests.
6. Health and hormonal changes. Obviously the more positive health habit and regular self-care you engage in, the more you will be prepared to mentally and physically deal with negative health changes.

7. Weather (gray winters and less light), holidays, and anniversaries of loss can be a trigger for many people. Ask yourself what you have learned about how to survive those times in a more positive manner. Also, consult a therapist to problem-solve and, once again, being socially connected is also important. It is also important for many people to honor the one(s) they have lost, but don't confuse the time of honoring with general isolation. That is a setup to spiral into depression.

SURVIVING THE HOLIDAY BLUES

For some, the holidays are an emotionally difficult time because of negative and hurtful childhood and adolescent experiences. For others, holidays emphasize the fact that the structure of everyone's life changes over time. These changes can be associated with children growing up, leaving home, and creating new rituals with a life partner, the modification of traditions as in-laws are incorporated into available holiday time, changes in health, death, or other crises. It is highly uncomfortable to face the holidays when they are anticipated with dread or distress. If, for any reason you feel out of sync with the holidays, consider the following:

1. *Develop new holiday traditions.* If you do this, start out with realistic expectations. Whatever you do, it is not going to feel the same way to you as the way it was. It may take repeating the new tradition several times before it begins to feel like something that you are really looking forward to. However, because many people do not have the resources of a large family or the money to travel far to see family, developing new traditions is something you have control over, so make the effort to create a special time.

2. *Choose to participate.* Do not withdraw from everything during the holidays. Do not isolate yourself. While it may be difficult to feel much enthusiasm for social gatherings, choose to do it. Chances are once you are in the midst of participating, you will be distracted and find yourself feeling better. Participate at a level that feels comfortable to you—but participate. Also, even participating a little may lift your spirits.

3. *Take care of you.* The commercialization of the holidays can be overwhelming. Do not let that influence how you choose to participate in the holiday season. This is also a time to reflect and give yourself a little tender loving care. Don't park yourself in front of the television and be in a trance or allow yourself to be filled with dread. Instead, choose a movie you have wanted to see, read a good book, listen to pleasing music, send cards, write letters, volunteer to help others or plan a new ritual like holiday vacation. You may be surprised to find that taking a little time for yourself can help you feel better.

4. *Volunteer.* Sometimes we get so focused on our losses or distress that we forget all we have to be grateful for. A lot of social service programs really try to reach out to those who have no resources and are destitute, as well as other holiday-oriented extras like special programs at museums. These organizations would be pleased to have the gift of some of your time. Sometimes helping others who are in a more difficult place than ourselves can fire up appreciation for the good things in our own lives. There are numerous ways to give some of your time: maybe there is something that you have wanted to get involved in for some time, call the volunteer bureau for ideas, look in the paper, and ask others.

5. *Talk about it.* The holiday blues are more common than you may realize. Do not suffer in silence. There is the risk that the blues could get worse and become depression. Take some time to think about why the holidays are distressful for you. Again, get informed about what is happening in your community. Churches and community centers often offer special programs for people who are alone or experiencing difficulty during the holidays. Also, if it seems to be getting worse, talk to your physician and seek advice from other professional resources. Talking about it is an important step to increased self-understanding, validation, and problem solving.

WHAT IS MANIA?

What to look for when coming down from mania is as varied as the people experiencing mania. However, for many the surge of energy and euphoria is not something they want to go away—especially if they fear bipolar depression. Common symptoms of mania include racing thoughts, sleeplessness, irritability, hyper-sexual, etc. It is so important to be a partner with your prescribing physician to manage and adjust medication as needed. Your physician depends on the information from self-reports and treatment compliance.

There are several types of bipolar disorder and all involve episodes of mania and depression—but to varying degrees:

1. With bipolar I, there are severe mood swings.
2. With bipolar II and cyclothymic disorder, there are milder versions of the illness.
3. Mixed bipolar is both mania and depression at the same time—a dangerous mix of grandiosity, racing thoughts, yet irritable, moody, angry.

What is the difference between hypomania and mania? Hypomania is a less severe form of mania. Hypomania is a mood that many don't perceive as a problem. It actually may feel pretty good. You have a greater sense of well-being, being goal directed and productive. However, for someone with bipolar disorder, hypomania can progress or evolve into mania or switch into "bipolar depression."

Maybe this is best understood by presenting the symptoms as if someone is sharing their experience:

1. *Hypomania.* At first, my mind is moving faster than usual, I am high and not repressed by much of anything. My social shyness disappears, and everything becomes more interesting and intense. I feel more sensual. I am seductive as well as being easily seduced. I feel powerful and euphoric.
2. *Mania.* My mind is racing "too many ideas too fast," I feel overwhelmed and confused. Who cares how much it costs. If I want to do, or I want to buy it I am. Seems like everything is funny…but then it can turn on a dime and I snap. I can become instantly irritable and then the out of control anger is there. My family and friends all say that I am scaring them.

When talking to your doctor about your experience, the following information may be helpful:

1. *Mood changes.* A prolonged period of a mood that's unusual for the person is required for a diagnosis of mania. The first two below are part of the specific diagnostic criteria for a manic episode; the others are descriptions of the way these moods may be expressed.
    A. Abnormally elevated or expansive mood (euphoric)
    B. Extreme and abnormal irritability
    C. Easily excited to enthusiasm, quick to anger, easily agitation
    D. Unusual hostility
2. *Increased energy.* Changes in energy may be observed by the person themselves or someone close to them. However, the change in sleep patterns won't be apparent in a person who lives alone, unless that person speaks about it to others to maintain their awareness, keeps a journal or monitors change in daily functioning. The following are the examples:
    A. Decreased need for sleep with little fatigue
    B. An increase in goal-directed activities
    C. Restlessness or being on edge
    D. Agitation
    E. Overreactivity

3. *Speech disruptions.* These symptoms are particularly easy for others to notice:
   A. Rapid, pressured speech
   B. Incoherent speech
4. *Impaired judgment.* The first three symptoms listed below are very much related to social situations, and are quite likely to be noticed by family members, friends, coworkers, etc. The last two are often obvious and can have particularly far-reaching consequences. In some cases, however, the manic or hypomanic person will try to hide those behaviors.
   A. Inappropriate humor and behaviors
   B. Increased impulsiveness
   C. Lack of insight and poor judgment
   D. Financial recklessness
   E. Hypersexuality
5. *Changes in thought patterns.* Some of these symptoms can't be observed by anyone but the person experiencing them, but he or she may tell friends and loved ones about them.
   A. Unusual distractibility
   B. Enhanced creative thinking and/or behaviors
   C. Flight of ideas
   D. Disorientation
   E. Disjointed thinking
   F. Racing thoughts
   G. Increased focus on religion or religious activities

*Sometimes there can be hallucinations, delusions, or paranoia. Additionally, there could be the possibility of periods of depression mixed with mania called "episodes."

10 POINTS FOR MANAGING MANIA

1. An accountability partner. A person that you speak to honestly in your support system.
2. Inform your prescribing physician when you become aware of mania-related changes taking place so that the two of you can monitor those changes and medication.
3. Create financial limits. For example, credit cards with low limits or not having any credit cards, having only a small amount of cash available, no ATM/debit card, bank account has a restriction/requirement of a 2- to 3-day transfer for online banking, etc.
4. Exercise is an excellent channel for manic energy, e.g., walking, running, cycling, hiking, swimming. Practice for a half-marathon!
5. Creative expression. A person could spend hours sketching, painting, or spending time at other areas of enjoyment and productivity (such as working in the yard).
6. Learn something new. Take a class at a local adult education or community center.
7. Volunteer to help someone less able. Maybe you have a neighbor who needs help with a yard project. Put your energy to work. Create a list when you are not manic regarding potential volunteer projects. Not everything would be a wise choice when manic.
8. Review what needs to be done at your house. You got it—clean, fix, and repair. Clean the webs, hose off the patio, fix the squeaky doors, clean baseboards, wash windows. There is always a lot to do so it may be helpful to keep a list going so it is right there when needed for reference.

9. Stay true to your beliefs and who you know yourself to be. Mania alters the way a person thinks. So write down information about yourself when you are doing well and when it begins to change use that information and your accountability partner to keep things in check.

10. What goes up must come down. That's right, it won't last forever. That is why the consistency of being compliant with treatment, working closely with your physician on any changes, and eliciting the support of your accountability partner are all necessary to keep doing as well as possible.

*Mania is temporary, but its consequences could be lasting.

ANXIETY SYMPTOM LIST

Anxiety can have an association to genetics, medication, or health issues such as thyroid dysfunction. Anxiety is also an issue of behavioral wellness. Few people with anxiety actually seek professional intervention for decreasing or eliminating anxiety symptoms. Life stress such as family challenges, a parent who demonstrated/role modeled (social learning) anxiety coping, and health problems is associated with a person having anxiety. Generalized anxiety disorder is one of the anxiety disorders and it involves excessive, unrealistic worry and tension, even if there is little or nothing to provoke the anxiety. Anxiety doesn't have to be a lifelong problem—but it can be if you don't do what needs to be done to change what you are thinking and doing. If the specific reasons underlying anxiety are not addressed, anxiety can unnecessarily continue. Most people struggle with anxiety because they don't

1. Understand anxiety and how it can affect the body
2. Seek professional help
3. Make the necessary changes in thinking patterns or behavioral changes to overcome a struggle with problematic anxiety

Common anxiety symptoms include the following:

1. Feeling nervous and on-edge
2. Feelings of fear, uneasiness, and panic
3. Shortness of breath
4. Numbness or tingling in the hands
5. Muscle tension
6. Easily tired, fatigues
7. Excess worry
8. Difficulty concentrating
9. Irritability
10. Stomach upset
11. Appetite disturbance
12. Sleep problems
13. Social avoidance and isolation

*When a person is presented with what they interpret as an anxiety-provoking situation the mind and body respond in a complicated interaction between physical reactions (physiology), thinking (cognition), behavior (performance), and emotion.

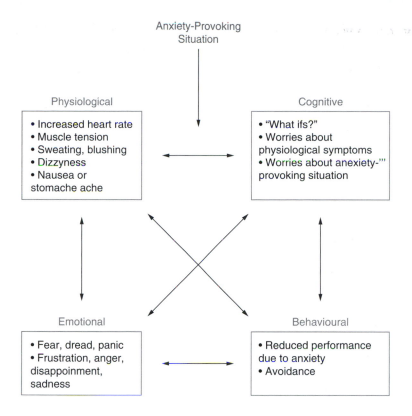

Anxiety-Provoking Situation

Physiological
- Increased heart rate
- Muscle tension
- Sweating, blushing
- Dizzyness
- Nausea or stomache ache

Cognitive
- "What ifs?"
- Worries about physiological symptoms
- Worries about anexiety-'" provoking situation

Emotional
- Fear, dread, panic
- Frustration, anger, disappoinment, sadness

Behavioural
- Reduced performance due to anxiety
- Avoidance

DECREASING OR ELIMINATING THE INTENSITY OF ANXIETY SYMPTOMS

1. Regular exercise (mediation, deep breathing, etc.).
2. Developing choices to increase trust in your ability to manage anxiety arousal. There are always options. Choose what works best for you.
3. Distraction or "time out" from daily activities. Let your mind and body rest.
4. Relaxation techniques.
5. Acknowledge when you are feeling anxious and that anxiety is like any other feeling.
6. Challenge irrational and negative thinking. Ask yourself such questions as:
   A. Is this worry realistic?
   B. Is this really likely to happen?
   C. If the worst possible outcome happens, what would be so bad about that?
   D. Could I handle that?
   E. What might I do?
   F. If something bad happens, am I trapped and unable to cope?
   G. Is this really true or does it just seem that way?
   H. What might I do to prepare for specific things I expect may happen?
7. Realize that your brain is playing tricks on you. For example, remind yourself that on another occasion you thought you were having a heart attack but you were thoroughly checked out and nothing was wrong with you physically. Knowing the fear is not based on reality and acknowledging that the symptoms don't last forever will be calming.
8. Use calming visualizations. Practice is important so that when you need it the calming visualization is easily accessible. For example, picture yourself sitting on the beach, the warm sun on your face, a gentle breeze, and the sound of the waves lapping on the beach.

9. Practice at refining your self-observations→thoughts, feelings, emotions, sensations, choices.
10. Develop and use beneficial social supports.

25 WAYS TO RELIEVE ANXIETY

1. Positive thinking. Look for the opportunity instead of the negative.
2. Task oriented. Feel good about your efforts and accomplishments.
3. Accept yourself. Don't be self-critical. If there is something you want to change then change it.
4. Be flexible. Not everything is black and white. Be open to the gray area of things.
5. Develop realistic goals. Evaluate what it will take to reach a goal.
6. Develop a positive view of life.
7. Nurture your spirituality.
8. Distract yourself from stressors. Sometimes you have to put everything aside to relax and have fun.
9. Deep breathing, relaxation, meditation, or visualization.
10. Finding humor in things.
11. Spending time with people you enjoy.
12. Keeping a journal for venting, and at the end of every entry closing with something positive.
13. Take time regularly to do activities that you enjoy.
14. Utilize your support system. This could be friends, family, individual therapy, group therapy, or community support groups.
15. Practice being assertive. You will feel better for taking care of yourself.
16. Good communication.
17. Take short breaks throughout the day. Take 5–10 min breaks throughout the day to relax and remove yourself from stressors or demands.
18. Regular exercise. Walking is excellent for decreasing body tension and alleviating stress.
19. Get adequate rest and sleep. If you don't get enough sleep you can't cope well.
20. Practice good nutrition.
21. Massage. A good way to relieve muscle tension and relax.
22. Choose to be in environments that feel good to you. Consider comfort, activity level, noise, color, scenery, etc.
23. Work on your financial security.
24. Practice good time management.
25. Do things that demonstrate respect, care, and nurturing of the self. That means take good care of you.

Develop a self-care plan. Incorporate these strategies and others to develop a plan of self-care behaviors, beliefs, and attitudes that can become a new and healthy lifestyle. That is practicing preventive medicine.

MANAGING ANXIETY

Anxiety is a part of everyday life. It is a normal emotional experience. However, in an anxiety disorder the anxiety is much more intense, it lasts longer, and it may be specific to people, places, or situations.

The goals in managing anxiety are to identify and understand personal reaction to anxiety-provoking situations, identify what your related concerns are, and to learn to "let go" of anxiety. You may need the help of a therapist to learn the skills useful for managing and eliminating anxiety disorder symptoms. You may also benefit from the use of antianxiety medications in conjunction with therapy to accomplish these goals. The hope is that, by reading that there are a number of strategies that are beneficial for managing anxiety, you will prioritize the goal of identifying which ones work well for you and learning to effectively manage the anxiety you feel.

As with almost everything, if you want things to be different then you need to be willing to do things differently. It takes a commitment to change and consistency in following through in the use of the strategies that you will develop to manage the distress of anxiety disorders. Some people experience anxiety in specific situations whereas others experience a certain level of anxiety all the time. To develop a treatment plan that will help you manage anxiety effectively requires that you clearly identify your symptoms, the thoughts you have about the anxiety you feel, the circumstances related to the onset of the symptoms if there are any, what resources and strategies you have used to cope with the distress of anxiety.

In identifying the possible issues related to anxiety you may have to pay better attention to the thoughts in your mind. People talk to themselves continually throughout the day. When you talk to yourself about the emotion or fear that you attach to it, you begin to have the needed insight on what is causing and maintaining anxiety. Increasing your awareness for what these self-talk statements are will allow you to begin to change and correct the thinking that has contributed to your unmanageable anxiety.

It is recommended that you keep a journal. A journal is useful for venting your feelings, clarifying what the problem is, and then problem-solving the situation by taking the appropriate action. To problem-solve the situations that you write about ask yourself if this is something that you have control over. If the answer is yes then consider the options for dealing with it, and make a decision after considering the various consequences or outcomes. Be prepared to try an alternative if the first attempt does not work effectively. If it is something that you do not have any control over then "let go." Learning to accept what you cannot change will relieve anxiety. It takes time to learn how to let go, but the increased energy, freedom, and relief that you will experience are well worth it.

During the course of your journal writing, you will become more aware of the internal self-talk and begin to understand the relationship between your thoughts and feelings. Thoughts affect feelings, and feelings affect actions. When you choose to think more positively about a situation you will feel better. Likewise, when you worry excessively, expect the worst to happen, and when you are self-critical you can expect to feel bad.

Now you know that beliefs affect emotion and behavior you will want to pay more attention to your own beliefs.

1. Do you feel an intense need for approval from others? People-pleasing behavior means that you put the needs of others before your own needs. This leads to frustration and, over time, resentment. Frustration and resentment are intense feelings that can contribute to chronic anxiety and tension.

2. Do you have an intense need for control? Do you worry about how you appear? Do you feel uncomfortable in letting other people be in charge of a situation? Do you believe that if you are not in control, that you are weak and a failure?

3. Do you tend to be perfectionistic and self-critical? Do you often feel that what you do is never enough or not good enough? Do you often criticize your own efforts and feel a constant pressure to achieve?

These patterns of beliefs and behavior are irrational. If this is your approach to life expect to experience chronic stress, anxiety, and low self-esteem. Who could feel calm and relaxed with this approach to life? Chances are that if you engage in any of these behaviors and beliefs that you also have a tendency to discount what you are experiencing physically. The mind and body function as one. When there is emotional distress you know it. Generally, there are physical symptoms as well, especially with chronic stress. Often when people ignore all of the ways that their body tries to tell them to slow down and take care of themselves the result is an escalation in symptoms that can feel so bad it makes you slow down. Deal with symptoms before it gets to this level of distress.

IMPROVING ANXIETY MANAGEMENT EFFECTIVENESS

Ineffective and dysfunctional approaches to relationships with others and with yourself need to be changed. To be the best that you can be in a relationship requires that you be the best you can be as an individual.

1. Develop good boundaries. This means having a realistic view of other people's approval, and that you don't depend on it to feel worthy or accepted. It also means learning to deal with criticism in an objective manner. Everyone is entitled to their opinion. If they offer information that is beneficial to you then use it. If not, then let go. If you have a tendency to put the importance of their needs above your own then recognize your codependency and take responsibility for changing it. This can be a big contributor to states of chronic anxiety and stress.

2. Develop realistic expectations and limitations. Change your belief that your worth is based on what you accomplish and achieve. Focus on what is right. You can drive yourself to the point of exhaustion with self-criticism. Once you develop realistic goals, you will have the time you need for other personal necessities such as spending time doing things that you find pleasurable and being with people you enjoy. Balance is the most important goal.

3. Recognize that not everything can be neat and predictable. Learning acceptance and patience will help you be more comfortable with the things that are not predictable. The next step is learning to trust that most problems eventually work out. One of two things will happen; either you will find a solution to the problem or you will see that it cannot be changed. If it cannot be changed, then you find a way to accept it or make some decision based on its influence in your life and do something else. Overall, things become clearer and coping is easier. The best policy is to deal with "what is" not "what if."

As previously discussed, people with chronic anxiety and stress tend to ignore their body's response to stress. This means that you may be ignoring physical symptoms. If this is the case, you will keep pushing yourself without slowing down to taking care of yourself. One consequence of pushing yourself with controlling, codependent, perfectionist standards is a chronic high level of stress that turns into panic attacks. A panic attack is also a warning sign. This warning sign is not as easy to ignore as others. If you have a panic attack, chances are that you have ignored taking good care of yourself for some time, are experiencing a lot of stress, and that irrational thinking is playing a role.

Learning to manage stress requires that you be able to identify your own symptoms of stress. Once you have this awareness, then you can determine the things you need to do to relieve your stress and anxiety. You are responsible for your own physical and emotional health. It is important to note that it is not uncommon for someone with an anxiety disorder to also be experiencing some level of depression.

DEALING WITH FEAR ASSOCIATED WITH ANXIETY

Fear is not a character flaw. It is a survival mechanism designed to protect you. It is meant to be a warning. However, it does more than just warn you, it makes the heart beat faster along with a lot of other changes as your body prepares itself for fight or flight. Fear may have benefit and be useful at times. However, when it becomes irrational and prevents you from doing normal things, it then becomes a problem. Use the following information to appropriately manage and recover from the problem of fear.

1. *Stop looking for the answer—when it comes from childhood.* It doesn't matter why you are afraid. When you think about something that scared you as a kid (and still does), does thinking about it take away the fear? The memory may not even be accurate. You don't need to know exactly how or when you developed your fear to put your fear to rest. Instead, work on ways to overcome the fear you experience.

2. *As an adult knowledge about the foundation of your fear can be used to help you.* Since fear is a protective mechanism, find out what you are afraid of. A powerful part of the experience of fear is unpredictability or uncertainty. Therefore, when the situation becomes predictable, fear decreases. The more accurate and realistic your information, the more prepared you will feel in dealing with it.

3. *Practice doing it.* The more you know how to do something or are clear about how you want to respond, the more fear seems to evaporate. If there is something you want to do but are afraid, train for it so that you develop a sense of "can do" and self-confidence.

4. *Find positive role models who you can learn from.* They are rational and accurate in what they do. Their courage is calming and contagious. They don't get stuck on things outside of their control.

5. *Talking helps.* Opening up about your fears can decrease distress even when you can't change the situation. Likewise, trying to keep your feelings of fear a secret isn't going to get you the help you need.

6. *Use your imagination.* Remind yourself that fear isn't the end of the world. For example, fear of public speaking is the number one phobia. There are numerous "mind tricks" for dealing with this fear, such as imagining you are speaking to children or that something is funny about everyone in the audience, which decreases the fear of being judged by them. Get creative in your problem solving. How you think about a situation makes a big difference.

7. *Focus on the little things.* Little things are always manageable. Figure out what you have to do and do it one step at a time.

8. *Give yourself permission to get help.* If the symptoms are severe, you may have an anxiety disorder that could be treated by medication and therapy. However, even if the symptoms are not severe, it may be useful to seek professional help.

9. *Find ways to decrease the physical and emotional stress associated with fear.* These may include exercise, positive self-talk, and progressive muscle relaxation or meditation.

10. Develop a hierarchy of experiences that range from not causing fear or/minimal fear leading up to the most feared experience that is the goal to overcome. This is called systematic desensitization, and a therapist can do this technique with you. Another technique is called "flooding," whereby you are continually exposed directly to the feared object or situation until the fear response is diminished.

STOPPING THE ANXIETY CYCLE

PLAN OF ACTION FOR DEALING WITH ANXIETY

1. Recognize and identify anxiety symptoms and situations related to it.

2. *Develop relaxation skills.* Most people will be able to feel relaxed by using progressive muscle relaxation. If you have made a good effort to use it and do not find that it is relaxing for you, then it is your responsibility to try other techniques until you find one that is effective for you. Other techniques include deep breathing, visualization, meditation, body scanning, and brief forms of progressive muscle relaxation. This is a very important part of managing anxiety. Because of the way the nervous system works, it is physically impossible to be stressed and relaxed at the same time. Learn a relaxation technique.

3. *Confront anxiety.* Make a commitment to understand and deal with the issues underlying your experience of anxiety.

4. *Problem-solve.* Once you have identified the underlying issues contributing to the anxiety you experience deal with the issues that you can do something about and let go of the issues that you cannot do anything about.

5. *Develop positive self-esteem.* If you do not accept and like who you are, how can you effectively manage the things that are causing your anxiety. The managing of anxiety is about lifestyle changes. This requires a commitment to yourself. To make this commitment and follow-through will depend on how important your well-being is to you.

6. *Exercise.* Aerobic exercise especially walking is a good stress reliever. It decreases muscle tension, increases energy, and can improve sleep. You will experience the benefits of walking after several weeks of commitment to this anxiety relieving strategy. It feels good to take care of yourself.

7. *Use positive self-talk.* How you talk to yourself will make a big difference in how you interpret things around you, how you choose to feel, and how you choose to respond. In other words, how you talk to yourself affects your entire life experience. Practice positive, rational self-talk and incorporate daily use of positive affirmations.

8. *Keep a journal.* A journal is a great tool for venting your feelings and thoughts. It takes emotional energy to keep all of this "stuff" inside. Get it out. Writing your thoughts and feelings can also clarify issues. Problem-solve these issues to alleviate distress and to unclutter your mind. A journal is also a great way to monitor your consistency and actual commitment to the changes necessary for managing your anxiety.

9. *Confront and change self-defeating behavioral patterns.* This means changing perfectionistic, controlling, codependent behaviors. These behaviors do not help you get your needs met and they do not make you feel better. Contrary, they generally leave you feeling stressed, frustrated, anxious, angry, and over time resentful.

10. *Desensitize phobias.* If there are specific situations that elicit extreme anxiety for you, then work with your therapist using a technique called systematic desensitization.

11. *Utilize your support system.* If you do not have a support system, then develop one. Start by identifying, and using, the supports that you need for confronting and dealing with your anxiety. A support system can include your therapist (individual or group), your physician, family members, friends, people at your church, etc. Generally the reason why a person lacks a support system is because they have made the choice to not allow others to help them. Instead, they have this distorted belief that it is only themselves who can be there to support other people.

12. *Energize yourself with pleasure and humor.* This means spending time with people you enjoy and doing activities that you like. Laughter is a great stress reliever. Have laughter in your life everyday.

13. *Practice good nutrition and get adequate sleep.* You must take care of yourself to live life fully including work, relaxation, and pleasure. Life balance is the key.

14. *Develop assertive communication.* Being able to say "no" and to otherwise effectively express yourself is a necessary skill. To get your needs appropriately met requires that you speak honestly and appropriately about what you want and need.

15. *Develop self-nurturing behaviors.* You are so good at taking care of the needs of others. The practice of doing things that feel good and self-nurturing will improve your mood.

If you have developed a program for managing anxiety and are consistently practicing it, you are probably feeling much better. Because change is difficult, you will need to make sure that you maintain the motivation to do things differently. Originally, it was the extreme distress and physical symptoms that facilitated your change. Sometimes when people start feeling better, they quit following through on the changes in their thinking and behaviors that got them to the feeling better place. This can lead to a relapse of symptoms. If a relapse happens to you view it as an opportunity to understand the importance of the components of your management program and the validation that if you do not make a commitment to take care of yourself your body will keep sending you the message that it needs to be taken better care of.

Some people experience relapse as a normal part of their recovery from extreme stress and anxiety. It could be that they are consistently practicing all of the parts of their program but reexperience some symptoms. This has likely happened because there was so much body tension that they may go through one or more stages of a readjustment. So if you are consistently doing what is prescribed in the way of changes—continue even if some symptoms reoccur. They will subside. Remember, it took a long time to get to this state, and it may take a while to alleviate all of the emotional and physical distress. Therefore, think of relapse as a normal, predictable part of recovery.

Be prepared to deal with the possibility of a relapse. If it does occur, it is likely that the symptoms will not be as intense or last as long as they did before. This is because you have developed skills to manage your anxiety and the level of distress is decreasing.

RELAPSE—SYMPTOM REOCCURRENCE

When you have a relapse, you fall back into old behaviors and old ways of thinking. When you started feeling better, you probably thought that you had conquered the anxiety and would not be bothered by those symptoms again. What happens in relapse is just a recycling of the old patterns. Relapse is a predictable and expected part of recovery.

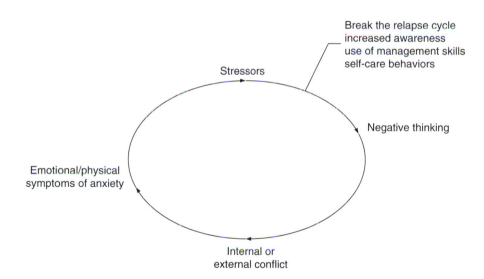

In preparing yourself for the management of a relapse remind yourself of the self-perpetuating cycle of extreme anxiety. If you experience any relapse, take the time to assess your reactions so that you can evaluate your feelings and behaviors. This will help you to appropriately intervene in the relapse cycle earlier and earlier. The result will be decreased setbacks and stronger progress and stabilization.

INTERVENING IN THE RELAPSE CYCLE

1. Managing stress
   A. Use strategies such as relaxation, meditation, exercise, utilization of support system, delegating tasks to others, etc.

2. Challenging negative/irrational thinking
    A. Use positive self-talk, remind yourself that the anxiety will not last forever, use positive affirmations, use your journal so that you can identify patterns of negative self-talk being initiated by specific situations and deal with it.
3. Resolving internal/external conflicts
    A. The conflicts were initiated by the stressors at the beginning of the cycle and then again through negative self-talk. Take the opportunity to understand the conflict and problem-solve it. This is an opportunity to resolve and let go of past issues and dysfunctional thinking patterns.

You will break the relapse cycle with your increased awareness, use of management skills (assertiveness, relaxation, spending time with people you enjoy, participating in activities that are pleasurable, improving your self-esteem, positive self-talk, etc.), and self-care behaviors (adequate rest/sleep, good nutrition, exercise, etc.).

Your consistency and repeated efforts to cope effectively with stressors using the strategies that you develop will pay off. Remember to use your journal or other source to monitor your efforts and consistency in changing your lifestyle to one in which you take care of yourself and avoid exhaustion.

You know that the progress that you have made is becoming more stable when you have learned to experience normal anxiety without panicking. Therefore, continue to be consistent in your efforts to overcome anxiety. You are responsible for your health.

WARNING SIGNS OF RELAPSE

1. Negative thinking
2. Controlling behavior
3. Excessive worrying/catastrophizing
4. Perfectionistic behavior
5. Codependent behavior
6. Change in appetite
7. Difficulty with sleep
8. Difficulty getting up in the morning
9. Fatigue/lethargy
10. Feeling bad about yourself
11. Feeling less hopeful about the future
12. Decreased exercise
13. Unwilling to ask for what you want or need
14. Procrastination
15. Social isolation
16. Withdrawal from activities
17. Use of alcohol or other drugs
18. Irritable/agitated
19. Impatience
20. Negative attitude
21. Lacking confidence
22. Feeling insecure
23. Poor judgment
24. Misperceptions

25. Self-defeating behaviors
26. Destructive risk-taking behaviors
27. Distrustful of others
28. Obsessive thoughts
29. Difficulty concentrating
30. Not experiencing pleasure in anything you do
31. Suicidal thoughts
32. Others

In the early stages of your recovery from anxiety you can use this item survey to regularly review for the presence of symptoms. If you are invested in making the necessary change in thoughts and behavior you are probably do well. However, anticipate that a relapse is inevitable. The use of self-monitoring will offer an early warning so that immediate intervention with management strategies will keep recovery on track. As your progress begins to stabilize, intermittently review this list to maintain awareness and to reinforce efforts and accomplishments. It will also keep you focused on positive lifestyle patterns that provide a natural deterrent to the development of acute anxiety.

SYSTEMATIC DESENSITIZATION

If your anxiety is fear or trauma based, then this CBT technique that can be used to alleviate and eliminate avoidance and recondition coping mechanisms. Systematic desensitization is a technique that couples progressive relaxation training and visual imagery for the extinction of maladaptive anxiety reactions.

To ensure that anxiety is inhibited by the counterresponse to anxiety, muscle relaxation, the anxious individual is instructed to imagine anxiety-provoking scenes arranged in a hierarchy. Hierarchies of anxiety-provoking situations are formulated as a range from mildly stressful or nonthreatening to very threatening. This imaging of scaled events occurs while the individual is deeply relaxed. Should any imaginary event in the hierarchy elicit much anxiety the individual is instructed to cease visualization and regain their feelings of relaxation. Depending on the situation, the hierarchy is adjusted accordingly (broken down into smaller steps or reorganized) or the imaginal representation of the event is repeated until the individual does not experience anxiety in response to the event image.

THE TEN STEPS OF SYSTEMATIC DESENSITIZATION

1. Identify the event that provokes the extreme anxiety.
2. Develop a hierarchy of 10 steps leading to the anxiety-provoking event. Begin with the least stressful aspect in the chain of events leading to the anxiety-provoking event that is avoided because of the associated distress.
3. Make sure that there will not be any disruptions or distractions as the process is initiated. Begin with 15–20 min of progressive muscle relaxation.
4. Once deep relaxation is achieved, present the first scene from the hierarchy. Talk the person through this scene with realistic detail, utilizing all senses if appropriate. Instruct the individual to picture fully this scene in their mind. Draw their attention to their emotional experience while visualizing this scene. Pause for 15–20 s while they visualize this scene.
5. Instruct the individual that if they experience any anxiety they are to signal by raising their right index finger. If there is an experience of intense anxiety or early symptoms of a panic attack instruct the individual to raise two fingers. If this occurs, instruct the individual to let go of distressful scene and to imagine a safe serene place (discussed and developed prior to the initiation of the systematic desensitization process). Instruct the individual to stay in that safe serene place until they feel relaxed again. When relaxation is achieved, proceed

again. If this happens in a later stage and the individual experiences difficulty regaining the relaxed state, back up to the previous imagined event and consolidate the mastery at that step or break down the event further if necessary before proceeding.

6. If there is a signal from the individual that they are experiencing anxiety, have them stay in the scene briefly. While they are still visualizing the scene instruct them to, "take a deep breath and exhale the anxiety, to imagine the tension and anxiety leaving their body. Let go of the anxiety and relax." Allow the person to remain in the relaxed state with the visualized image for 1 min.

7. Once relaxation has been achieved with that step of the hierarchy, instruct the individual to turn off that image and again enter a state of relaxation without a visualized event from the hierarchy. This relaxation period can be done with further relaxation statements or a guided imagery to a safe and relaxing place. Allow them to remain in the relaxed state for 1 min.

8. Have the individual signal with raising the right index finger when total relaxation has been achieved. Check in at intervals of 1 min monitoring the state of relaxation versus anxiety. When there is no anxiety present proceed to the next step.

9. Repeat the initial scene, going through the entire desensitization process. Continue to repeat this scene with desensitization until there is visualization of the scene without provoking anxiety. This can take two to four repetitions per scene.

10. Once anxiety has been eliminated at one step/event proceed onto the next imagined event, repeating the process as previously stated.

WHAT IS PANIC ANXIETY?

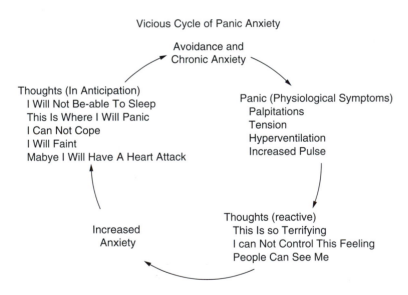

Panic attacks are generally related to the building process of stress along with other factors resulting in the escalation to panic anxiety. There is not a single answer to the question "what causes panic attacks?" However, biological, environmental, and genetic factors play a role.

1. It is possible that separation anxiety during childhood may be a predisposing factor for the development of panic anxiety later in life.

2. Imbalance in brain chemistry may be responsible.

3. Genetic predisposition may be evident when looking at family history of anxiety disorders.

4. Learned behaviors play a role—for example, continuously taking care of the needs of others while neglecting your own needs, buildup of stress over time, or the chronic feeling of being overwhelmed and not having enough time to get to everything that demands your attention.

5. The experience of losing someone close to you such as a family member can result in panic anxiety. A death can result in feelings of being helpless and out of control.
6. Physical trauma past or present may trigger panic anxiety.
7. Sexual trauma past or present may trigger panic anxiety.
8. Positive life events (marriage, job promotion, etc.) may also contribute to panic anxiety. This may be because there are feelings or concerns of some loss associated with the change. It could be that a person does not feel worthy or believes he/she does not deserve to be happy, which may result in negative ruminating and anxiety associated with the change.

SYMPTOMS OF PANIC ANXIETY

Panic attacks are a specific anxiety disorder with a significant level of distress that is overwhelming and provokes feelings of fear. Panic attacks are becoming more common as people feel overloaded and overwhelmed by stress. As lifestyle becomes more hectic the challenge of learning to cope with a variety of demands becomes increasingly important. The core of these necessary coping strategies is self-care. Better yet, make self-care an integral part of your lifestyle and experience increased quality of life and relationships.

Panic attacks are diagnosed when an individual experiences at least four of the following symptoms. Additionally, the symptoms develop and peak in a short period of time, which results in feelings of significant distress. Some might describe this degree of stress as fear of having a heart attack, going crazy or dying.

1. Palpitations/pounding heat/accelerated-racing heart rate
2. Chest pain/tightness
3. Vision problems
4. Sweating/chills/hot flashes
5. Trembling/shaking
6. Feeling short of breath/smothering
7. Feeling of choking
8. Nausea/abdominal distress
9. Feeling dizzy/lightheaded/faint
10. Numbness/tingling in hands or face
11. Derealization (feelings of unreality)
12. Depersonalization (feeling detached from oneself)
13. Fear of losing control/going crazy
14. Fear of dying

DEFEATING PANIC ATTACKS

The following are the traditional basics of treating panic attacks. Medication is a prevalent option combined with CBT. However, to defeat panic attacks requires a conscious approach to living differently—with a health focused lifestyle.

1. CBT
2. Medication
3. Health-focused lifestyle [exercise, decrease or eliminate caffeine and alcohol, develop a self-care plan that includes relaxation practices and meditation (also referred to as mindfulness)]

While all of the factors that define a health-focused lifestyle are important, once a person is experiencing panic attacks it becomes necessary to recondition the nervous system, thus how one thinks, so that there is a clear preference aside from anticipatory anxiety. Anticipatory anxiety is directly countered by the faithful practice of meditation. During the course of meditation brain waves are altered, allowing a person to feel calm physically and emotionally. This is a major key in defeating panic attacks. There are numerous ways to meditate. Prayer, listening to chanting monks, classical music, pan flute (Native American), focusing on one word, etc. will all calm the body and mind. An additional benefit of meditation is the impact that it has on other symptoms such as bad dreams or nightmares, upset stomach, migraines, and other symptoms.

Other important interventions that are essential to defeating panic attacks include exercise and challenging negative self-talk. Regular exercise is imperative to beating panic attacks. Exercise is a natural way to decrease muscle tension and clear the mind. Likewise, challenging negative self-talk is the cornerstone of decreasing and eliminating anticipatory anxiety. *The key to anticipatory anxiety is powerful fear in the absence of any danger.* This is the struggle to protect yourself from "fear" not an issue confronting you at the moment. So, it could happen which is a "what if." The only trouble is we can live a lot of stress and anxiety associated with "what if's," but the truth is we can only deal with the "what is." Therefore, quit being tricked into fearing that you're about to die, go crazy, or lose control of yourself. The fear may seem overwhelming. However, in all likelihood the feared situation is the panic attack itself, and fear is what drives it. *Anxiety thrives on anticipatory anxiety/fear.*

The ultimate intervention for overcoming panic attacks and the fear of fear (so that you don't develop phobias) is exposure therapy (ET). It has been identified as the most effective treatment for those who suffer anxiety disorders. ET helps you retrain or recondition your brain and nervous system. So, for those who are really motivated to resolve panic attacks demonstrate your motivation by using ET instead of trying to talk yourself out of panic attacks and phobias. This is how it works. If you have a fear of being in an elevator, exposure would be getting in an elevator and staying there until the anxiety goes away. It could take 20 min or more, but if you just choose to be there in the moment the anxiety will go away. The trigger or the situation (in this case being in an elevator) will have less power. Keep doing it and the intensity will be less and last for a shorter period of time. The anxiety may go away completely and no longer be frightening, unless you keep reminding yourself that it is scary instead of focusing on just doing it. If you don't notice any panic attack triggers (because it is the fear of the fear), deliberately induce a panic attack. This can be done by imagining all the symptoms and the associated sensations and encourage them (shallow slow breathing, rapid heart rate, muscle tension) and try to keep the anxiety as high as you possibly can. The anxiety will decrease eventually no matter how hard you try to maintain it.

EXPOSURE THERAPY

ET is a series of steps for challenging and overcoming panic attacks. Use the acronym AWARE to remind yourself of the five ET steps for overcoming anxiety. It also helps to keep a journal of your panic attacks and to take the opportunity to learn relaxation exercises and how to challenge negative self-talk. This is where recovery takes place:

Acknowledge and Accept is the most important step of overcoming anxiety.

1. I acknowledge that overcoming panic anxiety requires that I deal with "what is", by acknowledging my *current* reality. The anticipatory anxiety builds within me and I am afraid of having a panic attack. So, to overcome this fear and the panic attacks I need to acknowledge and accept that the thought of my fear of danger or having a health problem that my doctor has checked out and found nothing is just another symptom of panic anxiety. I need to quit being afraid of fear.

2. I accept that right now I am afraid. I don't need to fight the feeling of fear, or seek to be rescued by anybody else. I don't like it, I don't like the way it feel, but I don't like a migraine headache either. When I have a headache I don't fear that I am dying or going crazy. I deal with it. It is my reality in that moment. I know how it works and how to take care of myself. Having panic attacks isn't any different. Deal with it by using the skills that work and keep chipping away at it. I know that if I choose to worry about it that the fear grows and it gets worse. Therefore, I know something really important. That doesn't work. That means working with, not against, my panic and anxiety symptoms is how to defeat them.

3. Now I accept the fear I am currently experiencing is that I will have a panic attack. It is miserable but it is not dangerous—I am not going to die and I am not going crazy. I am ready to start dealing with panic attacks so that I can overcome them. *The more you resist, the more*

it persists. Panic attacks don't last forever so I just need to ride it out. "It is what it is." That means quit stressing and worrying about having a panic attack. If I don't I am going to keep the panic attacks happening. Instead I will continue to work on my acceptance that the worst that will happen is having a panic attack and it will pass. The better I get at acceptance, the closer I get to my goal of defeating panic attacks.

Wait and Watch (and if you are in the middle of a task—keep doing your task if possible while you watch and wait).

1. Okay. I have accepted that I have panic attacks, and panic attacks fill me with fear. Now I am learning to wait. I am preparing myself because I know when I feel fear and anxiety it robs me of the ability to think, concentrate, and remember how to manage. I will be ready and that will give me the time I need to just accept being in the moment so that I can take action. Wow! That is a demonstration that I am no longer making it worse by resisting. My acceptance allows me to think and deal with it instead of using all my energy to escape it! I am no longer helping panic attacks by being reactive, instead I am choosing how I want to respond. By taking the urge to escape away it is like using a fire extinguisher on flames. Stay in the situation. You don't need to run away to get relief. Let relief come to you.

*Panic attacks generally fade away once you lose the fear.

2. Now I can observe how my panic attacks work, and using a panic attack journal will help. Answer the following questions in your panic attack journal:
   A. Describe the panic attack. Start by describing your first panic attack and then your most recent panic attack
   B. How do your panic attacks occur?
   C. What symptoms are experienced?
   D. How long do panic attacks last?
   E. What helps panic attacks go away?
3. Each time you experience a panic attack write down the following information:
   A. Date and time (now).
   B. When did the panic attack happen? (date and time)
   C. Where were you when the panic attack started?
   D. The symptoms experienced.
   E. How long did it last?
   F. Triggers (anything that seemed to cause the panic attack).
   G. What were you doing when it started?
   H. What did you do during the panic attack?
   I. What were you doing when the panic attack ended?
   J. Did the panic attack begin gradually or suddenly? Did it end gradually or suddenly? How long did it take to go away?
   K. What did you think was happening? When did you realize that you were having a panic attack?
   L. Any additional information?
4. A panic attack journal can give you some important information that helps you master your management. The best time to write the journal is when you are having a panic attack. Write it or dictate it and transcribe later. Review your journal after 1–2 weeks to answer the following questions:
   A. How many panic attacks did you experience in a week?
   B. Longest panic attack.

C. Shortest panic attack.

D. What was the average length of time each panic attack lasted?

E. What were you usually doing when panic attacks started?

F. How did the panic attacks end?

G. Can you identify any patterns or triggers?

    1. Possible panic attack triggers (people, places, situations, thoughts).

    2. Times of day you experienced panic attacks (best or worst time of day).

    3. What decreased panic attacks?

    4. What did you find ends panic attacks?

    5. If you are in a relatively passive situation (sitting at a desk, passenger in a car, etc.), all you need to do is watch and wait. Don't fight it just be in the minute. "No fear, let it pass." If you are in the middle of a demand such as working, then do the best you can to watch and wait while you are doing what you need to do.

Actions (to make myself more comfortable and not resist).

1. So, you have gone through the two most important steps necessary for overcoming panic attacks. You know what you need to do, using *exposure* and *not resisting*, it is a relief knowing that your goal is not to end the panic attacks, but to make yourself more comfortable while having one (just like when someone has a migraine). Below is a basic list of effective coping strategies for making yourself more comfortable while going through a panic attack.

Repeat. Keep doing the same thing over and over again until you overcome panic attacks.

End. The job is done and it feels goods. Keep in mind. If you do not continue to maintain a good life balance with positive self-care as a core part of your lifestyle panic anxiety may pop up again as a reminder to resume those good basic behaviors.

If that happens to you choose to interpret it as an opportunity to live well and healthy.

EFFECTIVE COPING STRATEGIES FOR DEFEATING PANIC ATTACKS

1. *Don't resist* (don't fight panic attacks). Remember fighting panic attacks makes them stronger.

2. *Exercise.* Exercise is an important component of a self-care plan and balanced lifestyle.

3. *Humor.* Laughter should be a daily experience.

4. *Muscle relaxation.* Identify, and relax, the parts of your body that get most tense during a panic attack. This commonly involves first tensing, and then relaxing, the muscles of your jaw, neck, shoulders, arms, back and legs. Pay attention to be sure that you are not allowing yourself to stand rigid, muscles tensed, and holding your breath. All of that would be the feeling of a body stressed and tense by anxiety. That just makes you feel worse! There are a number of muscle relaxation techniques that can be supplied by your therapist (remind them the information is at the beginning of the skill building section)

5. *Belly breathing.* Regardless of what else you do, do belly breathing—also referred to as diaphragmatic breathing, but think "belly breathing" because it gives you a picture in your mind of what you are doing. Good belly breathing technique is a powerful strategy in the toolbox for defeating panic attacks!

6. *How to talk to yourself.* Everyone talks to themselves (silently in their head) about what is happening, and what they need to do. The quality of your self-talk will influence the quality or experience of your life. There is a big difference between being in danger versus being in discomfort. Panic attacks are uncomfortable, like other things that are uncomfortable. Take

responsibility for identifying negative self-talk and substituting it with realistic self-talk that will actually help you.

7. *Get involved in the present*. The more you live in the moment instead of worrying and anticipating the worst, the less you will experience panic symptoms. Another way to think about that is, people don't panic in the present. They panic when they dwell on their fear of the past and their anticipatory anxiety for the future. That is why recovery from panic attacks requires you to deal with "what is" not "what if." When you choose to be in the moment whatever you fear is not happening.

8. *Repeat*. It is important to remember that anxiety can sometimes creep back in and when it does go back and repeat everything associated with being aware of practicing your management skills. If that happens to you, choose to think of it as an opportunity to strengthen your management skills. Repeat the management skills as much as you need to, making yourself comfortable and being back in the moment instead of the past or the future.

9. *End*. Back on track again!

MAKING MY OWN TOOLBOX FOR DEFEATING PANIC ATTACKS

Below is a sample outline for taking the information read in this section and putting it together in a way that is most helpful to you because it is personalized. Use the sample in the spirit in which it is offered and create your *toolbox*.

1. Identify feared situations
2. List the things I can do to increase my comfort when I am experiencing a panic attack
3. Identify coping strategies I will practice regularly even when I am not experiencing panic attacks
4. Commit to my schedule or routines for practicing these coping strategies.

*I understand that this outline is provided to give me ideas so that I can create my own personal toolbox. Some of these ideas may not work for me and I may already have other skills for effectively coping— recommendations not on this list that I want to try. That is how a person makes a "personal" toolbox.

POSTTRAUMATIC STRESS DISORDER

WHAT IS POSTTRAUMATIC STRESS DISORDER?

When a person is given specific information that is traumatic and overwhelming, witnesses the trauma of another, or has an experience of a traumatic event, the person may experience anxiety, fear, distress, or relive the traumatic event for months and sometimes years after. Often the experience may have been life threatening or physically harming to themselves or others.

Actually, the percentage of people who are exposed to a trauma and develop PTSD is not a large number. Regardless, PTSD affects twice as many women as men. Half of all adults will experience a significant trauma, and some of them will develop posttrauma stress symptoms or PTSD. Immediately following a traumatic experience, a person may develop acute stress, which if treated may prevent the onset of the more enduring PTSD. Additionally, some individuals do not have an apparent acute stress reaction, but at a later date the trauma is triggered by some event or significant level of emotional distress and the person then experiences a delayed onset of PTSD. Keep in mind that the experience of posttrauma symptoms may be part of the body dealing with "processing" what it has been through. This is the case and the person goes through the experience, not dwelling on it (using natural distractions of regular daily demands, etc.) the symptoms will fade and the person will begin to acknowledge that the experience has faded. However, if the person begins to dwell on it, presses themselves to various forms of reexposure resulting in their disengagement from their current relationships and activities they are more likely to develop PTSD. Additionally, their intense focus on their symptom experience may complicate the extinction of the symptoms and recovery.

The following are the individuals most at risk for PTSD:

1. Victims of sexual assault
2. Victims of child sexual abuse
3. Victims of child neglect, emotional abuse, and physical abuse
4. Victims of spousal abuse
5. Victims of random acts of violence
6. Survivors or witnesses of
   A. Car accidents
   B. Plane crashes
   C. Fires
   D. Natural disasters
7. Veterans and victims of war
8. First responders
9. Family or friends of someone who has died suddenly
10. Individuals who experience a life-changing medical condition

*Genetics and brain structure are being recognized as predisposing factors. Research is taking place that developing some understanding about some differences in brain structures may play a role in vulnerability to the risk of developing PTSD and getting stuck.

Educate yourself about the difference between PTSD and a normal response to experiencing trauma. People are often confused about the normal reactions and do not know that it is common to experience bad dreams, feel fearful, and find it difficult to stop thinking about what happened. If these symptoms do not calm down and fade as part of "snapping back" to normal daily functioning it may be acute stress disorder or PTSD. Everyone has their own unique story and experience associated with trauma. Trauma is regulated by the nervous system in three ways:

1. Social engagement is a great strategy for self-calming and feeling safe. Engagement means actually interacting with another person and making eye contact, listening in an attentive way, and talking about here and now issues. It is a great way to calm down and avoid defensive responses like "fight or flight."
2. Mobilization, also known as the "fight-or-flight" response, can happen when a person is in a situation that isn't safe which means that it would not be appropriate to socially engage (like a natural disaster). You can feel your body going into survival mode—your heart pounds faster, muscles tighten, blood pressure rises, breath quickens, and your senses become sharper. These physical changes increase your strength and stamina and speed your reaction time. Once the danger has passed, your nervous system then calms the body, slowing heart rate, lowering blood pressure, and winding back down to its normal balance.
3. Immobilization describes what happens when the amount of stress experienced is overwhelming, and even when the danger passes you are "stuck" and your nervous system cannot reset, there is no snap back, you are out of balance and unable to move on from the traumatic experience. This is what described as PTSD.

Three major categories of symptoms are present when a person is diagnosed with a PTSD:

PTSD Symptom Cycle

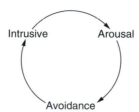

1. Reexperiencing the traumatic experience—intrusions
   A. Nightmares (of the event or other fear-provoking things)
   B. Intrusive thoughts or upsetting memories of the traumatic experience
   C. Flashbacks (reliving: acting or feeling like the traumatic experience is happening again)
   D. Intense and overwhelming physical reactions as reminders of the traumatic experience (pounding heart/palpitations, rapid breathing, muscle tension, sweating, nausea, etc.)
   E. Feelings of intense distress when reminded of the trauma

*These symptoms can result in physical reactions such as feelings of panic.

2. Avoidance behavior, loss of joy, and emotional numbing
   A. As thoughts of the trauma are pushed out of conscious awareness to some corner in one's mind the person may avoid anything that could trigger thoughts of the trauma. As a result, these individuals quit participating as they normally would and no longer find joy in previously enjoyed activities.
   B. Avoiding activities, places, thoughts, or feelings that remind you of the trauma
   C. Inability to remember important aspects of the trauma
   D. Loss of interest in activities and life in general
   E. Feeling detached from others and emotionally numb
   F. Sense of life limitations (you don't expect to live a normal life span, get married, have a career, etc.)
3. Increased anxiety and emotional arousal
   A. Feeling on-edge, jumpy, and easily startled
   B. Irritability or angry outbursts
   C. On high alert "hypervigilance"
   D. Difficulty concentrating
   E. Difficulty falling or staying asleep

There are also other common symptoms associated with PTSD:

1. Depression, hopelessness, helplessness
2. Substance abuse
3. Feelings of distrust/betrayal
4. Guilt (including survivor-guilt), shame, self-blame
5. Physical symptoms (aches and pains)
6. Suicidal thoughts and feelings

*People who have history of childhood abuses may find themselves unable to take action in some situations or with certain people. This is because of unconscious interpreted similarity of abuse factors that were present when they experienced abuse as a child. If this happens to you talk to your therapist about it. You can't heal and recover in the moment if you are not in the moment.

Treatment includes therapy and the consideration of medication. Other sources of information include the PTSD Alliance at 877-507-PTSD and the Moving Past Trauma hotline at 800-455-8300.

*It is possible to heal from PTSD.

TREATING POSTTRAUMATIC STRESS DISORDER

Treatment for PTSD is primarily therapy and often includes medication. Together, these two treatments can improve symptoms by teaching new strategies for coping and preparing you to deal effectively with symptoms when they arise. There are several techniques of therapy that have been particularly useful for treating trauma.

1. Cognitive therapy. This type of talk therapy helps you recognize the ways of thinking (cognitive patterns) that are keeping you stuck—for example, negative or inaccurate ways of perceiving normal situations. For PTSD, cognitive therapy often is used along with ET.
2. Exposure therapy. This behavioral therapy helps you safely face what you find frightening so that you can learn to cope with it effectively. One approach to ET uses "virtual reality" programs that allow you to reenter the setting in which you experienced trauma.
3. Eye movement desensitization and reprocessing (EMDR). EMDR combines ET with a series of guided eye movements that help you process traumatic memories and change how you react to traumatic memories.

All these approaches can help you gain control of lasting fear after a traumatic event. You and your health-care professional can discuss what type of therapy or combination of therapies may best meet your needs.

You are a key member of your own treatment team playing an important role in your own recovery from PTSD by the following:

1. *Learning about PTSD.* This knowledge can help you understand what you're feeling, and then you can develop coping strategies to help you respond effectively.
2. *Following your treatment plan.* Although it may take a while to feel benefits from therapy and/or medications, treatment can be effective, and most people do recover. Remind yourself that it takes time. Following your treatment plan will help move you forward in the healing process.
3. *Taking care of yourself.* Get enough rest, eat a healthy diet, exercise, and take time to relax. Avoid caffeine and nicotine, which can worsen anxiety.
4. *Don't self-medicate.* Turning to alcohol or drugs to numb your feelings isn't healthy, even though it may be a tempting way to cope. It can lead to more problems down the road and prevent real healing.
5. *Breaking the cycle.* When you feel anxious, take a brisk walk or jump into a hobby to refocus.

6. *Talking to someone.* Stay connected with supportive and caring people—family, friends, faith leaders, or others. You don't have to talk about what happened if you don't want to. Just sharing time with loved ones can offer healing and comfort.

7. *Considering a support group.* Ask your health professional for help finding a support group, or contact veterans' organizations or your community's social services system. Or look for local support groups in an online directory or in your phone book.

DEFEATING POSTTRAUMATIC STRESS DISORDER

1. The first stage is about "stabilization"—feeling "safe." This stage can include learning about PTSD and learning grounding techniques to cope with the symptoms. This is something that you can begin to do on your own.

2. The second stage is about making sense of what happened to you. This can involve talking about what happened and understanding how the events affected you. Evidence-based treatments at this stage include trauma-focused CBT and EMDR.

3. The third stage is about reclaiming your life. PTSD can be draining and result in living a shadow of your former life. Once the major symptoms of PTSD are resolved you need to claim back the life that you wanted to lead. An aspect of this stage is finding meaning in the trauma. *We don't waste anything that happens to us—especially the worst things. If we miss lessons that strengthen us we will undoubtedly have other opportunities to be tested.* Life is hard, that is just the way it is. However, maybe you will find meaning by helping other people who have less ability and resources than you do.

STABILIZATION AND GROUNDING TECHNIQUES

One of the common symptoms of PTSD is having memories of the trauma, feeling like the trauma is happening again, or becoming upset when you are reminded of the trauma. This can feel very overwhelming and exhausting. First, it is helpful to learn about PTSD so that you don't feel like you're going mad—there are actually very good reasons for the symptoms people with PTSD experience, and it is not your fault! Second it is helpful to begin practicing techniques to manage the memories, symptoms, and the distressing feelings that come along with them.

Grounding

Grounding is an important management tool to be used when you start to get distracted by intrusive thoughts or images/flashbacks. This is not the same as relaxation training. This is one of the most basic or simplest tools for helping you to be aware in the moment and that allows you to detach from difficult emotions.

1. *Open your eyes.* It is necessary to keep your eyes open so that you are able to look around where you are and focus on the details of your environment. Grounding is done by speaking out loud and describing what you see, hear, smell, touch, and are doing.

2. *Practice.* To be able to use a skill effectively requires that it be practiced. Therefore, don't wait to be in a flashback or other intrusion, practice this technique when you are calm and relaxed. That way when you need it you will already know how to use grounding.

3. *Support.* Teach those close to you, and trusted, about this technique and how it works. That will enable them to supportively remind you to use it, and do it with you, if you start to lose focus on the presence. You will need to decide what it is you would want them to say to you when they see you lose touch, such as "can you describe where you are and what you see?"

Some examples of grounding include the following:

1. Run water over your hands and describe how it feels
2. Touch any of the objects that surround you, i.e., a piece of furniture, drapes, carpet
3. Take note of the colors or sounds you hear in the moment
4. Naming lists of holidays, animals, colors, etc.

Be creative in finding ways to achieve grounding. Working with your therapist on this would be helpful. Grounding is a skill that you can use to help you find balance between the distress you are experiencing and numbing out. That is improved coping.

Grounding Exercise

Name three things:
You see
You smell
You hear
You feel
Breathe in and out slowly three times.

*It is not uncommon for people experiencing PTSD to abuse substances in an effort to numb distressing emotions. If you are numbing your symptoms with substances talk to your therapist/primary care physician about it.

IDENTIFYING TRIGGERS

Pay attention to what triggers feelings of fear, anger, distress, or threat. Some things you already know and some will be obvious. However, some things will be more subtle and not as easy to identify. Also, triggers can affect everyone of your senses, i.e., taste, touch, smell, vision, and hearing.

Triggers:

a. _____

b. _____

c. _____

d. _____

e. _____

f. _____

h. _____

i. _____

j. _____

k. _____

l. _____

m. _____

AVOIDANCE AND SAFETY BEHAVIORS

You have now identified triggers and are getting pretty good at observing how you feel, think, and react. Now pay attention to people, places, situations, activities, and things that you intentionally avoid. Also, pay attention to safety behaviors you use to try to protect yourself/control emotional distress.

What I Avoid (e.g., talking on the phone):

a. _____

b. _____

c. _____

d. _____

e. _____

f. _____

g. _____

h. _____

i. _____

j. _____

Safety Behaviors I Use (e.g., not going to new places alone):

a. _____

b. _____

c. _____

d. _____

e. _____

f. _____

g. _____

h. _____

i. _____

j. _____

LEARNING TO BREATH (EQUAL EFFORT BREATHING IN AND OUT)

Slowly

1. Slow breathing is a simple way to decrease stress and tension
2. This is about asserting your control to breath slowly—not deep breathing
3. Try the following steps:
    A. Take a normal breath slowly through your nose—keeping your mouth closed
    B. Exhale through slowly through your mouth

C. While exhaling say silently words such as "relax," "calm," "safe"

D. Count to four between each inhaling breath

E. Repeat on 10 min

Autogenic

1. Inhale through the nose deep into the diaphragm—count of four

2. Hold for count of four

3. Exhale through your mouth—count of four

4. Practice 3 min—3x's per day

LEARNING WHAT WORKS AND WHAT DOESN'T—REFINING INFORMATION TO USE IN YOUR PERSONAL POSTTRAUMATIC STRESS DISORDER TOOLBOX

1. It may make you feel better for the moment to avoid, escape, or use ineffective safety behaviors. But in the long run they could sustain or make your PTSD worse by preventing your brain's alarm system from learning what is really dangerous and what isn't.

2. Over time the use of the ineffective behavioral management techniques can actually increase feelings of fear, distress, and irritability.

3. Use repeated exposure to situations you fear and avoid while at the same time resisting ineffective safety behaviors (avoidance and escape). This allows healing and recovery from PTSD. This is because it allows your brain to reset its alarm system.

4. Exposure exercises must be used repeatedly for it to work. The alarm system is stubborn when it learns something, so it takes a lot of practice to reset that system.

MAKING MY OWN POSTTRAUMATIC STRESS DISORDER TOOLBOX

For those who feel like they will never get over what happened to them or feel normal again as a result of their battle with PTSD creating your personalized toolbox is a key to recovery. Use all of your resources; developing a positive working relationship with your therapist, consider a medication evaluation, develop and utilize beneficial/safe social supports, develop effective coping skills, do not self-medicate, and engage in daily positive self-care and balance.

1. Self-care
    A. Make relaxation a normal part of your daily schedule.
        1. Progressive muscle relaxation
        2. Deep breathing or controlled slow breathing
        3. Yoga
        4. Massage
        5. Meditation/mindfulness
    B. Don't self-medicate with substances. That will stand in the way of recovery and complicate your life in other ways.
    C. Eat balanced nutritious foods.
    D. Good sleep is essential for every facet of recovery for your mind and body.
    E. Engage in positive daily structure.
    F. Remain productive and creative. Living with purpose is essential to emotional and psychological health.

2. *Exercise clears your mind and can make you feel better physically and emotionally.* Be in the moment by focusing on the physical sensations. Choose exercise that uses your large muscles (arms and legs) and whenever possible do this by spending time in nature. Pushing yourself has the benefit of challenging a sense of helplessness and "resetting" your nervous system (getting unstuck). An added benefit could be found in seeking out local organizations that offer outdoor recreation or team building opportunities. When you can couple healing factors (i.e., exercise and social engagement), it creates a positive loading factor and positively impacts healing and recovery.

3. *Social engagement.* Developing and utilizing effective and positive social support is essential to PTSD recovery. Connecting is the opposite from the PTSD experience of feeling disconnected and withdrawn. While your nervous system is still stuck, it makes difficult to connect—even with those you feel really close to. Another way to think about it is that if you have a difficult time connecting with yourself how can you connect with others. You have to be in the moment to be emotionally available. If you are not emotionally available you are not connecting emotionally.

4. *Explore your resources for professional help (therapy, medication, systematic desensitization, conjoint/family therapy, EMDR).* A famous man (Winston Churchill) once said, "when you are going through hell – keep going." In other words, you cannot avoid or escape dealing with trauma if you are going to survive it—you have to go through it, which leads to a mindset of healing and recovery. A therapist will help you to:
   A. Process what you experienced and the emotions you had during the traumatic event and following
   B. Explore your thoughts and feelings (including interpretations) about the traumatic event
   C. Challenge any bias you have about PTSD (only weak people develop PTSD)
   D. Work through feelings of guilt, shame, self-blame, mistrust, and/or betrayal (e.g., survivor guilt)
   E. Learn necessary skills to effectively cope with difficult PTSD symptoms
   F. Identify and problem-solve how PTSD has negatively affected your life and personal relationships

5. *Strengthen resilience.* You probably have a lot of skills you used before the traumatic event that were effective for getting through difficult experiences. Feeling powerless and vulnerable can be challenged by using some of those old skills
   A. Gather with others struggling with similar issues. Joining a support group will allow you to clarify what things you are doing better with than you may think, decrease feelings of aloneness, and develop the additional skills you need to regain your feelings of personal power, get new information that is helpful, and to challenge perceived vulnerability by developing and/or using sound problem-solving skills.
   B. Allow yourself to feel strengthened by surviving the trauma and learning things that can only be learned by exposure to trauma. All self-knowledge is empowering. Even identifying a vulnerability or relative weakness is empowering because your awareness allows you to prepare for what you need to do using your strengths to avoid harm or learning new skills. This demonstrates the importance of interpretation. *What you survive makes you stronger.*
   C. Volunteer. It feels good and empowering to give to, and help, those who are less fortunate. It dilutes an over focus on the self.

6. *Coping with a breakup, divorce, or loss of friendship.* PTSD can be a selfish intruder in many relationships. Often it is due to withdrawal, lack of emotional availability or presence of additional stress that adds to an already troubled relationship. The loss of a relationship can leave you with a lot of negative emotions to understand, work through, and use as another opportunity to learn.
   A. You cannot control another person and the choices they make. *You only have control over how you choose to interpret what happens to you and how you choose to deal with it.* Therefore, don't waste time thinking about all of the things wrong with the other person.
   B. Find your self-esteem. A healthy relationship is one where both parties share a commitment and positive emotions. An additional factor is boundaries, i.e., you teach people how to treat you.
   C. The "golden rule"—you treat people the way you want to be treated.

7. Anger management is effective when self-responsibility is employed using the following strategies:
   A. Identifying triggers
   B. Identifying giving self-permission to behave badly
   C. Developing anger control plans
   D. Changing negative self-talk that promotes the anger cycle
   E. Learning conflict resolution

8. *Setting goals and self-monitoring.* Self-monitoring is self-explanatory. It is accomplished by keeping a journal of identified goals and the selected objectives (methods) for meeting those goals.

*I understand that this outline is provided to give me ideas so that I can create my own personal toolbox. Some of these ideas may not work for me and I may already have other skills for effectively coping or recommendations not on this list that I want to try.

*That is how a person makes a "personal" toolbox.

SUBSTANCE ABUSE, RELAPSE, AND CODEPENDENCY

SUBSTANCE ABUSE

People abuse substances such as drugs and alcohol for varied and complicated reasons. Substance abuse may begin in childhood or the teen years. Early recognition of drug or alcohol addiction increases chances for successful treatment. The longer addiction is a central part of life, the more damaging it is and the more difficult it is to treat because of the damage to your body, relationships, and life.

Addiction Cycle

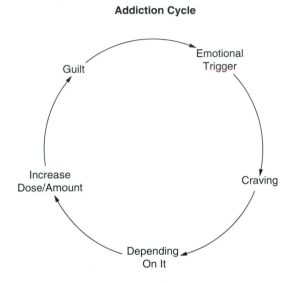

Substance Use Disorders Personal Evaluation

1. Age of first drug use?
2. What drug(s) did you use?
3. Who introduced you to drugs?
4. What drug(s) did you go on to use after that?
5. What was your reason for using drugs?
6. Did you ever try to stop?
7. If so, what is it like when you aren't using?
8. Do your friends use?
9. Are you easily influenced by others?
10. Family history of substance abuse?
11. Do you and your significant other use together?
12. How has drug abuse affected your life?
13. What do you see as your options?
14. What do you have to do to abstain from drug abuse?
15. Have you been to a treatment program before or attended 12-step meetings?
16. What do you feel like when you are using?
17. How do you think you benefit from using/or what do you get out of it?
18. Do you have or think you may have depression, anxiety, or PTSD?
19. How has choosing a substance(s) over relationships impacted your life?
20. How do you view drug screening in the workplace/school?

LIST OF SYMPTOMS LEADING TO RELAPSE

If you identified that you had a substance use disorder and entered treatment, then you have learned about "working a program." Working a program includes such factors as abstinence, refusal skills, relapse prevention, and attending self-help meetings such as AA/NA where your recovery is supported by the positive affiliation of other working on their recovery and having a sponsor or accountability partner that serves as a social support and mentor. Relapse prevention is very important to staying on track in your recovery. There are numerous signs and symptoms associated with the risk of relapse. The following are a list of possible risk factors.

1. *Exhaustion*. Allowing yourself to become overly tired. Not following through on self-care behaviors of adequate rest, good nutrition, and regular exercise. Good physical health is a component of emotional health. How you feel will be reflected in your thinking and judgment.

2. *Dishonesty*. It begins with a pattern of small, unnecessary lies with those you interact with in your family, social network, and at work. A pattern of dishonesty leads to lying to yourself or rationalizing and making excuses for avoiding working your program.

3. *Impatience*. Things are not happening fast enough for you. Or, others are not doing what you want them to do or think they should do.

4. *Argumentative*. Arguing small insignificant points indicates a need to always be right. This is sometimes seen as developing an excuse to drink.

5. *Depression*. Overwhelming feelings of loss, out of place/not fitting in, or despair may occur in cycles. If it does, talk about it and deal with it. You are responsible for taking care of yourself. Others cannot be mind readers—not matter how much they care about you.

6. *Frustration*. Finding yourself upset with people or situations because things may not being going your way. Remind yourself intermittently that things are not always going to be the way that you want them—or feel you need them to be.

7. *Self-pity*. Allowing yourself to feel like a victim, refusing to acknowledge that you have choices and are responsible for your own life and the quality of it.

8. *Cockiness*. "Got it made." Compulsive behavior is no longer a problem. Start putting yourself in situations where there are temptations to prove to others that you don't have a problem.

9. *Complacency*. Not working your program with the commitment that you started with. Having a little fear is a good thing. More relapses occur when things are going well than when not.

10. *Expecting too much from others*. "I've changed, why hasn't everyone else changed too?" All that you control is yourself. It would be great if other people changed their self-destructive behaviors, but that is their problem. You have your own problems to monitor and deal with. You cannot expect others to change their lifestyle just because you have.

11. *Letting up on discipline*, i.e., not working your recovery program (daily inventory, positive affirmations, 12-step meetings, sponsor, accountability partner, therapy, meditation, use of serenity prayer, etc.). This can come from complacency and boredom. Because you cannot afford to be bored with your program, take responsibility to talk about it and problem-solve it. The cost of relapse is too great, unless you need to relapse to appreciate a life of recovery. However, ultimately if you are going to recover, you must accept that you have to do something that are the routine for a clean and sober life and learn to deal with boredom as part of not using and being altered.

12. *The use of mood-altering chemicals*. You may feel the need or desire to get away from things by drinking, popping a few pills, etc., and your physician may participate in thinking that you will be responsible and not abuse medication(s) with addictive properties. This is about the most subtle and seductive way to enter relapse. Take responsibility for your life and the choices that you make. This will be additionally challenging if you like the feeling of being altered.

WORKING A PROGRAM AND MAKING MY RECOVERY TOOLBOX

Without the development of appropriate recovery social supports and the development of effective coping mechanisms the personal growth associated with the recovery process will be stunted. The person is abstinent but doesn't work a program that promotes personal growth and responsibility is referred to as a *dry drunk*. Coping skills are necessary to both manage and avoid the factors that increase the risk of relapse.

1. Professional support
   A. Individual, conjoint, family, and/or group therapy
   B. Medication evaluation
      1. Interventions for acute intoxication
      2. Medications used for stabilization
      3. Comorbid mental health issues (depression, bipolar disorder, anxiety, PTSD, etc.)
   C. Risk of self-injurious behaviors, aggressive behaviors (including homicide), or suicide requires effective interventions to be developed with a therapist, psychiatrist, primary care physician, and others who may play a critical role in safety
   D. Learning to effective cope with feeling emotionally overwhelmed (emotions were numbed and avoided by substance use)

2. Recovery supports are important to support you in your recovery goals
   A. Refusal skills
   B. Peer-to-peer services, mentoring, accountability partner, coaching
      1. Peer supports are essential to your recovery efforts and one that everyone is familiar with is the 12-step program(s). Celebrate recovery is another recovery program that offers numerous meetings in most communities. In general, active participation in self-help groups has been associated with better outcomes and is equally effective for males and females.
   C. Spiritual and faith-based support
   D. Parenting education
   E. Self-help and support groups
   F. Outreach and engagement
   G. Staffing drop in centers, clubhouses, respite/crisis services, or warm lines (peer-run listening lines staffed by people in recovery themselves)
   H. Education about strategies to promote wellness and recovery

3. Identifying triggers can be cue/trigger, stress, or substance induced and it is an education about relapse risk situations, thoughts, or emotions that increase vulnerability to relapse. The goal is to identify triggers for relapse and learn to manage unavoidable triggers without relapsing. Participation in AA or similar self-help group meetings that support sobriety and recovery can help you avoid relapse—if you use the resources. That is why at AA meetings they end with "keep coming back–it works"

4. Self-monitor emotion, thinking states, and behavioral patterns associated with craving and substance use.
   A. Identify patterns of thinking and behaving that play a role in substance using behavior
   B. Identify and modify/change dysfunction thought patterns

5. Developing behavioral self-control
   A. Set goals for substance reduction or cessation
      1. Develop refusal skills
   B. Monitor progress toward goals
   C. Build in rewards for progress
   D. Learn and use new coping skills that facilitate substance reduction (harm reduction) or abstinence
   E. Learn to break down behaviors associated with substance use to better understand all points of intervention

6. Developing alternative rewards or symptom relief to fill the place of substance use needed for effective management of depression, anger, sadness, anxiety, fear, feeling overwhelmed, and out of control, etc.

A. Recovery reinforcing activities

B. Create a list of pleasurable activities

C. Create a list of leisure activities

7. Social skills training

    A. Effective and meaningful communication and listening

    B. Empathy—being able to imagine what it is like in someone else's shoes

    C. Self-monitoring and modify what and how you say what you think and feel and how you behave

    D. Being able to make healthy adaptive changes/growth in relationships

    E. Assertiveness

8. Relaxation techniques to decrease the strength of substance related social cues and the intensity of craving

9. Cue exposure and relaxation training combined with drug refusal training to diminish or eliminate "triggered" craving

10. Developing a social support system that is reinforcing of sobriety and recovery

11. Lifestyle changes that are encouraging and supportive and creating a recovery lifestyle

12. Relapse prevention is developing the skills needed to develop improved self-control to avoid relapse

*I understand that this outline is provided to give me ideas so that I can create my own personal toolbox. Some of these ideas may not work for me and I may already have other skills for effectively coping—considerations not on this list that I want to try. That is how a person makes a "personal" toolbox.

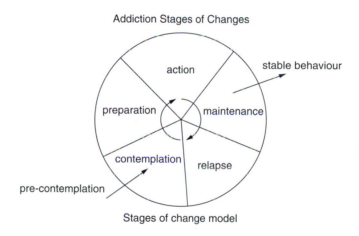

Addiction Stages of Changes

Stages of change model

ENABLING AND CODEPENDENCY

WHAT IS CODEPENDENCY?

Codependency is defined as when someone becomes so preoccupied with someone else that they neglect themselves. In a way it is the belief that something outside of themselves can give them happiness and fulfillment. The payoff in focusing on someone else is a decrease in painful feelings and anxiety.

Some people are in an emotional state of fear, anxiety, pain, or feeling like they are going crazy, and they feel these emotions strongly almost all the time. These people tend to think they can make those around them happy, and when they can't, they feel somehow less than others, they feel like they have failed. Codependency is ignoring the reality "that when you are the best you can be, then you are the best you can be for any relationship."

It is not uncommon for codependent individuals to tend to hold things in and then at inappropriate times they present as martyrs or overreact, or they just have a tendency to overreact (e.g., something frightening happens and instead of experiencing normal fear they panic or experience anxiety attacks) and are viewed more as the victims who are responsible for everything or others. However, another interpretation is one of manipulation and control. Codependents have their own recovery program to work. However, they often try to focus on the recovery of the substance using person-deflecting self-responsibility.

They live with the false belief that the bad feelings they have can be gotten rid of if they can just "do it better," if they can win the approval of certain important people in their life, or if they could successfully control what is wrong with significant people in their life. By doing this they make those people and their approval responsible for their own happiness. Often codependent people appear gentle and helpful. However, in this situation, two different things may be going on:

1. They may be struggling with a strong need to control and manipulate those around them into giving them the approval they believe they need to feel okay.
2. They minimize their emotions until they hardly experience any emotion at all. No fear, pain, anger, shame, joy, or pleasure. They just exist from one day to the next—numb.

*It was actually the families of alcoholics and other chemically dependent people who brought these two clusters of symptoms to the attention of professionals.

THE CLASSIC SITUATION

The codependents' efforts are apparently to get the alcoholic or chemically dependent person sober and free from drugs. If they could help the alcoholic, the family members would be free of pain, shame, fear, and anger. But it was found that doesn't really work because even when the alcoholic got sober the family stayed sick and sometimes even appeared to resent the sobriety. Sometimes they sabotaged it. It was as if the family needed the addict to stay sick and dependent on them so that they could maintain their dependence on the addict as a way of explaining their own experience and how they felt. In other words, the addict and the codependent are trying to solve similar basic symptoms of the same disease: the addict with alcohol or drugs and the codependent with the addictive relationship.

Codependency may be difficult to see from the outside because people who suffer from codependency generally appear adequate and successful—sometimes even victims in a difficult situation. However, they are (over) involved in a manner to win the all important approval they seek. Acknowledge the risk of being in a vicious cycle of addiction because it is common for the codependent to at some point turn to drugs to numb their discomfort. Codependents are set up to be alcoholics or other kinds of addicts themselves.

As you read these examples what do you identify with?

_____

_____

_____

_____

_____

_____

SOME CHARACTERISTICS OF CODEPENDENCE

1. My good feelings about who I am stem from being liked by you and receiving approval from you.
2. Your struggles affect my serenity. I focus my mental attention on solving your problems or relieving your pain.
3. I focus my mental attention on pleasing you, protecting you, or manipulating you to "do it my way."
4. I bolster my self-esteem by solving your problems and relieving your pain.

5. I put aside my own hobbies and interests, and instead spend my time involved in your interests and hobbies instead of developing my own.

6. Because I feel you are a reflection of me, my desires dictate your clothing and personal appearance.

7. My desires dictate your behavior.

8. I am not aware of how I feel. I am aware of how you feel.

9. I am not aware of what I want. I ask you what you want.

10. If I am not aware of something, I assume (I don't ask or verify in some other way).

11. My fear of your anger and rejection determines what I say or do.

12. In our relationship I use giving as a way of feeling safe.

13. As I involve myself with you, my social circle diminishes.

14. To connect with you, I put my values aside.

15. I value your opinion and way of doing things more than my own.

16. The quality of my life depends on the quality of yours.

17. I am always trying to fix or take care of others while neglecting myself.

18. I find it easier to give in and comply with others than to express my own wants and needs.

19. I sometimes feel sorry for myself, feeling no one understands. I think about getting help, but rarely commit or follow through.

20. A lot of my identity is associated with being a codependent.

THE RULES OF CODEPENDENCY

1. It's not okay to talk about problems.
2. Feelings are not expressed openly.
3. Communication is often not direct, having a person act as a messenger between two other people.
4. Unrealistic expectations: be strong, good, right, perfect. Make us proud.
5. Don't be selfish.
6. Do as I say, not as I do.
7. It's not okay to play.
8. Don't rock the boat.

*The rules of codependency create dysfunctional family system patterns. Examples of how this works is seen in the following section.

HOW DOES CODEPENDENCY WORK

Codependency creates a set of rules for communicating and interacting in relationships.

1. It's not okay to talk about problems.
   -"Don't air your dirty laundry in public."
   -We don't share our differences of opinion or argue (even though problems are denied, there is often a lot of tension).

*Belief; it is safer to avoid problems instead of confronting them.

2. Feelings are not expressed openly.
    -Take pride in being strong and not showing emotion.
    -"Big boys don't cry."

*Belief; it is better (safer) not to feel, eventually we get so cut off from the self that we are unsure what we feel.

3. Communication is often indirect, with one person acting as a messenger between two others.
    -Dad tells his son "I wish your mom was more understanding" (son talks to mom). Using someone else to communicate for you results in confusion, misdirected feelings, and an inability to directly confront personal problems.

*Belief; it is not safe to speak honestly and directly.

4. Unrealistic expectations: be strong, good, right, perfect, makes us proud.
    -Doing well and achieving is the most important thing.
    -Enough is never enough.
    -Results in creating an ideal in our head about what is good or right or best that is far removed from what is realistic and possible. This leads us to punish others because they don't meet our expectations. We may even blame ourselves for not pushing someone enough to meet our expectations.

*Belief; distorted reality of self-responsibility and self-actualization.

5. Don't be selfish.
    -Views self as wrong for placing their own needs before the needs of others.
    -Focus on feeling good by taking care of others.

*Belief; working on my own goals and sharing responsibility in relationship functioning means I don't care.

6. Do as I say … not as I do.
    This rule teaches us not to trust.

*Belief; a lack of understanding that the value of words are demonstrated by matching behaviors.

7. It's not okay to play.
    -Begin to believe that the world is a serious place where life is always difficult and painful.

*Belief: if you are happy and carefree something is wrong or you are not doing what you are supposed to do.

8. Don't rock the boat.
    -The system seeks to maintain itself. If you grow and change you'll be alone.

*Belief; the status quo must be maintained at all costs.

HOW CODEPENDENCY AFFECTS ONE'S LIFE

1. When I am having problems feeling good about myself and you have an opinion about me that I don't want you to have, I try to control what you feel about me so that I can feel good about myself.
2. I can't tell where my reality ends and someone else's reality begins. Leads to making assumptions, belief that you can read the thoughts of others, and as a result choosing your behavior based on your perception of what the other person's opinion of you is.
3. I have trouble getting my own needs and wants met because all of my energy goes into saving you from addiction.
4. Resenting others for the pain or losses they have caused you. This can lead to obsessively thinking about them and how to get back or punish them.
5. Avoid dealing with reality to avoid unpleasant feelings.
6. Difficulty in close or intimate relationships. Relationship implies sharing—one person giving and the other receiving (without trying to change each other). Also affects how we parent our own children and what we teach them in how to function in relationships.

THE ENABLER—THE COMPANION TO THE DYSFUNCTIONAL/SUBSTANCE-ABUSING PERSON

Substance abuse and substance dependency can have devastating consequences for the individual using the substances as well as for those closely associated with them. Of most concern is the individual who may reside with the substance-abusing individual or who spends a significant amount of time with them. Typically, they begin to react to the symptoms of the individual, which results in the "concerned person" unsuspectingly conspiring with the dysfunctional behavior/illness and actually enabling it to progress and get worse. This "enabling" behavior surrounds and feeds the dependency.

How does the dysfunctional behaviors/illness affect the dependent individual? For the substance-dependent individual they completely lose their ability to predict accurately when they will start and stop their substance use. Because of this they become engaged repeatedly and unexpectedly in such behaviors as follows:

1. Breaking commitments that they intended to keep.
2. Spending more money than they planned.
3. Driving under the influence violations.
4. Making inappropriate statements to friends, family, and coworkers.
5. Engaging in arguing, fighting, and other antisocial behaviors.
6. Using more of the substance(s) than they had planned.

These types of behaviors violate their internal value system resulting in feelings of guilt, remorse, and self-loathing. However, these feelings are blocked by rationalizations and projections. The rationalization is that "last night wasn't that bad." The projection causes the individual to believe that "anyone would be doing what I am doing if they had to put up with what I do." The result of such use of defenses is to progressively lead the individual to be out of touch with reality. This distortion becomes so solid that the individual using substances or engaging in other dysfunctional behaviors is the last to recognize that their behavior represents any type of personal problem.

What is an enabler? It is the person who reacts to the above symptom of illness/dysfunctional behavior in such a way as to shield and protect them from experiencing the consequences of their problem. Thus, the substance-abusing person loses the opportunity to gain insight regarding the severity of their behavior. Without this insight they remain a victim of the defenses and are incapable of recognizing the need to seek appropriate and necessary help. Tragically, the enabler's well-intentioned behavior plays an increasingly destructive role in the progression of the illness/dysfunctional behaviors.

The enabler continues their behavior because they see all that they have done as a sincere effort to help. While they see the negative behavior as isolated attempts to cope with difficult situations or something that just got a little out of hand, their behavior serves to reinforce the issues of rationalization, denial, and projections related to the substance abuse/dysfunctional behaviors.

The enabler may be in denial themselves about the significance or severity of the problem. Their thinking may be that the problem does not really exist or that it will disappear as soon as the real problem disappears. This makes the enabler highly vulnerable to developing beliefs and attitudes that victimize the individual engaging in substance-abusing/dysfunctional behaviors. The rationalizations of both persons are now supporting each other's misunderstanding of the true nature of the problem. The result is that they are both engaged in a successful self-deception that allows the disease to remain hidden and to progress to a more serious stage.

The substance abuse/dysfunctional behaviors continue to have an increasingly adverse effect on both individuals. To understand the progression of the type of thinking that the individual engaged in substance abuse/dysfunctional behavior, it is important to understand what a successful defense system projection serves:

1. They take the unconscious and growing negative feelings about the self and put them onto other people and situations. This relieves some of stress that they feel inside and allows them to continue to live in an increasingly painful situation. The individual does not have any insight, and as a result they continue to experience more pain that leads to further projections or putting it off on other. What a vicious cycle.

2. As the individual with the substance abuse/dysfunctional behavior problem continues to verbalize their projections on the other person, there is no realization from either party that this is being said out of hatred. Both believe that the individual hates the enabler and for good reason (because of the view that they are the source of the problem). The consequence is that they now both focus on the enabler's behavior and this allows the problem behavior to continue to go unseen as the central issue.

It is easy to see how this defense can have a significant emotional affect on the enabler. This becomes a pivotal point in the process of enabling. As the pain from the projections becomes more painful and uncomfortable, the enabler reacts by feeling hurt, injured, and guilty. The result is avoidance behavior. Less and less is expected of the individual with the substance abuse/dysfunctional behaviors because of the distress that it causes. These avoidant reactions only allow the progression of the problem. The individual with substance abuse/dysfunctional behaviors remains out of touch with reality and does not receive honest feedback about the behaviors causing the difficulties at home, work, school, etc. What develops is a "no talk" rule. By the enabler not directly expressing the issues, the individual with substance abuse/dysfunctional behaviors becomes more removed from any insight into their behaviors and its harmful consequences.

The enabler is not always able to avoid the individual with substance abuse/dysfunctional behaviors. Where relationships are very close, then the increasing projections create in the enabler a growing feeling of guilt and blame. They begin to feel responsible for the individual's self-defeating and self-destructive behavior. These feelings of self-doubt, inadequacy, and guilt continue to increase with the progression of the severity of the problem.

Unfortunately, the tendency is for the enabler's controlling behavior to escalate. The only way for them to feel positive is to "try to make sure that the behavior does not get out of control." "If there are things that I did to cause this, then I can make it go away." Most of their efforts are manipulative. They do things indirectly in an effort to get the behavior they want. These manipulations are destined to fail. Nothing is being confronted and dealt with. As the enabler's feelings of low self-worth increase, it triggers even more desperate attempts of control. The cycle continues and escalates as both parties become increasingly alienated and dysfunctional.

The way to break the cycle is through knowledge and understanding:

1. Learn about the dynamic of chemical dependency and other dysfunctional behaviors.
2. Learn about the characteristics and factors associated with being an enabler and the importance of self-care.
3. Become aware of the personal identification with the compulsive behavior of enabling.

With the development of this knowledge and insight the enabler can begin to respond to an individual with substance abuse/dysfunctional behavior in a meaningful and honest way versus control and manipulation (working their own recovery program). This will help the enabler let go of the responsibility for the behavior of others. The result is that the enabler becomes a person who lives life consciously and takes responsibility for themselves, thus becoming an agent of change who no longer reinforces dysfunctional behaviors through control and manipulation. This allows them to intervene directly in functional ways, which promotes change not maintains the status quo.

CHARACTERISTICS OF ADULT CHILDREN OF ALCOHOLICS

Adult children of alcoholics appear to have characteristics in common as a result of being raised in an alcoholic home. Review the characteristics listed. If you identify with these characteristics then seek appropriate sources of support to understand and resolve them. You will find many books at the bookstore on this subject. Additionally, there is Adult Children of Alcoholics 12-step self-help community meeting, individual therapy, and group therapy facilitated by a therapist.

1. Isolation, fear of people, and fear of authority figures.
2. Difficulty with identity issues related to seeking constantly the approval of others.
3. Frightened by angry people and personal criticism. This leads to becoming the mind reader. A heightened observance of others and what they need to avoid their negative reactions.
4. Becoming an alcoholic/addict, married to a chemically dependent person, or both. A variation would be the attraction to another compulsive personality such as a workaholic. The similarity is that neither is emotionally available to deal with overwhelming and unhealthy dependency needs.
5. Perpetually being the victim and seeing the world from the perspective of a victim. This interferes with the normal development of self-responsibility, growing stronger when confronted by adversity (resilience).
6. An overdeveloped sense of responsibility. Concerned about the needs of others to the degree of neglecting your own wants and needs. This is a protective behavior for avoiding a good look at yourself and taking responsibility to identify and resolve your own personal difficulties.
7. Feelings of guilt associated with standing up for your rights. It is easier to give into the demands of others and avoid adversity versus learning conflict resolution and accepting differences without being left in a one-down position.
8. An addiction to excitement. Feeling a need to be on the edge, and risk-taking behaviors. Much of this is experienced vicariously (being close to someone who takes risk).

9. A tendency to confuse feelings of love and pity. Attracted to people that you can rescue and take care of.

10. Avoidance or denial of feelings related to traumatic childhood experiences. An inability to feel or express feelings because it is frightening and/or painful and overwhelming experience.

11. Low self-esteem. This is a tendency to judge yourself harshly be perfectionistic and self-critical.

12. Strong dependency needs and terrified of abandonment. Will do almost anything to hold onto a relationship to avoid the fear and pain of abandonment.

13. Alcoholism is a family disease that often results in a family member taking on the characteristics of the disease even if they are not alcoholics (para-alcoholics). Dysfunctional relationships, denial, fearful, avoidance of feelings, poor coping, poor problem solving, afraid that others will find out that you are not who or what they think you are, etc.

14. Tendency to overreact to things that happen versus taking control and not being victim to the behavior of others or situations created by others.

15. A chameleon. This is a tendency to be what others want you to be instead of being yourself. It is a lack of honesty with yourself and others.

SYMPTOMS/EFFECTS IN CHILDREN OF CODEPENDENTS

1. Difficulty with self-esteem/inability to accurately and appropriately esteem children.
2. Difficulty setting boundaries/inability to avoid transgressing children's boundaries.
3. Difficulty owning and expressing our own reality and imperfections/inability to allow children to have their own reality and be imperfect.
4. Difficulty taking care of adult needs and wants along with inability to appropriately nurture children and teach them to appropriately meet their needs and wants.
5. Difficulty experiencing and expressing their reality along with an inability to provide a stable environment for children in a way that promotes personal growth and healthy boundaries.

CHALLENGING CODEPENDENCY

Codependency is a pattern of life that is particularly focused on key relationships and control. Therefore, it is necessary to objectively examine your life to see if you have codependent behaviors and are ready to let go of controlling those relationships and to focus on your own emotional health and well-being. If the answer is "yes" then you are ready to learn about boundaries, choices, and self-responsibility. Consider the most basic choices listed below to start your journey of change.

1. Education. There are many self-help books written on the subject.
2. Self-help groups such as Codependents Anonymous.
3. Getting a recovery sponsor and/or accountability partner
4. Initiating a journal to increase self-awareness, identify thinking and behavioral patterns that you will work on changing as part of your personal growth.
5. Male/female support groups (facilitated by a licensed therapist to objectively process gender issues, interdependence, working together).

6. Individual therapy.
7. Developing a self-care plan and positive daily structure.

GUIDELINES FOR FAMILY MEMBERS/SIGNIFICANT OTHERS OF ALCOHOLIC/ CHEMICALLY DEPENDENT INDIVIDUALS

1. Do not view alcoholism/chemical dependency as a family or social disgrace. Recovery can and does happen.

2. Do not nag, lecture, or preach. Chances are that they have already told themselves everything that you might say. People tune out to what they do not want to hear. Being nagged or lectured may lead to lying and may put them in a position of making promises they cannot keep or are not ready to keep.

3. Be careful that you do not come off sounding and acting like a martyr. Be aware, because you can give this impression without saying a word. Look at your own attitudes and behavior. Also, be honest about what your agenda is.

4. Do not try to control their behavior with "if you loved me." Because the individual using substances is compulsive in their behavior, such pleas only cause more distress. They have to decide to stop because it is their choice.

5. Be careful to guard against feelings of jealousy or feeling left out because of the method of recovery that they choose. Love, home, and family are not enough to support abstinence from substance abuse. Gaining self-respect is often more important in the early stages of recovery than other personal relationship responsibilities. They might spend a lot of time going to meetings and investing in relationships with other people in recovery. Don't focus on them— focus on your own journey of change.

6. Support responsible behavior in the chemically dependent individual. Do not do for them what they can do for themselves or do what they must do for themselves. Only they can work on their abstinence and recovery. Therefore, instead of removing the problem, allow them to see it, solve it, and deal with the consequences of it.

7. Begin to accept, understand, and to live *one day at a time*.

8. Begin to learn about the use of substances and what role it plays in an individual's life and what role you have played in the life of a substance abuser. Be willing to assume responsibility for your own life and totally give up any attempt to control the behavior and to change the substance abuser.

9. Participating in your own support group, like a 12-step meeting such as Alanon or Celebrate Recovery, etc. can help you in your own recovery from the dysfunctional behaviors in this relationship and possibly similar behaviors in other relationships as well.

10. Only monitor you own recovery efforts, positive daily self-care structure, and honesty are key.

11. Recognize and accept that whatever you have been doing does not work. Understand what your own behavior is about. Acknowledge that your life has become as unmanageable as the substance abuser's. It is time you to learn to live honesty and healthy boundaries instead of reacting to what is the responsibility of someone else. Know where you end and they begin.

12. Giving back. This is a significant factor of affiliation in a recovery environment. Passing on the gift of self-responsibility, self-understanding, and the added goal of personal development changes lives. We manage ourselves, not others. Everyone must work his/her own recovery program.

STAGES OF RECOVERY

1. The process actually begins by seeing yourself where you are right now. Before you start recovery you are in the mode of "survival and denial." This is existing, not living. There is a denial of having any problems or that behaviors are self-defeating.
2. Acceptance for the realization that you cannot change others and learning to deal with it.
3. Identifying and working through personal issues. This is where you see and understand more about yourself. Awareness is increasing. There is an understanding of the past, but living in the present. You are beginning to recognize that your most positive contribution to a relationship is your own emotional health and boundaries.
4. Reintegration. Learning to be okay with yourself—not identifying yourself by what you do for others. This prepares you for taking responsibility of self-care and getting your own needs met appropriately.
5. A new beginning. Living a new, emotionally healthy way of life.

DETACHING WITH LOVE VERSUS CONTROLLING

One of the hardest, but most important goals for people close to an individual in recovery to learn, is to detach from the behaviors/substance abuse process and continue to love the person without trying to control the situation.

What does detachment mean? It can sound frightening, given that everyone's life (especially family members) has revolved around the chemically dependent person—always trying to anticipate what will happen next, covering up for them, etc. Detaching with love is an attitude that is associated with behaviors that are not controlling.

What does controlling mean? Controlling behavior is the need to have people, places, and things, be "my way." Expecting the world to be what you want it to be for you. Living your life with "shoulds" and "ought to be." Not expressing your feelings honestly, but with self-centeredness and manipulation. Feeling okay if things are the way you want them to be regardless of the needs or desires of others. It is a behavior that comes from fear–fear of the unknown or of "falling apart" if people and situations are not the way you want them to be. It is a symptom of a family or systems dysfunction. It is a reaction to the substance abuse that evolves out of feeling increasing responsibility for the substance-abusing person.

As the illness within the substance-abusing individual progresses so do the projections: "If it were not for you I would not need to drink/use other substances." Statements like this contribute to a deterioration of self-worth with the result being that you believe that you are the key to change this awful mess by controlling your world, and the people in it. You become exhausted, frustrated, and resentful. Resentment comes from people not doing what you want them to do—and resentment kills love. It is necessary to accept the following:

1. Chemical dependency is an illness.
2. You did not cause it.
3. You cannot control it.
4. You cannot cure it.

Detaching from the illness and the substance-abusing individual's behaviors allows them to take responsibility for themselves—and allows you to be free to feel the love for the individual.

When you begin taking care of yourself and being responsible for yourself, you have the key to peace, serenity, sanity, and really feeling good about new ways of thinking. This personal recovery is supportive of others and their personal journey of recovery.

PERSONALITY DISORDERS

The following information is aligned with borderline, narcissist, and histrionic personality features and disorders. These nonpersonality disorders (NPDs) are the ones seen in therapy most often.

THE RELATIONSHIP BETWEEN A PERSON WHO HAS A PERSONALITY DISORDER AND A PERSON WHO DOESN'T (NONPERSONALITY DISORDER)

MAKING MY OWN TOOLBOX

The first distinction of a relationship between a person with a PD and another person who does not (NPD) is that of family relationships and chosen relationship (love relationship, business, or significant friend relationship). In the family relationship it is a mother or father who neglect, verbally/emotionally abuse, or hurt their children versus a child who hurts themselves or others. The unique quality of the family relationship with a PD is that it is not selected but by virtue of family—*unselected*. Contrary, are the relationships that are *selected* (marriage/love relationship, business partnership, or significant friendship). The context of these relationships are different in that there is a choice to be in the relationship with the following caveats; remaining committed, leaving/ending the relationship, coparenting (or trying to).

The above information may appear that it is pretty direct and cookie cutter but that is not accurate. Relationships are unique to the two people sharing that context and there is a lot of variation in addition to the common characteristics of the PD influence. However, there are also some common factors that can be used for problem solving, limit settings, and boundaries.

There have been numerous books written on PDs and what it is like to be in a relationship with someone who has a PD; feeling hostage, trapped, obligated, fear, anger, guilt, depressed, anxious, isolated, grief/loss, abused, walking on eggshells, etc. There is often a feeling of being paralyzed to take action, fearing, and avoiding the consequences of leaving or asserting their own rights to being treated respectfully. There is also a common experience shared by most people in a relationship with a person with PD and they first discover and understand the PD. It is a powerful "ah ha" moment. All of the sudden many things come into focus and they start putting together the angst of what they have been living with in that no-win irrational and or detached relationship.

Along with this newfound information and validation is the recognition of the mistakes they have made in an effort to cope with this difficult relationship. When someone is not rational or not able to be equally invested in common relationship goals and skill development, it is challenging to provide a positive outcome. Instead there are predictable landmines that can be used for generating a new view with associated expectations and limitations that can be utilized for problems solving, boundary clarification, and making personal choices.

LANDMINES IN PERSONALITY DISORDER RELATIONSHIP

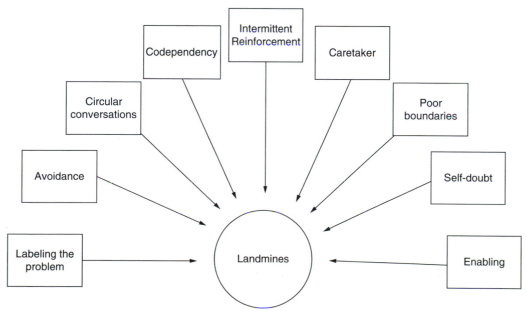

1. *Labeling the problem.* Confronting a PD individual believing that sharing this revelation of knowing what the problem is will result in rational discussion, effective problem-solving, and resolutions. Ever put kerosene on a smoldering fire?

2. *Avoidance.* Withdrawing from a relationship with a PD individual in an effort to buffer and defend against the fear of rejection, accountability, criticism, or exposure to pain and distress.

3. *Circular conversations.* Arguments that seem to never get resolved, i.e., repeating the same patterns with no resolution happen because of justifications, arguing, defending, and chronic explanations. These circular conversations along with many other characteristics listed contribute to learned helplessness or the belief that they have no control over a situation—even when they do.

4. *Codependency.* A codependent relationship is one in which a relatively mentally/emotionally healthy person is controlled or manipulated by a person who is affected by personal issues such as addiction or mental illness believing that by putting the needs of person struggling ahead of their own things will get better. Be honest and quit participating in problem.

5. *Intermittent reinforcement.* Intermittent reinforcement is the most common form of reinforcement—or making sure that undesired behavior will continue. It is when boundaries, rules, or rewards are not enforced consistently. This is a method of guaranteeing that the PD individual knows how to get what they want from you without changing their own behavior.

6. *Caretaker/rescuer.* An NPD individual frequently puts themselves in the position of a caretaker or rescuer. In other words the person who is responsible for compensating for the PD person's behaviors, cleaning up any problems created by their actions, and repairing any problems arising from their mental health issues. The NPD individual considers their own strengths, skill, and knowledge are enough to compensate for a PD individual's behavioral issues.

7. *Poor boundaries.* Poor boundaries means there is an absence of rules, limits, respect, and guidelines for acceptable and mutually respectful behavior. Inconsistent or intermittent reinforcement of consequences for inappropriate disrespectful behavior are common among both abusers and abuse victims.

8. *Self-doubt.* It's common for people who have lived a long time in a highly charged environment and emotionally distressed by trying to deal with a PD individual begin to question their own values or moral compass and their own mental health. When there is self-doubt you don't even trust your own actions.

9. *Enabling.* Enabling is a pattern of behavior (often seen by child abuse victims and those who raised by parents with an addiction) which seeks to avoid confrontation and conflict by taking the abuse without challenging it or setting/asserting boundaries. Thus enabling the abuser to continue their pattern of behavior.

TOOLBOX FOR THE NONPERSONALITY-DISORDERED INDIVIDUAL AND COPING IN A RELATIONSHIP WITH A PERSONALITY-DISORDERED INDIVIDUAL

MAKING MY OWN TOOLBOX

Whatever you try isn't going to work perfectly, but there are definitely the "do" and "don't do" (above) recommendations. Knowledge brings opportunity for growth and change. Take the time to learn all that you can about the personality disorder factors you are dealing with and then learn all you can about what made you so vulnerable to "selecting" it, or tolerating it. It is not all about pointing a finger—it is about looking in the mirror. You can only change yourself. The generally recommended responses for more effective coping and outcomes can be figured out by studying what not to do and includes the following:

1. *Family well-being comes first.* This translates to choices based on what is best for the children in the family.

2. *Self-responsibility rule—everyone cleans up and resolves their own problems.* This extends to being clear about what is your concern and under your control. Therefore, clarify what belongs to you and what belongs to the PD individual.

3. *Abuse is not allowed.* If necessary eliminate communication and contact if someone is verbally, emotionally, and/or physically abusive. Personal safety is a priority, and abuse is to be avoided or stopped immediately. The responses to abuse exist in a continuum from ending a conversation, leaving a room/environment to calling the police. Abuse is unacceptable.

4. *Taking time out is a decision made when you need to remove yourself from an irrational argument/conversation/situation or conflict.* *Do not participate in drama—that is when you become part of the problem.

5. *There is something called the 50% rule that means both people in a relationship share the responsibility for what happens in the relationship.*

6. *Therefore, strive to be objective about what you experience in relating to another person, but you are responsible for how you choose to interpret what happens and how you choose to deal with it.* That is your 50%.

7. *Add one more percent point and you have the 51% rule that means no matter how important someone is to you, you need to be the priority to yourself. Bottom line is that you are responsible for you and you need to be the best you can be in your relationships.*

8. *Make the best, well-thought-out choices you can.* Don't worry about "what if" deal with "what is."

9. *Self-care means investing in yourself.* Taking the time and energy to create a healthy balanced lifestyle. Only you are responsible for your emotional and physical well-being.

10. *Boundaries are reasonable, rational, and fair rules to assure that we are all safe and treated in a respectful manner.* Boundaries are realistic expectations of our behaviors and the behaviors of other. *Remember that you teach people how to treat you.

11. *Journaling is a valuable technique for understanding yourself, what is important to you, and what the best choices are for you to make to help you reach your goals.*

12. *Develop and utilize positive social support and consider the benefit of developing a positive relationship with a therapist so that you have an objective person to bounce things off of and help you develop the skills you need to effectively deal with challenging relationships and life situations.*

PERSONALITY DISORDER TOOLBOX

MAKING MY OWN TOOLBOX

1. The toolbox could actually be a container with objects that provide comfort and grounding in the moment (not consumed by the past or the future). Below are some examples that a "calm-box" might contain. Of course the contents need to be individualized to be what works for you.
   A. Flashcards with key reminders, list of safe people, affirmations, etc.
   B. List of emergency contact information.
   C. Stress ball.
   D. A timer (for time out. Even though "it seems really hard to do, I need self-calm and affirmations to encourage me").
   E. A metronome. Watching and focusing on the rhythm is a helpful distraction for calming.
   F. Journal.
   G. Sketch pad and other art supplies.
   H. Soothing stuffed animal.

2. Identify triggers.
3. Relaxation techniques.
    A. Breathing techniques. For example, breathe deeply by sitting or laying down somewhere quiet and focus on your breathing. Breathe evenly, deeply, and slowly. Watch you stomach rise and fall with each breath
    B. Yoga
    C. Meditation/mindfulness (take a class, or download a format you like so that it is always available to you)
4. Grounding exercises. Grounding exercises are used to help you focus your attention on the present by using everyone of your senses to focus on and describe where you are at in detail. You can be anywhere to practice grounding and self-calm by being in the moment.
5. Play music that helps you move to the opposite emotion you are fighting at the moment. For example, if you are feeling sad play happy upbeat music.
6. Call someone, maybe you have an accountability partner or you have written down a helpline (there are many). There are always choices.
7. Get active and do something that really gets you moving and distracts you from the pain and distress of the moment (dance, go for a power walk, do yard work, or housecleaning).
8. Take a warm bath or shower. Get focused on the sensation of the warm water and how it feels, use a soap that smells good to you (eucalyptus and lavender are calming).
9. Help someone else. Do something nice for someone else. Making small caring gestures for someone else can decrease your emotional pain.
10. Ride it out. The peak of emotional distress (where it is strongest) often brings with it urges to hurt yourself (drinking/drugs, cutting) last for a few minutes and then they begin to fade. Use an egg timer to take control of it and set it for 10 min to practice the skill of riding it out.
11. Practice increasing awareness and acceptance of strong emotions. Intense emotions are not good or bad (that's not the point). You can't deal with them effectively unless you are aware of what you feel, "create distance" from the overwhelming experience of such emotions and choosing techniques (such as mindfulness) that help you cope more effectively.
12. Journaling is a great tool for increasing awareness, identifying triggers, venting, and problem solving new ways of thinking and behaving.
13. Develop a safety plan. Work with your therapist to evaluate your risk and identify a stepwise progression of interventions/resources to use based on need. This list should include an accountability partner and suicide hotline.

*I understand that this outline is provided to give me ideas so that I can create my own personal toolbox. Some of these ideas may not work for me and I may already have other skills for effectively coping— recommendations not on this list that I want to try. That is how a person makes a "personal" toolbox.

DEMENTIA

Dementia is a term that describes a wide range of symptoms. Most of those diagnosed will be Alzheimer. The second most common dementia occurs after a stroke, vascular dementia. People with dementia may have memory problems, difficulty paying bills, planning and preparing meals, or traveling outside of their neighborhood. If you or a someone close to you is experiencing memory problems or other difficulties associated with changes in thinking skills it would be important to talk to their primary care physician about a professional evaluation to determine the cause and review treatment recommendations. Many dementias are progressive and gradually get worse so an early diagnosis is important.

TEN WARNING SIGNS OF ALZHEIMER DISEASE

We have an aging population and this is the most common dementia diagnosis. According to the Alzheimer's Disease and Related Disorders Association, we should familiarize ourselves with the following 10 warning signs of Alzheimer disease:

1. *Memory loss.* This is specifically most identifiable when it affects job skills. Everyone forgets a name or an assignment once in a while, but frequent forgetfulness with confusion in the home or workplace is definitely a sign that something is wrong. This symptom disrupts daily life.

2. *Difficulty performing normal and familiar tasks.* For example, preparing a meal and then forgetting to serve it. This is not an issue of getting distracted or forgetting one course of a meal. You could apply this type of situation to many different tasks and see the disconnection.

3. *Difficulty with language.* Everyone from time to time has the experience of not being able to find a certain word when speaking or thinking about something. However, people with Alzheimer's forget simple words and substitute inappropriate words making it difficult to understand what they are saying.

4. *Disoriented to time and place.* This issue creates great concern for the family members of someone who has Alzheimer disease. These individuals become lost in environments that have been familiar to them for years. They don't know where they are, how they got there, or how to get back home (such as their own street and neighborhood).

5. *Poor judgment.* They seem to lack the common sense of even self-care such as getting a sweater or coat on a cold day or wearing layers on a hot day. They do not dressing appropriately to go out on errands (such as wearing a bathrobe over clothes to the store).

6. *Difficulty with abstract thinking.* Recognizing numbers or performing elementary math operations may be impossible. *If this type of issue is evident difficulty with visual perception needs to be assessed.

7. *Misplacing things.* Unlike the situation where someone misplaces their keys, the Alzheimer patient may file away all kinds of items in totally inappropriate places and then not remember how they got there.

8. *Changes in mood or behavior.* A broad range of emotional expression is normal. Those with Alzheimer disease may display quick inappropriate changes in emotion for no known reason. There may be an expression of being blank, vacant, or flat.

9. *Changes in personality.* While it's not uncommon for our personalities to change as we age, the Alzheimer patient's personality can change dramatically over a short period of time or over a longer period of time.

10. *Loss of initiative.* Everyone loses interest and wants to shirk responsibilities every now and then. However, when the individual with Alzheimer disease has this experience, he/she may not reexperience or regain that interest and may remain uninvolved.

While symptoms of dementia vary, at least two of the following core symptoms/mental functions must be significantly impaired for dementia to be considered.

1. Memory
2. Communication and language
3. Ability to focus and pay attention
4. Reasoning and judgment
5. Visual perception

PREPARING FOR A DOCTOR VISIT

It is a good idea to maintain a current list of medications; name and dosage of the medication, directions (am, pm, how many times/day, etc.), what it was prescribed for, date the prescription was started, and name of the prescribing physician. Additionally, it is important to provide information regarding any changes you or a loved one has experienced, questions, etc.

1. Has your health, memory, or mood changed?
2. Describe the change.
3. When did you notice the change?
4. How often does it happen? Is it everyday?
5. Does it happen around the same time of day?
6. Does it happen in a specific situation?
7. What do you do when it happens?
8. Is it always the same?

The following are the questions to ask the doctor:

1. Do I need to be referred to a specialist?
2. Will I be taking any tests? If so, how long will they take?
3. Could any of the medications that I am taking be causing the difficulties that I am having?
4. If I am diagnosed with dementia what should I expect?

CAREGIVER EDUCATION

CAREGIVING OF ELDERLY PARENTS

This topic examines a situation when an adult child takes on the role of parent(s) caretaker. There is a common sense aspect of this section. Obviously, if a parent is experiencing dementia or physical disability there will likely be a significant shift in helping them to manage numerous life and care demands. However, there are also times when the caring role of the adult child is exploited to the detriment of both parties. We all benefit by managing the demands of our own lives. It keeps us stronger and current in making the best personal choices and fulfilling those choices. Therefore, it may be helpful to first clarify exactly what is taking place between you and your parents. Caregiving is a supportive role in which you are helping a parent(s) who is actively taking care of himself/herself. Caretaking involves doing for others what they are *not capable* of doing for themselves. If this is the case you will need to be thoughtful about how you will maintain balance as best possible in your own life.

However, if you find yourself in a caretaker role doing things for a parent(s) and they are things that your parent(s) is capable of doing for themselves then you are in a caretaking codependent relationship with your parent(s), and you are likely rescuing and helping them to be less capable. These behaviors may result from efforts to please or elicit some other response from your parents. Old family patterns that may have had a negative influence on early emotional development can resurface and intensify as you become more codependently involved in your parent's lives. There are many issues that require attention and management. Review the following:

1. The degree of help necessary
2. Medical appointments/treatment
3. Transportation
4. Living arrangements

5. Health care
6. Financial issues
7. Emotional support
8. Encouraging social involvement (as permitting)
9. Issues of loss
10. Legal issues/getting estate in order, etc.

*Legal issues also encompasses the importance of the caretaker having appropriate legal support via power of attorney for various legal issues (to be activated under specific circumstances), medical directives on file at the local hospital as well as a document maintained in the legal file, etc. It is beneficial to have a consultation with an attorney who specializes in elder care. They will provide you with information and recommendations for all major legal/economic topics confronting you and your parent(s).

The potential for blurred boundaries is significant. To avoid unnecessarily becoming a caretaker requires awareness and appropriate boundaries. Consider using the following information to create a healthy caregiving relationship while you continue to effectively live your own life:

1. Set appropriate boundaries
   A. Set limits
   B. Decide what you will, won't, and can't do
      1. Problem-solve alternatives
      2. Effectively utilize community resources
      3. Live in the here and now
2. Live in the here and now
   A Don't worry about what cannot be changed.
   B. Don't worry about "what if"—deal with "what is."
   C. Live the feelings of today, stop anticipating what you may feel later.
   D. Do what is right for you to do (for your heart and your conscience).
   E. Accept that parents may not follow medical recommendations (you can't control others).
   F. As best, possible focus on what is good and enjoyable. You don't want to miss on being able to enjoy good moments with those you love. *Laughter is the best medicine.*
3. Avoid excessive unnecessary worry
   A. This coincides with living in the here and now
   B. Don't second-guess decisions, acknowledge you are doing the best you can
   C. Stay focused on self-care and self-responsibility
   D. Find humor in everyday, laughter is a necessity

*If you are feeling anger and resentment, you may not be taking care of your own needs. This is your first responsibility. If you are not the best you can be it will eventually take a toll on your supportive care of others.

4. Cope with what needs to be done
   A. No "what ifs"—the circumstances are what they are
   B. When you do what needs to be done without overthinking, it doesn't feel so bad.
   C. Deal with it—even if that means the decision is to delegate, use other resources and assert your own limits
5. Avoid emotional blackmail
   A. Do not give into intimidation, tantrums, anger, silence, or being guilted into sympathy.
   B. If you give in to negative efforts to get you to respond, you are likely to feel resentful and that is not fair. Take responsibility for the choices you make.
   C. Give adequate, appropriate care.

6. Avoid the useless feeling of guilt
   A. Be clear about what you are doing and why you are doing it
   B. Recognize your own limitations
   C. Feel at peace by doing the best you can
   D. Don't self-criticize with "shoulds"
7. Exercise conservation of energy
   A. Avoid the stance of "I can do it all"
   B. Identify and utilize appropriate resources
   C. If you find yourself complaining a lot, use this awareness as an opportunity to make necessary changes
   D. If you find yourself experiencing physical fatigue or depression, you need to review your own needs and commitment to self-care and self-responsibility
8. Take care of yourself first
   A. If you are going to take care of some of the needs of another, it is imperative that you take care of yourself so that you have the physical and emotional energy to do what you feel is necessary.
   B. Utilize resources.
      1. Family
      2. Friends
      3. Professionals
      4. Community resources
   C. Get adequate rest, eat well, do things that you enjoy, spend time with people that are fun and who can distract you from your daily obligations. You need to laugh and to have fun.
9. Acceptance of current circumstances
   A. Don't waste your energy trying to think your way out—it won't change the situation
   B. Look realistically at the situation and make sensible choices
   C. Participate in a support group if one is available in your community, if not you will find numerous websites and blogs that offer information and support
   D. If there are not any support groups for caregivers in your community, read on the subject to reinforce your positive efforts
10. Self-review
    A. From time to time, take an inventory of your
       1. Emotions
       2. Use of time
       3. Self-care
       4. Personal goals
    B. Make amends when necessary
    C. Evoke self-responsibility
    D. Be honest with your parents about realistic limits
11. Obtain help for yourself
    A. It is painful to see those you love in pain and decompensating physically psychologically
    B. Find resources in your community that are helpful and healing to you
    C. Review personal losses
       1. Health
       2. Relationships
       3. Enjoyed activities
       4. Finances
    D. Problem-solve what must be done
    E. Participate in a caregiver support group
12. Grieve
    A. Grieving is a necessary part of letting go.
    B. Share your thoughts and feelings of grief with those who care about you.

C. This is often a time of painful losses and the acknowledgment of powerlessness.

D. Don't get stuck with immobilizing grief over difficult changes. Some losses simply leave a hole in your heart that doesn't go away or heal over. That does not mean that you do not continue to move on normally in your life. It means you will always miss that person and, if you choose, you can get in touch with those feelings

COMMON PROBLEMS EXPERIENCED BY CAREGIVERS

1. Concerns about medical advice and expense
2. Learning how to maintain positive social supports
3. The resulting strain on a marriage and other important relationships
4. Less time and energy for other important people in the person's life and for himself/herself
5. Balancing the pressures of additional obligations such as work, child care, school, managing home/yard, and so on

EFFECTIVE COPING STRATEGIES FOR THE CAREGIVERS

1. Find a support group of others facing similar issues.
2. Self-care. Stay active mentally and physically. Balance is essential to survival.
   A. Time for yourself
   B. Exercise
   C. Adequate sleep/nutrition
   D. Recreation
   E. Time with people you enjoy (laughter/distraction); stay involved with friends and activities
   F. Relaxation techniques
3. Ask for help from others when you need it.
4. Be honest with your parents about.
   A. Realistic limitations
   B. The need to feel appreciated
   C. Obtain the best possible medical care and always get a second opinion for serious diagnoses
5. Maintain a strong support system.
6. Maintain your own daily schedule apart from the person who is cared for.
7. Join a support group for caregivers.
8. Utilize therapy as a resource for reinforcing self-care and maintaining an objective eye on the situation.
9. Make an appointment with your primary care physician and get a thorough examination.
10. Keep a journal and self-monitor for how you are coping with the added stress/demands and for patterns that are not supportive of your own self-care.

ADVICE FOR OTHERS CLOSE TO THE SITUATION

1. Communicate
   A. Talk honestly about the situation
   B. Be realistic about limits
2. Problem-solve how to be supportive
3. Use available community resources
4. Maintain the mutual giving and sharing in relationships

*Remember, at some point in our lives we are likely to experience both roles. This thought may help to guide you in the decisions you make.

TEN WARNING SIGNS OF CAREGIVER STRESS

1. Anger and frustration. The person feels angry about the lack of effective medical treatment and diminishing feelings of hope. Frustration develops due to the lack of support available and insight with the experience.

2. Denial. The caregiver is in denial about the issues of loss, how things have changed, and how an illness has affected the person being cared for.

3. Fatigue and exhaustion. Fatigue is evident by never feeling like one adequately catches up with rest and sleep. Exhaustion makes even the smallest daily task seem impossible to complete. This chronic tiredness and feeling of ineffectiveness in one's own life takes a serious toll.

4. Sleep disturbance. Sleep is interfered with by continuous thoughts of what needs to be done and ongoing concerns.

5. Social withdrawal. Withdrawal from one's own support system occurs. What used to feel pleasurable no longer seems to matter.

6. Feeling irritable. Low frustration tolerance develops. These individuals become moody and restless. As a result, they seem to respond to others in a negative way more and more often. They make it clear by their tone of voice, what they say, and their body language that they would rather be left alone.

7. Difficulty with concentration and attention. Good concentration and attention require adequate rest and energy. If you cannot keep your mind on what you are doing, it becomes increasingly difficult to get even simple tasks completed.

8. Anxiety and stress. Anxiety begins to develop as stress is experienced by just thinking about facing the responsibilities of another day. It is difficult to have positive feelings and hopefulness for the future.

9. Depression. Depression affects a person's ability to cope and effectively manage the demands of life.

10. Health deterioration. With depression, anxiety, and exhaustion, the immune system is suppressed and a person becomes more vulnerable to health problems.

MENTAL HEALTH CRISIS PLANNING

DEVELOPING A WELLNESS RECOVERY PROGRAM (LIFESTYLE AND SELF-CARE)

Every goal requires a plan. A plan will serve the purpose of identifying how to accomplish your goal(s) and maintain the progress and benefits. The following will serve as a guide to help you develop your action plan for recovery and maintaining wellness. There is more benefit in working on the plan with your therapist as well as an accountability partner or other safe person who shares your life and is invested in your well-being.

YOUR SOCIAL SUPPORT NETWORK

Review who you currently list as your social support system and write them down with their phone numbers. This is important because while you are developing your crisis plan you also need to be practicing a healthy lifestyle that could include family members, close friends, and involvement in the community. Relationships are essential to successfully manage the entire continuum of crisis planning, dealing with a crisis and recovery.

Start by being a good family member and friend yourself. Remember, you treat others the way you want to be treated. Reaching out connecting with others and making plans for upcoming events feels good. Everyone that you have identified as key parts of your social support system (including your therapist) will be pleased to hear how hard you are working on your crisis plan. If you feel that there is no one you can trust to be there if you are having a hard time, you may need to work on developing some new relationships for your support system. If you find yourself needing to meet new people the following ideas may be useful to you. The goal is that all of us need to surround ourselves by people who care about us and want the best for us. Good people feel good to be around. You may not be able to do these things if you are not feeling well enough to do so, but if that is the case, use the time to identify all of the possibilities for when you feel better.

1. Every community has different support groups. Support groups are a great way to make new friends. Quite often that gives you an instant group of people who are there for the same reasons you are. Having things in common is a good basis for developing friendships. Also, your therapist might have some recommendations of specific groups that they think would be helpful for you. Check support group listings online and in the local newspaper.

2. Attend events in your community; concert in the park, fundraisers, art events, presentations, fairs, and concerts.

3. Join a special interest club. They generally don't cost anything and you will meet people that you have a shared interest with. It might be a group that is focused on maintaining walking trails, wildlife watching, DAR (Daughters of the American Revolution) stamp/coin collecting, book club, etc.

4. Take a class. Adult education programs, community center, parks and recreation, local college campus(s) offer a wide variety of courses that will help you improve/learn something new and meet potential friends at the same time.

5. Volunteer. Offer to assist a school library or crosswalk monitor, hospital guild, or other organization in your community. Every community needs help and most have a volunteer bureau that you can contact to find out more.

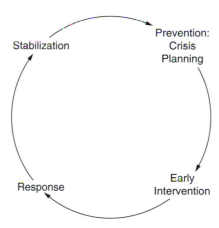

A NEW BEGINNING: GETTING STARTED

Whenever you are working on a project, it is helpful to create a binder where all of the information is stored. The following supplies are the basic materials that will be needed to develop a Wellness Recovery Action Plan:

1. Three-ring binder, 1-inch thick
2. Package of lined three-ring filler paper
3. Set of six dividers/tabs
4. Pen to write with and some different colored highlighters

5. Plastic/zippered pouch that is made to be used in a three-ring binder so that writing instruments and highlighters are always with the binder
6. Get started on your own, working with your therapist, an accountability partner, and/or a person close to you that can talk through your ideas and give you feedback

SIX-PART ACTION PLAN

1. *Daily maintenance list.* On top of the first section, place the list of your support system and their contact numbers. On the second page, keep a list of all of the medications, dosage, directions, and prescribing physician. Now→turn the section separator and you are in the first section of your six-step plan.
   A. Page 1 is a list of things that describe you when you are feeling well and doing well.
   B. Page 2 is about self-care and is a list of things you need to do for yourself everyday to keep yourself feeling good and doing well.
   C. Page 3 is a reminder list that should be reviewed daily to reassure that you stay on track for the things you need to do and you might need to.
   D. Be flexible. Add information to any of these pages if you think of additional information.

2. *Identifying triggers.* This section actually has two parts:
   A. It is important to write down a list divided into people, places, and situations that may result in you feeling like you are spiraling in a negative direction toward getting sick. These are all external things. This is challenging because some of the things you will probably write on your list are normal reactions to events. Therefore, the information is used to problem-solve how you choose to deal with them. Don't just avoid—problem-solve how you *choose* to manage whatever it is. You are in charge of your life. All of this information defines triggers and potential triggers.
   B. On the next page, write an action plan to use if triggers come up.

3. *Identifying warning signs of potential difficulties.* Warning signs are internal and the more you work on maintaining your plan, the more you will understand who you are and why. Knowledge = choices. Interestingly, early warning signs may not be related to reactions you experience to stressful situations. Therefore, even though you are making a good effort to decrease challenging symptoms, you may begin to experience early warning signs (subtle signs) of change that are telling you that you need to do more to deal with what is going on inside of you. This is an excellent time to use your support system to talk about what is going on inside of you.
   A. Make a list of the early warning signs you have identified. As you discover more early warning signs you can add them to your list.
   B. On the next page, write an action plan that goes with each trigger you identified. This becomes an important guide to maintaining wellness.

4. *Dealing with troubled waters.* Even though you work hard at staying well, you may find yourself in a hard place feeling like you are losing your strong footing. It could even be moving into the red zone of being a serious situation, but you are still able to make some good choices and take some actions on your own. Don't be foolish and think you can just tough it out. This may be a critical time—a very important time. Where immediate action is necessary to prevent slipping into a crisis. Preventive measures have two parts:
   A. Write down a list of symptoms that you need to pay attention to because if they get worse you may find yourself in a stage of crisis.
   B. On the next page, write an action plan to use to prevent decompensating.

*As your awareness improves, risk will decrease because even when you are going in a negative direction your plans of intervention will keep things from getting as bad as they would have previously.

5. *Prepared: the personal crisis plan.* In spite of your best efforts of self-care, planning, and assertive action, you may find yourselves in a mental health crisis. If this happens you will be benefited by your planning because in this circumstance others will likely need to take over at

least some responsibility for your care. But because you took the time to create active planning demonstrating that even in a difficult time, you are asserting some control.

Now you understand why writing a crisis plan when you are doing well is important. It is your opportunity to inform those on your social support network in how to care for you when you are not well. It is how you maintain control even when it seems like things are out of control. This works well for you and for those helping you. They will know exactly what you want them to do—there is no guesswork and that means less frustration for everyone. It is important to take the time, being thoughtful and thorough, to develop your plan. Also, discuss your plan with trusted individuals that age good to talk through things with. The crisis plan has the minimum information below written out:

A. Identify for your support network what symptoms that would indicate they need to take action on your behalf
B. Identify who you would want to take this action, or which people would do what
C. Place a copy of your current medications, if there are different ones that are to be used specifically when in a crisis, and those that should not be taken when in crisis.
D. Specify what treatments you prefer and those that are not desired or should be avoided
E. Develop a written workable plan for different levels home care/help
F. Specify acceptable and unacceptable treatment facilities
G. Specify (your permission, and to whom) actions that others can take that would be helpful
H. Clarify actions that should be avoided

**The list of instructions also needs to include at what level of functioning that the crisis plan no longer needs to be used and you resume all of the normal self-care activities.

1. *Reviewing and learning.* It is important to use any experienced crisis as an opportunity to glean new information that could be beneficial to you. Don't waste any experience as a potential for offering useful information. The results could lead to changes in what "to do" and what was previously designated as "don't do." Therefore, use this information to develop your *journal of change*: What works and what needs to be changed. This will serve as a personal guide of personal growth and change lived through self-responsibility.

SURVIVING THE CRISIS—WHAT TO DO AFTER A MENTAL HEALTH CRISIS

A mental health crisis, especially when others need to step in and take over some of your life management is very hard on a person and their self-esteem. Have a realistic expectation about the time it takes to recover. If you had surgery you would work consistently to get better everyday but you would accept that it is going to take a while. Just as when someone needs help when they have a surgery, it is fair to assume that some form of help will be needed following a mental health crisis. Likewise, such assistance/support can be expected to gradually decrease as you feel better and recover. Maybe now it makes even more sense that advanced planning for dealing with that critical time of a mental health crisis to assure the movement toward wellness and recovery. This plan allows those of us who experience psychiatric symptoms to maintain some degree of control over our lives, even when it feels like everything is out of control.

Developing a crisis plan takes time and you will need to come back to it several times and go through it with trusted social supports to make sure that you feel confident that should you find yourself in a crisis that things will go as you want them to. Work on it with family members or friends, or your therapist/case manager. Basically, whoever feels comfortable for you to work with on this project will be helpful in asking questions and making a thorough crisis plan.

Once the crisis plan has been completed, keep a copy for yourself, and give copies to all of your support network members. Consider the following basic outline to start with and you can modify or specialize it anyway that you feel better represents you and your needs/potential needs:

1. When I am feeling well and doing well this is what I look like and do during the course of the day
   →Describe yourself when you are feeling and doing well

2. When I am not doing well, I am experiencing the following symptoms
   → Write the symptoms
       When I am experiencing these symptoms I am no longer able to make responsible or appropriate decisions
3. If I am experiencing the symptoms in step 2, I want the following people to make decisions for me to make sure that I get appropriate treatment and to provide me care and support

a. _____

b. _____

c. _____

**I *do not* want the following people involved in anyway in my care or treatment. List names and (optionally) why you do not want them involved.

4. Preferred medications and why: Dosages that have worked best with minimal side effects
5. Acceptable medications and why: Dosages that have worked best with minimal side effects
6. Unacceptable medications and why: Provide side effects experienced

**You could take the time to create a spreadsheet of medication history to demonstrate your reasons for not taking some medications and why you prefer others.

7. Acceptable treatments and why: Provide history of benefit(s)
8. Unacceptable treatments and why: Provide history of negative experience(s) or other reasoning
9. Preferred treatment facilities/programs and why: Provide history of benefit(s)
10. Unacceptable treatment facilities/programs and why: Provide history of negative benefit(s) or other reasoning
11. What I want from my supporters when I am experiencing these symptoms: (list)
12. What I don't want from my supporters when I am experiencing these symptoms: (list)
13. Things I need others to do for me and whom I want to do what: Provide list
14. How I want disagreements between my social support network resolved:
15. Things I can do for myself: Provide list

*I give/do not give permission for my care providers to talk with each other about my symptoms and to make plans on how to assist me in accordance with my requests.

*Factors that demonstrate that my care providers no longer need to use this plan:

I developed this document myself with the help and support of:

Signed: _____ Date: _____

Attorney: _____ Date: _____

Witness: _____ Date: _____

Witness: _____ Date: _____

RECOVERING FROM A MENTAL HEALTH CRISIS

First, remember, you are not alone. Most people experience feelings or experiences like these at some time in their life. Some of them get help and treatment from health-care providers. Other people try to get through it on their own. Some people don't tell anyone what they are experiencing because they are afraid others will not understand and will blame them or treat them badly. While others feel safe in sharing what they are experiencing with trusted friends, family members, or coworkers. Sometimes these feelings and experiences are so severe that others know you have are having them even if you were trying to keep them private. Regardless of what your situation is, these feelings and experiences are very hard to live with. They can often interfere with you doing thing that you would otherwise do. Sometimes these symptoms and circumstances can also interfere in your ability to adequately care for yourself, make appropriate decisions, and/or doing things that are rewarding and enjoyable.

THINGS TO DO WHEN YOU ARE FEELING BETTER

When you have gotten through the crisis and are feeling better, make plans using the ideas in the previous section.

Identify things you can do right away. It will help you feel better, and that positive energy will contribute to your sense of well-being and health. It will be helpful to include simple basic lists:

1. To remind yourself of things you need to do everyday, such as getting a half hour of exercise, eating three healthy meals, picking up after yourself, not isolating, etc.
2. To remind yourself of things that need to be routinely, but not daily. However, if you miss them they will cause stress and problems in your life, like bathing, buying food, paying bills, or cleaning your home.
3. Of events or situations that, if they come up, may make you feel worse, such as a conflicts with family/friends, changes in health-care provider or therapist/case manager, financial distress, or loss of your job; and a list of things to do (leisure activities, relax, talk to a friend, play your guitar). It will support a strong recovery to engage in precrisis activities to resume feeling in control and normal.
4. Of early warning signs that you are starting to feel worse, such as always feeling tired, sleeping too much, overeating/under eating, isolating, dropping things, losing things, not keeping up your home, calling in sick, etc.; and a list of things to do (get more rest, take some time off, make an appointment with your therapist/case manager) to help yourself feel better and active in your recovery.
5. Of signs that things are getting much worse, such as you are feeling very depressed, you can't get out of bed in the morning, or you feel negative and hopeless about everything.
6. A list of things to do that will help you feel better quickly (get someone to stay with you, spend extra time doing things you enjoy, contact your doctor, attending church activities, etc.).

Key to successful recovery: A dependable social support network of family members and close friends. Socializing is one of the most effective ways to improve the way you feel. Therefore, maintaining positive social contacts by reaching out to a very good friend, family member, and/or health-care professional is an important part of your recovering from a mental health crisis. It is also important to have things to look forward to. If you feel that you don't have anyone you can depend on when you are having a difficult time, problem-solve the activities that you can participate in that will help you create the social support network that you need.

REGAINING CONTROL OF YOUR LIFE

Many people who experience psychiatric symptoms or have had traumatic things happen to them feel that they have no power or control over their own lives. Control of your life may have been taken over when your symptoms were severe and you were in a very vulnerable position. Family members, friends, and health-care professionals may have made decisions and taken action in your behalf because your symptoms were so intrusive you couldn't make decisions for yourself, they thought you wouldn't make good decisions or they didn't like the decisions you made. Even when you are doing much better, others may continue making decisions in your behalf. Often, the decisions that are made for you and the resulting action are not those you would have chosen.

Taking back control of your life by making your own decisions and your own choices is essential to recovery. It will help you to feel better about yourself and may even help you to relieve some of the symptoms that have been troubling to you.

There are several things you can do to begin this process. You can do these things in whatever way feels right to you. You may want use a journal to list or write your thoughts and ideas as a way to stay focused on what it is you want, to motivate yourself, and to record your progress. *Part of this process is developing a realistic vision of what you want your life to be, clarifying what you need to do to reach those goals, and then making that vision a reality.*

1. Think about what you really want your life to be like. Do you want to:
   A. Go back to school and study something of special interest to you?
   B. Enhance your talents in some way?
   C. Travel?
   D. To do a certain kind of work?
   E. Have a different home space or get your own apartment or home?
   F. Move to the country or the city?
   G. Have an intimate partner?
   H. Work with an alternative health-care provider on wellness strategies?
   I. Make your own decisions about treatment?
   J. Stop putting up with disabling side effects of treatment?
   K. Become more physically active?
   L. Lose or gain weight?
   Write down as many possibilities that you can think of. This would be great to enter in your journal. That way you can review it from time to time to update what is important to you.

2. Take the time to educate yourself about the possibilities so that you have all the information you need to make good decisions and to take back control of your life. Use resources such as the Internet, reentry counselor at a college, checking out classes, and certification programs at adult education, etc. Also, ask people whom you trust. Make your own decisions about what feels right to you and what doesn't.

3. The last stage of this process is to plan your strategies for making your life the way you want it to be. Figure out the best way for you to get what it is that you want or to be the way you want to be. Sometimes the answer is just finding a better way of being with your circumstance. Regardless, it is your responsibility to decide how you will move forward, and to what. It is the vision that you create. Then start working at it. Keep at it with courage and persistence until you have reached your goal and made your vision a reality.

SUICIDE

CONFRONTING AND UNDERSTANDING SUICIDE

Everyone is unique in the life crisis that they experience which can contribute or result in suicidal thoughts and behavior. We should all be educated about suicide. Suicide affects everyone, but the risk is higher for some more than others. According to the CDC (www.cdc.gov), men are 4x's more likely than women to die from suicide, but 3x's more women attempt suicide than men. Factors that increase risk include the following.

1. Health factors
    A. Mental health conditions
        1. Depression
        2. Bipolar (manic-depressive) disorder
        3. Schizophrenia
        4. Borderline or antisocial personality disorder
        5. Conduct disorder
        6. Psychotic disorders, or psychotic symptoms in the context of any disorder
        7. Anxiety disorders
    B. Substance abuse disorders
    C. Serious or chronic health condition and/or pain
2. Environmental factors
    A. Contagion would include exposure to another person's suicide, or to graphic or sensationalized accounts of suicide
    B. Access to lethal means including firearms and drugs
    C. Prolonged stress factors that may include harassment, bullying, relationship problems, and unemployment
    D. Stressful life events that may include a death, divorce, or job loss.
3. Historical factors
    A. Family history of suicide
    B. Family history of mental health conditions
    C. Previous suicide attempts
    D. Childhood abuse
4. Summary of common risk factors
    A. Mental illness
    B. Alcoholism or drug abuse
    C. Previous suicide attempts
    D. Family history of suicide
    E. Terminal illness or chronic pain
    F. Recent loss or stressful life event
    G. Social isolation and loneliness
    H. History of trauma or abuse

SUICIDE WARNING SIGNS (WWW.CDC.GOV)

People who commit suicide demonstrate one or more warning signs, either through what they say or what they do. The more warning signs identified, the greater the risk.

1. *Talk*. If a person talks about:
    A. Killing themselves
    B. Having no reason to live
    C. Being a burden to others
    D. Feeling trapped
    E. Unbearable pain
2. *Behavior*. A person's suicide risk is greater if a behavior is new or has increased, especially if it's related to a painful event, loss, or change
    A. Increased use of alcohol or drugs
    B. Looking for a way to kill themselves, such as stockpiling medication or searching online for materials or means
    C. Acting recklessly
    D. Withdrawing from activities

E. Isolating from family and friends

F. Sleeping too much or too little

G. Visiting or calling people to say goodbye

H. Giving away prized possessions

I. Aggression

3. *Mood*. People who are considering suicide often display one or more of the following moods

A. Depression

B. Loss of interest

C. Rage

D. Irritability

E. Humiliation

F. Anxiety

LEVEL OF SUICIDE RISK (WWW.CDC.GOV)

Suicide Prevention Tip: Respond Quickly in a Crisis

If a friend or family member tells you that he or she is thinking about death or suicide, it's important to evaluate the immediate danger the person is in. Those at the highest risk for committing suicide in the near future have a specific suicide *plan*, the *means* to carry out the plan, a *time set* for doing it, and an *intention* to do it.

Level of suicide risk

Low	Some suicidal thoughts. No suicide plan. Says he or she won't commit suicide.
Moderate	Suicidal thoughts. Vague plan that isn't very lethal. Says he or she won't commit suicide.
High	Suicidal thoughts. Specific plan that is highly lethal. Says he or she won't commit suicide.
Severe	Suicidal thoughts. Specific plan that is highly lethal. Says he or she will commit suicide.

The following questions can help you assess the immediate risk for suicide:

1. Do you have a suicide plan? (*plan*)

2. Do you have what you need to carry out your plan (pills, gun, etc.)? (*means*)

3. Do you know when you would do it? (*time set*)

4. Do you intend to commit suicide? (*intention*)

*For some, depression medication causes an increase—rather than a decrease—in depression and suicidal thoughts and feelings. Therefore, it is important to closely monitor someone taking antidepressant medication for 2–3 months to assure that they do not develop suicidal ideation. This time of observation is important because the risk of suicide is the greatest during the first 2 months of treatment with antidepressant medication.

If a suicide attempt seems imminent:

1. Call a local crisis center, dial 911, or take the person to an emergency room.

2. Remove all obvious objects that could be the instrument of suicide; guns, drugs, knives, and other potentially lethal objects from the environment.

3. Do not, under any circumstances, leave a suicidal person alone. If necessary, develop a rotation of family members or friends to assure monitoring/supportive coverage.

SUPPORTING A SUICIDAL PERSON

If a friend or family member is suicidal, the best way to help is by offering an empathetic, listening ear. Let your loved one know that they are not alone and that you care. Don't take responsibility, however, for making your loved one well. You can offer support, but you can't get better for a suicidal person. He or she has to make a personal commitment to recovery.

It takes courage and commitment to help someone who is suicidal. Seeing someone you care about dealing with the internal fight. Witnessing a loved one dealing with thoughts about ending his or her own life can stir up many difficult emotions. As you're helping a suicidal person, don't forget to take care of yourself. Find someone that you trust—a friend, family member, clergyman, or counselor—to talk to about your feelings and get support of your own.

Helping a suicidal person:

1. *Get professional help*. Do everything in your power to get a suicidal person the help he or she needs. Call a crisis line for advice and referrals. Encourage the person to see a mental health professional, help locate a treatment facility, or take them to a doctor's appointment.

2. *Follow-up on treatment*. If the doctor prescribes medication, make sure your friend or loved one takes it as directed. Be aware of possible side effects and be sure to notify the physician if the person seems to be getting worse. It often takes time and persistence to find the medication or therapy that's right for a particular person.

3. *Be proactive*. Those contemplating suicide often don't believe they can be helped, so you may have to be more proactive at offering assistance. Saying, "Call me if you need anything" is too vague. Don't wait for the person to call you or even to return your calls. Drop by, call again, invite the person out.

4. Encourage positive lifestyle changes, such as a healthy diet, plenty of sleep, and getting out in the sun or into nature for at least 30 min each day. Exercise is also extremely important as it releases endorphins, relieves stress, and promotes emotional well-being.

5. *Make a safety plan*. Help the person develop a set of steps he or she promises to follow during a suicidal crisis. It should identify any triggers that may lead to a suicidal crisis, such as an anniversary of a loss, alcohol, or stress from relationships. Also include contact numbers for the person's doctor or therapist, as well as friends and family members who will help in an emergency.

6. *Remove potential means of suicide, such as pills, knives, razors, or firearms*. If the person is likely to take an overdose, keep medications locked away or give out only as the person needs them.

7. *Continue your support over the long haul*. Even after the immediate suicidal crisis has passed, stay in touch with the person, periodically checking in or dropping by. Your support is vital to ensure your friend or loved one remains on the recovery track.

FEELING OVERWHELMED AND DESPERATE

When a person is depressed they often lack the energy to resolve problems as they arise. As a result, all of the new problems pile up on top of the difficulties that originally contributed to the state of depression. When this happens a person becomes overwhelmed. Being overwhelmed feels like there is just too much to deal with. They feel desperate because it seems like no matter what they do they will be unable to accomplish all that they have to. It may feel like there are no choices that can really help them. When this happens it may appear that suicide is the only way to escape from the awful, trapped feeling that they are experiencing.

Unfortunately, they are considering a permanent solution to temporary problems. There is always another way no matter how difficult the problems may be. If a person is at the point where they feel desperate and unable to cope the thing to do is to ask for help. If they are feeling that bad then they know that they are not emotionally well and it may require that others who care (family members, friends, therapists, ministers, physicians) are needed to break this downward spiral. Reach out to the people in your support system. If you don't have a support system tell your physician or call a hospital emergency room for help. Get whatever help is necessary to problem-solve the solutions that will create the support and structure to stabilize and manage the potentially destructive behavior. Sometimes someone else can offer a solution that a person in a state of being overwhelmed would not even be able to see because they are focusing only on how to escape these awful feelings.

If you have ever felt overwhelmed and desperate describe how you felt. _____

_____

_____

How did you resolve the situation? _____

_____

_____

What did you learn that could help you now? _____

_____

_____

FEELING LIKE YOUR LIFE IS OUT OF CONTROL

When a person feels like their life is out of control, their negative thinking increases, they feel overwhelmed and desperate, their self-esteem plummets, and there does not seem to be anything that they can do to get back in control. It is like having a lot of conversations in your head with yourself and you cannot turn it off. It is such a frightening feeling that suicide may appear like the only way to get away from it all. Most people experience this feeling a little bit when they have a lot of different things going on at one time and the demand is greater than what they can give to take care of everything.

It may not be what would be expected, but when a person is feeling like this they tend to engage in behaviors which contribute to feeling and being more and more out of control. It can be like a vicious cycle. The thing to do is to get help from someone who is trusted and can be objective. There are choices, but to effectively make good choices a person will have to slow things down, evaluate and define what the problems are, and then prioritize the identified issues so that they can be systematically resolved one by one. You can only do one thing at a time. When this process is followed it becomes possible to take one step at a time toward any goal that has been set. It helps to deal with "What Is" instead of "What If."

If you are feeling like your life is out of control describe it. _____

_____

_____

What are all of the things that you are feeling pressure from? _____

_____

_____

What resources can you use to help you slow things down to get a handle on your situation? _____

_____

_____

*Remember: Take 1 day at a time.

- You can only do one thing at a time.
- Give yourself credit for your efforts and accomplishments because every step you take contributes to regaining control over your life.

GUILT

A person who is experiencing feelings of guilt is focusing on something that they have done that is embarrassing, harmful to another person, or some other behavior which has contributed to negative consequences for themselves or someone else. Sometimes this feeling of guilt becomes so big that they feel an intense need to escape, and the only way out appears to be suicide.

Feelings of guilt and shame are very hard to deal with, mainly because it requires that you forgive yourself for whatever has happened. Forgiving yourself requires honesty and self-acceptance. When you own your behavior and confront it with appropriate problem solving, it will feel like a huge weight has been taken off of your shoulders.

If you regret your actions, do you attempt to learn from them so that your future behavior does not repeat the same mistakes? Or do you choose to suffer over the past and remain passively stuck in the patterns of behavior you know are not helpful or appropriate?

Self-forgiveness requires an understanding for the possibility of special circumstances, assuming the responsibility for the damage or consequences of your behavior, to make amends for your actions, and to make a firm commitment to do things differently in the future. If you do not make this commitment to change and follow through on it, you will not be free from guilt. In fact, you will very likely repeat the same dysfunctional behavior patterns.

Change can be difficult because there is some comfort in what is familiar to you. Who knows what life may confront you with if you did not have your depression, hopelessness, and self-loathing? Misery can provide its own kind of insulation from the rest of the world, whereas happiness, in its own way, is more demanding. Happiness requires energy, consciousness, commitment, and discipline. So it takes time, energy, and work to liberate yourself from guilt.

What have I done or said which makes me feel guilty? _____

_____

_____

How can I take responsibility for what I have done? _____

_____

_____

How can I make peace with what has happened, accept and forgive myself, and move on? _____

_____

_____

How does what has happened help me understand what my values are? _____

_____

_____

When I feel defensive about positives? _____

_____

_____

If I hide myself through fear, envy, or resentment. _____

_____

_____

_____

When I act against what I understand and know to be right. _____

_____

_____

_____

_____

_____

I will imagine how I would feel if I did things differently in the future. _____

_____

_____

_____

_____

_____

_____

LONELINESS

When a person feels that one cares or they really do not have anyone that they feel close enough to talk to and to get help this can contribute to thoughts of suicide. The factor of loneliness can work in two directions with severe depression. When a person feels depressed they may isolate and withdraw from their resources that leads to feelings of loneliness. Or, when someone lacks resources they may experience an increasing sense of isolation and loneliness. Both increase depression and the likelihood of suicide.

When trying to understand and deal with issues of loneliness consider, on the most basic level, that behavior has only two purposes: To bring people closer together or to push them apart. People who experience depression may find it difficult to maintain close relationships for several reasons.

1. They may not follow through on friendship behaviors because of their negative thinking and expectations of rejection and abandonment.
2. Because of their depressed mood people may feel helpless themselves and not know what to do.
3. People may get frustrated with the depressed person who talks about how bad they feel or who obviously looks like they are having a difficult time, but do not appear to follow through on behaviors to help themselves.

Even though you may think that no one cares about you, you probably do have friends and family who care and are genuinely concerned about you. Do you take advantage of community resources that can help you to establish or reestablish a feeling of belonging and connectedness? It is important that you feel that you are a part of life and the world.

Make a list of the people who care about you and the resources in your community that you could participate in to decrease your feelings of loneliness and isolation.

1. _____

2. _____

3. _____

4. _____

5. _____

6. _____

GENERAL MANAGEMENT SKILLS

There are a number of strategies that are useful for a variety of struggles. Therefore, this section, like Stress Management, can be used as an excellent resource for someone dealing with anxiety disorders and mood disorders. For example:

It is common that a person who has PTSD also suffers from depression and substance abuse. That is a lot to deal with, but the good news is that creating a healthy self-care play and living with balance will improve how you feel no matter what the symptoms are. The self-monitoring checklist can play a positive role in helping you to identify what you may already doing that is beneficial to your recovery as well as some things that can be added.

EMOTIONAL FIRST STEP

Taking the time to work on your emotional first step can be a very positive step toward understanding what you have lived and survived, how you have been affected, what are the inner resources you developed as a result of what you have lived, and what you need to work on to improve the quality of your life and relationships, skills, and knowledge. It is a personalized road to developing and increasing your resilience.

GUIDELINES FOR COMPLETING YOUR FIRST STEP TOWARD EMOTIONAL HEALTH

The first step is simply an honest look at how your life experiences have affected you. This includes how you perceive what you have experienced, how you react and respond to various situations and other people, your coping ability, problem-solving skills, conflict resolution skills, what motivates you, and the ability to form healthy relationships.

Answer all of the questions that follow as thoroughly as possible, citing specific incidents, the approximate date, how you felt, what you thought, and how you responded. It may be an emotional experience for you to review your life experiences in detail, but remind yourself that there is nothing that you will write about that you haven't already experienced and survived. This writing will help you understand yourself better, clarify what the problems are, and find what you need to do to solve these problems.

Part I: The Historical Review

1. Describe in detail your childhood home life. Include descriptions of relationships with family members, and extended family members that you view as significant.
2. What is your earliest memory? What emotion(s) does this memory evoke?
3. Share two of your happiest/pleasant and two of the most painful life experiences that you have had. Be specific in describing the experiences.

4. How did these experiences affect you then and now? How have these experiences shaped the life choices you have made? What did you learn?

5. What did you learn from your family about?
   A. What it means to be a family member?
   B. Relationship boundaries.
   C. Self-care and self-responsibility.
   D. How to be a partner to someone?
   E. How to resolve conflicts and problem solve issues?
   F. How to deal with anger and other emotions?

6. How do you function in social relationships?
   A. Are you friendly, reserved, distrustful, easily hurt?
   B. How do you respond to the ideas or opinions of others?
   C. Do you easily form acquaintances/friendships?
   D. Are you able to maintain relationships?
   E. Do you have any behaviors or attitudes that create difficulties for you?
   F. Do you assert clear boundaries, limitation and expectations?

7. How did your early life experience affect self-esteem and self-confidence?

8. When did you become aware that you have emotional and behavioral difficulties that contribute to negative life experiences?

9. Explain how your difficulties have prevented you from reaching desired goals and having fulfilling relationships.

10. What are your fears, and how do they affect your life?

11. Do your difficulties increase during times of stress or discomfort resulting from job, family, or personal problems? Give examples of each.

12. Discuss how your emotional and behavioral difficulties have had a negative impact on significant relationships, intimacy, trust, caused you social problems, such as loss of friends, inability to perform sexually, unreasonable demands on others, allowing yourself to be taken advantage of, etc. Tell how they interfered with your relationships. How do you feel about that now?

13. How have your emotional and/or behavioral difficulties affected your health?

14. List the emotional and behavioral problems that you have attempted to resolve. How successful have you been?

15. Review all that you have written. Use this information to take responsibility for your life. No matter what has happened to you or what others have done it is up to you to make yourself and your life what you want them to be. This requires that you live consciously maintaining a good awareness for what you are doing and why you are doing it. Making things right is an active process not just a thinking exercise.

Part II: Putting It Together and Increasing Resilience

You have taken the time to review the impact of your early life history. Now it is time to use that information to maximize your recovery and resilience. Consider the following:

1. *Don't interpret now based on the past.* You cannot change the past but you can learn from it and grow and improve your "snap back." You have identified the trauma and how it affected you. The first point of growth will be to write about other ways to express your thoughts and feelings. This will prepare you to talk through it—to process it. This will lead to new ways of thinking.

2. *Reframing.* You are not the child who was abused, neglected, or traumatized in some other way. You are an adult who has survived it. Reframing is a way of changing the way you look at something and, thus, changing your experience of it. Reframing can turn a stressful event

into either a major trauma or a challenge to be bravely overcome. It is a way that we can alter our perceptions of stressors and, thus, relieve significant amounts of stress and create a more positive life before actually making any changes in our circumstances.

3. *Asserting control*. Identify the areas of control and choice available to you. You have the ability to take the steps to create a safe and positive structure of daily activity. Being active decreases anxiety and reinforces a sense of control. As control is asserted the emotional and biological responses to stress are decreased.

4. *Engage a support system—personal and professional*. Reach out and accept the support from those you trust and feel good spending time with. From that group of personal social support, there is likely someone that you will be confident in talking to about your thoughts and feelings. It is important to also engage your therapist or other professional support to help you work through what you can take away that identifies and strengthens your resilience.

5. Learn about your physiology. There is a lot of information about how our mind and body responds to stress when we have been exposed to trauma. This is important because there is the feeling of being out of control. When you allow yourself to understand and accept your responses you can then begin to problem-solve how to change the way you think. The changes in thinking will help change the way you feel and help with positive problem solving.

   A. Fear stimulates vivid pictures of what's about to go wrong—and how to get out of the situation. Your focus narrows, your heart races, your senses perk up. Everything unrelated to your safety fades. The fear response is automatic and is very beneficial to survival. Without fear we might take unnecessary risks. However, when there is fear but we cannot adequately assess the risk *fear becomes anxiety*.

**However, anxiety can serve a corrective purpose, bringing us back to what is real and allow for purposeful problem solving.

6. Building confidence and self-esteem. It is essential to live the functionality of life fully. It reinforces daily "I can do it." The basics for strengthening confidence and self-esteem include the following:

   A. Choosing to be genuinely grateful for what is right and good in your life
   B. Setting goals and breaking down the steps to accomplish them
   C. Making choices—thinking through problem solving and decision making that engages the brain to function at its highest level. This process also reinforces self-reliance and learning from what works and what doesn't.
   D. Appropriate risk taking. Unforeseen opportunity for personal growth can come from risk taking. We learn from risk and sometimes those lessons provide new paths we would not have even considered possible. Risk taking can clearly be personally and professionally beneficial. It requires you to do your homework to clarify the degree of risk and the steps indicated for the outcome you are seeking. Risk could be as simple as going to a social gathering when you generally avoid them and finding that you have had a positive experience and you were invited to attend another gathering or activity as well.
   E. Develop new interest and stretch your personal growth. Developing new skills and knowledge are a positive aspect of personal development and are a functional distraction from dwelling on stress thinking traps.

7. Happiness increases positive moods and capitalizes on your strengths. According to Martin Seligman, happiness has three parts: pleasure, engagement, and meaning. Pleasure is the "feel good" part of happiness. Engagement refers to living a "good life" of work, family, friends, and hobbies. Meaning refers to using our strengths to contribute to a larger purpose. Seligman says that all three are important, but that of the three, engagement and meaning make the most difference to living a happy life.

8. Working through sadness and grief. Sadness is a response to loss (or potential loss) and can be a powerful motivator of change. Loss and grief are an expected and normal aspect of life. There are benefits to surviving hard times. Such as increased emotional strength and resilience, and being thoughtful about your own experiences can lead to an increased awareness for others who need help. When you have felt despair you know you have to find a foothold wherever you can—sometimes that can be holding onto the side of a cliff. At least you are holding and have the potential to pull yourself up—sometimes with the help of others. That is part of the opportunity for reset.

BUILDING A STRONG SUPPORT SYSTEM

DEVELOPING AND UTILIZING SOCIAL SUPPORTS

When someone lacks emotional health they tend to withdraw from pleasurable activities and socially isolate. One important way to regain emotional health is to develop and utilize social supports.

We all need several good friends to talk to, spend time with, and to be supported by with their care and understanding. For someone to be a part of your support system requires that you care for them and trust them. A partner or family member is a likely candidate for your support system. You may develop relationships with people through activities or interests that you share. These relationships could become strong enough to become part of your support system. Other resources could be clubs or other social group affiliations that you feel a part of and feel important to. Whoever the person or group is, it is necessary that there be mutual care, positive regard, and trust.

CHARACTERISTICS OF A SUPPORTIVE RELATIONSHIP

1. Objectivity and open-mindedness. They let you describe who you are and how you feel. They validate you.
2. They support and affirm your individuality and recognize your strengths. They validate and encourage your goals.
3. They empathize with you. They understand your life circumstances and how you are affected by your life experiences.
4. They accept you as you are without being judgmental. You can ask one another for help and support.
5. You can laugh with them and be playful. You will both enjoy it.
6. They are at your side, supporting you to do whatever is important to you.
7. List the people that make up your support system:

   A. _____

   B. _____

   C. _____

   D. _____

   E. _____

8. If you didn't have anyone to list as your support system or only one to two people don't feel bad about yourself and give up. What you have done is to accomplish the first step in understanding what you need to do: such as developing new resources and activities so that you develop new resources. The good news is that there are endless choices for connecting with people and increasing the potential for relationships/social.

9. What stands in your way of developing your support system (check the items that apply to you):
    A. you have a hard time reaching out
    B. you have a hard time making and keeping friends
    C. low self-esteem
    D. you tend to be very needy and draining to others
    E. you become overly dependent and wear people out
    F. you lack the social skills necessary to develop relationships
    G. you have inappropriate behaviors which embarrass others
    H. you are unreliable

10. What is it that you need and want from your support system (check the items that apply to you):
    __someone to talk to
    __understanding
    __someone to stand up for you
    __companionship
    __caring
    __sharing
    __someone to watch or monitor you
    __someone who will listen to you
    __someone to do things with
    __someone who writes to you or phones you
    __mutual support and positive regard

11. Are there other things that you would want or expect from a friend?

    _____

    _____

    _____

12. People who help you get started in making the changes necessary to develop a strong support system include your therapist, minister, and various support groups in your community. There are also many helpful books that have been written that you can find in the psychology or self-help sections of a bookstore. The main thing to do is make a commitment to yourself to develop a support system and to not give up.

HOW TO BUILD AND KEEP A SUPPORT SYSTEM

1. Requires being emotionally well and keeping moods stable. What do you do to maintain stable moods? _____

    _____

    _____

2. To take care of myself. List your self-care behaviors. _____

    _____

3. Define what you must do for yourself versus what is reasonable for others to do for you (avoid dependency). _____

    _____

4. Develop appropriate social skills. *Learn to listen.

This can be done by working with your therapist, reading and practicing the techniques you read about, participating in activities in the community or special groups, taking a class at adult education programs if available, watching what other people do, and what responses they get. Be involved.

5. What resources are available to you? _____

_____

6. Participate in volunteer work and be supportive of others.

Whether it is doing volunteer work or being supportive to people you know, it is good practice. Where could you volunteer? _____

_____

7. Who supports you and how can you be supportive back to them? _____

_____

_____

8. Make it a point to keep in touch with friends and acquaintances.

When was the last time you invited someone to do something or made an effort to get together? If it didn't work out was it the timing, the activity, or someone who really isn't capable of being a social support for you? What are you going to do to become more successful maintaining relationships? _____

_____

9. How will you know if you are making progress in developing a support system? _____

_____

10. Are you a helpful and positive participant in someone else's support system?

_____

SELF-MONITORING CHECKLIST

MANAGEMENT BEHAVIORS

__ getting up in the morning
__ getting dressed and ready for the day
__ practicing good hygiene
__ start the day off with a positive affirmation
__ thinking positive through the day
__ maintaining good awareness for my thoughts and behaviors
__ problem-solving issues instead of avoiding
__ attending work or school daily
__ participating in pleasurable activities
__ spending time with people I enjoy
__ getting my needs met appropriately
__ getting adequate sleep and rest

__ exercise
__ eating nutritionally
__ meditation or relaxation techniques
__ getting in touch with your spirituality
__ not engaging in self-defeating behaviors
__ not engaging in self-destructive behaviors
__ spending time outside
__ keeping busy
__ consistently taking medication as prescribed
__ maintaining a balance of rest and pleasurable activities
__ using my resources
__ attending support groups or meetings
__ attending therapy
__ Find something positive in everyday

What strategies have you found for decreasing or eliminating your depression?

_____

_____

_____

_____

_____

DAILY ACTIVITIES

Using a schedule of daily activities can alleviate the pressure of trying to get through a day in a positive and useful manner because it outlines expected activity.

A person who is feeling depressed may spend an entire day or many days doing nothing but existing. This inactivity and lack of accomplishment can maintain or contribute to your depression. Because self-esteem is an active process, when a person is lacking activity and accomplishments in their life they develop low self-esteem. When they have low self-esteem, they tend to devalue their efforts, viewing whatever they do as unimportant. To feel worthwhile will take a commitment to develop a self-care program that includes a positive attitude, adequate nutrition, exercise, relaxation, participation in pleasurable activities, and a daily structure for facilitating the development of a healthy and fulfilling lifestyle.

In everyone's life there are responsibilities that must be taken care of ranging from professional duties to housekeeping chores. Some of these tasks may be enjoyable while others are not. When you develop your daily activity schedule be sure to create a balance of pleasure and accomplishment. This will contribute to a sense of wellness. Some things may be both a pleasure and an accomplishment. Some examples are given so that you will have an idea of the types of things to include in your daily activity schedule.

__ get out of bed
__ get dressed
__ good hygiene
__ go to work
__ read the paper
__ have coffee/tea
__ balance the checkbook
__ go for a walk
__ paint/draw
__ talk with a friend

__ lunch with a friend/someone special
__ go to a support group
__ make dinner
__ wash the dishes
__ do the laundry
__ gardening
__ watch a movie
__ write a letter
__ journal writing
__ relaxation/meditation/affirmations
__ helping others
__ listening to music

DAILY ACTIVITY SCHEDULE

_____

DATE: _____

MOOD(S): _____

Time	Planned activity and expectations	Actual activity	How it felt
7–8 a.m.			
8–9 a.m.			
9–10 a.m.			
10–11 a.m.			
11–12 noon			
12–1 p.m.			
1–2 p.m.			
2–3 p.m.			
3–4 p.m.			
4–5 p.m.			
5–6 p.m.			
6–7 p.m.			
7–8 p.m.			
8–9 p.m.			
9–10 p.m.			

Keep a daily activity schedule until you feel that whatever is underlying your current struggle is manageable and you feel that you do not need the support of this strategy to remain focused and stable.

CHALLENGING NEGATIVE AND IRRATIONAL SELF-TALK

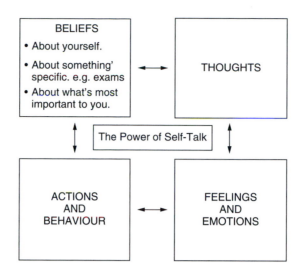

*Be careful how you talk to yourself because you are listening.

RATIONAL THINKING

Much of what a person feels is caused by what they say to themselves. People talk to themselves all day long with little awareness for it. This is because self-talk is automatic and carried out repeatedly. However, people generally have some idea for the type of self-talk they use once exploring the subject of self-talk begins.

When people are not sure why something is the way it is they often start looking outside themselves for the source of unhappiness or other form of emotional distress. They have the impression that what is happening around them is what "makes" them feel the way they do. While there is likely to be some contribution from their environment, it is really their thoughts and interpretation about the situation that causes the associated feelings.

$$\text{Situation or Experience} \rightarrow \text{Distorted-Negative Self-Talk} \rightarrow \text{Emotional Response}$$

Therefore, what a person thinks about a situation is likely the greatest factor influencing how they will feel and respond. The most positive aspect about this is that a person has choices. Choices combined with effort leads to change in the way they interpret events and think about them.

It is likely that if they do engage in negative self-talk that they have been doing it for a long time. It may have even started when they were very young. It starts by a person telling themselves negative things about themselves and their life situation. Not surprisingly, these types of internal messages could start when a person is young because they are unhappy, a negative thing may be repeatedly said to them which becomes part of their view of the world or identity, they didn't feel like they had control over their life, and/or they have not been taught good coping skills. All of this makes it easier for a person to externalize or blame the way that they feel and their responses to someone or something outside of themselves and their control instead of taking responsibility for their own feelings and actions.

As an adult, all of this negative self-talk is seen as perfectionism, chronic worrying, always being a victim, self-critical, low self-esteem, phobias, panic attacks, generalized anxiety, depression, and hopelessness. It is also possible that when people feel so bad emotionally that it affects them physically, e.g., headaches, abdominal distress, intestinal disorders, seems to be sick all the time.

If you experience physical symptoms, you should consult your physician. Examples:

Distorted Thinking—Negative Self-talk

1. What if I don't pass the employment exam (worrier)?
2. Am a weak person (critic)?

3. I will never get over this (victim).

4. I will be devastated if I don't get acceptance/approval (perfectionist).

List some negative self-statements that you are aware of:

1. _____

_____

2. _____

_____

3. _____

_____

4. _____

_____

5. _____

_____

6. _____

_____

7. _____

_____

8. _____

_____

9. _____

_____

10. _____

_____

The realization that you are mostly responsible for how you feel is empowering. When you take responsibility for your reactions you begin to take charge and have mastery over your life. Once you become aware of the distortions in your thinking you will be able to change negative thoughts to positive ones. Accomplishing this is one of the most important steps to living a happier, more effective and emotionally distressing free life.

THINKING DISTORTIONS

1. All-or-nothing thinking. You see things in black and white categories. If your performance falls short of perfect, you see yourself as a total failure.
2. Overgeneralization. You see a single negative event as a never-ending pattern of defeat.
3. Mental filter. You pick a single negative detail and dwell on it exclusively so that your vision of all reality becomes darkened, like the drop of ink that discolors the entire beaker of water.
4. Disqualifying the positive. You reject positive experiences by insisting that they don't count for some reason or other. In this way you can maintain a negative belief that is contradicted by your everyday experiences.
5. Jumping to conclusions. You make a negative interpretation even though there are no definite facts that convincingly support your conclusion.
   A. Mind reading. You arbitrarily conclude that someone is reacting negatively to you, and you don't bother to check it out.
   B. The fortune telling error. You anticipate that things will turn out badly, and you will feel convinced that your prediction is an already established fact.
6. Magnification, catastrophizing, or minimization. You exaggerate the importance of things (such as failure, falling short of the mark, or someone else's achievement), or you inappropriately shrink things until they appear tiny (your good and desirable qualities or someone else's limitations).
7. Emotional reasoning. You assume that your negative emotions necessarily reflect the way things really are, "I feel it, so it must be true."
8. Should statements. You try to motivate yourself with shoulds and shouldn'ts, as if you had to be whipped and punished before you could accomplish anything. "Musts" and "oughts" also fall into this faulty-thinking category. The emotional consequence is guilt. When you direct should statements toward others, you feel anger, frustration, and resentment.
9. Labeling and mislabeling. This is an extreme form of overgeneralization. Instead of describing your error, you attach a negative label to yourself, "I'm a loser." When someone else's behavior rubs you the wrong way you attach a negative label to him, "He's a jerk." Mislabeling involves describing an event with language that is highly colored and emotionally loaded.
10. Personalization. You see yourself as the cause of some problem, or take on someone's opinion as having more value than it does.

REALISTIC SELF-TALK

1. This too shall pass and my life will be better.
2. I am a worthy and good person.
3. I am doing the best I can, given my history and level of current awareness.
4. Like everyone else, I am a fallible person and at times will make mistakes and learn from them.
5. What is—is (It is whatever it is, deal with what is…).
6. Look at how much I have accomplished, and I am still progressing.
7. There are no failures only different degrees of success.
8. Be honest and true to myself.

9. It is okay to let myself be distressed for a while.

10. I am not helpless. I can and will take the steps needed to get through this crisis.

11. I will remain engaged and involved instead of isolating and withdrawing during this situation.

12. This is an opportunity, instead of a loss or a threat. I will use this experience to learn something new, to change my direction, to try a new approach or to help others.

13. One step at a time.

14. I can stay calm when talking to difficult people.

15. I know I will be okay no matter what happens.

16. He/she is responsible for their reaction to me.

17. This difficult/painful situation will soon be over.

18. I can stand anything for a while.

19. In the long run who will remember, or care?

20. Is this really important enough to become upset about?

21. Don't really need to prove myself in this situation.

22. Other people's opinions are just their opinions.

23. Others are not perfect, and I won't put pressure on myself by expecting them to be.

24. I cannot control the behaviors of others, I can only control my own behaviors.

25. I am not responsible to make other people okay.

26. I will respond appropriately, and not be reactive.

27. I feel better when I don't make assumptions about the thoughts or behaviors of others.

28. I will enjoy myself, even when life is hard.

29. I will enjoy myself while catching up on all I want to accomplish. I will find ways to stop and smell the roses, even when I am working hard.

30. Don't sweat the small stuff—it's all small stuff.

31. My past does not control my future.

32. I choose to be a happy person.

33. I am respectful to others and deserve to be respected in return.

34. There is less stress in being optimistic and choosing to be in control.

35. I am willing to do whatever is necessary to make tomorrow better.

THOUGHT STOPPING

Now that you are aware of negative self-talk and how it affects how you think, feel, and respond you are ready to learn some additional strategies to facilitate new ways of thinking.

Thought stopping is a technique that has been used for years to treat obsessive and phobic thoughts. It involves concentrating on the unwanted thoughts, and after a short time, suddenly stopping and emptying the thoughts from your mind. The command "stop" or a loud noise is generally used to interrupt the unwanted and unpleasant thoughts.

As previously discussed regarding negative self-talk, it has been well documented that negative and frightening thoughts invariably precede negative and frightening emotions. If the thoughts can be controlled, overall levels of stress and other negative emotions can be significantly decreased.

Thought stopping is recommended when the problem is primarily cognitive, rather than acted out. It is indicated when specific thoughts or images are repeatedly experienced as painful or leading to unpleasant emotional states. Assess which recurrent thoughts are the most painful and intrusive. Make an effort to understand the role that these thoughts have had on emotional functioning and how you experience your environment in general, based on the following statements.

Explore Your List of Stressful Thoughts (From Self-talk Section)

1. No interference. This thought does not interfere with other activities.

2. Interferes a little. This thought interferes a little with other activities, or wastes a little of my time.

3. Interferes moderately. This thought interferes with other activities, or wastes some of my time.

4. Interferes a great deal. This thought stops me from doing a lot of things, and wastes a lot of time everyday.

Thought-Stopping Practice

1. Close your eyes and imagine a situation where the stressful thought is likely to occur. Be honest about what your response would be and include the negative and/or distressing thought related to this situation.

2. Interrupt the thought

   A. Set a timer or alarm of some sort to go off in 3 min. Close your eyes and imagine the stressful thought as stated in step 1. When the alarm goes off, shout "stop." Let your mind empty of the stressful thoughts, leaving only neutral and nonstressful thoughts. Set a goal of about 30 s after the stop, with your mind remaining blank. If the stressful thoughts return during that brief period, shout "stop" again.

   B. Using a tape recorder, record yourself shouting "stop" at the varying intervals of 3, 2, 3, 1 min. Repeat the taped "stop" messages several times at 5-s intervals. Proceed the same way with your timer or alarm. The tape recording is beneficial to strengthen and shape your thought control.

   C. The next step is to control the thought-stopping cue without an alarm or tape recorder. When you are thinking about the stressful thoughts shout "stop." When you succeed in eliminating the thought(s) on several occasions by interrupting the thought with "stop" said in a normal voice, then start interrupting the thought by whispering the "stop" cue. When you are able to interrupt the thought with the whispered cue begin to use a subvocal cue of "stop" (moving your tongue as if you were saying it out loud). When you have success at this level, then you will be able to stop the thoughts alone or in public without making a sound and not calling attention to yourself.

   D. The final step of thought stopping involves thought substitution. In place of the distressing thought, use a positive, affirming, and assertive statement. For example, if you were afraid to go out on a lake in a boat you might say to yourself, "This is beautiful and relaxing out here." Develop several alternative statements to combat the negative one, since the same response may lose its power through repetition.

Special Considerations

1. Failure with your first attempt at thought stopping means that you have selected a thought that is very difficult to eliminate. In this situation choose a stressful thought that is either less stressful or intrusive than your first choice. Repeat the technique.

2. If the subvocalized "stop" is not successful, and saying "stop" out loud embarrasses you, then keep a rubber band around your wrist so that no one can see it and when the thought occurs snap it. Or pinch yourself, or press your fingernails into your palms. The idea is to interrupt and focus your awareness on changing negative self-talk.

3. You should be aware that thought stopping takes time. The thought will return and you will have to eliminate it again. The main idea is to stop the thought when it returns again, and to concentrate on something else. The thoughts will return less and less in most cases and eventually cease.

REFRAMING

You have learned about how negative self-talk affects how you think, feel, and respond. Now you are going to learn additional strategies for changing how you think and what you do related to how you will interpret situations and how you feel.

Often the way you interpret things is linked to irrational beliefs or negative self-statements. Reframing or relabeling is a technique you can use to modify or change your view of a problem or a behavior. You will also find it helpful in decreasing defensiveness and to mobilize your resources.

Therefore, reframing provides alternative ways to view a problem behavior or perception. Look for over-generalizations like never and always.

For example:

If labeled	Stubborn	Independent or persistent
	Greedy	Ambitious
	Anger	Loving or concern

When a behavior is labeled negatively ask the following questions:

1. Identify a situation that typically produces uncomfortable or distressing feelings.
2. Try to become aware of what you automatically focus on during the situation.
3. What are you feeling and thinking?

To challenge the long-term negative labeling ask the following questions:

1. Is there a larger or different context in which this behavior has positive value?
2. What else could this behavior mean?
3. How else could this situation be described?

STEPS TO SUCCESSFUL REFRAMING

1. To understand and accept an individual's belief that perceptions about a problem situation can cause emotional distress. The first step of reframing is to educate yourself about negative thinking patterns that may exacerbate your stress levels.
2. To become aware of what is automatically attended to or focused on in problem situations. Being aware of them is an important part of challenging and ultimately changing them. One thing you can do is just become more mindful of your thoughts, as though you're an observer. You can use imagery or role paying to reenact situations to become more aware of what thoughts and feelings are present. Keep a journal of your observations and start recording what's happening in your life and your thoughts surrounding these events, and then examine these thoughts through your new "lens" to get more practice in catching these thoughts. Another helpful practice is meditation where you learn to quiet your mind and examine your thoughts. When you identify your perceptions and feelings you will be able to be prepared for the next step.
3. Identification of alternative perceptions. Generally this means to attend to other features of the situation that have a positive or neutral connotation. The reframe must fit, be acceptable to the individual, and at least as valid as the perception they are reframing. An effective part of reframing involves examining the truth and accuracy (or lack thereof) of these thoughts. Challenge yourself to identify some other ways to interpret the same set of events.
4. Modifying the perceptions in a problem situation is designed to break the old patterns by creating new and more effective reframes. This requires commitment and practice. When you're looking at a potentially stressful situation see if you can view it as a challenge versus a threat. Look for the "gift" in each situation (meaning), and see if you can see your stressors on the more positive side of reality that still fits the facts of your situation, but that is less negative and more optimistic and positive.

5. Homework using real-life situations and recording it in your journal will reinforce desired change(s). The experience, perception with associated thoughts, feelings, and responses, and the chosen reframe (it may be helpful to list several possible alternative reframes). Reframing can actually decrease the discomfort.

PRACTICE REFRAMING HOW YOU INTERPRET SITUATIONS

You have a choice in how you view or interpret situations. If you tend to overgeneralize or focus on the negatives, you make it difficult to cope effectively, you decrease your opportunity for happiness, and you remain stuck instead of adjusting and adapting.

1. Identify several situations that typically produce uncomfortable or distressing feelings.

_____

_____

_____

_____

_____

2. What are your automatic focus, thoughts, and feelings in each situation?

_____

_____

_____

_____

_____

3. What is a more useful way to view each situation which offers you choices and the potential for growth?

_____

_____

_____

_____

DEFENSE MECHANISMS

Defense mechanisms, the way that people protect themselves from things they don't want to deal with. They are a part of everyday life. They are viewed as coping techniques that reduce anxiety. They are generally unconscious and may result in healthy or unhealthy consequences. The may also be used manipulate, deny, or distort reality. There is an immense list of defense mechanisms. It is beneficial to read more about defense mechanisms so that you can better understand your use of them. Below some of the most common defense mechanisms are listed with a basic definition.

DEFENSE MECHANISM DEFINITIONS

1. Denial — Protecting oneself from unpleasant aspects of life by refusing to perceive, acknowledge, or face them.

2. Rationalization — Trying to prove one's actions "made sense" or were justified: making excuses.

3. Intellectualization — Hiding one's feelings about something painful behind thoughts; keeping opposing attitudes apart by using logic-tight comparisons.

4. Displacement — Misdirecting pent-up feelings toward something or someone that is less threatening than that, which actually triggered the feeling response.

5. Projection — Blaming. Assuming that someone has a particular quality or qualities that one finds distasteful.

6. Reaction Formation — Adopting actions and beliefs, to an exaggerated degree that are directly opposite to those previously accepted.

7. Undoing — Trying to superficially repair or make up for an action without dealing with the complex effects of that deed, "magical thinking."

8. Withdrawal — Becoming emotionally uninvolved by pulling back and being passive.

9. Introjection — Adopting someone else's values and standards without exploring whether or not they actually fit oneself; "shoulds" or "ought to's."

10. Fantasy — Trying to handle problems or frustrations through daydreaming or imaginary solutions.

11. Repression — Unconsciously blocking out painful thoughts.

12. Identification — Trying to feel more important by associating oneself with someone or something that is highly valued.

13. Acting Out — Repeatedly doing actions to keep from being uptight without weighing the possible results of those actions.

14. Compensation — Hiding a weakness by stressing too strongly the desirable strength. Overindulging in one area to make up for frustration in another.

15. Regression — Under stress, readopting actions done at a less mature stage of development.

DEFENSE MECHANISMS

Defense mechanisms are a way of coping with anxiety, reducing tension, and restoring a sense of balance to a person's emotional experience. Defense mechanisms happen on an unconscious level and tend to distort reality to make it easier for the person to deal with. Everyone uses defense mechanisms as a way to cope with the everyday garden-variety mild to moderate anxiety. When defense mechanisms are used to an extreme, they interfere with a person's ability to tell the difference between what is real and what is not.

Defense mechanisms are used independently or in combination with one another. They are used to various degrees, depending on how well they meet a person's needs to alleviate distress or to avoid coping with the reality of a given situation.

Choose three defense mechanisms and describe how you use each. Additionally, describe how it prevents your personal growth. Identify constructive alternatives for coping that you could use instead of the defense mechanisms.

1. Defense Mechanism: _____

2. Defense Mechanism: _____

3. Defense Mechanism: _____

OVERCOMING WORRY

If a problem belongs to you do something about it… If there is a problem but it doesn't belong to you then let it go. Regardless, worrying does nothing to change it.

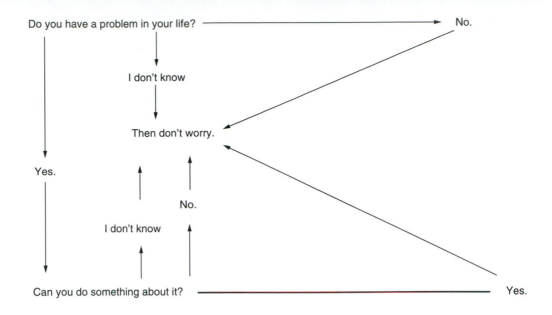

Worry plays a significant role in causing a number of psychological and health problems. Worry is very powerful, and if you worry constantly the quality of your daily life and relationships will be affected. Consider the following for changing the way you think about worry and deal with it.

1. Establish "worry time"
   It is common to hear that people find it difficult to stop worrying. Worry is an intruder—interfering with work and pleasure. A useful technique for dealing with this is to schedule your "worry time." Therefore, as you become aware of worry it can be acknowledged and put in the "worry file" to worry about at the scheduled worry time. Another option is creating a "delete file" for dispensing with worries.

2. Review the problem and ask, "does it belong to me" and "is it solvable?" If the problem doesn't belong to you let it go. If it does belong to you then identify the options for dealing with it. Thinking about a problem is part of the problem-solving process, but ruminative worry is not—it is simply worry and it does not help anything. But does contribute is stress, anxiety, and depression.

3. Develop realistic expectations. Aim for a reasonable resolution to problems not perfection. When a person is aware of what they are doing and they know the problem it causes them, the motivation for continuing to behave in a way that harms them needs to be questioned. So, merely evaluate the potential solutions and focus on what is right.

4. Challenging negative self-talk. An example is the focus on what is wrong or could go wrong, over estimating how likely things are to happen, catastrophizing, etc. The goal is to become more realistic in how you evaluate the possibilities and how you deal with them.

5. Be good to you. Generally, people tend to be kinder and more objective with their best friend than themselves. When talking with a friend it isn't negative, judgmental, or critical. Treat yourself the same way.

6. Think with your head and your heart. All you can do is the best you can do. If something doesn't really have a solution it means that you need to find some way to cope with it.

7. Remain calm. It is good for your mind and your body. If you don't practice balance and calm—choosing to remain a worrier, expect difficulty with concentration and attention, irritable, on-edge/snappy, sleep disturbance, etc. If you have forgotten how to achieve calm practice some relaxation techniques such as deep-belly breathy, muscle relaxation, visualizations, meditation, etc., and combine with regular exercise.

8. Mindfulness. This is another word for meditation and being in the moment "the now." Thinking about what is going on right now instead of what has already happened (past) or

may happen (future). Being in the moment requires your attention and that means worrying gets pushed down on the list. Consider taking a meditation class.

9. Recover is step 1 = sleep. Worry intrudes on quality sleep and may even interrupt sleep. Keep worry during your "worry time" and practice sleep regimen that prepares your mind and body for unwinding and letting go of the day so that you can get a good night sleep.

10. It's not all up to you. Remember be realistic, focused on positives and that it is important for you to take time for yourself.

ANGER MANAGEMENT

ANGER 101

Anger is an emotion that is viewed as neither good nor bad. It is a normal emotion.

Therefore, it is not the feeling that is the problem it is what you do with it. If you have a problem with anger management you can learn to appropriately express what you feel without intimidating others, hurting other or harming property. There is value in learning anger management. Anger is an emotion when experienced and expressed in an unhealthy and negative manner impairs judgment and thus, harms every possibility in your life. Mastering the art of anger management takes work, but the more you practice, the easier it will get. There are likely other benefits as well—improved relationships, less stress, improved focus on goals, and self-care. Overall, leading a healthier life.

UNDERSTANDING ANGER

1. What are the stressors, fears, and frustrations that are at the bottom of your anger?

   _____

   _____

2. Triggers: What do you think or say to yourself that increases anger?

   _____

   _____

3. Is anger effective in getting others to do what you want them to do? Explain.

   _____

   _____

4. What are more effective techniques you can use to get what you want and need?

   _____

   _____

5. What are resources or sources of social support you utilize when you are feeling angry?

   _____

   _____

6. What are you going to do differently to manage anger? How can you decrease or eliminate feelings of anger?

_____

_____

7. Are there things that you need to limit or eliminate from your life (obligations, relationships, saying yes to everyone, etc.)?

_____

_____

8. How can you get what you want and need through compromise and problem solving?

_____

_____

9. What are your goals of anger management and how are you going to go about the changes needed to reach your goals? (e.g., Goal: I choose to no longer feel angry about my husband's behavior. Object: Recognize and accept that he is responsible for his own behavior)

_____

_____

10. If you feel that you have tried everything and are unable to resolve issues with a person or situation the only thing left for you to do is to *let go*. How will you be able to make peace with such a situation?

_____

_____

11. How do you feel about having wasted so much of your energy, time, and life on anger?

_____

_____

12. Can you identify a role model in your life that demonstrates how you want to manage anger?

_____

_____

*Consider the following facts and beliefs about anger to increase your understanding about anger, and how your anger affects you.

1. Socialized to believe that anger is wrong.
2. Anger is associated with anxiety or fear of a person.
3. Anger is used to control and intimidate others.
4. Fear of anger.
    A. Fear of your own anger.
    B. Fear of the anger of others.
5. Anger is a normal reaction to a stimulus.
6. A belief that you are unable to control anger.
7. Physiological response associated with anger (survival emotion).
8. Pretending that you don't get angry can make you sick—it is called internalizing.
9. Blocked and unexpressed anger does not go away.
10. When not expressed assertively and appropriately, anger tends to pop up in destructive ways, such as resentment and hostility.

CONSEQUENCES FOR NOT EXPRESSING ANGER

1. Depression—experienced as feeling incompetent.
2. Anxiety—often experienced with fear.
3. Guilt—socialized to believe that it is wrong to feel angry.
4. Self-destructive activities and negative health consequences associated with the buildup.
    A. Drinking/drugs
    B. Eating to mask feelings
    C. Psychosomatic Illnesses
        1. Headache
        2. Gastrointestinal problems
        3. Hypertension
5. Aggression/violence.
6. Disguised anger.
    A. Hostile humor (sarcasm)
    B. Nagging
    C. Silence and withdrawal
    D. Withholding sex
    E. Displacement

STUCK ON ANGER

This is an explanation not an excuse. Use the information to increase your awareness and self-responsibility.

1. When a person is stressed and fatigued anger pops up more.
2. It not uncommon that a person does not even know why they are angry or mistakenly identify the reason for their anger
3. Some facets of anger are historical. That's right sometimes someone feels they were hurt, cheated or didn't get what they wanted as a child and they are carrying that with them
4. We often become angry when we see a trait in others we don't like in ourselves.
5. Underlying many current angers are old disappointments, traumas, and triggers.
6. We get angry when a current event brings up an old unresolved situation from the past.
7. Familiar disappointments or pain. We often feel strong emotion when a situation has a similar content, words, or energy that we have felt before.

ANGER AND SELF-RESPONSIBILITY

Anger is a normal, healthy emotion. When it is expressed appropriately you are letting go of the stress and frustration that you are experiencing, and those around you understand and accept that you are upset. When anger is expressed inappropriately with blame and aggression it can be a destructive force—both to the person experiencing it and for those subjected to it. Below is a diagram that shows the cycle of anger from the buildup through the explosive and postexplosive phase. With each phase the consequences increase for the person expressing inappropriate anger as well as the harm to others and/or property.

As with other things that are negative, there is a tendency to hold something or someone else responsible. When you hold someone else responsible for your stress, anxiety, or frustration you feel that you have the right to express it in an aggressive manner.

1. You are responsible for your own life, the choices you make, and the quality of your life experience.

2. Clarify your thoughts, feelings, needs, and wants. You are the only one who knows what goes on inside of you.

3. Compromise with others when wants or needs are in conflict, or an issue of some contention. It is unreasonable to always or rarely get what you want. Therefore, with mutual respect, compromise, and negotiation people can seek an equitable solution.

4. Develop effective skills for managing your life. Examine the difficulties that you experience, assess how you contribute to the difficulties, and decide what you are willing to do differently.

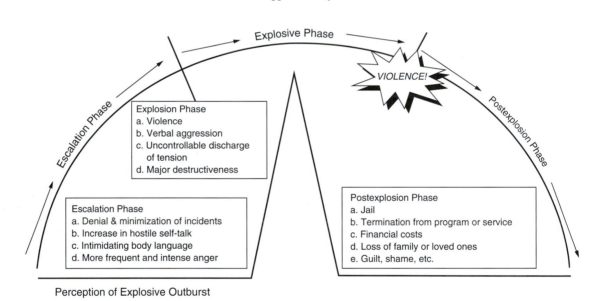

The Aggression Cycle*

One of the primary objectives of anger management treatment is to prevent reaching the explosion phase.

*Adapted from the Cycle of Violence by Lenore Walker (1979). *The Battered Woman.* New York: Harper & Row.

Source: SAMHSA; Anger Management for Substance Abuse and Mental Health. HSS Publication No. (SMA) 12-4210.

STEPS OF ANGER MANAGEMENT

1. Identify what underlies your anger.
   A. Anger is not always what it appears. It could be a cover-up for other underlying issues. This requires increased awareness for what the anger is hiding such as hurt, shame, vulnerability, insecurity, oppression, embarrassment, etc. Anger may be the safest emotion to express if you are

avoiding other negative emotions and fear. It could mean that you have practiced anger for a long time or that you are giving yourself permission to behave badly. Some possibilities that improve self-understanding if this is the case can be derived from observing your response patterns.

1. When a person has a different opinion than you, it feels like they are against you
2. It is difficult to express emotions other than anger
3. It is very difficult to compromise with others

2. Identify triggers and warning signs of anger. Contrary to what people often say, the explosions don't just come from nowhere. There are thoughts and feelings associated with how you *interpret* what is happening. Yes, it is your interpretation of what is said or done by others not their actual words or behaviors that trigger the anger you react with.

   A. Be careful of the following kinds of thinking patterns:
      1. Blaming. Everything is always someone else's fault.
      2. Overgeneralizing. Stay away from absolutes such as always and never.
      3. Obsessing. A lack of flexibility "must," "should."
      4. Assumptions. Assuming that you know what someone else is thinking or feeling.
      5. Focusing on negatives and letting them build up. Refusing to acknowledge what is positive to find the negative in everything.

*Avoid spending time with people, places, or situations that trigger your anger. If there is a pattern of a negative outcome/anger associated with anyone or anything then consider how to problem-solve or avoid these triggers.

3. Increased awareness for the warning signs of anger.
   A. Identify how anger feels
   B. Identify how your body language changes (nonverbal communication)
   C. How do others respond when you are angry (are they fearful, avoidant, or manipulate you into being angry)

4. Keeping anger in check by taking a time out or just cooling down. Once you are able to identify triggers and patterns associated with anger then you can work on developing the skills of dealing with anger to prevent it from escalating. Below are a few ideas:
   A. Deep breathing.
   B. Exercise. Physical activity can help reduce stress that can cause you to become angry. If you feel your anger escalating, go for a brisk walk or run, or spend some time doing other enjoyable physical activities.
   C. Identifying physical sensation associated with anger (knot in stomach, muscle tension, clenching fists, etc.)
   D. Be in the moment. Use your senses, listen to calming music, use soothing fragrances (aroma therapy), visualize a calm place to be (beach, mountains, lakeside, etc.)
   E. Time out. Give yourself short breaks during times of the day that tend to be stressful. A few moments of quiet time might help you feel better prepared to handle what's ahead without getting irritated or angry.
   F. Meditate or use other calming, body relaxing regimens
   G. Being clear. Do you even have control over what is taking place? Is it worth the negative emotion? Is your response appropriate to the situation? Is it even worth your time?
   H. Use humor to release tension. Lightening up can help diffuse tension. Use humor to help you face what's making you angry and, possibly, any unrealistic expectations you have for how things should go. Avoid sarcasm, though it can hurt feelings and make things worse.

5. When does anger become a problem? Anger becomes a problem when it happens too frequently, is too intense or is expressed inappropriately.
   A. List some ways that anger affects you physically

6. What about payoffs and consequences. The inappropriate expression of anger initially has apparent payoffs (i.e., releasing tension and controlling others). However, in the long term it can lead to negative consequences.

A. List three payoffs for using anger that are familiar to you

B. List three consequences for using anger (e.g., negative effect on relationships)

7. Develop healthy appropriate ways to express anger.

    A. Clarify what you are really angry about and then go do something else with the plan of coming back to identify the problem, react in a beneficial manner, and work toward a resolution. This is positive and constructive.

    B. Rules of engagement are important. There is nothing wrong with being upset with someone, but you still need to be respectful.

        1. Think before you speak. In the heat of the moment, it's easy to say something you'll later regret. Take a few moments to collect your thoughts before saying anything—and allow others involved in the situation to do the same.

        2. Don't bring up old issues. Stay with the current issue.

        3. Be respectful of the views of others.

        4. Carefully choose your battles. Not everything is worthy of being taken to task.

        5. Know when to let it go. There are times that it is better to just agree to disagree. If you hold your anger inside, it can lead to passive-aggressive behavior like "getting back" at people without telling them why or being critical and hostile.

8. Boundaries should be clear. Adhere to the golden rule and don't treat others in a manner in which you find unacceptable.

9. Don't hold a grudge. Forgiveness is powerful for you. Holding on to negative feelings can edge out positive ones.

10. The golden rule. Treat others the way you want to be treated. Let this be a motivation for acting responsibly and respectfully toward others the same way that you expect to be treated.

DECREASE THE INTENSITY OF ANGER

It is not uncommon for people to deny that they have any feelings of anger or to simply be unaware that they are angry until it escalates to a raging explosion. Once anger begins to intensify, this feeling may be carried over into your communication with others. Unfortunately, when this happens people do not listen to what you are trying to tell them; instead they either discount your message or become defensive to the display of anger. This could simply mean that your anger has built to a level that is overwhelming to you, and when it is expressed to someone else it overwhelms that person as well.

Start paying more attention to what you are thinking, feeling, and the physical changes you experience when you are angry. It would be expected that the more intense the feeling of anger, the more intense the emotional display and physical response associated with it. It is important to increase your awareness for anger so that it can be expressed at an earlier stage with less intensity and to decrease the impact on you physically. This is assuming that your anger is a rational and reasonable response. Ultimately, only you can accept responsibility for your anger and how you choose to express it. Regardless, if you are choosing to take responsibility to express yourself honestly and appropriately consider utilizing the following information:

1. Clarify your needs, thoughts, and feelings

    A. Express them

    B. If other are not supportive or caring, problem-solve appropriate ways to get your needs met

2. Take time out

3. Exercise or do relaxation techniques to decrease body tension

4. Write about your feelings

5. Decide how you are going to take responsibility for you, and take positive action.

    A. Acknowledge that inappropriate expression of anger is not acceptable

    B. Identify how your inappropriate expression of anger and behavior has affected and harmed others

    C. Prepare yourself for predictable times of increased risk of relapse into inappropriate expressions of anger (high level of stress, overwhelmed, tired, not feeling well, stuffing your emotions)

        1. How will you prepare yourself to express yourself appropriately?

2. What are your choices for appropriate management and expression of anger?
3. If you are feeling an escalation of anger what is your plan?

LETTING GO OF ANGER

1. Awareness of your feelings and behaviors.
2. Taking responsibility for your emotions and responses.
3. Attitude will greatly influence your success or failure. If you have a negative attitude, don't expect good things to happen.
4. Self-talk. What you say to yourself will determine how you think and feel. It is a choice.
5. Don't take responsibility for people and other things that you don't have control over.
6. Develop resources and a support system that encourages the positive changes in you and in your life.
7. Self-care behaviors. People who take care of themselves feel better about who they are, have more energy to deal with frustrating situations, and are more likely to be happy and respectful.
8. Develop positive self-esteem. People who have a positive opinion about themselves are not disrespectful to others.
9. Develop positive alternative responses to counter the older anger responses.
10. Practice rehearsing new appropriate responses. Keep a journal to track and reinforce change. A journal will also clarify issues that require further problem solving, or dysfunctional patterns that are keeping you from the progress and change that you desire.

HOW TO HANDLE ANGRY PEOPLE

Backlund and Scott (Assertiveness: Get What You Want Without Being Pushy) offer the acronym "BULLETS" to consider when dealing with people who are angry:

1. *Be seated*. Place yourself in a relaxed position sitting down and ask the other person to also sit down. This could slow behavioral reactiveness as well as maintain a measure of distance for personal space.
2. *Use the person's name*. Speak directly to someone who is angry in a calm and low tone of voice addressing them by name.
3. *Lower your voice*. With awareness for the tension that is present, systematically lower your voice and do not verbally react.
4. *Listen*. *Listen* and be validating about what the person has to say. Remember, validation does not mean agreement; it is only acknowledgment for the other person's thoughts or feelings. Listen thoroughly to what the person has to say and do not try to rush him/her out the door and minimize the anger that the person is experiencing. Learning to listen is a very important skill.
5. *Eliminate humor*. Do not try to make light of the situation when someone is upset. Such a response feels disrespectful and minimizing. It immediately conveys that the person is not being taken seriously, which would escalate anger.
6. *Talk, don't argue*. Arguing increases tension and escalates feelings of anger. When things have calmed down, share your ideas that you feel are important. Discussing things rationally requires people to be relatively calm and prepared to validate and problem-solve.

7. *Slow down.* Slowing the rate of speech is a way to initiate calm and role model to the other person the manner in which to speak without addressing it directly.

For problem solving and negotiation to take place, both parties must remain calm, rational, and mutually respectful.

BOUNDARIES

DEFINING BOUNDARIES

Unhealthy

1. Sharing too much too soon or, at the other end of the spectrum, closing yourself off and not expressing your needs and wants.
2. Feeling responsible for other's happiness.
3. Inability to say "no" for fear of rejection or abandonment.
4. Weak sense of your own identity. You base how you feel about yourself on how others treat you.
5. Disempowerment. You allow others to make decisions for you; consequently, you feel powerless and do not take responsibility for your own life.

Healthy

1. Have high self-esteem and self-respect.
2. Share personal information gradually, in a mutually sharing and trusting relationship.
3. Protect physical and emotional space from intrusion.
4. Have an equal partnership where responsibility and power are shared.
5. Be assertive. Confidently and truthfully say "yes" or "no" and be okay when others say "no" to you.
6. Separate your needs, thoughts, feelings, and desires from others. Recognize that your boundaries and needs are different from others.
7. Empower yourself to make healthy respectful choices and take responsibility for yourself.

Setting Healthy Boundaries

1. When you identify the need to set a boundary, do it clearly, calmly, firmly, respectfully, and in as few words as possible. Do not justify, get angry, or apologize for the boundary you are setting.
2. You are not responsible for the other person's reaction to the boundary you are setting. You are only responsible for communicating your boundary in a respectful manner. If it upsets them, know it is their problem. Some people, especially those accustomed to controlling, abusing, or manipulating you, might test you. Plan on it, expect it, but remain firm. Remember, your behavior must match the boundaries you are setting. You cannot successfully establish a clear boundary if you send mixed messages by apologizing.
3. At first, you will probably feel selfish, guilty, or embarrassed when you set a boundary. Do it anyway and tell yourself you have a right to self-care. Setting boundaries takes practice and determination. Don't let anxiety or low self-esteem prevent you from taking care of yourself.
4. When you feel anger or resentment or find yourself whining or complaining, you probably need to set a boundary. Listen to yourself, determine what you need to do or say, then communicate assertively.

5. Learning to set healthy boundaries takes time. It is a process. Set them in your own time frame, not when someone else tells you.

6. Develop a support system of people who respect your right to set boundaries. Eliminate toxic persons from your life—those who want to manipulate, abuse, and control you.

ESTABLISHING HEALTHY BOUNDARIES

1. Personal boundaries are the physical, emotional, and mental limits we establish to protect ourselves from being manipulated, used, or violated by others. They allow us to separate who we are, and what we think and feel, from the thoughts and feelings of others. Boundaries allow all of us to define ourselves as unique individuals as well as part of a greater community. Boundaries provide the guidelines for healthy relationships founded on assertive communication all within a package of individualized values, emotions, and goals. This is true for everyone, which is why, we offer the same respect to other that we expect for ourselves.

2. To set personal boundaries means to preserve your integrity, take responsibility for who you are, and to take control of your life. You are responsible for teaching others how to treat you and boundaries clarify every aspect of those parameters.

3. Boundaries buffer you from the harsh lines of other (because you have your own) and serves as a filter that allows what is acceptable in your life and what is not. If you don't have boundaries that protect and define you, as in a strong sense of identity, you tend to derive your sense of worth and direction from others. Therefore set clear and decisive realistic limits and expectations so that others will respect your boundaries. Additionally, be prepared to reassert your boundaries and reinforce them. Not surprisingly, those who do not have strong boundaries tend to violate the rights and boundaries of others.

4. Everyone's needs and feelings are equally important. It is an issue of mutual respect. If you don't assert your right to take good care of yourself, because you are putting other people first, leaving you worn out physically and emotionally, you not only put your own health at risk but you could also deprive those close to you (family and friends) of being fully engaged and emotionally available in their lives. Therefore, encourage everyone to prioritize the self-responsibility to take care of themselves. Putting themselves last is not something only women do, but many men as well.

5. Asserting your right to say "no." If you are a people-pleaser you are going to need to learn to not put the needs of other ahead of your own. Prioritizing the needs of others can be detrimental to your own well-being. It is not selfish to take care of yourself. If you are not the best you can be, then you are not the best you can be for the relationships that you share. Healthy personal boundaries are a necessity.

6. Just as it is important to identify what is right for you—it is equally important to identify the actions and behaviors that you find unacceptable. To effectively assert healthy boundaries requires you clarify the desired and undesired so that need are appropriately and effectively met. Do not hesitate clarifying when you need emotional and physical space. Allow yourself to be who you really are without pressure from others to be anything else. Be prepared to take action if your boundaries are not respected.

7. Trust yourself. Don't look to others to decide what is right for you. You know what is best for you. *You* know your values. You know what you need, want. Healthy boundaries promote you to respect your strengths, abilities, and individuality as well as offering the same to others. When boundaries are unhealthy, it breeds neediness and codependency instead of healthy individuality and interdependence.

THE CONSEQUENCES OF UNHEALTHY BOUNDARIES AND HEALTHY BOUNDARIES

Signs of Unhealthy Boundaries

1. Not protecting your personal values or rights to please others.
2. Giving as much as you can just to give and putting your needs aside.
3. Taking as much as you can for the sake of taking.
4. Being afraid to assert yourself and your values. Letting others define you.
5. Expecting others to be mind readers and to fill your needs without you taking the responsibility to speak honestly and directly about what you want and need.
6. Feeling bad or guilty when you say no instead of acknowledging that there are appropriate times for everyone to say "no."
7. Not speaking up when you are treated in an unacceptable manner.
8. Falling apart so someone can take care of you instead of directly asking for what you want or need.
9. Falling "in love" with someone you barely know, who reaches out to you or is nice to you.
10. Accepting advances, touching, and sex that you don't want. Telling yourself, that is was "no big deal."
11. Not practicing personal space of another and/or touching a person without asking.

Signs of Healthy Boundaries

1. We protect our values and express ourselves honestly
2. We have improved self-confidence and a healthy self-concept
3. We are more in touch with realistic expectations and limitations
4. We are better able to communicate with others about our values, wants, and needs
    A. Know what you want to say and why
    B. To express yourself honestly and appropriately
    C. Listen (there are two sides)
    D. Be able to reach an understanding or consensus
5. Have better, honest, and more fulfilling relationships
6. Have more stability and control over our own lives

**It is never too late to establish healthy boundaries.

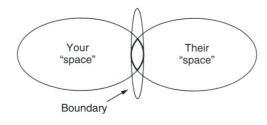

MARITAL BOUNDARIES

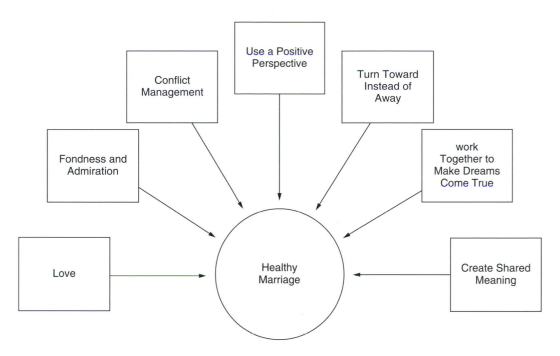

Adapted from Gottman Sound Relationship House

Boundaries define who we are along with limits, limitations, and responsibility. Having clear boundaries is the foundation for a healthy, balanced lifestyle as well as for growth through challenging times and for our ability to give and receive love. Boundaries provide the healthy tools to embrace new frontiers, hold each other close, heal wounds, protection from intruders, a place of safety and resolving conflicts, and a place of lifelong bonding. Both spouses take responsibility for their own issues instead of just reacting to one other, are not afraid of giving freedom to each other, and choose to continue to love the other person even when they feel their partner is hurting or disappointing them. Otherwise, spouses, who refuse to take ownership for their own feelings and behavior often end up in endless and meaningless arguments about all kinds of unimportant things. We are much better at identifying the infractions of other. Unfortunately, that skill does not bring desired change. We can only change ourselves and boundaries provide the rules for each one of us to be the best life partner that we can be. Woven into the following are the principles of marital boundaries offered by Dr. John Townsend as designated by (℘).

1. **Love**

   You may not think of love as a boundary but it is the most important value that nourishes a marriage and sustains it in difficult times. Love is a commitment of your entirety, i.e., for better or worse. Love in marriage is a promise that is not to be taken for granted and both parties are responsible for maintaining the health and resilience of this boundary. Marriage is meant to be a place of love, safety, trust, and growth.

   ℘ *We don't seek to change our partner—we each take responsibility for learning to change ourselves through self-examination and personal growth. Love is the core of marriage.*

2. **Honor**

   Honor in a marriage is a living statement that you are the most important person in my life. A loving marriage is a place where partners are able to freely express their feelings, ideas, and dreams—and they are shared.

   ℘ *A good marriage provides an environment of freedom and responsibility that reinforces love for each other by cultivating a psychological boundary of security.*

3. **Honesty**

Honesty is essential for an authentic and trustworthy marital relationship. A marriage without honesty is a marriage of self-centeredness, rife with major suspicions, lack of trust, and devoid of safety.

   ॐ Marriage is the merging of care, needs, partnership, and values between the husband and the wife. Such a union will overcome suffering, immature being, and selfishness. All of this will flourish with honesty.

4. **Faithfulness versus infidelity**

Fidelity is integral for a long term, committed, till death do us part kind of marriage. A commitment to faithfulness is a way to foster safety and trust within the relationship. It fosters protection, and paves the way for a deep and abiding trusting relationship. It guards the marriage from outside influences that could bring potential harm (intruders). It sets limits on outside relationships to preserve the bond between the couple. It brings assurance that this relationship, the marital relationship, is safe, nurturing, committed, and always "available." It allows each other to rest in the reliability of the relationship. It nurtures love, and guards against fear. It holds each other in high esteem and treasures each other's hearts, assuring each other "you are safe here." It always protects and preserves the bond between the both of you.

   ॐ Pay no price for your spouse's action: Each person is responsible for their own actions. Each is to carry their own load. A couple is to carry each other in their family life, but they cannot take responsibility for each other's feelings or behaviors. If you have trespassed on your partner you cannot seek to make them responsible for your choices. We ought to admit our fault and repent for the damage we have committed in our marriage. However, rarely does one party alone cause marital problems while the other party bears no responsibility. Most likely, both parties share responsibility.

5. **Forgiveness**

This is a part of the love and commitment that you have pledged by getting married. Marriage has a basic foundation of goodwill. It is a commitment to look out for the best interests of one another—to protect one another. Therefore, it is essential, in the act of protecting the integrity of the marriage covenant, to detect and solve problems *before* they start to avoid their destructive effects on us.

   ॐ Couples actively set boundaries seeking the truth, setting goals, and solving problems. Longing in a painful marriage situation is a desire to save the shattered relationship.

6. **Protection from intruders**

This addresses the couple and all other relationships. Boundaries include how close and connected you allow yourselves to become with outsiders to the relationship. This helps to guard against infidelity, affairs, or deep emotional connections with others that tears away at the intimacy between the couple. If you find yourself able to be close to someone outside the relationship that could potentially break down the strength of your committed marriage relationship. The values of honesty, faithfulness, and love protect the safety of your marital relationship. Marriage is an exclusive relationship that fosters the building of trust, safety, intimacy, and assurance that you are truly loved and protected in this most important relationship of your life.

   ॐ The goal of setting the boundaries in marriage is to seek for making the relationship work better. Investment in a healthy marriage comes before other relationships.

7. **Positive honest communication**

Communication is important and if you are a good respectful partner and you find communicating difficult then you must take responsibility for improving your communication skills instead of simply supplying the excuse that "I am not good at it." Remember, communication includes the verbal (words) and the nonverbal (body language) parts of conveying your thoughts and feelings. If either of you struggle with being able to voice your needs, or to identify your needs, this will affect your ability to communicate effectively. Don't expect your partner to be a mind reader. Good communication also includes thoughtful questions to verify understanding and clarify what is expected.

℘ Speak the truth with love, set goals, and solve problems as two people lifting each other and challenging each other with respect and commitment to work together with their words and thoughts.

8. **Being a team**

Marriage efforts are the effort of the team. It is two people working together to resolve conflicts, problem areas, weak areas, etc. to foster growth and health experienced in mature, deep, and committed relationship that will endure the test of time. If only one of you is committed to making it work, one of your pillars has broken down. If you are both invested in making it work, you both have work to do. One person cannot carry the entire relationship. Partners must be equally invested in making their marriage a place where both can thrive, their needs are met, and it is the safe port in a storm.

℘ Joy and satisfaction come from hard work or good deeds.

9. **Setting useful consequences in marriage**

A consequence is the result of an action. A consequence is to create some discomfort to promote the opportunity for self-reflection, self-responsibility, and making amends so that the action will not be repeated.

℘ A consequence protects you both with reality. The pain of irresponsibility brings with it the opportunity to repent, grow, and change.

10. **Living the golden rule**

Living the grateful marriage. There's just something about the hope that springs in the heart and soul of those in a marriage where positive regard, respect, care, and *love* are woven through the souls of partners. Leaving a marriage is not a choice so they are both responsible to make their marriage a place where they want to live.

℘ Wake up every morning and be grateful for your partner—no regrets. Every mistake had been a lesson learned, and that lesson was accepted as a gift. Feeling humbled by genuine gratitude as you treat the person you love as you desire to be treated.

DEATH OF A MARRIAGE

Just as the aforementioned marital boundaries build a strong marriage, there are also characteristics of marital destruction.

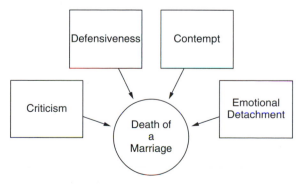

ASSERTIVE COMMUNICATION DEFINED

Being assertive is a core communication skill. Being assertive means that you express yourself effectively and stand up for your point of view, while also respecting the rights and beliefs of others. Assertive communication is the ability to express positive and negative ideas and feelings in an open, honest, and direct way. It recognizes our rights while respecting the rights of others. It allows us to take responsibility for our actions and ourselves without judging or blaming other people. And it allows us to constructively confront and find a mutually satisfying solution where conflict exists.

Assertiveness can help you control stress and anger resulting in improved coping skills. Recognize and learn assertive behavior and communication.

The Benefits of Assertive Communication

1. It helps us feel good about ourselves and others
2. It leads to the development of mutual respect with others
3. It increases our self-esteem
4. It helps us achieve our goals
5. It minimizes hurting and alienating other people
6. It reduces anxiety
7. It protects us from being taken advantage of by others
8. It enables us to make decisions and choices
9. It enables us to express, both verbally and nonverbally, a wide range of feelings and thoughts, both positive and negative

Practicing the Skill of Assertive Communication

1. Be factual, not judgmental, about what you don't like
2. Be accurate (don't judge or exaggerate) about the effects of behavior
3. Use "I Messages"
4. Make sure your body reflects confidence: stand up straight, look people in the eye, and relax.
5. Use a firm, but pleasant, tone.
6. Don't assume you know what the other person's motives are, especially if you think they're negative.
7. When in a discussion, don't forget to listen and ask questions. It's important to understand the other person's point of view as well.
8. Try to think win–win: see if you can find a compromise or a way for you both get your needs met.

PERSONAL BILL OF RIGHTS

1. I have a right to ask for what I want
2. I have a right to say "no" to requests or demands that I cannot meet
3. I have a right to express all of my feelings—positive and negative
4. I have a right to change my mind
5. I have a right to make mistakes and do not have to be perfect
6. I have a right to follow my own values and beliefs
7. I have the right to say "no" to anything if I feel that I am not (1) ready, (2) if it is unsafe, or (3) if it conflicts with my values

8. I have the right to determine my own priorities

9. I have the right not to be responsible for the actions, feelings, or behavior of others

10. I have the right to expect honesty from others

11. I have the right to be angry at someone I love

12. I have the right to be myself. To be unique.

13. I have the right to express fear.

14. I have the right to say, "I don't know."

15. I have the right not to give excuses or reasons for my behavior.

16. I have the right to make decisions based on my feelings.

17. I have the right to my own personal space and time.

18. I have the right to be playful.

19. I have the right to be healthier than those around me.

20. I have the right to feel safe, and be in a nonabusive environment.

21. I have the right to make friends and be comfortable around people.

22. I have the right to change and grow.

23. I have the right to have my wants and needs respected by others.

24. I have the right to be treated with dignity and respect.

25. I have the right to be happy.

If you are not familiar with your personal rights, then take the time to read this daily until you are aware of your rights and begin to assert them. It may be helpful to post a copy of this where you have the opportunity to see it intermittently for reinforcement.

ASSERTIVENESS INVENTORY

The following questions will help determine how passive, assertive, or aggressive you are. Answer the questions honestly and write out how you would handle each situation.

1. Do you say something when you think someone is unfair?

2. Do you find it difficult to make decisions?

3. Do you openly criticize the ideas, opinions, and behavior of others?

4. If someone takes your place in line do you speak up?

5. Do you avoid people or events for fear of embarrassment?

6. Do you have confidence in your own ability to make decisions?

7. Do you insist that the people you live with share chores?

8. Do you have a tendency to "fly off the handle?"

9. Are you able to say "no" when someone is pressuring you to buy or to do something?

10. When someone comes in after you at a restaurant and is waited on first do you say something?

11. Are you reluctant to express your thoughts or feelings during a discussion or debate?

12. If a person is overdue in returning something that they have borrowed from you do you bring it up?

13. Do you continue to argue with someone after they have had enough?

14. Do you generally express what you think and feel?

15. Does it bother you to be observed doing your job?

16. If someone's behavior is bothering you in a theater or lecture, do you say something?
17. Is it difficult for you to maintain eye contact while talking with someone?
18. If you are not pleased with your meal at a restaurant, do you talk to the waitress about correcting the situation?
19. When you purchase something that is flawed or broken do you return it?
20. When you are angry do you yell, name-call, or use obscene language?
21. Do you step in and make decisions for others?
22. Are you able to ask for small favors?
23. Do you shout or use bullying tactics to get your way?
24. Are you able to openly express love and concern?
25. Do you respond respectfully when there is a difference of opinion?

You can tell by your pattern of responses if you generally fall within the descriptor of being passive, assertive, or aggressive. Use this exercise to better understand yourself and to help you set a goal for change if necessary. Share the results with your therapist.

[Adapted from Alberti, R., & Emmons, M. (1975). *Stand Up, Speak Out, Talk Back*].

To further clarify what style of communication and behavior that you use, explore how you would handle the following situations.

1. You are standing in line and someone cuts in front of you, or it is your turn and the clerk waits on someone else.
2. Your doctor keeps you waiting for half an hour for your appointment.
3. You are not served something that you ordered at a restaurant.
4. Your neighbors are keeping you awake with loud music.
5. Your teenager is playing the stereo too loud.
6. Your friend borrowed some money from you. It is past the date that they promised to pay you back.
7. You receive a bill and it looks like there is an error on it.
8. You purchased something and decide that you want to return it to the store for a refund.
9. The people behind you at the theater are talking during the movie.
10. You realize that the person that you are talking to is not listening to you.
11. You are displeased by your partner's behavior.
12. The dry cleaners did a poor job on several articles of clothing.

This exercise will help you better understand yourself and help you determine appropriate and effective responses to normal, everyday experiences.

Passive: Failing to stand up for yourself or standing up for yourself ineffectively can lead to a violation of your rights.

Assertive: Standing up for yourself in a way that does not violate the rights of other. It is a direct, appropriate expression of thoughts and feelings.

Aggressive: Standing up for yourself in a way that violates the rights of another person. They may feel humiliated or put down by your response.

ASSERTIVENESS CHECKLIST

When you are preparing to respond to a situation or in a conversation that requires an honest constructive response demonstrating good boundaries:

1. Be specific in identifying your goal.
2. Decide what you want the other person to hear and understand, "What are the major points?"
3. Clarify your thoughts and feelings. If you are not clear about what you are thinking and feeling how can you assertively communicate to someone. Ask yourself.
    A. Am I holding onto resentments?
    B. Are my thoughts rational and objective?
    C. Am I holding onto would've, could've, should've?
    D. Am I imposing my perspective on someone else and trying to change them?
4. Anticipate positive and negative responses when you have asserted yourself.
    A. What is the best thing that could happen?
    B. What is the worst thing that could happen?
5. Identify your assertive rights and associated boundaries.
6. Identify the responsibilities that are associated with your rights and boundaries.
7. Be thoughtful about timing. Don't press or force a discussion when the time is not right.
8. Consider the risk—benefit analysis of being assertive.
9. Relax. Let go and choose to be in a positive, problem-solving mode.
10. Role-play practice encounters with a trusted person, in front of a mirror, or using the "empty-chair" technique (pretending that the person is sitting across from you in another chair and the conversation unfolds.

To Assure Your Success… Remember

1. Use "I" statements
2. Don't overexplain
3. Don't overapologize
4. Stay focused
5. Keep your goal in mind
6. Don't personalize
7. Focus on the behavior or situation, not the person
8. Be descriptive, don't take the role as the "evaluator"
9. Don't catastrophize or exaggerate
10. If the other person becomes aggressive, don't use their behavior to justify your own escalation
11. Set the tone and maintain it; you own your words and behaviors
12. Be sincere, conscious of expressing appropriate praise and positive feedback

ASSERTIVE COMMUNICATION

Assertiveness means to communicate your thoughts and feelings honestly and appropriately. Assertive communication is both verbal and nonverbal. To express yourself assertively requires self-awareness and knowing what you want and need. It means showing yourself the same respect that you demonstrate toward others.

If you do not assert yourself, by letting other people know what your thoughts, feelings, wants, and needs are then they are forced to make assumptions about you in those areas. Assumptions have about a 50% chance of being correct. That means you only have half a chance of people understanding you and responding to you in a way that you desire.

Once you begin to assert yourself you will find that you will feel better about yourself, have more self-confidence, that you get more of what you want out of life, and that others will respect you more.

Be prepared that not everyone will be supportive of your changes in thinking and behavior. Some people that you interact with, such as family members or a significant other, may even demonstrate some negativity toward these changes. This could be because change is difficult for them to accept, they are comfortable with what is familiar to them, they benefited from your passive, people-pleasing behavior, or they fear losing you through change. However, you can't give up who you are to please other people, or to keep certain people in your life. Take one day at a time, focus on the positive, and be the best that you can be.

To clarify the variations of responses and styles of communication/behavior review the following descriptions:

1. *Passive*: Always giving into what others want. Don't want to make waves. Don't express your thoughts or feelings. Afraid to say no. Discounting your own wants and needs.
2. *Aggressive*: Being demanding, hostile, rude, insensitive to the rights of others, intimidates others into doing what they want and are disrespectful.
3. *Passive–aggressive*: You tell people what they want to hear which avoids conflict. However, you really feel angry inside and you don't follow through on the expectations or requests that results in the other person feeling frustrated, angry, confused, or resentful.
4. *Manipulative*: Attempt to get what you want by making others feel guilty. Tend to play the role of the victim or the martyr to get other people to take responsibility for taking care of your needs.
5. *Assertive*: Directly, honestly, and appropriately stating what your thoughts, feelings, needs, and/or wants are. You take responsibility for yourself and are respectful to others. You are an effective listener and problem solver.

THE STEPS OF POSITIVE ASSERTIVENESS

1. Prepare for a neutral conversation by first diffusing your emotions and by waiting until the other person is likely to be least reactive and most receptive.
2. Deliver your message as briefly and directly as possible, without being sarcastic, condescending, or judgmental. Contribute to the interaction being a positive one.
3. Be respectful. Allow enough time for the other person to respond without pressure.
4. Reflectively listen. If the person becomes defensive reflect to them what you hear them saying and validate their feelings.
5. Reassert your message. Stay focused on the original issue, and do not be derailed.
6. Reuse this process, using a lot of reflective listening to decrease emotionality, debating, or arguing. It takes two people to escalate things. Don't participate.
7. Focus on the solution, without demanding that the person respond as you do. Because you brought it up, you have probably been thinking about it and resolved some aspects of the situation. Therefore, it is important that you facilitate their participation in problem solving the issue so that they don't feel like they have been railroaded.
8. Always treat others the way you want to be treated.

Nonverbal behaviors are as important as verbalizing your assertiveness. The signals that a person sends, as well as receives, are crucial to the success of assertive communication. Nonverbal cues include eye contact, body posture, personal space, gestures, facial expressions, tone of voice, inflection of voice, vocal volume, and timing. Other variables include smiling, head nodding, and appropriate animation.

Entering an ongoing conversation requires the observation of those already involved. Therefore, as you observe the body language of others, make eye contact, and become part of the group. Join in with appropriate statements and comments.

Ending a conversation can take place by stating a form of closure. "I've really enjoyed this discussion," or "I see someone I must say hi to that I haven't seen for some time." Other solutions could include a change in content, less self-disclosure, and fewer open-ended statements that encourage ongoing conversation. For body language, there is less eye contact, less head nodding, and increasing physical distance.

PRACTICING ASSERTIVE RESPONSES

1. Describe several problem situations. Arrange them of increasing discomfort or emotional distress that they cause you. In describing a problem situation include who is involved, when it happens, what bothers you about this particular situation, how you normally deal with it, and what fears you have about being assertive in this situation. Once you have fully described a problem situation then determine your goal. How would you like to deal with it, and what is the outcome you want.

2. Developing an assertive response
   A. Determine what your personal rights are in the situation.
   B. Speak directly with the person involved, clearly stating how the situation is affecting you. Use "I" statements so that your communication is not blaming or provokes defensiveness (e.g., I feel this way...when...happens).
   C. Express your thoughts and feelings honestly and appropriately. Respect demonstrates that you are taking responsibility for yourself and that you are motivated to cooperatively resolve issues.
   D. Clarify what it is that you want by requesting it directly. Stay focused on the issue and don't be sidetracked.
   E. Seek to make them aware of the consequences of having or not having their cooperation. Initiate it from a positive perspective of win–win, helping them to see that you will both benefit, e.g., "If you help me clean up the kitchen after dinner we can leave early for the game like you want to do."

3. Giving feedback
   A. Describe what you see or observe instead of making an evaluation or giving your judgment.
   B. Be specific instead of general. Specifics are helpful.
   C. Feedback should provide information about that which can be controlled and changed, otherwise it only adds to frustration.
   D. Timing is important—always consider it, but do not use it as an excuse.
   E. Check out what the person you were giving feedback interpreted you as saying. Assumptions cause problems and can lead to hard feelings.
   F. Check out the validity of your feedback with others.
   G. Encourage feedback, but do not pressure others or impose yourself on them if it is not wanted.
   H. Do not overwhelm others with a lot of information. Offer your feedback in small pieces.
   I. Own your own feedback and feelings by using "I" statements. After all, it is only your opinion.
   J. Share your feedback with others in a way that makes it easy for them to listen to what it is you want to express.

THE CONSEQUENCES OF "NO"

1. *Saying "no."* Many individuals find it difficult to say "no" or to accept someone saying "no" to them, without experiencing negative emotions. Saying "no" can be thought of as a way of taking care of oneself, not to make another individual feel rejected, or to experience feelings of guilt if you are the individual saying "no."

2. *How to overcome guilt in saying "no."* Ask yourself the following questions:
   A. Is the request reasonable?
   B. Ask for more information to clarify what all the facts are?
   C. Practice saying "no."
   D. Quit apologizing, if it is something that you do not want to do or cannot do. Therefore, quit saying, "I'm sorry, but…"

3. Review for yourself the consequences of saying "yes."
   A. End up angry with yourself for doing something you don't want to.
   B. Get in the way or distract from things you want to do.
   C. Resentment begins to develop and build up.
   D. Because you are doing something that you don't want to do, but aren't being honest, it leads to a lack of communication and dishonest communication.

4. *Accepting "no" for an answer.* Each time you hear someone saying "no" to a request that you have made, think to yourself, "I am not being rejected as an individual, it is my request that is being rejected." Rejection comes up emotionally because your need for approval is strong. You view accepting your requests as an acceptance and approval of you. It is not.

Remember, assertive communication does not mean getting what you want. Assertiveness means honest communication that contributes to respectful relationships.

TEN WAYS OF RESPONDING TO AGGRESSION

1. Reflection: Reflect back to demonstrate that the message has been received. If you like, add information, self-disclosure, or limit setting.

2. Repeated assertion: Instead of justifying personal feelings, opinions, or desires, repeat the original point. This requires ignoring issues that are not relevant or are meant to push buttons.

3. Pointing out assumptions of the aggressor's opinion or position: Do this and then wait for a response. Then state your own opinion or position.

4. Use "I" statement: "I think," "I feel," etc.

5. Ask questions: Questions are especially effective against nonverbal aggression. Questions help the individual become more aware of nonwarranted reactions and behaviors.

6. Paradoxical statements: Making a statement that will help others realize that their aggressive statement could backfire on them.

7. Time out: Stop and pause. You can do this by excusing yourself in some way, such as ending a phone conversation. This is helpful when you need time to think about how you want to respond, such as refusing a request or demand.

8. Repeat back: When you do not think that another individual is listening to you, ask a question such as, "What do you think I am asking for?" or "What is your understanding of what I just said?"

9. Feedback reversal: Clarify what you think is being said to you by restating what has been said, in your own words. For example, "Are you saying yes?"

10. Clipping: If you feel like you are under attack, do not want the discussion to be prolonged, and do not feel like you want to defend your position then answer directly: "yes" or "no."

BUILDING SELF-ESTEEM

Although they are linked, confidence and self-esteem are not the same thing. Confidence is the term we use to describe how we feel about our ability to perform roles, functions, and tasks. Self-esteem is how we feel about ourselves, the way we look, the way we think—whether or not we feel worthy or valued. People with low self-esteem often also suffer from generally low confidence, but people with good self-esteem can also have low confidence. It is also perfectly possible for people with low self-esteem to be very confident in some areas. Developing a positive sense of self is essential for building self-esteem.

CHARACTERISTICS OF SELF-ESTEEM

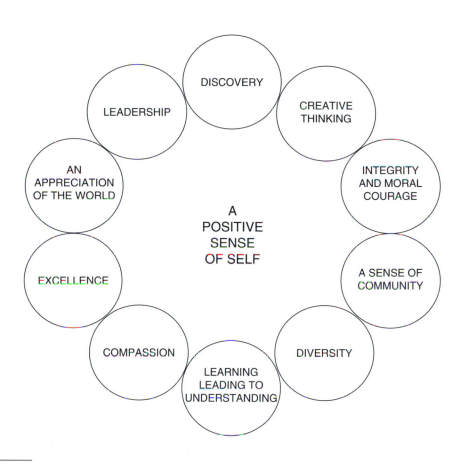

THE SELF-ESTEEM REVIEW

Directions: Review the following statements. Rate how much you believe each statement, from 1 to 5. The highest rating, 5, means that you think the statement is completely true, 0 means that you completely do not believe the statement.

	Rating
1. I am a good and worthwhile person.	_____
2. I am as valuable a person as anyone else.	_____
3. I have good values that guide me in my life.	_____
4. When I look at my eyes in the mirror, I feel good about myself.	_____
5. I feel like I have done well in my life.	_____
6. I can laugh at myself.	_____
7. I like being me.	_____
8. I like myself, even when others reject me.	_____
9. Overall, I am pleased with how I am developing as a person.	_____
10. I love and support myself, regardless of what happens.	_____
11. I would rather be me than someone else.	_____
12. I respect myself.	_____
13. I continue to grow personally.	_____
14. I feel confident about my abilities.	_____
15. I have pride in who I am and what I do.	_____
16. I am comfortable in expressing my thoughts and feelings.	_____
17. I like my body.	_____
18. I handle difficult situations well.	_____
19. Overall, I make good decisions.	_____
20. I am a good friend and people like to be with me.	_____

0   100

Total lack of self-esteem   High self-esteem

Your score_____

CHARACTERISTICS OF LOW SELF-ESTEEM

1. Fearful of exploring his/her real self
2. Believes that others are responsible for how he/she feels
3. Fearful of taking responsibility for his/her own emotions and actions
4. Fearful of assertively communicating wants and needs to others
5. Feels and acts like a victim
6. Judgmental of self and others
7. Does not live according to your his/her values (chameleon)
8. Covert, phony, "social personality"
9. Exaggerates, pretends, lies
10. Puts self down, shameful, blaming, self-critical, condemning
11. Nice person, approval seeking, people-pleaser, puts the needs of others first

12. Negative attitude
13. Triangulates by talking badly about one person to another
14. Rationalizes
15. Jealous/envious of others, has trouble being genuinely happy for the successes of others
16. Perfectionistic
17. Dependencies/addiction, compulsive, self-defeating thinking and behavior
18. Complacent, stagnates, procrastinates
19. Does not like the work one does
20. Focuses on what doesn't get done instead of what does
21. Leaves tasks and relationships unfinished and walks away without resolving issues
22. Judges self-worth by comparing to others, feels inferior
23. Does not accept or give compliments
24. Excessive worry or catastrophizing
25. Is not comfortable with self, hard to be alone with self
26. Avoids new endeavors, fears, mistakes, or failure
27. Irrational responses, ruled by emotions
28. Lack of purpose in life
29. Lack of defined goals
30. Feels inadequate to handle new situation, easily stressed
31. Feels resentful when doesn't win
32. Vulnerable to the opinions, comments, and attitudes of others
33. Feel like one's life is in the shadow of another
34. Gossips to elevate self
35. Continues to blame past experiences (or family) instead of dealing with the current self (the past is an explanation, not an excuse)

Identify your characteristic of low self-esteem. What have you learned from this self-review?

_____

_____

_____

_____

_____

_____

_____

_____

_____

_____

_____

_____

_____

_____

_____

_____

LOW SELF-ESTEEM

Self-esteem is composed of such factors as self-worth, self-competence, and self-acceptance. When a person is severely or chronically depressed their self-esteem is diminished. The cloak of depression perceives everything from the dark or negative side and offers little hope of change. This affects how a person views himself/herself. If their self-esteem has been lost they view themselves as worthless and cannot imagine what others could see in them. This feeling of unworthiness and failure as a person can play a large role in a person feeling hopeless, helpless, and despair.

If this is how you are feeling it is time to take an honest, objective look at your accomplishments. Your accomplishments will include the things you have done in efforts to obtain goals as well as things you have done to help other people. Self-esteem is an active process so it is related to behaviors and thoughts that are promoting growth and change. Another way of stating this is that a person with good self-esteem is a person who does not just talk about it—they do it. This activity affirms a sense of worthiness through accomplishment. It does not matter how small the step is as long as it is a step forward. If you have not set goals or have avoided taking responsibility for changing your life this is the time of opportunity.

People who take responsibility for their own existence tend to generate healthy self-esteem. They live an active orientation to life instead of a passive one without hope of change. They make change happen. They understand that accepting full responsibility for their life means growth and change. They recognize that they must make the decisions and use the resources presented to them. They also recognize that it is smart to ask for help when they need it, and for that help to benefit them they must use it. As a result, they have healthy self-esteem.

Avoiding self-responsibility victimizes people. It leaves them helpless and hopeless. They give their personal power to everyone except themselves. Sometimes when this occurs people feel frustrated and blame others for the losses in their life. When a person takes responsibility for their feelings they quit being passive and start taking the necessary action to reclaim their life. They recognize that nothing is going to get better until they change the way they look at things, the way they choose to feel about things, and the way they respond to things.

As you objectively evaluate the different areas of your life you may find that you are more responsible in some areas and less responsible in other areas. It is likely that the areas where you practice greater responsibility are the same areas that you like most about yourself. To accept responsibility for your existence is to recognize the need to live productively. It is not the degree of productivity that is an issue here, but rather the choice to exercise whatever ability you do have. Living responsibly is closely associated with living actively that translates into healthy self-esteem.

If you wish to raise your self-esteem you need to think in terms of behaviors. If you want to live more responsibly you need to think in terms of turning your thoughts into behaviors. For example, if you say that you will have a better attitude describe how that will be seen in behaviors.

Describe the behaviors associated with having a positive attitude. _____

_____

_____

List the resources you can use for the support of developing healthy self-esteem. _____

_____

_____

Making the changes to improve self-esteem requires increased awareness and understanding of myself. Complete the following sentences to initiate this process:

1. As I learn to accept myself _____

_____

_____

2. If no one can give me good self-esteem except myself _____

_____

_____

3. What follows is an honest and objective evaluation about the positive and negative things in my life.

   A. Negatives_____

   B. Positives_____

4. The things that I can do to raise my self-esteem include _____

_____

_____

TEN SELF-ESTEEM BOOSTERS

1. Be realistic
   A. Do not compare yourself to others
   B. Be satisfied with doing your best
2. Focus on your accomplishments
   A. Each day review what you have done
   B. Give yourself credit for what you do
3. Use positive mental imagery
   A. Imagine success
   B. Mentally rehearse confidence
4. Look inside not outside
   A. Avoid being materialistic or identifying yourself by what you have
   B. Identify your sense of purpose
5. Actively live your life
   A. Set goals and follow through
   B. Think strategically
6. Be positive
   A. Substitute negative thoughts with realistic positive thoughts
   B. Acknowledge that how you think affects how you feel
7. Have genuine gratitude
   A. Be grateful for all that you have
   B. Appreciate your life as a gift
8. Meditate
   A. Think of peaceful, pleasant things
   B. Learn to relax and let go of stress
   C. Use positive affirmations
9. Develop positive self-care as a lifestyle
   A. Believe you are worthy of taking care of yourself
   B. Take care of your health
10. Appropriately get your needs met
    A. Identify what you need
    B. Identify your choices for getting those needs met

Positive self-esteem is an active process. Daily efforts will make a difference in your life experience.

AFFIRMATIONS FOR BUILDING SELF-ESTEEM

1. I am a valuable and important person, and I'm worthy of the respect of others.
2. I'm optimistic about life; I look forward to and enjoy new challenges.
3. I am my own expert and I am not affected by negative opinions or attitudes of others.
4. I express my ideas easily, and I know others respect my point of view.
5. I am aware of my value system and confident of the decisions I make based on my current awareness.
6. I have a positive expectancy of reaching my goals, and I bounce back quickly from temporary setbacks.
7. I have pride in my past performance and a positive expectancy of the future.
8. I accept compliments easily and give them freely to others.
9. I feel warm and loving toward myself, for I am a unique and precious being, ever doing the best I can, and growing in wisdom and love.
10. I am actively in charge of my life and direct it in constructive channels. My primary responsibility is for my own growth and well-being (the better I feel about myself, the more willing and able I am to help others).
11. I am my own authority, and I am not affected by the negative opinions or attitudes of others.
12. It is not what happens to me but how I handle it that determines my emotional well-being.
13. I am a success to the degree that I feel warm and loving toward myself.
14. No one in the entire world is more or less worthy, more or less important, than me.
15. I count my blessings and rejoice in my growing awareness.
16. I am an action person; I set priorities and do one thing at a time. I like living my life effectively.
17. It feels good to live my life with purpose and working toward accomplishments that are important to me.
18. I am kind, compassionate, and gentle with others and myself.
19. I make every effort to live the golden rule. I treat others respectfully and I expect to be treated respectfully.
20. I am a genuine person who lives consciously.

SELF-NURTURING: A COMPONENT OF SELF-ESTEEM

You will know that you are developing self-care and self-love when you feel worthy, confident, and secure about who you are. The following are demonstrations of progress in self-nurturing:

1. You spend a day alone and are able to enjoy your own company and peacefulness.
2. You are able to make choices and do things to make yourself feel better.
3. You are able to be objective and loyal to yourself. You are able to hear the opinions of others while maintaining your own point of view.

4. While you strive to avoid becoming materialistic, you also feel worthy of giving yourself things that are important to you.

5. You take care of your health and well-being.

6. You do not engage in self-destructive behaviors or choices.

7. When you laugh, you laugh deeply and you laugh often.

8. You feel good about all of your successes large and small. You feel good about all that you achieve. You always strive to be the best you can be.

9. If someone is rejecting or hurtful, you do not take it personally. You are objective and honest with yourself. You realize that the problem may belong to the other person. Likewise, you are honest with yourself about you, take responsibility, and make changes as needed.

10. You are assertive in asking for what you need and want in your relationships with others. You set appropriate boundaries in relationships.

Adapted from a handout by J. Hays, author of Smart Love.

CHARACTERISTICS OF HIGH SELF-ESTEEM

1. Live authentically
2. Demonstrate self-responsibility—does not blame others
3. Take responsibility for life and consequences of actions
4. Set goals and is committed
5. Has purpose in life
6. Is emotionally and intellectually honest with self and others
7. Confronts and deals with fears
8. Is aware of both strengths and weaknesses (self-objective)
9. Is self-respectful and sets appropriate limits and boundaries
10. Does not lie about the choices he/she makes
11. Self-accepting and self-soothing (does not seek external sources to "make it okay")
12. Self-sufficient (thinks and makes decisions independently)
13. Does not hold grudges
14. Is persistent in all efforts
15. Is genuinely grateful
16. Positive attitude (cup is half full not half empty)
17. Accepts others
18. Genuinely pleased for the success of others
19. Does not compare oneself to others
20. Direct efforts toward being the best he/she can be (recognizes that life is about continual personal growth with an aim for excellence not perfection)
21. Live according to one's own internal values, principles, and standards
22. Choose to see opportunity and challenges instead of problems
23. Is spontaneous and enthusiastic about life
24. Is able to praise oneself and others for efforts and accomplishments
25. Is able to see the big picture versus being trapped by stumbling blocks (mistakes have value)
26. Appropriately asks for help and utilizes resources

27. Is an active participant in life
28. Is comfortable with self and can enjoy alone time
29. Is true to oneself
30. Has quiet self-confidence

Identify your characteristics of high self-esteem. What have you learned from this self-review?

_____

_____

_____

SELF-CONFIDENCE

BUILDING SELF-CONFIDENCE

Confidence is a state of mind. It means believing in yourself and your capabilities. It is the power of positive thinking and the willingness to actively live a purpose driven life. Positive thinking is a mental and emotional attitude that focuses on the bright side of life and expects positive results. A positive person anticipates happiness, health and success, and believes he or she can overcome any obstacle and difficulty.

Choosing to think positively does not mean that you never have any negative thoughts. The truth is sometimes bad things do happen, and when they do you feel bad/down about it. However, the self-confident, resilient person also has "possible thinking" which is another way of saying "I will get through this difficult time today and tomorrow will be better." This describes reality-based optimism, or "deal with what is not what if."

*Negative thinking is a habit, something you can train your brain to change with intention. Constant negative thinking can make you much more likely to be stressed and can lead to more serious problems, such as depression, anxiety, etc. Challenge yourself to change negative thinking patterns by reconditioning your mind to positive thinking.

Four Ways to Reinforce the Practice of Positive Thinking

1. Positive self-talk (that internal dialogue in your head) is the embodiment of self-love and self-acceptance.
2. Meditation. Mindfulness is the meditation of "being in the moment." Being in the moment tends to be positive in comparison to negative focus on what has been or what will be. It is the self-knowledge of feeling confident to live each moment as it comes as positive and productively as possible.
3. Journal. Engage in the simple practice of writing about positive experiences in your journal. It will leave you with a positive mood. An added benefit is that it will leave you feeling better physically as well.
4. Leisure time. Everyday should carry with it laughter and light heartedness, playfulness, time with a friend, etc.

Positive thinking underlies positive self-concept that is practiced daily. If this is something you need to work on, then train for it by practicing, educating yourself (knowledge through experience, reading, etc.), and talking to other people. These are all useful ways to help improve your self-confidence. Confidence comes from feelings of well-being, self-esteem (acceptance of your body and mind also known as self-concept), and belief in your own abilities and resilience. Self-confidence is what it takes to hit home runs, to meet your goals, and dare to dream. Instead of being afraid it is the self-knowledge that you will deal with whatever happens. In other words, self-perception is powerful because it makes you indomitable, and it has an immense impact on how others perceive you as well. Perception is reality—the more self-confidence you have, the more likely it is you'll succeed. Additionally, confident people inspire confidence in others. To reinforce your self-confidence:

1. *Identify your strengths*.
2. *Change your behavior*. Change your feelings by changing your behavior. Just putting a smile on your face makes you feel happier. You can speed up your journey to increase self-confidence by changing your behavior. Be thoughtful about what you show the world to be you. How do you want to be known?
   A. Smile more. This is a great way to counter negativity.
   B. Be positive about others. Compliment others on their strengths. Positive will result in reflections of positive from others. Everyone likes to hear good things about themselves.
   C. Be generous and kind. Offer the best of yourself to others. It is another reinforcement for self-confidence.
   D. Exercise and get enough sleep. These behaviors improve our mood and our ability to deal effectively with whatever confronts us.
   E. The close of the day is a time to reflect and reconcile what the day has brought you and to prepare for your best tomorrow. By being thoughtful about what is ahead of you it will decrease missteps, disappointments, the ineffective choices.
3. *Take action*. Get it done. Just do it! No procrastination.
4. *Face your fear*—and demonstrate your confidence.
5. *Be prepared*. Most of what we experience is in the predictable realm and we are relatively prepared.
6. *Realize that failures are empowering opportunities for learning*. Some of the best lessons come from situations that don't turn out the way we expected or wanted. We generally call those failures. But failures can be tremendously positive in so many ways.
7. *Get to know who you are and what you want out of life*. "Who am I and why?" "What is important to me?" and "What do I want?" The more you can answer the questions about the "self" the more empowered and confident you will be.
8. *Stay away from negativity*. It will have an impact on you and bring you down.
9. *Focus on the positive and enthusiasm*.
10. *Change your body language and image*. It is helpful to ask yourself, "How do I want to be known?" and "How do I want to be seen?"
11. *Failure is not an option*. Accept the challenge and be tenacious in meeting your goals. Eliminate any negative voices in your head—only positive self-talk!
12. *Self-monitor*. From time to time review and reinforce your confidence.

PROGRAMMING SELF-CONFIDENCE (RICHARD BANDLER, ALESSIO ROBERTI, AND OWEN FITZPATICK)

HOW TO TAKE CHARGE OF YOUR LIFE: THE USER'S GUIDE TO NLP

Neuro-Linguistic Programming, or NLP, is a practical thinking process. Remember you have control over two things (1) how you choose to interpret what you experience and (2) how you choose to deal with it. Well, NLP is the choice of interpretation. It shapes your mind and belief system by providing practical ways of changing the way that you think, view past experiences, and your general approach to life—by taking responsibility and control of your mind so that you can focus on thinking and living life positively with intention.

1. Setting goals. Goals are always to be positive. If a goal is pleasing and satisfying, it will increase your motivation.
2. Inquisitive. There is never a bad question or too many questions. Questions are necessary for clarifying what you want and why.
   A. What is good and right?
   B. What are my strengths?
   C. Why am I seeking change?
   D. When I achieve change how will it affect my life?
   E. What do I need to be prepared for?
   F. What will change look like?
3. Power of images. Images are effective tools for dealing with negative annoyances and positive goals.
   A. Positive images create positive feelings. Make it bigger so that it will metaphorically embrace you.
   B. Imagine someone or something that bothers you. Take the color out of it (make it black and white) and make it small, smaller, insignificant.
4. Challenging and eliminating the negative voice.
   A. Challenge it. "That's not even me."
   B. Imagine that negative voice as a squeaky little voice you could never take seriously.
   C. Name the negative and put it in its place, like locking it in the closet because it has no place in your mind/thoughts. Negative thoughts waste tie and energy.
      1. Take note, that when you don't take that negative voice seriously or value it you feel better and are better able to direct your efforts toward positive thoughts.
5. Play the movie backwards. This technique is useful when you have experienced something that you are having a hard time letting go of.
   A. Start at the end. Then take it all the way to *before* whatever it is happened
   B. Repeat it several times to increase the familiarity with the backward play
   C. Now give it the focus it deserves—make it smaller and smaller and smaller
   D. The last piece is to give it a different ending—one that puts a smile on your face and makes you happy
6. "Brilliance Squared." What works here is that you have successfully trained and conditioned your mind to associate an image with a feeling. By calling upon the image the feeling comes with it. Once again you are reinforcing the focus on positive.
   A. Take a desired emotion like feeling "confident." Identify the color you associate with that emotion. Then imagine a square in front of you filled with the color that you associate with that emotion.
   B. Now imagine yourself standing in that square—filled with the chosen emotion. Notice every detail about you, how you stand, the look on your face, the square of your shoulders, etc.
   C. Next, step into that square taking on the color/emotion like a blanket wrapped around you. Feel the feeling washing over you—filling you. Repeat this step over and over until you can easily do it. Repetition is conditioning.
   D. Last, imagine the colored square on its own and step into it being wrapped in the emotion.

PERSONAL EMPOWERMENT

Personal empowerment is about self-awareness, self-examination, and identifying your own unique individual qualities and personal strengths. Most important is valuing your skill set. This self-valuing is essential to determine your relative strengths as the source of taking your relative weaknesses and minimizing their influence or turning them into strengths. The foundation of personal empowerment is based on such factors as follows:

1. Taking control of your circumstances and identified goals in your personal and working life.
2. Becoming more aware of your strengths and weaknesses and therefore being better equipped to deal with problems and the unpredictable.
3. Enhancing the contribution you make as an individual and as a member of a team.
4. Taking opportunities to enhance personal growth and a sense of fulfillment.

The qualities comprising personal empowerment are derived from the belief that the greater the range of skills or coping responses that a person can develop, the greater the possibility that they will cope effectively with anything that they are challenged by. Acknowledging that successfully coping with adversity is strengthening (empowering):

1. Self-awareness or understanding your strengths and character along with how you will likely respond to various situations. This enhances your assets and increases awareness for any negative traits that could interfere with effectiveness and diminish them. This embodies learning from your experiences.
2. Values are your beliefs/opinions that are important to you and guide you—but you are not always aware of them. It is what you prefer or may choose—but not necessarily knowing why. You can't be truly self-aware without knowing your values. Therefore, it is imperative to explore and examine your values as part of your individuality.
3. Skills provide you the ability to achieve your desired goals. Skills can be obtained and refined through experience, practice, education, and training. Skills are what allow you to take your values and turn them into action. Skills are the "can" in "can do."
4. Use positive and active language that acknowledges strengths and weaknesses in a positive way to empower yourself. It is self-affirming, "I can," "I will."
5. Define your identity. Always be clear about who you are and what your values and goals are. You define you—others don't.
6. Knowledge is the information required in the development of self-awareness and skills. Information gathering is an incredible skill itself. Without information (quality information, not general Internet information) all of your choices will be limited therefore an ever-growing fund of information that is accurate and reliable must be sought. We never get to a point where we no longer need to seek knowledge. Choose to enjoy learning and to never quit growing.
7. Goals clearly define and describe how each individual takes charge of the direction of their life. Again all of this is a process. To set a goal requires thinking about your values and the direction that you want your life to take. What is important for you to accomplish? What will that life look like? Reflect on your ideas and then take action.

Goals need to be realistic and specific → Goals provide a sense of direction in life → Life direction is essential to personal empowerment.

RESILIENCE

RESILIENT LIVING

Generally resilience is defined as the ability to snap back in the face of adversity. Resilience is common—not uncommon. It is the process of learning and adapting in the face of adversity, trauma, tragedy, threats, or significant sources of stress. Instead of being taken down they find themselves stronger and moving forward with more knowledge of themselves and the world. Just because a person is resilient does not mean that they do not experience feeling of disappointment, loss, or sadness like everyone else. Emotional pain is common in people who have suffered major stressor or trauma in their lives is expected. In fact, strengthening resilience involves exposure to considerable emotional distress, resolving it, and moving on.

People that are resilient all share some basic common factors:

1. Having mutually caring and supportive relationships
2. Healthy relationships that create love, trust, and encouragement
3. Provide role modeling and are able to learn from mentors
4. Able to develop realistic expectations and limitations
5. Choose to participate instead of isolating
6. Are able to formulate and take calculated risks
7. Have the ability to make realistic plans and carry them out
8. Have a positive view of themselves and their abilities
9. Have confidence in their strengths and ability to deal with adversity
10. Possess good communication skills and problem solving
11. Demonstrate the capacity to manage strong feelings and impulses

*If someone does not possess these characteristics they can develop them if they are invested, motivated, and tenacious.

Strategies for building resistance can be natural or learned and include the following:

1. Acknowledging that resilience is a personal journey with ups and downs
2. Accepts that everyone reacts in their own unique way to traumatic exposure and stressful life events
3. There is variation among individuals with regards to what skills will work effectively for them in difficult circumstances
4. The ability to learn from losses and mistakes
5. Good relationships with family and friends
6. Being able to accept help/goodwill from others when in need
7. Being flexible and accept that change is a part of living
8. Develop and remain focused on their own goals
9. Able to take decisive action
10. Practice good self-care behaviors
11. Able to keep things in perspective
12. Nurture a positive self-view
13. Feel confident in managing difficulties and avoid seeing crises as insurmountable problems
14. Maintain a relatively stable optimistic view of life and what it bring
15. Tend to be happy with a perspective of the glass half full versus half empty

RAISING RESILIENT CHILDREN

1. *As a parent set the example of resilience.* Like any self-improvement program, increasing resiliency takes both commitment and practice. This is even more important when you are trying to lead by example. If your children see you applying positive interpretations to difficult circumstances, actively problem-solving, expressing how good it feels to take

responsibility, and snapping back from a crisis they will easily and intuitively follow your lead. Parents can offer the positive education that encourages their children to identify and embrace their strengths.

2. *Take responsibility.* Self-responsibility is a gift for choosing self-direction. Responsibility means that you are in control of your life. That doesn't mean that you can control everything. It means that you control yourself—how you interpret and respond to the things you experience. When you are resilient you know the difference. There are explanations, but resilient people do not make excuses or blame other people. We are all responsible for our own actions. Watch children and you can the see the personal power and joy in being industrious—doing it themselves.

3. *Always fulfill your own responsibilities, but also seek to serve or help others.* We are like a pebble in a pond. We are the first ring where the pebble hits the water. The next ring is our family and friends, and the following ring our community. We are self-responsible and active participants in improving the quality of life around us. When we give to others it helps to increase resourcefulness and empathy. It is important for children to know that they are valued members of their family and community. It is a powerful lesson in life to realize that you have something to offer. Watch a child's face when they have effectively contributed to a need.

4. *Practice daily gratitude.* People who are successful and do the right thing for the right reason practice genuine gratitude daily. They do not take things for granted. Genuine gratitude creates a positive environment and enhances leadership performance. A leader who practices genuine gratitude appreciates the participation and contribution of all. They appreciate what they are given and recognize that even when they are going through a difficult time they do not have to look far to see someone else having a much more difficult time.

5. *Demonstrate respect for others by allowing them to solve their own problems.* This does not mean letting other people suffer—especially your own children or other family members. However, there's often as much to be gained in learning how to solve problems as there is in solving the problems themselves. If you have healthy relationships, then they know that you are always there for them. But everyone should be afforded the opportunity to feel empowered by solving their own problems.

6. *Be a mentor and example—not a rescuer.* Sometimes the worst thing that can happen in a situation is really the best thing that can happen, and it means living with the consequences. There can be so much learned from really big mistakes. When a child makes a big mistake the consequences are generally short term. Therefore, childhood is a highly valued time for being allowed to make mistakes so that many important lessons can be learned without long-term and far-reaching consequences. Other reasons for learning more when you are young is that it allows them to understand the importance of beneficial interpretations such as things are rarely as bad as they might appear at first and that sometimes good can be gained bad.

7. *Be challenged to learn and improve from failure.* Often failure is a prerequisite to success. The weak are not going to make it unless they learn and get tougher. Nobody accomplishes anything important if they are afraid to fail. Failure allows children to learn how to struggle with adversity and how to confront fear—and survive with increased feeling of strength and understanding (knowledge). By reflecting on failure, children begin to see how to correct themselves and then try again with better results.

*Practice is empowering.

8. *Positive self-talk.* It is essential to teach kids how to identify the association between self-talk→their feelings, and→behaviors. Negative self-talk creates a negative placebo or self-fulfilling prophecy. For example, "I am not a very good reader." That sets up a child to not even try and

their skill level gets worse as this negative self-talk is associated with not expecting a positive outcome with effort. This is further reinforced when parents echo "yeah, reading isn't your thing." This is actually an opportunity for a child to learn about problem solving. The question should be "what do I need to do to improve my reading." Opportunity…

A. First of all, challenge their negative self-talk (self-concept).

B. Help them to see disappointment from a different perspective.

C. Developing or improving problem solving by encouraging kids to identify the negative thinking patterns that stand in the way of improvement and success, and how to best challenge the problem.

D. To understand how thinking positively can increase happiness. Some people are born happy (50% genetics). But about 40% of happiness comes from how a person chooses to think/interpret what happens, choosing to be happy in your life and what you have (gratitude), and the motivation to be happy. *Happiness takes effort!

E. Create an internal thinking competition; for every negative emotion, come up with three positive emotions (remember the connection between thoughts→feelings→behaviors). *Negative emotions are normal but if there are more negative emotions than positive emotions a person isn't going to feel happy.

F. Practice on identifying what is working or what is right versus the negatives.

9. *Sometimes it is easy to be a victim.* Especially with the numerous social messages that state and reinforce "how could you ever be successful with what has happened to you, that you were born into poverty, or didn't get the breaks that *rich* people do?"

A. A troubled family where there has been neglect or abuse can inflict significant harm on its children. But resilient people are challenged by such problems and go on to respond actively and creatively. They learn how to prepare for life's adversity and it becomes incorporated into how they live and is one of their most important strengths. Unfortunately, society keeps telling people that they are not capable of helping themselves or changing their lives, and that the government or others will have to help them. This has resulted in several generations of people who are waiting to be given a better life and resources. *Only you can create the life you earn.* You can be given numerous opportunities but if you don't do the right thing with those opportunities nothing will be different. How are you going to learn to read, write, and do math if you don't go to school and don't study. Parents play a crucial role in establishing self-responsibility and respect versus entitlement, a lack of motivation, and a lack of self-investment to develop and reach reasonable goals.

B. Talking about how other people make you feel or do what you do removes the obligation to change "its their fault." Sympathy can feel good and it can be used as a validation for not changing. Society and the excuses it provides (e.g., if you are born poor you cannot escape it) has created the "damage model" or a false belief that you cannot make your life better.

C. *Challenging the damage model.* The reality is that there are two major factors that determine success: (1) Parents are married—creating a family system of commitment, team work, creating a positive environment, self-responsibility, etc. (2) You go to school. How do you think the drop out rate influences a recycling of negative excuses?

D. Talk of resilience can make some feel that no one is really appreciating exactly how much they have suffered. **Resilience is not the ability to escape harm, loss, hurt, or disappointment→those are real scars to learn from and not intended to result in being a lifetime victim. "Resilience is about rebounding, learning, and becoming stronger, better and smarter at being you!" Resilient people don't waste anything that happens to them and they grow from adversity.

E. Moving beyond trauma, loss, and disappointments of surviving coming from a troubled family. This requires a more balanced perspective about their past. For example, adult children who come from families troubled by social angst such as chronic mental illness, racial discrimination, marital discord, poverty, or survived parents who were alcoholics/addicts more often than not "do not repeat their parent's pattern of behavior or allow themselves to limited by the ignorance of others."

F. Effort. The people who choose to work hard at creating a good life and learn from their experiences, rebound versus immobilized, learn how to move forward with their tenacious efforts, and emerge as strong adults who are genuinely grateful living fulfilling lives. We deserve the right to pursue, not the right to be given because it should be fair. Lots of things in life aren't fair or don't feel fair. That is supposed to challenge you and how important something is to you that you will work past the obstacles.

10. *Reframing is an essential skill for resilience.* It is the ability to focus on what is right, useful, or beneficial. In other words the *cup is half full not half empty.* Everyone has a life story.

Think about your life story and how it helps you or leaves you stuck. For the person coming from discrimination and poverty to stay in school and become educated, create positive relationships with healthy positive people who have good values, developing skills and knowledge to effectively live a challenging life with a good career—promotes a person to look at where they come from and find strengths, build self-esteem, and build self-confidence in their abilities and achievements. A life story filled with "I have…" "I am…" and "I can…"

A. I have strong healthy relationships with boundaries, rules at home, positive role models.

B. I am person who has hope, faith and expect that I can deal with whatever life brings me, care about others, proud of myself for how I choose to deal with the hardships of life, by how I choose to interpret my experiences, deal with them and move forward with reinforced inner strengths that continue to develop and grow.

11. *Ask yourself questions.* "Who am I?" "Who do I choose to be?" "How do I want other people to know me—based on my accomplishments?" Life is a journey. We are meant to grow our whole lives and enjoy continued self-understanding that brings with it continued growth and accomplishments. Life is hard and there are always difficult circumstances challenging us. That is a common life. The quality of your life will depend on the following:

A. How you interpret what happens to you

B. How you choose to deal with it

C. What knowledge and skills you *invest yourself* in learning to help you deal more effectively with the adversity of life

12. *Encourage risk-taking.* Risk-taking and failure go hand-in-hand. Risk taking and success go hand-in-hand. People who are afraid to make a mistake or lose what little they have will likely never achieve very much more.

13. *Choose healthy relationships.* Relationships foster resilience. Resilient people engage in active give-and-take work necessary to get emotional gratification from others. The result is the development of positive relationships of pleasure and laughter, helping each other, and trust.

14. *Parents need to assert their authority where it's sensible.* Parents and children are not equal. Children depend on parents to be parents. If you want to increase children's resilience, then as a parent in the leadership role there are times you have to apply your authority over others' actions—as a boss, a coach, or a mentor. A good risk is one with distinct possibilities for a positive and desired outcome. That doesn't mean it is a guarantee—that is the risk. However, there are times we all need an experienced, more authoritative person to show us the better way. Those are important lessons too.

15. *Express your love generously for the people you care about.* Resilient people know that they rely on the love and care of others in their communities. One of the best ways to reinforce this is to express when you experience positive feelings. Good sharing and caring relationships are reciprocal. It feels good to give and to receive. Doing so both reassures them and reminds you about the importance of your relationships.

SELF-DETERMINATION

Self-determination is standing up for yourself. Getting your wants and needs appropriately met. Self-determination is related to motivation and the freedom to live as one chooses without seeking counsel from someone else, i.e., settling for what someone else tells you is good for you. It can also be thought of as self-advocacy. Characteristics of self-advocacy include the following:

1. Self-awareness

   A. Interests and strengths

   B. Goals and dreams

    C. Need for support

    D. Self-responsibility

2. Knowledge of rights

    A. Personal rights (human rights/consumer rights/educational rights/knowledge of resources)

    B. The right to pursue what is important to you

3. Communication

    A. Assertiveness

    B. Nonverbal/body language

    C. Listening and reflective

    D. Compromise/negotiation

4. Leadership

    A. Knowledge of resources

    B. Self-responsibility

    C. Advocating for others, etc.

BUILDING SELF-ADVOCACY SKILLS IN CHILDREN

1. For your children (or others you are helping) requires an individual learn to:

    A. Effectively communication

    B. Assert their rights

    C. Assert their needs/wants

    D. Learning to make informed decisions

2. The following recommendations for learning these skills may be beneficial:

    A. Be a mentor to your children

    B. Role-play important skills

    C. Help them understand their place and their rights. We have an over entitled society. To respectfully assert your "right" requires that you also know your place. How to be respectful, an effective communicator, persistence, asking for information and/or resources, etc.

    D. Facilitate the earning of effectively communicating their wants and needs. As well as their strengths and weaknesses.

    E. Facilitate the learning of social cues and social process. A great way to do this is with books that have a specific theme or lesson. Use it as an opportunity to talk about what they have learned and how they would use that knowledge themselves.

    F. Stay positive.

    G. Practice at home. The best lessons of life are learned with the family at home. Practice, practice, practice

    H. Building self-esteem. This comes from the development of skills and accomplishment.

    I. Go out into the world. Real-life practice. Be prepared for a learning curve where we take the opportunity to understand what works and what doesn't.

*For all of us recognizing that we are lacking useful skills, it is our responsibility to learn those skills. We can read, ask others for mentoring who possess the skills we are seeking or we can learn the skills by "silently being mentored." Silent mentoring takes place when we have identified someone who does something really well that we want or need to learn. Demonstrate the skill and the right way to do it, i.e., if asserting yourself it should be calm, direct, respectful, patient, and persistent. Treat others in the manner in which you wish to be treated.

GOALS AND MOTIVATION

WHAT MOTIVATES ME?

To set meaningful goals, it is necessary to understand what motivates you.

1. First, identify the life goals for which you are striving. If you do not identify your goals on the list below, write them down.

   → wealth, security, love, self-acceptance, power, status, achievement, success, peace, fulfillment, truth, contribution, social change, personal growth, excellence, lasting relationships, comfort, challenge.

2. What values guide you in the pursuit of your goals?

   → commitment, marriage quality/experiences, excitement, self-discipline, integrity, honor, self-respect, pain, avoidance, leisure, cooperation, decency, kindness, meaning, sexual gratification, serving others, happiness, education, friendship, affection, instant gratification, actualization, honesty, health, control, anger, independence, noncommitment, anger, revenge, adventure, travel, children, family position, superiority, self-importance, laziness, freedom, self-sacrifice, substance use, isolation, job satisfaction, intimacy, assertiveness, accountability, pain seeking, advantage, dishonesty (getting away with it), selfishness, irresponsibility, pleasure, justice, self-serving, resentment, insecurity, vulnerability, play, shyness, equality, hatred, compulsiveness, conflict, curiosity, self-confidence, illness, affluence, resisting change.

QUESTIONS TO ASK YOURSELF

1. Suppose someone who used to know you well, but has not seen you for sometime, sees you when you complete a thorough review of changes to be made to your level of motivation and goal development. What would be different about you then now?
2. When you are successful, what will you be doing differently?
3. How would you like to benefit from the program, and how will you make that happen?
4. What do you want to be thinking, feeling, and doing?
5. How much control do you have over making this happen?
6. What changes will these goals require of you?
7. Can these goals be achieved without the help of anyone or anything else?
8. To whom is this goal most important?
9. Who, specifically, is responsible for making this happen?

*It is important that goals be feasible and realistic.

Part of self-monitoring includes the following:

1. Goal setting
2. Accomplishment
3. Listing strengths
4. Resources

SETTING PRIORITIES

Once you have set major goals and decided on your plan of action, you need to determine how important it is for you to reach your goal. This is what is meant by "setting priorities." Sometimes people get frustrated with themselves because they start things that they never finish. It is important to explore the reason behind the lack of accomplishment. It could be that motivation is low, avoidance is at work, or that it is simply not a priority for you.

STEPS FOR SETTING PRIORITIES

1. *Develop a strategy*. This relates back to the steps of clearly defining your goals. Once the goal is decided, you then break it down into steps that will ensure that you are able to reach it. Because you remain focused on your goal the steps to getting there are each a priority set in sequence.

2. *Know what is important*. To be satisfied with the outcome of your goal, it is important to be aware of all of the issues related to it. In some ways your goal may open the door for other opportunities, or it may present some limitations. Understand where you are going and how things may change for you over time. Changes may alter priorities.

3. *Investigate alternatives*. Use your resources, take the time to educate yourself, and ask as many questions as possible. Because goals can include investments of time, money, and effort thoroughly investigate the different paths for getting to the same goal. Then, when it comes time to put your plan into action, you will know if there is more information that you need to update yourself or if you feel assured that you are ready to proceed.

4. *Reach your goal*. By having a clearly defined goal and a plan that is broken down into manageable steps, you will be able to reach your goal. When you put your priorities into place you will be on your way to accomplishing your goal.

JOURNAL WRITING

Sometime changes can occur just by recognizing the source of the problem. However, most changes come from an accumulation of changes in beliefs, priorities, and behaviors over a period of time. Consistency and an investment in yourself (self-knowledge, recovery/healing, skill development) are necessary. Journal writing can be useful for keeping track of a wide variety of things that can help you achieve your goals. Use your journal to record your thoughts and feelings. "Just doing it" can make a difference. Acknowledging underlying thoughts and feelings and writing about them can help increase self-understanding and self-awareness that can make it easier to change old patterns of behavior and to start new ones. Consistently keeping a journal is a strong message to yourself that you want to change and that you are committed to make it happen.

People often experience greater successes when they have established goals. Unpredictable situations do occur which can cause setbacks, but they can also allow for a reevaluation of your problems and can offer unforeseen opportunities. However, when goals are clearly defined and the unexpected happens, you are more likely to reach them even if you are initially thrown off course. Most people don't clearly establish their goals, let alone write them down and think about what it will take to accomplish them.

STEP 1

Write down the goals you want to accomplish in the next 12 months. Make them as specific as possible. They should be realistic, but also challenging.

STEP 2

Write down 10 goals you want to accomplish this month. These should help you move toward some of your goals for the year. The monthly goals should be smaller and more detailed than the yearly goals.

STEP 3

Write down three goals you want to accomplish today. Goals need to be accompanied by plans to make them happen. If your goals are too large, you are likely to stop before you start. Better to start small and build upward. Small successes build big successes.

STEP 4

Self-monitoring: Keep track of where you are now. Create realistic plans that can get you to your goals.

STEP 5

Begin observing which self-talk has been maintaining the old patterns you want to change. List at least 5–10 negative self-statements that feed into your old patterns.

STEP 6

List 5–10 positive statements that are likely to help create the new patterns you want to create.

STEP 7

Create challenges that will replace the negative self-talk you listed in Step 5.

STEP 8

Program positive and affirming self-talk. Each day, say at least 10 positive self-statements to yourself.

STEP 9

Imagination and visualization: Five times each day, take 1 min to visualize a positive image.

STEP 10

Building self-esteem: Use your journal to list good things about yourself. Be supportive to yourself.

STEP 11

Each day record three of the days successes—big or small. Praise yourself. Plan small rewards for some accomplishment each week.

STEP 12

In your journal, frequently ask what parts of yourself you are involved with. The various issues you face (e.g., the needy child, the rebellious adolescent, etc.).

STEP 13

Each day, forgive yourself for something you have done. Like self-esteem, forgiveness is one of the keys to successful change. Forgiving yourself for past actions allows you to learn from what you have experienced and take responsibility for what happens in the future.

STEP 14

List the fears of success that the different parts of you may have. Work on making success safe. For example, the needy adolescent doesn't want to be given information/direction from others but is fearful and insecure.

STEP 15

Be willing to do things differently. If you don't, nothing is going to change.

SELF-MONITORING

Self-monitoring is the process of observing and recording your thoughts, feelings, and behaviors. It is used to:

1. Define or redefine the problem or target of change as needed.
2. Increase or decrease desired target behaviors, thoughts, or feelings.
3. Evaluate the progress toward your goal(s).

Self-monitoring is important for increasing your awareness for which management skills and behaviors have been most helpful, and in planning the steps you will take to ensure continued progress and success. Initiate self-monitoring by:

1. Identify
   A. Target behaviors, thoughts, and/or feelings to be changed
   B. Desired behaviors
   C. Goals
2. Identify methods supportive of making desired changes and reaching your goals
   A. Objectives
   B. Strategies
3. What has been most helpful, and how do you plan to maintain positive changes

GOAL DEVELOPMENT

Before a person can reach goals they must set goals. Often, people have a lot of different things on their mind that they would like to see happen. However, they have not taken the time to sit down and thoroughly think through all that is required to see those things happen. Strategizing for success is an easy process, doesn't take much time to do, and when you are completed you will have a much clearer idea of what you want and how you are going to go about making it happen.

STEPS FOR DEVELOPING GOALS

1. *Keep it simple.* Define goal(s) as clearly as possible. If you are not sure of exactly what you want, the course to get there will be bumpy, and it will take more time and energy than necessary.
2. *Break it into small steps.* Once you have clearly defined the goal, break it down into small steps that you take to reach your goal. Small steps are helpful because they are manageable, require the least amount of stress, and allow you to see the progress that you are making toward your goal.
3. *Choose a starting point.* Once you have broken your goal down into steps, the next thing to do is to choose a starting point. When will you begin working on your goal? This is a question that clarifies how much of a priority it is to you. Life is about choices, and everyone is responsible for the quality of their own life.
4. *Redefine the goal.* Sometimes it becomes necessary to redefine a goal that you have set. Maybe it was an unrealistic goal because you lacked the resources to reach it, it is not as important to you as it once was, or maybe as time has gone on you have learned some new

information which changes the way that you are looking at things. In redefining the goal you go through the same steps as setting the original goal. Redefining goals is often related to personal growth.

5. *Act on your plan.* By the time you actually initiate a formal starting point of your goal you will already have completed several of the steps toward it. You will have thought it through and actually planned it out. Accomplishing steps toward your goal will reinforce positive self-esteem, and following through on other important changes in your life—if that is your choice.

GOAL SETTING

To accomplish the tasks that will make the most difference in the quality of your life experience it is required that you develop appropriate goals. To successfully reach your goals requires that you develop a plan using objectives or steps that will lead to the completion of your selected goal(s).

1. Goal: _____

    Objectives: _____

    _____

    _____

2. Goal: _____

    Objectives: _____

    _____

    _____

3. Goal: _____

    Objectives: _____

    _____

    _____

4. Goal: _____

    Objectives: _____

    _____

    _____

5. Goal: _____

    Objectives: _____

    _____

    _____

ACCOMPLISHMENTS

From the time that you begin your program of change and personal growth it is important to keep a log of what you accomplish in how you think, how you manage your feelings and the difficulties in your life, and behavioral changes.

_____

_____

_____

_____

_____

_____

_____

_____

_____

_____

STRENGTHS

As you continue to work toward your goals of personal growth you will learn more about yourself, your abilities, and your assets. Identify your strengths and write them down. Your strengths contribute significantly to how you manage your life. When you combine your strengths with your skills and your resources you will experience yourself as much more effective in how you choose to live your life as well as effectively collaborating with others when necessary.

1. _____

2. _____

3. _____

4. _____

5. _____

6. _____

7. _____

8. _____

9. _____

10. _____

RESOURCES

Developing a list of resources can be very helpful. It will have to be updated from time to time. Write down whatever resources you are aware of at this time and continue to add to it as you go through this program. Examples of resources include trusted individuals, community meetings, sponsors, etc.

1. _____

2. _____

3. _____

4. _____

5. _____

6. _____

7. _____

8. _____

9. _____

10. _____

PROBLEM SOLVING

PREPARING TO LEARN PROBLEM-SOLVING SKILLS

Preparing yourself to learn this skill is critical and requires motivation and commitment along with practicing the components of problem solving. This challenge is not simple because marital partners and family members typically view themselves as victims of unreasonable and offensive behavior on the part of other significant members of their family system. Failing to see how they contribute to their difficulties, they perceive the solution as consisting of favorable changes by the "offending" person. Therefore, they see no need for collaborative problem solving or changing themselves. Often having assumed an adversarial quality, their interactions tend to be characterized by arguments, mutual recriminations, put-downs, and power struggles.

Begin by clarifying what the problem-solving process is all about. Basically, it is a process of defined stages that will help you collaborate in the effort to solve problems and effectively reach decisions. It involves a number of steps that will assist you to define problems accurately and to generate several possible solutions so that you can select the best possible option(s). The best option is the one that best meets your needs, so another step involves helping you to identify and understand each other's needs (when collaborating). The process also involves guidelines that will assist you to work together as a team and avoid needless and unproductive hassles.

The process is effective and you can succeed in applying it, but only if you commit to following the steps and guidelines.

MANAGING INTERACTION DURING PROBLEM SOLVING

As individuals prepare to begin practicing problem-solving steps, they need to observe the following guidelines:

1. Be specific in relating problems.
2. Focus on the present problem rather than on past difficulties.

3. Focus on only one problem at a time.

4. Listen attentively to the concerns and feelings of others who are sharing identified problems.

5. Share problems in a positive and constructive manner.

DEVELOPING GOOD PROBLEM-SOLVING SKILLS EQUIPS INDIVIDUALS TO

1. Identify the causes of emotional difficulties.

2. Recognize the resources they have to deal with their difficulties.

3. Give them a systematic way to overcome their current problems.

4. Enhance their sense of control.

5. Prepare them to deal more effectively with future problems.

STAGES OF PROBLEM SOLVING (AS THERAPIST FACILITATES SKILL DEVELOPMENT IN INDIVIDUAL)

1. To acknowledge and define the problem.

2. Identify their resources—assets and supports.

3. Obtain information from other sources (if available) if helpful.

4. Decide on practical arrangements—who will be involved.

5. Establish a therapeutic contract that clarifies the individual and therapist's responsibilities in problem solving.

Implementing the process does not ensure that resultant decisions and solutions will always produce desired results. However, using the process does avoid discord and substantially enhances the chances of achieving favorable outcomes.

STEPS FOR PROBLEM SOLVING

1. Acknowledge/identify the problem.
   A. Focus on the solution—not the problem.
   B. View problems neutrally. It's just feedback on a current situation.
2. Analyze the problem and identify needs of those who will be affected.
3. Employ brainstorming to generate possible solutions.
   A. Have an open mind
   B. Use language that creates possibility (imagine if…)
4. Evaluate each option, considering the needs of those affected.
   A. Have the courage to say no when appropriate. For example, if the problem cannot be solved in the time frame allowed or with available resources, then address it immediately and change plans accordingly.
5. Implement the option selected.
6. Evaluate the outcome of problem-solving efforts.

*Problem solving is an ongoing process.

PROBLEM-SOLVING PROCESS

Take a few minutes to focus on yourself. Are you (1) a person who generally copes well but is having current difficulties associated with a specific situation or (2) a person who experiencing difficulty coping?

If you identified yourself as generally experiencing difficulty coping, be prepared to be patient as you learn to improve your problem-solving skills and use the necessary resources for reaching this important goal.

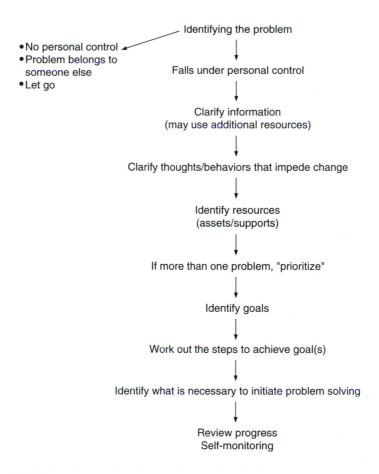

Identifying the problem

• No personal control
• Problem belongs to someone else
• Let go

Falls under personal control

↓

Clarify information
(may use additional resources)

↓

Clarify thoughts/behaviors that impede change

↓

Identify resources
(assets/supports)

↓

If more than one problem, "prioritize"

↓

Identify goals

↓

Work out the steps to achieve goal(s)

↓

Identify what is necessary to initiate problem solving

↓

Review progress
Self-monitoring

ASSIGNMENT 1

SAMPLE PROBLEMS

1. "I wish you would ask me in advance about taking the car. When you wait until the last minute, it really annoys me and puts me in a bind because sometimes I need the car. I would like to be considered when you think about taking the car."

_____

_____

_____

_____

2. "I don't like you going to the bar with your buddies several nights in a row. I feel unimportant to you when you spend so little time with me. I would like to share more evenings with you."

_____

_____

_____

_____

3. "It humiliates me when you get on my case in front of my friends. I would like to feel I could bring my friends home without fear of being embarrassed."

_____

_____

_____

Make a list of your own problems and how you plan to resolve them.

ASSIGNMENT 2

_____

1. Discuss a situation that you have experienced that was easy to get into, but difficult to get out of.
   A. Why was the situation so difficult to get out of?
   B. What have you learned from your experience, has it changed you, and what would you do differently next time or in a similar situation?

ASSIGNMENT 3

_____

Taking Risks

1. What is the meaning of risk?
2. Discuss a "risk" you need to take in your life.
3. What keeps you from taking the risk?
4. Why do you feel this risk should or should not be taken?
5. What is possible positive outcome(s) if the risk is taken?

RISKS

_____

Nothing ventured, nothing gained.

A venture is a risk. It is trying something new or approaching the same problem in a different way.
There are many times when we must take certain risks to bring about desired change, growth, and learning. By avoiding risk you may avoid suffering and sorrow. However, you will also avoid learning, feeling, change, growth, love—living. To avoid risk is to remain a prisoner of fear and doubt.

1. What does the statement, "nothing ventured, nothing gained" mean?

   _____

   _____

2. Do you live your life taking well thought out risks or do you fear risk and remain stuck?
   Explain.

   _____

   _____

3. Does the way you approach problems offer you few choices or more choices with alternatives
   in case something doesn't work out the way you planned?

   _____

   _____

4. Explain how you currently live your life, and what you want to try to do differently.

   _____

   _____

DECISION MAKING

Life is about choices. Decision making is a skill that can help you to make choices that are necessary and right for you. It is an active process that requires you to take responsibility for yourself, your life, and your own happiness. People who are good at making decisions have the self-confidence that comes from knowing how to make good choices in their life.

STEPS FOR DECISION MAKING

1. *Isolate the problem.* Sometimes things are not what they seem. Be careful in not just looking at the surface issues and making a decision based on minimal information. Instead, try to understand any underlying issues that may actually be the source of the problem. If you allow yourself to examine the problem from a number of different perspectives or angles, you may find yourself defining the problem in a number of different ways. The more options you have the better your chance of making the best choice.

2. *Decide to take action.* Once you have identified and isolated the problem, the next step is deciding whether or not you need to take action now. Sometimes the best decision is to do nothing. However, there is a difference between making a choice to do nothing versus procrastination, and avoidance of dealing with an uncomfortable situation.

3. *Gather resources.* Ideally it is best to gather as much information as possible about the situation. Sometimes this may even mean consulting with a professional or expert could be beneficial. Gather as much information as you can, but use common sense. Gathering information could be a way to delay taking any action based on the premise that you don't have all the information that you know its out there.

4. *Make a plan.* In other words, "make a decision." You have analyzed the problem, looked at it from all the different angles. Now it is time to decide how you will carry out your decision.

5. *Visualize your plan of action.* It is not possible to anticipate the exact outcome of any decision you make, because making a decision involves some degree of risk. However, you can do a test run on your plan by visualizing the potential outcome of your decision. Use your gut feeling or intuition. If it doesn't feel right, don't ignore it, and try to understand the source of your discomfort with the decision.

6. *Take action.* You have successfully completed all the steps required for good decision making. Now it is time to take action and put your decision to work. At this point you should feel confident about the work you have done in making this decision, and you will be able to maintain that feeling of self-confidence as you take action.

TIME MANAGEMENT

Time is defined by how we use it. If you feel like you are constantly rushing, don't have enough time, are constantly missing deadlines, have many nonproductive hours, lack sufficient time for rest or personal relationships, feel fatigues, and feel overwhelmed by demands, it is likely that you suffer from poor time management.

FOUR CENTRAL STEPS TO EFFECTIVE TIME MANAGEMENT

1. *Establish priorities.* This will allow you to base your decisions on what is important and what is not, instead of wasting your time.

2. *Create time by realistic scheduling.* People tend to misjudge how much time tasks will really take to accomplish. Therefore, give yourself adequate time to accomplish a given task and eliminate low-priority tasks.

3. *Develop the skill of decision making.* A lot of time is wasted procrastinating. Problem solving and decision making are essential skills for effective time management.

4. *Delegate tasks to others.* If you tend to control everything or believe that only you can do whatever it is, then realistically evaluate all the tasks that you do and you will be surprised to find that many people in your life are capable of doing some of the things that you do.

STARTING YOUR TIME MANAGEMENT PROGRAM

1. Making an initial assessment of how you spend your time takes approximately 3 days of observation. Keeping a journal specifically to log how you spend your time will clarify your time management or lack thereof. This will be easy to manage if you break up the day into three parts:
   A. From waking through lunch.
   B. From the end of lunch through dinner.
   C. From the end of dinner until you go to sleep.

2. It will take one day to define and prioritize your goals and activities.

3. To adequately develop a habit of effective time management will take between 3 and 6 months.

Once you begin your time management program continue to do a weekly review to monitor your consistency and progress. Maintain an awareness of what you are doing and why. You will find that effective time management will significantly reduce your stress. Keep in mind—nothing is going to change unless you decide to change it. Therefore, you have been provided clear steps to starting the change of more effective time management. Don't just talk about it do it.

EXAMPLES OF INDIVIDUALIZED TIME MANAGEMENT OPTIONS

Effective time management contributes to a balanced lifestyle. Review the following list and choose some time management tips that you can incorporate into your life to accomplish more and to feel less stress.

1. Be realistic with yourself regarding how much you can actually accomplish in a given span of time.
2. Say "no" to additional responsibilities that infringe on personal/leisure or work time.
3. Prioritize your tasks, because they are not equally important. Set priorities on a daily, weekly, and monthly basis for maximizing accomplishments.
4. Develop an awareness for your peak energy periods and plan to do the activities with the highest energy demand at that time.
5. On a regular basis, review what the best use of your time is currently.
6. Striving for perfection is generally not necessary and can burn up time better spent in another way. Complete tasks well enough to get the results that you really need.
7. Delegate tasks and responsibilities to others whenever appropriate. Just be sure to communicate your expectations clearly.
8. Don't waste time thinking and rethinking the decisions for basic issues. Make those decisions quickly and move on.
9. If you have a difficult task to do that you are not looking forward to, do yourself a favor and approach it with a positive attitude. You will be surprised about how much stress that can relieve. Additionally, don't procrastinate—just do it. You will feel both relieved and accomplished.
10. Break big overwhelming tasks into small manageable ones so that way it is easier to keep track of your progress and achievements—which is reinforcing.
11. Be prepared to make good use of "waiting" time by having small tasks or activities to do. Another way to deal with it is to always be prepared to take advantage of potential relaxation time when there are no demands on you.
12. When you need time to focus on your goals without interruption then request it. Take responsibility for creating an encouraging work environment at home and at work.
13. Set goals and reward yourself when you have accomplished them. If it is a big goal, you may want to build in rewards at certain milestones of effort and accomplishment as a reinforcer.
14. From time to time, remind yourself how good it feels to accomplish tasks, what the benefits of accomplishment are, and the relief of having that weight off your shoulders.
15. Good use of time means more than completing "necessary" tasks. It means building in time for self-care such as leisure activities and exercise. You being the best that you can be is a priority.

MINDFULNESS

There are many kinds of meditation. Mindfulness is just one. If you want to develop the skill of meditation, pick just one form and practice it a lot.

Mindfulness takes time and patience to learn. Some who are considered master of mindfulness might say that it is a lifelong process. There are two principles of mindfulness:

1. Your focus and full attention should be on the present moment.
2. Your emotions, thinking, and observations should be unbiased and without judgment.

If you are interested in learning mindfulness, find out if there is a group in your community. If there isn't go online and see who offers guidance and support that works for you. Jon Kabat-Zinn is likely the most well known and his institute has numerous resources. But in the meantime, there are simple basic ways to practice mindfulness in daily exercises. In many ways, mindfulness is similar to transcendental meditation that asserts the idea to reach a place of "restful or concentrated" alertness that allows a person to let negative thoughts and distractions pass by without upsetting calm and balance.

Mindfulness practice is "self-directed neuroplasticity" that changes the brain and transforms neural networks that support unhealthy patterns, such as pervasive anxiety, depressive thoughts, anger, and self-judgment. Those are big words that mean the practice of mindfulness transforms negative emotional states into positive ones. This is a very important skill for those dealing with depression, anxiety, substance use disorders, and PTSD. Mindfulness is a great skill for countering the emotional hijacking by core negative beliefs. Practicing mindfulness means that you are actively paying attention to the moment that you are in right now.

1. Set intention
   A. Stabilizing intention means "what is it that I want to remember at this moment" or the active process of situational awareness
   B. Staying in the moment means not thinking about or remembering the past or thinking about and planning the future. You can look into the past or future without shifting your focus away from the present moment you are in now.
2. Cultivate witnessing awareness
   A. Means to cultivate an attitude of acceptance, openness, and curiosity about life as it unfolds in each moment. Less autopilot.
   B. You become an observer of life and an observer of yourself placed in life. This is focused attention like a fully absorbed state of concentration on an object like breathing.
3. Regulate attention
   A. Creates the understanding that one's experience is not based on their life, but what they pay attention to or focus on.
   B. Regulating attention is a critical component of the emotion regulatory process.
   C. Mindfulness and meditation are among the best methods to boost your ability to focus. Ideally, start out your day with a mindfulness "exercise," such as focusing on your breathing for 5 min before you get out of bed.
   D. As the day goes on, try to minimize multitasking, as this is the opposite of mindfulness.
   E. End your day with a 10- or 15-min meditation session to help stop your mind from wandering and relax into a restful sleep.
4. Strengthen self-regulation (use a work or color as the mind–body connection)
   A. Increased strengthened self-regulation = decrease in emotional hijacking. Therefore, you may notice negative emotion but you no longer dwell, thus wasting emotional energy and time.
5. Loving kindness for self and others
   A. Let go of judgments and criticisms about yourself and others. JCZ would say, "there is no perfect way to do this, no 'standard' to judge yourself against." Be on the best terms possible with others.
6. Personal journal of the journey of understanding mindfulness
   A. Goal of practice (formal or informal) is to get better at being mindful in daily life—to train the untrained mind.
   B. Observe thoughts and feelings.
   C. Ask reflective questions, keep open mind, let go of preconceived assumptions.

HOW TO PRACTICE MINDFULNESS

Jon Kabat-Zinn was one of the first people to lead the way in the field of mindfulness. He defined mindfulness as "paying attention in a particular way: on purpose, in the present moment, and nonjudgmentally." This refers to consciously paying attention to all of our senses and feelings without judgment. An example of mindfulness would be to focus on the sensation of water rushing over our hands as it falls from the faucet or the sensation of our body in water as we relax in the pool.

It means accepting the sensation and feelings without pushing it away or evaluating it—just being in the moment of the meditation experience. Mindfulness is mental training to reduce stressful reactive thoughts and emotional distress.

Research has linked mindfulness meditation with decreased anxiety, increased positive emotions, and when practiced enough, permanent structural changes in the brain that sustains the described benefits of mindfulness, referred to as neuroplasticity. Practice is required to develop a useful skill level of mindfulness meditation. At first it will be difficult to challenge unwanted intrusive thoughts that continually pop up. Everyone struggles with intrusions and part of the learning process is to gently push them away by refocusing on *being in the moment*. However, with time and practice your ability to meditate will improve. Below are the step-by-step instructions for practicing mindfulness meditation.

PLANNING

For the best results, meditation should be part of your daily schedule. Meditating for 30 min a day would be a recommended goal, even if it would be challenging with your lifestyle. Try to build up to it by using a progression of:

$$10 \, min \rightarrow 15 \, min \rightarrow 20 \, min \rightarrow 25 \, min \rightarrow 30 \, min.$$

Create a schedule that you will be consistent with.

POSTURE

Make sure to sit in a comfortable position, but don't position yourself to be so relaxed that you fall asleep. Therefore, don't lie down, keep your spine straight up.

THOUGHTS

Be peaceful and allow your thoughts to come and go. The more you try to control them (resist), the more the intrusion persists. Some intrusive thoughts are viewed as normal. Simply acknowledge them and allow them to drift away as you redirect yourself back to meditation. *The more you resist it persists*.

BREATHING

Focus on your breathing, taking full but gentle breaths. Inhale through your nose deeply into your lungs and exhale out your nose. Equal effort in and out. Breathing is the key to mindfulness meditation. Focus on the rhythm not the sensation of breathing. When you are in a relaxed mindful state you do not want to connect the body and the mind—you want the mind to let go of processing as much as possible.

SEVEN BASIC AND EASY MINDFULNESS EXERCISES

As you examine the exercises, one thing they all have in common is that they challenge you to do something different than you normally do it. This makes your brain develop new neural pathways (neuroplasticity which is a very good thing) in addition to demanding that you pay attention to the moment that you are in which is meditation.

1. Fully pay attention to the detailed experience of breathing: the sounds, the rhythm, sensations, smells, etc. (this is an easy and great way to get into a deep meditative state).
2. Change your routine. Drive a different way to work, reverse the order in which you get ready in the morning, be thoughtful about reversing the order on house and garden tasks, and eat something different for breakfast. Change up your routine anytime and often.
3. Reverse the order in which you do things. Be involved in the awkwardness of reversing the order in which you towel yourself off, get dressed and put on your socks and shoes in the morning.
4. Pay attention to the full experience of walking: the sensations, fine and gross motor movement, how objects seem to move past you, the temperature, the wind, the sounds, and colors, etc.
5. Write with the opposite hand; use the mouse with the opposite hand; brush your hair with the opposite hand, brush your teeth with the opposite hand.

6. Purposefully choose to stop and smile. Use your awareness to feel the immediate physiological response to your body. Smiling "feels" good.

7. Take a deep breath and while you hold it, notice and name five things you can see, feel, and hear.

DEALING WITH LOSS AND GRIEF

ADJUSTING/ADAPTING: LIFE CHANGES

Basic factors contributing to personality and social development include heredity, social learning, family factors, peer factors, SES, experience history, and age. It can be helpful to understand what experiences have contributed to how you respond to your environment because if there are difficulties such information offer indications of necessary change and growth. Looking at your past for information and understanding can be emotionally painful, but it can also help you take responsibility for making the changes that will help you resolve old wounds and reach your goals.

Because a significant review of your life experience will be related to parental interaction it is important to maintain awareness for what you are trying to accomplish. Don't get stuck blaming your parents or other people for what is wrong. As an adult, only you can take responsibility for your choices and behavior.

There are common stages of development that everyone experiences. There are also unique or defining experiences that have a significant impact on your life, how you define yourself, and how you deal with things.

Some Common Life Changes Which Require Adjusting and Adapting

1. Selecting a mate.
2. Learning to live with a partner.
3. Starting a family.
4. Rearing children.
5. Getting started in an occupation, and then changing and growing professionally.
6. Developing a support system/peer group affiliation.
7. Developing healthy adult leisure time activities.
8. Relating oneself to one's partner as a person.
9. Accepting and adjusting to physiological changes.
10. Altering one's role in family as appropriate and necessary.

What are all the life changes that you have experienced?

Understanding Your Skill of Adjusting and Adapting

1. Write about a difficult or challenging experience you had in which you were able to adjust.

_____

_____

_____

_____

_____

2. What did you do, and how were you able to accomplish it?

_____

_____

_____

_____

3. What is something that you have experienced that you have had difficulty adjusting to or have not been able to adjust to?

_____

_____

_____

4. What has prevented the necessary adjustment?

_____

_____

_____

ADJUSTING/ADAPTING: DEVELOPMENTAL PERSPECTIVE

The basic view of development begins with a look at your family experience. There are five specific aspects of family functioning to consider:

1. *Leadership*. The parents serve as models. The parental modeling is determined by each parent's personality, the relationship between the parents, the presence or absence of mutual support and esteem, the effectiveness of their communication, absence of mutual support and esteem, the effectiveness of their coping, their way of relating to relatives and others in the community, power, and discipline.

2. *Boundaries*. Family boundaries include the individual's self-boundaries, the boundaries between generations, and the boundaries between the family and the community. Boundaries need to be semipermeable. Boundaries serve as a guideline to appropriate interaction between individuals and between generations. The family–community boundary needs to become increasingly permeable. As children grow, they need to cross it more freely to participate in community. Boundaries that are inadequate, overly rigid, or overly loose present a risk because they interfere with optimal family functioning as an open system (vs. closed system).

3. *Emotional climate*. Emotional forces are the glue that holds the family together. No family can function well unless its family members care for and support each other. The family needs to be a place where intimacy and anger can be tolerated (to a greater extent than in the community and where people can relax more freely than they can outside the home). Discipline and how parents exercise their power are related to and often determine the emotional climate of the family. *There are also wide cultural variations in emotionality and its expression.

4. *Communication*. Language, the basis for social interaction, is learned initially in the family. Language develops best when children are talked to, read to, sung to, and encouraged to respond to others and to express feelings and experiences verbally. Communication consonant with the thinking and values of the community and culture underlies an important aspect

of sociocultural development. Any communication handicap is a potential risk factor, and communication difficulties and deviance are significant risk indicators in children's development.

5. *Family goals and tasks.* The understanding of family goals and tasks throughout the life cycle is the most important component of family functioning to decrease risk. Society expects families to nurture and socialize the young to become productive members of society with an appropriate value system and morality. The family life cycle begins with marriage and family formation and passes through many stages. Each stage offers life lessons and skill development.

LEARNING HISTORY

1. What did you learn from your family that you have carried on in how you interact with other people, the community (*positive and negative*)?

_____

_____

2. How do you deal with your emotions?

_____

_____

3. How do you deal with anger?

_____

_____

4. How would you rate your self-esteem?

_____

_____

5. How do you take care of yourself?

_____

_____

6. What are the consequences of your behaviors?

_____

_____

7. What are your choices? For example, are people and the community safe or feared?

_____

_____

8. What changes do you need to continue working on to reach your goals?

_____

_____

LOSSES/OPPORTUNITIES

Sometimes changes in life, even positive changes, result in losses. When you experience a loss, it is important to work through the associated thought and feelings. This working through is called grieving. Grief is a normal and natural response to loss. People grieve over the death of someone they love and sometimes over life changes including changes in family patterns or behavior. Grieving is related to adjusting and adapting.

Examples of situations that may facilitate grieving include the following:

1. Children starting school
2. Children going away to school
3. Marriage
4. Divorce
5. Addictions
6. Retirement

The negatives or losses in each of these situations seem pretty easy to pick out. Can you pick out the potential positive(s)? Quite often with losses also comes opportunity, and you need to be prepared to look for it.

There are stages that many people experience when engaged in to the grieving process. Think through a significant loss experience and explore how you worked through your loss. Did you experience the following five stages or was it different for you. If it was different, how?

1. Denial
2. Anger
3. Bargaining
4. Despair
5. Acceptance

*These stages do not occur in the same order for everyone.

GRIEF

Grief is intense emotional suffering caused by a loss. When unresolved, it can lead to acute anxiety and depression. Usually when we think of loss and the grief process, we think of someone very close to us dying or leaving. When this happens, we experience intense emotional pain (hurt, sadness, abandonment). So we can say that grief is the natural, normal, inevitable process that all human beings experience when they lose something that is important to them. The common stages of grief are denial, anger, bargaining, depression, and acceptance.

The varying things that a person can experience during the course of their life that can result in feelings grief and loss are identified in the list below. Journal about some of your grief experiences and what you learned as well as how it affects you now.

1. Death of a loved one.
2. The ending of an important relationship (boyfriend–girlfriend).
3. Loss of relationship with a parent through divorce.
4. Feelings of loss for a friend that moved away (or you moved away).
5. Feelings of loss associated with school, neighbors, house, etc. because you moved away.
6. Loss of job due to restructuring, lack of transportation, drinking, etc.
7. Loss of your special place in the family because another child was born.
8. Damaged reputation due to someone who doesn't like you, your own poor judgment, mistakes, etc.
9. Physical impairment—accident, illness.
10. Loss of a pet.
11. Not being able to return to school, friends, family, or spouse for some reason.
12. Recognizing that life dreams will not be realized.
13. Others _____

*What are the things that you may have wanted to happen that never occurred and you feel hopeless about.

NEVER HAPPENED

1. Happy childhood.
2. Normal or happy home perhaps like a friend has or you saw on TV or a movie.
3. To belong to and be accepted by a certain social group.
4. Get a particular person to care about you.
5. Parents you didn't have.
6. A beautiful or great body (according to the narrow and damaging social perspective that slim is okay and any variation from that is not as good as…).
7. A smooth and clear complexion (this can be a painful experience).
8. Color of hair or eyes (not accepting of self).
9. Parents that were home or spent time with you or didn't get drunk and abusive.
10. Grandparents.

From this place of pain, hurt, and disappointment comes a wall of protection called *denial*:

1. I don't care.
2. It's not really that.
3. Who wants it anyway?
4. Everyone does it.
5. There's no problem.
6. Drugs aren't my problem.

When we quit denying our loss, we move into the next stage: *ANGER*. Your anger may be reasonable or unreasonable and it may be felt in varying degrees.

Hate	Rage	Anger	Frustrated
Hurt	Upset	Irritated	

This is a stage where blaming occurs. Perhaps distrust, revenge, or get even. Externalization takes place—"It's all his fault."

Make a list of all the people, places, and things that you are angry about to some degree.

BARGAINING

When anger begins to calm down there is an attempt to bargain with:

1. Life
2. Ourselves
3. Another person
4. God
   A. I'll try harder to please…
   B. Maybe if I had…
   C. Bargaining in an attempt to postpone the inevitable in an attempt to prevent it.

DEPRESSION

It begins when there is realization that bargaining has not worked, the struggle toward off reality fails, and the belief that the experience has been unfair and overwhelming. If not identified and effectively coped with depression can take over. This is when the full force of the loss is experienced and is accompanied by crying, intense emotional pain, and not being able to move forward. Feelings associated with this stage include the following:

1. Helpless/hopeless.
2. Powerlessness.
3. Self-pity—Why me?
4. Sadness.
5. Guilt.
6. Suicidal thoughts.
7. Self-destructive or self-defeating thoughts and behaviors.

ACCEPTANCE

This is the last stage of the grieving process. Acceptance is not necessarily a happy stage. It is almost void of feeling. It is as if the pain is healing and the struggle is over. There is peace, but it does not mean that healing is complete or the feelings of pain and emptiness are gone. Some words/phrases to describe acceptance are as follows:

1. At peace
2. Learned coping skills
3. Accept our past
4. Accept life as it is

5. Accept our present circumstances
6. Accept our loss
7. Free to go on with life
8. Begin to feel comfortable with life again
9. Adjusting
10. Set new goals
11. May strive for some understanding "meaning" of the loss
12. Stop avoiding issues associated with the loss or rumination about the loss

Are you or someone in your life going through this grief process for a major loss? If it is you, what stage do you think you are in? Review your life and consider the major losses and changes you have gone through. Recall your experiences with the grief process. Write about your feelings as you remember them.

WHAT IS MEANT BY RESOLVING GRIEF/LOSS?

1. Claiming your circumstances instead of them claiming you (discuss what this means).
2. Being able to enjoy fond memories without having the precipitation of painful feelings of loss, guilt, regret, or remorse.
3. Finding new meaning in the moment and living without fear of future abandonment/loss.
4. Acknowledging that it is okay to feel sad from time to time and to talk about those feelings.
5. Being able to forgive others when they say or do things that you know are based on a lack of knowledge and understanding.

COMMON SYMPTOMS OF GRIEF

People are affected by grief in different ways but the following is a list of common symptoms for those experiencing grief/loss:

1. Overwhelmed by emotion—with the result of difficulty concentrating and getting started
2. Shock and disbelief. Right after a loss, it can be hard to accept what happened. You may feel numb, have trouble believing that the loss really happened, or even deny the truth. If someone you love has died, you may keep expecting him or her to show up, even though you know he or she is gone.
3. Sadness. Profound sadness is probably the most universally experienced symptom of grief. You may have feelings of emptiness, despair, yearning, or deep loneliness. You may also cry a lot or feel emotionally unstable.
4. Lack of direction. There could be difficulty getting started or not even knowing where to start.
5. Guilt. You may regret or feel guilty about things you did or didn't say or do. You may also feel guilty about certain feelings (e.g., feeling relieved when the person died after a long, difficult illness). After a death, you may even feel guilty for not doing something to prevent the death, even if there was nothing more you could have done.

6. Anger. Even if the loss was nobody's fault, you may feel angry and resentful. If you lost a loved one, you may be angry with yourself, God, the doctors, or even the person who died for abandoning you. You may feel the need to blame someone for the injustice that was done to you.

7. Depression. This may be seen with social withdrawal, lack of pleasure in activities previously experienced as pleasurable, and physical symptoms such as sleep and appetite disturbance.

8. Fear. A significant loss can trigger a host of worries and fears. You may feel anxious, helpless, or insecure. You may even have panic attacks. The death of a loved one can trigger fears about your own mortality, of facing life without that person, or the responsibilities you now face alone.

9. Physical symptoms. We often think of grief as a strictly emotional process, but grief often involves physical problems, including fatigue, nausea, lowered immunity, weight loss or weight gain, aches and pains, and insomnia.

WHAT ARE THE MYTHS OF DEALING WITH LOSS?

Myth: The pain will go away faster if you don't think about it.

Fact: Trying to ignore your pain/grief or keep it from surfacing will stand in the way of healing and make it worse over time. For real healing it is necessary to face your loss/grief and actively deal with it.

Myth: It's important to be "be strong" when you experience a loss.

Fact: Feeling sad, lonely, frightened, or that others don't understand are all normal reaction to loss. Crying and needing to talk about it with others doesn't mean you are weak. You don't need to "protect" your family or friends by putting on a brave front. Showing your true feelings can help them and you. Also, someone you trust doesn't have to "understand your emotional experience" they only need to be available.

Myth: If you don't cry, it means you aren't grieving about the loss.

Fact: Crying is a normal response to sadness, but there are other emotional expressions of loss/grief. Those who don't cry may feel the pain just as deeply as others. They may simply have other ways of showing it.

Myth: Grieving doesn't last very long, maybe about a year.

Fact: There is no right or wrong time frame for grieving. Everyone has their own journey of working through loss/grief. Some people start to feel better in weeks or months. For others, the grieving process is measured in years—possibly endured over their lifetime.

Grieving is as individual as people are. Grieving can sometimes be like an emotional roller coaster of ups and downs. Commonly in the beginning the down times are longer and deeper. However, as time goes by these difficult periods should become less intense and not last as long. Not because the value of the loss has decreased, but because we need to fully resume living our life and being emotionally available to other important people in our life. Some losses are so challenging that we get better living with it but the pain remains and may be triggered by the anniversary of loss or other unforeseen events. Consider the following to help you understand your personal experience of grief and loss.

1. Growing awareness—that issues are unresolved
2. Accepting responsibility—for resolving the loss
3. Identifying—what you need to do to resolve the loss
4. Taking action—to resolve the loss
5. Moving beyond loss—through sharing with others and taking action that facilitates resolution and growth. Finding meaning in what you had as well as the loss is a key challenge to the grieving process

GRIEF CYCLE (WHERE ARE YOU STUCK?)

DEFINITION: THE NATURAL EMOTIONAL RESPONSE TO THE LOSS OF A CHERISHED IDEA, PERSON, OR THING

1. DENIAL (isolation)
   A. Powerlessness
   B. Psychological buffer (defense)—protects knowledge or awareness of thoughts or feelings that you are not ready to deal with mentally, emotionally, or spirituality
   C. Denial of reality
      1. The more you have depended on the last object, the stronger your denial

2. ANGER (self-disappointment, self-hatred)
   A. Anger over loss and not being able to find it
      1. Regrets
   B. Can become destructive if not expressed in healthy ways
      1. Out of control anger = rage, violence
      2. Held in, stuffed anger = out of control physical illness
         a. Anger turned inward toward self = depression
         b. Despair, suicide

3. BARGAINING (postponing the inevitable. Attempts to control the uncontrollable)
   A. "What if's" and "if only"
   B. Desperate attempts to regain control
   C. Keeps you from facing reality
   D. Destructive if one gets stuck here

4. DEPRESSION (sorrow, despair)
   A. Anger channeled back into self, turned inward against self
   B. Response typically associated with grief but actually only one part of the whole process
      1. Tears, reminiscing, sad music.
      2. Trapped (stuck) sorrow = self-pity leads to destructive behavior.
      3. Can be immobilizing = total helplessness.
      4. Crying is a good way to express sorrow. It washes away sadness. It heals. It is a sign of strength when used as part of the grieving process, but if stuck crying can become a chronic behavior that does not effectively promote grieving.

5. ACCEPTANCE
   A. Final goal with achieving resolution of grief
   B. Belief that it is possible to heal and recover
   C. Surrender to reality
   D. Recognition of responsibility = ACTION
   E. Finding meaning

HISTORY OF LOSS GRAPH

On your graph write:

1. What happened?
2. When did it happen?

Below your graph write about:

1. How did it affect your life?
2. What issues do you now have to resolve?
   Example:

year	1977	1980	1981	1987
Loss	Lost job	Father died	Son left for college	Spouse had affair

3. What events were never acknowledged or discussed?
4. Did you become aware of other unspoken communications, either things you wish you had heard or things you wish you had said?

Think about the meaning of the following statements:

LIFE WHAT YOU MAKE IT SOMETHING

LOST—SOMETHING GAINED IS

YOUR CUP HALF EMPTY OR HALF FULL

1. Write about what the statements mean.
2. Do you apply this type of attitude/perspective to your life?
   If yes—how do you apply it to your life?
   If no—how do you go about changing it?

COPING WITH LOSS AND GRIEF

1. *Social support.* Not surprising, the important factor in healing from loss is having the support of other people. Whether it is to trusted family/friend, someone you don't know well but is easy/comfortable to talk to, or a grief group it is important to express your feelings and thoughts when grieving. Connecting with others is an important factor for healing.
   A. Utilize your resources. Don't avoid those who care about you or deflect from talking about what you are going through.
   B. Join a support group. Grief can feel very lonely, even when you have loved ones around. Sharing your sorrow with others who have experienced similar losses can help. To find a bereavement support group in your area, contact local hospitals, hospice, funeral homes, and counseling centers.
   C. Use social media for support. Memorial pages on Facebook and other social media sites have become popular ways to inform a wide audience of a loved one's passing and to reach out for support.
   D. Seek spiritual guidance/support. If you belong to a church or share a philosophy of a certain faith it could be comforting to reach out.
   E. Get professional help. If you feel overwhelmed or stuck obtain some names of therapists who specialize in loss and grief. They can help you work through intense emotions and overcome obstacles to your grieving.

2. Self-care
   A. Confront your emotions. You can put off dealing with emotions and "stuff" them—but not forever. Suppressing your grief only prolongs it. Not confronting normal grief issues and allowing your grief to remain unresolved can lead to depression, anxiety, substance use disorders, and/or health problems.
   B. Be respectful of the emotions of other's, likewise don't let anyone tell you how you should feel. It is also important to not tell yourself how you feel either. Instead make the effort to identify what it is.
   C. Find creative ways of expressing your feelings and thoughts (journal about your loss or fear, if you have lost a loved one write them a letter, make a photo album or scrap book celebrating their life and shared times, get involved in an organization that was important to them, or create a fundraiser for a scholarship, etc.).
   D. Exercise and strive to develop physical activities that you enjoy (walking, running, cycling). Feeling good physically often improves emotional states. Eat well, get good sleep, drink a lot of water and minimize the use of alcohol or drugs to numb the distress, pain and grief or for a false lift that will result in a spiral as the substance influence fades.
   E. Relapse prevention. Identify as many "triggers" as possible such as anniversaries, holidays, specific environments, sounds, odors, noises, etc. They are normal and they "trigger" PTS symptoms that are also normal. But you can still plan for triggers by having strategies to manage them. It won't be perfect so one of the backup plans must be for when the "unplanned" happens.

3. *Complicated grief.* When grief doesn't get any better and doesn't go away it is referred to as complicated grief. Keep in mind that it is normal that the sadness of losing someone you love never goes away entirely, but it shouldn't continue to be the center either. If the pain of the loss remains severe and constant as to consume you—you may have complicated grief. Complicated grief has been described as being stuck in an intense state of grieving. Symptoms of complicated grief include the following:
   A. Intense longing for the deceased
   B. Intrusive thoughts and images of the deceased
   C. Sense of disbelief or denial of the death
   D. Searching for the person in familiar places
   E. Imagining that your loved one is alive
   F. Feeling life is empty or meaningless
   G. Extreme anger or bitterness over the loss

4. The difference between grief and depression is not always easy to define. They share symptoms, but there also differences. If you experience any of the following symptoms talk to your doctor immediately and seek professional help.
   A. Feelings of hopelessness or worthlessness
   B. Inability to function at work, home, or in relationships
   C. Slow speech and body movements
   D. Intense and pervasive sense of guilt
   E. Thoughts of suicide or preoccupation with dying
   F. Seeing or hearing things that aren't there

LOOSING A FAMILY MEMBER OR FRIEND TO SUICIDE

1. Shock: "I feel numb." Feelings of being dazed or detached are a common response to trauma. Shock can protect the mind from becoming completely overwhelmed, allowing the person to function.
2. Denial: "I feel fine." Sometimes people can consciously or unconsciously refuse to accept the facts and information about another's death. This process can be even more challenging when there is little information or explanation about a loved one's suicide. Eventually, as you gather

information and accept that you may not be able to know everything, you can begin to process the reality of this tragic event and all the emotions that come with it. In time, however, our minds become more able to analyze the tragic event, and this allows the denial to give way to less troubling emotions.

3. Guilt: "I think it was my fault." Feelings of guilt following a suicide are very common. Guilt comes from the mistaken belief that we should have, or could have, prevented the death from happening. Guilt can also arise if there are unreconciled issues with the deceased or regret about things said or not said. In truth, no person can predict the future, nor can they know all the reasons for another person's actions. It is human nature to blame oneself when experiencing a loss, rather than accepting the truth that some things were out of our control.

4. Sadness: "Why bother with anything?" Once the initial reactions to the death by suicide have lessened in intensity, feelings of sadness, and depression can move to the forefront. These feelings can be present for some time and can, at times, be triggered by memories and reminders of the loved one who was lost. Feelings of hopelessness, frustration, bitterness, and self-pity are all common when dealing with a loss of a loved one. Typically, you gradually learn to accept the loss and embrace both your happy and sad memories.

5. Anger: "How could they do this to me?" Feelings of anger toward the person you have lost can arise. Many who mourn feel a sense of abandonment. Others feel anger toward a real or perceived culprit. These feelings can be complex and distressing when they are directed at the person who died. It is important to know that it is possible to both be angry with someone, and to still hold them dear in your heart. Sometimes anger is needed before you can accept the reality of the loss.

6. Acceptance: "I can miss them and still continue living." The ultimate goal of healing is to accept the tragic event as something that could not have been prevented and cannot be changed—or simply cannot be changed. Acceptance is not the same as forgetting. Instead, acceptance is learning to live again and to be able to reopen your heart, while still remembering the person who has passed away.

7. Complicating challenges: Suicide can feel different than other losses and that can make the healing process more difficult. Below are a few of the complex thoughts and feelings following suicide.

   A. Confusing mixed emotions: After a death by illness or natural causes, the bereaved's feelings may be less complicated than when the death is by suicide. When a death is by suicide, you might both mourn the person's passing while also hold intense feelings about the circumstances of their death. Feelings such as anger, abandonment, and rejection can all occur after a suicide as well as positive feelings about the deceased. Sorting through all of these diverse feelings can make the healing process more challenging.

   B. Stigma of suicide and the associated isolation: Talking about suicide can be difficult for those who have experienced the loss. Different cultures view suicide in different ways, and sometimes discussing it can be a challenge. This can also be made more difficult when the act of suicide conflicts with religious views. Suicide can be isolating as communities of friends each struggle differently to make sense of the loss they all experienced. Finding the right people in your support network who are able to help you experience your loss is important. Sometimes, this may mean seeking professional help to help you cope with your loss. In those situations, it is recommended that you contact a counselor at the UT Counseling and Mental Health Center, or find a trusted therapist in the community.

   C. Driving need to understand why: This need to understand "why" may be a difficult path, as the circumstances surrounding the loved one's death could be unclear or not easily known/not shared. Some questions may never be answered, while you may find other answers that make sense. Sometimes you will find answers to your questions, while other times, you must learn to accept the fact that there are some things no one can know. You will be confronted to find a way to "think" about such a loss with compassion.

   D. Risk for survivors: People who have recently experienced a loss by suicide are at increased risk for having suicidal thoughts themselves. After experiencing the loss of a loved one, it's not uncommon to wish you were dead or to feel like the pain is unbearable. Remember that having suicidal thoughts does not mean that you will act on them. These feelings and thoughts will likely decrease over time, but if you find them too intense, or if you're considering putting your thoughts into action, seek support from a mental health professional.

8. Healthy ways to cope
   A. Immediately seek support from those who listen and talk with you, could be a family member, friend, therapist, or minister. Consider joining a support group for survivors of suicide. Do not isolate, reach out for support when you feel like you need it.
   B. Acknowledge your experiences and express your feelings. Be thoughtful about maintaining some balance and purposefully doing other things. Also create a pattern of ending the day in a pleasant and peaceful manner.
   C. Stay in the moment experiencing your emotions without being overwhelmed. This can be accomplished by using your social supports, journaling, meditating, or other relaxation techniques (deep breathing, progressive muscle relaxation, etc.).
   D. Everyone close to the person who completes suicide is going to be sorting through their feelings. Be patient and take time to heal and be true to yourself by setting limits, saying "no," and taking time for exercise and other forms of self-care. If you feel like crying, do so but be wise to not isolate and indulge in loss.
   E. Identify your positive memories and how you will honor your relationship.
   F. Identify what you learned in sharing a relationship with them.
   G. Identify how you may share information about the loss of your loved one in a manner that may be helpful to others.
   H. Maintain balance as best you can by establishing a routine. This structure can help you manage your emotions of grief and provide some reassuring sense of normal life patterns. A very important part of life routines is fun and laughter. Laughter is the best medicine. As previously stated for effective coping, eat well as you can, exercise when you can, and avoid alcohol and other drugs that will make it harder for you to work through your feelings.

PHYSICAL HEALTH

HEALTH INVENTORY

Use the following list to identify basic health-related habits:

1. Exercise regularly.
2. Maintain good nutrition.
3. Do not smoke.
4. Avoid excessive snacking.
5. Get 7–8 h of sleep per night.
6. Maintain normal weight.
7. Avoid having more than two to three drinks in at a given time to prevent substance abuse. If you drink everyday—think about what you are doing, why you are doing it, and what negative consequences may be associated (i.e., weight gain, poor nutrition, not being emotionally available, etc.).
8. Maintain regular health checkups.
9. Avoid overeating or weight gain.
10. Be aware of chronic stress or anger.

Other health concerns:_____

Take some time to consider the impact of your self-care/health behaviors.

1. What are your assets, and what is the current and potential benefit?
2. What are your problem areas, and what are the current and potential liabilities?
3. What areas of change are necessary?
4. What are you willing to change?

Plan: _____

_____

_____

_____

ASSESSING LIFESTYLE AND HEALTH

A. Current risk factors

__hypertension   __elevated triglycerides   __elevated cholesterol

__overeating   __excess salt, sugar, fat __lack of exercise

__chronic stress   __smoking   __overweight

__alcohol abuse   __sleep disturbance   __prescription medication abuse

B. Nutrition

When you review your diet and compare it to 1 year ago and 5 years ago, is it the same, less healthy, or more healthy?

1. The positive changes made are _____

_____

_____

2. Changes that need to be made are _____

_____

_____

C. Stress management

1. Current level of stress is _low _moderate _high

   To the following, respond never (N), sometimes (S), often (O), or always (A):

2. In an effort to deal with stress

   a. Exercise is used to decrease tension __
   b. Relaxation techniques are help for releasing tension __

3. Characteristics I have in common with those who manage stress well:

   a. Daily moments of peace and solitude __
   b. Playfulness and humor to improve mood __
   c. Positive relationships with family and friends __
   d. Distracting activities __
   e. Good level of frustration tolerance __
   f. Good ability to manage criticism __
   g. An ability to avoid overloaded scheduling __
   h. A good balance of work and pleasure __

D. Answer each of the following questions regarding your negative lifestyle habits:
   1. How is it a problem?
   2. How did it begin and develop?
   3. What could be some appropriate substitutes?
   4. What do you want to change?
E. Plan of change

ASSUMING THE PATIENT ROLE: THE BENEFITS OF BEING SICK

With real or perceived symptoms of chronic illness, an individual may experience real or perceived benefits. This is called "secondary gain." To better understand yourself and your potential motivation to change, thoroughly think through the following issues:

Accidents, illnesses, symptoms (please list)

Car

Choose an accident, illness, or symptom from your list to complete the following statements:

1. It happens when _Don't pay attention_
2. It feels like _I've been wounded, embarrassed, financial struggle_
3. It prevents _Going to work_
4. It results in _Less Money_
5. It encourages _Low Self-Esteem, Lack of Courage_
6. It demonstrates that I have a deep need for _Rest and relief from some duties_
7. It benefits me with _Support care of family friends_
8. An appropriate way to get this need met would be to _Text or call everyone let them know about situation._

My plan for dealing with this issue:
Take my time, get up earlier, no rushing

IMPROVING YOUR HEALTH

Ready to turn your life around? It may require that you make some changes in basic health behaviors, but the results are worth it. It's simple.

1. Eat right ✓
2. ~~Quit smoking~~
3. ~~Decrease or eliminate alcohol~~ consumption
4. Exercise and get fit ✓
5. Learn to relax ✓
6. Get adequate sleep ✓
7. Live authentically (be honest, learn from life, and be true to yourself) ✓

Even small changes can lead to significant health improvements. According to an article in *Time* (February 2001), 50 million Americans still smoke and 60% of the American population is obese or overweight:

1. Eating right

   Educate yourself about the types of fat and their health consequences (for example, omega-3 from cold water fish is good and certain nuts are good; sparingly consume saturated fats, watch out for trans-fatty acids, which are found in crackers and cookies).
   A. Emphasize fruits and vegetables
   B. Promote low-fat dairy
   C. Promote high-fiber grains
   D. Promote modest portions of lean meat
   E. Reduce sodium intake
   F. Reduce alcohol intake (some studies demonstrate a health benefit for small portions of red wine; again, take responsibility and educated yourself)

2. Smoking N/A
   A. The day you quit smoking, carbon monoxide levels in your blood drops significantly
   B. Within 1 week, blood becomes less sticky and death by heart attack declines
   C. After 4–5 years of not smoking, risk of heart attack is decreased to nearly the same as someone who has never smoked

   Most can use it but not abuse it.

3. Alcohol consumption

   First of all, clarify why you are drinking. Is a glass of wine part of enjoying a good meal, or do you drink to relax, sleep, get high, or numb out? Be honest with yourself, and if you are not able to substitute positive health behaviors for self-medication, or if you cannot decrease drinking or stop drinking on your own, then seek professional help. Remember, some people can drink alcohol and experience some health benefits, others, not necessarily alcoholics, cannot tolerate alcohol use. Be honest and smart.

4. Exercise

   A 40-year-old sedentary individual who starts walking briskly for half an hour a day, 4 days a week, has almost the same low risk of heart attack as the person who has always exercised.

5. Learning to relax

Adequate rest includes getting enough hours of rejuvenating sleep and reconditioning your body to know what it feels like to be relaxed. With the fast pace of life and daily demands, people sometimes forget what it feels like to not be making lists in your head, stressing about deadlines today, and worrying about the tasks of tomorrow. Exercise, soothing music, being creative/art, hobbies, pleasure reading, formal relaxation, and meditation are all choices for relaxing. Make sure to throw in a healthy dose of laughter everyday. Genuine laughter, smiling, and happy/pleasing thoughts are healing. Likewise, attitude influences health, emotional functioning, and how you share your life with others. Are you honest, friendly, kind, and optimistic, or sour, angry, hostile, and negative? Guess what is good for health and happiness and which isn't?

6. Sleep

Research continues to confirm the importance of sleep in optimal physical, emotional, and psychological functioning. If you are experiencing difficulty sleeping, talk with your physician to make sure that there are not any physical reasons contributing to sleep disturbance (such as sleep apnea). Also, it is important to have a regular schedule, which conditions your body to wind down and prepare for sleep.

7. Living authentically

Be true to yourself. Take responsibility for your own thoughts and feelings. Don't live in the past or hold grudges. If there are issues that you need to resolve do so, learn, heal, and move forward integrating whatever you learn into your life experience—it is a part of who you are and cannot be erased. Consciously choose how you think about things, and respond in the way that is best for you. Self-responsibility is the only way to successfully bring sustaining positive changes to your life.

As you review your life and health, use a journal to record the following:

1. Identify what is good (be genuinely grateful) *My spirit walk*
2. Identify what needs to be changed
   A. Why? *Read bible more.*
   B. What is the goal? *Spend more time reading*
   C. What steps need to be taken?
   D. How can change be reinforced and maintained? *Mark on calendar, set a reminder*
   E. What will you need to self-monitor? *Daily Calendar log checked on weekend*
3. Clarify and understand why you have chosen negative health behaviors or emotional responses
   A. Self-medication *Never took responsibility*
   B. Lack of insight and awareness
   C. Lack of motivation/self-responsibility
   D. What motivates the decision to change now?
4. What resources may be helpful in reaching you goals?
   A. Gym, walking, jogging, cycling, exercise videos, organized sports
   B. Yoga or other classes
   C. People who are supportive of positive health behaviors
   D. Maintaining a journal
5. Educate yourself on the role of emotions on health, harmful thinking, or feeling:
   A. Anger
   B. Hostility
   C. Anxiety

SLEEP

SLEEP DISORDERS

Sleep Disorders can be present due to factors such as physiological changes, changes in environment, distressing experiences, emotional difficulties, stress, or changes in daily routine. In dealing with sleep disorders, there is a single goal: improved sleep accompanied by increased feelings of restfulness.

TREATMENT FOCUS AND OBJECTIVES

1. Identify the nature and extent of the sleep disturbance
   A. Have the individual keep a sleep journal to more accurately determine the number of hours of sleep per night
   B. Assess the need to refer to specific support resources or for further evaluation
2. Rule out presence of concomitant impairment in physiological/psychological/emotional state that is contributing or responsible for the sleep disturbance
3. Evaluate and refer for psychopharmacological treatment
4. Devise and implement a behavioral management program for treating the sleep disturbance

Individuals who experience sleep disturbance may develop a "phobic"-type reaction that exacerbates their sleep difficulties and further negatively impacts their coping with lack of sleep because of self-defeating internal dialogue. Rule out substance abuse, medication reactions, menopause, pain, and excessive caffeine use.

TEN TIPS FOR BETTER SLEEP AND RECOVERY

People suffer from insomnia for different reasons. Sleep disturbance can be related to physiological changes such as menopause, medical problems such as hyperthyroidism, emotional distress such as depression or anxiety, changes in lifestyle such as having a baby or any other change that may influence daily patterns, and general life stressors. Take a few minutes to review what may possibly be related to the difficulty that you are experiencing with sleep. If it has been some time since your last physical examination or you think that there may be a relationship between the sleep disturbance and physiological changes or a medical problem make an appointment with your physician to identify or rule out health-related issues. If health-related issues are definitely not a factor then consider the following ways to improve your sleep.

If you are not able to identify the exact symptoms of your insomnia keep a sleep journal for 2 weeks and write down your sleep–wake cycle, how many hours you sleep, and all the other details related to your sleep disturbance.

1. *Establish a regular time for going to bed, and be consistent.* This helps to cue you that it is time for sleep. Going to sleep at the same time and awakening at the same time daily helps stabilize your internal clock. Having a different sleep–wake schedule on the weekends can throw you off. For the best results be consistent.

2. *Do not go to bed too early.* Do not be tempted to try to go bed earlier than you would normally need to. If you have started doing this then identify the reason why (depression, stress, boredom, pressure from your partner). When people go to bed too early it contributes to the problem of fragmented sleep. Your body normally lets you sleep only the number of hours it need. If you go to bed too early you will also be waking too early.

3. Determine how many hours of sleep you need for optimal functioning and feeling rested. Consider the following to determine the natural length of your sleep cycle.
   A. How many hours did you sleep on the average as a child?
   B. Before you began to experience sleep difficulty how many hours of sleep per night did you sleep on the average?
   C. How many hours of sleep do you need to awaken naturally, without an alarm?
   D. How many hours of sleep do you need not feel sleepy or tired during the day?

4. *Develop rituals that signal the end of the day.* Rituals that signal closure for the day could be tucking the kids in, putting the dog out, and closing up the house for the night … then … it's time for you to wind down by watching the news, reading a book (not an exciting mystery), having a cup of calming herbal tea, evening prayers, or doing something such as meditation, deep breathing exercises, or progressive muscle relaxation. All of these behaviors are targeted for shifting your thinking from the daily stressors to closure that the day is over and it is time for rest so that you can start a new day tomorrow.

5. *Keep the bedroom for sleeping and sex only.* If you use your bedroom as an office or for other activities your mind will associate the bedroom with those activities that are not conducive to sleep.

6. *A normal pattern of sex can be helpful.* However, it is only helpful if you are engaging in sex because you are interested in being close to your partner. Sexual stimulation releases endorphins that give you a mellow, relaxed feeling. Be careful to avoid trying to use sex to fall asleep. It can backfire because you are taking a pleasurable, intimate, and ultimately relaxing behavior and putting expectations on it that can lead to pressure and feeling upset.

7. *Avoid physical and mental stimulation just before sleep time.* Exercising, working on projects, housecleaning, watching something exciting on television, or reading something that has an exciting plot just prior to going to bed can energize you instead of helping you to have closure at the end of the day.

8. *Be careful of naps.* Some people are able to take naps and feel rejuvenated by them without interfering with their sleep–wake cycle. Other people may be overtired for various reasons and benefit from an hour nap early in the afternoon. However, for others it can be sabotaging. If you take naps skip them for a week. If you find that you are sleeping better without the naps then stop napping.

9. *Get regular exercise.* Regular aerobic exercise such as walking can decrease body tension, alleviate stress, alleviate depressive symptoms, and contribute to an overall feeling of well-being. Less stress and regular exercise = better sleep.

10. *Take a warm bath one to two hours before bedtime.* Experiment with the time to determine what works best for you. A good 20 min soaking in a warm bath (100–102°F) is a great relaxer. It raises your core body temperature by several degrees that naturally induce drowsiness and sleep.

Be careful not to obsess about sleep. When someone is experiencing sleep disturbance they can become so focused on the issue of sleep that they nearly develop a phobia about not getting it, which creates a lot of stress and tension for them at the end of the day instead of relaxation which is necessary for the natural sleep rhythms to be initiated. Instead, try to relax and think about something pleasant. If, after 20 min, that does not work get up and go to another room to meditate, or engage in some other ritual that you find helpful to inducing feelings of drowsiness so you can sleep.

EATING AND NUTRITION

EATING HISTORY

To increase your awareness for eating patterns and behavioral patterns associated with eating, please use the following to write your eating history. Use this as an opportunity to better understand and be honest about your loss of control in regard to food use or rituals and practices surrounding your food use. Share your eating history with a trusted person or with your therapist.

Consider the following:

1. Kinds, amounts, and frequency of food use
2. Foggy memories or difficulty concentrating after eating too much
3. Feeling high after vomiting or starving
   A. Feeling powerful when "choosing to withhold food or correcting food mistakes" by throwing up (fully of power in demonstrating this self-control to self others.)
4. Behavior changes
   A. Mood swings with eating/not eating
   B. Withdrawal from others to eat or starve
   C. How relationships change and why
5. Rituals surrounding food use
   A. Overeating or binge eating on certain foods
   B. Frequent eating out
   C. Sneak eating/eating in secret
   D. Weighing self daily or more often
   E. Eating/not eating certain food(s)
6. Preoccupation
   A. Thinking about eating/not eating
   B. Eating for relief from problems, boredom, frustration, and so on
   C. Protecting your food supply; hiding food
   D. Preoccupation with body size
7. Attempts to control eating or weight
   A. Doctor's diets
   B. Fad diets
   C. Diet pills or shots
   D. Starving, vomiting, laxative use, diuretics, or manual extraction of stool
   E. Diet clubs or fat farms
   F. Hypnosis, acupuncture, stomach stapling, or gastric bypass surgery
   G. Spending money to control eating or weight
8. Family/friend response
   A. To your eating patterns
   B. To changes in your appearance

STOP USING FOOD AS A COPING MECHANISM

Some people experience difficulty expressing their emotions and resolving associated issues. Over time, they may identify food as the source of comfort they are looking for. By this time it is quite possible that they are experiencing depression. Therefore, their use of food as a mechanism to cope has (1) created a cycle of conditioned behavior that maintains depression and (2) become a demonstration of self-medication.

Emotional distress → Internalizes distress → Thinks about food/eating → Engages in compulsion → Numbs out → Feels guilty/bad

The irony of this cycle is that these individuals often do not even notice the taste or how much they are eating. The distress and emptiness cannot be alleviated with food. The foods often eaten under these conditions are sugars and starches. These foods increase serotonin in the brain and temporarily alleviate emotional distress. Therefore, these two issues must be confronted: (1) reconditioning, which involves learning new ways to cope and take care of yourself and (2) understanding the role of your specific brain chemistry. Consider the following information as resources for developing new coping mechanisms:

1. Increase self-understanding and self-awareness. Keep a self-awareness journal that records what you are doing and why you are doing it. Keep a food journal. Write down exactly what you eat, when, and how you felt.

2. Create a habit of asking yourself why you feel like eating. If you are not hungry, take responsibility for making a better choice. Create a list of behaviors you can do in an effort to get redirected.

3. Identify what you are feeling. Identify what the feeling is associated with (thoughts and experiences), and identify your choices for "dealing" with the feeling.

4. Acknowledge that life is never without issues to deal with. Don't ruminate about it, don't worry about it, and don't procrastinate. Whatever it is, deal with it (without food) and move on.

5. Be assertive about how you feel instead of using food as a coping mechanism. Compulsive eating is a negative way of expressing feelings that are being stuffed.

6. Develop realistic expectations about working through emotional distress that has built up over a period of time. Just because you have identified the problem and are practicing positive health behaviors and improved coping does not mean that everything is immediately resolved. Continue to journal for increased clarity and problem solving, and practice appropriately and honestly expressing your thoughts and feelings.

7. Focus on what is working in your life, use positive self-talk, and develop genuine gratitude. Find the silver lining in clouds. What positive things have you learned through difficult experiences? You often do not have any control over things that happen, but you do have control in how you choose to deal with them.

8. Identify triggers. What thoughts, feelings, and situations serve as setups for a relapse? This would be a good topic for putting your journal to good use. Be prepared and be self-responsible. Life is about choices, so use choices that help you.

9. Consider joining a support group that reinforces positive health behaviors and self-care.

10. Talk with your doctor about health changes and medications that increase serotonin.

PREVENTING WEIGHT AND BODY IMAGE PROBLEMS IN CHILDREN

Increased stress, ever-present media, convenience food and soda, and decreased physical activity have led to an overconcern about physical appearance with decreased tolerance for all the normal variations in body types and an epidemic of obesity in children. Children have become more concerned about their weight and body image at an earlier age (as early as 6–9 years old). However, children who are obese do not necessarily have lower self-esteem than nonobese children.

Obesity among children has now become a health concern that can make some medical issues worse and lead to others (such as diabetes, joint problems, hypertension, premature onset on periods and irregular periods, etc.). Both genetic and environmental factors affect a child's potential for obesity. Therefore, it may be important for both you and your child to change some habits. Consult with your family physician or nutritional specialist, attend nutrition classes, and educate yourself by reading about how to eat healthfully. Continuously bringing up exercise and dieting to children and adolescents can create conflicts, resistance, and negatively affect self-esteem. Therefore, problem-solve what changes you will make that sets the tone for nutrition and exercise. Your children will learn from you. Be a more active family. Make activity fun an important part of your lifestyle.

OBSESSION WITH WEIGHT

While being obese is not necessarily related directly to lower self-esteem, there is still warranted concern:

1. Peer cruelty
2. Parental focus on weight
   A. May cause a child to develop feelings of inadequacy
   B. A develop potential precursor to eating disorders
3. Media continuously portraying the cultural perception of thin as attractive

OBESITY AND SELF-ESTEEM

1. Obesity is not always related to the lowering of self-esteem
2. Self-esteem is more likely to be associated with how
   A. Family members respond to weight issues
   B. Social experiences
   C. Development of effective coping skills

*However, juvenile obesity is not a good thing. It is a parent's responsibility to provide nutritious food and an activity-based lifestyle for children. Be a role model.

WHAT PARENTS CAN DO

1. Set a healthy example
   A. Physical activity
   B. Nutrition
   C. Not being negatively judgmental about different body types

*Children develop adult perceptions of attractiveness as early as age 7.

2. Make sure that children know and feel they are loved regardless of their weight
   A. Do not focus on their weight
   B. Focus on spending time with them
   C. Focus on teaching them effective life-management skills

GUIDELINES TO FOLLOW IF SOMEONE YOU KNOW HAS AN EATING DISORDER

1. Don't pretend that everything is okay when it is not. Anorexia and bulimia are serious illnesses. These eating disorders are self-destructive behaviors (starving, bingeing, purging). They scream for help with underlying problems such as depression, and they can become life threatening. So don't be silent—be honest and address your concerns.

2. Approach you family member or friend in a gentle, caring manner, but be persistent. Listen without interrupting. However, let your family member know how concerned you are. Do not expect an admission of a problem or changes just because you address your concern.

3. Pay attention to what you witness or experience in the way of changes in your family member or friend, such as anorexia, which is indicated by significant weight loss, obsessive dieting, hyperactivity, distorted body image (seeing oneself as fat when the person is thin) or bulimia, indicated when someone eats a lot of food and then rushes to the bathroom or uses laxatives.

4. Do not focus on the eating habits of those you are concerned about. Instead, try to encourage an understanding of why they are engaging in eating disorder behaviors.

5. Encourage them to get help because of their unhappiness. If you have noticed increased fatigue, irritability, depression, anxiety, or compulsiveness, be supportive in their getting help.

6. Being supportive is the best that you can offer. It is important to show you believe in them. Be emotionally available and do not judge.

7. If possible, offer a written list of resources in your community, online, and in books. Again, do not expect an admission of a problem, just share the resources.

8. Do not keep this to yourself and deal with alone. Colluding with secrecy is not helpful—things are likely to get worse. Confide in someone that you trust. Be honest about not keeping it a secret and say that you are speaking out because you care.

9. Deal with your own emotions. How have you been affected by this experience? Talk to someone about your own feelings.

10. Be clear that you are not responsible for your family member or friend. You can only encourage these loved ones to help themselves.

RELATIONSHIPS

RELATIONSHIP QUESTIONNAIRE

This questionnaire is intended to estimate the current satisfaction with your relationship. Circle the number between 1 (completely satisfied) and 10 (completely unsatisfied) beside each issue. Try to focus on the present and not the past.

1. List the things that your partner does that please you:
2. What would you like your partner to do more often?
3. What would your partner like you to do more often?
4. How do you contribute to difficulties in the relationship?
5. What are you prepared to do differently in the relationship?

6. Is there a problem of alcohol/substance abuse?
7. Do you often try to anticipate your partner's wishes so that you can please them?
8. What are your goals or what do you hope to accomplish?

	completely satisfied									completely unsatisfied
General relationship	1	2	3	4	5	6	7	(8)	9	10
Personal independence	(1)	2	3	4	5	6	7	8	9	(10)
Spouse independence	(1)	2	3	4	5	6	7	8	9	10
Couples time alone	1	2	3	4	5	6	7	(8)	9	10
Social activities	1	2	(3)	4	5	6	7	8	9	10
Occupational or Academic progress	(1)	2	3	4	5	6	7	8	9	10
Sexual interactions	(1)	2	3	4	5	6	7	8	9	10
Communication	(1)	2	3	4	5	6	7	8	9	10
Financial issues	1	2	3	4	5	6	7	8	9	(10)
Household/yard Responsibility	1	2	3	4	(5)	6	7	8	9	10
Parenting	1	(2)	3	4	5	6	7	8	9	10
Daily social interaction	(1)	2	3	4	5	6	7	8	9	10
Trust in each other	1	2	(3)	4	5	6	7	8	9	10
Decision making	(1)	2	3	4	5	6	7	8	9	10
Resolving conflicts	(1)	2	3	4	5	6	7	8	9	10
Problem solving	(1)	2	3	4	5	6	7	8	9	10
Support of one another	(1)	2	3	4	5	6	7	8	9	10

HEALTHY ADULT RELATIONSHIPS: BEING A COUPLE

Just as people change over time so do their relationships. When two people initially get together there is the excitement, hope, and passion of a new relationship. Then they make a lifetime commitment to one another. During the early stage of commitment each person has an expectation that things will feel wonderful forever. This *honeymoon* period of relationship development lasts for 1–2 years. During this time, they begin to notice that there are differences in beliefs and how each would like to handle various situations. However, they continue to put their best foot forward, feeling close, and enjoying one another.

As this period of discovery continues, there are disagreements and differences of opinion, but a relatively new couple may not talk about it. They tend to hold back fearing an increase in disagreements. They are struggling to find a way to go beyond being two people in a relationship to being two people who are sharing their lives together and building a future.

Unfortunately, avoiding conflicts don't make them go away. In fact, if issues are being talked about a lot but it is not accompanied by problem solving, there can be increased frustration and distancing from one another. The two people struggling to be a couple earlier in their relationship may now be doing things separately. With this drifting there are questions that arise regarding the stability of the relationship. This leads to a fork in the road for them. They can choose one of two courses of action: (1) being disillusioned and increasingly pulling away from one another and ending it in a separation or (2) recognize that they have not been making the necessary efforts to strengthen their relationship and making a commitment to invest themselves in creating a successful partnership.

With a recommitment to each other a couple can feel as if they have found that excitement that they originally experienced. If this is the case they have found out some very important things about themselves and their relationship:

1. To feel good about your partner you must have positive thoughts about them in your heart and in your head.

2. For a successful relationship there must be an enduring commitment to get through the good and the bad as partners.

3. There must be an effort to share their lives cooperatively.

4. As they leave their family of origin to begin their own new family:
   A. Recognize that now it is your partner who comes before others.
   B. From the positive perspective, your parents have gained your partner not lost you. Make sure they include your partner as they would include you. Also, be respectful of their gifts to you and include them in the new family you are creating.

5. Since life is very hectic make sure that you are spending adequate time together, focusing on one another and your relationship.

6. Validate your partner. Listen without interrupting when your partner is talking to you. Reflect to them your understanding of what they have shared. Accept and acknowledge how they feel.

IMPROVED COPING SKILLS FOR HAPPIER COUPLES

There is no way to eliminate all conflicts between two people. However, by improving your coping skills, you can go a long way to alleviate the distress of seeing things differently. By evaluating your problems, learning effective ways to resolve them, and knowing when to seek professional help, you and your partner can ensure the lifelong loving relationship you want. Keep in mind, both people must be prepared to take responsibility, work at becoming aware of their contribution to positive and negative outcomes and be prepared to make changes when needed. This is a demonstration of mutual respect and responsibility.

EVALUATE THE PROBLEM

Just bringing two lives together quickly highlights basic differences:

1. Lifestyle
2. Values and beliefs
3. Love language
4. Process of how to accomplish tasks
5. Skills for problem solving, conflict resolution, etc.
6. Parenting
7. Family expectations

8. Traditions
9. Priorities and prioritizing (what's important)
10. Goals (short/long term, personal development, and family achievements)

Differences may initially play a role in mutual attraction, but over time they may become sources of frustration. Therefore, while differences or complementarity may bring you together, it is commitment, the sharing of common goals, mutual respect, and collaboration that keeps you together.

COUPLE'S CONFLICT: RULES FOR FIGHTING FAIR

1. Do not use threats during the argument. Stay focused on the issue(s).
2. Do not use blanket or labeling judgments such as "You never…" or "You are…" Doing and saying hurtful things is not helpful. Be respectful and treat others as you wish to be treated.
3. Stay on the topic. Save other topics for a later discussion. Focus on specific problem, behaviors, or situations that you are striving to resolve.
4. It is not fair to interrupt. Stay at the same eye level. Take responsibility for being a good listener and being sure that you understand what the message is before you respond with your own thoughts and feelings. How you act will be a demonstration of your own agenda or goal. Do you want to work through a problem and resolve it or keep the conflict going?
5. Do not use "always" or "never." Be realistic and honest. Exaggerating prolongs and intensifies a conflict.
6. Stay in the present tense. Bringing up past issues is usually utilized to "win" or prove a point. Just because someone acted in certain in the past does not mean that they will always do the same thing. What is in the past cannot be changed. Also, if you are held hostage by the past, your partner may start to think that no matter what he/she does, it will not make a difference. This does not mean, however, that one should not take responsibility for past actions and make amends.
7. Do not argue in the dark or in bed.
8. It is not fair to walk away or leave the house while you are in the midst of a conflict. Be respectful and responsible for your own behavior. If tempers are escalating, then make a mutual decision to cool off and come back to resolve the conflict.
9. Avoid finger pointing, which will seem like lecturing. Pay attention to your body language. People pay more attention to how a message is delivered than the words said. What do you want to communicate?
10. Take responsibility for change. Always do your part. Take the high road. Be true to yourself.
11. Take responsibility for your own feelings. Rather than saying, "You make me mad," take responsibility for your emotions by saying, "I am mad." You are responsible for your own thoughts, feelings, and behaviors.
12. If you suspect that a conflict is brewing, write down the issue or problem before it evolves into an emotional volcano. This helps a couple to stay in control and more effectively problem-solve the issues at hand. Also, taking the time to write it down can slow the building of tension and clarify the problem.
13. Drama and exaggeration are not helpful. Being dramatic is likely to escalate the situation. Take responsibility to do your part honestly and in a straightforward manner.
14. Both partners have the right to take time to calm themselves and to think about their thoughts and feelings so that they can express them appropriately.

15. Be sure that you know what you are having conflict about. What is the real issue? Choose your battles carefully. Don't sweat the small stuff. What is worth fighting about?

16. Approach conflict with a problem-solving attitude. Be honest about your own agenda and take responsibility for how you choose to deal with it. Ultimately, you have to be a team that finds a way to make it work.

17. Don't say things that are critical, hurtful, or attacking that offers your partner no recourse but to avoid or retaliate. You can't erase hurtfulness. This is akin to "nails in the fence"— when the nails are removed a hole (damage) remains.

18. Don't store up feeling and then erupt like a volcano with your accumulated resentments. This is overwhelming and confuses the current issue. Deal with important issues as they come up.

19. Be honest even when it hurts. Avoid making assumptions. When you make assumptions, you run the risk of totally being off base 50% of the time. It is always easier to see what is wrong with the other person than it is to see what is wrong with yourself. Be honest about your own shortcomings and contributions to relationship difficulties. People grow and change. Also, just because someone loves you does not mean that the person knows what you want or need. It is your responsibility to express your wants and needs directly, clearly, and respectfully.

20. Does it matter who is right? Is it about winning? If you answered yes to either of these questions, you are not investing yourself in a conflict resolution process that is best for your partnership. You are investing yourself in what you think is best for you. When you approach conflict resolution, it must be from a position that both partners win, both must benefit, and neither will be harmed. When issues are resolved, it is a win–win situation. You are going to have to decide if you are two teams or one. With two teams, each has its own agenda. A single team works together toward a common goal.

PROBLEM RESOLUTION

Every couple has differences in opinion. However, people who feel respected, loved, and appreciated experience less conflict. Make it a point everyday to say positive and supportive things to your partner. Simply saying, "I love you" is reassuring and feels good—especially when you take a moment to look in their eyes and touch them. Give compliments about how the other looks or what he/she has done. Compliments are a nice way to say, "I noticed," "I am aware of all that you do."

Talk to each other about fears, concerns, plans, goals, ideas, and financial management. Explore different solutions to the issues that confront you. That will give you more information into the discussion of what the two of you can do to reach your desired outcome. Use the basic problem-solving outline for approaching issues:

1. Identify the problem (agree on what the problem is)
2. Generate all the different ways that are available for resolving the problem
3. Make a mutually agreed on method for resolving the problem
4. Do it!
5. Be supportive and prepared to go to plan B without blaming if it is necessary.

If you have baggage from the past that you (as an individual) have seen interferes with positive outcomes, take responsibility for working through it. If there are couple's issues that you don't seem to be able to resolve to your satisfaction or feel that there is increasing distance in what was a loving and sharing relationship, seek professional help. Also check into community presentations or activities that may improve your functioning as a couple. Many churches also offer helpful groups or programs to the community. Do whatever you need to give your relationship the opportunity to get back on track.

BE CLEAR ABOUT WHAT YOU WANT

1. Everyone should occasionally take the time to review where they are with consideration to goals, interests, and friendships.
2. Consider goals, interests, and friendships as an individual.
3. Consider goals, interests, and friendships as a couple.

*Are there conflicts between step 2 and 3 that need to be worked out?

Be Clear in Communicating What You Want

1. A successful couple is one that works hard at making decisions that are acceptable to both parties.
2. Establish a good time to talk over issues.
3. Remain on one topic until it has been resolved. Then move on to the next topic of discussion.
4. Avoid criticizing, judging, or coercing your partner into what you want and they don't. It may feel like you get what you want in the short run, but you will both pay for it later because your partner will feel hurt and cheated.
5. Avoid stating things from a position of what you don't want. Instead, state what your goals are.
6. Stay focused, respectful, and concentrate on the discussion topic.
7. Avoid bringing up negative experiences from the past. Remain focused on the here and now.
8. Own your actions. Avoid using your partner as an excuse for your making poor choices. Instead engage in productive problem solving if you are experiencing difficulties. Whatever a person does it affects the partnership.

How Can Both of You Get What You Want

1. If there is a difference in what you both want be prepared to negotiate to increase understanding and consensus in decision making.
2. If there is something you need or want from your partner, request it, don't make a demand for it. It may not be an important issue to them, but if you own it as a personal struggle they may be more willing to help or accommodate.
3. When negotiating be prepared to offer something that your partner wants if you want them to give you what you want. There must be balance. Both partners must feel that they get out what they put into the relationship.
4. Don't hold back waiting to see how your partner is going to help you. Instead, show them how they can assist in completing any task. Remember, balance is key. Each must feel like they get out what they put in. That also means demonstrating appreciation when your partner responds to requests for help. Likewise, whenever possible, ask if you can help when you see your partner needing assistance. Better yet, when you can see normal household maintenance tasks that need to be done—don't wait to be asked. Be a partner and help.
5. Self-monitor. Make short-term agreements with a built-in time for reviewing what has been accomplished.
6. Always reinforce the efforts and accomplishments of your partner in assuring that your needs are met. Therefore, when you get what you want make sure you let them know in a loving and appreciative manner.

Be Clear About Mutual Principles That Cannot Be Allowed to Guide Your Marriage

1. *Nonesteeming.* When you share your life with someone who not have a high regard or respect for you, it is clear that they do not honor you. Honor being a statement that "you are the most important person to me" is in direct opposition and results in tremendous emotional pain.

2. *Criticism.* This is the literal tearing apart of the person you share your life with. It is a statement that devalues them and offers a negative belief about them that strikes at the core.

3. *Contempt.* This can be communicated in numerous pain causing ways; being mean, calling names, negative body language (eye-rolling, looking away, etc.), being sarcastic, ridiculing. This is a purely toxic behavior that has no place in a healthy relationship.

4. *Defensiveness.* This is a very damaging to a committed relationship. When someone feels accused of something and offers their partner an excuse for whatever the behavior was instead of validating what your partner has expressed about their concern, it is a clear statement that you are ignoring their expressed concern. If you are guided by the golden rule and always take responsibility for your behaviors, it will be the moral compass that maintains a healthy partnership.

5. *Stonewalling.* Don't avoid conflict out of fear of discussing a problem. Avoidance results in "piling on" and that results in negative feelings and more avoidance. Avoidance can be seen by not listening, tuning-out, being too busy, or engaging in obsessive behavior

6. *Being Unworthy.* This is about being respectful and responsible to the committed relationship in the most basic and enduring ways. Never engage in behaviors while away from your partner that would be hurtful or humiliating to them.

DOMESTIC VIOLENCE

HOW TO PREDICT THE POTENTIALLY VIOLENT RELATIONSHIP

At the core of any violent relationship is the use of power and control. Women often express interest in how they might be able to predict if a potential partner may be someone who is emotionally, sexually, or physically abusive. While women are predominantly the focus of domestic violence (DV), men can also be the victims of DV. Consider the following points in increasing awareness for concern:

1. *Controlling behavior.* Where they are allowed to go, who they are allowed to see or talk to, how they dresses, and how they do their hair and makeup.

   This behavior tends to escalate under the guise of trying to be protective or to prevent someone from being harmed by their poor judgment—therefore, they need to be told what to do and how to do it.

2. *Jealousy.* Defines jealousy as a sign of love and concern. There may be accusations of flirting or being questioned for talking to someone. A major indicator is being isolated from family and friends. As jealousy intensifies, they will be monitored by frequent phone calling and will not be allowed to make personal decisions. Ultimately, they may not be allowed to do anything without the permission of their partner.

3. *Neediness.* Insecurity is expressed as "I have never felt like this about anyone or I have never been able to talk to someone or trust someone like you." There is pressure to commit quickly to an exclusive relationship. There may be pressure to have sex or to move in together.

4. *Isolation.* There is an attempt to isolate the abused person from family and friends. There will likely be efforts to sabotage close relationships and accuse others of causing difficulties in the relationship. There may also be efforts to limit phone contact, use of a car, or even from going to school or work.

5. *Projecting blame onto others.* Almost anything that goes wrong will be blamed on the controlled partner or other people.

6. *Unrealistic expectations.* Expectations of the perfect partner, who is expected to meet all needs regardless of how unrealistic.

7. *Blaming others for the abuser's feelings.* They do not take responsibility for their own emotions. Blames the controlled partner or others for how they feel and may use it as a means to manipulate. Makes light of abuse through minimizing, denying, and blaming ("if you would just…").

8. *Verbal and emotional abuse.* Saying things to be hurtful and cruel—minimizing ability, accomplishments, and overall degradation. There may be awakening during the night out of sleep to be verbally assaulted, questioned, and called names. There may be added manipulation such as threats to end the relationship, harm themselves, abandonment, or kick the person out of their home. There is game playing, resulting in the abused experiencing low self-esteem and feeling crazy.

9. *Rigidly traditional roles.* Expectation of the woman being in the home, being the central caretaker, being submissive, being unable to make decisions independently and seen as inferior. This can be a part of economic abuse. The abused may become totally financially dependent on the abuser. This situation can be exacerbated by the abuser utilizing children as an instrument to provoke guilt in the abused partner when they strive for personal growth and accomplishments or using children to relay messages as a sign of disrespect to the controlled partner. There are numerous ways to assert male privilege, such as treating her like a servant, or creating biased gender rules that exemplify a double standard. Likewise, if the male is the victim of DV, they can never do enough, often turn over their check, often work outside of the home, and then come home and continue to do work that partners should share, etc.

10. *Coercion and threats.* Cruelty to children or pets. Having unrealistic expectations about children's abilities. Pets may be harmed or even killed.

11. *Using force sexually.* Desires to act out fantasies during sex in which a partner is forced, bound, or hurt. There is little concern about what the partner wants or needs. They may use manipulative behavior such as withdrawal, anger, or guilt to get the woman to comply. There may be no empathy for illness, and they may make demands for sex or initiate sex while they are sleeping.

12. *Using force during conflicts.* The use of force such as being prevented from leaving a room, held down, or restrained. Being held against one's will.

13. *History of violence in a relationship.* History of physically hurting a past partner but blames them for what happened.

14. *Threats of violence.* Making or carrying out threats of harm, threatening to leave, or to harm self. Coercing someone into illegal behavior. This is meant to control. There may be excuses later, such as "I was just upset because of what you did. I wouldn't do that."

15. *Throwing or breaking things.* This behavior is threatening and is often used as a punishment and to terrorize another person into submission.

16. *Mood swings.* This is the confusing behavior where 1 min the person is nice and the next minute the person is upset, angry, or out of control.

DOMESTIC VIOLENCE: SAFETY PLANNING

Depending on where you live, much of the following information may not be necessary for you to do. For example, in California the law has changed to protect those who have experienced DV whereby it is the *State v. Perpetrator.* If that were the case it would be recommended that you make contact with a local women's shelter and talk to them about your situation or call the police department to file a complaint/report about the abuse.

MOST IMPORTANT TO REMEMBER

1. Help is available.
2. You are not alone.
3. You are not to blame.

*No one deserves to be controlled or physically abused!

Even if you do not believe that there will be a "next time," decide now what you will do and where you will go.

DOCUMENT THE ABUSE

1. Keep a journal. Make sure that it is hidden in a secret place.
2. Take photos of any physical harm to yourself or to property.
3. If you are physically harmed, show bruises or injuries to a friend, neighbor, or family member.
4. Make the following copies and keep them in your secret place.
   A. Hospital bills.
   B. Property damage bills.

*In part, this evidence is kept so that the victim cannot minimize or deny what they have experienced.

FIND A SAFE PLACE TO GO

1. A shelter.
   A. Know how to get there.
   B. Memorize the phone number.
2. Make arrangements to stay with family or a friend.
   A. Make friends with a neighbor.
   B. Ask neighbors to call the police if they hear suspicious noises from your home.
3. Decide ahead of time if you plan to take the children with you. Always try to take the children to get yourself and them out of an unsafe environment. An abusive environment may teach your children things about behavior and relationships that you don't want them to learn.
4. Develop a code word with your children, neighbor, friends, or supportive family that lets them know that you need to get out or you need them to call the police.

*If there have been serious threats to your safety and you are fearful, contact local law enforcement.

5. Make sure that your phone has GPS on it so that you can be tracked.

CREATE A SAFE ROOM IN YOUR HOME

1. Choose a room with a window.
2. Get a cordless phone for that room.
3. If possible, arrange a signal system for help with a neighbor.
4. Plan a barricade.
5. Install interior locks on the door (ask about locks at the local hardware store).

6. Make sure that there are not any weapons in the room.
7. Call the police immediately should you need to use the safe room.

*If things are building up, try to leave immediately to prevent the situation from getting out of control. If you can't get out, don't get backed into a corner. Try to keep your back toward an opening such as a door or window.

HAVE MONEY AND KEYS

1. Make duplicate keys for your vehicles, house, safety deposit box, post office box, and so on.
2. Start hiding money in amounts that will not be missed.
3. Open your own bank account.
4. Save paystubs and other important receipts.

CREATE A FILE WITH YOUR IMPORTANT DOCUMENTS (IF YOU ARE TAKING YOUR CHILDREN, ALSO PUT THEIR DOCUMENTS)

1. Temporary restraining order
2. Driver's license
3. Car title and registration
4. Social security card(s)
5. Birth certificate(s)
6. Immigration paper(s)
7. Social services documents
8. Prescriptions
9. Tax records/receipts for property purchases
10. Bank statements
11. Address book

PACK A SUITCASE

1. Pack basic clothing
   A. Shoes
   B. Socks
   C. Underwear
   D. Nightclothes
   E. Change of clothes
   F. Toiletries
   G. Special children's needs such as diapers
2. Pack keepsakes that cannot be replaced
   A. Photos
   B. Documents
3. Hide it in a safe place
   A. At a neighbor's house
   B. Under the bed
   C. At church
   D. In the garage
   E. In a public locker
   F. At a family member's home

KNOW WHEN AND HOW TO LEAVE

1. Leave while the offender is away.
2. Ask the police to help you and seek guidance from a local shelter.
3. If your children are in danger, contact child protective services or the police.
4. Consult an attorney or legal resource at a shelter about your parental rights if you are leaving your children while you seek safety.

*Safety is the priority.

WHY VICTIMS OF DOMESTIC VIOLENCE STRUGGLE WITH LEAVING

1. *Fear in general.* Often they have been cut off from all of their resources and have lived under threat and control, not being able to rely on their own decision making.
2. *Low self-esteem.* People who have been emotionally beaten down over a period of begin to see themselves as failures at everything they do. Offenders reinforce this belief to maintain their control.
3. *Self-blame/responsibility.* Victimized people often blame themselves for the abuse. This may be reinforced by an offender who blames the victim for the abuser's own violent behavior.
4. *Holding the family together.* Women are raised and socialized to see themselves as the center of family cohesiveness—for keeping their families safe and together. Women often believe they must do this at any cost to themselves, while at the same time questioning their parenting abilities.
5. *Fear of being crazy.* When you are told you are crazy often enough you begin to believe it. As a result, these victims question their ability to cope with all of the responsibilities of the outside world.
6. *Dependence.* Victim of domestic violence have likely had their worlds made very small so that they could be controlled. As a result, they lack experience in making their own decisions and acting independently.
7. *Isolation.* One of the most common things done to victims of domestic violence is to isolate them from family and friends, physically and emotionally. The more isolated they are, the less likely they will seek help or be aware of the help available in their community.
8. *Traditional values.* Traditional male–female roles are in conflict with separation and divorce and support the notion of "keeping the family together at all costs." There may also be strong religious influences and unsupportive family members that reinforce a victim's belief that they must stay in an abusive relationship.
9. *Learned behavior.* When you live in an isolated and abusive environment, over time the experience takes on a normalcy because there is nothing else to compare it to. When combined with a lack of belief in oneself, the victim may come to believe that the situation is impossible to change. This may be further embedded if the victim grew up in an abusive home.
10. *The honeymoon stage and promises of change.* Victims often love their partners and want a good marriage and a stable family life for their children. With the promise of change is the hope that all of these things are possible. In the hopes that the promise of change will be kept, the victims will forgive and give the relationship another chance for a new beginning.

*Deal with what is, not what if. If things were going to change on their own they would have. If there is to be any chance of hope for change, for the victim and the victim's family, it is necessary to take action.

SURVIVING DIVORCE

Divorce is not an event, it is a process. It is one of the most stressful life experiences to endure. However, as with all times of crisis it can also be a time of opportunity and new beginnings. It is a time to learn, to grow personally, and to develop new relationships and discover community resources. The first step in learning how to deal with divorce is to understand how it is affecting you emotionally and physically. Once you have an increased awareness for how you are being affected, you can then acknowledge and accept your feelings and work on developing a lifestyle that includes exercise, good nutrition, social supports, etc. Therefore, you can use this time for learning new ways to take care of yourself. This is a very stressful time, but you will learn that you can deal with an overwhelming change in your life and even go on to thrive. Time is a healer. And laughter is the best medicine.

You need to give yourself the opportunity to explore and consciously make choices about the life you want to lead postdivorce. This may be more challenging for the person who didn't want the divorce, but it doesn't change the healing and personal growth that needs to take place dealing with such a significant loss. Envision what you would like life to look like when you are ready to start moving on and think about what you need to do to get there. Don't procrastinate! Only you can change and make your life what you want it to be. Whatever choices you identify self-care needs to be at the top of the list. Set a goal to create a better life today than the one you had before.

There are numerous issues that you will need to cope with following a divorce. The number one coping strategy is to get yourself in a position of wanting very little from your ex-spouse. The less you want from him/her, the less frustrated you will be. You know your ex better than anyone else. You know who you are dealing with and if you couldn't change them when you were married, you certainly aren't going to change them now. Accept that you will never get the vindication, validation, or apology you want and may even deserve. Let go and move on. Taking control of your life, getting organized and making informed decisions will be empowering.

You may be struggling with feelings of anger, grief, and resentment toward your ex. However, you have to be careful to not put the children in the middle of your anger and grief. There may also be conflict stressors associated with custody and child support. You may have worries about your children being alienated from you. You will likely have to get used to the fact that your children are not going to be with you 24/7. They will be spending part of their time with your ex and part with you. You can't control what goes on when your kids are with the other. Learn to let go and don't worry about what you can't control.

Use the time when your kids are not with you productively. Pursue your dreams and your interests. Also, use this time to build up your social support—reconnect with old friends. Consider expanding your circle of support and journey of personal growth by volunteering, seeking a new hobby, or taking skill building classes if there are specific issues you are challenged by such as a group dealing with narcissistic or controlling partners, codependence anonymous, or divorce care.

SELF-CARE

1. Recognize your feelings and find positive ways to deal with them.
2. Do not self-medicate. You need a clear mind and good judgment—substance abuse can work against you.
3. Reach out to others, use your social resources.
4. Find social support in your community with groups dealing with divorce and other activities.
5. Take good care of your body (sleep, nutrition, laughter, exercise).
6. Take healthy risks such as trying new activities and getting distracted from your problems.
7. Nurture yourself, do things that feel good and do not have a harmful side. Doing these things can make you stronger, more confident, and more content.
8. Make sure that you laugh everyday. Choose to be happy.

LETTING GO OF THE PAST

If a lot of your energy is going to fighting your ex, instead of getting on with your life, you have a serious problem. Swallow your pride and break into any denial about how your angry acting out does not hurt your child. If your conflict with your ex-spouse causes problems in your new relationship, get help. If you and your new love can't get it together on discipline, take a stepparenting class or at least read some books on stepparenting. If you can't work out your frustration on your own, get help. If you have been trying to calm your anger, but it's not working, that's a signal you need someone to help you get a handle on it.

Use your anger to make a positive difference in your future. Anger is a momentum that gives energy for change. Use it to get off dead center and invest it in making a difference. Go to divorce recovery classes or anger management counseling.

You get only one chance in raising a child. The childhood years cannot be taken back and redone. If you blow it, your child suffers for life! Professional help is available. There are agencies that have a sliding scale for counseling to fit your circumstances. Even if it costs some money, get help. Money is not the object here. Your child's success in life is the important thing. You are worth it. Your kids are worth it.

Make your goal to get a working relationship with the other parent of your child. If you are willing to see how your angry actions affect your child and do something about it, your child has the best chance for a happy future. The pain of the divorce can start to heal for everyone. Your life will become happier and get back on even keel. Remember, the best revenge for the misery of divorce is making a good life for yourself! And your child will be the better for your investment in his and your future. *The greatest gift that parents can give a child when they are no longer together is to assure that a child does not experience stress or fear associated with parents being in the same room or at an activity for them (the child).

FAMILIES AND CHILDREN

PARENTING A HEALTHY FAMILY

CREATING EFFECTIVE FAMILY RULES

1. Rules hold the family together. They create a foundation for learning responsibility, developing mutual respect, and encouraging age-appropriate independence. It is essential for preparing a child to effectively deal with the expectations of dealing with society.

2. Create rules from a positive perspective. Make rules that facilitate what you want and creates opportunity for learning.

3. Have as few rules as possible, be clear, and be specific.

4. Choose consequences that are logical, and that you are willing to enforce.

5. Take the time to educate the child of each rule and the associated consequences. Life is about choices, and early on this is how a child learns responsibility.

6. Have the child reflect to you in their own words the understanding of the rules and consequences.

7. Whenever possible and appropriate include children in making rules as well as other decision-making situations. It is great practice.

8. Be consistent in adhering to rules.

9. Be aware when it is appropriate to change a rule because of developmental changes and increased maturity, to facilitate responsible behavior and reinforce personal growth.

EFFECTIVE COPARENTING

1. Make rules together. Agreement on the rules is important so that children receive consistent information from both parents.
2. If you don't agree on certain rules negotiate until there is agreement so that there is consistency in working with children.
3. Be supportive of each other. Remember, this was a joint decision and children will be confused if there is conflict between parents over rules. Not being consistent and supportive can lead to manipulation and power struggles.
4. If one parent intervenes in a situation and the other disagrees with the intervention, do not voice the disagreement and undermine the intervening parent. Instead, discuss and resolve later when not with children.

MAINTAIN THE PARENT ROLE

1. Be specific in telling a child exactly what actions are expected.
2. Be flexible in how a child accomplishes a task. If you want your child to be aware of different ways of doing something show them. It is important for a child to work effectively, to have accomplishments, and to master skills associated with the various environments they engage. That includes being given the space to complete the task without being scrutinized or criticized.
3. Don't lecture. Talk less, act more.
4. Give positive feedback, rewards, and reinforcement for efforts and accomplishment of the behaviors you want.
5. Be consistent, and don't argue.
6. Follow through with rewards and consequences to shape the behaviors you want.

BE AN ACTIVE PARENT

1. Help your child learn by teaching how to do things "their way." Don't expect them to have the same level of expertise as someone older.
2. Be aware that you are always a role model to your child. They learn by watching and copying what they see.
3. Demonstrate your love through actions. Words lack meaning and value if your child doesn't feel the love from a parent through attention, affectionate, and caring behaviors. Feeling loved and secure are essential.
4. Develop routines. Routinely create an environment that feels dependable, predictable, and safe to you child.
5. As part of the family routine have regular one to one activities and conversations with your child. Playful time with children is very important.

A HEALTHY FAMILY MEANS ALL OF ITS MEMBERS ARE INVOLVED

1. The development of self-esteem is an active process. Empower children by their demonstrated importance in family functioning. Interdependence means that a family functions at its best when everyone is contributing.
2. The best way to teach values and build skills is by doing things with a child.
3. Identify a child's contributions to family life and reinforce their efforts.
4. Laugh and be playful with a child. They will enjoy and appreciate it. It would also be a time of positive bonding and making memories.

5. Include a child in appropriate family decision making. While only the parents are voting partners in family management children are encouraged to share their thoughts and feelings.

ENCOURAGE COMMUNICATION

1. Be interested in a child's life and their experiences. It is through talking about things that happen that children are able to learn valuable lessons and better understand themselves along with appropriate choices.
2. Encourage a child to talk to you about things that are important to them. To effectively facilitate this requires that daily scheduling include time for sharing.
3. When a child shares their experiences, thoughts, and ideas with you actively listen and encourage their problem solving of issues confronting them.
4. Avoid criticizing and giving directions. Respect them. Ask them what they think.
5. Give a child the time and attention required to understand their point of view. They are individuals. Expect them to have their own ideas.
6. Use active listening behaviors (face them and use eye contact) and reflect to them what you hear them saying. When you repeat to them what you think they are saying it demonstrates interest, respect, and that they are important. Likewise, asking questions demonstrates interest and encourages practice in expressing their thoughts and feelings.
7. When there is an opportunity to teach values to a child in a meaningful way take advantage of it. It will feel natural instead of contrived. Don't forget, learning values is reinforced by good parent role models.

GUIDING YOUR CHILD TO APPROPRIATELY EXPRESS ANGER

Anger is a normal emotion that requires learning how to express it honestly and appropriately. Being aggressive to another person or destroying property is not an acceptable way to express anger. At the extreme, everyone is familiar with the devastating situations in which children have killed other children as an expression of their intense anger with being treated badly and being humiliated. While it is imperative that bullies and cruel social behaviors be dealt with, it is also important that children be taught how to appropriately express feelings of anger. Learning how to effectively problem-solve and deal with difficult emotions is a preventive measure for positive mental health and preventing violent behavior. Young people turn to violence when they don't see other ways of managing difficult situations. They may be reacting to the moment without anticipating the consequences of their actions. The following tips can help a child to learn internal management, use of resources, and self-responsibility.

1. *Be a good listener*. Pay attention to what your children are saying about what they feel and how they are thinking about things in their life. Unfortunately, children are confronted at an earlier age about more adult-oriented issues such as relationships, sex, and romanticizing. Failure and rejection are also difficult issues to deal with. Young people are not prepared mentally or physically to effectively manage many of these issues and can find themselves overwhelmed and in trouble.
2. *Be comforting and reassuring*. Tell your children that you care about what they think and feel. Show confidence in them by helping them to explore their choices for managing the issues confronting them.
3. *Normalize the experience of anger*. Everyone gets angry. Share the positive ways that you have found to deal with anger and other difficult feelings. Encourage them to also express ideas they have about how they can deal with anger appropriately.

4. *Encourage children to express their feelings honestly and appropriately*. Validate the emotions underlying their feeling. Help them to learn that you can't control others, and when they express their feeling to someone who isn't interested it could be quite frustrating. However, if they are prepared for such experiences where there is a lack of resolution they will have a realistic expectation. The next step in this process is to move on to fun and interesting activities. Distracting oneself with other activities helps to refocus on other things and not get stuck and miserable with anger. *It is also a lesson in personal control. We can't control others—only our own interpretation for what we experience and how we choose to deal with it.

5. *Teach problem solving and conflict resolution skills*. Give your children some ideas about how to deal with difficult situations and encourage them to talk about what they try to do in those situations, what works, what doesn't, and what they may do next time they are confronted with a similar situation. It is a skill building process that requires practice.

6. *Catch them being good*. It is always important to reinforce good behavior by acknowledging it. When your children deal with their anger in positive ways, reinforce their positive choices. Use every opportunity to build and reinforce strengths and skills.

*If you do not feel that your efforts are successful, or you need support to improve your skills investigate books, research websites, talk to a professional about community resources (such as anger management classes) and consider therapy.

THE FAMILY MEETING

The Family Meeting is a regularly scheduled meeting of all family members. It creates the opportunity to promote healthy family functioning by the following:

1. Providing time for clarifying rules or establishing new rules as a family goes through new stages of growth and change.
2. Making decisions and problem solving. List any family problems. Choose one to solve. State the result that is desired. List and discuss all possible solutions. Choose one solution and make a plan to carry it out. Set a date to review it.
3. Acknowledging and appreciating good things that happen to the family or a family member.
4. Identifying strength of individual family members, and of the family as a whole.
5. Creating a list of fun activities for the family.
6. Encouraging all family members to share their ideas when discussing family issues. Try to see and understand each other's point of view as a means of building self-esteem and self-confidence.
7. Using it as a time to practice assertiveness and democracy. Parents role-model respectful and effective communication skills as well as reflective listening, "I" messages, and problem solving so that children can learn.
8. Promoting commitment of all family members to the functioning of the family. This reinforces the value of each family member and that each person's efforts are appreciated.
9. Providing an opportunity for all family members to be heard.
10. Expressing feelings, concerns, and complaints.
11. Distributing chores and responsibilities fairly among family members.
12. Expressing positive feelings about one another and giving encouragement.

GUIDELINES FOR THE FAMILY MEETING

1. Meet at a regularly scheduled time that is convenient for everyone. Provide a brief and useful agenda.
2. Share the responsibility of the meeting by taking turns in chairing the meeting.
3. Reserve an hour for the family meeting. If the children are young, try 20–30 min.
4. Each person has a chance to speak.
5. One person speaks at a time.
6. Listen when others are speaking.
7. No one is forced to speak, but participation is encouraged.
8. No criticism or teasing. Do not allow the meeting to become a regular gripe session.
9. All family members must have an opportunity to bring up what is important to them.
10. Focus on what the family can do as a group rather than on what anyone member can do.
11. Share things that are going well. Recognize efforts and accomplishments.
12. The goal of the family meeting is communication and agreement. Be sure to accomplish plans for family fun.
13. End the meeting by summarizing the decisions and clarifying commitments. Thank everyone for respectfully attending and participating.

DEVELOPING POSITIVE SELF-ESTEEM IN CHILDREN AND ADOLESCENTS

*Strong self-esteem, a solid sense of self, is essential to being a resilient individual.

1. Demonstrate a positive perspective rather than a negative one. "Catch" your children doing something good. This communicates love, care, acceptance, and appreciation. Be careful not to undo a positive statement. For example, "you did a great job of cleaning your room—when you do your job it makes our family run better. Thank you for being a good family member."
2. Keep your promises. This facilitates trust in parents. It is also role modeling for being respectful and responsible. Consistency is important.
3. Create opportunities out of your children's mistakes. For example, "what did you learn? What would be helpful next time?"
4. Show appreciation, approval, and acceptance. Listen for the feelings behind the words. Active listening to what a child says shows respect and is a way to reflect their worthiness. Being genuinely interested fosters mutual care and respect.
5. Have reasonable and appropriate consequences. Discipline should be a part of learning and encouraging responsible behavior. If a consequence is too long or severe, it creates feelings of hopelessness and a feeling that they have nothing to lose. As a result, it is likely to lead to more opposition and acting out.
6. Ask your children for their opinions, involve them in family problem solving and decision making whenever possible and appropriate.
7. Help your children develop reasonable age-appropriate goals for themselves and help them recognize their progress toward goals. This encourages appropriate risk taking along with realistic expectations and limitations.
8. Avoid making comparisons between siblings or peers. Each person is unique and has something special to offer. Recognizing individual attributes is a good thing because it helps a child or adolescent to become more aware of their strengths or assets. It

is important for everyone to have an objective view of their relative strengths and weaknesses.

9. Support your children in activities in which they feel accomplished and successful. Everyone feels good about themselves when they are successful.

10. Spend time doing things with your children. The amount of time as well as the quality of time is important. Remember, your children grow quickly and time that has past can never be recaptured. Be sure to take time to have fun and enjoy your children.

11. Encourage your children's efforts and accomplishments. Genuine encouragement of efforts, progress, and accomplishments can be internalized and become self-reinforcing. Children learn to accept themselves, identify their assets and strengths, build self-confidence, and develop a positive self-image.

12. Communicate your love by saying it and demonstrating it. Feeling loved is feeling secure. Love is communicated by mutual respect, which is a cornerstone in the development of independence and responsibility.

13. Accept your children for who they are. This facilitates self-acceptance, self-like, and self-love.

14. Have faith in your children so that they can learn to expect the best in themselves.

15. Focus on contributions, assets, and strengths so that children feel that they are important and have something to offer. Let them know that what they offer counts.

FAMILY FACING A CRISIS

A crisis can be defined as a person's evaluation of an experience as dangerous, threatening, traumatic, outside of anything they have ever experienced, and with an uncertainty of how they will handle it. A crisis is unique to the individual. What is experienced as a crisis for one person will not necessarily be a crisis for another. It involves a person's interpretation and feelings about an experience along with speculation and questions regarding why it happened and what the consequences of it will be.

Losses such as death, divorce, relocation, job change, and new or frightening experiences such as a physical trauma or hospitalization are frequently thought of in terms of what a crisis means. However, some positive events such as a marriage, birth of a child, job promotion, and acceptance to a desired college can also be experienced as stress. With any experience that is new there is some level of stress, expectation of performance, concern of how to deal with it, and questions about what may happen as a result of it. This can be just as overwhelming for a person as an event interpreted as a negative experience. When a person experiences a crisis in relation to a positive experience they may also feel guilty or upset with themselves expressing that they are confused because this should be a happy or pleasing experience.

Recognizing and understanding that the crisis is the event, but the individual's interpretation of the event allows insight into why two different people may react differently to the same event. One child may begin school confident, secure, and grown up, while another child may feel fearful, rejected, or punished. Other events that may trigger a crisis include loss, loneliness, independence, sexuality, high expectations of performance (by self or others), and feeling overwhelmed by a situation that is interpreted as being out of their control. Therefore, everyone has different areas of vulnerability to sensitivity resulting from their past experiences and disposition which will influence their interpretation and response to situations. Each person will interpret and react to life experiences in their own unique manner as a result of personality, disposition, coping ability, support, issues of emotional security, and previous life experiences.

All of the aforementioned issues and information associated with experiencing a crisis are important for parents to spend some time considering. Apply thought about how parents would work together, and if you are a single parent be thoughtful about your resources as an individual. If parents have not taken the time to be thoughtful regarding how they face life challenges, how they would use resources and identify relative strengths and weaknesses then how they help children to feel secure and reframe a crisis as an opportunity to learn and grow from. Adversity of any kind is an opportunity to reinforce resilience.

WHAT HAPPENS DURING A CRISIS

When an event precipitates a crisis, there is a disruption in equilibrium and stability. Anxiety and tension begin to rise. The person tries to understand what is happening and why it is happening. The less a person is able to understand the situation, the more tension and anxiety they experience. This can lead to feeling overwhelmed, out of control, and helpless. With this psychological and emotional experience, there may also be feelings of shame, depression, anger, or guilt. A child may be unable to verbally express their fears or may be afraid to express them. The confusion of fear, anxiety, and other emotions is the crisis.

When preparing yourself to help children deal with life events that they may interpret and experience as a crisis, it is helpful to consider the following:

1. Children tend to be self-centered/focused. This is especially true of young children and adolescents. They seem to interpret things as if the world revolves around them—everything is taken personally. Because of this they may interpret themselves as being the cause of something that they have no power or control of, which can be overwhelming.

2. Children tend to interpret things in a literal or concrete manner. This can cause a crisis via misunderstanding. For example, telling a child that death is like sleep, or having a medical or dental procedure, won't hurt because they will be sleeping. What the parent means and what the child interprets such statements as meaning are likely to be different.

3. Fantasy is reality for young children. This could be a situation in which one parent is seeking divorce and the child fears that they will also be abandoned or divorced by this parent. Sometimes a child experiences a form of fantasy called magical thinking, which means that a child has a belief that they had the power to make something happen by thinking it. An example of this is when a child is angry and thinks or says, "I wish you were dead" and someone is harmed in some way. They may believe that harm came to the person because of their thoughts or wish.

4. The effect of childhood loss or separation. Most of the crises experienced by a child involve a loss or separation of some kind. The loss or separation can be fantasy or real. There are direct losses such as divorce or death, or indirect losses such as starting school, a hospitalization, or staying for a brief period with a relative. Losses are a threat to predictability, feeling safe, and feeling secure. Losses can involve feelings such as sadness, depression, loneliness, rejection, abandonment, anger, guilt, and confusion.

Because life has a normal level of stress and changes, it would be impossible to hide from children the problems that confront a family. Children are very sensitive and can feel when things are not right at home. Therefore, instead of allowing a child to interpret what is going on, it is better to give them age-appropriate information in a manner that helps them maintain their feelings of safety and security.

UNDERSTANDING AND DEALING WITH LIFE CRISES OF CHILDHOOD

Everyday family life is full of stressors, crises, and necessary adjustments. An aspect of general growth and development includes the experience of being exposed to difficult/stressful situations and learning to cope with them. Growing up means learning to cope effectively with a full range of life experiences—both good and bad. Your child's ability to effectively cope with any given situation is related to the amount of distress it elicits, if they previously have experienced anything similar they were able to resolve, and how supportive parents and other adults are in facilitating the effective management of stressors. As an adult, you probably have had years of experience in dealing with all kinds of crises and have probably learned to cope with them. If this is not the case it is recommended that you consult with a therapist on the issues of problem solving, conflict resolution, and crisis resolution. If you are unable to cope effectively with stressors and crises, it will be very difficult for you to help a child successfully resolve and learn to cope with the stressors in their life.

A central task for all parents is teaching your child how to deal with stressors, pressures, and demands so that as they move into each successive developmental stage of life they are able to cope effectively. How your child responds to difficult circumstances will be influenced by how you help them deal with the life crises they experience. While crises are often associated with emotional distress, it is also a time of opportunity. It is a time of learning. The very essence of a crisis demands that a person search and explore new methods of coping and developing alternatives for dealing with it. As a result, a crisis presents a person, child or adult, an opportunity for growth and increased effectiveness in coping.

Parents are confronted with two major problems in helping children face and cope with stress:

1. To deal with their own reactions to the stress.
2. Facilitate optimal coping of the child by giving adequate support, encouraging and helping with the development of alternatives to deal with difficult situations, and by giving positive feedback and reinforcement for efforts toward management and resolution of stressors and crises.

CRISIS RESOLUTION

1. *Promoting objectivity.* Help the child see the situation for what it is. For example, while the child is at school, parents won't forget about them or did not divorce because the child was bad, etc. There are numerous prior life experiences to draw from to help feeling both understand and assured.
2. *Validate feelings.* Recognize and accept how the child feels about a given situation. Denying their feelings is a rejection and is also confusing. When feelings are denied it leads to a misinterpretation of feelings later on and undermines the development of instincts.
3. *Elicit their thoughts and feelings about what has happened.* Encourage them to vent their thoughts and feelings appropriately instead of keeping them inside.
4. *Facilitate problem solving and taking appropriate action.* This means identifying exactly what the problem is, what the alternatives are for managing it or resolving it and then taking action. It also includes utilizing resources and self-care behaviors such as getting adequate rest/sleep, nutrition, exercise, and balance in their life—not just being focused on the crisis.

Helping the child to understand what has happened, why it happened, how it is happening, what it means to them, and how it affects them are the objectives for facilitating resolution of the crisis for the child. The efforts of understanding and support to the child early in life when faced with crises pays off later because it lays the foundation of coping skills for dealing with crises later in life.

HELPING A CHILD DEAL WITH A CRISIS

1. As with any relationship interaction you need to be the best you can be before you can offer healthy support, guidance, and facilitate problem solving for effective coping. This means that you need to understand and cope with your own reactions to events before you can help a child learn to cope. When a child experiences a crisis, parents experience their own personal reactions. Additionally, the body language or nonverbal communication your child experiences from you will have a significant impact on how they interpret an event. A child tends to reflect their parents reaction to an event. An example of this is the parent who is a chronic worrier. Children quite often adopt the same way of coping with whatever they are anticipating to worry about it instead of learning to deal with "what is."

2. A parent's first impulse may be to protect their child from the stress of a crisis and manage it for them. Resist this impulse. Doing so would deny them the opportunity to learn useful skills and to learn about their own abilities.

3. Attempt to understand the child's experience of the event. Remember the tendency of the child to be self-centered. This will give you insight into how the child might personalize a given experience. Does the child fear loss, rejection, or abandonment? Is the situation frightening or do they feel that they are to blame for what has occurred? What kind of feelings might the child be trying to express?

4. Validate the child's feelings. Acknowledge and accept the feelings that the child is experiencing. For the child to master the situation they must be able to understand and effectively express what it is they are feeling. Reflecting the child's emotional experience ("I understand that you feel sad because we could not keep the kitten") because it offers acceptance and a label to their emotion, which allows them to connect their feelings to the event and lets them know that having such a feeling for that experience is okay.

5. Understand the stage of loss that a person experiences—even children need to work through a loss and/or death even though it will be different than how an adult would process (age/ develop expected). Consider the following:
   A. Denial that the event is happening.
   B. Anger that the event happened, or that they have been abandoned.
   C. Depression (and guilt) often experienced as sadness and loneliness associated with the object, or feeling guilty that something has happened to another and harboring a belief that somehow they could have prevented it.
   D. Bargaining as an attempt or as a plea to not accept what has happened, or being willing to do anything to take it back.
   E. Acceptance of the reality of what has occurred.

*Everyone goes through these stages in their own unique way based on how they grieve and cope. However, everyone seems to go through this sequence of feelings in coping with a loss, and children seem to go through these stages in general when coping with a crisis.

6. Accept the child's efforts to deal with the crisis. Be careful to not put them down or shame them. Instead, offer acceptance and support to facilitate the resolution of the crisis. In other words, meet the child where they are at emotionally and guide them by responding appropriately to what they need in moving toward resolving the crisis.

7. Make an effort to hear what the child is trying to express.

8. Respond verbally to the child at their level of understanding. Be direct and keep it simple.

9. Don't push the child to talk about the event. This can result in distressing the child more and leading to withdrawal.

10. Be empathic. Try to understand what the child's experience is. Often, a child experiences a crisis because they believe that they are somehow responsible for what has happened (divorce, death), they are being punished for being bad (a new baby takes their place in the family, they are sent to school), or they are being rejected and abandoned. Be consistent and reassuring by what you say and what you do. Give the child adequate time and support to work it out.

11. Whenever possible, prepare a child for a difficult event such as an impending change, loss, or death. It is much easier to cope with something when there is some expectation and understanding for what is happening. This will often reduce the intensity of the crisis or avert it all together. A child can be prepared for predictable changes by talking with them, using age-appropriate books, drawing, dolls, etc. Also, if possible avoid too many changes within a given period of time. This could be overwhelming for an adult with good coping skills, let alone a child who is striving to develop the skills necessary to adequately cope with difficult situations.

YOUR CHILD'S MENTAL HEALTH

When a parent has any health concerns, he/she seeks medical advice. Mental health problems may be more difficult to recognize. According the Center for Mental Health Services, one in five children has a diagnosable mental, emotional, or behavioral problem. Sometimes these problems lead to family conflict, divorce, school problems and academic failure, violence, or suicide. Even though help is available, two-thirds of the children with mental health problems do not get the help that they need.

Don't confuse normal responses with an illness. It is common for children to at times feel sad or to behave badly. However, if you are not sure, talk to their primary care physician/pediatrician or a therapist about your concerns. Overall, if you see severe and persistent troubling behaviors, immediately seek help. The following questions will help to clarify if there is a problem and help you to effectively communicate your concerns to a therapist.

1. Is the child extremely fearful? Is this worry and fear is excessive in comparison to other children your child's age?
2. Does the child want to be alone all the time?
3. Do he or she avoid family and friends?
4. Does the child seem to have lost interest in things he or she formerly enjoyed?
5. Is the child angry most of the time?
6. Does he or she cry a lot?
7. Does the child overact to things?
8. Is the child easily distracted and does he or she seems to have poor concentration?
9. Does he or she have trouble making decisions?
10. Has the child's school performance gone down?
11. Is the child obsessed about his or her looks?
12. Are there unexplained changes in the child's sleeping or eating habits?
13. Does he or she complain about headaches, stomachaches, or other physical problems?
14. Does the child feel that life is too hard to manage or is he or she easily overwhelmed?
15. Does the child talk about suicide?

*If you answered yes to any of these questions, seek professional help.

WARNING SIGNS OF TEEN MENTAL HEALTH PROBLEMS

The teen years can be tremendously fun and interesting. They can also be tough for both the parent and child. Adolescents experience a lot of stress:

1. To be liked
2. To do well in school
3. To get along with their family (when they are trying to separate)
4. To define who they are
5. To plan their future
6. To manage negative peer pressure (substance use, etc.)

7. To deal with continual physical and emotional changes
8. Bullying
9. Cyber bullying or harassment
10. Discrimination

Most of these pressures cannot be avoided, and worrying about them is natural. However, if your teen is feeling sad and depressed, hopeless, worthless, or overwhelmed, these could be warning signs of a mental health problem. These problems are real, painful, and can become severe. They can lead to increased difficulty and stress, such as family conflict, school problems, and academic failure. Consider the following review of possible problems:

1. Experiences significant changes
    A. Grades go down
    B. Loses interest in things usually enjoyed
    C. Wants to be alone all the time
    D. Avoids family and friends or doesn't get things done
    E. Daydreams a lot
    F. Feels that life is too hard and is overwhelmed
    G. Talks about suicide
    H. Hears voices
    I. Is not taking care of his/her hygiene
    J. Is giving prize possessions away
    K. Is very moody
2. Emotional changes
    A. Feels extremely sad and hopeless with or without reason
    B. Is angry a lot of the time
    C. Is often tearful
    D. Overreacts to things
    E. Feels worthless or guilty
    F. Worries excessively
    G. Has excessive anxiety
    H. Cannot get over grief from a death of someone he/she was close to
    I. Is extremely fearful
    J. Is overly concerned about physical appearance
    K. Is overly concerned about physical problems
    L. Is fearful of his/her own thinking
    M. Feels like he/she is out of control (his/her mind is out of control/someone is controlling him/her)
    N. Has poor concentration
    O. Has difficulty making decisions
    P. Fearful of the future
    Q. Is constantly fidgeting
    R. Has difficulty remaining seated
    S. Has a fear of harming self or others
    T. Displays compulsive, ritualistic behavior
        1. Need to wash/clean things
        2. Hand washing
        3. Need for specific order
        4. Other similar behaviors
    U. Has racing thoughts
    V. Has persistent nightmares

W. Has a sleep disturbance

X. Has a appetite disturbance

3. Self-defeating behaviors
   A. Substance use
   B. Truancy
   C. Lying/stealing
   D. Eating excessive amounts of food
   E. Forced vomiting
   F. Abusing laxatives
   G. Excessive exercise/dieting
   H. Obsessiveness about weight (bone-thin)
   I. Destroying property
   J. Breaking the law
   K. Hurting people or animals
   L. Fascinated with fire/starts fires
   M. Engaging in risky, life-threatening activities

If you identify any of these issues of concern, seek professional help for your teen.

TALKING TO CHILDREN

A parent communicating with their child is an important interaction. It provides a time of sharing and understanding, and it holds the opportunity for building self-esteem, encouragement, feeling understood, and feeling accepted. Accept the child as a unique individual separate from yourself. They have their own ideas and special way of looking at things. When a child experiences your acceptance they are more open to you, your support, and your encouragement for learning skills such as problem solving. In other words, they feel respected. Acceptance can be communicated verbally as well as nonverbally. If your verbal communication is accepting but your nonverbal communication is not it will be confusing to a child.

DEMONSTRATING RESPECT

Respect and interest is interwoven. Demonstrating your respect to your child is a wonderful opportunity to provide support and encouragement.

1. Taking an interest in the child's activities, hobbies, and interests.
2. Listening to the child, and encouraging them to give details, to express their thoughts and feelings about it, and reflecting to them what you are hearing.
3. Allow and encourage the child to do thing for themselves. They are capable beings with their own ideas and abilities.
4. Be careful to avoid lecturing, repeating, ordering, preaching, criticizing, and shaming.

Always make an effort to hear what a child has to say. This means taking the time to listen. If you are in a hurry or have limited time, let a child know and make sure that you follow up later to complete the conversation. For example, the morning can be rushed trying to get everyone ready for work and school. If this is not a good time for discussing things or sharing, then clarify and offer other time frames for quality sharing. Be accepting of a child's feelings. Treating a child as a unique, worthwhile person requires genuine positive regard and respect.

RULES FOR LISTENING

1. When a child is talking to you face them physically and use eye contact.
2. Avoid shaming, criticizing, preaching, nagging, threatening, or lecturing.
3. Treat a child in the respectful manner that you would treat a friend.
4. Be accepting and respectful of their feelings.
5. Restate in your own words the child's feelings and beliefs. Reflective listening is a demonstration of interest and understanding in what they are saying.
6. Be open and encouraging.
7. Allow and facilitate the child's learning. Resist jumping in with your own solutions.
8. Encourage a child to identify solutions to problems, "what do you think would help?" This supports the development of self-esteem and self-confidence.

RULES FOR PROBLEM SOLVING AND EXPRESSING YOUR THOUGHTS AND FEELINGS TO CHILDREN

1. Communicate your feelings with "I" messages. When you use "I" messages you are making a statement about how their behavior affects you and how you feel about it. "You" messages are blaming and disrespectful.
2. When there is a conflict:
    A. Decide who owns the problem.
    B. Limit your talking to perception of feelings and answering questions.
    C. Initiate problem solving. Invest the child in understanding the conflict and what to do about it.
        1. Identify the problem
        2. Identify potential solutions to the problem
        3. Review the possible consequences of each solution
        4. Choose a solution
        5. Take action
3. Communicate belief in the child by what you say, how you say it, and with body language.
4. Always be encouraging. People learn from their mistakes. Encourage a child to interpret mistakes as an opportunity to learn.
5. Be patient. Allow children the time to think and to express their responses to what it is you are sharing with them. Pressuring them will create unnecessary stress and anxiety.
6. Admit that as an adult you do not have all the answers, but together you can explore alternatives and find solutions to their questions or difficult situations.
7. Engage in purposeful conversation, talking with one another to understand what the other means. This is valuable sharing time.
8. Offer a nonjudgmental attitude that demonstrates respect.
9. Avoid pressure, sarcasm, ridicule, laughing at them, put-downs, and labeling.

DO'S

__ Take an interest in what a child is interested in.
__ Allow a child to do things for himself/herself.
__ Encourage a child to try new things.
__ Be accepting of their feelings.
__ Encourage their expression of thoughts and ideas.
__ Talk to the child honestly, simply, and at their level.
__ Ask one question at a time and listen to their answer.

DON'TS

__ Do not tell a child that their fears are stupid.

__ Do not lie or make false promises.

__ Do not invade their privacy. Don't push them to talk about something that causes them to clam up more.

__ Do not redo tasks that they have completed. Be encouraging.

__ Do not deny their feelings, "you shouldn't feel that way."

__ Do not be controlling. Clarify rules, boundaries/limits, and safety issues. Children need room to grow.

BOUNDARIES WITH CHILDREN

Boundaries are the foundation of healthy relationships. Children depend on parents to set boundaries and to consistently reinforce them. Just go to a grocery store or to a child-friendly restaurant if you are uncertain about the difference between good parent child boundaries and poor one. When parents set and reinforce appropriate boundaries, they are teaching them skills of emotional and social intelligence required to live a productive life.

We expect children test limits and push boundaries in their effort to get what they want (without consideration to others) and as part of growing up and learning to be a part of social exchanges. The role of the parent is to educate, be a role model of appropriate (respectful and responsible) behavior, and discipline inappropriate behavior. Boundaries are a fundamental part of parent–child interactions. Parenting with boundaries allows children to develop their own sense of right versus wrong and moral development.

1. Children feel loved and secure by the *consistent* use of positive boundaries. Giving in from time to time will undermine your hard work at other times. It is called "intermittent reinforcement" and is the most powerful form of reinforcement. This means that you are actually teaching your children to not follow boundaries or rules when you are inconsistent.

2. Parents need to be on the same page with family rules and limits so that they can be consistent with behavior management. This also prevents children from manipulating parents.

3. Set down with children from time to review boundaries. Boundaries don't change, but the context may change as children grow. An example of this is curfew. Initially, curfew may feel restrictive and there are likely to be complaints. However, use the situation as a learning tool to accomplish two things.

   A. Engage a child in a conversation about "why" the time frame is given, i.e., their age, it's a school night, or general reasons associated with safety, etc.

   B. Frame it as an opportunity for them to demonstrate that they are a respectful and responsible family member, and to practice following rules—even one they don't agree with. "It's not all about you." Without boundaries anarchy would be everywhere.

4. Consequences are earned and consistency is required. It is essential for children to learn that life is about choices and every choice has a consequence. Make sure that children know what the consequences will be if they violate rules. If boundaries have been violated the child, in all likelihood, knew they were not following rules and they also knew they might get in trouble. A parent is encouraging and reinforcing such risk taking (braking rules) because it could pay off. Unfortunately, if violating rules is done at home without consistent consequences, children are also being taught that they might get away with not following the rules at school and in other situations. It makes it harder on everyone.

5. Be firm—not wimpy or weak. Being firm strengthens the relationship between parents and children. Parents are the authority not the friend. Being firm is not cruel and harsh, it is being a parent who wants their children to grow up and be effective people.

*Be fair, firm, and consistent.

GUIDELINES FOR DISCIPLINE THAT DEVELOPS RESPONSIBILITY

For discipline to be a learning experience that shapes positive, appropriate, and responsible behavior requires that the consequences be the following:

1. Logically related to the misbehavior. The central reasons of discipline are to assist children to develop responsibility, to learn and develop skills to control themselves, and to take responsibility for their own behavior.

2. Given in a manner that treats a person with dignity. Also separate the behavior from the person. Recognize that positive attitudes of encouragement, understanding, and respect by parents are the basic conditions for desirable behavior in children—avoid the use of threats, put-downs, embarrassing statements, and criticisms to control children's behavior.

3. Based on the reality of the social order with clarification on its importance for community living. In other words, parents and children are not equal. However, remember that discipline is a learning and mentoring process. Therefore, create an environment where children are encouraged to make choices and are actively involved in planning activities for the day.

4. Concerned with present and future behavior, not bringing up the past. Learning from the mistakes of violating rules is important.

5. Verbally expressed in a way that communicates respect and goodwill. Recognize that positive attitudes of encouragement, understanding, and respect by parents are the basic conditions for desirable behavior in children. Avoid the use of threats, put-downs, embarrassing statements, and criticisms to control children's behavior.

6. Tied to choices, i.e., all choices have a consequence, some are positive and some are negative. Choosing a certain behavior is acknowledging a willingness to accept the associated consequences. Parents don't do a child any favor by protecting them from their consequences. Consequences teach a child about themselves and what is right as well as responsible.

7. A defining factor for telling the difference between a privilege and a right. Positive discipline fosters a sense of self within a community versus being entitled. Privileges are earned.

HELPFUL HINTS

1. Don't look at discipline as a win or lose situation. The goals are as follows:
   A. To provide children the opportunity to make one's own decisions and to be responsible for their own behavior.
   B. To encourage children to learn the natural order of community life (rules are necessary to promote optimal freedom of choice for all and to maintain safety).
   C. To encourage children to do things for themselves for the development of self-respect, self-esteem, and taking responsibility for their own behavior.
2. Be both firm and kind.
3. Don't lecture. Be brief, clear, and respectful.
4. Don't argue.
5. Don't be worn down or manipulated.
6. Be consistent.
7. Be patient. It takes time for natural and logical consequences to be effective.
8. Don't be reactive. Parents' responses often reinforce children's goals for power, attention, revenge, or displays of inadequacy. Be calm and respectful when you intervene.

CHILDREN SURVIVING DIVORCE

It is tough to be a child of divorced parents. A separation or divorce often leaves parents angry with each other, and children feeling confused and sometimes even blaming themselves. This can cause friction, tension, and just generally bad relations between the two parents. What's even worse is that in these situations children are put in the middle and sometimes used as pawns. Divorce hurts. It is a terrible thing to have happen to a family. Everyone gets hurt, but children remain scarred for years when parents continue the war. Research shows that negative behaviors from parents after a divorce can cause more problems to a child than the divorce itself. Children will progress through the challenging adjustments to their feeling of loss and insecurity when they get the best possible experiences at both parent's homes and both parents are respectful and don't act angry toward one another. Therefore, consider the following and be thoughtful about what is in the best interest of the children:

1. If you want to do something invaluable for your child, create a positive relationship with your ex. If you can't be positive, at least be civil. Remaining civil, in the face of great anger, shows that you are letting go and moving on. Someday when your child is grown, they will thank you for keeping a cool head during the difficult times. Children are a witness to what is said and done between parents. Be thoughtful.

2. Reassure your child that both parents love them. This is a must. Remind your children that the other parent loves them just as much as you do. That they are sad about the situation too, but that they will always love them.

3. With all of the questions and feelings of insecurity, they need to know what's coming. As awkward as it may be, parents should let children know in advance that they are contemplating divorce. Just how to say this depends how old a child is. Young children may simply be told that Mommy and Daddy are not going to be living together/in the same house but that the child will be with one or the other parent at all times.

4. Don't use your child as a confidant. Never discuss your ex with your child. Do not talk about your ex when your child can overhear it. Your child wants to be loyal to both mom and dad. Hearing one parent trash the other sets up confusion and not knowing what to believe. If what you say is inaccurate, based on your feelings of hurt and betrayal, your child will eventually figure it out and distance from you. Children bond with parents with whom they feel safe. Your child will not feel safe to talk about unhappy feelings if you are bashing the other parent. Children need to have a healthy relationship with both parents.

5. Don't use your child as a messenger. Do not ask your child to carry messages between you and your ex. That puts the child in the middle and creates confusion. Be adults and work out some neutral way of discussing situations with your ex. Be the bigger person and insist on being straightforward to calm things between you and your ex.

6. Don't force your child to pick sides. Expect a child to have loyalties to both parents. Requiring them to "side with you" is unfair to the child. They should not even be involved enough to have the opportunity to choose sides.

7. Do not involve your child in your disagreements. It is never ok to include a child in an argument. Keep them out of it. If they have a question about what is going on, try answering as openly and honestly as you can, without divulging too much information and assure them that parents are taking care of it.

8. Remember, you chose this person to be the mother or father of your child. There must have been good points for you to choose them for this most important role. Think back and focus on the good aspects of your former spouse. Look for ways that they are being an effective parent. Keep your mind on their positive points, not on what they are doing wrong.

9. Never allow your child to hear you say anything bad about the other parent (even if it is true). We need to teach our children sympathy and compassion. Discuss instead with your child, that everyone is different and that sometimes that two people who got married are so different that they cannot remain married.

10. Don't ask your child about what the other parent does. It is none of your business and may signal some hidden jealousy on your part. Don't check up on them or feel that you have a right to make judgments about what they are doing. Divorce took away that right. Having to report on or answer questions about the absent mother or father puts your child in a lose–lose situation. Grilling your child will backfire on you—you will lose their trust

11. Your ex's decisions and behavior are totally their own responsibility unless, of course, your child is placed in a harmful situation. Then you are obliged to speak up. Do a reality check with a neutral third party to see if there is actual harm to your child or you are just upset. If your child complains about things at your ex's house, and your ex is unable to hear about from you, tell your child that he must address it with that parent. You can't troubleshoot for them in this situation. If they can't speak up, get him into counseling so that he can become more assertive or at least learn to deal with the situation.

12. Stop and think of each demand that you make on the mother or father of your child and the direct consequences it will have on your child. Follow visitation times to the letter. Not following the legal arrangements or asking to change visitation dates only causes more conflict for your child.

13. Do not make choices that hurt your child. You play games with your child's mind if you do not show up on time or not at all or if you do not bring your child home at the agreed upon time or you make excuses/refuse to support their extracurricular activities to get back at the other parent. Your child will keep score on this. Some children sit by the window for hours waiting for a parent who doesn't show up. They may pretend they don't care, but they will feel abandoned if you don't keep your word.

14. Don't lie to your child. Their anger about being lied to may take years to surface, but it will come out at you at some time in the future. Your lifelong relationship with your child is at stake. Do what you say you will do. You brought this child into the world and now you have a responsibility to be the grown-up and a stable parent.

15. Taking your hurt and anger out on your ex-spouse *will* damage your child. How you deal with your ex is another indicator of your self-esteem and maturity. If you are raging, then you have lots of problems to work out. Do a self-inventory—maybe you are acting as if you are still in a bad marriage instead of letting go and moving on. If this is the case talk to a professional and get help. If you blow it and act out with anger, apologize to your ex and to your child. Then make a resolution to better in the future. Keep working by keeping your temper under control. Acting badly is your choice—let your conscience be your guide, not your bruised ego or righteous indignation.

THE CHILDREN'S BILL OF RIGHTS IN A DIVORCE

1. To be told that my mother and father still love me and will never divorce me.
2. To be told that the divorce is not my fault and not to be told about the adult problems that caused it.
3. To be treated as a human being, not as another piece of property to be fought over, bargained over, or threatened.
4. To have decisions about me based on my best interest, rather than past wrongs, hurt feelings, or parent's needs.
5. To love both my parents without being forced to choose or feel guilty.
6. To know both my parents through regular, frequent involvement in my life.

7. To have the financial support of both my father and mother.
8. To be spared hearing bad hurtful comments about either of my parents which have no useful purpose.
9. Not to be asked to tell a lie or act as a spy or messenger.
10. To be allowed to care about others without having to choose or feel guilty.

(author unknown)

PARENT-CENTERED STRUCTURE

A couple's bond needs to be strong. When there is a healthy couple relationship, there is greater success in dealing with difficult family issues.

HELPING CHILDREN COPE WITH SCHEDULING CHANGES

A schedule change could be a return to work following a long leave of absence, change from a traditional lifestyle (mom has been at home), or family/parent adjustments of any kind, which present a disruption to a child's schedule or learned expectation of parental contact. The following are some suggestions to consider:

1. Talk with your child in age-appropriate terms. Talk factually about the change and explain in age-appropriate language what that means. Remain focused on the positive aspects and assure your child that any rough spots will be managed. Likewise, what you see as positive may be stressful to your child. Explain what you will be doing and how important it is.

2. If possible, take your children to your place of work (or familiarize them with whatever is associated with change) so that they have a picture of where you will be or what is involved. If there is a receptionist, introduce them for added comfort should there be a time they need to call you. If at all possible, call them at predetermined times to check in.

3. Outline changes that will improve your lives and make things easier. This is an opportunity to develop positive family behaviors. Family members should all have a contribution in self-responsibility and home maintenance. Children are likely to feel empowered when they feel that they have positive contributions. Consider age-appropriate ways that children can help around the house. Reinforce their participation and development of self-responsibility by using a reward system

4. Make sure that your children know that you are thinking of them without repeatedly reinforcing how much you miss them or how sad you are. They may begin to feel responsible for making you happy or develop other negative feelings about work or change. Instead, do sweet things like leaving them fun notes.

5. Be emotionally available to your children when you are with them. Sitting in front of the television or being busy with chores when you are home is not a demonstration of taking the time to be with them. Talk to and listen to your children. Keep the lines of communication open so you will know what is happening in their lives and how they feel about it. This way you will know what are they interested in, what do they like at school, what are they struggling with, who their friends are, and so forth.

6. Each day, allot specific child time where there is no phone, no television, and no interruptions of any kind. Even if it is only a short period of time, you are telling your child how important they are, which reinforces positive self-esteem. This is an investment in your child. One thing you can do is to read to your child. Reading with children is a special time; it fosters reading

as being enjoyable, a quiet time, laughing and learning, and it can be used as a nonstressful means for working on difficult issues. Think of the possibility that reading may facilitate children to be more open to learning life lessons.

7. Demonstrate a focus on the positives and what is working. Demonstrating genuine gratitude for what one has improves coping with limitations and encourages letting go or accepting what cannot be changed. A perspective of genuine gratitude is a healthy and resilient way of thinking.

8. If you feel that your child is keeping difficult emotions inside or you just want to stimulate the sharing of thoughts and feelings, play the "finish the sentence" game. Create sentence stems where the child gets to complete the sentence. This game not only creates the opportunity to understand what your child is thinking and feeling, it is also an opportunity for your child to find out that you have similar feelings about some things. Examples include the following:
   A. "I wish…"
   B. "I feel happy when…"
   C. "I feel unhappy when…"
   D. "I don't understand…"
   E. "When I grow up I will never…"
   F. "When I grow up I will…"

9. Even when you find yourself tired and frustrated, don't give into blaming your significant other for hardships created by the changes associated with necessary adjustment. If you talk in terms of feeling punished for taking responsibility for what needs to be done, consider the effect on children and how they may be reinforced to view their own issues of responsibility.

10. Remember, you are the role model for positive self-talk and self-care. Your child is learning from watching you:
   A. How to interact with the world
   B. How to simply do what needs to be done without negativity and procrastination
   C. How to problem-solve and resolve conflicts
   D. How to appropriately get needs met

IS YOUR BEHAVIOR IN THE BEST INTEREST OF YOUR CHILDREN?

Though we often consider a separation or divorce to be a time when parents engage in behaviors that may be emotionally and psychologically damaging to children, the concern of children could be expanded in general to marital distress as well. Therefore, carefully consider the following, and if you do any of the things listed, stop immediately. Try to put yourself in the shoes of your child, who needs a healthy relationship with both parents.

1. Do not put your child in the middle.
   A. Children should not be placed between two parents communicating information from one to the other. Parents need to act like adults and communicate directly.

2. Do not put your child in the position of having to choose to be with one parent over the other.
   A. Parents are supposed to be in the family leadership role. This means that children are supposed to be able to rely on parents to make the decisions that are best for them.
   B. Allow your children to be children, not to take on adult worries and stress.
   C. Parents are supposed to protect, nurture, and encourage children.

3. Do not use your child as a confidant.
   A. Do not speak to your children about the adult issues that you struggle with.
   B. Do not speak to your children about your view of the faults of other parents.
   C. Do not try to get children "on your side" against the other parent.

4. Do not allow your child to be responsible for you emotionally.
   A. When your children are exposed to your emotional displays of sadness, fear, anger, and so on, they may come to believe that they are responsible for protecting you and making you feel better because of the following:
      1. They see you as fragile and unable to fulfill all aspects of your parent role.
      2. They see you as a victim of the other parent.

If you are doing any of these behaviors, then something is wrong. As a parent, you need to stop thinking about yourself and your needs and take responsibility for what you are doing to your children. If you need support, understanding, and to problem-solve how to deal with your own difficult feelings, get help so that you can learn to do things differently before you damage your children and their relationship with the other parent.

Your children are entitled to the following:

1. To be a carefree child who does not have to worry about you or adult issues.
2. To have a healthy relationship with both parents.
3. To be able to trust that their parents will protect them and their emotions.
4. To be encouraged and supported in their lives.

SUCCESSFUL STEPFAMILY CHARACTERISTICS

Differences between biological families and stepfamilies

Biological family	Stepfamily
Marriage is a new beginning	Marriage brings together two families
Traditions and history develops	Different traditions and history—not shared
Couple's relationship comes before new marital relationship (stress)	Biological parent–child relations come before relationship with children
Family lives in same home	Children spend time in two parental homes
Couple develops parenting role and skills gradually and together	Couple brings their own individual parenting ideas and skills to marriage

Since approximately 50% of first marriages and approximately 60% of second marriage end in divorce, understanding what happens in marriage is important if you want to improve the outcome of your marriage when stepfamily issues complicate it. As with all marriages, the factors necessary for success are the following:

1. Honor
2. Validation
3. Respect
4. Responsibility
5. Communication
6. Discipline
7. Parent-centered structure

HONOR

Honor embodies the meaning of marriage vows. It is the feeling demonstrated to a marital partner that he/she is the most important person in your life.

VALIDATION

Validation means to listen, acknowledge, and accept that everyone is entitled to their own thoughts and feelings. There are few things that feel as bad as when we share our thoughts and feelings with someone important to us and the reaction is that they are denied as real, accurate, or important by someone important.

RESPECT

One never minimizes how their choices and behavior affect the people that they love, especially their life partner. Treat others as you desire to be treated. Respect is the foundation of trust.

RESPONSIBILITY

Responsibility describes how one thinks and behaves in a way that demonstrates doing what is right. It is the recognition that we have obligations and values, which clarifies how to take care of and nurture a couple's relationship.

COMMUNICATION

Open and honest communication is the foundation of a successful stepfamily. Do not avoid talking about difficult issues. Instead problem-solve the issues that confront you as a couple and a family (children) together.

DISCIPLINE

It is imperative that a couple approach parenting issues as a team. The children in a family need the consistency offered by the team approach. Likewise, the couple benefits from being able to depend on an alliance with their team member.

Chapter 4

Professional Practice Forms
Clinical Forms
Business Forms

The documents offered in this section provide a selection of forms utilized in a general behavioral health practice. Some documents are presented in several variations allowing the clinician to select the format that best suits their specific needs. Clinicians may find themselves in professional realms of utilization management, case reviewer, or case consultant. These areas of professional engagement carry an expectation of specific documentation to address the prescribed need. Additionally, the forms are designed to be used with a therapist's own letterhead.

Therapist's Guide to Clinical Intervention. http://dx.doi.org/10.1016/B978-0-12-811176-5.00004-8

Clinical Forms

CASE FORMULATION

As many as 70% of primary care physician appointments have a psychological component, thus signifying that behavioral health factors play a significant role in prevention, diagnosis, and treatment in the primary care setting. Therefore, behavioral health consults are valuable to physicians. If you are preparing to consult with a treatment team, insurance case reviewer, or referring physician, consider the following informational format:

1. Identifying information
   A. Provider name and identification (ID) number (social security number or tax ID)
   B. Member name, identification, and date of birth (DOB), date of injury (DOI) if relevant
2. Treatment modality
   A. Type of session (individual, conjoint/family, or group)
   B. Number of sessions to date and session frequency
   C. Number of additional sessions needed to complete treatment

GENERAL CONSULT INFORMATION

1. Diagnostic information
   A. Diagnosis
      1. General examples of issues defining diagnosis include the following:
         a. Problems with primary support group
         b. Economic problems
         c. Housing problems
         d. Educational problems
         e. Occupational problems
         f. Problems with access to health care
         g. Problems in interaction with legal/criminal system
         h. Problems related to social environment
         i. Problems related to stage of life issues
         j. Other psychosocial and environmental problems
2. Medical history presentation
   A. Psychotropic medications
   B. Substance use disorders
   C. Medical diagnoses (*including presence of any allergies)
      1. Management problems
      2. Medical instability
      3. Factors associated with medical issues influencing emotional/psychological functioning
3. Clinical presentation
   A. Crisis issues
      1. Harm to self
      2. Harm to others
      3. Gravely disabled (inability to care for oneself)
      4. Child abuse/neglect
      5. Elder abuse
      6. Domestic violence
      7. Other related issues

B. Symptoms/behavior

C. Stability and compliance

D. History of abuse/neglect/assault

E. Treatment history (including hospitalizations) and course of associated treatment

F. Family history and involvement in treatment

4. Relevant history of presenting problem(s)

5. Current status

A. Descriptive current level of functioning

B. Situational issues impeding or facilitating improvement

6. Treatment goals and objectives

A. Integrating evidence-based best practice interventions

INITIAL PATIENT EVALUATION CONSULTATION NOTE TO PRIMARY CARE PHYSICIAN

_____

Date: _____

Patient: _____ DOB: _____ Age: _____

Primary Care Physician: _____ Ph./Fax: _____

Reason for Referral: _____

(Presenting Problem) _____

Medications currently prescribed: _____

Medical problems currently experiencing: _____

Previously seen by therapist or psychiatrist: _____

Symptoms:

__depression	__anxiety	__hopeless/helpless
__tearful	__fears/phobias	__anger/frustration
__sleep disturbance	__shakiness/trembling	__depersonalization
__appetite disturbance	__palpitations	__derealization
__difficulty concentrating	__sweating/flushes/chills	__obsessive thoughts
__memory problems	__dizziness/nausea	__compulsive behaviors
__social isolation	__fatigue	__relationship problems
__activity withdrawal	__irritability/on edge	__family problems
__headaches	__hypervigilance	__issues of loss
__abdominal distress	__intrusive thoughts	__stress
__suicidal ideation	__bowel problems	__difficulty relaxing
__homicidal ideation	__asthma/allergies	__work problems
__sexual abuse/assault	__mania	__legal/financial problems
__eating disorder	__school problems/truancy	__hyperactive
__defies rules	__annoys others	__easily annoyed

__spiteful/vindictive   __blames others   __argues

__uses obscene language   __excessive drinking   __drug use

__somatic concerns

History of Current Problem (Relevant History, Reason for Treatment):

_____

_____

_____

_____

_____

_____

Mental Status:

Mood	__Normal __Depressed __Elevated __Euphoric __Angry __Irritable __Anxious
Affect	__Normal __Broad __Restricted __Blunted __Flat __Inappropriate __Labile
Memory	__Intact __Short-term Problems __Long-term Problems
Processes	__Normal __Blocking __Loose Associations __Confabulations __Flight of Ideas __Ideas of Reference __Grandiosity __Paranoia __Obsession __Perseverations __Depersonalization __Suicidal Ideation __Homicidal Ideation
Hallucinations	__None __Auditory __Visual __Olfactory __Gustatory __Somatic __Tactile
Judgment	__Good __Fair __Poor
Insight	__Good __Fair __Poor
Impulse Control	__Good __Fair __Poor

Initial Diagnostic Impression:

DSM 5/ICD 10: _____

Initial Treatment Plan:

__Brief psychotherapy	__Medication evaluation with PCP
__Supportive psychotherapy	__Medical referral
__Decreased symptomatology	__Improve coping
__Stabilize	__Utilization of resources
__Cognitive restructuring	__Social skills training
__Specialized group	__Problem solving/conflict resolution
__Child Protective Services	__Stress management
__AA/Alanon	__Behavior modification
__Chemical dependency treatment	__Pain management

___Self-esteem enhancement   ___Suicide alert

___Parent counseling   ___Impatient Program/Partial HP

___Grief resolution   ___Legal alert

___Psychological testing   ___Potential violence

Next Appointment _____

_____   _____

Therapist's Signature   Date

BRIEF CONSULTATION NOTE TO PHYSICIAN

Dear Dr. _____ Ph./Fax: _____

Patient: _____ DOB: _____ Age: _____

Date of Assessment: _____

Purpose of visit: _____

_____

_____

Preliminary findings reveal: _____

_____

_____

Tentative diagnosis: _____

_____

_____

Next appointment: _____

If you have further questions please feel free to contact me. Authorization to share information attached.

Sincerely,

GENERAL CLINICAL EVALUATION

The general clinical evaluation systematically reviews all domains associated with understanding an individual and his/her level of functioning. Depending on the presentation of a given area, the assessment will vary in intensity as needed. Areas of evaluation include the following:

1. Presenting problem/reason for evaluation
2. Referral source with associated information

3. History of the presenting problem
4. Psychiatric history
   A. Chronology of episodes of mental illness and associated course of treatment including medication, treatment programs, and treatment providers
   B. Responses to prior treatment (medication, dosage, duration, side effects, benefits, complaints)
5. Medical history
   A. Medical illness (medication(s), treatment, procedures, hospitalizations)
   B. Undiagnosed health problems
   C. Injuries, trauma
   D. Sexual/reproductive history
   E. Headaches/chronic pain
   F. Allergies/drug sensitivities
   G. Disease(s), infection
   H. Health-related behaviors (exercise, nutrition, use of substances, etc.)
6. Substance use history
   A. Specific substances
   B. Frequency/amount
   C. Route of administration
   D. Pattern of use (episodic/continual/single/recreational/mood management)
   E. Association between substance use and mental illness
   F. Perceived benefits
7. Personal history
   A. Developmental milestones/stage-of-life experiences
   B. Response to transitions/adjustments
   C. Genetic influences (inherited/consequences, potential of passing on to children)
   D. Psychosocial issues
      1. Family (experiences and genogram)
      2. Education
      3. Religion/spiritual beliefs
      4. Culture/ethnicity (immigration, political repression, war experience, natural disaster)
      5. Legal issues (past, current)
   E. Current level of functioning in the following areas
      1. Mood management
      2. Family (marriage, parenting)
      3. Personal relationships/resources
      4. Work
      5. School
      6. Social environment
   F. Past level of functioning
      1. Mood management
      2. Family (marriage/parenting)
      3. Personal relationships/resources
      4. Work
      5. School
      6. Social environment
8. Mental status examination (MSE)
   A. The MSE is a systematic review of observed information collected during the interview. A good report is brief and addresses the following issues:
      1. Appearance
      2. Behavior/psychomotor activity

3. Attitude toward examiner (interviewer)
4. Affect and mood
5. Speech and thought
6. Perceptual disturbances
7. Orientation and consciousness
8. Memory and intelligence
9. Reliability, judgment, and insight
9. Diagnostic tests
    A. There may be the use of paper-and-pencil tests or inventories, which may be used later to assess improvement in patient functioning or to monitor other areas of progress
10. Initial diagnostic impression and diagnoses to be ruled out
11. Initial treatment plan
12. Recommendations or requests of the treatment team members are to follow up on in establishing a comprehensive treatment plan

TREATMENT PLAN

Name: _____   Date: _____

DOB: _____   SS No./Patient No.: _____

Referral source: _____

Current medications:
(and purpose of medications)

Prescribing physician: _____

_____   Primary care physician: _____

_____   Current health problems: _____

_____   _____

_____   _____

_____   _____

_____   Date of last physical exam: _____

Approximate date and time frame of treatment

Prior inpatient and/or outpatient treatment (Reason for treatment, Provider, Outcome of treatment) physical and emotional reasons

_____

_____

_____

Is there a family history of the following? (If yes, explain)

Alcoholism: _____

Drug abuse/dependency: _____

Emotional/psychological problems: _____

Health issues (hypertension, diabetes, cardiac, allergies, others): _____

_____

_____

Do you use substances (daily basis, bingeing/party, other patterns, how much)?

_____

_____

Is there a history of sexual abuse or sexual assault?

_____

_____

Is there a history of anger problems or domestic violence?

_____

_____

DIFFICULTIES EXPERIENCED

Thoughts/Feelings/Mood

__ Depression
__ Anxiety
__ Sadness
__ Fear
__ Fatigue
__ Euphoria
__ High energy
__ Financial stress

__ Intrusive thoughts
__ Anger/frustration
__ Not liking self
__ Not liking others
__ Sudden mood changes
__ Obsessive/ruminative thoughts
__ Thought of hurting yourself
__ Legal worries/problems
__ Hear things other people don't

__ Dissociation
__ Depersonalization
__ Derealization
__ Thoughts of hurting others
__ Excessive worry/stress
__ Negative thoughts
__ Believing you are better than others
__ Confusion
__ Memory difficulties
__ Difficulty with attention and concentration
__ Suspicious (distrustful)
__ See things other people don't

Behaviors

__ Compulsive behavior/rituals
__ Difficulty with daily routine
__ Difficulty getting to appointment on time
__ Let others take advantage of you
__ Using alcohol/drug to cope
__ Dependency upon others

__ Angry/hostile
__ Withdrawal from other
__ Isolation
__ Self destructive/sabotaging
__ Abuse of others
__ Hyperactivity
__ Not able to relax

__ Lying
__ Stealing
__ Reactive
__ Avoidant
__ Controlling
__ Argumentative
__ Decrease/lack of sexual interest
__ Preoccupation with sex

Experience in Workplace

__ Pattern of tardiness   __ Negative feelings about work
__ Absenteeism   __ Difficulty with supervision
__ General performance   __ Difficulty with coworkers
__ General satisfaction   __ History of work problems

Physical Functioning

__ Ulcers   __ Colitis/irritable bowl   __ Chest pain
__ Bowel problems/changes   __ Headache   __ Shakiness/trembling
  in habit   __ Hearing/vision problems   __ Hypertension
__ Abdominal pain/   __ Sweating/flushes   __ Hypoglycemia
  vomiting   __ Hyperventilation   __ Thyroid dysfunction
__ Changes in urinary   __ Shortness of breath   __ Sleep disturbance
  patterns   __ Easily fatigued   __ Appetite disturbance
__ Changes in menstrual   __ Back pain   __ Hypoglycemia
  problems   __ Joint pain   __ Skin problems
                               __ Swelling legs/ankles/feat

Presenting problem identified by client (why is the person coming to therapy and why now?): As stated by client

_____

_____

_____

_____

_____

PRESENTING PROBLEMS PERCEIVED BY CLINICIAN

Personal
Depression
Anxiety
Stress
Grief
Self-esteem

Interpersonal
Significant other
Marital
Family
Child
Divorce
Friendships

Work/School
• Career/vocational
• Performance
• Interpersonal
• Authority

Addictions
Alcohol
Smoking
Amphetamine
Cocaine
Hallucinogens
Huffing
Opeatis
Sedatives
Tranquilizers
Eating
Gambling
Sex
Stealing

Health
Weight
Appetite
Sleep
Pain
Other

Crisis Issues
Suicidal ideation/death wish
• H/o suicide attempts
Self-destructive behavior
• Homicidal ideation
• H/o violent behavior
• Potential for violent behavior
Child abuse
Domestic violence
Dependent adult abuse/neglect
Elder abuse

DSM 5/ICD 10 Diagnosis: _____

	Problem	Goal	Interventions	Time frame to complete goal	How progress monitored
1					
2					
3					
4					
5					
6					

_____   _____

Therapist's signature   Date

_____   _____

Client's signature   Date

MENTAL STATUS EXAM

The mental status exam serves as the basis for diagnosis and understanding of the dynamic elements that contribute to an individual's current level of psychological and emotional functioning.

A satisfactory assessment should include objective behavioral observation as well as information elicited through selected questioning of the individual. Sensitivity, tact, and respect to the individual and their reactions will facilitate cooperation. Several MSE formats have been provided in this section to choose from for the desired format.

The following outline for the mental status exam breaks down the type of information needed for a thorough evaluation. To foster feelings of interest and compassion from the therapist (therapeutic alliance), it is best to begin the evaluation by discussing the present difficulties or primary complaint and then proceed in a natural manner. This is accomplished by blending specific questions into the general flow of the interview.

MENTAL STATUS EXAMINATION CONTENT

1. Appearance, Behavior, and Attitude
   A. Appearance—apparent age, grooming, hygiene/cleanliness, physical characteristic (build/weight, physical abnormalities, deformities, etc.), appropriate attire. The description of appearance should offer adequate detail for identification. It should take into consideration the individual's age, race, sex, educational background, cultural background, socioeconomic status, etc.
   B. Motor Activity—gait (awkward, staggering, shuffling, rigid), posture (slouched, erect), coordination, speed/activity level, mannerisms, gestures, tremors, picking on body, tics/grimacing, relaxed, restless, pacing, threatening, overactive or underactive, disorganized, purposeful, stereotyped, repetitive.
   C. Interpersonal—rapport with the interviewer. Evaluation process, cooperative, opposition/resistant, submissive, defensive.
   D. Facial Expression—relaxed, tense, happy, sad, alert, daydreamy, angry, smiling, distrustful/suspicious, tearful.
   E. Behavior—distant, indifferent, evasive, negative, irritable, labile, depressive, anxious, sullen, angry, assaultive, exhibitionistic, seductive, frightened, alert, agitated, lethargic, somnolent.

2. Characteristics of Speech
   A. Descriptors—normal, pressured, slow, articulate, amount, loud, soft, dysarthric, apraxic, accent, enunciation.
   B. Expressive Language—normal, circumstantial, anomia, paraphasia, clanging, echolalia, incoherent, blocking, neologisms, perseveration, flight of ideas, mutism.
   C. Receptive Language—normal, comprehends, abnormal.

3. Mood and Affect
   A. Mood—a symptom as reported by the individual describing how they feel emotionally, such as normal, euphoric, elevated, depressed, irritable, anxious, angry.
   B. Affect—observed reaction or expressions. Range of affect includes broad, restricted, blunted, flat, inappropriate, labile, mood congruent, mood incongruent.

4. Orientation and Intellectual Ability
   A. Orientation—time, person, place, and self. The individual should be asked questions such as the day of the week, the date, where he lives, where he is at, and if he knows who he is.
   B. Intellectual Ability—above average, average, below average
      1. General information—the last four presidents, governor of the state, the capital of the state, what direction does the sun set, etc.
      2. Calculation—serially subtracting 7 from 100 until he can go no further. Simple multiplication word problems such as, "if a pencil costs 5 cents, how many pencils can you buy with 45 cents?"
      3. Abstract Reasoning—proverbs. This is the ability to make valid generalizations. Responses may be literal, concrete, personalized, or bizarre. For example, "still waters run deep," "A rolling stone gather no moss."
      4. Opposites—slow/fast, big/small, hard/soft.
      5. Similarities—door/window, telephone/radio, dog/cat, apple/banana.
      6. Attention—digit span, trials to learn four words.
      7. Concentration—months of the year or days of the week backward.
      8. Reasoning and Judgment—is able to connect consequences to choices and behaviors.

5. Memory—immediate (10–30 s)
   short term (up to 1½ h)
   recent (2 h to 4 days)
   recent past (past few months)
   remote past (6 months to lifetime)

6. Thought Processes/Content—deals with organization and composition of thought. Examples include normal, blocking, loose associations, confabulation, flight of ideas, ideas of reference, illogical thinking, grandiosity, magical thinking, obsessions, perseveration, delusions, depersonalization, suicidal ideation, homicidal ideation.

7. Hallucination—none, auditory, visual, olfactory, gustatory.

8. Insight—good, fair, poor. Understanding, thought, feeling, behavior.

9. Impulse Control—good, fair, poor. The ability/tendency to resist or act on impulses.

A Mental Status Exam review form is an adjunct to the initial assessment report.

MENTAL STATUS EXAM

Appearance: Grooming   __Normal   __Disheveled   __Unusual
               Hygiene   __Normal   __Body Odor   __Bad Breath
               __Other _____

Motor Activity   __Relaxed   __Restless   __Pacing   __Sedate
                  __Threatening   __Catatonic   __Posturing
                  __Mannerisms __Psychomotor Retardation
                  __Tremors   __Tics   __Other _____

Interpersonal   __Cooperative   __Oppositional/Resistant
                 __Defensive   __Other _____

Speech   __Normal   __Pressured   __Slow   __Dysarthric   __Apraxic
   Expressive Language   __Normal   __Circumstantial   __Anomia
                        __Paraphasia   __Clanging   __Echolalia
                        __Incoherent   __Neologisms
   Receptive Language   __Normal   __Abnormal _____

Mood   __Normal   __Euphoric   __Elevated   __Depressed   __Angry
        __Irritable   __Anxious

Affect   __Broad   __Restricted   __Blunted   __Flat
          __Inappropriate   __Labile

Orientation   __Normal   __Abnormal _____

Estimated IQ   __Above Average   __Average   __Below Average

Attention   __Normal   __Distractible   __Hypervigilant

Concentration   __Normal   __Brief

Memory   Recent Memory   __Normal   __Abnormal _____
          Remote Memory   __Normal   __Abnormal

Thought Processes   __Normal   __Blocking   __Loose Associations
                     __Confabulation   __Flight of Ideas
                     __Ideas of Reference   __Grandiosity
                     __Paranoia   __Magical Thinking   __Obsessions
                     __Perseveration   __Delusions
                     __Depersonalization   __Suicidal Ideation
                     __Homicidal Ideation   __Other _____

Hallucination   __None   __Auditory   __Visual   __Olfactory
                 __Gustatory

Judgment   __Good   __Fair   __Poor

Insight   __Good   __Fair   __Poor

Impulse Control   __Good   __Fair   __Poor

BRIEF MENTAL STATUS EXAM FORM

_____

1. Appearance	☐ casual dress, normal grooming and hygiene ☐ other (describe):
2. Attitude	☐ calm and cooperative ☐ other (describe):
3. Behavior	☐ no unusual movements or psychomotor changes ☐ other (describe):
4. Speech	☐ normal rate/tone/volume w/out pressure ☐ other (describe):
5. Affect	☐ appropriate to content ☐ normal range ☐ reactive and mood congruent ☐ depressed ☐ labile ☐ constricted ☐ tearful ☐ flat ☐ blunted ☐ other (describe):
6. Mood	☐ euthymic ☐ anxious ☐ irritable ☐ depressed ☐ elevated ☐ other (describe):
7. Thought Processes	☐ goal-directed and logical ☐ disorganized ☐ other (describe): ☐ circumstantial ☐ tangential

8. Thought Content	**Suicidal ideation:** **Homicidal ideation:**
	☐ None ☐ passive ☐ active ☐ None ☐ passive ☐ active
	If active: yes no If active: yes no
	    plan ☐ ☐ plan ☐ ☐
	    intent ☐ ☐ intent ☐ ☐
	    means ☐ ☐ means ☐ ☐
	
	☐ delusions ☐ obsessions/compulsions
	☐ phobias
	☐ other (describe):

9. Perception	☐ no hallucinations or delusions during interview ☐ other (describe):
10. Orientation	Oriented: ☐ time ☐ place ☐ person ☐ self ☐ other (describe):
11. Memory/ Concentration	☐ short term intact ☐ long term intact ☐ other (describe): ☐ distractable/inattentive
12. Insight/Judgement	☐ good ☐ fair ☐ poor

_____   _____

Practitioner's Signature   Date

_____   _____

Patient Name   ID#

MENTAL STATUS EXAM

_____

Date: _____

Name: _____

INITIAL INTERVIEW

Presenting problem:

Sleep patterns:

Appetite change:

Drug/alcohol use:

Marital status:

Marriage quality:

Children:

APPEARANCE
Clothing
   Clean
   Dirty
   Disheveled
   Atypical

Physical hygiene
   Good
   Fair
   Poor

BEHAVIOR
Posture
   Normal
   Slumped
   Rigid
   Unsteady
   Atypical

Facial expression
   Anxious
   Sad
   Hostile
   Cheerful
   Inappropriate
   Other _____

General body movements
   Accelerated
   Slowed
   Appropriate
   Inappropriate
Speech (speed and volume)
   Increased/loud
   Decreased/slowed
   Normal
   Mute
   Atypical
Relationships with others
   Domineering
   Submissive
   Provocative
   Suspicious
   Uncooperative
   Cooperative
   Physically/emotionally abusive

FEELINGS (AFFECT AND MOOD)
   Appropriate
   Inappropriate
Range of affect
   Broad
   Restricted
Lability of affect
   Labile
   Stable
Prominent mood
   Euphoria
   Hostility
   Anxiety
   Sadness
   Fearful
   Other _____

PERCEPTION
Illusions
   Present
   Absent
Hallucinations
   Absent
   Present
   Visual
   Olfactory
   Tactile
   Responding to hallucinations
   Not responding to hallucinations
Thought processes
Orientation
Disoriented
X-4 Person/place/time/situation

Memory
Impaired
Not impaired
Immediate
Recent
Remote
Comments:

Thought content
   Obsessions
   Compulsions
   Phobias
   Derealization

Depersonalization
Suicidal ideation
Homicidal ideation
Delusions
No thought disorder
Sexually preoccupied
Associational disturbance
   Present
   Absent
Judgment
   Impaired
   Not impaired

Comments:

_____

_____

_____

_____

_____

_____

_____   _____

Therapist's Signature   Date

INITIAL CASE ASSESSMENT

Name: _____ Date of 1st Contact: _____ Date of 1st Session: _____

IDENTIFYING INFORMATION:

_____

_____

_____

PRESENTING PROBLEM:

_____

_____

_____

SITUATION STRESSORS:

_____

_____

_____

MENTAL STATUS EXAM:

_____

_____

_____

SYMPTOMS OF IMPAIRED FUNCTIONING:

_____

_____

_____

PATIENT'S STRENGTHS AND ASSETS:

DSM 5/ICD 10 DIAGNOSIS:

_____

_____

_____

DIAGNOSTIC COMMENTS:

_____

_____

_____

_____

_____

TREATMENT GOALS:

_____

_____

_____

_____

_____

_____

TREATMENT PLAN:

_____

_____

_____

_____

_____

_____

_____

_____   _____

Therapist's Signature   Date

INITIAL EVALUATION

Person(s) present at interview:

_____

1. Presenting problem
   A. Presenting problems and precipitating events
   B. History of problems
   C. Medications/prescribed by whom
   D. Primary care physician (PCP)

2. Interpersonal relationships
   A. Current living arrangement
   B. Present family relationships
   C. Relationships in family-of-origin (past emphasis)
   D. Marital/significant other relationships (past and present)
   E. Peers and social relationships

3. Medical and developmental history

_____

_____

_____

4. Vocational and educational information

_____

_____

_____

5. Other mental health and community agency involvement (past and present)

_____

_____

_____

_____

6. Diagnostic impression
   A. Client mental status
   B. Strengths and weaknesses
   C. Diagnosis

_____

   D. Observations about other family members and relationships

7. Treatment disposition
   A. Goals (what will be accomplished)
   B. Objectives (what interventions to reach goals)

Therapist _____   Date _____

BRIEF MENTAL HEALTH EVALUATION REVIEW

Name: _____   DOB: _____

Date first examined: _____

Type of Service
__ Outpatient
__ Case management

Date of most recent visit: _____

Presenting Problem: _____

_____

Diagnosis:

_____

Medications: _____

_____

Current mental status examination (circle and comment on abnormal findings)

Appearance and Behavior

Grooming: well-groomed   disheveled   eccentric   poor hygiene

Motor activity: normal tremor,   retarded agitated   hyperactive

Speech: normal   slow   rapid   pressured   slurred   mute   delayed   soft loud   stuttering   aphasia

Interview behavior: cooperative   guarded   evasive

Behavior disturbance: none   irritable   aggressive   violent/poor   impulse   control   manipulative   apathetic

Comment:_____

_____

Sensorium and Cognitive Functioning

Orientation: oriented ×4   disoriented (person, place, time, situation)

Concentration: intact slight distracted   impaired (mild, moderate, severe)

Memory: normal   impaired (immediate, recent, remote) and degree (mild, moderate, severe)

Intelligence: above average   below average   borderline   developmentally disabled

Comment:_____

_____

Mood and Affect

Mood: normal   anxious   depressed   fearful   elated   euphoric   angry

Affect: appropriate   labile   expansive   blunted   flat

Perception

Hallucinations: none   auditory   visual   olfactory   gustatory

Illusions: none   misidentified

Thought Processes

Associations: goal directed   blocking   circumstantial   tangential   loose   neologisms

Content-delusions: none   persecution   somatic   broadcasting   grandiosity   religious   nihilistic   ideas of reference

Judgment: good   fair   poor

Insight: good   fair   poor
Impulse control: good   fair   poor

Comment: _____

_____

Substance Abuse

    Current alcohol use: none   social   abuse (occasional, binge, pattern, daily)

        Specify type, amount, frequency: _____

        _____

        _____

    Current illicit drug use: none   abuse (occasional, episodic, daily)   cannabis
                cocaine   heroin   amphetamines   sedatives
                hallucinogens   hypnotic   inhalants

        Specify drug, amount, frequency: _____

        _____

        _____

    History of substance abuse: _____

    _____

    _____

    Detox, treatment program, tox screen (specify date): _____

    _____

    _____

History of sexual abuse or assault: _____

_____

_____

Suicidal Ideation: __Yes __No

Homicidal Ideation: __Yes __No

Progress in Treatment and Prognosis: _____

_____

_____

_____
Therapist's Signature

_____

LIFE HISTORY QUESTIONNAIRE

The purpose of this questionnaire is to obtain a comprehensive understanding of your life experience and background. Completing these questions as fully and as accurately as you can, will benefit you through the development of a treatment program suited to your specific needs. Please return this questionnaire when completed, or at your scheduled appointment.

PLEASE COMPLETELY FILL OUT THE FOLLOWING PAGES

Date _____

Name _____

Address _____

Telephone numbers (day) _____ (evenings) _____

DOB_____ Age _____ Occupation _____

By whom were you referred? _____

_____

With whom are you now living? (list people) _____

_____

Where do you reside? __house __hotel __room __apartment __other

Significant relationship status (check one)
__single
__engaged
__married
__separated
__divorced
__remarried
__committed relationship
__widowed

　If married, husband's (or wife's) name, age, occupation?

_____

1. Role of religion and/or spirituality in your life:

   A. In childhood _____

   B. As an adult _____

2. Clinical

   A. State in your own words the nature of your main problems and how long they have been present:
   B. Give a brief history and development of your complaints (from onset to present):

C. On the scale below please check the severity of your problem(s):
___mildly upsetting
___moderately severe
___very severe
___extremely severe
___totally incapacitating

D. Whom have you previously consulted about your present problem(s)? _____

_____

_____

E. Are you taking any medication? If "yes," what, how much, and with what results?

_____

_____

3. Personal data

A. Date of birth _____ Place of birth _____

B. Mother's condition during pregnancy (as far as you know): _____

_____

C. Check any of the following that applied during your childhood:

___Night terrors	___Bed-wetting	___Sleepwalking
___Thumb sucking	___Nail biting	___Stammering
___Fears	___Happy childhood	___Unhappy childhood

Any others:

D. Health during childhood?

List illnesses _____

E. Health during adolescence?

List illnesses _____

F. What is your height? _____ Your weight _____

G. Any surgical operations? (Please list them and give age at the time)

_____

_____

H. Any accidents:

_____

_____

I. List your five main fears:

1. _____

2. _____

3. _____

4. _____

5. _____

J. *Underline* any of the following that apply to you:

headaches	dizziness	fainting spells
palpitations	stomach trouble	anxiety
bowel disturbances	fatigue	no appetite
anger	take sedatives	insomnia
nightmares	feel panicky	alcoholism
feel tense	conflict	tremors
depressed	suicidal ideas	take drugs
unable to relax	sexual problems	allergies
don't like weekends and vacations	overambitious	shy with people
can't make friends	inferiority feelings	can't make decisions
can't keep a job	memory problems	home conditions bad
financial problems	lonely	unable to have a good time
excessive sweating	often use aspirin or painkillers	concentration difficulties

Please list additional problems or difficulties here.

_____

_____

_____

_____

K. Circle any of the following words which apply to you:
Worthless, useless, a "nobody," "life is empty"
Inadequate, stupid, incompetent, naive, "can't do anything right"
Guilty, evil, morally wrong, horrible thoughts, hostile, full of hate
Anxious, agitated, cowardly, unassertive, panicky, aggressive
Ugly, deformed, unattractive, repulsive
Depressed, lonely, unloved, misunderstood, bored, restless
Confused, unconfident, in conflict, full of regrets
Worthwhile, sympathetic, intelligent, attractive, confident, considerate, dependable, responsible, analytical
Please list any additional words:

_____

L. Present interests, hobbies, and activities. _____

_____

M. How is most of your free time occupied? _____

_____

N. What is the last grade of school that you completed? _____

O. Scholastic abilities: strengths and weaknesses _____

_____

P. Were you ever bullied or severely teased? _____

Q. Do you make friends easily? _____

Do you keep them? _____

4. Occupational data

A. What sort of work are you doing now?

B. List previous jobs.

C. Does your present work satisfy you? (If not, in what ways are you dissatisfied?)

D. How much do you earn? _____

How much does it cost you to live? _____

E. Ambitions/Goals _____

Past _____

_____

Present _____

_____

5. Sex information

A. Parental attitudes toward sex (e.g., was their sex instruction or discussion in the home?)

B. When and how did you derive your first knowledge of sex?

C. When did you first become aware of your own sexual impulses?

D. Did you ever experience any anxieties or guilt feelings arising out of sex or masturbation? If "yes," please explain.

E. Please list any relevant details regarding your first or subsequent sexual experience.

F. Is your present sex life satisfactory? (If not, please explain).

G. Provide information about any significant heterosexual (and/or homosexual) reactions.

H. Are you sexually inhibited in any way? _____

6. Menstrual history

Age of first period? _____

Were you informed or did it come as a shock? _____

Are you regular? _____ Duration _____

Do you have pain? _____ Date of last period _____

Do your periods affect your moods? _____

7. Marital history _____

   How long did you know your marriage partner before engagement? _____

   How long have you been married? _____

   Husband's/wife's age _____

   Occupation of husband or wife _____

   A. Describe the personality of your husband or wife (in your own words)

   B. In what areas is there compatibility?

   C. In what areas is there incompatibility?

   D. How do you get along with your in-laws? (This includes brothers and sisters-in-law.)

      How many children do you have? _____

      Please list their gender and age(s). _____

      _____

   E. Do any of your children present special problems?

   F. Any history of miscarriages or abortions?

   G. Comments about any previous marriage(s) and brief details.

8. Family data
   A. Father
      Living or deceased? _____

      If deceased, your age at the time of his death. _____

      Cause of death. _____

      If alive, father's present age. _____

      Occupation: _____

      Health: _____

B. Mother

Living or deceased? _____

If deceased, your age at the time of her death. _____

Cause of death. _____

If alive, mother's present age. _____

Occupation: _____

Health: _____

C. Siblings

Number of brothers: _____ Brothers' ages: _____

Number of sisters: _____ Sisters' ages: _____

D. Relationship with brothers and sisters:

Past: _____

_____

Present: _____

_____

E. Give a description of your father's personality and his attitude toward you (past and present):

_____

_____

F. Give a description of your mother's personality and her attitude toward you (past and present):

_____

_____

G. In what ways were you punished by your parents as a child?

H. Give an impression of your home atmosphere (i.e., the home in which you grew up, including compatibility between parents and between parents and children).

I. Were you able to confide in your parents? _____

_____

J. Did your parents understand you? _____

_____

K. Basically, did you feel loved and respected by your parents? _____

_____

If you have a step-parent, give your age when parent remarried: _____

_____

L. Describe your religious training:

M. If you were not raised by your parents, who did raise you, and between what years?

N. Has anyone (parents, relatives, friends) ever interfered in your marriage, occupation, etc.?

O. Who are the most important people in your life?

P. Does any member of your family suffer from alcoholism, epilepsy, or anything which can be considered a "mental disorder"?

Q. Are there any other members of the family about whom information regarding illness, etc. is relevant?

R. Recount any fearful or distressing experiences not previously mentioned?

S. What do expect to accomplish from therapy, and how long do you expect therapy to last?

T. List any situations which make you feel calm *or* relaxed.

U. Have you ever lost control (e.g., temper or crying or aggression)? If so, please describe.

V. Please add any information not brought up by this questionnaire that may aid your therapist in understanding and helping you.

9. Self-description (Please complete the following):

   A. I am a person who _____

   B. All my life _____

   C. Ever since I was a child _____

   D. One of the things I feel proud of is _____

   E. It's hard for me to admit _____

   F. One of the things I can't forgive is _____

   G. One of the things I feel guilty about is _____

   H. If I didn't have to worry about my image _____

   I. One of the ways people hurt me is _____

J. Mother was always _____

K. What I needed from mother and didn't get was _____

L. Father was always _____

M. What I wanted from my father and didn't get was _____

N. If I weren't afraid to be myself, I might _____

O. One of the things I'm angry about is _____

P. What I need and have never received from a woman (man) is _____

Q. The bad thing about growing up is _____

R. One of the ways I could help myself but don't is _____

10. A. What is there about your present *behavior* that you would like to change?

   B. What feelings do you wish to alter (e.g., increase or decrease)?

   C. What sensations are especially:

      1. pleasant for you?

      2. unpleasant for you?

   D. Describe a very pleasant image of fantasy.

   E. Describe a very unpleasant image of fantasy.

   F. What do you consider your most irrational thought or idea?

   G. Describe any interpersonal relationships that give you:

      1. joy

      2. grief

   H. In a few words, what do you think therapy is all about?

11. With the remaining space and blank sides of these pages, give a brief description of you by the following people:
   A. Yourself
   B. Your spouse (if married)
   C. Your best friend
   D. Someone who dislikes you

This has been adapted from Lazarus (1977).

ADULT PSYCHOSOCIAL

_____

IDENTIFYING INFORMATION (age, gender, ethnicity, marital status):

_____

_____

Presenting Problem:

_____

_____

Current Social Information:

1. Describe the present living arrangements (include with whom you are living with, and a brief description of these relationships):

_____

_____

2. How long have you been married/dating/living together? Describe this relationship (include occupation and age of significant other): _____

_____

_____

3. How many children do you have? (name, sex, age): _____

_____

_____

4. Are there any significant problems with any of these children? (describe): _____

_____

_____

_____

5. Give details of previous relationships/marriages: _____

_____

_____

6. Any history of abuse (emotional, physical, sexual) in current or previous relationships:

_____

_____

_____

FAMILY HISTORY

1. Describe your childhood and adolescence (include home atmosphere, relationship with parents):

_____

_____

_____

2. State any history of significant life events such as death, abuse (physical, emotional, sexual) divorce, separation, other: _____

_____

_____

_____

3. List mother and father by age, include occupation: _____

_____

_____

_____

4. List siblings by age and describe how you relate to them (past and present): _____

_____

_____

_____

5. Have any family members been treated for/have emotional problems? Describe:

_____

_____

_____

DRUG AND ALCOHOL ABUSE

1. Any family history of drug and/or alcohol usage? List and describe: _____

_____

_____

_____

2. Any personal history of drug/alcohol usage? List and describe: _____

_____

_____

EDUCATIONAL HISTORY

1. Describe all school experiences, high school, college, vocational school. Were there any problems with truancy, suspensions, special education, vocational training, etc.? _____

_____

_____

EMPLOYMENT HISTORY

1. Present employment status and where (positive and negative aspects of what is going on at work):

_____

_____

2. If on leave of absence or disability, will you return to present job: _____

_____

_____

SOCIALIZATION SKILLS

1. List clubs and organizations you belong to: _____

_____

_____

2. What do you do for pleasure and relaxation? _____

_____

_____

SUMMARY

This _____ year old (include sex, marital status, ethnicity) is currently participating in outpatient treatment for_____(summary of reasons for treatment).

1. What/who seems to be placing the most stress on you at this time?: _____

   _____

2. Are there any legal issues pending? _____ Yes _____ No (describe): _____

   _____

3. Are you having financial problems at this time?: _____

   _____

4. Describe your plans regarding any help you would like to have with your living arrangements:

   _____

   _____

TREATMENT PLANS AND RECOMMENDATIONS

1. _____

2. _____

3. _____

4. _____

_____   _____
Therapist's Signature   Date

CHILD/ADOLESCENT PSYCHOSOCIAL

IDENTIFYING INFORMATION

Date of assessment: _____

Name of child _____ Sex: (M) _____ (F) _____

Birth date _____ Place of birth _____ Age _____

Address (number and street) _____

(city) _____ (state) _____ (zip code) _____

Telephone ( ) _____ Religion (optional) _____

Education (grade) _____ Present school _____

Referral Source: _____

I give permission for (therapist) to contact (physician/teacher/etc.) regarding treatment issues, symptoms, behaviors, or other information necessary for the treatment of (minor patient).

Parent's Signature _____ Date _____

CHIEF COMPLAINT

Presenting Problems: (check all that apply)

__Very unhappy
__Irritable
__Temper outbursts
__Withdrawn
__Daydreaming
__Fearful
__Clumsy
__Overactive
__Slow
__Short attention span
__Distractible
__Lacks initiative
__Undependable
__Peer conflict
__Phobic

__Impulsive
__Stubborn
__Disobedient
__Infantile
__Mean to others
__Destructive
__Trouble with the law
__Running away
__Self-mutilating
__Head banging
__Rocking
__Shy
__Strange behavior
__Strange thoughts

__Fire setting
__Stealing
__Lying
__Sexual trouble
__School performance
__Truancy
__Bed-wetting
__Soiled pants
__Eating problems
__Sleeping problems
__Sickly
__Drugs use
__Alcohol use
__Suicide talk

Explain:

How long have these problems occurred? (number of weeks, months, years)

_____

What happened that makes you seek help at this time? _____

_____

Problems perceived to be: __very serious   __serious   __not serious

What are your expectations of your child? _____

_____

What changes would you like to see in your child? _____

_____

What changes would you like to see in yourself? _____

_____

What changes would you like to see in your family? _____

_____

PSYCHOSOCIAL HISTORY

CURRENT FAMILY SITUATION

Mother—Relationship to child   __natural parent   __relative
                                    __step-parent   __adoptive parent

Occupation _____

Education _____   Religion _____

Birthplace _____   Birth date _____

Age _____

Father—Relationship to child   __natural parent   __relative
                                    __step-parent   __adoptive parent

Occupation _____

Education _____   Religion _____

Birthplace _____   Birth date _____

Age _____

Marital History of Parents:
    Natural Parents: __married   when _____   age _____
                         __separated   when _____
                         __divorced   when _____
                         __deceased   M or F _____
    Step-parents: __married   when _____

If child is adopted:

Adoption source:

_____

Reason and circumstances:

_____

Age when child first in home:

_____

Date of legal adoption:

_____

What has the child been told?

_____

LIVING ARRANGEMENTS: Places   Dates

    Number of moves in child's life _____   _____   _____
                                        _____   _____
    Present home __renting   __buying   _____   _____
              __house   __apartment   _____   _____

    Does the child share a room with anyone else?   __Yes __No

    If yes, with whom? _____

    If no, how long has he/she had own room? _____

Was the child ever placed, boarded, or lived away from the family?   __Yes   __No

Explain: _____

What are the major family stresses at the present time, if any? _____

_____

What are the sources of family income? _____

_____

BROTHERS and SISTERS: (indicate if step-brothers or step-sisters)

Name	Age	Sex	School or Occupation	Present Grade	Living at home (yes or no)	Use drugs or alcohol (yes or no)	Treated for drug abuse (yes or no)
1. _____	__	__	_____	_____	_____	_____	_____
2. _____	__	__	_____	_____	_____	_____	_____
3. _____	__	__	_____	_____	_____	_____	_____
4. _____	__	__	_____	_____	_____	_____	_____
5. _____	__	__	_____	_____	_____	_____	_____
6. _____	__	__	_____	_____	_____	_____	_____

List all other extended family members by their relation to the patient who have drug and/or alcohol problems (legal or illegal), history of depression, self-destructive behavior, or legal problems.

    1. _____

    2. _____

    3. _____

    4. _____

    5. _____

    6. _____

Others living in the home (and their relationship):

    1. _____

    2. _____

HEALTH OF FAMILY MEMBERS: (excluding patient)

Name	Relationship to Child	Type of Illness	When Occurred	Length of Illness
1. _____	_____	_____	_____	_____
2. _____	_____	_____	_____	_____
3. _____	_____	_____	_____	_____
4. _____	_____	_____	_____	_____

Does or did any member of the child's family have any problems with:
__reading   __spelling   __math   __speech
(if yes, please explain)

Is there any history in the child's family of:
__mental retardation   __epilepsy   __birth defects   __schizophrenia
(if yes, please explain)

CHILD HEALTH INFORMATION

Note all health problems the child has had or has now.

	Age		Age
__High fevers	_____	__Dental problems	_____
__Pneumonia	_____	__Weight problems	_____
__Flu	_____	__Allergies	_____
__Encephalitis	_____	__Skin problems	_____
__Meningitis	_____	__Asthma	_____
__Convulsions	_____	__Headaches	_____
__Unconsciousness	_____	__Stomach problems	_____
__Concussions	_____	__Accident prone	_____
__Head injury	_____	__Anemia	_____
__Fainting	_____	__High or low blood pressure	_____
__Dizziness	_____	__Sinus problems	_____
__Tonsils out	_____	__Heart problems	_____
__Vision problems	_____	__Hyperactivity	_____
__Hearing problems	_____	__Other illnesses, etc.	_____
__Earaches	_____	(Explain)	_____

Has the child ever been hospitalized?   __Yes   __No
If yes, please explain.

Age	How Long	Reason
_____	_____	_____

Has child ever been seen by a medical specialist?   __Yes   __No

Age	How Long	Reason
_____	_____	_____

Has child ever taken, or is he/she taking presently any prescribed medications?   __Yes   __No

Age	How Long	Reason
_____	_____	_____

Name of Primary Care Physician_____

DEVELOPMENTAL HISTORY

Prenatal—Child wanted?   __Yes __No   Planned for?   __Yes   __No
Normal pregnancy?   __Yes __No

If mother ill or upset during pregnancy, explain: _____

Length of pregnancy:
Paternal support and acceptance: (explain)

Birth

Length of active labor: __hrs   __Easy   __Difficult
Full term: __Yes   __No

If premature, how early: _____

If overdue, how late: _____

Birth weight: __lbs   __oz
Type of delivery: __spontaneous   __cesarean   __with instruments
                       __head first   __breech
Was it necessary to give the infant oxygen?   __Yes   __No   If yes, how long: _____
Did infant require blood transfusions?   __Yes   __No
Did infant require X-ray?   __Yes   __No
Physical condition of infant at birth:
(If yes explain)   Anorexia   __Yes   __No
                      Trauma   __Yes   __No
                      Other complications   __Yes   __No
Did mother abuse alcohol/drugs during pregnancy?   __Yes   __No

Newborn Period

			How Long
irritability	__Yes	__No	_____
vomiting	__Yes	__No	_____
difficulty breathing	__Yes	__No	_____
difficulty sleeping	__Yes	__No	_____
convulsions/twitching	__Yes	__No	_____
colic	__Yes	__No	_____
normal weight gain	__Yes	__No	_____
was child breast fed	__Yes	__No	_____

DEVELOPMENTAL MILESTONES

Age at which child:

sat up: _____

crawled: _____

walked: _____

spoke single words: _____

sentences: _____

bladder trained: _____

bowel trained: _____

weaned: _____

Describe the manner in which toilet training was accomplished:

EARLY SOCIAL DEVELOPMENT

Relationship to siblings and peers:

                  __individual play   __group play
                  __competitive   __cooperative
                  __leadership role   __a follower

Describe special habits, fears, or idiosyncrasies of the child:

EDUCATIONAL HISTORY

Name of School	City/State	Dates attended: from	to	Grades completed at this school
Preschool _____	_____	_____	_____	_____
Elementary _____	_____	_____	_____	_____
Junior high _____	_____	_____	_____	_____
High school _____	_____	_____	_____	_____

Types of classes: __regular   __learning disability   __continuation
                       __emotionally handicapped   __opportunity   __other
Did child skip a grade?   __Yes __No   Repeat a grade? __Yes __No
If yes, when and how many years appropriate grade level at present time?

_____

Did child have any specific learning difficulties?   __Yes __No
Has child ever have a tutor or other special help with school work?   __Yes __No
Does child attend school on a regular basis?   __Yes __No
Does child appear motivated for school?   __Yes __No
Has child ever been suspended or expelled?   __Yes __No

ACADEMIC PERFORMANCE

Highest grade on last report card? _____

Lowest grade on last report card? _____

Favorite subject? _____

Least favorite subject? _____

Does child participate in extracurricular activities?   __Yes __No (explain)

In school, how many friends does child have: __a lot __a few __none

What are child's educational aspirations?   __quit school

__graduate from high school

__go to college

Has child had special testing in school? (If yes, what were the results?)

Psychological   __Yes   __No   Vocational __Yes __No

List child's special interests, hobbies, skills:

_____

_____

_____

_____

_____

Has the child ever had difficulty with the police?   __Yes   __No   (if yes, explain)

Has child ever appeared in juvenile court?   __Yes   __No   (if yes, explain)

Has child ever been on probation?   __Yes   __No

From To	Reason	Probation Officer
_____	_____	_____
_____	_____	_____

Has child ever been employed?   _Yes   _No

Job	Employed	How long
_____	_____	_____
_____	_____	_____

ADDITIONAL COMMENTS

_____

_____

_____

_____

_____

_____

_____

_____

_____

_____

_____

_____

_____

Therapist's Signature   Date

PARENT'S QUESTIONNAIRE

Name of child: _____ Date: _____

Name of parent (filling out form): _____

Answer all of the questions by indicating the degree of the problem. Write "N" for never, "S" for sometimes, or "O" for often in front of the number for each question.

QUESTION

_____1. Picks at things (nails, fingers, hair clothing)
_____2. Talks back to authority figures (attitude)
_____3. Has problems with making or keeping friends
_____4. Excitable, impulsive
_____5. Wants to run things
_____6. Sucks or chews (thumb, clothing, blankets, etc.)
_____7. Cries easily/often
_____8. Emotionally reactive
_____9. Has a chip on his/her shoulder
___10. Tendency to daydream
___11. Difficulty learning
___12. Always squirming, restless, and moving around
___13. Experiences fear and anxiety in new situations/meeting new people
___14. Breaks things/destructive
___15. Lies, makes up stories
___16. Does not follow rules
___17. Gets into trouble more than peers
___18. Shy and does not assert self
___19. Has problems with speech (stuttering, hard to understand, baby talk)
___20. Denies mistakes and is defensive
___21. Blames others for mistakes
___22. Steals
___23. Argumentative
___24. Disrespectful
___25. Pouts and sulks
___26. Obeys rules but is resentful
___27. When hurt or angered by someone, holds a grudge
___28. Develops stomachache or headache when stressed
___29. Worries unnecessarily
___30. Does not finish tasks
___31. Emotionally sensitive and easily hurt
___32. Bullies others
___33. Cruel and insensitive
___34. Clingy and in need of constant reassurance
___35. Easily distracted
___36. Frequent headaches or stomachaches
___37. Rapid mood changes
___38. Fights a lot and creates conflicts

___39. Power struggles with authority

___40. Childish or immature (wants help when should be able to do it independently)

___41. Does not get along well with siblings

___42. Easily frustrated

___43. Perfectionism prevents trying new things

___44. Problems with sleep

___45. Problems with eating

___46. Has bowel problems

___47. Vomiting, nausea, or other complaints of pain or physical distress

___48. Feels he/she is treated differently in the family than siblings

___49. Passive and gets pushed around

___50. Self-centered, brags, little understanding of others

SELF-ASSESSMENT

_____

What is happening in your life which resulted in this appointment? _____

_____

What would you like to see accomplished in therapy? _____

_____

CHIEF COMPLAINT (CHECK ALL THAT APPLY TO YOU)

__ Depression
__ Low energy
__ Low self-esteem
__ Poor concentration
__ Hopelessness
__ Worthlessness
__ Guilt
__ Sleep disturbance (more/less)
__ Appetite disturbance (more/less)
__ Thoughts of hurting yourself
__ Thoughts of hurting someone
__ Isolation/social withdrawal
__ Sadness/loss
__ Stress
__ Anxiety/panic
__ Heart pounding/racing
__ Chest pain
__ Trembling/shaking
__ Sweating
__ Chills/hot flashes
__ Tingling/numbness
__ Fear of dying
__ Fear of going crazy
__ Nausea
__ Phobias
__ Obsessions/compulsive behaviors
__ Thoughts racing
__ Can't hold onto an idea
__ Easily agitate
__ Excessive behaviors (spending, gambling)
__ Delusions/hallucinations
__ Not thinking clearly/confusion

__ Feeling that you are not real
__ Feeling that things around you are not real
__ Lose track of time
__ Unpleasant thoughts won't go away
__ Anger/frustration
__ Easily agitated/annoyed
__ Defies rules
__ Blames others
__ Argues
__ Excessive use of drugs and/or alcohol
__ Excessive use of prescription medications
__ Blackouts
__ Physical abuse issues
__ Sexual abuse issues
__ Spousal abuse issues
__ Other problems/symptoms:

_____

_____

_____

_____

_____

_____

_____

Previous outpatient therapy? _____Yes _____No, with _____

What was accomplished? _____

__medications, list: _____

Previous hospitalization? ___Yes ___No Number of hospitalizations ___ECT? _____

If yes, when _____

BRIEF MEDICAL HISTORY

_____

Name: _____ Age: _____ DOB: _____ Date: _____

Primary Care Physician: _____

Last medical exam: _____

_____

List any medical problems that you are currently experiencing: _____

Name of the physician monitoring this condition(s): _____

List any medications you are currently taking: _____

_____

Who prescribed the medication(s): _____

Have you ever seen a psychiatrist or counselor before?

Yes _____ No _____ When: _____

Please Explain: _____

_____

Check any of the following problems that you experience:

__ lack of appetite	__ sleep disturbance	__ depression
__ excessive drinking	__ headaches	__ bowel problems
__ anger management	__ sexual problems	__ bladder control problem
__ problem drug use	__ appetite disturbance	__ difficulty relaxing
__ nervousness	__ stomach problems	__ fears/phobia
__ fatigue	__ pain (where)	__ obsessive thoughts
__ panic attacks	__ low self-esteem	__ compulsive behaviors
__ anxiety	__ relationship problems	__ marital/family problems
__ loneliness	__ difficulty concentrating	__ poor impulse control
__ nightmares	__ feelings of unreality	__ confusion
__ intrusive thoughts	__ flashbacks	__ difficulty trusting

ILLNESSES AND MEDICAL PROBLEMS

Please mark with an "X" any of the following illnesses and medical problems you have had and indicate the year when each started. If you are not certain when illness started, write down an approximate year or age it occurred.

ILLNESS	X	YEAR	N/A	ILLNESS	X	YEAR	N/A
Eye or Eyelid Infection				Venereal Disease			
Glaucoma				Genital Herpes			
Other Eye Problems				Breast Disease			
Ear Condition				Nipple Drainage			
Deafness or Decreased Hearing				Headaches			
Thyroid Problems				Head Injury			
Strep Throat				Stroke			
Bronchitis				Convulsions/Seizures			
Emphysema				Black Outs			
Pneunomia				Dizziness			
Allergies, Asthma, or Hayfever				Mental Problems			
Nose Bleeds				Arthritis			
Tuberculosis				Gout			
Other Lung Problems				Cancer or Tumors			
Difficulty Breathing				Bleeding Tendency			
High Blood Pressure				Diabetes			
High Cholesterol				Measles/Rubeola			
Arteriosclerosis (hardening of arteries) .				German Measles/Rubella			
Heart Attack				Polio			
Chest Pain				Mumps			
Irregular Heart Beat				Scarlet Fever			
Heart Murmur				Chicken Pox			
Other Heart Conditions				Mononucleosis			
Stomach/Duodenal Ulcer				Eczema			
Nausea				Psoriasis			
Vomiting				Skin Rash			
Weight Loss				Open Wounds			
Weight Gain				Infection			
Difficulty Swallowing				Muscle Stiffness			
Diverticulosis				Muscle Weakness			
Colitis				Muscle Pain			
Other Bowel Problems				Bone Fracture			
Blood in Stools				Bone Stiffness			
Diarrhea				Others			
Hemorrhoids				. . . .			
Easily Fatigued				. . . .			
Hepatitis				. . . .			
Liver Problems				. . . .			
Gallbladder Problems				. . . .			
Hernia				. . . .			
Kidney or Bladder Disease				. . . .			
Prostate Problem (male only)				. . . .			
Ovarian Problem (female only)				. . . .			
Last Menstrual Period				. . . .			
Last Pregnancy				. . . .			
Menstrual Flow Pattern							

MEDICAL REVIEW CONSULT REQUEST FOR PRIMARY CARE PHYSICIAN OF AN EATING DISORDER PATIENT

Dear Attending Physician:

This patient has presented for psychological treatment for an eating disorder (EDO). For effective, comprehensive treatment to be rendered, all professionals involved must share information, including the screening and monitoring of medical complications associated with the EDO. Before psychological treatment proceeds, a physical examination is required, which includes the following routine lab work. If abnormalities are presented, a list of selected studies may be required. Please forward the results of your examination and lab studies. Your consultation is appreciated.

Laboratory Studies for Evaluation of Eating Disorders

Routine:

    Complete blood count

    Electrolytes, glucose, and renal function tests

    Chemistry panel

        Liver function tests

        Total protein and albumin

        Calcium

        Amylase

    Hormones

        Thyroid function tests

        A.M. plasma cortisol

        Luteinizing hormone

        Follicle-stimulating hormone

        Estrogen (female)

        Testosterone (male)

    Chest X-ray

    Electrocardiogram

    Dual photon absorptiometry

Selected:

    Magnetic resonance imaging for brain atrophy

    Abnormal X-ray for severe bloating

    Lower esophageal sphincter pressure studies for reflux

    Lactose deficiency tests for dairy intolerance

    Total bowel transit time for severe constipation

Regards,

_____

Therapist's Signature

Adapted from E. Anderson (1991). *Medical complications of eating disorders.*

SUBSTANCE USED AND PSYCHOSOCIAL QUESTIONNAIRE

(To be filled out by client)

Client Name: _____

Sex: _____   Date of Birth: _____   Age: _____   Marital Status: M/D/S

Living Arrangements: _____

Referral Source: _____

Presenting Problems: _____

_____

1. Use of alcohol and/or drugs

   Type   How used   Age started   Amount   Frequency   Last time used

   _____

   _____

   _____

   _____

   _____

   _____

2. Has there been any change in the pattern of alcohol/drug use in the last
   6 months to 1 year __Yes __No. If yes, describe: _____

   _____

   _____

3. Preferred alcohol or drug: _____

   _____

   _____

4. Preferred setting for alcohol/drug use (home, work, bars, alone, with friends):

   _____

   _____

5. Longest period of time you have gone without using alcohol or drugs?_____

   _____

6. What medication(s) are you currently being prescribed, what are you taking it for, and who is
   prescribing it?

   _____

   _____

7. Do you use alcohol or drugs to get started in the morning? _____

_____

_____

8. Have you ever felt annoyed when other people criticize your substance use?_____

_____

9. Has your physician ever told you to cut down or stop using alcohol/drugs? _____

_____

10. Have you ever felt the need to cut down on the use of alcohol/drugs (if yes, explain):

_____

_____

11. Has the use of alcohol/drugs caused you to be late to or miss work? _____

12. Has the use of alcohol/drugs affected your home life or relationships? _____

13. How do you feel about your use of alcohol/drugs? _____

_____

14. Have you ever attended AA/NA meetings? _____

_____

TREATMENT HISTORY

1. Number of attempts to stop alcohol/drug use _____. By what means? _____

_____

2. Length of time you abstained from alcohol/drug use: _____
   Why did you start again? _____

3. Previous experiences with detox: _____

_____

_____

4. Previous treatment experiences (list problems, type of treatment, location, and what you learned and accomplished): _____

_____

_____

FAMILY HISTORY

1. Alcoholism and/or drug dependence of mother, father, siblings, or grandparents?

_____

2. High blood pressure? _____

3. Diabetes? _____

4. Liver disease? _____

SOCIAL HISTORY

1. Occupation: _____

2. Level of education completed: _____

_____

Symptoms (If Yes, Please Explain)	Yes/No	Explain
Depression	_____	_____
Fatigue/decreased activity level	_____	_____
Sleep problems	_____	_____
Appetite problems or changes	_____	_____
Memory problems/changes	_____	_____
Suspicious	_____	_____
Anxiety	_____	_____
Fever, sweaty	_____	_____
Shortness of breath	_____	_____
Chest pain/discomfort	_____	_____
Palpitations	_____	_____
Dizziness	_____	_____
Indigestion/nausea	_____	_____
Vomiting (with blood)	_____	_____
Abdominal pain	_____	_____
Diarrhea	_____	_____
Black "tarry" stools	_____	_____
Trouble getting an erection	_____	_____
Tremors	_____	_____
Blackouts	_____	_____

Symptoms (If Yes, Please Explain)	Yes/No	Explain
Periods of confusion	_____	_____
Hallucinations	_____	_____
Staggering/balance problems	_____	_____
Tingling	_____	_____
Headaches/vision changes	_____	_____
Muscle weakness	_____	_____
Suicidal attempts/thoughts	_____	_____

MEDICAL PROBLEMS

Has your physician told you that you have any of the following:

Diabetes	__Yes	__No
Cirrhosis	__Yes	__No
Hepatitis	__Yes	__No
Anemia	__Yes	__No
Gout	__Yes	__No
High blood pressure	__Yes	__No
Delirium tremens	__Yes	__No
Gastritis	__Yes	__No
Pancreatitis	__Yes	__No

Goals of participating in treatment at this time? _____

_____

_____

_____

_____

_____

_____

CHEMICAL DEPENDENCY PSYCHOSOCIAL ASSESSMENT

_____

Date: _____   Age: _____

S.O. Name _____   Phone: _____

Religious/ethnic/cultural background: _____

_____

Marital Status: _____   Children: _____

Living with Whom: _____

Present Support System (family/friends): _____

Chemical History:

Chemical Use	Route	Age Started	Amt.	Freq.	Last Dose? Last Used	Length of Use

Description of Presenting Problems (patient's view):_____

_____

Previous Counseling:

When	Where	Therapist/Title	Response To

Family/S.O. Relationships/History of Chemical Use: _____

_____

_____

_____

S.O. Relationships and History of Chemical Use: _____

_____

_____

_____

Effects of on Family/Support System: _____

_____

_____

_____

Daily Activities that: A. support abstinence:_____

                     B. encourage usage: _____

History of Sexual/Physical Abuse (victim/abuser): _____

_____

Sexual Orientation: _____

Education: _____

Vocational History: _____

Leisure/Social Interests: _____

_____

Current Occupation: _____

Current Employer: _____

Impact of on Job Performance: _____

_____

EAP? Yes__ No__ Name: _____ Phone: _____

Socioeconomic/Financial Problems: _____

_____

_____

Legal: _____ DWI: Yes__ No__ Court Ordered: Yes__ No__

Patient's Perceptions of Strengths and Weaknesses: _____

_____

_____

Preliminary Treatment Plan: List presenting problems based on initial assessment of the client's physical, emotional, cognitive, and behavioral status.

Detox: Yes__ No__ Explain: _____

Rehab: Yes__ No__ Explain: _____

Problem #1: _____

Problem #2: _____

Problem #3: _____

Immediate treatment recommendations to address identifying problems: _____

_____

_____

_____

_____

_____   _____
Therapist   Date

BRIEF CONSULTATION NOTE TO PHYSICIAN

Dear Dr. _____;

_____was seen on _____.

Purpose of visit:

Preliminary findings reveal:

I tentative diagnosis:

Return appointment: _____
If you have further questions please feel free to contact me.

Sincerely,

OUTPATIENT TREATMENT PROGRESS REPORT

Name: _____   Date: _____

SS#: _____   DOB: _____

Date of initial interview: _____   Number of sessions: _____

Describe treatment motivation and compliance: _____

_____

_____

Current Risk Factors
- Suicidality: ☐ None   ☐ Ideation   ☐ Plan   ☐ Intent w/o means   ☐ Intent with means
- Homicidality: ☐ None   ☐ Ideation   ☐ Plan   ☐ Intent w/o means   ☐ Intent with means
- If risk exists: Client is able to contract not to harm: ☐ Self   ☐ Others
- Impulse control: ☐ Sufficient   ☐ Moderate   ☐ Minimal   ☐ Inconsistent   ☐ Explosive
- Substance abuse: ☐ None   ☐ Abuse   ☐ Dependence   ☐ Unstable Remission
- Medical risks: ☐ Yes   ☐ No   If "yes," explain: _____

Risk History (Explain significant history of behaviors that may affect the current level of risk.)

Functional Impairments (Explain how symptoms impact current functioning or place client at risk.)

Diagnosis

_____

Current Medication
   ☐ None ☐ Psychiatric ☐ Medical ☐ No information _____

Specify (*include dosage, frequency, and compliance*): _____

_____

A. **Measurable Behavioral Goals with Target Dates for Resolution**

    1.

    2.

    3.

B. **Planned Interventions**

    1.

    2.

    3.

C. **Objective Outcome Criteria by Which Goal Achievement Is Measured**

    1.

    2.

    3.

D. **Progress Since Last Update**

E. **Referrals**

F. **Discharge Planning**

Comments:

_____

_____

_____

_____

_____

_____

_____

_____

_____

_____

_____

_____   _____

Therapist's Signature   Date

_____

Patient

PROGRESS NOTE FOR INDIVIDUAL WITH ANXIETY AND/OR DEPRESSION

Symptoms List: Check off any symptoms that have been most bothersome or have occurred frequently during the past week.

Date: _____

Name: _____

General Symptoms

❏ Acute stress
❏ Repetitive, senseless thoughts
❏ Repetitive, senseless behaviors
❏ Fainting or feeling faint
❏ Tremors, trembling, or shakiness
❏ Unexplained physical problems (body aches/pain)
❏ Social isolation/withdrawal
❏ Anger (thoughts/feelings/outbursts)
❏ Violent behavior

❏ Constant worry
❏ Irritability
❏ Tension
❏ Headache
❏ Feeling in a dreamlike state
❏ Fearful feelings
❏ Fear of losing control
❏ Jumpiness
❏ Restlessness
❏ Sweating
❏ Dizziness/lightheadedness
❏ Keyed up/on edge

Section 1: If constant worry plus three other symptoms in Section 2 are checked, consider a diagnosis of persistent anxiety.

❏ Agitation
❏ Nervousness
❏ Trouble concentrating
❏ Insomnia/trouble sleeping
❏ Decrease in sex drive
❏ Trouble making decisions

Section 2: If any symptoms are checked in this section, plus either of the first two symptoms in Section 3, consider a diagnosis of depression with associated anxiety.

❏ Sad/depressed/down in the dumps
❏ Lack of/loss of interest in things
❏ Helpless feelings
❏ Fatigue, lack of energy
❏ Weakness
❏ Increase or decrease in appetite
❏ Increase or decrease in weight
❏ Frequent crying or weeping
❏ Frequent thoughts of death or suicide
❏ Worthless feelings
❏ Excessive feelings of guilt

Section 3: If six or more symptoms in this area are checked, consider a diagnosis of depression.

- ❏ Hopeless feelings
- ❏ Feeling life is not worth living
- ❏ Sleeping too much
- ❏ Frequent negative thinking
- ❏ Memory problems
- ❏ Fear of doing something uncontrollable
- ❏ Fear of dying
- ❏ Chills
- ❏ Seeing or hearing things that are not real
- ❏ Fear of going crazy

Please list medications and dosages Do you smoke?   _No   _Yes. How much?
Do you drink or use other substances?   _No   _Yes. How much and how often?

Do you have thoughts of harming yourself? _____

Do you have thoughts of harming another person? _____

*May be used as a progress note. Have patient check off symptoms. Remove the printing on the right side of page and line to write progress note.

Adapted from Bristol Meyer Squibb Well Being Chart.

CLINICAL NOTES

1. Mental Status:
    A. Appearance: WNL__   Unkempt__   Dirty__   Meticulous__   Unusual__
    B. Behavior: WNL__   Guarded__   Withdrawn__   Noncompliant__   Hostile__
         Uncooperative__   Provocative__   Manipulative__   Hypoactive__   Hyperactive__
         Suspicious__   Cooperative__   Pleasant__   Under the influence__
    C. Mood/Affect: WNL__   Flat__   Depressed__   Euphoric__   Anxious__   Fearful__   Irritable__
         Angry__   Labile__   Incongruent__
    D. Cognitions: WNL__   Loose__   Scattered__   Blocked__   Illogical__   Dilusional__
         Paranoid__   Hallucinations__   Grandiose__   Fragmented__   Somatic__
    E. Safety: Danger to self/others?   Yes__   No__
         If yes, describe:_____
         Safe to return home?   Yes__   No__
         If no, state planned intervention below.

2. Clinical Intervention and/or Educating/Bibiotherapy:

_____

_____

_____

3. Patient Response/Participation:

_____

_____

_____

Signature: _____   Date:_____

* *

Printed by permission from Cosette Taillac-Vento, LCSW

WNL = within normal limits

OUTLINE FOR DIAGNOSTIC SUMMARY

DIAGNOSTIC SUMMARY

Date: _____

Patient: _____ M/F   DOB:_____   Age:_____

Sources of Information (includes but not limited to, mental status exam, history and physical, psychiatric evaluation, psychosocial and treatment plan).

Identification of the Patient (demographic information, include but not limited to, age, race, marital status, etc.):

_____

_____

_____

_____

_____

Presenting Problems (includes, but not limited to, why was the patient hospitalized, drug of choice, route of admission, frequency of use, pattern of use, medical problems, mood, affect, mental status, legal problems, etc.):

_____

_____

_____

_____

_____

Treatment Plan/Recommendations/Goals (includes problem list, therapeutic interventions and goals):

_____

_____

_____

_____

_____

Discharge Plan (includes, but not limited to, follow-up with therapy, a physician, a sponsor, a 12-step recovery program, vocational guidance, etc.):

_____

_____

_____

_____

_____

_____

_____

Therapist's Signature

DISCHARGE SUMMARY

NAME OF PATIENT:_____ DOB: _____

IDENTIFICATION OF PATIENT:

_____

_____

PRESENTING PROBLEM:

_____

_____

TREATMENT GOALS: WERE GOALS MET? (yes/no)

_____   _____

_____   _____

_____   _____

DISPOSITION/CONSULTS/REFERRALS/PROGNOSIS:

_____

_____

_____

_____

INITIAL DIAGNOSIS: DISCHARGE DIAGNOSIS:

_____   _____

_____   _____

_____   _____

Date of 1st session: _____ Date of last session: _____# of sessions: _____

_____
Therapist's Signature

REPORTS ASSOCIATED WITH DISABILITY OR WORKERS' COMPENSATION

There may be instances when it is necessary to develop a specific report associated with disability or workers' compensation. It could be as simple as a circumstance involving your patient leading to the need to evaluate them following an industrial injury. Below there are several such reports to choose from.

DISABILITY/WORKER'S COMPENSATION

Patient Name: _____ M/F   DOB_____ Age:____

Address: _____Phone:_____

Occupation: _____

SS#: _____ Date of Injury:_____ Case No.:_____

Date Last Worked: _____ Date Disability Commenced: _____

Approximate date patient may resume work: _____

Has patient previously been treated at this office? _____Yes _____No

If yes, give dates/circumstances: _____

_____

Description of patient complaint: _____

_____

_____

Symptoms experienced: _____

_____

Diagnosis (including DSM 5/CPT 10 code): _____

_____

Type of treatment rendered and frequency: _____

_____

Referral to Specific/Residential Treatment Facility: _____Yes _____No

If yes, where and for what purpose: _____

_____

Profession: _____ Practice in the State of: _____

Name on License: _____ License No.: _____

Signature: _____ Date: _____

Address:_____

Phone: _____ Fax: _____

SOCIAL SECURITY EVALUATION MEDICAL SOURCE STATEMENT, PSYCHIATRIC/ PSYCHOLOGICAL

Please evaluate, give examples, and provide comments on the patient's ability in the following categories:

1. Ability to relate and interact with supervisors and coworkers.

2. Ability to understand, remember, and carry out an extensive variety of technical and/or complex job instructions.

3. Ability to understand, remember, and carry out simple one-or-two step job instructions.

4. Ability to deal with the public.

5. Ability to maintain concentration and attention for at least 2 h increments.

6. Ability to withstand the stress and pressures associated with an 8 h workday and day-to-day work activity.

7. Please comment on the patient's ability to handle funds.

8. Please comment on expected duration and prognosis of patient's impairments.

9. Please comment on the onset and history of the patient's impairments, as well as response to treatment.

10. Specify any side effects from medication and restrictions related thereto.

11. Does patient require any additional testing or evaluations? Please specify.

_____   _____

Therapist's Signature   Date

WORKER'S COMPENSATION ATTENDING THERAPIST'S REPORT

_____

Employee: _____   Claim/Case Number: _____

Employer: _____   Date of Injury:_____ Date of Next Appt:_____

Patient Social Security No: _____   Date of This Exam: _____

Current Diagnosis (DSM 5/ICD 10): _____

_____

PROGRESS

Since the last exam, this patient's condition has:

__progressed as expected   __progressed slower than expected

__not progressed significantly   __worsened

__plateaued. No further progress expected   __been determined to be nonwork related

Briefly describe any change in objective or subjective complaint: _____

_____

TREATMENT

Treatment Plan: (only list changes from prior status): __No change __Patient is/was

discharged from care on: _____

Est. Discharge Date: _____Medications: _____

Therapy Type _____ Duration _____ Frequency _____

Diagnostic Studies: _____

Hospitalization/Surgery: _____

Consult/Other Services: _____

WORK STATUS

The patient has been instructed to:

__ return to full duty with no limitations or restrictions

__ remain off the rest of the day and return to work tomorrow

__ with no limitations __with limitations listed below

__ return to work on _____

Work limitations (if applicable): _____

Remain off work until _____

Estimated date patient can return to full duty: _____

DISABILITY STATUS

__ Patient discharged—reached maximum medical benefit

Please supply a brief narrative report if any of the following apply:

__ Patient will be permanently precluded from engaging in his/her usual and customary occupation

__ Patient's condition is permanent and stationary

__ Patient will have permanent residuals   __Patient will require future medical care

Therapist Name: _____   Address: _____

Signature: _____   Date: _____

BRIEF PSYCHIATRIC EVALUATION FOR INDUSTRIAL INJURY

Date: _____

Name: _____

Date of first examination: _____

Date of most recent visit: _____

Frequency of visits:_____

Diagnosis (DSM/ICD):_____

Type of service
- Outpatient psychotherapy
- Intensive outpatient
- Urgent care
- Case management

Medication

1. _____   2._____

3. _____   4._____

Current Mental Status Exam (circle and comment if abnormal findings)

Appearance and Behavior
Grooming: Well-groomed, disheveled, eccentric, poor hygiene
Motor activity: Normal, tremor, retarded, agitated, hyperactive
Speech: Normal, slow, rapid, pressured, slurred, mute, delayed, soft, loud, stuttering, aphasia
Interview behavior: Cooperative, guarded, evasive
Behavioral disturbance: None, irritable, aggressive, violent, poor impulse control, manipulative, apathetic
Comments: _____

Sensorium and Cognitive Functioning
Orientation: Oriented in all spheres, disoriented (person, place, time, situation)
Concentration: Intact, slightly distracted, impaired (mild, moderate, severe)
Memory: Normal, impaired (immediate, recent, remote) and degree (mild, moderate, severe)
Intelligence: Above average, average, below average, borderline, mental retardation
Comments: _____

Mood and Affect
Mood: Normal, anxious, depressed, fearful, elated, euphoric, angry
Affect: Appropriate, labile, expansive, blunted, flat
Comments: _____

_____

_____

Perception
Hallucinations: None, auditory, visual, olfactory
Illusions: None, misidentification
Specify: _____

Thought Process
Associations: Goal directed, blocking, circumstantial, tangential, loose, neologisms
Content-Delusions: None, persecution, somatic, broadcasting, grandiosity, religious, nihilistic, ideas of reference
Content-preoccupations: None, obsessions, compulsions, phobias, sexual, suicidal, homicidal, depersonalization
Comments:_____

Judgment: Intact, impaired (mild, moderate, severe)
Comments:_____

TREATMENT PROGRESS AND PROGNOSIS

_____

_____

ALCOHOL AND DRUG ABUSE

Current alcohol use: None, social, abuse (occasional, binge pattern, daily)
Current illicit drug use: None, social, abuse (occasional, binge pattern, daily)
Detox, drug program, or tox screen: (Specify dates and results) _____

_____

_____

History of alcohol/drug abuse:_____

CURRENT WORK-RELATED SKILLS

(Comment on reason for limitation and degree of limitation, if there is impaired ability.)

Able to understand, remember, and perform simple instructions:_____

_____

Able to understand, remember, and perform detailed, complex instructions:_____

_____

Able to maintain concentration for 2-h periods:_____

Able to interact with coworkers and supervisors: _____

_____

Able to sustain an ordinary routine without special supervision: _____

_____

Able to handle the responsibilities common to a basic work environment:_____

_____

Do you believe this patient is capable of managing funds in his/her own best interest?

Yes_____No_____ Comments:_____

_____   _____
Therapist   Date

BRIEF LEVEL OF FUNCTIONING REVIEW FOR INDUSTRIAL INJURY

_____

Name: _____   Date: _____

DOB: _____ M/F Age: _____   SS No.: _____

Date of Injury:_____   Case/Claim No.:_____

Mental Status Assessment <u>based on last office visit</u>

Provide assessment based on last office visit. Circle response.

1. Sensorium: Alert   Clear   Clouded   Drowsy   Other _____

2. Orientation: Normal   Disoriented as to: Time   Place   Person   Situation

3. Behavioral attitudes: Cooperative   Hostile   Withdrawn   Guarded/Resistant
   Indifferent/Passive

4. Appearance: Well-groomed   Adequate   Unkempt   Inappropriate
   Other _____

5. Attention and concentration: Good   Fair   Distractible   Other

6. Speech: Rate   Normal   Slow   Rapid   Halting   Pressured
   Other _____
   Quality   Clear   Mumbled   Slurred   Other _____
   Tone   Normal   Low   Inaudible   Loud   Other _____

7. Psychomotor activity: Normal   Retarded   Accelerated   Restless   Agitated

8. Mood: Euthymic   Depressed   Elevated   Hypomanic   Manic
   Anxious   Angry   Irritable   Labile

9. Affect: Congruent w/mood and thought   Incongruent w/mood and thought
   Intensity: Full   Bland   Blunted   Flat
   Range: Constricted   Normal

10. Thought Process: Goal Directed/Relevant   Tangential   Circumstantial
    Loose Associations   Flight of ideas

11. Thought Content   Obsessions   Preoccupations   Grandiose   Paranoid
    Somatic religious   Phobia   Fears
    Hallucinations: Auditory (Command Type   Y   N)   Visual
    Tactile   Olfactory
    Delusions: _____
    Suicidal Ideation: No   Yes   Plan/Intent: No   Yes
    Risk: Low   Moderate   High
    Homicidal Ideation: No   Yes   Plan/Intent   No   Yes
    Risk: Low   Moderate   High

12. Insight and psychological mindedness   Excellent   Good   Fair   Poor

13. Evidence of possible organic/neurological pathology   No   Yes   Comments:

14. Vegetative symptoms:

_____

_____

Circle the response that applies to the patient's ability to perform ADL's

	Performance Areas	ADL's	Performance of ADL's			
1	Mathematical skills	Balance checkbook	Yes	No	N/A	?
2	Word processing skills	Operate personal computer at home	Yes	No	N/A	?
		Write letters	Yes	No	N/A	?
3	Problem solving/judgment	Schedule day	Yes	No	N/A	?
		Schedule children's day	Yes	No	N/A	?
		Driving	Yes	No	N/A	?
4	Attention/concentration	Read newspaper or books	Yes	No	N/A	?
		Follow movie/TV shows	Yes	No	N/A	?
5	Initiate work	Shopping	Yes	No	N/A	?
		Planning/cooking meals	Yes	No	N/A	?
		Initiate and complete domestic chores (washing dishes, laundry, yard work, etc.)	Yes	No	N/A	?
6	Memory	Remember doctor's appointments	Yes	No	N/A	?
		Recalling phone conversations	Yes	No	N/A	?
		Remembering medications/dosages	Yes	No	N/A	?
7	Social interactions	Socialize with family/friends	Yes	No	N/A	?
		Attend social outings/church	Yes	No	N/A	?
		Pariticipate in hobbies	Yes	No	N/A	?
		Participate in exercise /sports	Yes	No	N/A	?
		Take trips/vacations	Yes	No	N/A	?
8	Maintain personal hygiene	Bathe/shower regularly	Yes	No	N/A	?
		Neat grooming	Yes	No	N/A	?
		Dressed appropriately	Yes	No	N/A	?
9	Supervise others	Supervise children/family members	Yes	No	N/A	?
		Organize home activities	Yes	No	N/A	?
10	Understand and carry out instructions	Medication compliant	Yes	No	N/A	?
		Manage physical health needs	Yes	No	N/A	?
		Return phone calls	Yes	No	N/A	?

How are these functions assessed?

_____

_____

_____

_____

What are the treatment plan target dates?

Goal: _____Target date: _____

Goal: _____Target date: _____

Goal: _____Target date: _____

What are the current:	Medications	/Dosage	/Frequency	/Response

DSM 5/ICD 10 Diagnosis:_____

Current symptoms:

_____

_____

_____

_____

Released to return to work: _____ or Estimate for return to work:_____

The patient is unable to return to work at this time because he/she is unable to perform the following job-related duties: _____

_____

_____

The reason(s) that he/she is unable to return to work:_____

_____

_____

_____

_____

_____

Circumstances that have contributed to the patient's recovery taking longer include the following: _____

_____

_____

_____

_____

_____

_____

The patient could return to work with the following modifications or restrictions:_____

_____

_____

_____

_____

_____

_____
Therapist's Signature

Business Forms

PATIENT REGISTRATION

(PLEASE PRINT)   Today's Date: ___/___/_____

Patient's full name: _____ SS No./Pt ID: _____

Home Address: _____ City: _____ State: _____ Zip: _____

Home Phone: ( )_____Sex: _____ Age: _____ Date of Birth: ___/___/_____

Patient Employer: _____ Phone Number: ( )_____

If Student: Grade Level_____ College: _____

Family Physician:_____ Referred By: _____

Person to Contact in Emergency: _____ Phone: ( )_____

INSURED/RESPONSIBLE PARTY INFORMATION

Please complete this section regardless of insurance coverage.

Full Name of Insured: _____ Relationship: _____ Occupation: _____

Home Address:_____Phone:( )_____

Employer and Address: _____Phone: ( )_____

Insured's SS#_____ Driver's License No._____State_____

Full Name of Spouse: _____ SS#:_____

Spouse's Employer: _____ Phone: ( )_____

Insured's Primary Ins. Co.: _____ I.D.No.: _____ Group No.: _____

Secondary Ins. Co.: __No   __Yes; Company: _____ Policy No.: _____

Job Related Injury-Workmens Comp. Co.: __No   __Yes; Company: _____

OFFICE BILLING AND INSURANCE POLICY

1. I authorize us of this form on all of my insurance submissions.
2. I authorize the release of information to my insurance company(s).
3. I understand that I am responsible for the full amount of my bill for services provided.
4. I authorize direct payment to my service provider.
5. I hereby permit a copy of this to be used in place of an original.

Name:_____I.D.#_____

Signature:_____Date:_____

It is your responsibility to pay any deductible amount, co-pay, co-insurance amount or any other balance not paid by your ins. the day and time serviced provided.

There will be a $25.00 service charge on all returned checks.

In event that your account goes to collections, there will be a 20% collection fee added to your balance.

There is a 24-h cancellation policy that requires that you cancel your appointment 24 h in advance between the hours of 8 a.m. to 4 p.m. Monday through Friday to avoid being charged.

Signature _____ Date _____

CONTRACT FOR SERVICES WITHOUT USING INSURANCE

Financial Agreement

I have agreed to pay privately for my therapy.

The agreed upon charge is $_____ for the first visit and then $_____ per session thereafter. Paperwork or other requests will be a separate cost if not done during the allotted time. Additionally, I acknowledge that my insurance will not reimburse me for my decision to see _____ privately. _____ is not to bill my insurance.

Name: _____ Date: _____

FEE AGREEMENT FOR DEPOSITION AND COURT APPEARANCE

Date:

To:

From:

Re:

When served with a subpoena *duces tecum* for my appearance in person or a deposition subpoena for my appearance, the following fee policies will be in effect. This is the case unless you receive a signed, written amendment from me.

My fee for scheduled appearance is $_____/hour paid in advance. The fee is due with the subpoena. If the fee is not paid at that time, arrangements for payment are the duty of the party requesting the appearance and must be made on receipt of this communication.

The fee is required for my scheduling the day or any fraction of the day. The fee is due whether or not I am actually called on that day. The fee is due even if the appearance is canceled by anyone other than me for any reason and at any time. These are my usual and customary fee arrangements.

Further required attendances will be charged at additional daily rates under the same circumstances. These terms are not negotiable.

Please determine the number of days you need me, specify same, and send me a check for $_____ per day by return mail if you want me to obey your subpoena. Then I will get back to you with my availability.

For payment purposes, my Federal Tax Identification Number or my Social Security Number is _____.

_____

Signature of Therapist

LIMITS ON PATIENT CONFIDENTIALITY

We are required to disclose confidential information if any of the following conditions exist:

1. You are a danger to yourself or others.
2. You seek treatment to avoid detection or apprehension or enable anyone to commit a crime.
3. Your therapist was appointed by the courts to evaluate you.
4. Your contact with your therapist is for the purpose of determining sanity in a criminal proceeding.
5. Your contact is for the purpose of establishing your competence.
6. The contact is one in which your psychotherapist must file a report to a public employer or as to information required to be recorded in a public office, if such report or record is open to public inspection.
7. You are under the age of 16 years and are the victim of a crime.
8. You are a minor and your psychotherapist reasonably suspects you are the victim of child abuse.
9. You are a person over the age of 65 and your psychotherapist believes you are the victim of physical abuse. Your therapist may disclose information if you are the victim of emotional abuse.
10. You die and the communication is important to decide an issue concerning a deed or conveyance, will or other writing executed by you affecting as interest in property.
11. You file suit against your therapist for breach of duty or your therapist files suit against you.
12. You have filed suit against anyone and have claimed mental/emotional damages as part of the suit.
13. You waive your rights to privilege or give consent to limited disclosure by your therapist.
14. Your insurance company paying for services has the right to review all records.

*If you have any questions about these limitations, please discuss them with your therapist.

Signature: _____ Date: _____

I am consenting to my (or my dependent) receiving outpatient treatment.

Signature: _____ Date: _____

RELEASE OF INFORMATION

I authorize _____ to contact my primary care physician (name) _____ regarding an appointment being made for follow-up, as well as information pertaining to psychological and emotional function.

Signature: _____ Date: _____

TREATMENT CONTRACT

The therapist and I have discussed my/my child's case and I was informed of the risks, approximate length of treatment, alternative methods of treatment, and the possible consequences of the treatment which includes the following methods and interventions. For the purpose of

__Stabilization

__Decrease and relieve symptomatology

__Improve coping, problem solving, and use of resources

__Skill development

__Grief resolution

__Stress management

__Behavior modification and cognitive restructuring

__Other _____

While I expect benefits from this treatment I fully understand and accept that because of factors beyond our control, such benefits and desired outcomes cannot be guaranteed.

I understand that the therapist is not providing emergency service and I have been informed of whom/where to call in an emergency or during the evening or weekend hours.

I understand that regular attendance will produce the maximum possible benefits but that I or we am/are free to discontinue treatment at any time in accordance with the policies of the office.

I understand that I am financially responsible for any portion of the fees not covered or reimbursed by my health insurance.

I have been informed and understand the limits of confidentiality, that by law, the therapist must report to appropriate authorities any suspected child abuse or serious threats of harm to myself or another person.

I am not aware of any reason why I/we/he/she should not proceed with therapy and I/we/he/she agree to participate fully and voluntarily.

I have had the opportunity to discuss all of the aspects of treatment fully, have had my questions answered, and understand the treatment planned. Therefore, I agree to comply with treatment and authorize the above named clinician(s) or whomever is designated to administer the treatment(s) to me or my child.

Name of Patient: _____

Signature of Patient/Parent/Guardian: _____

Therapist's Signature: _____ Date: _____

CONTRACT FOR GROUP THERAPY

1. As a group member I expect to benefit from participation, I recognize that I have rights and responsibilities as a group member.
2. The goals of this group are:

    A. _____

    B. _____

    C. _____

3. I will attend all group meetings and be on time. If there is an emergency that prevents me from attending, I will contact the group facilitator as soon as possible. If for some other reason I am not able to attend a group meeting, I will let the group know at least 1 week in advance.
4. If for some reason I decide to not continue to participate in group or I am unable to, I will let the group know 2 days before the last group meeting that I attend.
5. I agree to not socialize with group members outside of group.
6. I have been informed and understand the limits of confidentiality, that by law, the group facilitator must report to appropriate authorities any suspected child abuse and any serious threats of harm to myself or another person.
7. The cost of group is $ _____, or $ _____ per session, which begins at_____ am/pm and ends at _____ am/pm on _____ days. The first group meeting is scheduled for _____.
8. Respectfully and with full understanding I accept the following rules:

    A. Only first names will be used.

    B. There will be no side conversations or comments, whoever is speaking will be given full attention and respect.

    C. Children or other unauthorized visitors are not allowed in group.

    D. Recording of the group meetings is not allowed.

    E. I agree to not disclose information/problems of any group member outside of group.

    F. I will not disclose the identity of any group member outside of group.

    G. No food or drink will be allowed in group.

    H. I will not abuse any substances on the day of a group meeting.

Name: _____ Date: _____

AUTHORIZATION FOR THE RELEASE OR EXCHANGE OF INFORMATION

Patient Name: _____ DOB: _____

Information To Be Released By Or Exchange With:

Name: _____

Address: _____

Information To Be Released By Or Exchanged:

__ History and Physical
   Exam
__ Court/Agency
   Documents
__ Family Systems Eval
__ Discharge Summary
__ Mental Status
__ Nursing Notes
__ Psychiatric
   Evaluation

__ Treatment Plans
__ Consultation
   Reports
__ Psychological Test
   Results
__ Progress Notes
__ Educational Records
__ Chemical Recovery
   History
__ Therapist Orders

__ Educational-Tests
   and Reports
__ Dates of
   Hospitalization
__ Diagnoses Reports
__ Crisis Intervention
__ Attendance Record
__ Psychosocial Report
__ Medical Records
__ Lab results

Other (specify) _____

_____   _____
Patient's Signature   Date

PEDIATRIC PATIENT REGISTRATION

This outline is adapted from S. Johnson (2013). *Therapist's Guide to Pediatric Affect and Behavior Regulation.*

Filled out by: _____ Date: _____

Child's Name: _____ Child's Date of Birth: _____ Age: _____

Sex: __Male __Female   Child's Ethnic Group/Race: _____

Child's Address: _____

Child's Health Insurance: __None __Medicaid __Private Insurance __Other: _____

CLIENT INFORMATION

1. Persons of legal custody of child
   A. Name
   B. Relationship to child
   C. Address
   D. Home phone
   E. Cell phone
   F. Work phone
   G. Birth date
   H. Age
   I. Highest education completed
   J. Ethnicity
   K. Occupation
   L. Employer
   M. Work schedule
   N. Okay to contact at work?
      1. If so, when?
   O. Is the child adopted?
   P. Who does the child live with on a regular basis?
2. Other adults and children living in the child's home
   A. Name
   B. Age
   C. Gender
   D. Relationship to child
3. Child's full or half-siblings that do not live in the same house with the child
   A. Name
   B. Age
   C. Gender
   D. Relationship to child
4. Contact person for appointments
   A. Name
   B. Relationship to child
   C. Address
   D. Home phone

    E. Cell phone

    F. Work phone

    G. If the child's birth parents do not have legal custody

       1. Mother's name

         a. Date of birth

         b. Address

         c. Occupation

         d. Employer

         e. Reason for not having custody of child

         f. How often does she see the child?

         g. If deceased, when?

         h. Cause of death

       2. Father's name

         a. Date of birth

         b. Address

         c. Occupation

         d. Employer

         e. Reason for not having custody of child

         f. How often does he see the child?

         g. If deceased, when?

         h. Cause of death

5. Presenting concerns about child

    A. What concerns do you have about the child?

    B. What are the child's strengths?

    C. What are you wanting to happen for the child?

6. Child's preschool/school history (if yes, describe)

    A. Identified learning problems?

    B. Behavior problems?

    C. Identified suicidal problems?

    D. Are they receiving special help (special education, tutor help in school plan, speech pathologist, occupational therapist, school psychologist, counselor, etc.)?

    E. Other school problems?

7. Child's medical history

    A. Child's physician/pediatrician

       1. Phone

       2. Address

       3. Date of last doctor visit

         a. Reason

         b. Outcome

    B. Does the child take medication for other reasons (illness, allergies, disability)?

       1. Name of medication

       2. Dose

       3. Purpose

       4. Effect

       5. Prescribing doctor

    C. If the child has allergies—to what (please describe food, pets, etc.)?

    D. Are there concerns about the child's health? (Describe)

8. Pregnancy and newborn stages

    A. Medical problems during mother's pregnancy with this child (bleeding, high blood pressure, infections, diabetes, convulsions, extra weight gain, etc.)?

    B. Did the mother take medications during the pregnancy?

C. Did the mother smoke during pregnancy?

D. Did the mother drink alcohol during pregnancy?

E. Did the mother experience high stress during the pregnancy (marital problems, domestic violence, financial problems, job problems, problems with other relationships)?

F. Were there any problems with labor delivery (prolonged labor, bleeding, breech birth, forceps used, C-section, etc.)?

G. Was the child born prematurely?

H. Did the child have any problems as a newborn (born blue, jaundice, birth defects, seizures, infections, injuries, feeding, or sleep problems)?

I. Was the child difficult to care for as a baby?

9. Developmental delays

A. Have any developmental delays been identified?

B. Was the child slow or have problems with any of the following?

1. Walking alone
2. Speaking
3. Bowed training
4. Bladder training
5. Staying dry at night
6. Tying shoes
7. Riding bike
8. Reading
9. Writing

C. Child's temperament

1. Is the child overactive?
2. Does the child have trouble paying attention?
3. Does the child have trouble staying with one activity?
4. Does the child go from happy to sad quickly (without any obvious cause)?
5. Does the child get frustrated easily?
6. Does the child get upset by changes?
7. Are the child's emotional responses unpredictable?
8. Does it take the child a long time to warm up to new people and/or new situations?
9. Does the child overreact to physical pain?
10. Does the child react strongly to other things?

10. Child's early behavior

A. Has the child demonstrated any problems with the following?

1. Discipline
2. Temper
3. Fighting
4. Moods
5. Relationships with others
6. Other behaviors

11. Family history

A. Has any relative of the child had any of the following problems?

1. Neurological disease (seizures, spills, etc.)?
2. Chronic disease (diabetes, thyroid, heart disease, stroke)?
3. Mental illness (schizophrenia, bipolar disorder, depression, anxiety, etc.)?
4. Learning problems?
5. Behavior problems?
6. Excessive use of alcohol?
7. Drug problems/drug addiction?
8. Trouble with the law?

9. Trouble holding a job?
10. Suicidal behavior?
11. Violent behavior?
12. Other problems?
   B. Has anyone in the child's family seen a psychologist, psychiatrist, or other mental health provider?
12. Current living situation
   A. Are any of the following a part of the child's current living situation?
      1. Marital/relationship problems between the child's major caregivers?
      2. Problems with a sibling or other people in the house?
      3. Problem with work?
      4. Financial problems?
      5. Recent major changes or stressors in the child's living situation or family?
      6. Violence in the home or neighborhood?
      7. Alcohol or drug problems in the home or neighborhood?
      8. Other problems?
   B. Please write down anything else that you think is important to this evaluation.

CLINICAL INTAKE FORM (FOR CHILDREN)

Intake packet to be filled out prior to appointment and returned to office.

1. Child information form
   A. Name
   B. Date
   C. Date of birth
   D. Referred by
   E. Grade
   F. School
   G. District
   H. Person completing form
   I. Relationship to child
2. Mother (or guardian)
   A. Name
   B. Street address
   C. City
   D. State
   E. Home phone
   F. Cell/work phone
   G. Date of birth
   H. Marital status
   I. Education
   J. Occupation
   K. Employer
3. Father
   A. Name
   B. Street address
   C. City
   D. State
   E. Home phone
   F. Cell/work phone
   G. Date of birth

4. Members of household
    A. Name
    B. Age
    C. Sex
    D. Relationship
5. Ethnicity (check all that apply)
    A. Caucasian
    B. Hispanic/Latino(a)
    C. African American
    D. Native American
    E. Other
6. Is the child currently on medication?
7. Reason for currently seeking services
8. Previous therapy/evaluation: yes/no
    A. If yes, where/when
9. Referral questions
    A. Describe the reasons for referral. Please include specific behaviors or problems that you would like help with.
    B. What services or interventions have been previously performed (if any)?
10. Family history
    A. Please indicate any family members on either side who have had any of the following
        1. Medical problems
            a. Learning disabilities/problems
            b. Hyperactivity/attention problems
            c. Speech/language problems
            d. Seizures
            e. Headaches
            f. Genetic disorders
            g. Miscarriages
            h. Multiple sclerosis
            i. Tourette's syndrome
            j. Thyroid problems
            k. Other medical problems
        2. Psychiatric problems
            a. Depression/suicide
            b. Bipolar (manic depression)
            c. Anxiety disorder
            d. Panic attacks
            e. Obsessive-compulsive disorder
            f. Phobias and fears
            g. Attention deficit/hyperactivity
            h. Autism spectrum disorder
            i. Schizophrenia
            j. Hallucinations
            k. Alcohol/drug abuse (specify)
            l. "Nervous breakdowns"
            m. Other
11. Pregnancy delivery and birth
    A. During pregnancy, mother (check all that apply)
        1. Drank alcohol or used drugs
        2. Smoked

3. Suffered any illness, infection, trauma, fevers
4. Had toxemia
5. Experienced vaginal bleeding/spotting
6. Almost miscarried
7. Took medication (which?)
8. Had other significant events occur

B. During labor and delivery, mother and/or baby (check all that apply and describe)
1. Went into early labor
2. Suffered fetal distress
3. Had induced labor
4. Suffered complications (breach birth, cord around neck, lack of oxygen, C-section, forceps, required oxygen, etc.)
5. Required special care (ICU, incubator, etc.)

Length of pregnancy _____ weeks   Baby's APGAR score: _____

Baby's weight_____ lbs _____ oz   Baby's length _____

C. After birth did the baby have problems with (describe)
1. Breathing
2. Jaundice
3. Sucking or feeding
4. Food, milk, or other allergies
5. Other problems

D. Describe the child's personality, mood, and temperament as an infant and toddler

12. Development history
A. At what age did the child:
1. Crawl
2. Sit up
3. Walk alone
4. Say first word
5. Speak in sentences
6. Become potty trained

B. Please indicate if the child suffered any of these problems as an infant or young child and describe:
1. Delayed development or growth
2. Ear infections, tube placement
3. Head banging
4. Repetitive or unusual movements
5. Restlessness or overactivity
6. Attention problems
7. Aggression (hitting, biting, kicking)
8. Difficulty making or keeping friends
9. Shunned by peers
10. Defiance, resistance to authority

C. Describe the child's current friendships
D. What types of discipline is used with the child? Is it effective?
E. What type of rewards are used with the child? Are they effective?

13. School history
A. Child began school at age
B. Describe the child's preschool/kindergarten experience

14. Medical history
    A. When was the child last tested for:
        1. Vision
        2. Hearing
        3. Does the child wear/need glasses or contacts?
        4. Does the child wear/need hearing aids?
    B. List any medications prescribed for the child, dosages, and reason for the medication:
        1. Medication
        2. Dosage
        3. Reason
    C. Please indicate and describe the child's current and past health problems:

	Age and Duration	Treatment
1. Headaches		
2. Seizures		
3. Head injury		
4. Loss of consciousness		
5. Meningitis		
6. Encephalitis		
7. Brain tumor		
8. Paralysis		
9. High fever		
10. Fainting spells		
11. Coma		
12. HIV infection/AIDS		
13. Near drowning		
14. Electric shock		
15. Drug/alcohol exposure		
16. Psychiatric hospitalization		
17. Psychological counseling		
18. Other		

    D. If the child has suffered head injury, please describe the incident:
        1. Date of the incident
        2. Did the child suffer loss of consciousness? How long?
        3. Did the child have amnesia of events before the incident? After?
        4. Did the child remember the incident itself?
        5. Was the child treated by a doctor? Hospitalized?
        6. Describe the length and course of the hospitalization
    E. Indicate the neurological procedures performed:

	Date	Date/Hospital	Result (if known)
1. CT or brain scan			
2. MRI of brain			
3. EEG			
4. Lumbar puncture (spinal tap)			
5. Other (PET, SPECT, etc.)			

    F. Physician(s) currently caring for the child?

15. Please indicate and describe whether your child currently or in the past has experienced or complained of the symptoms listed below. Please indicate whether the problem has been resolved or is ongoing.
    A. Physical symptoms
        1. Sensitivity to noise
        2. Sensitivity to light

3. Ringing in the ears

4. Dizziness

5. Nausea/vomiting

6. Blurred vision

7. Double vision

8. Hearing problems

9. Problems with taste or smell

10. Numbness or tingling in the extremities

11. Sleep problems

12. Fatigue

B. Psychological symptoms

1. Depression

2. Mood swings

3. Irritability

4. Anger

5. Aggression

6. Low frustration tolerance

7. Can't handle stress

8. Anxiety

9. Hates to be in crowds

10. Social withdrawal/social problems

11. Difficulty with change

C. Cognitive symptoms

1. Memory

a. Poor short-term memory

b. Poor long-term memory

2. Reasoning

a. Reasoning problems

b. Takes things too literally

c. Difficulty understanding consequences of actions

3. Language

a. Problems understanding of what other say

b. Says "what" a lot

c. Needs frequent repetition to understand

d. Can't follow a 3-step command

e. Trouble expressing self-verbally

f. Talks too much/too little

g. Problems finding the right word to say

h. Stutters

4. Visuospatial

a. Gets lost frequently

b. Has trouble with directions

c. Trouble with visual tasks (puzzles, games, etc.)

d. Poor drawing ability

e. Poor penmanship

5. Other

a. Attention problems

b. No concept of time

c. Clumsy, poor motor skills

d. Drop in school performance (which subjects?)

16. Strengths/interests
    A. Please describe the child's strengths
    B. Please describe the child's interests
    C. Addition information
        1. Please provide any other information or describe any other concerns which have not been covered in this questionnaire.

RELEASE FOR THE EVALUATION AND TREATMENT OF A MINOR

_____

As parent or legal guardian of _____. I authorize his/her evaluation and treatment. As parent or legal guardian, I have the right to request information concerning the above minor's evaluation and treatment.

Signature _____   Date _____

Witness _____   Date _____

CLIENT MESSAGES

In-Chart Log

Client's name: _____

Phone calls/messages

Date: _____ Time: _____ am/pm

Content: _____

_____

Response: _____

_____

Date: _____ Time: _____ am/pm

Content: _____

_____

Response: _____

_____

Date: _____ Time: _____ am/pm

Content: _____

_____

Response: _____

_____

Date: _____ Time: _____ am/pm

Content: _____

_____

Response: _____

_____

AFFIDAVIT OF THE CUSTODIAN OF MENTAL HEALTH RECORDS TO ACCOMPANY COPY OF RECORDS

I, _____ declare that:
(custodian of records)

1. I am the (a) duly authorized custodian of the mental health records of and have the authority to certify said records; and
2. The copy of the mental health records attached to this affidavit is a true copy of all the records described in the subpoena duces tecum; and
3. The records were prepared by _____ in the ordinary course of business; and
4. The documents contained herein are subject to privilege and may be subject to confidentiality provisions. They are to be reviewed by a judge of competent jurisdiction prior to further distribution.

I declare under penalty of perjury that the foregoing is true and correct.

_____
(Signature of custodian)

REFERRAL FOR PSYCHOLOGICAL

Evaluation Testing Therapy (<u>circle one</u>)

Date: _____

Patient: _____Age: _____ Sex: _____

Telephone # (H) ( )_____ (W) ( ) _____

Address: _____

Referral Sources: _____Agency _____

PSYCHIATRIC HISTORY

1. Nature and length of client involvement with referral source:

   _____

   _____

   _____

2. Background information regarding client and family:
   A. Household members and ages.
   B. Behavioral description of client/family interactional style.

   _____

   _____

3. Is client presently taking medications: _____Yes _____No _____DK

   If yes, specify medication: _____

   Dosage level: _____

   Medical/psychiatric condition: _____

4. Behavioral description of client:

   _____

   _____

   _____

   _____

5. Questions to be addressed by, and purpose of this referral?

   _____

   _____

   _____

   _____

6. What has client been told about this referral?

_____

_____

_____

7. What is the client's attitude toward and expectation of this referral?

_____

_____

_____

_____

_____

8. List other agencies involved:

_____

_____

_____

_____

_____

_____

_____
Therapist's Signature

RELEASE TO RETURN TO WORK OR SCHOOL

Date _____

This is to certify that _____ has been under my care and has been unable

to attend work/school since _____. They are released to return to work/school on

_____.

Remarks/Limitations/Restrictions:

_____

_____

_____

_____
Therapist's Signature

NOTICE OF DISCHARGE FOR NONCOMPLIANCE OF TREATMENT

Date:

Dear

This letter is to inform you that I am discharging you from further professional attendance because you have not complied with appropriate recommendations throughout the course of your treatment.

Since you have the need of professional services it is recommended that you promptly seek the care of another mental health professional to meet your needs. If for some reason you are unable to locate another mental health practitioner, please let me know and I will try to assist you.

Effective 14 days from the date, I will no longer be available to attend to your mental health needs. This period will give you ample time to find another mental health professional.

When you have selected another mental health professional, I will, upon your written authorization, provide a summary of your chart to the new provider.

Sincerely,

_____

Therapist's Signature

DUTY TO WARN

Although confidentiality and privileged communication remain rights of all clients of mental health practitioners according to the law, some courts have held that if an individual intends to take harmful acts or dangerous action against another human being, or against themselves, it is the practitioner's duty to warn the person or the family of the person who are likely to suffer the results of harmful behavior, or the family of the client who intends to harm himself of such an intention.

I, as a mental health practitioner, will under no circumstances inform such individuals without first sharing that intention with the client, unless it is not possible to do so. Every effort will be made to resolve the issue before such a breach of confidentiality takes place.

_____
Therapist's Signature

I have read the above statement and understand the therapist's social responsibility to make such decisions when necessary.

Name _____ Date _____

MISSED APPOINTMENT

_____

It appears that circumstances have prevented you from meeting with me for an appointment on_____ at _____. Please contact me if you are interested in rescheduling the appointment. If I do not hear from you I will assume that you are not interested in my services at this time. In that event, please feel free to call again in the future if I can be of service to you.

Sincerely,

RECEIPT

_____

RECEIPT

Date of service: _____

Name: _____

DOB: _____ SS#: _____

Service provided: _____

Diagnosis code: _____

Amount paid: _____

RECEIPT
_____

(letterhead)

RECEIPT

Date of service: _____

Name: _____

Service provided: _____

Amount paid: _____

BALANCE STATEMENT

Date: _____

Name:_____

    Our records show that you have a balance due for _____ in the amount

of_____.

    Date of service was_____.
    Please bring your account current.

CLIENT SATISFACTION SURVEY

To be completed by client or parent/guardian if client is a minor.

1. The problems, feelings, or situation that brought me to the therapist are:
   __Much improved
   __Improved
   __About the same
   __Worse
   __Much worse

2. Because of therapy, I understand the problems well enough to manage them in the future:
   __Strongly agree
   __Agree
   __Not certain
   __Disagree
   __Strongly disagree

3. My therapist was
   __Very helpful
   __Somewhat helpful
   __Neither helpful nor unhelpful
   __Somewhat unhelpful
   __Very unhelpful

4. If I needed help in the future, I would feel comfortable calling this therapist:
   __Definitely yes
   __Probably yes
   __Maybe
   __Probably not
   __Definitely not

5. I would recommend this therapist to others who need help:
   __Definitely yes
   __Probably yes
   __Maybe
   __Probably not
   __Definitely not

6. The interest shown by my therapist in helping me to solve my problems was:
   __Very satisfactory
   __Satisfactory
   __Neither satisfactory nor unsatisfactory
   __Unsatisfactory
   __Very unsatisfactory

7. How long has it been since your last visit?
   __Less than 1 month
   __1 or 2 months
   __3 to 5 months
   __6 months or more (how many) _____

8. Treatment ended with this therapist because:

__The concerns which brought me to the therapist were worked out to my satisfaction.

__Most of the significant concerns which brought me to seek therapy were worked out satisfactorily. There are some minor problems which we can now handle.

__We reached the number of sessions set by the therapist at the beginning of treatment. Significant problems remained that were not dealt with adequately.

__I felt that more treatment would not be helpful at this time, even though significant problems remained.

__The therapist felt that more treatment would not be helpful at this time, even though significant problems remained.

__There was a change in a work or school schedule that made it impossible to arrange further appointments.

9. After you received counseling with this therapist, have you or any members of your family received any counseling elsewhere for the same problems you came here for?

_____Yes _____No

10. Additional Comments:

_____

_____

_____

_____

_____

_____

Thank you for your time.

_____   _____

SIGNATURE (OPTIONAL)   DATE

FORM FOR CHECKING OUT AUDIO CDS, DVDS, AND BOOKS

Date: _____

_____ has borrowed the following:

_____

_____

_____

_____

The tape(s) will be returned by _____. It is understood that for each tape or book not returned during this period of time I will be charged $10.00.

Signature _____

MENTAL HEALTH RECORD REVIEW

CHART CONTENT REVIEW

This form, chart content review, demonstrates the comprehensive information that should comprise the content of a patient's chart. It can also be used as a review form to assure that all areas have been documented and provide the therapist with a quality assurance self-monitoring tool.

BEHAVIORAL HEALTH - MENTAL HEALTH RECORD REVIEW FORM

Clinician Name: _____ Date: _____

GENERAL INFORMATION, CONSENTS AND DISCLOSURES	YES	NO	N/A
1. Patient identification and relevant demographics:			
Name			
Address			
Phone			
Employer/School			
Age			
Sex			
Marital status			
Guardianship info			
2. Consent for treatment, signed by patient			
3. Release of information, signed by patient			
4. Other disclosure forms:			
Limits of confidentiality			
Financial responsibility			
Cancellation policy			
5. Patient's name and date on each chart entry			
6. Clinician's signature, with professional degree & date of service on each chart entry			
7. Record is legible			
TOTAL FOR GENERAL INFORMATION				(16)

ASSESSMENT	YES	NO	N/A
1. Presenting problem and symptoms			
2. Relevant history affecting or precipitating current symptoms			
3. Prenatal & developmental hx for children & adolescents, incl academic & social history			
4. Medical history:			
Primary care physician			
Relevant medical conditions			
Current medications and dosages			
Allergies/adverse reactions to medications			
5. Previous mental health treatment history			
6. Substance abuse history incl alcohol, illicit drugs, prescription meds, cigarettes			
7. Assessment of suicidal and homicidal ideation			
8. Mental status exam:			
Orientation			
Affect			
Speech			
Mood			
Thought content			
Judgment			
Insight			
Attention			
Concentration			
Memory			
Impulse control			

9. Diagnosis using DSM-5/ICD-10			
All five axis, consistent with presenting problem and assessment			
TOTAL FOR ASSESSMENT				(22)

TREATMENT PLAN	YES	NO	N/A
1. Treatment plan consistent with diagnosis			
2. Measurable treatment goals and objectives			
3. Time frame for attaining goals and objectives			
4. Treatment interventions consistent with goals and objectives			
5. Notation of referrals to other professionals/community support groups			
6. Evidence of patient involvement in and/or acceptance of treatment plan			
7. Treatment plan signed by clinician			
TOTAL FOR TREATMENT PLAN				(7)

PROGRESS NOTES	YES	NO	N/A
1. Progress note for each date of service			
2. Each note has patient's name and date of service			
3. Each note signed and dated by the clinician			
4. Notes reflect progress & pt's strengths/weaknesses/limitations in meeting goals & obj			
5. Notes reflect communication with other hlth care professionals involved in pt's care			
6. Increased level of treatment/referral to more intense care (if patient's level of functioning declines significantly, or suicidal/homicidal ideation is present)			
TOTAL FOR PROGRESS NOTES				(6)

TOTAL FOR GENERAL INFORMATION			
TOTAL FOR ASSESSMENT			
TOTAL FOR TREATMENT PLAN			
TOTAL FOR PROGRESS NOTES			
GRAND TOTAL				(51)

TOTAL POSSIBLE	51
MINUS TOTAL "N/A"	
EQUALS TOTAL POSSIBLE FOR THIS CHART ("TP")	
TOTAL YES SCORES FOR THIS CHART ("YES")	
"YES" DIVIDED BY "TP" X 100 = PERCENT SCORE FOR THIS CHART	

Extremely Low: 0-2%	
Borderline: 3-9%	
Low Average: 10-25%	
Average: 26-76%	
High Average: 77-93% *****PASSING=80%*****	
Superior: 94-98%	
Very Superior: 99-100%	

REFERENCES

Academy of Nutrition and Dietetics. (May 18, 2015). *5 Ways to promote a positive body image*. Retrieved from www.eatright.org/resource/health/weight-loss/your-health-and-your-weight/promoting-positive-body-image-in-kids.

AHRQ. (2008, reaffirmed 2011). *Putting evidence into practice*. Retrieved from www.guideline.gov/content.aspx?id=15692.

Alberti, R., & Emmons, M. (1975). *Stand up speak up talk back: The key to self-assertive behavior*. New York: Pocket Books.

Alzheimer's and Dementia Caregiver Center. (2015). *Anxiety and agitation*. Retrieved from the web 9/25/2015 www.alz.org/care/alzheimers-dementia-agitation-anxiety.asp.

American Association of Matrimonial Lawyers (AAML). (2011). *Child custody evaluation standards*. Retrieved from www.aaml.org.

American Council on Exercise. (2014). *My hunger scale*. Retrieved from http://www.acefitness.org/healthcoachre-sources/pdfs/16_MyHunger.

American Foundation of Suicide Prevention. Retrieved from http://www.afsp.org.

American Psychiatric Association DSM-III-R. (1987). *Diagnostic and statistical manual of mental disorders* (3rd ed.). Washington DC: American Psychiatric Association.

American Psychiatric Association. (1994). *Diagnostic and statistical manual of mental disorders* (DSMIV) (4th ed.). Washington DC: American Psychiatric Association.

American Psychiatric Association. (2000). *Practice guidelines for the treatment of psychiatric disorders*. Washington DC: American Psychiatric Association.

American Psychiatric Association. (2004). Practice guidelines for the assessment and treatment of patients with suicidal behaviors. In *Practice guidelines for the treatment of psychiatric disorders compendium* (2nd ed.) (pp. 835–1027). Arlington: VA.

American Psychiatric Association (APA). (October 2010). *Practice guideline for the treatment of patients with major depressive disorder* (3rd ed.). Arlington (VA): American Psychiatric Association (APA). Retrieved from. www.guideli-ine.gov/content.aspx?id=24158. 152 p.

American Psychiatric Association (APA). (2013). *Diagnostic and statistical manual of mental disorders* (5th ed.). Arlington: American Psychiatric Association. Retrieved from www.DSM5.org.

American Psychiatric Association. (2015). *Help with bipolar disorders*. Retrieved from www.psychiaty.org/patients-families/bipolar-disorders.

American Psychological Association (APA). (December 2010). Guidelines for child custody evaluations in family law proceedings. *American Psychologist*. Retrieved from www.apa.org.

Anastopolous, A. D., & Shelton, T. L. (2001). *Assessing attention deficit/hyperactivity disorder*. New York: Kluwer Academic Plenum.

Anxiety and Depression Association of America. (2015a). *Suicide and prevention*. Updated August 2015 www.adaa.org/understanding-anxiety/suicide.

Anxiety and Depression Association of America. (2015b). *Childhood anxiety disorders*. Updated 9/2015 www.adaa.org/living-with-anxiety/children/childhood-anxiety-disorders.

APA Autism Spectrum Disorder. (2013). Retrieved from www.dsm5.org/Documents/Autism%205Spectrum%20Disorder%20Fact%20Sheet.pdf.

Australian Psychological Society. (2015). *Understanding and managing psychological trauma*. Retrieved from www.psychology.org.au/publications/tip_sheets/trauma/#top.

Baller, J., Kestner, T., Witthoft, M., Diener, C., Mier, D., & Risk, F. (2016). Health anxiety and hypochondriasis in the light of DSM-5. *Anxiety Stress Coping, 29*(2), 219–239. http://dx.doi.org/10.1080/10615806.2015.1036243. Epub May 11, 2015.

Barone, N. M., Weitz, E. I., & Witt, P. H. (2005). Psychological bonding evaluations in termination of parental rights cases. *Journal of Psychiatry and Law, 33,* 387–412.

Beautrais, A. L. (2003). Subsequent mortality in medically serious suicide attempts: A 5 year follow-up. *Australian and New Zealand Journal of Psychiatry, 37,* 595–599.

Beck, J. S. (1995). *Cognitive therapy: Basics and beyond*. Chapter 3. New York: Guilford Press.

Beck, J. (2011). *Cognitive behavior therapy: Basics and beyond*. New York, NY: The Guilford Press.

Beirne-Smith, M., Patton, J. R., & Kim, S. H. (2006). *Mental retardation*. New Jersey: Pearson.

Bell, N. S., Harford, T. C., Fuchs, C. H., McCarroll, J. E., & Schwartz, C. E. (2006). Prevalence, correlates, and comorbidity of DSM-IV antisocial personality syndromes and alcohol and specific drug use disorders in the United States. Results from the national epidemiology survey on alcohol and related conditions. *Journal of Clinical Psychiatry, 66,* 677–685.

Bhaumak, S., Gangadharan, S., Hiremath, A., & Russell, S. S. P. (May 2011). Psychological treatments in intellectual disability: The challenges of building a good evidence base. *The British Journal of Psychiatry, 198*(6), 428–430. http://dx.doi.org/10.1192/bip.bp.110.085084.

Bird, M. (2000). Psychosocial rehabilitation for problems arising from cognitive deficits in dementia. In R. D. Hill, L. Bäckman, & A. S. Neely (Eds.), *Cognitive rehabilitation in old age*. Oxford: Oxford University Press.

Bond, F. W., & Dryden, W. (2002). *Handbook of brief cognitive behavioral therapy*. San Francisco: Wiley.

Borja, B., Borja, C. S., & Gade, S. (2007). Psychiatric emergencies in the geriatric population. *Clinics in Geriatric Medicine, 23,* 391–400.

Brand, B. L., Armstong, J. G., Loewenstein, R. J., & McNary, S. W. (2009). Personality differences on the Rorschach of dissociative personality disorder, borderline personality disorder and psychotic inpatients. *Psychological Trauma: Theory, Research, Practice & Policy, 1,* 188–205.

Brown, G. K., Henriques, G. R., Sosdjan, D., & Beck, A. T. (2004). Suicide intent and accurate expectations of lethality: Predictors of medical lethality of suicide attempts. *Journal of Consulting and Clinical Psychology, 72,* 1170–1174.

Brown, S. (1985). *Treating the alcoholic: A developmental model of recovery*. NY: John Wiley & Sons.

CDC. Centers for Disease Control and Prevention. (2015). *Treatment: Autism spectrum disorder (ASD)*. Page last reviewed August 12, 2015. www.cdc.gov/ncbddd/autism/treatment.html.

CDC. Youth Risk Behavior Survey. (2005). Morbidity and mortality weekly. *Surveillance Summaries, 55*(SS-5), 1–108 (June 6, 2006).

Clare, L. (2008). *Neuropsychological rehabilitation and people with dementia*. Hove: Psychology Press.

Clinical concerns: Dementia, depression, or both? differentiating in older patients. *The Canadian Journal of Diagnosis* (October 2012).

Cohen-Kettenis, P., & Pfafflin, F. (2009). The DSM diagnostic criteria for gender identity disorder. *The Archives of Sexual Behavior*. http://dx.doi.org/10.1007/s10508-009-9562-y.

Department of Health and Human Services, Substance Abuse and Mental Health Services Administration, Center for Mental Health Services. (2004). *National consensus statement on mental health recovery*. For the complete report, see: http://mentalhealth.samhsa.gov/publications/allpubs/sma05-4129/.

DHS. (2000a). *Federal definition of foster care and related services.* Retrieved from www.dhs.state.mn.us/main/groups/county_access/documents/pub/dhs_id.

DHS. (2000b). *Guide for assessing attachment and bonding.* Retrieved from www.dhs.vic.gov.au.

DuPaul, G. J., Power, T. J., Anastopolous, A. D., & Reid, R. (1998). *ADHD Rating Scale IV checklists, norms and clinical interpretation.* New York: Guilford Press.

Dutton, D. G., & Golant, S. K. (1995). *The batterer: A psychological profile. Basic Books (A division of Harper Collins).*

Feeney, J. A., Pasmore, N. L., & Peterson, C. C. (2007). Adoption, attachment and relationship concerns: A study of adult adoptees. *Personal Relationships, 14*, 129–147. Printed in the United States of America. Copyright Ó 2007 IARR. 1350-4126/07.

Florette O. G. Establishment of maximum medical improvement in injured workers: Perception, truth and fallacy. Workers' Compensation Institute. 1/16/13 www.wci360.com.

Foote, B., Smolin, Y., Neft, D. I., & Lipschitz, D. (2008). Dissociative disorders and suicidality in psychiatric outpatients. *Journal of Nervous & Mental Disease, 196*, 29–36.

Frankenburg, F. R., et al. (2015). *Schizophrenia treatment & management.* Retrieved from www.emedicine.medscape.com/article/288259-treatment#d11.

Gardner, R. A. (1999). Guidelines for assessing parental preference in child-custody disputes. *Journal of Divorce & Remarriage, 30*(1/2), 1–9.

Gardner, R. A. (2001). Parental Alienation Syndrome (PAS): Sixteen years later. *Academy Forum, 45*(1), 10–12. Reference with www.rachelfoundation.org.

Geffner, R., & Mantooth, C. (2000). *Ending spouse/partner abuse: A psychoeducational approach for individuals and couples.* New York: Springer.

Geller, B., Craney, J. L., Bolhofner, K., et al. (2002). Two year prospective follow-up on children with a prepubertal and early adolescent bipolar disorder phenotype. *American Journal of Psychiatry, 159*, 927–933.

Gerg M. J., Raptosh D., Fick F. & Kaskutas V. The American Occupational Therapy Association. Copyright © 2012 by the American Occupational Therapy Association. This material may be copied and distributed for personal or educational uses without written consent. For all other uses, contact copyright@aota.org.

Giles-Sims, J. (1983). *Wife battering: A systems theory approach.* New York: The Guilford Press.

Gluck, S. (2014). *HealthyPlace neurodevelopmental community.* Created 5/21/2014, last updated 6/12/2014. www.healthyplace.com/neurodevelopmental-disorders/intellectual-disability/mild-moderate-severe-intellectual-disability.

Greenspan, S. I. (2001). *The affect diathesis hypothesis: The role of emotions in the core deficit in autism and in the development of intelligence and social skills.* Retrieved from www.floortime.org/downloads/affect_diathesis_hypothesis.pdf.

Grey, I. M., & Hastings, R. P. (September 2005). Evidence-based practices in intellectual disability and behavior disorders. *Current Opinion in Psychiaty, 18*(5), 469–475 PMID:16639193 (PubMed). www.ncbi.nim.nih.gov/pubmed/16639103.

Guidi, J., Rafanelli, C., Roncuzzi, R., Sirri, L., & Fava, G. A. (March–April 2013). Assessing psychological factors affecting medical conditions: Comparison between different proposals. *General Hospital Psychiatry, 35*(2), 141–146. http://dx.doi.org/10.1016/j.genhosppsych.2012.09.007. Epub October 31, 2012.

Hettema, J., Steele, J., & Miller, W. R. (2005). Motivational interviewing. *Annual Review of Clinical Psychology, 1*, 91–111.

Horowitz, M. J. (1986). *Stress response syndromes* (2nd ed.). Northvale, NJ: Jason Aronson.

Horowitz, L. M., Bridge, J. A., Teach, S. J., Ballard, E., Klima, J., Rosenstein, D. L., et al. (December 2012). Ask Suicide-screening Questions (ASQ). A brief instrument for the pediatric emergency department. *Archives of Pediatrics and Adolescent Medicine, 166*(12), 1170–1176.

Housekamp, B. M., & Foy, D. W. (1991). The assessment of post-traumatic stress disorder in battered women. *Journal of Interpersonal Violence, 6*, 367–375.

IDEA. (2004). *Laws & Guidance/Special Education & Rehabilitative Services.* Retrieved from http://idea.ed.gov.

Jacobson, J. W. (1982a). Problem behavior and psychiatric impairment within a developmentally disabled population: I. Behavior frequency. *Applied Research in Mental Retardation, 3*, 121–139.

Jacobson, J. W. (1982b). Problem behavior and psychiatric impairment within a developmentally disabled population: II. Behavior severity. *Applied Research in Mental Retardation, 3*, 369–381.

Javit, D. C., & NIH (2009). Sensory processing in schizophrenia: Neither simple nor intact. *Schizophrenia Bulletin*, *35*(6), 1059–1064.

Johnson, S. L. (2004). *Therapist's guide to clinical intervention*. San Diego: Academic Press.

Johnson, S. L. (2013). *Therapist's guide to pediatric affect and behavior regulation*. San Diego: Academic Press.

Keeton, C. P., Kolos, A. C., & Walkup, J. T. (2009). Pediatric generalized anxiety disorder: epidemiology, diagnosis and management. *Pediatric Drugs*, *11*(3), 171–183. http://dx.doi.org/10.2165/00148581-200911030-00003. Retrieved from www.ncbi.nim.nih.gov/pubmed/19445546.

Kessler, R. C., Borges, B., & Walters, E. E. (1999). Prevalence of and risk factors for lifetime suicide attempts in the National Comorbidity Survey. *Archives of General Psychiatry*, *56*, 617–626.

Kirk, S. A., Gallagher, J. J., Anastasiow, N. J., & Coleman, M. R. (2006). *Educating exceptional children* (11th ed.). Boston MA: Houghton Mifflin.

Kleber, H. D., et al. (2010). *Treatment of patients with substance use disorders* (2nd ed.). Retrieved from www.psychiatryonline.org/pb/assets/raw/sitwide/practice_guidelines/guidelines/substances.pdf.

Kleiman, K. R., & Ranskin, V. D. (1994). *This isn't what I expected*. New York: Bantam Books.

Korzewa, M. I., Del, P. F., Links, P. S., Thabane, L., & Fougere, P. (2009). Dissociation in borderline personality disorder: A detailed look. *Journal of Trauma & Dissociation*, *10*, 346–367.

Kroop, P. R., & Hart, S. D. (1997). Assessing risk for violence in wife assaulters: The spousal assault risk guide. In C. D. Webster, & M. A. Jackson (Eds.), *Impulsivity, theory, assessment and treatment* (pp. 302–325). NY: Guilford Press.

Lee, M.-Y. (2007). Female domestic violence survivors: An application of Roberts' continuum of the duration and severity of woman battering. *Brief Treatment and Crisis Intervention*, *7*, 102–114.

Lowenstein, R. J. (2007). Dissociative identity disorder: Issues in the iatrogenesis controversy. In E. Vermetten, M. Dorahy, & D. Spiegel (Eds.), *Traumatic dissociation* (pp. 275–299).

Mago, R. (December 11, 2009). Sleep disorders, sleep wake transition, alcohol abuse. *Psychiatric Times*. www.psychiatrictimes.com/sleep-disorders/sleep-hygiene.

Martin, B. (2013). In-depth: Cognitive behavior therapy. *Psych Central*. Retrieved 5/7/16 http://psychcentral.com/lib/in-depth-cognitive-behavioral-therapy.

Mateer, C. (2005). Fundamentals of cognitive rehabilitation. In P. W. Halligan, & D. T. Wade (Eds.), *Effectiveness of rehabilitation for cognitive deficits* (pp. 21–29). Oxford: Oxford University Press.

Maxmen, J. S., & Ward, N. G. (1995). *Essential psychopathology and its treatment*. NY: WW Norton & Co.

Mayo Clinic. (January 31, 2014). *Personality disorders*. www.mayoclinic.org/diseases-conditions/basics/treatment/cn-20030111.

MedlinePlus. (2015). *Somatoform pain disorder*. www.nlm.nih.gov/medlineplus/article/00922.htm.

Medscape. (August 13, 2015). *Oppositional defiant disorder: Defining ODD*. emedicine.medscape.com/article/918095-overview.

Meichenbaum, D. H., & Turk, D. (1976). The cognitive-behavioral management of anxiety, anger, and pain. In P. O. Davidson (Ed.), *The behavioral management of anxiety, depression, and pain*. New York: Brunner/Mazel.

Melton, G., Petrila, J., Poythress, N., & Slobogin, C. (2007). Psychological evaluations for the (dis)agreements on risk assessment measures in sexually violent predator proceedings. Evidence of adversarial allegiance in forensic evaluation? *Psychology, Public Policy and Law*, *15*(1), 19–53.

Meyer, C. 6 Signs of parental alienation syndrome. Last updated 3/8/2016 www.divorcesupport.about.com.

MHS. PANSS – positive and negative syndrome scale. Retrieved from the web 5/27/2016. www.mhs.com/panss.

Miller, W. R., & Rollnick, S. (2002). *Motivational interviewing: Preparing people for change* (2nd ed.). New York: Guilford Press.

Mitchell, J. T., & Everly, G. S. (2000). Critical incident stress management and critical incident stress debriefings: Evolutions, effects, and outcomes. In B. Raphael, & J. P. Wilson (Eds.), *Psychological debriefings: Theory, practice and evidence* (pp. 71–90). New York: Cambridge University Press.

Morgan, J. F., Reid, F., & Lacey, J. H. (March 2000). The SCOFF questionnaire: A new screening tool for eating disorders. *Journal of Medicine*, *172*(3) PMC1070794.

Najavits, L. (2015). *Detaching from emotional pain (grounding)*. Retrieved from the web 9/24/15. www.e-tmf.org/downloads/Grounding_Techniques.pdf.

NAMI: National Alliance on Mental Illness. Schizophrenia. Retrieved from the web 5/28/2016. www.nami.org.

NAMI. (November 2012). *Borderline personality disorder*. http://www2.nami.org/Content/NavigationMenu/Inform_Yourself/About_Mental_Illness/By_Illness/Borderline_Personality.

National Action Alliance for Suicide Prevention: Youth in Contact with the Juvenile Justice System Task Force. (2013). *Screening and assessment for suicide prevention: Tools and procedures for risk identification among juvenile justice youth*. Washington, DC: Author.

National Guidelines Clearinghouse. (2013). *Treatment of schizophrenia*. Retrieved from www.guidelines.gov/content.aspx?id=43956&search=schizophrenia.

National Institute for Health and Clinical Excellence (NICE). (February 2011). *Clinical guideline; no. 115*. 54 p.

NHS. Personality disorder – symptoms. Last review 21/08/2014. Retrieved from www.nhs.uk.

NHS.uk Personality disorder – treatment. www.nhs.uk/Conditions/Personality-disorders/Pages/Treatment.aspx.

NIAAA. (April 2015). *Alcohol overdose: The dangers of drinking too much*. www.pubs.niaaa.nih.gov/publications/AlcoholOverdoseFactsheet/Overdosefact.htm.

NICE. CBT Assessment Process. Retrieved from the web 5/5/16. www.evidence.nhs/search?q=cbtassessmentprocess.

NIH. Mental disorders. Retrieved 9/21/2015 http://www.nim.nih.gov/medlineplus/mental disorders.html.

NIM/NIH. (2015). *Paranoid personality disorder*. National Library of Medicine. Retrieved from the web 10/24/15 www.nim.nih.gov/medlineplus/ency/article/000938.htm.

NIMH. (2014a). *Substance use disorder*. Updated 2/24/2014 www.nim.nih.gov/medlineplus/ency/article/001522.ht.

National Institute of Mental Health (NIMH). (2014b). *Substance Use and Mental Health*. Updated May 2016. Retrieved from www.nimh.nih.gov.

NIMH. Statistics – National Institute of Mental health. Retrieved from the web 9/21/2015 www.nimh.nih.gov/health/statistics/index.shtml.

Nordentoft, M. (2007). Prevention of suicide and attempted suicide in Denmark. Epidemiological studies of suicide and intervention studies in selected risk groups. *Danish Medical Bulletin*, *54*, 306–369.

NQF (National Quality Forum) APA. (2005). *Evidence-based treatment practices for substance use disorders*. www.apa.org/divisions/div50/doc/Evidence_Based._TreatmentPractices_for_Substance_Use_Disorders.pdf.

O'Leary, K. D., Vivian, D., & Malone, J. (1992). Assessment of physical aggression against women in marriage: The need for multimodal assessment. *Behavioral Assessment*, *14*(1), 5–14.

Office of Disability Employment Policy (ODEP). Disability employment policy resources by topic (retrieved from the web 6/18/16) www.dol.gov/odep/pubs/fact/employ.htm.

Oregon Child Welfare Data Book. (2009). www.oregon.gov/DHS/abuse/publications/children/index.shtml.

Owens, D., Horrocks, J., & House, A. (2002). Fatal and non-fatal repetition of self-harm. Systematic review. *British Journal of Psychiatry*, *181*, 193–199.

Pace, C. S., & Zavattini, G. C. (January 2011). Adoption and attachment theory' the attachment models of adoptive mothers and the revision of attachment patterns of their late-adopted children. *Child: Care, Health and Development*, *37*(1), 82–88. http://dx.doi.org/10.1111/j.1365-2214.2010.01135.x. www.ncbi.nim.nih.gov/pubmed/20637017.

Perry, S., Frances, A., & Clarkin, J. (1985). *A DSM-III casebook of differential therapeutics*. New York: Brunner/Mazel.

Peterson, G. (2010). Dissociative disorders: Assessment and treatment tools for dissociative disorders. *Clinical Lecture Series. Univ. North Carolina –CH School of Social Work*. Retrieved from www.cls.unc.edu.

Phillips, R. (June 2012). Predicting the risk of future dangerousness. *AMA Journal of Ethics*, *14*(6), 472–476.

Pollin, I., & Golant, S. K. (1994). *Taking charge: Overcoming the challenges of long term illness*. NY: Times Books.

Pollin, I., & Kanaan, S. (1995). *Medical crisis counseling: Short-term therapy for long-term illness*. New York: Norton.

Pope, S. J. (2002). Nonadherence with mood stabilizers: Prevalence and predictors. *Journal of Clinical Psychiatry*, *63*, 384–390.

Practice guidelines: Core elements for responding to mental health crises. HHS Pub. No. SMA-09–4427. (2009). Rockville, MD: Center for Mental Health Services, Substance Abuse and Mental Health Services Administration.

Rada, R. (1981). The violent patient: Rapid assessment and management. *Psychosomatics*, *22*, 101–109.

Rasgon, N., Bauer, M., Glenn, T., & Whybrow, P. (2002). Gender differences in mood patterns in bipolar disorder. In *Research presented at 155th Annual Meeting of the American Psychiatric Association, Philadelphia, May 2002.*

Regier, D. A., Kuhl, E. A., & Kupfer, D. J. (June 2013). The DSM-5: Classification and criteria changes. *World Psychiatry, 12*(2), 92–98. http://dx.doi.org/10.1002/wps.20050. Published online June 4, 2013.

Regier, D. A., Narrow, W. E., Clarke, D. E., Kraemer, H. C., Kuramoto, S. J., Kuhl, E. A., et al. (2013). DSM-5 field trials in the United States and Canada, part II: Test-retest reliability of selected categorical diag- noses. *American Journal of Psychiatry, 170,* 59–70.

Roberts, A. R. (2000). An overview of crisis theory and crisis intervention. In A. R. Roberts (Ed.), *Crisis intervention handbook: Assessment, treatment and research* (2nd ed.) (pp. 3–30). New York: Oxford University Press.

Roberts, A. R. (2005). Bridging the past and present to the future of crisis intervention and crisis management. In A. R. Roberts (Ed.), *Crisis intervention handbook: Assessment, treatment, and research* (3rd ed.) (pp. 3–34). New York: Oxford University Press.

Roberts A. R., & Otten, A. J. The seven-stage crisis intervention model: A road map to goal attainment, problem solving, and crisis resolution. Online ISSN 1474–3329, Print ISSN 1474–3310. Copyright © 2007 Oxford University Press.

Rollnick, S., Mason, P., & Butler, C. (1999). *Health behavior change. A guide for practitioners.* Chapters 3, 4, 5. New York: Churchill Livingstone.

Root, M. P. P. (1992). Reconstructing the impact of trauma on personality. In L. S. Brown, & M. Ballon (Eds.), *Personality and psychopathology: Feminist reappraisals* (pp. 229–265). NY: Guilford Press.

Ross, C. A., & Norton, G. R. (1989). Suicide and parasuicide in multiple personality disorder. *Psychiatry, 52,* 365–371.

Royal College of Psychiatrists. (October 2013). *Good practice guidelines for the assessment and treatment of adults with gender dysphoria.* Royal College of Psychiatrists. Retrieved March 14, 2014, from http://www.rcpsych.ac.uk/files/pdfversion/CR181.pdf.

Rudd, M. D., Berman, A. L., Joiner, T. E., Nock, M. K., Silverman, M. M., Mandrusiak, M., et al. (2006). Warning signs for suicide: Theory, research and clinical applications. *Suicide and Life Threatening Behavior, 36,* 255–262.

SAMHSA. (June 2012). *Presentation by Pam Hyde: Behavioral Health Evidenced Based and Recovery Practices.* Pub ID: SM1A2PHYDE061312.

SAMHSA. (2013). *How to prevent opioid overdose and overdose-related death.* SAMHSA. Updated 08/28/2013 content.govdelivery.com/accounts/USSAMHSA/bulletins/88c847.

SAMHSA. (2014). *Evidence-based practices WEB GUIDE.* Last updated 08/29/2014 www.samhsa.gov/ebp-web-guide.

SAMHSA. (2015). *Treatment for substance use disorders.* Updated 7/28/2015 www.samhsa.gov/treatment/substance-use-disorders.

Sar, V., Kundakci, T., Kiziltan, E., Yargic, I. L., Tutkun, H., Bakim, B., et al. (2003). The axis I dissociative disorder comorbidity of borderline personality disorder among psychiatric outpatients. *Journal of Trauma and Dissociation, 2*(2), 119–136.

Schalock, R. L., Verdugo, M. A., Gomez, L. E., Claes, C., Buntinx, W., Bonham, G., et al. (2010). Evidence-based practices in the field of intellectual and developmental disabilities: an international consensus approach. *Evaluation and Program Planning.* http://dx.doi.org/10.1016/j.evalprogplan2010.10.004.

Seligman, M. (1990). *Learned optimism: How to change your mind and life.* New York: Pocket Books.

Silver, J. M., Kramer, R., Greenwald, S., & Weissman, M. (2001). The association between head injuries and psychiatric disorders: Findings from the New Haven NIMH Epidemiological Catchment Area Study. *Brain Injury, 15*(11), 935–945.

Simpson, G., & Tate, R. (2002). Suicidality after traumatic brain injury: Demographic, injury and clinical correlates. *Psychological Medicine, 32,* 687–697.

Smith, T., Polloway, E., Patton, J., & Dowdy, C. (2012). *Teaching students with special needs in inclusive settings* (6th ed.). Columbus: Prentice Hall.

Soer, R., van der Schans, C. P., Groothoff, J. W., Geertzen, J. H., & Reneman, M. F. (2008). Towards consensus in operational definitions in functional capacity evaluation: A Delphi survey. *Journal of Occupational Rehabilitation, 18,* 389–400. See more at: http://www.aota.org/About-Occupational-Therapy/Professionals/WI/Capacity-Eval.aspx#sthash.64d3Hkg1.dpuf.

Sonkin, D. J. (2000). *Count-mandated perpetuator assessment and treatment handbook.* CA: Author.

Stahl, P. (March 1999). Alienation and alignment of children. *California Psychologist*, 23–29.

Stein, D. S., Blum, N. J., & Barbaresi, W. J. (2011). Developmental and behavioral disorders through the life span. *Pediatrics*, *128*(2), 364–373.

Stetka, B. S., & Correll, C. U. (May 21, 2013). A guide to DSM-5. *Medscape*.

Taiwo, O. A., Cantley, L., & Schroeder, M. (June 15, 2008). Impairment and disability evaluation: The role of the family physician. *American Family Physician*, *77*(12), 1689.

Tang, B., Byrne, C., Friedlander, R., McKibbin, D., Riley, M., & Thibeault, A. (July, August 2008). The other dual diagnosis: Developmental disability and mental health disorders. *Issue: BCMJ*, *50*(6), 319–324.

Tartakovsky, M. (2013). Top relapse triggers for depression & how to prevent them. *Psych Central*. Retrieved on September 27, 2015, from http://psychcentral.com/lib/top-relapse-triggers-for-depression-how-to-prevent-them/.

Teasdale, T. W., & Engberg, A. W. (2001). Suicide after traumatic brain injury: A population study. *The Journal of Neurology, Neurosurgery, and Psychiatry*, *71*(4), 436–440.

Walker, L. (1979). *The battered woman*. NY: Harper and Row.

WebMD, Recognize the warning signs of suicide. Reviewed by Joseph Goldberg, MD on August 31, 2014. www.webmd.com/depression/guide/depression-recognizing-signs-of-suicide

WebMD. Bipolar disorder in children and teens – Treatment overview. Last updated November 14, 2014 www.webmd/bipolar-disorder-in-children-and-adolescence-htm.

Wehmeyer, M. L., & Obremski, S. (2010). Intellectual disabilities. In J. H. Stone, & M. Blouin (Eds.), *International encyclopedia of rehabilitation*. Available online: http://cirrie.buffalo.edu/encyclopedia/en/article/15/.

Weider, S., & Greenspan, S. I. (2001). The DIR approach to assessment and intervention planning. *Bull Zero to Three*, *21*(4), 11–19. National Center for Infants, Toddlers and Families. www.stanleygreenspan.com.

Wenzel, A., Brown, G. K., & Beck, A. T. (2009). *Cognitive therapy for suicidal patients: Scientific and clinical applications*. Washington. DC: APA Books.

Wiger, D. E., & Haroski, K. J. (2003). *Essentials of crisis counseling and intervention*. Hoboken NJ: Wiley & Sons.

Wilson, C. P., & Mintz, I. L. (1989). *Psychosomatic symptoms: Psychodynamic treatment of underlying personality disorders*. New York: Jason Aronson.

Wright, B., Williams, C. J., & Garland, A. (2017). Using the five areas cognitive–behavioural therapy model in psychiatric in-patients. *Advances in Psychiatric Treatment*, *8* (in press).

Zwi, M., Jones, H., Thorgaard, C., York, A., & Dennis, J. A. (2011). Parent training interventions for attention deficit hyperactivity disorder (ADHD) in children aged 5 to 18 years. *Cochrane Database of Systematic Reviews* (12). http://dx.doi.org/10.1002/14651858.CD003018.pub3. Art. No.: CD003018. Link to Cochrane Library. [PubMed].

FURTHER READING

Ackerman, R., & Michaels, J. (1990). *Recovery source guide* (4th ed.). Deerfield Beach, FL: Health Communication.

Agras, W. S. (1965). An investigation in the decrements of anxiety responses during systematic desensitization therapy. *Behaviour Research and Therapy*, *2*, 267–270.

Agras, W. S., Barlow, T. H., Chapin, H. N., Abel, G. G., & Leitenberg, H. (1974). Behavioral modification of anorexia nervosa. *Archives of General Psychiatry*, *30*, 279–286.

Aguilera, D., & Messick, J. (1982). *Crisis intervention: Therapy for psychological emergencies*. New York: New American Library/Mosby.

Alban, L. S., & Nay, W. R. (1976). Reduction of ritual checking by a relaxation-delay treatment. *Journal of Behavior Therapy and Experimental Psychiatry*, *44*, 656–664.

Alexander, J. F., Barton, C., Schiavo, R. S., & Parsons, B. V. (1976). *Systems-behavioral intervention with families of delinquents: Therapist characteristics, family behavior, and outcome*. Monterey, CA: Brooks/Cole.

Allport, G. (1961). *Pattern and growth in personality*. New York: Holt, Rinehart & Winston.

Alexander, J. F., & Parsons, B. V. (1982). *Functional family therapy*. Monterey, CA: Brooks/Cole.

Altmaier, E. M., Ross, S. L., Leary, M. R., & Thornbrough, M. (1982). Matching stress inoculation's treatment components to client's' anxiety mode. *Journal of Counseling Psychology, 29*, 331–334.

American Association of Suicidology. Retrieved from http://www.suicidology.org.

Anderson, P. K. (1988). *Adult children of alcoholics: Coming home*. Seattle: Glen Abbey Books.

Anthony, J., & Edelstein, B. (1975). Thought-stopping treatment of anxiety attacks due to seizure-related obsessive ruminations. *Journal of Behavioral Therapy and Experimental Psychiatry, 6*, 343–344.

APA. www.healthyminds.org.

APA. www.psychiatry.org.

Aranoff, G. M., Wagner, J. M., & Spangler, A. S. (1986). Chemical interventions for pain. *Journal of Consulting and Clinical Psychology*.

APA Fact Sheet: Developmental Disabilities. Society of pediatric psychology (Div. 54). Retrieved from the web September 15, 2015. www.apadivisions.or/division-54/evidence-based/developmental-disabilites.aspx.

Arrick, M., Voss, J. R., & Rimm, D. C. (1981). The relative efficacy of the thought-stopping covert assertion. *Behaviour Research and Therapy, 19*, 17–24.

Ascher, L. M., & Phillips, D. (1975). Guided behavior rehearsal. *Journal of Behavior Therapy and Experimental Psychiatry, 6*, 215–218.

Association of Family and Conciliation Courts (retrieved from the web 06/17/2016). Preparing for your custody evaluation. Retrieved from https://www.afccnet.org/resource-center/resources-for-families/pamphlet-information/categoryid/1/productid/9.

Association of Reproductive Health Professionals. (Updated online July 2013). Postpartum counseling. Retrieved from www.ahrp.org.

Atwood, J., & Chester, R. (1987). *Treatment techniques for common mental disorders*. New Jersey: Jason Aronson, Inc.

Auerswald, M. C. (1974). Differential reinforcing power of restatement and interpretation on client production of affect. *Journal of Counseling Psychology, 21*, 9–14.

Austad, C. S., & Berman, W. H. (1991). *Psychotherapy in managed health care: The optimal use of time and resources*. Washington, DC: American Psychological Association.

Azrin, N. H., Gottlieb, L., Hugart, L., Wesolowiski, M. D., & Rahn, T. (1975). Eliminating self-injurious behavior by educative procedures. *Behaviour Research and Therapy, 13*, 101–111.

Baker, S. B., & Butler, J. N. (1984). Effects of preventative cognitive self-instruction training on adolescent attitudes, experiences and state anxiety. *Journal of Primary Prevention, 5*, 10–14.

Baker, S. B., Thomas, R. N., & Munson, W. W. (1983). Effects on cognitive restructuring and structured group discussion as primary prevention strategies. *School Counselor, 31*, 26–33.

Baldwin, C. (1977). *One on one: Self-understanding through journal writing*. New York: M. Evans.

Bandura, A. (1969). *Principles of behavior modification*. New York: Holt, Rinehart & Winston.

Bandura, A., Jeffrey, R. W., & Gajdos, E. (1975). Generalizing change through participant modeling with self-directed mastery. *Behaviour Research and Therapy, 13*, 141–152.

Barlow, D. H. (Ed.). (1981). *Behavioral assessment of adult disorders*. New York: Guilford Press.

Barlow, D. H. (1992). Cognitive-behavioral approaches to panic disorder and social phobia. *Bulletin of the Menninger Clinic, 56*(Suppl. 2), A29–A41.

Barsky, A. J., & Klerman, G. L. (1983). Overview: Hypochondriasis, bodily complaints, and somatic styles. *American Journal of Psychiatry*.

Bauer, G., & Kobos, J. (1984). Short-term psychodynamic psychotherapy: Reflections on the past and current practice. *Psychotherapy, 21*, 153–170.

Bauer, G., & Kobos, J. (1987). *Brief therapy: Short-term psychodynamic intervention*. New Jersey: Jason Aronson, Inc.

Beattie, M. C. (1987). *Codependant no more*. Center City, MN: Hazelden.

Beck, A., Rush, J., & Emery, G. (1979). *Cognitive therapy of depression*. New York: Guilford Press.

Beck, A. T. (1976). *Cognitive therapy and emotional disorders*. New York: International Universities Press.

Bell, J. (June 1977). Rescuing the battered wife. *Human Behavior*, 16–23.

Bellak, A. S., Hersen, M., & Himmelhoch, J. (1981). Social skills training, pharmacotherapy, and psychotherapy for unipolar depression. *American Journal of Psychiatry*, *138*, 1562.

Bellak, L., & Small, L. (1965). *Emergency psychotherapy and brief psychotherapy*. New York: Grune & Stratton.

Bemis, K. (1980). Personal communication. In P. C. Kendall, & S. D. Hollon (Eds.), *Assessment strategies for cognitive-behavioral interventions*. New York: Academic Press.

Bepko, C., & Krestan, J. A. (1985). *The responsibility trap: A blueprint for training the alcoholic family*. New York: The Free Press.

Berman, A. (1991). *Adolescent suicide: Assessment and intervention*. Washington, DC: American Psychological Association.

Bernstein, N. (1979). Chronic illness and impairment. *Psychiatric Clinics of North America*, *2*, 331–346.

Biere, J. (1996). *Trauma symptom checklist for children (TSCC)*. Odessa, FL: PAR.

Bishop, G. D. (1987). Lay conceptions of physical symptoms. *Journal of Applied Social Psychology*.

Bodin, A. M. (1996). Relationship conflict–verbal and physical: Conceptualizing an inventory for assessing process and content. In F. W. Kaslow (Ed.), *Handbook of rotational diagram and dysfunctional family patterns* (pp. 371–393). NY: Wiley.

Bolby, J. (1973). *Attachment and loss: Separation, anxiety, and anger*. New York: Basic Books.

Bolstad, O. D., & Johnson, S. M. (1972). Self-regulation in the modification of disruptive classroom behavior. *Journal of Applied Behavior Analysis*, *5*, 443–445.

Bonger, B. (1991). *The suicidal patient: Clinical and legal standards of care*. Washington, DC: American Psychological Association.

Boon, S., Steele, K., & Van der Hart, O. (2010). *Coping with trauma related dissociation: Skills training for clients and therapists*. New York, NY: W.W. Norton.

Booth, G. K. (1984). Disorders of impulse control. In H. H. Goldman (Ed.), *Review of general psychiatry*. Los Altos, CA: Lange Medical Publications.

Borck, L. E., & Fawcett, S. B. (1982). *Learning counseling and problem solving skills*. New York: Haworth Press.

Borman, L. D., Borck, L. E., Hess, R., & Pasquale, E. L. (Eds.). (1982). *Helping people to help themselves*. New York: Self-Help and Prevention.

Bowen, M. (1978). *Family therapy in clinical practice*. New York: Jason Aronson.

Brammer, L. M., & Shostrom, E. L. (1982). *Therapeutic psychology: Fundamentals of counseling and psychotherapy*. Englewood Cliffs NJ: Prentice-Hall.

Brown, J. (1991). *The quality management professional's study guide*. Pasadena, CA: Managed Care Consultants.

Brown, S. (1988). *Treating adult children of alcoholics: A developmental perspective*. New York: Wiley.

Brownell, K., Colleti, G., Ersner-Hershfield, R., Hershfield, S., & Wilson, G. (1977). Self-control in school children: Stringency and leniency in self-determined and externally imposed performance standards. *Behavior Therapy*, *8*, 442–455.

Bruch, H. Psychotherapy of anorexia nervosa and developmental obesity. In R. K. Goldstein (Ed.), *Eating and weight disorders*. New York: Springer.

Budman, S. H., & Gurman, A. S. (1988). *Theory and practice of brief therapy*. New York: Guilford Press.

Budman, S. H., Hoyt, M. F., & Friedman, S. (1992). *The first session of brief therapy: A book of cases*. New York: Guilford Press.

Budman, S. H. (Ed.). (1981). *Forms of brief therapy*. New York: Guilford Press.

Buggs, D. C. (1975). *Your child's self-esteem*. New York: Doubleday.

Campbell, O. C. (Ed.). (1995). *Assessing dangerousness: Violence by sex offenders, batteries and child abuseness*. Newbury Park, CA: Sage Publications.

Campbell, J. (Ed.). (2007). *Assessing dangerousness: Violence by batterers and child abusers*. New York: Springer.

Canino, I. A., & Spurlock, J. (2000). *Culturally diverse children and adolescents*. New York: Guilford Press.

Cantwell, D. P., et al. (1978). In M. Rutter, & E. Schopler (Eds.), *Autism: A reappraisal of concept and treatment*. New York: Plenum Press.

Carkhuff, R. R., & Pierce, R. M. (1975). *Trainer's guide: The art of helping*. Amherst, MA: Human Resources Development Press.

Carrington, P. (1978). *Learning to meditate: Clinically standardized meditation (CSM) course workbook*. Kendall Park, NJ: Pace Educational Systems.

Carter, L., & Minirth, F. (1995). *The freedom from depression workbook*. Nashville: Thomas Nelson Publishers.

Cautela, J. R. (1969). *Behavior therapy and self-control: Techniques and implications*. New York: McGraw Hill.

Cautela, J. R., & Groden, J. (1978). *Relaxation: A comprehensive manual for adults, children, and children with special needs*. Champaign IL: Research Press.

Cermak, T. L. (1986). *Diagnosing and treating codependence*. Minneapolis, MN: Johnson Institute Books.

Chiauzzi, E. (1991). *Preventing relapse in the addictions: A biopsychosocial approach*. New York: Pergamon Press.

Claiborn, C. D. (1982). Interpretation and change in counseling. *Journal of Counseling Psychology, 29,* 439–453.

Cohen, D. J., & Volkmar, F. R. (Eds.). (1997). *Handbook of autism and pervasive developmental disorders* (Rev. ed.) New York: Wiley.

Cormier, W. H., & Cormier, L. S. (1975, 1985). *Interviewing strategies for helpers: Fundamental skills and cognitive behavioral interventions* (2nd ed.). Monterey, CA: Brooks/Cole.

Craske, M. (1988). Cognitive-behavioral treatment of panic. In A. J. France, & R. E. Hales (Eds.), *American psychiatric press review of psychiatry* (Vol. 7) (pp. 121–137). Washington, DC: American Psychiatric Press.

Daley, D. (1989). A psychoeducational approach to relapse prevention. *Journal of Chemical Dependency Treatment, 2(2),* 105–124.

Daley, D. (1993). *Preventing relapse*. Minnesota: Hazelden.

Daley, D., & Sproule, C. (1991). *Adolescent relapse prevention workbook*. Holmes Beach, FL: Learner Publications.

Davanloo, H. (1978). *Basic principles and techniques in short-term dynamic psychotherapy*. New York: Spectrum Publications.

Davis, A., Rosenthal, T. L., & Kelley, J. E. (1981). Actual fear cues, prompt therapy, and rationale enhance participant modeling with adolescence. *Behavior Therapy, 12,* 536–542.

Davis, M., Eshelman, E. R., & McKay, M. (1988). *The relaxation and stress reduction workbook*. Oakland, CA: New Harbinger Publications.

Day, R. W., & Sparacio, R. T. (1980). Structuring the counseling process. *Personnel and Guidance Journal, 59,* 246–250.

Deffenbacher, J. L., & Suinn, R. M. (1982). The self-control of anxiety. In P. Karoly, & F. H. Kanfer (Eds.), *Self-management and behavior change*. New York: Pergamon Press.

Department of Health and Human Services 200 Independence Avenue, S.W.Washington, DC 20201. Website URL http://www.mentalhealth.gov/.

DeShazer, S. (1985). *Keys to solutions in brief therapy*. New York: Norton.

DeWitt, K. N. (1984). Adjustment disorder. In H. H. Goldman (Ed.), *Review of general psychiatry*. Los Altos, CA: Lange Medical Publications.

DHHS (retrieved from the web 6/16). Child placement services. Retrieved from http://.www.Info.dhhs.state.nc.us/olm/manuals/dss/csm-10/man/CSs1201c4-05.html.

Docherty, N. M., DeRose, M., & Andreasen, N. C. (1996). Communication disturbances in schizophrenia and mania. *Archives of General Psychiatry, 53,* 358–364(E).

Doenges, M., Townsend, M., & Moorhouse, M. (1989). *Psychiatric care plans: Guidelines for client care*. Philadelphia: F. A. Davis.

Drabman, R. S., Spitalnick, R., & O'Leary, K. D. (1973). Teaching self-control in disruptive children. *Journal of Abnormal Psychology, 82,* 10–16.

Dutton, D. G. (1993). A scale for measuring propensity for abusiveness. *Journal of Family Violence, 10(2),* 203–221.

Dyer, W. W., & Friend, J. (1975). *Counseling techniques that work*. Washington DC: American Personnel and Guidance Association.

Eberle, T., Rehm, L., & McBurrey, D. (1975). Fear decrement to anxiety hierarchy items: Effects of stimulus intensity. *Behavioral Research Therapy, 13*, 225–261.

Edelstein, M. G. (1990). *Symptom analysis: A method of brief therapy*. New York: Norton.

Egan, G. (1976). *Interpersonal living: A skills contract approach to human-relations training in groups*. Monterey, CA: Brooks/Cole.

Eisenberg, J. M. (June 26, 2012). *Attention deficit hyperactivity disorders in children and adolescents. Comparative effectiveness review summary guides for clinicians (internet)*. Houston, Texas: Baylor College of Medicine. Retrieved from www.ncbi.nlm.nih.gov/pubmedhealth/PMH0047799/.

Eisenstein, S. (1980). The contributions of Franz Alexander. In H. Davanloo (Ed.), *Short-term dynamic psychotherapy*. New York: Jason Aronson.

Eisler, R. M., Hersen, M., & Miller, P. M. (1973). Effects of modeling on components of assertive behavior. *Journal of Behavior Therapy and Experimental Psychiatry, 4*, 1–6.

Eisler, R. M., Hersen, M., Miller, P. M., & Blanchard, E. F. (1975). Situational determinants of assertive behavior. *Journal of Consulting and Clinical Psychology, 43*, 330–340.

Emery, G., & Campbell, J. (1986). *Rapid relief from emotional distress*. New York: Rawson Associates.

Erickson, L., Bjornstad, S., & Gotestam, K. G. (1986). Social skills training in groups for alcoholics: One-year treatment outcome for groups and individuals. *Addictive Behaviors, 11*, 309–329.

Evans, I. M. (1974). A handy record-card for systematic desensitization hierarchy items. *Journal of Behavior Therapy and Experimental Psychology, 5*, 43–46.

Everstine, D. S., & Everstine, L. (1983). *People in crisis: Strategic therapeutic interventions*. New York: Brunner/Mazel.

Falloon, I. R. H. (1985). *Family management of schizophrenia: A study of the clinical, social, family and economic benefits*. Baltimore, MD: Johns Hopkins University Press.

Fawcell, J. M. D. (Ed.). (1993). *Predicting and preventing suicide. Psychiatric Anals: Vol. 23*. (p. 5).

Ferster, C. B. (1961). Positive reinforcement and behavior deficits of autistic children. *Child Development, 32*, 437–456.

Filsinger, E. (1983). *Marriage and family assessment: A sourcebook for family therapy*. Beverly Hills, CA: Sage.

Fisch, R., Weakland, J., & Segal, L. (1982). *The tactics of change: Doing therapy briefly*. San Francisco: Jossey-Bass.

Fishman, S. T., & Lubetkin, B. S. (1983). *Office practice of behavior therapy*. New York: Grune & Stratton.

Flegenheimer, W. (1985). History of brief psychotherapy. In A. Horner (Ed.), *Treating the oedipal patient in brief psychotherapy*. New York: Jason Aronson.

Flor, H., Kerns, R. D., & Turk, D. C. (1987). The role of spousal reinforcement, perceived pain, and activity levels of chronic pain patients. *Journal of Psychosomatic Research, 31*(2), 251–259.

Foccaro, E. F., Kramer, F., Zemishlanz, Z., Thorne, A., Rice, C. M., II, Giordano, B., et al. (1990). Pharmacological treatment of noncognitive behavioral disturbances in elderly demented patients. *American Journal of Psychiatry, 147*, 1640–1645.

Fordyce, W. E. (1976). Behavioral concepts in chronic pain and illness. In P. O. Davison (Ed.), *Behavioral management of anxiety, depression and pain*. New York: Brunner/Mazel.

Fredricksen, L. W. (1975). Treatment of ruminative thinking by self-monitoring. *Journal of Behavior Therapy and Experimental Psychiatry, 6*, 258–259.

Fremouw, W. J., & Brown, J. P., Jr. (1980). The reactivity of addictive behaviors to self-monitoring: A functional analysis. *Addictive Behaviors, 5*, 209–217.

Fremouw, W. J., & Heyneman, N. (1983). Obesity. In M. Hersen (Ed.), *Outpatient behavior therapy*. New York: Grune & Stratton.

Friedman, S., & Fanger, M. T. (1991). *Expanding therapeutic possibilities: Getting results in brief psychotherapy*. New York: Lexington Books.

Galassi, M. D., & Galassi, J. P. (1977). *Assert yourself: How to be your own person*. New York: Human Sciences.

Gambrill, E. (1981). *Behavior modification: Handbook of assessment, intervention, and evaluation*. San Francisco: Jossey-Bass.

Gardner, R. A. (1989). *Family evaluation in child custody, mediation, arbitration and litigation*. Creskill, NJ: Creative Therapeutics.

Garvey, W., & Hegrenes, J. (1966). Desensitization techniques in the treatment of school phobia. *American Journal of Orthopsychiatry*, 36,147–152.

Giovacchini, P. (1986). *Developmental disorders: The transitional space in mental breakdown and creative integration*. New Jersey: Jason Aronson.

Glaister, B. (1982). Muscle relaxation training for fear reduction of patients with psychological problems: A review of controlled studies. *Behavior Research Therapy*, 20, 493–504.

Goldfried, M. R. (1982). *Behavioral assessment: An overview*. New York: Plenum Press.

Goodman, F., & Jamisin, K. (1990). *Manic-depressive illness*. New York: Oxford University Press.

Goodman, M., Brown, J., & Deitz, P. (1992). *Managing managed care: A mental health practitioner's survival guide*. Washington DC: American Psychiatric Press.

Goodwin, S. E., & Mahoney, M. J. (1975). Modification in aggression through modeling. *Journal of Applied Behavior Analysis*, 9, 114.

Gorski, T., & Miller, M. (1988). *Staying sober workbook*. Independence, MO: Independence Press.

Goulding, M. M., & Goulding, R. L. (1979). *Changing lives through redecision therapy*. New York: Brunner/Mazel.

Gresham, F. M., & Nagle, R. J. (1980). Social skills training with children: Responsiveness to modeling and coaching as a function of peer orientation. *Journal of Consulting and Clinical Psychology*, 48, 718–729.

Grisso, T. (1988). *Competency to stand trial evaluations: A manual for practice*. Sarasota, FL: Professional Resource Exchange, Inc.

Grotstein, J. S., Solomon, M. F., & Lang, J. (Eds.). (1987). *The borderline patient*. Hillsdale, NJ: Analytic Press.

Gustafson, J. P. (1986). *The complex secret of brief psychotherapy*. New York: Norton.

Hackett, G., & Horan, J. J. (1980). Stress inoculation for pain: What's really going on? *Journal of Counseling Psychology*, 27, 107–116.

Haley, J. (1961). *Control in brief psychotherapy*. New York: Grune & Stratton.

Haley, J. (1977). *Problem-solving therapy*. San Francisco: Josey-Bass.

Haley, J., & Hoffman, L. (1967). *Techniques of family therapy*. New York: Grune & Stratton.

Hamby, S. (1995). *Dominance scale*. Durham NH: University of New Hamphire Press.

Hay, W. M., Hay, L. R., & Nelson, P. O. (1977). The adaptation of covert modeling procedures to the treatment of chronic alcoholism and obsessive-compulsive behavior. *Behavior Therapy*, 8, 70–76.

Hays, V., & Waddell, K. J. (1976). A self-reinforcing procedure for thought stopping. *Behavior Therapy*, 7, 559.

Helfer, R., & Kempe, R. (1987). *The battered child*. Chicago: The University of Chicago Press.

HelpGuide.Org. Last updated August 2015. www.helpguide.org/articles/add-adhd/attention-deficit-disorder-adhd-treatment-in-children.

HelpGuide.Org. Last updated August 2015. www.helpguide.org/articles/bipolar-disorders-treatment.htm Bipolar Disorder Treatment.

Hersen, M., & Bellack, A. S. (1976). A multiple baseline analysis of social-skills training in chronic schizophrenia. *Journal of Applied Behavior Analysis*, 9, 239–246.

Hersen, M., Eisler, R. M., Miller, P. M., Johnson, M. D., & Pinkston, J. G. (1973). Effects of practice, instructions, and modeling on components of assertive behavior. *Behavior Research and Therapy*, 11, 443–451.

Horner, A. (1985). *Treating the oedipal patient in brief psychotherapy*. In A. Horner (Ed.), New York: Jason Aronson.

Horowitz, M. J. (1976). *Stress response syndromes*. New York: Aronson.

Horowitz, M. J., et al. (1984). *Personality styles and brief psychotherapy*. New York: Basic Books.

Hoyle, C. (2008). "Will she be safe? A critical analysis of risk assessment in domestic violence cases". In *Children and youth services review* (30) (pp. 323–337).

Hoyt, M. F. (1979). Aspects of termination in a brief time-limited psychotherapy. *Psychiatry, 42,* 208–219.

Hoyt, M. F. (1985). Therapist resistance to short-term dynamic psychotherapy. *Journal of the American Academy of Psychoanalysis, 13,* 93–112.

Hoyt, M. F. (1986). Mental-imagery methods in short-term dynamic psychotherapy. In M. Wolpin, et al. (Ed.), *Imagery 4.* New York: Plenum.

Hoyt, M. F. (1987). Notes on psychotherapy with obsessed patients. *The Psychotherapy Patient, 3*(2), 13–22.

Hoyt, M. F. (1989). Psychodiagnosis of personality disorders. *Transactional Analysis Journal, 19,* 101–113.

Hoyt, M. F. (1990). On time in brief therapy. In R. A. Wells, & V. J. Gianetti (Eds.), *Handbook of brief psychotherapies.* New York: Plenum Press.

Hoyt, M. F. (1991). Teaching and learning in short-term psychotherapy within an HMO: With special attention to resistance and phase-specific parallel process. In C. S. Austad, & W. Berman (Eds.), *The handbook of HMO psychotherapy in prepaid health care setting.* Washington DC: American Psychological Association.

Hoyt, M. F. (1995). *Brief therapy and managed care: Readings for contemporary practice.* San Francisco: Jossey-Bass.

Institute for the Advancement of Human Behavior. Child abuse and the mental health professional (manual). P.O. Box 7226, Stanford, CA 94309.

Institute of Medicine. (2006). *Committee on crossing the quality chasm: Adaptation to mental health and addictive disorders, recommendation 3-1,* 126.

International Society for the Study of Trauma and Dissociation (ISSTD). (2011). Guidelines for treating dissociative identity disorder in adults, third revision. *Journal of Trauma and Dissociation, 12*(2), 115–187. http://dx.doi.org/10.1080/15299732.2011.537247.

International Society for the Study of Trauma and Dissociation (ISSTD). (2015). *Adult treatment guidelines.* Retrieved from www.isst-d.org/default.aspx?contentID=49.

Jacobs, D., & Brown, H. (Eds.). (1989). *Suicide understanding and responding.* Madison, CT: International University Press.

Jacobson, G., Strickler, M., & Morley, W. E. (1968). Generic and individual approaches to crisis intervention. *American Journal of Public Health, 58,* 339.

James, J., & Cherry, F. (1988). *The grief recovery handbook.* New York: Harper and Row.

Jarvinen, P. J., & Gold, S. R. (1981). Imagery as an aid in reducing depression. *Journal of Clinical Psychology, 37,* 523–529.

Johnson, S. L. (1997). *Therapist's guide to clinical intervention: The 1,2,3's of treatment planning.* San Diego: Academic Press.

Jones, M. C. (1924). The elimination of children's fears. *Journal of Experimental Psychology, 7,* 383–390.

Kandal, D., & Faust, R. (1975). Sequence and stages in patterns of adolescent drug use. *Archives of General Psychiatry, 32,* 923–932.

Kanfer, F. H. (1980). *Self-management methods.* New York: Pergamon Press.

Kaplan, H. (1979). *Disorders of sexual desire and other new concepts and techniques in sex therapy.* New York: Brunner/Mazel.

Kaplan, H. (1985). *Comprehensive evaluation of disorders of sexual desire.* Washington, DC: American Psychiatric Press.

Kaplan, H. I., & Sadock, B. J. (1981). *Modern synopsis of comprehensive textbook of psychiatry III* (3rd ed.). Baltimore: Williams & Wilkins.

Kashdan, T. B., Uswatte, G., Steger, M. F., & Julian, T. (2006). Fragile self-esteem and affective instability in post traumatic stress disorder. *Behavior Research and Therapy, 44,* 1609–1619.

Kazdin, A. E. (1974). *Self-monitoring and behavior change.* Monterey, CA: Brooks/Cole.

Keefe, F. J., & Williams, D. A. (1989). New direction in pain assessment and treatment. *Clinical Psychology Review,* 549–568.

Kellner, R. (1987). Hypochodriasis and somatization. *Journal of the American Medical Association.*

King, S. H. (1962). *Perceptions of illness and medical practice.* New York: Russell Sage Foundation.

Kolodny, R., Masters, W., & Johnson, V. (1979). *Textbook of sexual medicine*. Boston: Little, Brown and Company.

Kozloff, M. A. (1973). *Reaching the autistic child: A parent training program*. Champaign IL: Research Press.

Krumboltz, J. D., & Krumboltz, H. B. (1972). *Changing children's behavior*. Englewood Cliffs, NJ: Prentice-Hall.

Kubler-Ross, E. (1969). *On death and dying*. New York: MacMillan.

Lacy, J. I. (1967). Somatic response patterning and stress: Some revisions of activation theory. In M. H. Appley, & R. Trumbull (Eds.), *Psychological stress: Issues in research*. New York: Appleton-Century-Crofts.

Lange, A., & Jakubowski, P. (1976). *Responsible assertive behavior: Cognitive/behavioral procedures for trainers*. Champaign, IL: Research Press.

Lazarus, A. A., Davidson, C. G., & Polefka, D. A. (1965). Classical and operant factors in the treatment of a school phobia. *Journal of Abnormal Psychiatry*, 70, 225–229.

Lazarus, A. A. (1976). *Multi-modal behavior therapy*. New York: McGraw-Hill.

Lazarus, A. A. (1981). *Multi-modal behavior therapy. Part 3*. New York: Springer.

Lazarus, R. (1966). *Psychological stress and the coping process*. New York: McGraw Hill.

Lehrer, P. M., & Woolfolk, R. L. (1982). Self-report assessment of anxiety: Somatic, cognitive, and behavioral modalities. *Behavior Assessment*, 4, 167–177.

Lewinsohn, P. M. (1974). A behavioral approach to depression. In R. J. Friedman, & M. M. Katz (Eds.), *The psychology of depression*. Washington DC: V. H. Winston and Sons.

Lewis, J. A., Dana, R. Q., & Blevins, G. A. (1994). *Substance abuse counseling: An individual approach* (2nd ed.). Pacific Grove, CA: Brooks/Cole Publishing.

Liberman, R. P., King, L. W., DeRisi, W. J., & McCann, M. (1975). *Personal effectiveness: Guiding people to assert themselves and improve their social skills*. Champaign, IL: Research Press.

Linehan, M. (1987). Dialectical behavior therapy for borderline personality disorder. *Bulletin of the Menniger Clinic*, 51(3), 261–276.

Linehan, M. (1995). *Treating borderline personality disorder: Dialectical approach program manual*. New York: Guilford Press.

Linton, S. (1994). Chronic back pain: Integrating psychological and physical therapy—an overview. *Behavioral Medicine*, 20, 101–104.

Lion, J. (1972). *Evaluation and management of the violent patient*. Springfield, IL: Charles C. Thomas.

Lovaas, O. I., & Newsom, C. D. (1976). *Behavior modification with psychotic children*. Englewood Cliffs, NJ: Prentice Hall.

Mace, N., & Rabins, P. (1981). *The 36 hour day*. Baltimore: John Hopkins University.

Malan, D. (1979). *Individual psychotherapy and the science of psychodynamics*. Boston: Butterworths.

Maltsberger, J. (1986). *Suicide risk: The formulation of clinical judgment*. New York: New York University Press.

Mann, J. (1973). *Time-limited psychotherapy*. New York: McGraw-Hill.

Marlatt, G. A., & Gordon, J. R. (Eds.). (1985). *Relapse prevention: Maintenance strategies in the treatment of addictive behaviors*. New York: Guilford Press.

Mash, E. J., & Barkley, R. A. (1989). *Treatment of childhood disorders*. New York: Guilford.

Mayo Clinic. Schizotypal personality disorder. Retrieved from the web 10/24/15 www.mayoclinic.org/diseases-conditions/schizotypal-personality-disorder/basics/definition/con-20027949.

Mayo Clinic. (February 6, 2015). *Oppositional defiant disorder*. www.mayoclinic.org/diseases-conditions/oppositional-defiant-disorder/basics/symptoms/con-20024559.

McCracken, J. (1985). Somatoform disorders. In J. Walker (Ed.), *Essentials of clinical psychiatry*. Philadelphia: Lippincott.

McFall, R. M., & Dodge, K. A. (1982). *Self-management and interpersonal skills learning*. New York: Pergamon Press.

McGlashen, T. H., & Fenton, W. S. (1997). The positive/negative distinction in schizophrenia: Review of natural history validators. *Archives of General Psychiatry*, 49, 63–72(F).

McHugh, R. K., Hearon, B. A., & Otto, M. W. (September 2010). Cognitive-behavioral therapy for substance use disorders. *Psychiatric Clinics of North America*, 33(3), 511–525. http://dx.doi.org/10.1016/j.psc.2010.04.012. Author manuscript; available in PMC September 1, 2011. Published in final edited form as: Psychiatric Clinics of North America.

McKay, M., & Fanning, P. (1992). *Self-esteem*. Oakland, CA: New Harbinger Publications.

McKay, M., Fanning, P., & Paleg, K. (1994). *Couple skills*. Oakland, CA: New Harbinger Publications.

McKay, M., Rogers, P., & McKay, J. (1989). *When anger hurts: Quieting the storm within*. Oakland, CA: New Harbinger Publications.

Medicare Preventive Services. Interactive tool at http://www.cms.gov/Medicare/Prevention/PrevntionGenInfo/Downloads/MPS_QuickReferenceChart_1.pdf or for the text only version, visit http://www.cms.gov/Medicare/Prevention/PrevntionGenInfo/Downloads/MPS-QuickReferenceChart-1TextOnly.pdf.

Medscape. Pediatric generalized anxiety disorder. Last reviewed 8/2015 www.emedicine.medscape.com/article/916933-overview.

Medscape. Adjustment disorders treatment and management (retrieved from the web 10/15/2015) http://emedicine.medscape.com/article/2192631-treatment.

Meichenbaum, D. H. (1976). A cognitive-behavior modification approach to assessment. In M. Hersen, & A. S. Bellack (Eds.), *Behavioral assessment: A practical handbook*. New York: Pergamon Press.

Meichenbaum, D. H. (1985). *Stress-inoculation training*. New York: Pergamon Press.

Meichenbaum, D. H., & Goodman, J. (1971). Training impulsive children to talk to themselves: A means of developing self-control. *Journal of Abnormal Psychology*, 77, 115–126.

Melton, G., Petrila, J., Poythress, N., & Slobogin, C. (1987). *Psychological evaluations for the courts: A handbook for mental health professionals and lawyers*. New York: Guilford Press.

Meyer, R. G. (1983). *The clinician's handbook: The psychopathology of adulthood and late adolescence*. Boston: Allyn & Bacon.

Miller, A. (1988). *The enabler: When helping harms the one you love. Claremont*. CA/Ballantine, NY: Hunter House.

Miller, W. (1989). *Matching individuals with interventions: Handbook of alcoholism treatment approaches*. New York: Pergamon Press.

Mirin, S., & Weiss, R. (1983). Substance abuse. In E. Bassuk, S. Schoonover, & A. Gelenberg (Eds.), *The practitioner's guide to psychoactive drugs* (pp. 221–290). New York: Plenum Press.

Monti, P. M., Abrams, D. B., Kadden, R. M., & Cooney, N. L. (1989). *Treating alcohol dependence: A coping skills training guide*. New York: Guilford Press.

Morrison, J., & Anders, T. F. (1999). *Interviewing children and adolescents: Skills and strategies for effective DSM IV diagnoses*. New York: Guilford.

Murphy, L., & Moriarty, A. (1976). *Vulnerability, coping, and growth from infancy to adolescence*. New Haven, CT: Yale University Press.

Murphy, L. B. (1974). Coping, vulnerability, and resilience in childhood. In G. V. Coehlo, et al. (Eds.), *Coping and adaption*. New York: Basic Books.

N. H. consensus development panel on depression in late life. *Journal of the American Medical Association*, 268, (1992), 1018–1024 (G).

NASW (National Association of Social Workers retrieved from the web 7/2/16) Domestic violence assessment and intervention provided by the family violence prevention fund www.socialworkers.org.

National Association of Anorexia Nervosa and Associated Disorders. Important changes in eating disorder diagnoses in DSM V. Last reviewed 2015 www.anad.org/news/important-changes-in-eating-disorder-diagnoses-in-dsm-v.

National Institute for Health and Clinical Excellence (NICE). Alcohol-use disorders. Diagnosis, assessment and management of harmful drinking and alcohol dependence. London (UK).

National Institute of Health. Borderline personality disorder. Retrieved from the web 10/24/15 www.nimh.nih.gov/health/topics/borderline-personality-disorder/index.shtml.

National Institute of Mental Health. (2011). *A parent's guide to autism spectrum disorder*. Retrieved March 8, 2012, from http://www.nimh.nih.gov/health/publications/a-parents-guide-to-autism-spectrum-disorder/index.shtml. [top].

National Mental Health Association (NMHA). 1021 Prince Street. Alexandria, VA. 22314–22971.

National Mental Health Consumer Self-Help Clearinghouse Phone Number: (215) 751–1810. Toll Free Number: (800) 553-4539. Fax Number: (215) 636-6312. Email address info@mhselfhelp.org. Website URL http://www.mhselfhelp.org/.

Nay, W. R. (1979). *Multi method clinical assessment*. New York: Gardner Press.

Neimeyer, R., & Feixas, E. (1990). The role of homework and skills acquisition in the outcome of cognitive therapy for depression. *Behavior Therapy*, 21, 281–292.

Neimiah, J., & Sifneos, P. (1970). Affect and fantasy in patients with psychosomatic disorders. In O. W. Hill (Ed.), *Modern trends in psychosomatic medicine* (Vol. 2) (pp. 26–34). New York: Appleton-Century-Crofts.

Nelson, R. O. (1983). Behavioral assessment: Past, present, and future. *Behavioral Assessment*, 5, 195–206.

NIH, & Medline. (9/1/2015). *Bipolar disorder*. www.nim.nih.gov/medlineplus/bipolardisorder.html.

NIH, & MedLinePlus. (2013). *Intellectual disability*. U.S. National Library of Medicine. www.nim.nih.gov/medlineplus/ency/article/001523.htm.

NIH. SLOF: A behavioral rating scale for assessing the mentally ill. Retrieved from the web 5/27/2016 www.ncbi.nim.nih.gov/pubmed/17454281.

NIH. (2013). *What are the treatments for autism spectrum disorder (ASD)?*. www.nichd.nih.gov/health/topics/autism/conditioninfo/pages/treatment.aspx.

NIH/NIMH. (2014). *Eating disorders: About more than food*. U.S. Department of H.H.S. National Institutes of Health. NIH Publication No. (TR 14-4901) www.nimh.nih.gov/health/topics/eating-disorders/index.shtml.

NIMH. Bipolar Disorder in Children and Adolescents. Retrieved from the web 9/19/2015 www.nimh.nih.gov/health/publications/bipolar-disorder-in-children-and-adolescents/htm.

NJCLD (National Joint Commission on Learning Disabilities). (2005). www.readbag.com.

NJCLD (National Joint Commission on Learning Disability). (2016). www.idonline.org.

O'Hanlon, W. H., & Weiner-Davis, M. (1988). *In search of solutions: A new direction in psychotherapy*. New York: Norton.

O'Leary, K. D., Heyman, R. E., & Neidig, P. H. (1999). Treatment of wife abuse: A comparison of gender specific and conjoint approaches. *Behavior Therapy*, 30, 475–506.

Othmer, E., & DeSouza, C. (1985). A screening test for somatization disorder (hysteria). *American Journal of Psychiatry*, 142, 1146–1199.

Patsiokas, A. J., et al. (1979). Cognitive characteristics of suicidal attempts. *Journal of Consulting and Clinical Psychology*, 47, 478–484.

Peterson, L., & Brownlee-Duffeck, M. (1984). Prevention of anxiety and pain due to medical and dental procedures. In M. C. Roberts, & L. Peterson (Eds.), *Prevention of problems in childhood: Psychological research and application* (pp. 195–308). New York: Wiley.

Pruder, R. S. (1988). Age analysis of cognitive-behavioral group therapy for chronic pain patients. *Psychology and Aging*, 3(2), 204–207.

Psychcentral. Somatization disorder symptoms. Last reviewed: By J. M. Grohol, PsyD. on 18 March 2016 Published on www.PsychCentral.com.

Roberts, A. R. (2002). Assessment, crisis intervention and trauma treatment: The integrative ACT intervention model. *Brief Treatment and Crisis Intervention*, 2(1), 1–21.

Rosenbaum, R. (1990). Strategic psychotherapy. In R. A. Wells, & V. J. Giannetti (Eds.), *Handbook of the brief psychotherapies*. New York: Plenum Press.

Rosenbaum, R., Hoyt, M. F., & Talmon, M. (1990). *The challenge of single-sessions therapies: Creating pivotal moments*. New York: Plenum Press.

Rosenberg, K. (1993). *Talk to me: A therapist's guide to breaking through male silence*. New York: Plenum Press.

Rosenberg, L. (1983). The technique of psychological assessment as applied to children in foster care and their families. In M. Hardin (Ed.), *Foster children in the courts* (pp. 550–574). Boston: Butter-worth.

Rosenberg, M.S., Westling, D.L., & McLeskey, J. (2013). *Primry characteristics of students with intellectual disabilities*. Pearson Allyn Bacon Prentice Hall. Updated July 24, 2013 www.education.com/reference/article/characterisitcs-intellectual-disabilities/.

Russell, M. L., & Thoresen, C. E. (1976). Teaching decision-making skills to children. In J. D. Krumboltz, & C. E. Thoresen (Eds.), *Counseling methods*. New York: Holt, Rinehart, and Winston.

SAFE-T: Originally conceived by Douglas Jacobs, MD, and developed as a collaboration between Screening for Mental Health, Inc. and the suicide prevention Resource Center.

Samaan, M. (1975). Thought-stopping and flooding in case of hallucinations, obsession, and homicidal-suicidal behavior. *Journal of Behavior Therapy and Experimental Psychiatry*, 6, 65–67.

SAMHSA. (June 13, 2012). *Behavioral health – Evidence-based treatment and recovery practices*. http://www.store.samhsa.gov/product/Behavioral-Health-Evidence-Based-Treatment-and-Recovery-Practices/SMA12-PHYDE061312.

Schetky, D. H., & Slader, D. L. (1980). Termination of parental rights. In D. H. Schetky, & E. P. Benedek (Eds.), *Child psychiatry and the law*.

Seligman, M. E. P. (1991). *Learned optimism*. New York: Knopf.

Sifneos, P. (1972). *Short-term psychotherapy and emotional crisis*. Cambridge, MA: Harvard University Press.

Sifneos, P. E. (1987). *Short-term dynamic psychotherapy*. New York: Plenum.

Simos, B. G. (1979). *A time to grieve: Loss as a universal human experience*. New York: Family Services Association of America.

Simpson, J. R. (2014). DSM-5 and neurocognitive disorders. *Journal of the American Academy of Psychiatry and the Law*, 42(2), 159–164. www.ncbi.nlm.nih.gov/pubmed/24986342.

Small, L. (1979). *The briefer psychotherapies*. New York: Brunner/Mazel.

Smith, R. E., & Sarason, I. G. (1975). Social anxiety and the evaluation of negative interpersonal feedback. *Journal of Consulting and Clinical Psychology*, 43, 429.

Social Security Disability. (retrieved from the web 06/18/16) Disability Evaluation Under Social Security. www.ssa.gov/disability/professionals/bluebook/evidentiary.htm.

Sonkin, D., Martin, D., & Auerbach Walker, L. (1985). *The male batterer: A treatment approach*. New York: Springer Publishing Company.

Spates, C. R., & Knafer, F. H. (1977). Self-monitoring, self-education, and self-reinforcement in childrens learning: A test of a multistage self-regulation model. *Behavior Therapy*, 8, 9–16.

Spitzer, R., Williams, J., & Gibbon, M. (1987). *Structured clinical interview for DSM III-R, personality disorders module*. New York: Guilford (BMA Audio Casettes a Division of Guilford Publications, Inc.).

StopPain. org, & Department of Pain Medicine and Palliative Care. (July 2, 2016). *Definitions and types of pain*. www.healingchronicpain.org.

Stoudemire, G. (1988). Somatoform disorders, factitious disorders, and malingering. In J. Talbott, R. Hales, & S. Yudofsky (Eds.), *Textbook of psychiatry*. Washington DC: American Psychiatric Press.

Strupp, H. H., & Binder, J. (1984). *Psychotherapy in a new key: A guide to time limited dynamic psychotherapy*. New York: Basic Books.

Suicide Prevention Action Network (SPAN). Retrieved from http://www.spanusa.org.

Suicide Prevention Resource Center. Retrieved from http://www.sprc.org.

Tatarsky, A., & Washton, A. (1992). *Intensive outpatient treatment: A psychological perspective*. New York: Brunner/Mazel.

Taylor, C. B. (1983). DSM-III and behavioral assessment. *Behavioral Assessment*, 5, 5–14.

Terman, M., Williams, J., & Terman, J. (1991). Light therapy for winter depression: Clinician's guide. In P. Keller (Ed.), *Innovation in clinical practice: A source book* (pp. 179–221). Sarasota, FL: Pro-Resources.

The Center for Implementation-Dissemination of Evidence-Based Practices among States (IDEAS). Updated September 20, 2015 www.ideas.4kidsmentalhealth.org.

The Forensic Panel: Assessment of Dangerousness – Risk Assessment – The … www.forensicpanel.com/.../assessment_of_dangerousness.html. Risk assessments from the Forensic Panel carefully incorporate the latest insights into forensic psychiatry and corrections that reflects on recidivism risk.

The National Alliance for the Mentally Ill (NAMI). 200 North Glebe Road, Suite 1015, Arlington, VA 22203–23754.

Turk, D., & Genest, M. (1979). Regulation of pain: The application of cognitive and behavioral techniques for prevention of remediation. In P. Kendall, & S. Hollon (Eds.), *Cognitive-behavioral interventions: Theory, research, and procedures*. New York: Academic Press.

Turner, R. M. (1983). Cognitive-behavior therapy with borderline personality disorder. *Carrier Foundation Letter, 88*, 1–4.

Turner, R. M. (1988). The cognitive-behavioral approach to the treatment of borderline personality disorder. *International Journal of Partial Hospitalization, 5*, 279–289.

Turpin, J. (1975). Management of violent patients. In R. Shader (Ed.), *Manual of Psychiatric Therapeutics*. Boston: Little Brown.

US Department of Health and Human Services, Substance Abuse and Mental Health Services Administration (SAMHSA). Retrieved from www.samhsa.gov.

Vaillant, G., & Perry, J. (1985). Personality disorders. In H. Kaplan, & B. Sadock (Eds.), *Comprehensive textbook of psychiatry* (4th ed.). Baltimore: Williams & Wilkins.

Veinot, T. (2001). *Who is the abuser? A screening challenge*. Website http://www.womenabuseprevention.com/ht.screening.html.

Wachtel, P. L. (Ed.). (1982). *Resistance: Psychodynamic and behavioral approach*. New York: Plenum Press.

Waldinger, R. (1986). *Fundamentals of psychiatry*. New York: American Psychiatric Press.

Walls, R. T., Werner, T. J., Bacon, A., & Zanc, T. (1977). Behavioral checklists. In J. D. Cone, & R. P. Hawkins (Eds.), *Behavioral assessment: New directions in clinical psychology*. New York: Brunner/Mazel.

Washton, A. M. (1989). *Cocaine abuse: Treatment, recovery, and relapse prevention*. New York: Norton.

Washton, A. M. (1995). *Psychotherapy and substance abuse: A practitioners handbook*. New York: Guilford Press.

Watson, D., & Tharpe, R. (1981). *Self-directed behavior: Self-modification for personal adjustment*. Monterey, CA: Brooks/Cole.

Watzlawick, P., Weakland, J., & Fisch, R. (1974). *Change: Principles of problem formation and problem resolution*. New York: Norton.

WebMD. (2015a). *Autism spectrum disorders*. Reviewed May 19, 2015 www.webmd.com/brain/autism/autism-spectrum-disorders.

WebMD. (2015b). *Separation anxiety in children*. Last reviewed 8/2015. www.webmd.com/children/guide/separation-anxiety.

Weiner, H. (1977). *Psychobiology and human disease*. New York: Elsevier.

Weiner, I., & Hess, A. (1987). *Handbook of forensic psychology*. New York: Wiley.

Weissman, H. N. (1991). The child custody evaluation: Methodology and assessment. *Family Law News, 14*, 2.

Weissman, M. M., Klerman, G. I., Markowitz, J. S., & Ouellette, R. (1989). Suicidal ideation and attempts in panic disorders and attacks. *New England Journal of Medicine, 321*, 1209–1214 (C).

Wells, R. A., & Giannetti, V. J. (1990). *Handbook of brief psychotherapies*. New York: Plenum Press.

Wells, R. A., & Phelps, P. A. (1990). *The brief psychotherapies: A selective overview*. New York: Plenum Press.

Wernick, R. L. (1983). *Stress inoculation in the management of clinical pain: Application to burn pain*. New York: Plenum Press.

West, D. (1979). The response to violence. *Journal of Medical Ethics, 5*, 128–131.

Wetzel, R. D. (1976). *Hopelessness, depression, and suicidal intent*.

Wexler, D. (1991). *The adolescent self: Strategies for self-management, self-soothing, and self-esteem in adolescents*. New York: Norton.

Whitfield, C. L. (1992). *Boundaries and relationships in recovery*. Deerfield Beach, FL: Health Communications.

Williams, R., & Williams, V. (1993). *Anger kills*. New York: Harper Perennial.

Wills-Brandon, C. (1990). *Learning to say no: Establishing healthy boundaries*. Deerfield Beach, FL: Health Communications.

Winokur, M., & Dasberg, H. (1983). Teaching and learning short-term dynamic psychotherapy. *Bulletin of the Menninger Clinic, 47,* 36–52.

Woititz, J., & Garner, L. (1991). *Lifeskills for adult children.* Deerfield Beech, FL: Health Communications.

Wolberg, L. R. (1980a). Crisis intervention. In L. R. Wolberg (Ed.), *Handbook of short-term psychotherapy.* New York: Grune & Stratton.

Wolberg, L. R. (1980b). *Handbook of short-term dynamic psychotherapy.* New York: Grune & Stratton.

Wolff, P. (1972). Ethnic differences in alcohol sensitivity. *Science, 125,* 449–451.

Wolpe, J. (1982). *The practice of behavior therapy* (3rd ed.). New York: Pergamon.

Wolpe, J., & Lazarus, A. A. (1966). *Behavior therapy techniques.* New York: Pergamon.

Woolfolk, R. L., & Lehrer, P. M. (Eds.). (1984). *Principles and practice of stress management.* New York: Guilford Press.

Wooten, V. (1994). Medical causes of insomnia. In M. H. Kryger, T. Roth, & W. C. Dement (Eds.), *Principles and practice for sleep medicine* (2nd ed.). (pp. 509–522). Philadelphia: Saunders.

Yager., et al. (2012). *American psychiatric association eating disorders guidelines* (3rd ed.). www.psychiatryonline.org/pb/assets/raw/sitewide/practice_guidelines/guidelines/eatingdisorders-watch.pdf.

Yamagami, T. (1971). The treatment of an obsession by thought-stopping. *Journal of Behavior Therapy and Experimental Psychiatry, 2,* 133–135.

Yapko, M. (1990). *When living hurts: Directives for treating depression.* New York: Brunner/Mazel.

Zorick, F. (1994). Overview of insomnia. In M. H. Kryger, T. Roth, & W. C. Dement (Eds.), *Principles and practice of sleep medicine* (2nd ed.). (pp. 483–485). Philadelphia: Saunders.

Zweben, J. E. (1992). Issues in the treatment of the dual diagnosis patient. In B. C. Wallace (Ed.), *The chemically dependent: Phases of treatment and recovery.* New York: Brunner/Mazel.

INDEX

'*Note*: Page numbers followed by "f" indicate figures, "t" indicate tables and "b" indicate boxes.'